CROSS-BORDER INVESTMENTS WITH GERMANY – TAX, LEGAL AND ACCOUNTING
In Honour of Detlev J. Piltz

CROSS-BORDER INVESTMENTS WITH GERMANY - TAX, LEGAL AND ACCOUNTING

In Honour of Detlev J. Piltz

Published by the
**Partners of
Flick Gocke Schaumburg**

Editorial Team:
Prof. Dr. Thomas Rödder,
Dr. Jochen Bahns
&
Dr. Jens Schönfeld

2014

 Flick Gocke Schaumburg

Flick Gocke Schaumburg is a tax-focused
Partnership of Lawyers, Tax Advisors and Public
Auditors with Offices in
Bonn, Berlin, Frankfurt, Munich and Zurich.

ottoschmidt

*Bibliografische Information
der Deutschen Nationalbibliothek*

Die Deutsche Nationalbibliothek verzeichnet diese Publikation in der Deutschen Nationalbibliografie; detaillierte bibliografische Daten sind im Internet über http://dnb.d-nb.de abrufbar.

Verlag Dr. Otto Schmidt KG
Gustav-Heinemann-Ufer 58, 50968 Köln
Tel. 02 21/9 37 38-01, Fax 02 21/9 37 38-943
info@otto-schmidt.de
www.otto-schmidt.de

ISBN 978-3-504-26007-1

©2014 by Verlag Dr. Otto Schmidt KG, Köln

Das Werk einschließlich aller seiner Teile ist urheberrechtlich geschützt. Jede Verwertung, die nicht ausdrücklich vom Urheberrechtsgesetz zugelassen ist, bedarf der vorherigen Zustimmung des Verlages. Das gilt insbesondere für Vervielfältigungen, Bearbeitungen, Übersetzungen, Mikroverfilmungen und die Einspeicherung und Verarbeitung in elektronischen Systemen.

Das verwendete Papier ist aus chlorfrei gebleichten Rohstoffen hergestellt, holz- und säurefrei, alterungsbeständig und umweltfreundlich.

Einbandgestaltung: Jan P. Lichtenford, Mettmann
Satz: WMTP, Birkenau
Druck und Verarbeitung: Kösel, Krugzell
Printed in Germany

Authors

Dr. Jochen Bahns
Lawyer, Tax Advisor

Dr. Johannes Baßler
Lawyer, Tax Advisor

Prof. Dr. Hubertus Baumhoff
Public Auditor, Tax Advisor

Dr. Martin Cordes
Tax Advisor, Diplom-Finanzwirt, Diplom-Kaufmann

Dr. Holger Dietrich
Lawyer, Tax Advisor

Dr. Xaver Ditz
Tax Advisor

Dr. Jens Eggenberger LL.M.
Lawyer, Attorney-at-Law

Dr. Torsten Engers
Lawyer, Tax Advisor, Expert Advisor on International Tax Law

Dr. Michael Erkens
Lawyer, Tax Advisor

Dr. Arne von Freeden LL.M.
Lawyer, Certified Tax Lawyer, Tax Advisor

Dr. Lambertus Fuhrmann
Lawyer, Tax Advisor

Dr. Jan C. Giedinghagen LL.M.
Lawyer

Dr. Stephan Göckeler
Lawyer, Attorney-at-Law

Dr. Jens Eric Gotthardt
Lawyer, Tax Advisor

Dr. Markus Greinert
Tax Advisor, Diplom-Kaufmann

Dr. Ulrich Grünwald
Lawyer, Tax Advisor

Dr. Jens Hageböke
Public Auditor, Tax Advisor, Diplom-Finanzwirt, Diplom-Kaufmann

Prof. Dr. Frank Hannes
Lawyer, Certified Tax Lawyer, Tax Advisor

Prof. Dr. Michael Hendricks
Lawyer, Tax Advisor, Diplom-Finanzwirt

Prof. Dr. Joachim Hennrichs
Professor of Civil Law (Of Counsel)

Prof. Dr. Dr. h.c. Norbert Herzig
Public Auditor, Tax Advisor (Of Counsel)

Dr. Oliver Hötzel
Public Auditor, Tax Advisor

Jesco Idler
Public Auditor, Tax Advisor, Diplom-Kaufmann

Dr. Torsten Kohl
Public Auditor, Tax Advisor

Dr. Florian Kutt
Lawyer, Tax Advisor

Dr. Dieter Leuering
Lawyer, Certified Commercial and Corporate Lawyer, Certified Tax Lawyer

Dr. Jörg W. Lüttge
Lawyer, Tax Advisor

Dr. Marcus Oliver Mick LL.M.
Lawyer, Tax Advisor

Dr. Tobias Nießen
Lawyer

Dr. Bernd Noll
Lawyer, Certified Tax Lawyer

Dr. Christian von Oertzen
Lawyer, Certified Tax Lawyer, TEP

Dr. Martin Oltmanns LL.M.
Lawyer, Tax Advisor,
Attorney-at-Law

Dr. Karsten Randt
Lawyer, Certified Tax Lawyer,
Certified Criminal Lawyer

Prof. Dr. Thomas Rödder
Public Auditor, Tax Advisor

Prof. Dr. Matthias Rogall
Tax Advisor, Diplom-Ökonom

Dr. Philipp Rulf
Lawyer

Dr. Jörg Schauf
Lawyer, Certified Tax Lawyer

Dr. Stephan Schauhoff
Lawyer, Certified Tax Lawyer

Dr. Stefan Schloßmacher
Lawyer, Tax Advisor

Dr. Carsten Schlotter
Lawyer, Tax Advisor

Marc Schmidt
Public Auditor, Tax Advisor,
Diplom-Kaufmann

Prof. Dr. Joachim Schmitt
Lawyer, Certified Tax Lawyer, Public
Auditor, Diplom-Kaufmann

Dr. Helder Schnittker LL.M.
Lawyer, Certified Tax Lawyer

Dr. Jens Schönfeld
Lawyer, Certified Tax Lawyer,
Diplom-Kaufmann

Dr. Christoph Schulte
Lawyer, Tax Advisor

Prof. Dr. Andreas Schumacher
Tax Advisor

Dr. Klaus Sieker
Tax Advisor

Prof. Dr. Stefan Simon
Lawyer, Tax Advisor

Prof. Dr. Andreas Söffing
Tax Advisor, Diplom-Kaufmann

Prof. Dr. Ingo Stangl
Tax Advisor

Prof. Dr. Dr. h.c.
Franz Wassermeyer
Lawyer, Tax Advisor (Of Counsel)

Dr. Wolf Wassermeyer
Lawyer, Tax Advisor, Expert Advisor
on International Tax Law

Dr. Michael R. Wiesbrock
Lawyer, Diplom-Kaufmann

Dr. Michael Winter
Lawyer, Tax Advisor

Foreword

For over 40 years, the partnership Flick Gocke Schaumburg has been advising German and foreign corporate groups, major family businesses operating nationally and internationally, high-net-worth individuals, foundations, and public and nonprofit organizations, specializing in tax law and corporate law. With more than 200 professionals at our offices in Bonn, Frankfurt, Berlin, Munich and Zurich, Flick Gocke Schaumburg is one of the leading law firms on the German market. The firm's defining features are its independence and focus on tax advice given by professionals in interdisciplinary teams. Specialist publications view Flick Gocke Schaumburg as the leading German tax law firm.

Flick Gocke Schaumburg has provided expert advice on international tax and corporate law from the outset. As markets and therefore our clients have become increasingly global, our focus has become markedly more international. A large part of our work involves advising clients on the tax and legal aspects of inbound and outbound investments from a German perspective.

This book stems from the international development of our daily work and covers selected current tax and legal questions on cross-border investments with Germany; the topics represent a cross-section of our work as practitioners. Considering the primarily foreign readership of this book, its writers have departed from their usual approach to their subject matter. The main thrust of publications by Flick Gocke Schaumburg takes the form of in-depth academic discourse, but the topics covered here are intended to be of practical use to our readers.

The success of Flick Gocke Schaumburg particularly in international tax law would not have been conceivable without our team of highly qualified and motivated partners and employees. Our long-serving colleague Prof. Dr. *Detlev J. Piltz* was one of the first partners to specialize in international tax law. Since joining the firm as a lawyer and certified tax lawyer in 1991, he has helped to shape the international development of Flick Gocke Schaumburg. *Detlev Piltz* celebrated his 70th birthday in 2014. The first edition of this book is dedicated to him.

Tax law has left a very significant mark on *Detlev Piltz's* professional career. After studying law in Freiburg, Bonn and Mannheim, he completed his dissertation on 'Partnerships in the International Tax Law of the Federal Republic of Germany' in 1980. The title alone points to the international focus of this publication in which *Detlev Piltz* addressed the challenging issues of international tax law that still engage practitioners, the judiciary and the administration to a considerable degree.

Detlev Piltz's areas of specialization are many and varied. His main fields of expertise include national and international corporate and business taxation in addition to (cross-border) estate planning and business planning. Tax litigation and business valuation also form part of his core competence. *Detlev Piltz* is greatly valued by clients and colleagues alike, which is reflected in the unchanged listings in national and international legal directories. He remains active in the firm (on weekends as well). As a result, younger colleagues have the opportunity to share ideas with an experienced partner at a very sophisticated level. The discussions in his office are legendary; some are even reputed to have lasted for hours.

Apart from being a tax law practitioner, *Detlev Piltz* has also devoted much of his time to academic work. He has been an honorary professor at the University of Mannheim since 1992 and lectured at other universities as well. Additionally, he was President of the German Branch of the International Fiscal Association (IFA) for many years. It is essentially due to his efforts in this capacity that the annual IFA congress will take place in Berlin in 2021. Moreover, he was Chairman of the German professional body *Fachinstitut der Steuerberater* for a number of years. He is still an active member of the advisory board of the professional association *Deutsche Steuerjuristische Gesellschaft*. In particular, his academic activities include his work as co-editor of the journals *'Zeitschrift für Erbrecht und Vermögensnachfolge'* and *'Internationales Steuerrecht'*. *Detlev Piltz* has also earned an outstanding reputation through numerous treatises, contributions to specialist publications and editorships in virtually all areas of German and international tax law. He continues to be held in high esteem in the world of academia. He is one of the few tax law practitioners to be accepted by tax law academics as an equal.

We would like to extend our thanks to the partners and of counsels at Flick Gocke Schaumburg whose contributions have made this book possible. Our thanks also go to *Fiona Penny-Brüll*, *Jennifer Knudsen* and *Anna Hentschel* for their coordination and editing support of the project from start to finish.

Bonn, Berlin, Frankfurt, Munich and Zurich in the late summer of 2014

On behalf of the partners of Flick Gocke Schaumburg

Thomas Rödder   Jochen Bahns   Jens Schönfeld

Content

Authors	V
Foreword	VII
Glossary	XIII

I. Tax

1. Taxation of Inbound and Outbound Investments

Wolf Wassermeyer
   Tax Classification of Foreign Legal Entities ('Comparability Test') 1

Jörg W. Lüttge
   The Taxation of German Corporations and Partnerships
   by Comparison. 11

Thomas Rödder
   International and Domestic Aspects of German Group Taxation 25

Jens Schönfeld
   Controlled Foreign Company Legislation 41

Jochen Bahns
   Repatriation by Foreign Investors of Profits from
   German Investments. 53

Helder Schnittker
   Cross-Border Investments in German Private Equity Funds 67

Martin Oltmanns
   Typical Transaction Structures for Buyout Investments
   in Germany 81

Franz Wassermeyer
   Taxation of Partnership Income Under German
   International Law 93

Klaus Sieker
   German Income Taxation of Foreign Partners in German
   Trading Partnership. 103

Florian Kutt
   German Tax Aspects in M&A Transactions 113

Torsten Engers
   Taxation of Real Estate Investments in Germany................. 125

Matthias Rogall
   Tax Aspects of Corporate Financing. 139

Marcus Mick
    The German Investment Tax Act.............................. 155

2. Transfer Pricing

Hubertus Baumhoff
    Taxation of Royalties Between Affiliated Companies............... 165

Xaver Ditz
    German Transfer Pricing Documentation Requirements............ 177

Markus Greinert
    Business Restructurings 187

3. Reorganization Tax

Ingo Stangl
    An Overview of Reorganizations Under German Tax Law........... 199

Holger Dietrich
    Tax-Neutral Contributions in Kind of Business Units 215

Jens Hageböke
    Share-for-Share Transactions 225

Andreas Schumacher
    Foreign Reorganizations with a Connection to the
    German Tax Net 235

4. Tax Accounting

Joachim Hennrichs
    Provisions in German Income Tax Law........................... 245

Norbert Herzig
    Specific Features of Tax Accounting in Germany 257

5. VAT, Trade and Real Estate Transfer Tax

Ulrich Grünwald
    Subordination or Close Links................................... 267

Arne von Freeden
    International Aspects of German Trade Tax 281

Oliver Hötzel
    The Cornerstones and Quirks of Real Estate Transfer Tax.......... 293

6. Tax Procedure

Michael Hendricks
Tax Disputes and Litigation in Germany........................ 309

Stefan Schloßmacher / Joachim Schmitt
Tax Audits in Germany.. 321

Martin Cordes
Ruling Practice in Germany – Achieving Legal Certainty on Taxation. 331

II. Private Clients and Succession Planning

Frank Hannes
Unlimited and Limited Inheritance Tax Liability of Individuals and Business Entities.. 343

Bernd Noll
Foundation and Trust in Succession Planning................... 353

Christian von Oertzen
Inheritance and Gift Tax Planning Strategies for Individuals Subject to Nonresident Taxation (Foreigners)................ 367

Johannes Baßler
Immigration and Emigration of Individuals...................... 379

Stephan Schauhoff
Using German Tax Incentives for Nonprofit Organizations Across National Borders.. 393

Carsten Schlotter
Taxation of Sportsmen and Artists................................ 403

III. Corporate, M&A and Labor/Employment Law

Christoph Schulte
Legal Forms in German Corporate Law........................... 415

Jens Eggenberger
Private M&A in Germany.. 429

Stephan Göckeler
M&A Involving Listed Corporations................................ 443

Philipp Rulf
Cross-Border Reorganizations..................................... 453

Michael Erkens
Corporate Reorganizations in Germany.......................... 467

Michael R. Wiesbrock
    Legal Aspects of Investments in German Real Estate............... 481

Dieter Leuering
    Delisting as a Component of Taking Private Transactions........... 493

Jens Eric Gotthardt
    German Corporate Governance Code 501

Stefan Simon
    Recent Developments in Corporate and Financial Restructuring 513

Lambertus Fuhrmann
    Corporate Litigation in Germany............................... 523

Jan Christian Giedinghagen
    Forms of Distribution Under German Commercial Law 539

Tobias Nießen
    Matrix Structures as a Means of Steering Groups Under Corporate
    Law and Labor-and-Employment Law 553

Michael Winter
    Corporate Codetermination and Its Avoidance 565

IV. Tax Crime

Jörg Schauf
    Voluntary Disclosure of Tax Evasion Under German Law 579

Karsten Randt
    Changed Criminal Tax Law Framework 591

V. Public Auditing, Accounting and Business Valuation

Torsten Kohl
    A Comparison of Valuation Principles in Germany and
    Internationally... 603

Marc Schmidt
    Financial Statements: Disclosure Requirements and Ways of Avoiding
    Them 615

Andreas Söffing
    Accounting for Advertising Spots................................ 631

Jesco Idler
    Tax Compliance – A Challenge for Tax Departments................ 641

Index 655

Glossary

German Terms	English Terms
Abgabenordnung	General Tax Code
Abgeltungsteuer	final withholding tax
Abspaltung	spin-off
Aktiengesellschaft = AG	stock corporation
Aktiengesetz	Stock Corporation Act
Allgemeine Geschäftsbedingungen	general terms and conditions
Amtshilferichtlinie-Umsetzungsgesetz	Act Implementing the Mutual Assistance Directive
Anfallsberechtigte	beneficiaries or persons entitled on dissolution
Anfechtungsklage	action for annulment
Anleihen	bonds
Anschlusserklärung	notification of joinder
Antrag auf verbindliche Auskunft	request for a binding ruling
Anwachsung	accrual
Anwendungserlass zur Abgabenordnung	General Tax Code Application Decree
Arbeitnehmerüberlassung	temporary hiring-out of employees
Arbeitnehmerüberlassungsgesetz	Temporary Employment Act
Auflassung	agreed title conveyance
Auftrag	engagement
Aufspaltung	split-up
Ausgliederung	hive-down
Außensteuergesetz	Foreign Tax Act
Außensteuerreformgesetz	International Transactions Tax Reform Act
außergerichtlicher Sanierungsvergleich	out-of-court restructuring scheme
Beherrschungsvertrag	control agreement
Beibringungsgrundsatz	principle of party presentation
Berichtigungsverbund	system of adjustments
Besteuerungsgrundlage	basis of taxation

Glossary

Beteiligungsgesetz für Europäische Genossenschaften	SCE Participation Act
Betrieb	undertaking
Betriebsaufspaltung	operational split
Betriebskostenverordnung	Operating Costs Regulation
Betriebsrat	works council
Betriebsstätte	permanent establishment (PE)
Betriebsverfassungsgesetz	Works Constitution Act
Betriebsvorrichtungen	fixtures and other nontaxable equipment
Betriebszugehörigkeit	affiliation with an organizational unit
Beurkundung	formal recording by a German notary
Beweismittel	proof
Bewertungsgesetz	Valuation Act
Bezugsberechtige	persons entitled to income
Börsengesetz	Stock Exchange Act
Bundesamt für Justiz	Federal Office of Justice
Bundesanstalt für Finanzdienstleistungsaufsicht	Federal Financial Services Supervisory Agency
Bundesdatenschutzgesetz	Federal Data Protection Act
Bundesfinanzhof	Federal Tax Court
Bundesgerichtshof	Federal Court of Justice
Bundessteuerblatt	Federal Tax Gazette
Bundestag	Lower House of the German Parliament
Bundesverfassungsgericht	Federal Constitutional Court
Bundesverfassungsgerichtsgesetz	Federal Constitutional Court Act
Bundeszentralamt für Steuern	Federal Central Tax Office
Bürgerliches Gesetzbuch	Civil Code
Dauerschuldverhältnis	continuing obligation
Deutsche Prüfstelle für Rechnungswesen	German Financial Reporting Enforcement Panel
Deutsche Vereinigung für Finanzanalyse und Asset Management	Society of Investment Professionals in Germany

Glossary

Deutschland AG	large corporations in Germany
Dienstvertrag	service contract
Dispositionsmaxime	principle of party control
Doppelbesteuerungsabkommen	double taxation treaty
Drittanfechtung	action for annulment
Drittbeteiligungsgesetz	One-Third Participation Act
echter Handelsvertreter	genuine commercial agent
echter (Teil-)Betriebsführungsvertrag	genuine agreement on management of a business (unit)
Eigengeschäft	contract with the entrepreneur, in his own name and for his own account, i.e. through his own business
Einbringender	contributor
Einbringungsvertrag	contribution and subscription agreement
eingetragene Genossenschaft	registered cooperative
Eingliederung	formal integration
Eingliederungskonzern	integrated corporate group
Einheitswert	assessed value
Einkommensteuer-Durchführungsverordnung	Income Tax Implementation Regulation
Einkommensteuergesetz	Income Tax Act
Einkünfte aus selbständiger Arbeit	income from independent personal services
Einkünfte mit Kapitalanlagecharakter	profit deemed as investment income
Einspruch	administrative appeal
Einspruchsentscheidung	administrative appeal decision
Einspruchsverfahren	administrative appeal procedure
Eintragungssperre	suspension of registration
Einzelrechtsübertragung	singular succession
Entlastung	discharge
Entscheidungen der Finanzgerichte	decisions of the tax courts
Entsprechenserklärung	Declaration of Conformity
Entstrickung	exit taxation

Glossary

Erbbaurechte	hereditary leasehold rights
Erbersatzsteuer	substitute inheritance tax
Erbschaft- und Schenkungsteuergesetz	Inheritance and Gift Tax Act
Erfüllungsgeschäft	legally consequential act that discharges the obligation
Ergänzungsbilanz	supplementary balance sheet
Erstausstattung	initial transfer
erweiterte Gewerbesteuer-Kürzung	extended trade-tax relief
erweiterte unbeschränkte Steuerpflicht	extended unlimited tax liability
Europäische Gesellschaft	Societas Europaea — European Company
Festsetzungsfrist	assessment deadline
Feststellungsbescheid	determination notice
Feststellungsklage	action for a declaratory judgment
Finanzgerichtsordnung	Tax Court Code
Forderungsverzicht mit Besserungsschein	waiver subject to restoration
Formwechsel	change of legal form
Franchisenehmer	franchisee
Freigabeverfahren	release proceedings
Freiverkehr	free market
Funktionsabschmelzung	downsizing of a function
Funktionsabspaltung	separation of a function
Funktionsausgliederung	hive-down of a function
Funktionsverdoppelung	duplication of a function
Garantiedividende	guaranteed dividend
Gegenstände des Handelsverkehrs	commercial objects
Gemeinschaftsbetrieb	joint organizational unit
Genossenschaft	cooperative
Gerichtskostengesetz	Court Costs Act
Gesamtrechtsnachfolge	universal succession
Gesamtschuld	joint and several debt
Geschäftsbesorgungsvertrag	management agreement

Geschäftsführer	manager
Geschäftsführung	management
geschäftsleitende Holding	managerial holding company
Geschäftsleitungsbetriebsstätte	management PE
Gesellschaft bürgerlichen Rechts	partnership constituted under civil law
Gesellschaft mit beschränkter Haftung	privately held corporation
Gesetz gegen die Steuerflucht	Tax Evasion Act
Gesetz gegen Wettbewerbsbeschränkungen	Antitrust Act
Gesetz über die Mitbestimmung der Arbeitnehmer	Employee Codetermination Act
Gesetz zur weiteren Erleichterung der Sanierung von Unternehmen	Act for the Further Facilitation of the Restructuring of Companies
gesonderte und einheitliche Gewinnfeststellung	separate and uniform determination of profits
Gewerbebetrieb	trade or business
Gewerbeertrag	trade tax base
Gewerbesteuer	trade tax
Gewerbesteuergesetz	Trade Tax Act
gewerbesteuerliches Schachtelprivileg	trade tax participation exemption
Gewerbesteuermessbetrag	trade tax base value
Gewerbesteuer-Richtlinien	Trade Tax Guidelines
gewerblich geprägte Personengesellschaft	deemed business partnership
gewerblich tätige Personengesellschaft	partnership carrying on a trade or business
Gewinnabführungsvertrag	profit and loss transfer agreement
Gewinnabgrenzungsaufzeichnungsverordnung	Profit Allocation Documentation Regulation
Gewinnfeststellungsbescheid	notice of assessment
Gewinnvorab	profit advance
GmbH & Co. KG	type of limited partnership in Germany
Grunderwerbsteuer	real estate transfer tax

Grunderwerbsteuergesetz	Real Estate Transfer Tax Act
grunderwerbsteuerliche Organschaft	tax group for real estate transfer tax purposes
Grundgesetz	Federal Constitution
Grundkapital	capital stock
Grundpfandrechten	in rem security interests
Grundsatz der Ämterkontinuität	principle of officer/director continuity
Grundsätze der Verwaltung zum Datenzugriff und zur Prüfbarkeit digitaler Unterlagen	principles of data access and the verifiability of digital documents
Grundsätze ordnungsmäßiger datengestützter Buchführungssysteme	generally accepted principles of computerized accounting systems
grundsätzliche Bedeutung	question of fundamental significance
Grundschuld	land charge
Grundsteuer	land tax
Grundstockvermögen	basic property
grundstücksgleiche Rechte	rights equivalent to real estate
Handelsgesetzbuch	Commercial Code
(Handels-)Makler	(commercial) broker
Handelsregister	commercial register
Handelsvertreter	commercial agent
Hauptfachausschuss	Auditing and Accounting Board
Hauptversammlung	shareholders' meeting
Hebesatz	multiplier
Hereinverschmelzung	inbound merger
Hinausverschmelzung	outbound merger
Hinzurechnungsbesteuerung	add-back taxation
Inhaberaktie	bearer share
Inländer	tax resident
Inlandsvermögen	domestic property
Insolvenzausfallgeld	compensation for lost wages due to insolvency
Insolvenzgeldvorfinanzierung	insolvency payment prefinancing

Insolvenzordnung	Insolvency Code
Insolvenzplan	insolvency scheme
Insolvenzquote	insolvency quota
Institut der Wirtschaftsprüfer	Institute of Public Auditors in Germany
Investitionsgesellschaft	investment corporation
Investmentaktiengesellschaft	investment stock corporation
Investmentkommanditgesellschaft	investment limited partnership
Investmentsteuergesetz	Investment Tax Act
Investmentvermögen	investment assets
Jahressteuergesetz	Annual Tax Act
Kammer der Wirtschaftstreuhänder	Chamber of Public Accountants
Kapitalanlagegesellschaft	investment entity
Kapitalanlagegesetzbuch	Capital Investment Code
Kapitalertragsteuer	withholding tax on capital investments
Kapitalkonto der Gesamthandsbilanz	capital account of the partners
kapitalwertorientierte Verfahren	income approach methods
Kaufmann	merchant
Kleinstkapitalgesellschaften-Bilanzrechtsänderungsgesetz	Act Amending Accounting Law for Microcorporations
Kommanditaktionär	limited-liability shareholder
Kommanditgesellschaft	limited partnership
Kommanditgesellschaft auf Aktien	partnership limited by shares
Kommanditist	limited partner
Kommissionär	commission agent
Kompensationsverbot	nonrecognition of expenses
Komplementär	general partner
Komplementär-Kapitalgesellschaft	general partner corporation
Koordinationsverfahren	coordination proceedings
Körperschaftsteuer	corporate income tax
Körperschaftsteuergesetz	Corporate Income Tax Act
Kreditwesengesetz	Banking Act
Länder	federal states

Glossary

Landesholding/Funktionsholding	national or functional holding company
Landgericht	regional court
Leitung	directional management
Leitungsverantwortung	directional management duties
Lohnsteuerabzugsverfahren	wage-tax deduction procedure
Lohnsteueranmeldung	wage-tax report
Lohnsteueranrufungsauskunft	wage-tax ruling
Lohnsumme	aggregate wages
Markengesetz	Trademark Act
Maßgeblichkeitsgrundsatz	authoritative principle
Mehrerlösabschöpfung	refund of excess fees charged by network operators
Mehrheitsidentität	identical majority shareholders
Mehrkapital	surplus capital
Mitbestimmung	codetermination
Mitbestimmungsgesetz	Codetermination Act
Mittelstand	small and medium-sized enterprises
Mitunternehmer	co-entrepreneur
Mitunternehmeranteil	interest in a partnership
Mitunternehmerschaft	co-entrepreneurship or partnership for tax purposes
Montan-Mitbestimmungsergänzungsgesetz	Supplementary Codetermination Act
Montan-Mitbestimmungsgesetz	Codetermination Act for the Coal, Iron and Steel Industry
Namensaktie	registered share
Nennbetragsaktie	par-value share
Nichtzulassungsbeschwerde	appeal against denial of leave to appeal
Nießbrauch	usufruct
Nutzungsberechtigter	beneficiary owner
Oberlandesgericht	higher regional court
offene Handelsgesellschaft	general partnership
Ordnungswidrigkeitsgesetz	Administrative Offenses Act

Organgesellschaft	controlled entity
Organhaftung	liability of directors and officers
Organkreis	tax group
Organschaft	tax group
Partenreederei	ship-owning partnership
partielle Gesamtrechtsnachfolge	partitioned universal succession
Partnerschaftsgesellschaftsgesetz	Professional Partnership Act
Personengesellschaft	partnership
Personenvereinigung	association of individuals
persönliche Entlastungsberechtigung	individual relief entitlement
persönlicher Strafaufhebungsgrund	personal grounds for exemption from punishment
Pflanzenschutzgesetz	Plant Protection Act
Qualifikationskonflikt	conflict of classification
Rechtsbehelfsstelle	Legal Remedies Office
Rechtstypenvergleich	comparison of legal forms
regulierter Markt	regulated market
Reichsfluchtsteuer	Reich flight tax
Rentenschulden	annuity charges
Rückstellungen	provisions
Sachenrechte	rights in rem
sachenrechtliche Bestimmbarkeit	obligation under property law to provide sufficient identifiability
sachliche Entlastungsberechtigung	factual relief entitlement
Sachwalter	examiner
Satzung	bylaws, constitution, statutes
Schachtelbeteiligung	significant holding
Schachteldividenden	significant-holding dividends
Schachtelprivileg	participation exemption
Schuldverschreibung	debenture
Schuldverschreibungsgesetz	Debenture Act
Schutzschirmverfahren	umbrella proceedings
Schwarzgeldbekämpfungsgesetz	Act for Combatting Unreported Income

SE Ausführungsgesetz	SE Implementation Act
SE-Beteiligungsgesetz	SE Employee Participation Act
selbständiger Gewerbetreibender	independent person carrying on a trade or business
Selbstanzeige	voluntary disclosure
Selbstorganschaft	principle of self-governance
Solidaritätszuschlaggesetz	Solidarity Surcharge Act
Sonderbetriebsausgaben	special business expenses
Sonderbetriebsbilanz	special balance sheet
Sonderbetriebseinnahmen	special business income
Sonderbetriebsvermögen	special business assets
Sondervergütung	special income
Sondervermögen	separate assets
Spaltung	division
Spaltung zu null	zero division
Spaltung zur Aufnahme	division for absorption and transfer into an existing entity
Spaltung zur Neugründung	division which involves a transfer to a newly formed entity
sperrfristbehaftete Anteile	tainted shares
Spezial-Sondervermögen	special fund
Spiegelbildmethode	mirror-image method
Spruchgesetz	Act on Judicial Valuation Proceedings
Spruchverfahren	judicial valuation proceedings
Standortsicherung	safeguarding of locations
Statusfeststellungsverfahren	status-determination procedure
Steuer-Auskunftsverordnung	Tax Information Regulation
Steuerbescheid	tax assessment notice
Steuerfestsetzung	setting the amount of tax
Steuerinländer	resident in Germany for tax purposes
steuerliche Einlagekonto	tax reserve account
Steuermessbescheid	basic nonpersonal tax assessment notice
Steuermessbetrag	base value

Steuermesszahl	base rate
Steuerung	steering
Steuerveranlagung	tax assessment
Stiftung	foundation
Stiftungsgeschäft	act of formation
Strafgesetzbuch	Criminal Code
Stückaktien	shares without a par value
subjektiver Fehlerbegriff	doctrine of subjective error
tatsächliche Verständigung	mutual agreement
Teilbetrieb	business unit
Teilbetriebsvoraussetzung	partial business unit qualification requirement
Teileinkünfteverfahren	partial income taxation method
Teilschuldverschreibung	securitized bonds and receivables
Teilselbstanzeige	partial voluntary disclosure
Tendenzunternehmen	entities that directly or predominantly serve political, religious, educational, charitable, scientific or artistic purposes
Transparenz- und Publizitätsgesetz	Transparency and Disclosure Act
Treu und Glauben	good faith
Treuhandverhältnis	trust relationship
Umsatzsteueranwendungserlass	Rules for the Application of the German VAT Act
Umsatzsteuer-Durchführungsverordnung	VAT Implementing Regulation
Umsatzsteuergesetz	VAT Act
Umwandlungsgesetz	Reorganization Act
Umwandlungsteuergesetz	Reorganization Tax Act
unechter Handelsvertreter	ungenuine commercial agent
Unternehmensgegenstand	statutory purpose
Unternehmergesellschaft (haftungsbeschränkt)	entrepreneurial company (limited liability)
Urheberrechtsgesetz	Copyright Act
Verfahrensfehler	procedural error
Vermögensanfall	succession of property

Vermögensinteressen	pecuniary interests
Vermögensmasse	pool of assets
Vermögenssphäre	private-property sphere
Vermögensübertragung	transfer of assets
vermögensverwaltende Personengesellschaft	private asset management partnership
Vermögensverwaltung	asset management
Verpflichtungsgeschäft	a legally consequential act that creates an obligation
Verschmelzung	merger
Verschmelzung im Wege der Aufnahme	merger by way of absorption
Verschmelzungsbescheinigung	merger certificate
Vertragshändler	authorized dealer
Vertragskonzern	group affiliated by contract
Verwaltungsakt	administrative act
Vorstand	executive board, management board
Wegzugsteuer	exit tax
Werkvertrag	contract for work and services
Wertpapiererwerbs- und Übernahmegesetz	Securities Acquisition and Takeover Act
Wertpapierhandelsgesetz	Securities Trading Act
wirtschaftlicher Geschäftsbetrieb	commercial business
Wirtschaftsprüfer	auditor
Zinsschranke	earnings stripping rule, interest barrier
Zivilmakler	civil broker
Zivilprozessordnung	Code of Civil Procedure
Zurechnungsbesteuerung	add-back taxation
Zuwendung	contribution
Zwischenberechtigter	person entitled in the interim

I. Tax

1. Taxation of Inbound and Outbound Investments

Tax Classification of Foreign Legal Entities ('Comparability Test')

by Wolf Wassermeyer

Contents

I. Introduction
II. Entity Classification of Foreign Legal Entities under German Tax Law
  1. Clear Classification of Foreign Entities for German Tax Purposes
  2. Classification of Foreign Entities for German Tax Purposes According to the Comparability Test
  3. Factors of the Comparability Test
    a) Centralization of Management and Representation of the Entity
    b) Limited Liability for its Owners
    c) Free Transferability of the Ownership Interests in the Entity
    d) Discretion to Access Profits
    e) Equity Contributions
    f) Unlimited Life for the Entity
    g) Profit Allocation
    h) Formation Requirements
    i) Nonrelevant Criteria
  4. Practical Advantages of the Eight-Factor Test
III. Tax Consequences of the Classification
  1. Foreign Entity as a Partnership for German Tax Purposes
  2. Foreign Entity as a Corporation for German Tax Purposes
IV. Conclusion

I. Introduction

The German income taxation of a legal entity depends on its classification for tax purposes. The main types of German legal entities are corporations and partnerships. There are significant distinctions between these entities for German income tax purposes. Most importantly, corporations are treated as independent legal persons and are liable to pay corporate income tax (on undistributed as well as distributed profits). Distributions of the profits as dividends are also taxed at the level of the shareholders. By contrast, partnerships are treated as tax-transparent. There is only one taxation level as the income of the partnership 'flows through' to its partners. The partners are subject to tax on their *pro rata* share of income from the partnership. Their income is taxed with their individual income tax rate.

It should be mentioned that both corporations and partnerships are treated as taxable entities for certain German taxes: municipal trade tax, which is imposed by the local municipalities, and value-added tax. They will be disregarded in this chapter.

Business activities of foreign investors and companies with operations in Germany are often conducted through a German legal vehicle such as a German corporation, a German partnership or a permanent establishment. But due to business reasons or other considerations foreign investors also conduct their investments in Germany through foreign entities. 'Hybrid' entities can play an important role in this context. They are subject to corporate tax in one jurisdiction while being classified as partnerships and therefore qualifying for tax-transparent treatment in another. Under certain circumstances, the different classifications of foreign entities enable the investor to benefit from the advantages of a corporation (such as the limited liability) and still benefit from the tax-transparent treatment of a partnership.

The following describes the classification procedure of foreign entities with a particular focus on foreign hybrid entities for German tax purposes.

II. Entity Classification of Foreign Legal Entities under German Tax Law

The German tax authorities classify foreign legal entities either as partnerships or corporations in order to apply the corporate or the partnership tax regime to those entities' business income from German sources or the income of their German-resident partners. In the first case, the classification particularly affects the double taxation treaty entitlement of the foreign entity. In the second case, the classification has particular significance for the German taxation of the shares of profits, distributions and special remunerations.

In Germany, the tax treatment follows the civil law treatment. This means that legal entities that according to civil law have the status of a partnership are treated as (transparently taxed) partnerships for tax purposes. Legal entities that have the (civil law) status of a corporation are subject to corporate income tax.

However, the classification of entities under foreign tax law sometimes differs from the German perspective. Other countries might conduct the tax treatment of entities without reference to their civil law regime. For example, a US limited liability company (LLC) can choose its preferred tax treatment (check-the-box procedure) without reference to its classification according to the applicable provisions of US civil law.

Germany has no check-the-box regulations or other comparable tax concepts, even for trusts. For that reason the German classification of an LLC for tax purposes can differ from the chosen tax treatment classification in the US. Generally, it has to be noted that the tax treatment of the foreign tax authorities has no bearing on the German entity classification. Of course, this may mean that an entity is classified differently in Germany and the foreign state. But there are practical reasons for that, and also reasons related to fair competition among foreign and domestic entities.

However, most of the classifications of entities in other countries are based on either the corporation or the partnership type, which makes the classification for German tax purposes uncomplicated.

1. Clear Classification of Foreign Entities for German Tax Purposes

Many of these uncomplicated classifications are published in a (binding) ruling letter issued by the Federal Finance Ministry. An overview of which worldwide foreign entity is comparable to a German entity can be found in Tables 1 (entities of international companies except Eastern Europe) and 2 (entities of Eastern European companies) of the administrative guidelines for permanent establishments published by the Federal Finance Ministry.[1] For example:

State	Legal form of the entity	Comparable with
UK	Private company limited by shares (Ltd.)	GmbH (corporation)
	Public company limited by shares (PLC)	AG (corporation)
	Limited partnership	KG (partnership)
	Partnership	OHG (partnership)
US	Business corporation (public corporation, stock corporation) (Corp.)	AG (corporation)
	Limited partnership	KG (partnership)
	General partnership	OHG (partnership)

The list classifies the main types of foreign entities for German tax purposes. The classification of a foreign entity provided in the ruling letter is binding for local tax assessment and German tax treaty purposes.

2. Classification of Foreign Entities for German Tax Purposes According to the Comparability Test

Many foreign entities, especially entities that can be treated as corporations or partnerships for tax purposes, (e.g. the above-mentioned US LLCs; also foundations) are not mentioned in these tables. In some cases (e.g. business trusts) the tables do not provide a clear classification.

These foreign entities have to be classified on a case-by-case basis. The German Federal Tax Court established a 'comparability test' (*Rechtstypenvergleich*) for this purpose. This test is based on a structural comparison of the foreign entity with the main German civil law types of entities (partnerships and corpora-

---

[1] 24 Dec. 1999, IV B 4 – S 1300 – 111/99, Federal Tax Gazette Part I, p. 1076.

tions). The German tax treatment of the comparable type of entity is applied to the foreign entity for German tax purposes.

The comparison rests on an overall assessment of whether the applicable (foreign) state law and any relevant agreement relating to the organization or structure of the foreign entity legally and economically resemble those of a German corporation or those of a partnership more closely. If the foreign company more closely resembles a German corporation, it is taxed as a corporation for German tax purposes.

3. Factors of the Comparability Test

To substantiate the comparability test, which was established by Germany's Federal Tax Court, the Federal Finance Ministry published another ruling letter on 19 March 2004 concerning the entity classification of a US LLC. This letter lists decisive criteria for classifying hybrid entities in the form of a US LLC for German tax purposes. The German tax authorities apply these criteria strictly. The criteria can be guidelines not only for classifying a US LLC but also for classifying any other foreign entity for German tax purposes. The Federal Tax Court approved the criteria.

The test laid down in the ruling letter is similar to the former US entity classification rules (four-factor test). These rules were replaced by a set of new regulations (check-the-box regulations) that became effective on 1 Jan. 1997 in response to concerns and uncertainties about the previous rules. Despite the concerns of the US tax authorities, the German tax authorities made the judicial comparability test more specific by adopting the US four-factor test and incorporating additional factors. They then applied an 'eight-factor test' to determine whether to treat a US LLC as a partnership or a corporation for German tax purposes. The following criteria for the comparison are taken into account:

a) Centralization of Management and Representation of the Entity

A clear distinction between an autonomous acting management and the ownership of the company is characteristic for corporations. Corporations are typically managed and represented by people who are not necessarily shareholders (the management board). In contrast, a partnership is usually managed and represented by its partners.

b) Limited Liability for its Owners

The shareholders of a corporation are not liable for debts of the corporation or charges against the corporation, whereas the partners of a partnership are.

c) Free Transferability of the Ownership Interests in the Entity

An essential characteristic of a corporation is the free transferability of its shares. In contrast, the transferability of interests in a partnership is often ruled out or restricted by the terms of the company agreement and subject to the consent of one or more partners.

d) Discretion to Access Profits

The distribution or retention of profits in a corporation depends on a formal resolution of the shareholders. In a partnership, disposing of profits is at the discretion of the partners.

e) Equity Contributions

In a corporation, the shareholders are obliged to make equity contributions. In a partnership, equity contributions are not required by law. The partners may contribute services to the partnership if this is provided for in the partnership agreement. It is not possible for shareholders of a corporation to make their equity contribution by contributing services.

f) Unlimited Life for the Entity

'Unlimited life' of a corporation means that it continues as a legal person regardless of the shareholder structure. Generally, the 'life' of a company is limited if the company is dissolved upon the fulfillment of certain conditions without any action by its members. If either the foreign law or the corporation agreement provides at least one condition for dissolution, this would be assumed as a factor for an entity to be classified as a partnership. The occurrence of this condition has to be realistically expected.

g) Profit Allocation

The profit allocation in a corporation is based strictly on the subscribed equity of the shareholders. In a partnership, not only the contributed capital but also other aspects such as specialist knowledge or business experience of a partner can be taken into consideration for the profit allocation.

h) Formation Requirements

The incorporation of a corporation requires a registration (with the Commercial Register). The company agreement or the articles of association have to be confirmed by a governmental institution. Partnerships are established by merely signing a partnership agreement. The registration with the Commercial Register is relevant only with respect to the company's business relations with third parties.

i) Nonrelevant Criteria

Neither the legal capacity of an entity under a foreign jurisdiction nor the number of members is a relevant criterion for the classification of a foreign entity.

As mentioned above, the classification is subject to an overall assessment. First, each of the criteria listed above has to be weighted by its relevance. No single criterion is decisive or controlling. If the analysis does not yield a clear conclusion, the Federal Finance Ministry instructed the tax authorities to treat a US LLC (and other foreign entities as can be assumed) as a corporation for German tax purposes if the majority of the criteria (1) to (5) listed above indicate the corporate status of the foreign entity. Criterion (6) should be included in certain cases only.

4. Practical Advantages of the Eight-Factor Test

At first glance it seems quite complex to properly structure a foreign entity based on this test. Additionally, by fulfilling the requirements of the German factor test certain terms may be included in the structure of an entity which would otherwise not be present (e.g. limited life, (non)transferability of interests). This may lead to distortions in the relationship of the shareholders/partners. But despite these concerns the German factor test creates significant tax planning opportunities for international investors with German tax reporting obligations because it enables them to include these factors prior to their investment in the structure of terms of the entity in order to benefit from a specific tax treatment. Before this test was published, investors had to file a request for an advance letter ruling (*Antrag auf verbindliche Auskunft*) in order to avoid disputes with the German tax authorities or litigation concerning the classification of a foreign entity. Now the criteria laid down in the ruling letter enable them to conduct exact tax planning for their investments without filing a request for an advance letter ruling (which is subject to a fee). However, previous business conducted with a foreign entity that is not structured in accordance with the German factor test may deliver a surprising result at the tax audit. Foreign investors are therefore well advised to consult a tax counsel prior to the investment to determine the best planning measures. Knowledge of the tax requirements prevents investors from experiencing surprises at tax audits in the future.

III. Tax Consequences of the Classification

If there is no difference between the classification of a foreign entity from the perspective of Germany and the relevant foreign state, the corresponding German tax treatment of a partnership or a corporation applies. However, the classification of foreign entities becomes especially relevant in cross-border cases if the German classification of the entity differs from the classification of the other state. The different classification of these hybrid entities has particular effects on the application of the double taxation treaty (DTT) between these two states. DTTs, in principle, enable the tax authorities of the contracting states to avoid double taxation of income which is taxable in both states by granting an exemption or taxation at a reduced rate on dividends, interests, royalties and so on, or by crediting the foreign tax paid in the state of residence. Germany is a signatory to DTTs with more than 90 states. For the following it should be assumed that a DTT based on the Model Convention drafted by the Organization for Economic Cooperation and Development (OECD-MC) between Germany and the other state is in place and that the taxpayer is a German resident. If a DTT is applicable, the different entity classification may lead to the two states applying different DTT provisions. Below is a brief overview of the general tax consequences of this situation. It is oriented toward the legal opinion of the German tax authorities.

1. Foreign Entity as a Partnership for German Tax Purposes

Insofar as a foreign hybrid entity is treated as a partnership for German tax purposes, but as a corporation under the tax regime of the other state, it is treated as tax-transparent. Therefore, such an entity is disregarded for DTT purposes.[2] On this basis it has to be examined whether the DTT in general, and which article of a DTT in particular, can be applied to its partners. Provided that the foreign entity maintains a permanent establishment in the other state that generates business income (see Art. 7 of the OECD-MC), the income is generally exempt from German tax safeguarding progression (exemption method)[3] as far as the income can be allocated to the permanent establishment.

In general, a DTT tax exemption might be restricted by particular subject-to-tax clauses which require that the particular income is actually taxed in the other state (otherwise the tax exemption is withdrawn). Another way to ensure one-time taxation is by means of switchover clauses, whereby Germany 'switches' from the exemption to the tax credit method in the case of a non- or limited taxation in the other state due to a classification conflict that leads to the two states applying different treaty provisions. Many DTTs and domestic tax law provide those regulations.

To the extent that the income is not exempted from German tax under the articles of a DTT (for example because the entity generates interest, dividend or royalty income from sources located in the other state), Germany will provide a tax credit for the corporate taxes paid in the other state to the member of the entity who is taxed in Germany. But as the other state may classify the entity as a corporation, foreign withholding tax on 'dividends' may be applicable. In this case, there is no tax credit for any withholding taxes imposed by the other state because from a German perspective no dividends, but only nontaxable 'distributions' from a partnership, exist.

---

2 Note that some DTTs contain divergent regulations.
3 Note that the application of the progression clauses has been restricted for particular income from EU sources since 2009.

2. Foreign Entity as a Corporation for German Tax Purposes

If a foreign entity is treated as a corporation for German tax purposes, but not for those of the foreign state, its distributions are subject to German taxation pursuant to Art. 21 para. 1 of the OECD-MC ('other income'). Its distributions will be fully taxed in Germany, and no withholding tax on distributions imposed by the other state should apply. The German rules concerning the taxation of dividend income with the domestic tax exemptions (40% in the case of a natural person or 95% in the case of corporations as recipients of dividends) at the personal tax rate or a flat taxation of 25% without any tax exemptions will apply.[4] As the other state treats the entity as tax-transparent it will generally tax the members of the entity on their share in profit as far as the business income can be allocated to a permanent establishment located in that state. Double taxation might occur because in the case of the distribution of business income from a German perspective different tax subjects are taxed and therefore no tax credit is provided.

IV. Conclusion

It has been shown in this chapter that a number of factors relating to the structuring of the terms of a foreign entity have to be considered before using it as a business vehicle. A well-structured foreign (hybrid) entity might enable the investor to combine the tax advantages of a partnership with the limited liability of a corporation at a reasonable tax level. The particular factors that are relevant for the classification of the entity for German tax purposes are laid down by ruling letters of the German tax authorities. These factors can be used as guidelines for structuring the terms of a foreign entity. They give legal certainty for tax planning. Of course, good tax planning also considers pitfalls that might lead to double taxation.

---

4 It is assumed that the corporation has sufficient substance and is therefore not considered as abusive from a German tax perspective.

Dr. Wolf Wassermeyer

Lawyer, Tax Advisor, Expert Advisor on International Tax Law

Areas of Specialization

- International tax law
- Exit taxation
- Taxation of capital investments, investment funds and fund structures
- Taxation of partnerships

Telephone (ext.) +49 89/80 00 16-21

Email: wolf.wassermeyer@fgs.de

The Taxation of German Corporations and Partnerships by Comparison

by Jörg W. Lüttge

Contents

I. Introduction
  1. Fundamental Differences in the Taxation of Corporations and Partnerships
  2. Differences in Taxation as a Result of Determining Profits

II. Comparison of Tax Burdens: Underlying Facts and Assumptions
  1. Foreign Parent: Corporation
    a) Taxation in Germany
    b) Taxation at Parent Company Level

  2. Foreign Parent: Partnership
    a) Taxation in Germany
    b) Taxation at Parent Partnership Level

III. Means to Reduce the German Income Tax Burden

IV. Offsetting German Losses?

V. Taxation of the Sale of Shares vs. Interests

I. Introduction

A key factor in deciding on an investment in a foreign business is the after-tax result of its operations. The German tax burden on income essentially depends on the legal form of the investment: A subsidiary[1] is taxed differently from a partnership[2] or a permanent establishment. The differentiation is particularly important as partnerships have a long and established tradition in Germany and are more widely spread, also for large businesses, than in many other countries. The picture would be incomplete without taking into account the tax treatment of the German-sourced income in the investor's home country. The following text combines both views in that it considers, from a potential foreign investor's perspective, the typical tax effects of setting up or acquiring a German subsidiary vs. an interest in a German partnership in the cases of (1) current profits, (2) losses and (3) capital gains from a later sale of the shares or interests.

1. Fundamental Differences in the Taxation of Corporations and Partnerships

A **corporation** is an independent legal entity and, as such, a taxpayer of its own. Where its shareholders are resident is not relevant. The profits of a corporation

---

1 Limited company *(Gesellschaft mit beschränkter Haftung = GmbH)* or stock corporation *(Aktiengesellschaft = AG)*.
2 Limited partnership *(Kommanditgesellschaft = KG or GmbH & Co. KG)* or, rarely used for business purposes, general partnership *(Offene Handelsgesellschaft = OHG)*.

registered in Germany are subject to corporate income tax *(Körperschaftsteuer)* of 15.825%[3] and municipal trade tax *(Gewerbesteuer)* at the level of the corporation. The amount of the trade tax varies within Germany because the municipalities influence the final tax burden by setting their own trade tax multiplier (200–520%). The distribution of dividends from the corporation is subject to income tax at the level of the shareholder. If the shareholder is an individual the dividend will be taxed at a preferential rate of 26.375%.[4] If the shareholder is a German juridical person and holds at least 10% of the distributing company, only 5% of the dividend is included in the parent's tax base.[5] In cross-border cases, Germany as the source country generally levies a withholding tax on the dividend. The amount of taxation in the foreign country depends firstly on any double taxation treaties and secondly on the tax level of the recipient's country of residence abroad.

A **partnership**, in contrast, is treated as transparent under German income tax law. This means that for tax purposes the partnership is regarded not as generating its own income, but as attributing its income proportionately to the partners as profits of their permanent establishments. Germany does not have an equivalent to the US check-the-box rules under which the partners can elect to be taxed as a transparent or an opaque entity. As natural persons the partners are subject to income tax; as legal persons they are subject to corporate income tax. The distribution of profits to the partners does not trigger any additional taxation.[6]

If the partnership carries out a commercial business it is also subject to trade tax which, in contrast to income tax, is levied from the partnership itself, rather than from its partners. It is then credited against the partners' income tax in proportion to their interests in the partnership.[7]

2. Differences in Taxation as a Result of Determining Profits

The amount of taxation depends not only on the tax scale, but also on the system of profit determination used. Furthermore, the amount of an enterprise's taxable profit depends on which gains are subject to taxation and on which expenditures and other transactions are permitted to reduce the tax base. Differences can also arise from the profit determination provisions of the countries involved. The taxable profit of a foreign investor from a German permanent establishment can differ depending on whether it is determined in accordance with German regulations or with those in the investor's country of residence.

---

[3] The CIT rate is 15% to which a 'solidarity surcharge' of 5.5% of the CIT is added.
[4] Incl. solidarity surcharge. The preferential rate will be definitive unless the taxpayer's personal marginal rate is lower, in which case the personal rate will apply.
[5] If the stake is less than 10% the dividend is fully taxed at parent level.
[6] For details on the taxation of partnerships in Germany see below *Sieker*, German Income Taxation of Foreign Partners in a German Trading Partnership, p. 103.
[7] On trade tax see below *von Freeden*, International Aspects of German Trade Tax, p. 281.

Under German tax law, the GAAP applied for financial accounting are, as a starting point, also authoritative for tax accounting. However, the profit determination regulations under tax law provide for deviations from the provisions of commercial law. Until 2009, rights to opt for a certain tax treatment were required to be exercised in accordance with the commercial balance sheet. This 'inverse authoritative principle' was abolished in law with effect from 2010, with the result that commercial accounting and tax accounting can now deviate from each other.

As to reporting and valuation provisions, we find many differences between commercial and tax accounting law. To name a few:

- For tax accounting only purchased intangible assets may be activated. For the commercial balance sheet, the entity drawing up the statements can choose to also activate internally generated intangible assets.
- The commercial balance sheet must contain a provision for anticipated losses from pending transactions. This is not permitted in the balance sheet prepared for tax purposes.
- Upon the sale of certain assets (plots of land, buildings, inland water vessels), the taxpayer can roll built-in gains over to surrogate assets. An amount up to the amount of the capital gain can be deducted from the selling price. The taxpayer can either deduct this amount from the acquisition or manufacturing costs of the surrogate asset in the same financial year or set up a profit-reducing reserve for up to four years and transfer it to a surrogate asset during this period. Neither is allowed in the commercial balance sheet.

Other differences arise in particular from the transparent taxation of partnerships. In addition to the partnership's tax accounting, which must be derived from the commercial balance sheet, each partner can have a supplementary tax balance sheet and a special-purpose tax balance sheet that must contain those transactions that concern only the domain of the individual partner (e.g. acquisition or financing costs for the interest in the partnership). Differences between corporations and partnerships can also be found in the amortization of goodwill. The goodwill of corporations is amortized over 15 years in tax accounting. In contrast, the goodwill in the acquisition of a partnership must be distributed, due to its income tax transparency, among its various assets and amortized in accordance with their respective remaining lives. In terms of amortization, acquiring a partnership is therefore generally more attractive than acquiring a corporation.

International accounting standards have to date had a minor direct influence on profit determination in Germany. Certain regulations have been adapted in line with the IFRS, but the international standards are not expected to be fully applied in Germany in the foreseeable future. At the European level, the proposed Common Consolidated Corporate Tax Base is an initial attempt to harmonize the determination of the corporate income tax base for companies operating in multiple EU states.⁸ The proposal does not take the IAS/IFRS as its starting point; instead it is more of a collection of best practices from individual member states. It is not expected to be implemented in the near future.

The following comparisons of tax burdens assume that the assessment base as stipulated by German regulations is no different from that used in determining profit generated abroad.

II. Comparison of Tax Burdens: Underlying Facts and Assumptions

This section compares the tax burden of a current income of 100 points for a foreign investor resident in a country that has concluded a double taxation treaty with Germany when this income is generated in a German subsidiary vs. in a German commercial partnership. The comparison distinguishes between the investor being a corporation or a partnership. In the latter case, it is assumed that all partners are individuals resident outside Germany and that the foreign partnership does not maintain a permanent establishment of its own in Germany – except the one constituted by the German partnership.

This produces the following matrix:

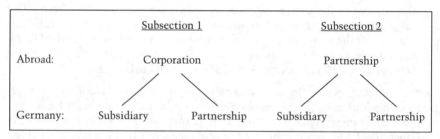

The interests in the German entities should each be 100% and financed in full with equity.

The German marginal rate for income tax in the highest bracket is 47.475%. As shown above, the corporate income tax rate is 15.825%.⁹ With a multiplier of 400%, the trade tax burden is 14%.¹⁰ It must be pointed out that the bases of corporate income tax and of trade tax are not necessarily identical since the taxable business profit for trade tax purposes may be determined by making certain adjustments to the profit accounted for income tax purposes. For the

---

8 Commission Proposal for a Council Directive on a Common Consolidated Corporate Tax Base, COM(2011) 121/4.
9 Both rates include solidarity surcharge.
10 The trade tax is calculated in two steps. The trade tax base value *(Gewerbesteuermessbetrag)* is calculated by applying the basic rate *(Steuermesszahl)* of 3.5% to the taxable business profit *(Gewerbeertrag)*. The competent municipality applies a multiplier to the base value that must be at least 200%. The average multiplier in Germany is 400%.

tax calculations below, it is assumed that the income of 100 points does *not* require such adjustments.

In cross-border cases, Germany retains a withholding tax on the gross dividends of a domestic corporation. Let us assume that the withholding tax is 5% if the dividend is distributed to a foreign parent corporation with at least a 25% stake in the German entity, and 15% in the case of a foreign natural person or partnership.[11] Within the EU/EEA, the parent-subsidiary directive normally obligates both the source state and the recipient state to fully exempt dividends from taxation.

In Germany the withholding tax is initially levied regardless of the restrictions mentioned. However, the foreign parent corporation can submit evidence to the German Federal Central Tax Office (*Bundeszentralamt für Steuern*) that it is entitled to a lower rate of withholding tax. In this case the Federal Central Tax Office will issue an exemption certificate allowing the subsidiary to not retain the excess amount. Without this certificate the parent corporation would have to apply for reimbursement of the amounts withheld. (Below we provide the effective tax deductions taking bilateral restrictions into account.)

Finally it is assumed that the foreign income tax rate for natural persons/partnerships is 40% and that the foreign corporate income tax rate is 15%. The foreign country also grants a reduced income tax rate of 25% on dividends paid to natural persons (shareholder relief).

1. Foreign Parent: Corporation

a) Taxation in Germany

	Subsidiary		Partnership
Profit	100.000		100.000
Trade tax (400 x 3.5)	./. 14.000		./. 14.000
CIT (15.285%)	./. 15.825		./. 15.825
Profit after taxes/gross dividend	70.175		70.175
German WHT (5%)	./. 3.509		–
(Parent in EU/EEA)		–	
Net dividend/net profit	**66.666**	**(70.175)**	**70.175**

Explanation: At the level of the German entity the legal form makes no difference to the tax burden – but it does make a difference to who owes the tax. Assuming a subsidiary corporation is in place, (only) this entity is subject to unlimited corporate tax liability. In the case of an interest in a partnership, the parent corporation is directly subject to limited corporate tax liability with the

---

11 The solidarity surcharge is not levied on withholding taxes that are reduced pursuant to a double tax treaty.

profits of the partnership as permanent establishment profits (Art. 7 of the OECD Model Convention).

Unlike the transfer of profits from the partnership, dividends from the German subsidiary corporation are additionally subject to withholding tax. The participation exemption regulated in double taxation treaties with a withholding tax rate of 5% applies to dividends paid to legal persons that hold a certain minimum stake in the subsidiary for a minimum period of time. As explained above, Germany grants the reduced rate of withholding tax on application.

If the German subsidiary is held by an EU/EEA corporation, the Parent-Subsidiary Directive applies. This directive requires the share in nominal capital to be at least 10% for an uninterrupted period of 12 months. Under these conditions, and again upon application, Germany fully exempts the dividends from withholding tax. The parent's EU/EEA home state will not tax it either.

For the participation exemption to be granted – vis-à-vis non-EU as well as EU countries – Germany requires a minimum substance from the parent corporation in order to prevent treaty abuse (anti-treaty-shopping rule). The required substance is generally defined to exist if the parent acts as a managerial holding company *(geschäftsleitende Holding)*. However, the German financial authorities apply strict criteria for acknowledging a holding company as 'managerial'.[12]

Non-EU/EEA parent corporations that are not entitled to a full exemption from the withholding tax due to their home country's double taxation treaty with Germany can in some cases secure the zero tax rate by placing the German subsidiary under an intermediate holding company in another EU/EEA member state which has concluded a more generous treaty with the parent's home country. Thus, in a first step, the corporation can utilize the Parent-Subsidiary Directive to receive exemption from withholding tax for the dividends paid to the intermediary in the EU/EEA member state. Then the dividends are passed on, again with no withholding tax retained, if the EU/EEA member state has agreed a dividend exemption in its double taxation treaty with the third country.

An investor domiciled in the US, for example, can consider Belgium, the Netherlands or Luxembourg as holding company locations. These countries do not impose withholding tax on the US. The exemption is generally subject to a minimum stake and duration and requires compliance with a limitation-on-benefits clause. In accordance with this clause, direct or indirect holding corporations that have a certain proportion of publicly traded shares are generally exempted from withholding tax. However, for this model to work, the conditions of the German anti-treaty-shopping rule must also be met.

---

[12] German Federal Finance Ministry circular on the authorization of relief for foreign companies (Sec. 50d(3) of the Income Tax Act) of 24 Jan. 2012, Federal Tax Gazette Part I, 2012, p.171. On the prerequisites of the anti-treaty-shopping rule cf. below *Bahns*, Repatriation by Foreign Investors of Profits from German Investments, p. 57.

b) Taxation at Parent Company Level

	Subsidiary		Partnership	
	Exemption Method	Credit Method	Exemption Method	Credit Method
Profit after German taxes	66.666	66.666	70.175	70.175
Taxable profit domestically	0.000	100.000	0.000	100.000
Domestic CIT (15%)	–	./. 15.000	–	./. 15.000
Domestic tax burden:	0.000		0.000	
Direct credit		+ 3.509		+ 29.825
		./. 11.491		0.000
Indirect credit		+ 29.825		
		0.000		
Profit after all taxes:	66.666		70.175	
After direct credit		55.175		70.175
After direct + indirect credit		66.666		

Explanation: In accordance with standard double taxation treaties[13] the foreign parent corporation may be taxed on the (gross) dividend in its country of residence. Some countries apply the exemption method to fully exempt intra-group dividends from taxation (Art. 23 of the OECD Model Convention). At the level of the parent corporation, the profit after (German only) taxes is therefore 66.666[14]. Profits from the German partnership, which in international tax law is regarded as the permanent establishment of the foreign partner, are also exempted in the receiving country in accordance with many double taxation treaties.

In some cases double taxation is avoided by applying the credit method. If the foreign person is a shareholder in a corporation, the withholding tax retained in Germany is credited to the foreign tax due on the German-sourced dividends. If the foreign person invests in a German partnership, the taxes paid in Germany are credited to the foreign tax levied on the gross profits (**direct credit**).

In the case of intra-group dividends, some countries (e.g. the US and Canada) also apply a credit method to taxes paid in Germany by the subsidiary corporation if they fall on profits from which the dividend is paid (income tax, corporate income tax, trade tax; **indirect credit**).[15] The indirect credit breaches the

---

13 Art. 10 para. 1 OECD MC.
14 Within the EU, the amount of profit after German taxes would be 70.175.
15 cf. Art. 23 para. 1 sentence 2 in conjunction with Art. 2 para. 1(b) DTT-USA.

protective shield of the corporation. The parent company can credit taxes paid by someone else (namely by its subsidiary) to its own tax liability. To calculate the foreign tax, the taxes paid by the subsidiary are added to the gross dividend paid. The parent corporation is therefore treated as though it had received the dividend, including taxes, and paid the tax itself.[16]

If the applicable tax rates are higher in Germany than in the foreign country, the indirect credit method has the same effect as an exemption. The table above also describes the impact of the credit methods.

2. Foreign Parent: Partnership

a) Taxation in Germany

	Subsidiary	Partnership
Profit	100.00	100.00
Trade tax (400 x 3.5%)	./. 14.000	./. 14.000
CIT/income tax	./. 15.285	./. 34.175
Profit after taxes/gross dividend	70.175	51.825
German WHT (15%)	./. 10.526	–
Net dividend/net profit	59.649	51.825

Explanation: If the foreign top-level entity is a natural person/partnership, rather than a corporation, the German tax burden differs considerably. This applies to shares held in a German subsidiary as well as to interests held in a partnership.

Again, the German subsidiary is subject to corporate income tax and trade tax. Withholding tax is also levied on dividends paid to a partnership abroad. Since foreign partnerships cannot take advantage of the participation exemption on dividends unless they are classified as corporations in Germany by way of exception, the withholding tax rate is 15%.

If the foreign partnership holds an interest in a German partnership, the profits, as permanent establishment income, are subject to the personal unlimited income tax liability of the partner(s) of the foreign partnership. The domestic income tax rate of 34.175% is obtained by deducting the trade tax rate from the applicable income tax rate. However, the reduction is limited to a multiplier of 380%. Assuming a marginal rate of tax of 47.475%, the income tax is therefore reduced by 13.3% to 34.175%. If the trade tax multiplier exceeds the 380% limit, the trade tax burden in Germany becomes definitive.

---

16 For instance US-IRC Sec. 78, 902(a).

b) Taxation at Parent Partnership Level

	Subsidiary		Partnership	
	Exemption Method	Credit Method	Exemption Method	Credit Method
Profit after German taxes	59.649	59.649	51.825	51.825
Taxable profit domestically	0.000	70.175	0.000	100.000
Domestic income tax (25% / 40%)	–	./. 17.544	–	./. 40.000
Domestic tax burden:	0.000		0.000	
Direct credit		+ 10.526		+ 48.175
		./. 7.018		0.000
Profit after all taxes:	59.649	52.631	51.825	51.825

Explanation: Unlike a parent corporation, a partnership can offset only the direct credit of the withholding tax retained in Germany (15%) against the domestic income tax. The parent partnership cannot claim the indirect credit granted in some countries (the US, Canada and the UK) for the taxes paid by the German subsidiary corporation in Germany. Partnerships do not benefit from the participation exemption on dividends.

III. Means to Reduce the German Income Tax Burden

As the corporation is regarded as an independent legal entity, it can conclude contracts with its shareholders. This can enable it to reduce its profit by, for example, taking out a loan from the shareholder that is not required to treat the interest payments as dividend payouts. Similar conditions apply to the transfer of intangible assets (IP) to affiliated companies.

Structures in the EU/EEA can utilize the EU Interest and Royalties Directive. The directive stipulates that the member states are not permitted to tax cross-border interest payments between affiliated companies under certain conditions. Vis-à-vis third countries (such as the US), interest and royalties are in some cases exempt from taxation in the source country due to double taxation treaties.

The limits of financing arrangements are set out by thin capitalization rules, which vary widely from country to country. The main difficulty with the interest barrier in Germany is that it is not only restricted to excessive interest payments to affiliated or associated persons, but also includes interest paid on bank loans. This can make the financing more difficult. At the bilateral level, double taxation treaties provide for arm's length assessments with regard to the amount of the interest or royalties.[17]

It should also be noted that part of the interest and royalties payable is added to the corporation's trade earnings when the trade tax is calculated. This is not in breach of European law even in the scope of the EU Interest and Royalties Directive.[18]

In contrast to transactions between the corporation and its shareholders, German tax law does not recognize service contracts between a partnership and its partners. If the partner grants a loan to the partnership, the interest payments of the partnership are treated as co-entrepreneur income, i.e. as a withdrawal from the partnership.

IV. Offsetting German Losses?

Tax losses in Germany can be offset interperiodically. This applies both to permanent establishments/partnerships and to corporations. In the case of income tax and corporate income tax, a loss not in excess of EUR 1 million from a given year can be offset against profits from the previous year (loss carryback). Any additional losses may be carried forward with no time restriction – without limitations up to EUR 1 million, but beyond that limit restricted to 60% of the total amount of income (minimum taxation). Loss carrybacks do not apply to trade tax.

Whether losses of a German **partnership** can be offset across national borders depends on the method provided for by the double taxation treaty between Germany and the contracting state. With the credit method, the parent entity can directly offset the losses of its German partnership against other profits. With an exemption for the income of a foreign permanent establishment, however, losses cannot be offset domestically. This also applies within the EU.[19]

A foreign shareholder may not offset losses of a German **corporation** against its own profits because they are incurred by a different legal subject. Losses can only be utilized interperiodically by the subsidiary. If the applicable double taxation treaty for profits of a permanent establishment selects the credit method, electing a hybrid corporate form can in some cases enable losses to be offset at home. For example, a German GmbH (closely held corporation) can be treated as transparent in the US due to the check-the-box options that apply there.

If the foreign investor maintains other, profit-making, German corporations in addition to the loss-making entity, it may be useful to establish a tax group under trade tax and corporate income tax law to offset the losses against the

---

17 cf. e.g. Art. 11 para. 4 and Art. 12 para. 4 of the DTT-D/USA.
18 European Court of Justice of 21 July 2011 – C-397/09, Federal Tax Gazette Part II, 2009, p. 528.
19 European Court of Justice of 15 May 2008 – C-414/06, Federal Tax Gazette Part II, 2009, p. 692.

profits from the other investments. This does not, however, enable the investor to offset losses over the border. Pursuant to the German regulations on cross-border tax groups, the profit or loss of a controlled company is attributed not directly to the controlling company, but through a German permanent establishment[20] with which the foreign controlling company in Germany is subject to limited tax liability.

If a corporation has already carried forward considerable losses, the investor must bear in mind that acquiring a substantial stake can cause losses to be forfeited.[21] With an acquisition of more than 25% the loss forfeiture is in line with the scope of the stake acquired; with an acquisition of more than 50% the losses are forfeited in full. This also applies to the purchase of a shareholding through an increase in capital. Multiple subsequent acquisitions within a five-year period are added together to calculate the critical mass. The loss forfeiture cannot be prevented even if several affiliated partnerships coordinate the acquisition of a majority stake.

By way of exception, and under very strict conditions, the European Court of Justice provides for cross-border loss utilization when an entity wishes to exit a loss-making activity in the EU. The Court considers losses from a foreign permanent establishment or subsidiary to be tax-deductible in another member state providing it is certain that the taxpayer or a third party (such as another subsidiary) in the other country will definitely no longer be able to utilize them in the future.[22] In this matter the ECJ is positioned against the treaty regulations, common between EU member states, on the exemption of corporate and permanent establishment profits. However, the threshold for losses to be recognized as final is high. In the *A Oy*[23] case the ECJ clarified that simply discontinuing a permanent establishment or merging a corporation with the parent does not amount to loss finality. If it is possible to carry losses back or forward, or to disclose built-in gains, the loss is not yet final. In addition, according to the ECJ, the finality of losses must be based on actual circumstances only. Therefore, if losses are forfeited as a result of local law, loss utilization in another country will not come into consideration.[24]

V. Taxation of the Sale of Shares vs. Interests

The sale of a German subsidiary by a foreign corporation is not a taxable event under German tax law. If the shares in the subsidiary are held by a foreign partnership[25], the sale is taxable pursuant to the German ITA. At treaty level, how-

---

20 Sec. 14(1) sentence 1 no. 2 sentence 6 of the Corporate Income Tax Act (*KStG*).
21 Sec. 8c of the Corporate Income Tax Act.
22 European Court of Justice of 13 Dec. 2005 – C-446/03 – Marks & Spencer, EU: C: 2005: 763.
23 European Court of Justice of 21 Feb. 2013 – C-123/11 – A Oy, EU: C: 2013: 84.
24 European Court of Justice of 23 Oct. 2008 – C-157/07 – Krankenheim Ruhesitz am Wannsee, EU: C: 2008: 588.
25 ... whose partners, as assumed above (cf. II., p. 14), are all resident outside Germany and which does not have a German permanent establishment.

ever, Germany is normally not entitled to tax the capital gain (cf. art. 13 para. 5 OECD Model Convention).[26] A problem of withholding tax arises only if a bank is involved in the transfer/payment process. In such a situation, the seller would have to recur to the mechanism of a certificate of exemption, as shown sub II., p. 15 above.

A capital gain from the sale of an interest in a German commercial partnership – irrespective of whether held by a foreign corporation or by a partnership – is part of the income of the permanent establishment maintained by the partner via the German partnership. It is therefore taxable in Germany without any exception.

If the interest in a partnership was acquired by the investor in a purchase transaction, its subsequent divestment is reflected in a supplementary balance sheet to the investor's interest. This supplementary statement contains the original acquisition costs for the interest to the extent that they exceed the book value of the investor's interest in the partnership's equity. For the subsequent divestment these acquisition costs reduce the amount of the capital gain that is subject to tax in Germany. The investor's taxable capital gain is recorded in addition to the current profits of the German partnership in its uniform and separate determination of profits.

Provided that the investor does not urgently depend on repatriating the appreciation of his interest in the partnership, he can avoid taxation on the capital gain by converting his interest into a share in a corporation. This can be done by means of a contribution of the partnership interest to a corporation in return for granting shares, or by changing the legal form into a corporation, both in a tax-neutral way. The tax neutrality of such a conversion requires that the acquirer of the shares in the corporation retain them for a minimum of seven years from the transaction. Not until after this time would a divestment be tax-free.

---

26 For further means of repatriation of profits in the case of exit see below *Bahns*, Repatriation by Foreign Investors of Profits from German Investments, p. 60.

Dr. Jörg W. Lüttge

Lawyer, Tax Advisor

Areas of Specialization

- International tax law
- Structuring of cross-border investments
- Mergers & acquisitions and corporate reorganizations
- Tax and corporate-law advice for family-owned businesses
- Estate planning and succession planning

Telephone (ext.) +49 228/95 94-311

Email: jwl@fgs.de

International and Domestic Aspects of German Group Taxation

by Thomas Rödder

Contents

I. Basics
  1. Introduction
  2. Conditions for the Creation of a Tax Group
     a) Tax Group for Corporate Income Tax Purposes
     b) Tax Group for Trade Tax Purposes
  3. Implications of a Valid Tax Group
     a) Tax Group for Corporate Income Tax Purposes
     b) Tax Group for Trade Tax Purposes
  4. Implications of an Invalid Tax Group
II. Pitfalls and Schemes
  1. Special Issues Involved Tax Groups with an International Dimension
     a) Controlled Entity with Two Locations
     b) Requirements for a Foreign Controlling Entity
     c) Prevention of Double Recognition of Losses
  2. Formulation of Assumption of Losses in a PLTA with a *GmbH*
  3. Execution (Application) of the PLTA
  4. Section 8b of the Corporate Income Tax Act in the case of a Tax Group
  5. Interest Barrier in the Case of a Tax Group
  6. Tax Groups and Sec. 8c of the Corporate Income Tax Act
  7. Disposal of a stake in a Controlled Entity
III. Conclusion

I. Basics

1. Introduction

In Germany, all corporations are assessed individually for corporate income tax and trade tax on the basis of their taxable income even if they belong to a corporate group. Accordingly, no provision exists for consolidating the income of different affiliated group entities for tax purposes (or indeed for any elimination of profits resulting from intercompany transactions). In view of the economic dependence of affiliated companies, this presents problems. Under current German law governing income tax, these problems are taken into account exclusively through the *'Organschaft'* approach, which involves attributing the income of a controlled entity to the entity that controls it for tax purposes. The controlling entity and one or more controlled entities together constitute a tax group.

2. Conditions for the Creation of a Tax Group

a) Tax Group for Corporate Income Tax Purposes

aa) Controlled Entity

The conditions governing tax groups formed for corporate income tax purposes are contained in Sec. 14 of the German Corporate Income Tax Act (*Körperschaftsteuergesetz*). Although Sec. 14(1) of the Corporate Income Tax Act mentions only stock corporations (*Aktiengesellschaft*) and partnerships limited by shares (*Kommanditgesellschaft auf Aktien*), a German privately held corporation (*GmbH*) can also qualify as a controlled entity pursuant to Sec. 17 of the Corporate Income Tax Act. According to this legislation, a corporation's management must be based in Germany for it to qualify as a controlled entity.

bb) Controlling Entity

Essentially, any trade or business undertaking can qualify as a controlling entity (Sec. 14(1) of the Corporate Income Tax Act). A controlling entity can therefore be a private individual or a corporate body, association or special-purpose fund that is not exempt from taxation within the meaning of Sec. 1 of the Corporate Income Tax Act or a partnership within the meaning of Sec. 15(1) sentence 1 no. 2 of the German Income Tax Act (*Einkommensteuergesetz*) (Sec. 14(1) sentence 1 no. 2 sentence 1 of the Corporate Income Tax Act).

If a controlling entity is a partnership within the meaning of Sec. 15(1) sentence 1 no. 2 of the Income Tax Act, the shares in the controlled entity must be included in the jointly held assets of the partnership (Sec. 14(1) sentence 1 no. 2 sentence 3 of the Corporate Income Tax Act). In addition, the trade or business activity of a controlling entity that is a partnership must meet specific requirements. A partnership can qualify as a controlling entity only if involved in an activity within the meaning of Sec. 15(1) no. 1 of the Income Tax Act (Sec. 14(1) sentence 1 no. 2 of the Corporate Income Tax Act).[1] Activity of a deemed trade or business nature (Sec. 15(3) no. 2 of the Income Tax Act) does not suffice.

cc) Profit and Loss Transfer Agreement and Financial Integration

The existence of a tax group also presupposes financial integration of the controlled entity into the controlling entity and requires that the controlled entity agree to and actually transfer its entire profit to the controlling entity for a period of at least five years under a profit and loss transfer agreement (hereinafter 'PTLA') within the meaning of Sec. 291(1) of the Stock Corporation Act (*Aktiengesetz*).

Financial integration means that a controlling entity has held a majority of the voting rights from its shareholding in a controlled entity without interruption

---

[1] Questions arise as to the necessary scope of trade or business activity, recognition of a management holding company, etc.

as of the beginning of the financial year in question (Sec. 14(1) sentence 1 no. 1 of the Corporate Income Tax Act). Indirect shareholdings are taken into consideration when interests in pass-through entities account for a majority of the voting rights.

Under a PTLA within the meaning of Sec. 291(1) of the Stock Corporation Act, a controlled entity agrees to transfer its entire profit to the controlling entity, which in principle means the transfer of the entire maximum amount mentioned in Sec. 301 of the Stock Corporation Act.[2] Section 302 of the Stock Corporation Act also requires that the controlling entity assume any net losses incurred in a given year by the controlled entity during the term of the agreement.

Section 14(1) sentence 1 no. 3 of the Corporate Income Tax Act stipulates that PTLAs must be entered into for at least five years and that their provisions must actually be carried out during the entire term of the agreement. There are no disadvantages associated with premature termination of a PTLA as long as the termination takes place for good cause.[3] Termination or rescission of a PTLA in the course of a financial year of a controlled entity takes effect retroactively as of the beginning of that year (Sec. 14(1) sentence 1 no. 3 of the Corporate Income Tax Act).

b) Tax Group for Trade Tax Purposes

The conditions discussed above that must be satisfied to qualify as a tax group for corporate income tax purposes also apply accordingly in respect of trade tax (see Sec. 2(2) sentence 2 in conjunction with Secs. 14 and 17 of the Corporate Income Tax Act).

3. Implications of a Valid Tax Group

a) Tax Group for Corporate Income Tax Purposes

Once the conditions for recognition as a tax group have been met, the taxable income of the controlled entity is attributed to the controlling entity. Conversely, the profit shown in the controlling entity's financial statements is eliminated when determining its taxable income.[4]

Attribution of such income means in particular that the tax profit or tax loss of the controlled entity or entities is consolidated with that of the controlling

---

2 Established intragroup capital reserves have to be distributed; see Federal Tax Court of 8 Aug. 2001, DB 2002, p. 408. The dependent corporation may transfer amounts to revenue reserves insofar as this can be economically justified on the basis of sound business judgment.
3 See on this in greater detail R 60(6) of the Corporate Income Tax Guidelines. See also the more stringent decision of the Federal Tax Court of 13 Nov. 2013, Federal Tax Court/NV 2014, p. 783.
4 This implication is not explicitly mentioned in the text of the law, but is obvious. See, for example, Federal Tax Court of 18 Dec. 2002, Federal Tax Gazette Part II, 2005, p. 49.

entity. In addition, a single entity exists for the purposes of the application of the interest barrier. The attribution of income to a controlling entity also means that the actual transfer of profit cannot be considered a dividend, which permits avoidance of dividend tax in particular, but can also prove relevant as regards Sec. 3c(2) of the Income Tax Act.[5]

The income of a controlled entity is determined according to the general rules applicable to independent corporations, which means in particular that intercompany profits on transactions carried out within the group are not eliminated. However, the special provisions contained in Sec. 15 of the Corporate Income Tax Act must be observed. That also means in particular that the exemption of income or profits (or, seen the other way around, the nondeduction of losses) pursuant to Sec. 8b of the Corporate Income Tax Act does not apply when determining the income of a controlled entity (see Sec. 15 sentence 1 no. 2 of the Corporate Income Tax Act).[6] It must be applied to the corresponding portion of income attributed to the controlling entity when determining its income if the controlling entity is eligible to benefit from this provision. Section 15 sentence 1 no. 3 of the Corporate Income Tax Act stipulates that all interest expense and income (as well as depreciation and amortization) must be attributed to the controlling entity for the purposes of applying the interest barrier.

PTLAs must cover and be applied to the entire profit of a controlled entity. As a result, Sec. 304 of the Stock Corporation Act gives nonrelated shareholders who hold a stake in a controlled entity a right to receive appropriate compensation for the loss incurred through the transfer of all profit to a controlling entity.[7]

The attribution of a controlled entity's income to a controlling entity is independent of the treatment of the actual transfer of profit for accounting purposes. In the case of any discrepancy between the two amounts, positive or negative differences may trigger different tax consequences depending on the reasons for such differences.[8]

---

5 An advantage of a tax group that should be taken into account is the avoidance of retention of capital gains tax. Moreover, the 'danger' of the burdensome results from the disclosure of a hidden distribution of dividends is in many cases eliminated since a hidden distribution of dividends is treated as an advance transfer of profit in the context of a tax group formed for the purposes of corporate income tax (see also R 61(4), 62(2) of the Corporate Income Tax Guidelines.
6 Exception: Sec. 8b(7) of the Corporate Income Tax Act. See also Sec. 15 sentence 2 of the Corporate Income Tax Act on the corresponding regulation relating to favorable double taxation treaty treatment (participation exemption).
7 The details of taxation are governed by Sec. 16 of the Corporate Income Tax Act in this case.
8 See Sec. 14(3) and (4) of the Corporate Income Tax Act.

b) Tax Group for Trade Tax Purposes

Once the conditions for recognition as a tax group have been met, a controlled entity is classified as a (dependent) permanent establishment of its controlling entity under trade tax law ('permanent establishment fiction', Sec. 2(2) sentence 2 of the German Trade Tax Act – *Gewerbesteuergesetz*). The trade tax base of the controlling entity and that of the controlled entity must, however, be determined separately without eliminating profit from intercompany transactions. The trade tax base of the controlled entity is then added to that of the controlling entity.

The use of the permanent establishment fiction means that consolidation of the trade tax bases that are determined separately cannot result in a double trade tax burden or unwarranted relief. Accordingly, for example, interest on liabilities that exist between entities belonging to a tax group is not taken into account for potential addbacks for trade tax purposes.[9]

The single tax base of a controlling entity is allocated to the municipalities in which the permanent establishments of the various members of the tax group are located on the basis of the allocation key contained in Sec. 29 of the Trade Tax Act. In the case of differences in municipal multipliers (*Hebesätze*) and/or differences in the relationships between trade or business income and wages, the formation of tax groups may result in changes in the absolute amount of the trade tax liability. In addition, the allocation of trade tax to the respective municipalities may be affected.

4. Implications of an Invalid Tax Group

If the conditions for a valid tax group pursuant to Secs. 14 and 17 of the Corporate Income Tax Act are not met, it can be assumed that a valid *Organschaft* does not exist. In such cases, the corporate income tax liability of the controlled entity will be assessed on the basis of the generally applicable provisions of tax law. In particular, the possibility of consolidating the income of a controlled entity with that of its controlling entity is then precluded. The transfer of profit to a controlling entity under a PTLA in place may not be allowed to reduce the income of its controlled entity. Such profit will regularly be considered a hidden distribution (Sec. 8(3) sentence 2 of the Corporate Income Tax Act). If, on the other hand, a controlling entity assumes the losses of a controlled entity, such losses will be considered to represent constructive equity contributions (Sec. 8(3) sentence 3 of the Corporate Income Tax Act) that are not allowed to increase the income of the controlled entity. Such constructive contributions to equity increase the tax book value of the controlling entity's stake in the tax group.

---

9 R 41(1) of the Trade Tax Guidelines (*Gewerbesteuer-Richtlinien*).

II. Pitfalls and Schemes

1. Special Issues Involved Tax Groups with an International Dimension

a) Controlled Entity with Two Locations

A controlled entity can be an entity that maintains its registered seat and place of management in Germany, but also one whose management is based in Germany and whose registered seat is in another EU/EEA country (Sec. 14(1) sentence 1 of the Corporate Income Tax Act).[10] At the practical level, the latter case is of very limited importance.[11]

b) Requirements for a Foreign Controlling Entity

The revision of Sec. 14(1) sentence 1 no. 2 of the Corporate Income Tax Act, which is a response to the Federal Tax Court decision of 9 Feb. 2011[12], is of greater importance. The Federal Tax Court is of the opinion – grounded in the prohibition of discrimination under treaty law – that a corporation having its place of management and registered seat in Germany may be the controlled entity of a controlling entity that is a trade or business enterprise located in the UK in the context of a trade tax group. One possible result is that the income and trade tax base would be attributed to a foreign controlling entity that is not taxable in Germany.

Section 14(1) no. 2 of the Corporate Income Tax Act no longer makes provision for any restrictive prerequisites as far as the location of controlling entities is concerned. The controlling entity can maintain its place of management and registered seat anywhere. What is determinative is that it has to be possible to assign the stake in a controlled entity (during the entire existence of a tax group) to a domestic permanent establishment and that the income tax and trade tax base as well as the income attributable to the permanent establishment are attributed to that location. Only if these conditions are met will a parent qualify as a suitable controlling entity.

The vaguely formulated revised legislation stipulates that a permanent establishment must validly exist under both national law and the relevant double taxation treaty and that Germany must have the right under both national law and the relevant double taxation treaty to tax the 'income to be attributed' to the permanent establishment. This can actually only mean recognition of the attributed income and the trade tax base of the controlled entity. The wording of the revised legislation could, however, be understood to mean that a prerequisite for the existence of a tax group is that all income to be attributed to a

---

10 The reverse scenario as regards the registered seat and place of management is not yet covered.
11 Since, for example, the problems of cross-border PLTAs remain unchanged.
12 Federal Tax Court of 11 Feb. 2011, Federal Tax Gazette Part II, 2012, p. 106; nonapplication decree of 27 Dec. 2011, Federal Tax Gazette Part I, 2012, p. 119.

permanent establishment must also otherwise be taxable in Germany. This would make no sense at all.[13]

The problem is compounded in actual practice, especially in the case of controlling entities in the form of partnerships that have the status of management holding companies and also have partners termed 'co-entrepreneurs' (*Mitunternehmer*) who are based in other countries. According to the view taken here, when a co-entrepreneur based in another country does not maintain a foreign business location but only resides abroad, the investment in the controlled entity should be functionally attributed to the domestic permanent establishment. In that regard the need for clarification is urgent in actual practice.

c) Prevention of Double Recognition of Losses

Section 14(1) no. 5 of the Corporate Income Tax Act stipulates that losses of a controlling entity or a controlled entity are not considered for the purposes of domestic taxation if they are taken into account in a foreign state in connection with taxation of the controlling entity, the controlled entity or some other person. The practical importance of this provision has also not yet been conclusively clarified. It could mean a very far-reaching limitation of loss recognition for domestic tax groups, the purpose of such a restriction would in many respects not be readily understandable. The wording of the law goes too far since the actual intention was to limit application to cases of two locations outside the EU and the EEA. There is a danger of unreasonable taxation (with profits being recognized twice, but losses only once).

According to the wording, this could also affect even the loss of a permanent establishment of a controlled entity taxed using the credit method. This could also be taken to include the loss from a permanent establishment of a controlling entity taxed using the credit method that is not attributed within the tax group. It could also be taken to mean the loss from an inbound investment made by a corporation that is subject to limited tax liability and qualifies as a controlling entity by virtue of the domestic permanent establishment.

Such a broad construction of the wording of the new rule should, however, be clearly rejected. The sole purpose of the provision is to prevent recognition of a loss in two jurisdictions for tax purposes.

It is likely that, for example, the new rule covers the case of double deduction of special business expenses (*Sonderbetriebsausgaben*) by controlling entities that are partnerships. Simply referring to the credit method, on the other hand, could not be justified. Avoiding double taxation by applying the credit method does not constitute a loss double dip within the meaning of Sec. 14(1) no. 5 of the Corporate Income Tax Act (New Version). Insofar as it might seem necessary, construction of the law would require purposive interpretation.

---

13 Income of permanent establishments exempted in accordance with a double taxation treaty can in no case be affected by the requirement.

It would be correct to again limit the provision to entities with two locations (management in Germany, and registered seat in another country) in non-EU/EEA cases.[14]

2. Formulation of Assumption of Losses in a PLTA with a *GmbH*

According to Sec. 17 sentence 2 no. 2 of the Corporate Income Tax Act (Old Version), provisions of PLTAs governing the assumption of losses from controlled entities in the form of a *GmbH* are (were) required to comply with the provisions contained in Sec. 302 of the Stock Corporation Act. This means that it is (was) necessary not only to agree to assume losses pursuant to Sec. 302(1) of the Stock Corporation Act, but also to comply with the provisions contained in Sec. 302(3) and Sec. 302(4) of the Stock Corporation Act.[15] The Federal Tax Court has adopted this view in its established case law[16] although application of Sec. 302 of the Stock Corporation Act is also, by analogy, compulsory in legislation governing *GmbHs*.

The new version of Sec. 17 sentence 2 no. 2 of the Corporate Income Tax Act that followed requires that PLTAs with controlling entities contain reference to the most recent version of Sec. 302 of the Stock Corporation Act in its entirety in order for a tax group to be valid.[17]

If this makes it advisable or necessary to modify a PLTA[18], such modification must take place before 1 Jan. 2015 unless the tax group is dissolved prior to that date. In each case the correct amount of loss must actually have been assumed in the years preceding the change in the PLTA or the dissolution of the tax group.[19] If the required contractual amendment is made, the change is not considered to represent the beginning of a new five-year minimum term for the

---

14 And clearer purposive information on when losses in other countries are 'taken into account'. Whether or not the provision is also of importance for trade tax should be clearly defined; in anticipation of Federal Finance Ministry of 29 May 2013, *GmbH* Guidelines, 2013, p. 728.
15 According to the Federal Finance Ministry of 16 Dec. 2005, Federal Tax Gazette Part I, 2006, p. 12, only for PLTAs as of 1 Jan. 2006. See now, however, also Federal Tax Court of 24 July 2013, DStR 2013, p. 1939; reference to Sec. 302(2) of the Stock Corporation Act is (was) not necessary.
16 For example, in Federal Tax Court of 3 March 2010, Federal Tax Court/NV 2010, p. 1132.
17 Possible formulation: "The provisions contained in Sec. 302 of the Stock Corporation Act as most recently amended apply accordingly." See also Federal Finance Ministry of 29 May 2013, *GmbH* Guidelines 2013, p. 728.
18 There is some question as to whether the new transitional solution will remedy all PLTA references to Sec. 302 of the Stock Corporation Act that are deficient because of the previous understanding of requirements. This is in fact the case according to current prevailing opinion. See also Federal Tax Court of 24 July 2013, DStR 2013, p. 1939.
19 Only if there were losses. See Federal Tax Court of 24 July 2013, DStR 2013, p. 1939.

PLTA. The prevalent opinion currently found in scholarly literature and in practice is that this is also the case if there is actually no need for any change.[20]

In practice, the reform may potentially require considerable work to comply with formalities since most PLTAs currently include no reference to the most recent version of Sec. 302 of the Stock Corporation Act and as a rule must or should be changed accordingly by the end of 2014. This is especially inconvenient for stock-listed controlling entities since PLTAs must be approved by the shareholders.

3. Execution (Application) of the PLTA

The requirement contained in Sec. 14(1) sentence 1 no. 3 of the Corporate Income Tax Act on transfers of profit means that the entire profit of a controlled entity must be transferred during the term of a PLTA; the amount transferred may neither exceed nor be less than the actual profit. This follows in particular from Sec. 301 of the Stock Corporation Act, which specifies the upper limit to the transfer of profit, and Sec. 14(1) sentence 1 of the Corporate Income Tax Act, which stipulates that a controlled entity must transfer its entire profit.

In this context, profit is generally taken to mean net profit for the year as determined under trade or business law taking into account Sec. 301 of the Stock Corporation Act and other restrictions of such transfers contained in provisions of commercial and corporate law. According to the case law of the Federal Court of Justice, net profit for the year as determined objectively through proper application of generally accepted accounting principles is determinative in such cases; the actual financial statements – even if they have legal effect and are not invalid – are not determinative.[21] It is, however, unclear whether every deviation from the provisions of the German Commercial Code (*Handelsgesetzbuch*) results in the transfer of an incorrect amount. The tax administration has considered immaterial errors to be irrelevant in individual cases.[22]

According to the view taken here, what is referred to as the 'doctrine of subjective error' (*subjektiver Fehlerbegriff*) is a significant element of the German generally accepted accounting principles. This is why any accounting operation or valuation that would have been considered acceptable by a conscientious and diligent businessman at the time of preparing the financial statements for accounting purposes also results in correct financial statements for the purposes of compliance with commercial law even if it should subsequently be found that certain factual or legal assumptions made by the businessman were incorrect.

However, according to the view taken here, execution (i.e. actual application) of a PLTA could conceivably be a problem due to a lack of proper financial

---

20 See also Federal Finance Ministry of 29 May 2013, *GmbH* Guidelines 2013, p. 728.
21 Federal Court of Justice of 14 Feb. 2005, Federal Law Gazette, 2005, p. 1104.
22 Forgotten accrual of interest: Federal Finance Ministry, Federal Tax Gazette Part I, 2008, p. 280; Corporation income tax credit balance erroneously established by controlling entity: Hanover Regional Tax Office, DStR 2009, p. 325.

statements that comply with commercial law or failure to conform to corporate law (e.g. in the form of a PLTA, the Stock Corporation Act or the Commercial Code). In particular, such noncompliance includes failure to offset losses that predate a tax group against profit (see Sec. 301 of the Stock Corporation Act) and failure to observe other restrictions governing the transfer of profit.

The only way to rectify such cases in the past was to adjust incorrect financial statements prepared for accounting purposes retroactively 'at the source', which in practice could (can) remedy the past situation. The details are, however, to some extent unclear and are not handled uniformly in practice.

The revision of Sec. 14(1) sentence 1 no. 3 of the Corporate Income Tax Act that became law against this background contains a fiction ('is deemed') of the proper execution of a PLTA. The following assumptions are made:

- the annual financial statements contain accounting errors[23], but have been validly adopted;[24]
- the error was not discernible (as defined by the doctrine of subjective error); this prerequisite can be replaced by an unqualified audit opinion or similar;
- the error is corrected after detection by the tax administration unless the error need not be corrected in the financial accounts.

If the prerequisites for the new fiction do not apply, the only alternative is to resort to the options for adjustment mentioned above (retroactive adjustment of statements prepared for financial reporting purposes) from previous practice.

4. Section 8b of the Corporate Income Tax Act in the Case of a Tax Group

Under certain conditions, 95% of a corporation's dividend income and profits from the disposal of shares are exempt from taxation pursuant to Sec. 8b of the Corporate Income Tax Act.

The possibility of applying Sec. 8b of the Corporate Income Tax Act is, however, generally precluded by Sec. 15 sentence 1 no. 2 of the Corporate Income Tax Act in the case of controlled entities belonging to an existing tax group for the purposes of corporate income tax[25]. If the income of a controlled entity that is attributed to a controlling entity includes income and profits within the meaning of Sec. 8b of the Corporate Income Tax Act as well as expenses or losses related to such amounts within the meaning of Sec. 8b(3) of the Corporate In-

---

23 The requirement based on 'accounting errors' in the annual financial statements is as it were the door to the 'rectifying' fiction, which is why the question of the interpretation of this term is of considerable importance in practice. An entry in financial statements is an error if it does not comply with generally accepted accounting principles. Incorrect valuations (breaches of valuation rules) are clearly included the same way.
24 Valid ratification of the annual financial statements is the norm and will seldom tend to present problems in practice.
25 Section 8b(7) of the Corporate Income Tax Act is applied at the level of the controlled entity.

come Tax Act, Sec. 8b of the Corporate Income Tax Act does, however, apply to the determination of the income of the controlling entity if the latter is eligible for such treatment; otherwise Sec. 3 no. 40 of the Income Tax Act applies in conjunction with Sec. 3c(2) of the Income Tax Act.

This 'gross method' permits uniform determination of the income of a controlled entity while taking into account the situation of the controlling entity. This is likely to result in simplification, especially in the case of controlling entities that are partnerships consisting of both corporations and private individuals. Section 15 sentence 1 no. 2 of the Corporate Income Tax Act applies accordingly to shares of profits from stakes in foreign entities that are tax-exempt under the provisions of a double taxation treaty.

Application of Sec. 3c(2) of the Income Tax Act pursuant to Sec. 15 sentence 1 no. 2 of the Corporate Income Tax Act can refer only to expenses included in the income of a controlled entity attributed to a controlling entity. This does not pertain to expenses that are related to the investment in a controlled entity (e.g. finance costs for the acquisition of a stake in a controlled entity, which in turn generates income within the meaning of Sec. 8b of the Corporate Income Tax Act). There is, however, some question as to whether Sec. 3c(2) of the Income Tax Act applies to such expenses of controlling entities that are partnerships when dividends received by a controlling entity are partially exempt from taxation pursuant to Sec. 3 no. 40 of the Income Tax Act.

5. Interest Barrier in the Case of a Tax Group

Under German law, finance costs are generally deductible business expenses. What is referred to as an 'interest barrier' (Sec. 4h(1) sentence 1 of the Income Tax Act) may cause restrictions. According to this provision, an undertaking may deduct interest expense in an amount equal to that of its interest income (in that regard the two items initially offset each another), but expense deducted in excess of that amount may not exceed 30% of the corresponding taxable profit (or income in the case of corporations) plus special depreciation and amortization and less interest 'EBITDA'.

According to Sec. 15 sentence 1 no. 3 of the Corporate Income Tax Act, controlled entities and their controlling entity are treated as a single undertaking in terms of the interest barrier. This also applies to trade tax.

Application of the interest barrier means that interest is (ideally only temporarily) not deductible at the level of the payer. Nondeductible interest is not reclassified at the level of the recipient of the interest or the shareholder.

According to Sec. 4h(1) sentences 2 and 3 of the Income Tax Act, interest expense that is not deducted is carried forward to ensuing financial years (interest carryforward). It then increases the interest expense for those financial years, but not the corresponding profit.

Interest expense affected by the interest barrier is therefore only temporarily considered a nondeductible business expense. It can be carried forward to future financial years and then deducted in compliance with the rules governing the application of the interest barrier.[26]

An interest carryforward that is not used is forfeited in the event of dissolution or disposal (Sec. 4h(5) sentence 1 of the Income Tax Act)[27]. According to Sec. 8a(1) sentence 3 of the Corporate Income Tax Act, Sec. 8c of the Corporate Income Tax Act (see below) also applies to interest carryforwards.

An EBITDA carryforward is a carryforward to the following five financial years of EBITDA that has not been completely used. That means that interest expense in an amount not to exceed an EBITDA carryover from previous years can be deducted in cases where interest expense has not been deducted because of the basic 30% rule, in which case the least recent EBITDA carryforwards must be used first. EBITDA carryforwards that are not used are forfeited after five financial years. EBITDA carryforwards are also forfeited upon dissolution and disposal.[28]

The following cases should be noted:

- The interest barrier does not apply if interest expense in excess of interest income is less than EUR 3 million (Sec. 4h(2) sentence 1(a) of the Income Tax Act). The limit applies for all undertakings; it also applies to undertakings subject to payment of corporate income tax.[29]
- The interest barrier does not apply to undertakings that do not belong to a group (Sec. 4h(2) sentence 1 (b) of the Income Tax Act). In actual practice, however, nongroups are seldom found in cases involving *Organschaft*.
- The interest barrier does not apply unless the equity ratio of the undertaking is worse than that of the group, in which case a tolerance of only 1% is allowed. The comparison of equity ratios must be made on the basis of financial statements for the end of the previous financial year (Sec. 4h(2) sentence 1(c) of the Income Tax Act). The equity ratios must be determined in accordance with IFRS for both the undertaking and the group.[30]

---

26 In the case of a tax group, the carryover is at the level of the controlling entity. Interest carryforwards of the controlled entity that predate the tax group should be 'frozen' at the level of the tax group (Federal Finance Ministry of 4 July 2008, Federal Tax Gazette Part I, 2008, p. 718 marginal no. 48).
27 The dissolution or assignment of business units should also be harmful although the wording of the law does not support this. According to the Federal Finance Ministry of 4 July 2008, Federal Tax Gazette Part I, 2008, p. 718 marginal no. 47, the departure of a controlled entity from the tax group also had to be considered as a partially harmful dissolution of a business unit.
28 Termination of a tax group does not result in *pro-rata* forfeiture of the EBITDA carryforward established during the term of the agreement if viewed properly.
29 It also applies for the tax group only once (Federal Finance Ministry of 4 July 2008, Federal Tax Gazette Part I, 2008, p. 718 marginal no. 57).
30 If necessary, financial statements have to be prepared for the tax group as a subgroup.

6. Tax Groups and Sec. 8c of the Corporate Income Tax Act

The offsetting of previous and current losses of a corporation may under certain conditions be disallowed (Sec. 8c of the Corporate Income Tax Act[31]). If more than 25% of the issued capital, membership rights, shareholder rights or voting rights of a corporation is/are assigned, directly or indirectly, to a purchaser or to a related party of the purchaser or in the event of any similar occurrence (harmful acquisition) within five years, any deficit (unused losses) that has not been covered or deducted as of the time of such an acquisition is no longer deductible. Regardless of the above, any losses unused prior to the occurrence of the harmful acquisition are no longer deductible in their entirety if within five years more than 50% of the issued capital, membership rights, shareholder rights or voting rights of a corporation is/are assigned, directly or indirectly, to a purchaser or to a related party of the purchaser or in the event of any similar occurrence within five years. A group of purchasers with similar interests also qualifies as a purchaser in this context.

The provision covering nonrecognition of losses is in practice accompanied by important simplifications in the form of a 'group provision' and a 'hidden reserves provision'. According to the group provision, losses are not forfeited if the same person holds, directly or indirectly, 100% of both the entity assigning the interest in the loss-making company and the entity acquiring it. According to the hidden reserves provision, the loss is forfeited in the case of a harmful acquisition only if the unused losses exceed the *pro-rata* share or all the taxable hidden reserves of the domestic operating assets of the entity incurring the loss.

In the disputed opinion of the tax administration, the hidden reserves of controlled entities should not be taken into account for the purposes of determining hidden reserves at the level of the controlling entity[32] even if it would have been possible to offset them against a loss (carryforward) of the controlling entity if they had been realized without the occurrence of a harmful acquisition in the meantime.

Section 8c of the Corporate Income Tax Act means that losses that are not covered or deducted prior to a harmful acquisition are no longer deductible. The legal implication of Sec. 8c of the Corporate Income Tax Act thus affects in particular the assumption and carryforward of the loss of the affected entity.

If a shareholding is acquired in the course of the year[33], Sec. 8c of the Corporate Income Tax Act also affects the cumulative loss incurred up to the time of the relevant purchase. Profit realized up to the time of the acquisition of the share-

---

31 Section 8c of the Corporate Income Tax Act also applies to trade tax, see Sec. 10a sentence 10 of the Trade Tax Act. Section 8c of the Corporate Income Tax Act also applies to a trade tax shortfall of a party to a partnership insofar as this can be attributed to a partnership directly through a corporation or indirectly through a partnership.
32 Marginal no. 61 *et seq.* of the draft circular of the Federal Finance Ministry (*BMF-E*).
33 Acquisition at the 'stroke of midnight' does not qualify as an acquisition in the course of the year.

holding can be used to offset losses that have not yet been used.[34] Section 8c of the Corporate Income Tax Act then applies to the remaining unused loss carry-forwards.

Special questions arise in the case of a harmful acquisition of a controlling entity in the course of a year.[35] In the opinion of the administration, the *pro-rata* share of negative income that has not been attributed should be subject to the fiscal implication of Sec. 8c(1) of the Corporate Income Tax Act.[36] The administration argues that the loss sustained by a controlled entity and a controlling entity must be reduced in the case of an acquisition in the course of the year in each case prior to attribution of income at the level of the respective entity according to their relative shares of the profit or loss in the year in question.

Moreover, the tax administration is of the opinion that the rule according to which profit realized up to the time of the acquisition of the shareholding can be used to offset losses should not apply to controlled entities.[37] According to the administration, controlled entities cannot have as yet unused losses from previous years that could be offset against profits generated up to the time of the harmful acquisition due to the attribution of the income of a controlled entity to a controlling entity. The administration takes the view that losses incurred before the creation of the tax group may not be offset against profits arising within the group (Sec. 15 sentence 1 no. 1 of the Corporate Income Tax Act).

7. Disposal of a stake in a Controlled Entity

If a stake in a controlled entity is sold, it is often in the interests of the purchaser to create a tax group with the acquired subsidiary with effect as of the date of the acquisition of the shareholding. From the point of view of the seller, on the other hand, an existing tax group should as a rule – in line with the sale – end precisely with the disposal of the shareholding.

In view of the timing requirements – the prerequisite for integration must exist as of the beginning of the financial year of the controlled entity (Sec. 14(1) sentence 1 no. 1 of the Corporate Income Tax Act) – what is referred to as the 'midnight rule' comes to mind as a structuring option[38] that would in the indi-

---

34 Federal Tax Court of 30 Nov. 2012, Federal Tax Gazette Part II, 2012, p. 360. Dis. opin. also Federal Finance Ministry of 4 July 2008, Federal Tax Gazette Part I, 2008, p. 736 marginal no. 31. According to this opinion, one effect of Sec. 8c(1) of the Corporate Income Tax Act is that unused loss carryforwards cannot be offset against profit accrued in the course of the year in the case of a harmful acquisition of a shareholding in the course of a year.
35 In the case of the acquisition of shares in a controlled entity, on the other hand, only loss carryforwards that predate creation of the tax group and a current loss of the controlled entity can be affected.
36 Federal Finance Ministry of 4 July 2008, Federal Tax Gazette Part I, 2008, p. 736 marginal no. 33.
37 Marginal no. 33 of the Federal Finance Ministry circular.
38 See also R 59(2) sentences 1 and 2 of the Corporate Income Tax Guidelines.

vidual case make possible a seamless transition in terms of chronological requirements from the seller to the purchaser through disposal with effect as of the turn of the year. Termination of an existing PLTA and conclusion of a new one would in this case also present no problems as regards fiscal considerations.[39] The situation can also be facilitated in the individual case by changing the financial years of the controlled entity.[40] In this context it must be kept in mind that the required amendments to bylaws must be entered in the commercial register prior to the end of the short financial year.

III. Conclusion

The provision governing *Organschaft* for income tax purposes ranks among the most important in German corporate tax law. A valid *Organschaft* can produce numerous tax advantages, including in particular the possibility of consolidating the profit or loss of fiscally independent legal entities. Due to these tax advantages, tax auditors tend to focus on the validity of such tax groups. Not least due to the many cases of very formal – and occasionally disputed and unclear – requirements for such tax groups, it is frequently necessary to seek clarification from the courts. The German legislature would therefore be well advised to revive the original plans of the current government for modern group taxation that were dropped due to the lack of funding.

---

39 Pursuant to R 60(6) sentence 2 of the Corporate Income Tax Guidelines, the tax administration always views the disposal of the shares in a controlled entity as good cause for the termination of a tax group. See, however, Federal Tax Court of 13 Nov. 2013, Federal Tax Gazette Part I 2014, p. 486.
40 See R 59(2) sentence 3(3) of the Corporate Income Tax Guidelines.

Prof. Dr. Thomas Rödder

Public Auditor, Tax Advisor

Areas of Specialization

- Taxation of corporate groups
- Taxation of family-owned businesses
- Mergers & acquisitions and corporate reorganizations
- Structuring of German investments abroad
- Tax accounting
- Tax litigation

Telephone (ext.) +49 228/95 94-227 /-251

Email: thomas.roedder@fgs.de

Controlled Foreign Company Legislation

by Jens Schönfeld

Contents

I. Introduction
II. Definition of a CFC
III. Definition of Control
IV. Definition of Low Taxation
V. Attributed Income and Calculation of Income
   1. Transactional Approach for Passive Low-Taxed Income
   2. German Tax Rules for Calculating Attributed Income
VI. Domestic Taxpayers to Whom the Income of a CFC is Attributed
VII. Exemptions from CFC Taxation
   1. Active Income Test
   2. De minimis test
   3. EU Test
   4. Publicly Traded Company Test
VIII. Relief Provisions
   1. Foreign Taxes
   2. Losses
   3. Subsequent Dividends and Capital Gains
IX. CFC Legislation and Transparent Entities
X. Tax Treaty Issues

I. Introduction

Germany's Controlled Foreign Company (CFC) legislation was introduced in 1972 with the International Transactions Tax Reform Act (*Außensteuerreformgesetz*).[1] The corresponding provisions are still in effect in sections 7–14 of the German Foreign Tax Act (*Außensteuergesetz*).

Initially, the idea behind the CFC legislation was to prevent deferral of taxation that resulted from having CFCs retain income. This was achieved by lifting the corporate veil of CFCs and attributing their income to their shareholders, who then had to declare this income in Germany regardless of whether it was actually distributed. The original idea behind the CFC legislation must be seen in view of the fact that income from interests in foreign associated or subsidiary undertakings was fully subject to taxation. The sole purpose of the CFC legislation was therefore to advance the time of distribution for tax purposes. This was justified by arguing that shareholders were able to determine the time of distribution by CFCs. Even at that time, this argument was, however, not very convincing because of the German concept of control.

Dividend income received by German companies from interests in domestic and foreign entities has not been taxable since the beginning of this century.

---

1 *Gesetz zur Wahrung der steuerlichen Gleichmäßigkeit bei Auslandsbeziehungen und zur Verbesserung der steuerlichen Wettbewerbslage bei Auslandsinvestitionen* of 8 Sept. 1972 (Federal Law Gazette Part I 1972, p. 1713).

CFC legislation also took on a new purpose in the context of this paradigm change. Unilateral exemption from taxation was supposed to apply for foreign income from interests in associated or subsidiary undertakings only if that income had already been subject to adequate taxation or was derived from business activities that produce active income. The purpose of the CFC legislation is to negate any benefit from excessively low taxation. This is achieved by attributing passive low-taxed income of CFCs to their domestic shareholders. Active income and passive high-taxed income are not subject to CFC taxation (referred to as the "transactional approach"). Shareholders incur a tax liability from income attributed to them regardless of whether that income is actually distributed. CFC legislation previously had an effect on timing only, since it eliminated deferred taxation, but it also increases the taxpayer's tax base.

II. Definition of a CFC

A CFC presupposes the existence of an entity that is a company within the meaning of the German Corporate Income Tax Act (*Körperschaftsteuergesetz*) (Sec. 7(1) of the Foreign Tax Act) for the purposes of German tax law. This involves an initial assessment of the effective nature of the foreign entity for the purposes of application of German law. Whether the undertaking is a partnership or a corporate entity under foreign civil law is therefore immaterial. It is also irrelevant whether the taxation of the company under foreign tax law is transparent or opaque. Only the perspective of German tax law is relevant.

Both the registered office and management of the CFC must be located in another country (Sec. 7(1) of the Foreign Tax Act). If one of them is located in Germany, the CFC legislation is not applicable. This is understandable since the entity in Germany would in that case be fully taxable. The location under a double taxation treaty is also immaterial.

Classification as a CFC does not depend on the foreign country in which the undertaking is located. German CFC legislation relies on no official black, gray or white list of specific countries that would be relevant for the purposes of determining treatment as a CFC. Certain peculiarities apply in the case of EU/EEA countries, but they concern legal consequences only.

III. Definition of Control

The normal CFC legislation assumes that more than 50% of the shares or the voting rights in a CFC can be attributed to resident German taxpayers (exclusively or with nonresident German taxpayers within the meaning of Sec. 2 of the Foreign Tax Act) (Sec. 7(2) of the Foreign Tax Act; hereinafter referred to as 'domestic shareholders'). It is therefore of no importance whether more than 50% of the shares in the CFC are held by a single domestic shareholder. In fact, a stake of less than 50% held by a domestic shareholder also suffices if domestic shareholders together hold an aggregate stake of more than 50% of the shares or voting rights in the CFC. This can also happen by pure chance, which calls into question the justification behind the CFC legislation, for it is thoroughly conceivable that individuals holding a stake in a CFC who are unaware of one another's existence could be subject to CFC taxation without knowing it. There is also, quite correctly, some doubt as to whether an individual who has no significant control over a CFC would even be able to fulfill the duties associated with CFC taxation (such as determination of income and determination of amount of low tax paid).

Indirect stakes are also taken into account for the purposes of determining aggregate stakes (Sec. 7(2) sentence 2 and Sec. 7(3) of the Foreign Tax Act). The situation prevailing at the end of the financial year of the foreign entity is determinative for the purposes of establishing ownership. Changes in the course of the year are therefore irrelevant as regards ownership of stakes for tax purposes. The sole criterion is whether domestic shareholders hold more than 50% of the shares or voting rights in a foreign entity as of the end of its fiscal year.

If the CFC receives what is referred to as 'financial investment income', control by a domestic shareholder is not a necessary prerequisite. In fact, even a stake of 1% held by a domestic shareholder is sufficient (Sec. 7(6) sentence 1 of the Foreign Tax Act) for such purposes. Financial investment income is defined as income derived from holding or managing currency, receivables, securities, investments and similar assets or from the increase in value thereof (Sec. 7(6)a of the Foreign Tax Act). This income may under exceptional circumstances be considered to constitute active income if the taxpayer can demonstrate that it derives from activities that support the pursuit of active business activity by the foreign entity.

When a CFC receives exclusively or nearly exclusively (90%) financial investment income, even a stake of less than 1% can result in CFC taxation. This does not, however, apply if the shares of such a CFC are regularly traded on a recognized stock exchange (Sec. 7(6) sentence 3 of the Foreign Tax Act).

IV. Definition of Low Taxation

Taxation is considered to be low if the passive income of a CFC is subject to an effective burden of less than 25% (Sec. 8(3) sentence 1 of the Foreign Tax Act). As a result the nominal foreign tax rate to be applied to the CFC is unimportant. Effective foreign taxation is solely determinative.

In the case of CFCs that receive both active and passive income, the low-tax limit applies only to their passive income. The amount of passive income is determined by applying the German rules for the determination of earnings and profits. As a result, taxation may be found to be lower even if the effective foreign tax burden exceeds 25%. According to the German tax authorities, mere timing differences (e.g. due to differences in respect of depreciation and amortization between German and foreign law) should not result in a finding of low taxation. The same applies if foreign taxation lies under 25% only because losses from active business activities or passive high-taxed activities are offset against passive income. This also applies across legal entities in the case of CFCs that are subject to a foreign group taxation system.

A special provision was introduced to counteract what is referred to as the 'Malta model'. This model involves applying a high tax rate to the passive income of Maltese companies to escape the application of CFC legislation. When dividends are then distributed, they are accompanied by tax credits. That means that the dividends constitute low-taxed income, but dividend payments to a CFC qualify as active income. The tax credits must then be taken into account when determining the foreign tax burden (Sec. 8(3) sentence 2 of the Foreign Tax Act).

It must be borne in mind here that foreign taxes must not only be legally due, but also actually remitted. As a result, taxation can also be low if foreign income is subject to a high tax rate but the tax is not remitted, for example in the case of tax evasion.

No binding black, gray or white lists exist for the purposes of identifying low-tax jurisdictions.

The low-tax limit of 25% corresponded to the corporate income tax rate prior to the enactment of the 2008 corporate income tax reform. Currently there is no explicit parallel between the low-tax limit and the level of German taxation. It would at best be possible to argue that the low-tax limit is based on the sum of corporate income tax (15%) and typical trade tax (approximately 15%). However, that fails to convince since foreign tax can be offset only against corporate income tax. According to current law, foreign tax cannot be offset against trade tax. This can result in distortions.

V. Attributed Income and Calculation of Income

1. Transactional Approach for Passive Low-Taxed Income

Only passive low-taxed income of CFCs is attributed to their domestic shareholders for the purposes of CFC taxation. Active income and passive high-taxed income are not subject to CFC taxation. What constitutes active income is defined in a conclusive, highly complex catalog (Sec. 8(1) of the Foreign Tax Act). If a given activity of a CFC cannot be subsumed under one of the activities in the catalog, the corresponding income is considered passive. The structure – in very simplified form – of the catalog is described below.

All income from agriculture and forestry (Sec. 8(1) no. 1 of the Foreign Tax Act) is considered active. The same applies to income from the production and processing of goods as well as from the extraction of mineral resources (Sec. 8(1) no. 2 of the Foreign Tax Act). The operation of a financial institution or insurance undertaking is on principle also considered an active business activity unless most business is conducted with domestic German shareholders or parties related to them (Sec. 8(1) no. 3 of the Foreign Tax Act).

Trading activities also qualify as active business. This principle does not, however, apply to transactions between CFCs and domestic shareholders or a party related to such shareholders. Nevertheless, a taxpayer may also submit proof to the effect that a CFC disposes of an operational facility that was set up for trading purposes and is generally involved in the conduct of such business and that such business is conducted without the tainted involvement of a domestic shareholder or any party related to a domestic shareholder (Sec. 8(1) no. 4 of the Foreign Tax Act). Essentially the same also applies in the case of services (Sec. 8(1) no. 5 of the Foreign Tax Act).

The commercial exploitation of IP, on the other hand, qualifies as an active business activity only if the IP is the product of the CFC's own research and development activity (Sec. 8(1) no. 6(a) of the Foreign Tax Act). The rental of real estate qualifies as an active business activity only if the proceeds would be exempted from taxation in Germany under a double taxation treaty if received directly (without the CFC) (Sec. 8(1) no. 6(b) of the Foreign Tax Act). The rental of movables qualifies as an active business activity only if the CFC disposes of an operational facility that was set up to conduct such rentals and is generally involved in the conduct of such business and the activity is carried out without the tainted involvement of a domestic shareholder or any party related to a domestic shareholder (Sec. 8(1) no. 6(c) of the Foreign Tax Act).

Interest may qualify as active income only under exceptional circumstances, namely if evidence is provided that the CFC borrowed the capital in another country and made it available to foreign entities involved in an active business activity, or to domestic entities. Given the many flows of capital found in practice, it is hardly likely that it would be possible to provide such evidence (Sec. 8(1) no. 7 of the Foreign Tax Act).

Dividends that a CFC receives from its own subsidiaries qualify as active income without any reservations (Sec. 8(1) no. 8 of the Foreign Tax Act). The reason for this is that the CFC legislation also applies at the level of a foreign subsidiary of a CFC (and lower tiered entities). That ensures adequate taxation at level of the foreign associate or subsidiary of the CFC, which permits the exemption of subsequent dividends from taxation. The same applies in principle to any capital gains that the CFC would realize upon disposal of its stake in such a subsidiary (Sec. 8(1) no. 9 of the Foreign Tax Act). This would not, however, apply to that share of the capital gains that derives from the financial investment assets of the subsidiary.

The proceeds from a foreign transformation that the CFC is involved in would also essentially constitute active income. However, this requires – in very simple terms – that the transformation could have been carried out at book values if it had taken place in Germany. In addition, no company that has tainted financial investment assets may be involved in the transformation (Sec. 8(1) no. 10 of the Foreign Tax Act).

In the event that an activity cannot be subsumed under one of the subparagraphs of the catalog of activities, but this passive activity constitutes part of an active business activity in terms of functional considerations, the corresponding income for the passive activity also qualifies as active (referred to as the 'functional approach'). This becomes important, for example, if a foreign production entity terminates its activity by selling off the assets used for its production activity. The 'sale' itself constitutes a passive activity since it cannot be subsumed under any of the paragraphs of the catalog of activities. On the other hand, the disposal of active assets constitutes the final act of active production, which means the sale can be assigned to the active production under the functional approach. The same applies to interest on the investment of surplus liquidity, as long as the investment does not constitute a dedicated activity within the undertaking. In practice, it is difficult to draw clear lines in many cases.

The catalog mentioned above essentially dates from the time the CFC legislation was adopted and therefore no longer reflects the reality of a modern industrial and service society. Calls to revise the catalog have quite rightly been issued, but the German legislature has failed to respond to date.

2. German Tax Rules for Calculating Attributed Income

Attributed income is calculated on the basis of the German rules for determining earnings and profits (Sec. 10(3) of the Foreign Tax Act). How income is determined in host countries is of no relevance. In practice, income for the purposes of German tax law is derived from income calculated on the basis of the corresponding foreign rules. This involves making appropriate adjustments.

The CFC legislation also applies for lower-tiered foreign companies of CFCs (Sec. 14 of the Foreign Tax Act). As regards domestic subsidiaries of a CFC, this applies only to REIT companies. In practice, the income of a lower-tiered company is attributed to the CFC tier above it. This income increases the income attributed to the CFC.

VI. Domestic Taxpayers to Whom the Income of a CFC is Attributed

CFC income is attributed to the fully taxable shareholders of the CFCs in Germany. Unlike other foreign CFC regimes, no minimum interest is required on the part of the shareholder other than domestic control. In practice, income is attributed in the form of a deemed dividend (Sec. 10(1) of the Foreign Tax Act). The deemed flow of funds takes place a logical second after the end of the financial year of the CFC (Sec. 10(2) of the Foreign Tax Act). Deemed dividends do not benefit from the general tax exemption for intercorporate dividends. The recipients are liable for payment of corporate income tax and trade tax on deemed dividends. Partners of a CFC who are subject to income tax are also subject to CFC taxation, but this is of no significant practical relevance in the present context of groups of companies.

CFC taxation does not apply in cases in which both the shareholder and the CFC are domiciled in Germany for tax purposes. It is, however, conceivable that German income received by a CFC located abroad will be subject to CFC taxation. It is unlikely that this was the intention of the legislature, but it has become possible due to the fact that the reduction in the corporate income tax rate makes it lower than the low-tax limit under the CFC legislation since a taxation of less than 25% can also result for German income. This entails the possibility of significant unusable foreign tax credits.

VII. Exemptions from CFC Taxation

1. Active Income Test

Due to the use of the transactional approach, the essential exception from CFC taxation involves providing proof that CFC income derives from active business.

2. De minimis test

Provision is also made for a *de minimis* rule, which is, however, virtually irrelevant when dealing with groups of companies. Under this rule, gross passive income of a CFC may not exceed 10% of its total gross income. The attributable income from this CFC may also not exceed EUR 80,000 (Sec. 9 of the Foreign Tax Act).

3. EU Test

CFC legislation is applicable only to foreign undertakings, not to domestic entities. This discriminatory effect very soon led to conjecture that the CFC legislation was in violation of EU law.

The German legislature ignored these reservations until the European Court of Justice's ruling in the Cadbury Schweppes case.[2] The German tax authorities reacted to the court's ruling with an exhaustive ministerial decree.[3] This decree gives domestic shareholders of CFCs located within the EU or EEA the opportunity to provide proof to the effect that the CFCs are involved in the pursuit of a genuine economic activity in their countries of domicile. It provides a very detailed description of the proof that must be furnished for such purposes. However, in its final judgment in the Columbus Container Services matter, the Federal Tax Court found that the burden of proof called for by the ministerial decree did not satisfy the standards set out by the European Court of Justice in the Cadbury Schweppes case.[4] The requirements of the ministerial decree are therefore to be applied with reservation.

With the 2008 German Annual Tax Act (*Jahressteuergesetz*), the legislature legally anchored the necessity for counterevidence required under EU law (Sec.

---

2 European Court of Justice of 12 Sept. 2006 – C-196/04 – Cadbury Schweppes, ECR 2006, p. I-7995.
3 Federal Finance Ministry, Decree of 8 Jan. 2007, Federal Tax Gazette Part I, 2007, p. 99.
4 Federal Tax Court of 21 Oct. 2009 – I R 114/08, Federal Tax Gazette (2010) Part II, p. 774.

8(2) of the Foreign Tax Act). This allows a taxpayer to provide proof to the effect that a CFC is involved in a genuine economic activity in its country of domicile. Unlike the decree issued by the Federal Finance Ministry, this legislation does not address in greater detail the question of what constitutes genuine economic activity or the form in which proof of the pursuit of such an activity must be provided. It does, however, suggest that the question be answered on the basis of functional aspects, taking into account the actual activity of the company. If one complies with this, then the requirements are not very high, in particular in the case of CFCs involved in a spectrum of mobile activities centered on the production factor of capital. This tendency can be found in the case law of the Federal Tax Court;[5] on the other hand, it is also possible to discern a tendency on the part of well-known contributors to the German legal literature to consider even limited economic substance to be sufficient in the case of mobile financial activities. This is also justified since it is in the nature of these activities to require only little substance. In that regard, the exaggerated 'operational presence' of an investment company, which would theoretically be possible, could take on artificial dimensions. It will be necessary to await further developments in this regard.

It must be borne in mind that the 'EU test' applies only to CFCs located in an EU or EEA country. CFCs in other countries are excluded, although protection under the free movement of capital is being discussed. The same applies to third-country permanent establishments of CFCs. As regards Switzerland, protection by virtue of the freedom of movement treaty between the EU and Switzerland is under consideration.

It is also necessary to ensure the exchange of information between Germany and the countries in which CFCs are located through an EU directive or other agreement. In the EU this is achieved through the EU Mutual Assistance Directive. Within the EEA, the exchange of information with Norway and Iceland is ensured on the basis of the major information clauses in the respective double taxation treaties. The Tax Information Exchange Agreement with Liechtenstein fulfills the same purpose.

4. Publicly Traded Company Test

CFCs that receive income exclusively or nearly exclusively from financial investments are subject to CFC taxation even if they are not controlled by domestic shareholders, but a domestic shareholder holds a stake of less than 1%. An exception is made for CFCs whose shares are regularly traded on a recognized stock exchange. This does not apply, however, if a domestic shareholder controls 1% or more of the shares in the CFC. CFCs also do not qualify for this exceptional treatment if they are controlled by domestic shareholders. The possibilities for application are therefore limited.

---

[5] Federal Tax Court of 21 Oct. 2009 – I R 114/08, Federal Tax Gazette Part II, 2010, p. 774; of 13 Oct. 2010 – I R 61/09, Federal Tax Gazette Part II, 2011, p. 249.

VIII. Relief Provisions

1. Foreign Taxes

The option of deducting foreign taxes is intended to provide relief from foreign taxes paid by the CFC on the attributed income (Sec. 10(1) of the Foreign Tax Act). Taxpayers may also obtain permission to opt for the credit method, which will regularly be more advantageous (Sec. 12(1) of the Foreign Tax Act). Tax withheld from subsequent dividends of the CFC may also be credited (Sec. 12(3) of the Foreign Tax Act). Taxes paid under a foreign tax regime by a lower-tier company controlled by a CFC are also creditable.

It must be remembered in this context that foreign taxes can be applied only against German corporate income tax. Offsetting against trade tax is not possible although the attributed income shall be subject to trade tax. The amount that can be offset is therefore currently limited to a maximum of 15%. If the foreign tax liability exceeds this amount, an unusable foreign tax credit results that cannot be applied against trade tax. Such unusable foreign tax credits may not be carried forward or backward. The possibility of offsetting such credits against trade tax is currently under discussion due to the double taxation this entails.

2. Losses

Losses from passive low-taxed activities are not attributed to the shareholder. Such losses can generally be used only at the level of CFCs, i.e. carried forward indefinitely (Sec. 10(3) sentence 5 of the Foreign Tax Act in conjunction with Sec. 10d of the Income Tax Act). The possibility of a carryback is of no significant practical importance due to the limitation of the amount. Losses can be offset against the income of other CFCs only in the case of entities that are controlled by the same CFC.

3. Subsequent Dividends and Capital Gains

Subsequent dividends received by domestic shareholders are exempt from taxation for a period of seven years (Sec. 3(41)(a) of the Income Tax Act). If the shareholder is a domestic entity, the otherwise usual taxation in the amount of 5% of the dividend does not apply during this period (Sec. 8b(5) of the Corporate Income Tax Act). If the shareholder is a natural person, subsequent dividends will generally be subject to taxation upon expiration of the seven-year period (flat-rate withholding tax or partial income rule). This can result in significant excess taxation for no objective reason. The comments on subsequent dividends apply accordingly to subsequent capital gains (Sec. 3(41)(b) of the Income Tax Act).

IX. CFC Legislation and Transparent Entities

German tax law contains a unilateral switchover clause by virtue of Sec. 20(2) of the Foreign Tax Act. The purpose of that provision is to rule out exemption of foreign income under German double taxation treaties in the case of income from passive low-taxed sources. The typical case will regularly involve income received by a foreign permanent establishment or by a foreign transparent entity that would not normally be subject to taxation in Germany by virtue of the exemption provision contained in the procedural article. If such income derives from passive activities and is subject to a low tax rate, exemption is unilaterally denied. At the procedural level, the provision achieves this by making direct reference to the CFC legislation. This involves a hypothetical test based on the assumption that the foreign company qualifies as a foreign permanent establishment. If the income of this hypothetical foreign entity would be subject to CFC taxation, the credit method is substituted for the exemption method for the purposes of taxation of the actual income of the permanent establishment.

X. Tax Treaty Issues

The question of the extent to which German CFC legislation embodies a treaty override that negates provisions of German double taxation treaties was addressed in the German scholarly literature very early.

The German legislature anticipated the above reservations in 1992 by adding a provision to CFC legislation to the effect that CFC rules are not to be affected by German double taxation treaties (Sec. 20(1) of the Foreign Tax Act). This must be seen as an explicit attempt to lend legitimacy to the treaty override resulting from CFC legislation. On the other hand, such treaty overrides are increasingly considered to infringe constitutional principles. The principal idea behind this position is that a state predicated upon the rule of law may not derogate an international treaty without good reason. The advocates of this initiative rely on various decisions of the Federal Constitutional Court, which did not, however, fall into the area of tax law. The question of treaty overrides in connection with tax issues has not yet been resolved. The Federal Tax Court did, however, recently submit this matter to the Federal Constitutional Court pursuant to Art. 100(1) of the Federal Constitution (*Grundgesetz*).[6] A decision is expected to be issued soon.

It is, however, also to be mentioned here that German double taxation treaties increasingly contain provisions that explicitly allow CFC legislation to be applied. No treaty override can exist in such cases, and there would be no restrictions regarding the application of CFC taxation.

---

6 Federal Tax Court of 10 Jan. 2012 – I R 66/09, *Entscheidungssammlung des Bundesfinanzhofs*, Volume 236, p. 304.

Dr. Jens Schönfeld

Lawyer, Certified Tax Lawyer, Diplom-Kaufmann

Areas of Specialization

- Corporate tax
- International and European tax law
- Cross-border reorganizations
- Taxation of family-owned businesses
- Tax litigation (e.g. European Court of Justice, German Federal Fiscal Court)

Telephone (ext.) +49 228/95 94-266 /-383

Email: jens.schoenfeld@fgs.de

Repatriation by Foreign Investors of Profits from German Investments

by Jochen Bahns

Contents

I. Introduction
II. Investment via a German PE or a German Partnership
  1. Permanent Establishment
    a) Current Income
    b) Capital Gains
  2. Partnership
    a) Current Income
    b) Capital Gains

III. Investment via a German Corporation
  1. Direct Stake in a German Corporation
    a) Current Income
    b) Repatriation of Capital Gains
  2. Investment via a German Partnership
    a) Current Taxation
    b) Tax Burden upon Exit
IV. Conclusion

I. Introduction

An essential element of any tax-optimized structure for an investment in Germany by a foreign investor is the possibility of the tax-neutral repatriation of its profits generated in Germany as well as of the equity added over the course of the investment. Such repatriation can occur either by way of profit distributions or by disposing of the investment. In this context, the tax consequences of repatriation depend significantly on the type of investment in Germany. More specifically, the contrast is between an investment (a) via a German permanent establishment (PE) or partnership and (b) via a German corporation. For the purposes of this article, it is assumed that the German investment is made by a foreign corporation.

In cross-border scenarios, from a German perspective, the tax position hinges especially on where the domestic investor has its tax residence (notably its (actual) place of management, Sec. 10 of the German General Tax Code *(Abgabenordnung)*, Art. 4 para. 3 of the OECD MC) and whether the assets held by the PE or the interest/shares in the partnership/corporation can be attributed to that investor as the legal and/or beneficial owner (in this respect cf. Sec. 39 of the General Tax Code).

By way of precaution, the investor should also, in the context of its foreign structure, observe the German general anti-abuse rule of Sec. 42 of the General Tax Code. Based on the case law[1] of the highest German fiscal court, it seems fair to say that employing a foreign corporation as an intermediary – ultimately just like employing a domestic entity – has to be denied recognition from a tax perspective only if it is exclusively motivated by tax considerations. Against this background, employing a foreign corporation as an 'intermediary' should be recognized from a tax perspective at least if the entity is established on a lasting basis and bears the economic consequences in connection with the business's assets. A minimum degree of substance in terms of human and physical substance should enable the entity to effectively discharge the functions it is obligated to carry out under its corporate objective. For practical purposes, the general anti-abuse rule should only affect genuine 'letter-box' constructions; in this connection, the developments in the context of the BEPS project[2] by the OECD should be closely monitored.

Any tax-optimized repatriation focuses in particular on relief from German withholding tax (*Kapitalertragsteuer*, abbreviated as WHT) and on avoiding a tax burden on capital gains.

II. Investment via a German PE or a German Partnership

1. Permanent Establishment

a) Current Income

Given that a PE (Sec. 12 of the General Tax Code) constitutes a dependent part of a foreign enterprise, in legal terms, that enterprise is directly entitled to any profits and losses. The enterprise is subject to limited German tax liability on the profits derived from the German PE (Sec. 49(1) no. 2(a) of the German Income Tax Act (*Einkommensteuergesetz*); Art. 7 in conjunction with Art. 5 of the OECD MC). In this regard, there is no profit distribution. Accordingly, no German WHT is levied on the repatriation to the head office of proceeds realized by the PE, so that the repatriation can be effected in a tax-optimized way.

b) Capital Gains

A capital gain realized upon disposal of a German PE by a foreign investor is subject to German taxation (Sec. 49(1) no. 2(a) of the Income Tax Act; Art. 13 para. 2 of the OECD MC). No additional German WHT is levied, however.

---

1 cf. German Federal Tax Court of 25 Feb. 2004 – I R 42/02, Federal Tax Gazette Part II, 2005, p. 14; Federal Tax Court of 31 May 2005 – I R 74/04, Federal Tax Gazette Part II, 2006, p. 118.
2 See Action Plan on Base Erosion and Profit Shifting 2013 of the OECD, available at http://www.oecd.org/ctp/BEPSActionPlan.pdf.

2. Partnership

a) Current Income

If the foreign investor invests in Germany via a German partnership – e.g. a *GbR* (*Gesellschaft bürgerlichen Rechts* – civil-law association), *OHG* (*Offene Handelsgesellschaft* – a general partnership), *KG* (*Kommanditgesellschaft* – a limited partnership) or *GmbH & Co. KG* (a limited partnership with a *Gesellschaft mit beschränkter Haftung* – privately held corporation – as its general partner) – which carries on a trade or business *(gewerblich tätig)*, there are no differences from a German tax perspective to the taxation of a PE. The partnership constitutes an entity with partial legal capacity which from a legal perspective derives the profits. That is why profit distributions are subject, as a general rule, to a partners' resolution approving such distributions.

From a tax perspective and as a general rule, however, the German partnership constitutes a transparent entity which is not subject to taxation on income. Rather, it is the partners who are subject to tax in relation to their partnership's profits (cf. Sec. 15(1) sentence 1 no. 2 of the Income Tax Act). A partnership carrying on a trade or business establishes a PE for tax purposes for each of its foreign partners (Art. 7 of the OECD MC).[3] Accordingly, for tax purposes, the profits are attributed – like in the case of a PE – directly to the foreign investor. These profit withdrawals are not subject to any German WHT.[4]

b) Capital Gains

Due to the 'transparency principle' applicable to German partnerships, profits derived from the disposal of partnership interests are subject to taxation in Germany. No German WHT is levied thereon.

Under certain circumstances, the partnership interest may be transferred in a tax-neutral manner to another entity (e.g. to a corporation pursuant to Sec. 20 of the German Reorganization Tax Act (*Umwandlungsteuergesetz*)). With respect to PEs cf. item 1. b) above.

III. Investment via a German Corporation

There is a fundamental difference between (a) the taxation of profit distributions and capital gains at the level of a German corporation and (b) the treatment as regards the PE and the partnership carrying on a trade or business, because the corporation itself is a taxable entity.

---

[3] cf. e.g. Federal Tax Court of 17 Oct. 2007 – I R 5/06, Federal Tax Gazette Part II, 2009, p. 356.
[4] For stakes of a German partnership in a German corporation, cf. item III.2.

1. Direct Stake in a German Corporation

If the foreign investor holds a direct stake in the German corporation, then the following applies with regard to repatriation:

a) Current Income

The distribution of profits by a corporation with its registered seat (Sec. 11 of the General Tax Code) or place of management (Sec. 10 of the General Tax Code) located in Germany leads to the foreign investor becoming subject to limited tax liability in Germany (Sec. 49(1) no. 5(a) of the Income Tax Act).

aa) General Obligation to Deduct WHT

Profit distributions (Sec. 20(1) no. 1 of the Income Tax Act) to a foreign investor are subject to German WHT (Secs. 43(1) no. 1, and 43a(1) sentence 1 no. 1 of the Income Tax Act). The WHT rate is 25% (plus solidarity surcharge of 5.5% thereon, leading to an effective WHT of 26.375%). As a general rule, the WHT deduction is deemed to settle finally the income tax or corporate income tax of the foreign shareholder who is subject to limited tax liability in Germany (Sec. 50(2) sentence 1 of the Income Tax Act or Sec. 32(1) no. 2 of the Corporate Income Tax Act (*Körperschaftsteuergesetz*)), i.e. no tax assessment is carried out in the course of which the WHT could be credited against possible lower tax liability of the foreign shareholder and, where appropriate, be refunded.

bb) Relief from German WHT

Tax-optimized profit-repatriation strategies must aim at countering any definitive German WHT burden. A WHT reduction to 15% may be achieved under the special provision of Sec. 44a(9) of the Income Tax Act. A further reduction down to as little as 0% is achievable subject to the prerequisites of a double taxation treaty (DTT) (cf. Art. 10 in conjunction with Art. 23 of the OECD MC) or the EU Parent-Subsidiary Directive.

Of primary importance in practice is relief from WHT under the Parent-Subsidiary Directive, which was transposed into German law by way of Sec. 43b of the Income Tax Act. Under that provision and on application, WHT is not levied on dividends (Sec. 20(1) no. 1 of the Income Tax Act) that accrue to a parent which has neither its registered seat nor its place of management in Germany (cf. Sec. 43b(1) sentence 1 of the Income Tax Act). 'Parent' means each entity that fulfills the requirements set out in Annex 2 to Sec. 43b of the Income Tax Act and, at the point in time at which the WHT arose pursuant to Sec. 44(1) sentence 2 of the Income Tax Act, demonstrably held a direct stake of at least 10% in the capital of the subsidiary (minimum participation; Sec. 43b(2) sentence 1 of the Income Tax Act) pursuant to Art. 3 para. 1(a) of Council Directive 2011/96/EEC of 30 Nov. 2011 on the common tax system for parent and subsidiary companies from different Member States[5]. If this holding period is completed after WHT has arisen, then the WHT deducted and paid to the tax office has to be refunded pursuant to Sec. 50d(1) of the Income Tax Act; the exemption procedure under Sec. 50d(2) of the Income Tax Act is excluded.

cc) Anti-Treaty-Shopping Rule of Sec. 50d(3) of the Income Tax Act

Any reduction of or relief from German WHT under Sec. 44a(9) of the Income Tax Act, under DTTs or under the Parent-Subsidiary Directive is only conceivable, however, if such benefit is not barred by the anti-abuse rule of Sec. 50d(3) of the Income Tax Act, a provision which is very important in practice. This rule is meant to prevent the possibility of claiming tax privileges by means of improperly involving a foreign entity.[6] If the prerequisites of this special anti-abuse rule are fulfilled, then it takes precedence over the general anti-abuse rule (Sec. 42 of the General Tax Code).[7]

By way of overview, the special anti-abuse rule of Sec. 50d(3) of the Income Tax Act is applied as follows:

(1) Shareholder Test

A foreign entity is entitled to full or partial relief (Sec. 50d(1) or (2) of the Income Tax Act) to the extent that its shareholders include persons who would also be entitled to a refund or exemption were they to derive the income directly (*persönliche Entlastungsberechtigung* or 'personal entitlement to relief').

If the foreign entity is directly or indirectly held by a corporation whose main class of shares is subject to substantial and regular trade at a recognized stock exchange, then this is sufficient to preclude application of Sec. 50d(3) of the Income Tax Act (Sec. 50d(3) sentence 5 of the Income Tax Act). The term 'recognized stock exchange' means an organized market within the meaning of Sec. 2(5) of the German Securities Trade Act (*Wertpapierhandelsgesetz*) and comparable markets with their registered seats outside the European Union and the European Economic Area. In that case, further requirements in terms of activity or substance are irrelevant.

Besides, the shareholder of the foreign entity is disregarded, to a certain degree, if the shareholder is a corporation which is personally entitled to relief under a DTT or the EU Parent-Subsidiary Directive. To the extent that the entity holding an indirect stake is not entitled – on the merits – to relief, what then needs to be examined is whether some other entity holding a stake in the first one – to the extent that that other entity is personally entitled to relief – fulfills, on the merits, the prerequisites in terms of functions exercised of Sec. 50d(3) sen-

---

[5] OJ L 345 of 29 Dec. 2011, p. 8.
[6] For details cf. letter issued by the Federal Finance Ministry on 24 Jan. 2012, Federal Tax Gazette Part I, 2012, p. 171.
[7] cf. letter by the Federal Finance Ministry of 3 April 2007, Federal Tax Gazette Part I, 2007, p. 166.

tence 1 of the Income Tax Act. With respect to entities within a chain, in each instance, each entity within the chain must be personally entitled to relief.[8]

(2) Business-Income and Business-Purpose Test

In the absence of personal entitlement to relief, the foreign entity can claim relief from WHT solely if it is entitled, on the merits, to relief (*sachliche Entlastungsberechtigung*), which is known as 'harmless earnings'. The prerequisites, in terms of functions exercised, for harmless earnings are met to the extent that:

- the gross earnings realized by the foreign entity in the relevant fiscal year were derived from its own business activity, or,
- with regard to any earnings not derived from its own business activity, there are economic or otherwise substantial grounds for involving the foreign entity, and

the foreign entity participates in general economic dealings through a business establishment that is organized appropriately in relation to its business objective.

(a) Business-Income Test

According to the intention of the legislature, merely hinted at in the wording of the rule, the provision of Sec. 50d(3) of the Income Tax Act is an 'apportionment clause'[9]. This means that the treaty benefits are granted to the extent that the gross earnings originate from the relevant person's own business activity. In principle, this means that the gross earnings derived by the foreign entity are split into active and passive earnings. Depending on their amount, the foreign entity may be entitled to partial or full relief from WHT.

Earnings derived from subsidiaries (dividends, interest and royalties) are to be recognized as active earnings only to the extent that the foreign entity has to be classified as a 'management holding entity'.[10] This is usually the case if the foreign entity becomes actively involved in the management of two or more entities. To that extent, the foreign holding entity should exercise a certain degree of influence over the subsidiaries and take certain long-term strategic as well as fundamental decisions with regard to the subsidiaries.[11]

---

8 cf. letter issued by the Federal Finance Ministry on 24 Jan. 2012, Federal Tax Gazette Part I, 2012, p. 171, marginal no. 4.2.
9 *Bundestag* (Lower House of the German Parliament, printed matter no. 17/7524, p. 17.
10 cf. Federal Tax Court of 29 Jan. 2008 – I R 26/06, Federal Tax Gazette Part II, 2008, p. 978.
11 cf. letter issued by the Federal Finance Ministry on 24 Jan. 2012, Federal Tax Gazette Part I, 2012, p. 171, marginal no. 5.3.

(b) Business-Purpose Test

Finally, the foreign entity is entitled to WHT relief with respect to passive earnings if employing the foreign entity as an intermediary is justified by economic or otherwise substantial grounds and the foreign entity participates in general economic dealings through a business establishment that is organized appropriately in relation to its business objective.

It is unclear under which circumstances such economic or otherwise substantial grounds exist. In practice, as a general rule, an activity such as a financing or cash-pooling entity is recognized in this regard.[12] Circumstances ensuing from the situation of the affiliated group – such as grounds of coordination, organization, development of client relationships, costs, local preferences, overall entrepreneurial concept – do not constitute economic or otherwise substantial grounds.[13]

An appropriately organized business establishment requires in particular that, in its state of residence, the foreign entity has at its disposal qualified personnel, business premises and technical means of communication,[14] i.e. there needs to be a demonstrable 'tangible presence'. The following constitute indicators for a 'tangible presence':[15]

- in its state of residence, the entity employs both management and other personnel on a permanent basis in order to carry out its activity;
- the entity's personnel possess the qualifications necessary to autonomously and independently fulfill duties delegated to the entity, and
- the transactions between related persons are at arm's length (i.e. as between unrelated third parties).

(3) Interim Conclusion

In relation to a tax-optimized structure that ideally avoids any WHT burden altogether, it is essential that the foreign entity as a shareholder of the German corporation has sufficient activity and substance. This requirement might be dispensed with only in cases where personal entitlement to relief exists.

---

12 cf. also Federal Tax Court of 23 Oct. 1991 – I R 40/89, Federal Tax Gazette Part II, 1992, p. 1026.
13 cf. letter issued by the Federal Finance Ministry on 24 Jan. 2012, Federal Tax Gazette Part I, 2012, p. 171, marginal no. 6.
14 cf. Federal Tax Court of 20 March 2002 – I R 38/00, Federal Tax Gazette Part II, 2002, p. 819.
15 cf. letter issued by the Federal Finance Ministry on 24 Jan. 2012, Federal Tax Gazette Part I, 2012, p. 171, marginal no. 7.

b) Repatriation of Capital Gains

aa) Exit

If a foreign corporation sells its stake in a German corporation to a third party, realizing a profit in the process, then as a general rule it is subject to limited corporate income tax liability on its capital gains (Sec. 2 no. 1, and Sec. 8 of the Corporate Income Tax Act in conjunction with Sec. 49(1) sentence 1 no. 2(e)(bb) of the Income Tax Act). The capital gains are tax-free, while a fixed portion of 5% of the gains is subject to corporate income tax at a rate of 15% (Sec. 23(1) of the Corporate Income Tax Act) as a nondeductible business expense (cf. Sec. 8b(2) and (3) sentence 1 of the Corporate Income Tax Act). Effectively, this means a tax burden of 0.75% (plus solidarity surcharge). Unlike in the case of dividends, this tax exemption does not (at least to date) require a minimum level of participation or minimum holding period. Given the absence of a German PE, a direct investment by the foreign investor does not normally trigger a trade-tax burden (cf. Sec. 2(1) of the German Trade Tax Act – *Gewerbesteuergesetz*).

However, the German DTTs usually provide that it is not Germany, as the source state, which taxes the capital gains but instead the state in which the seller is tax-resident (state of residence) (cf. Art. 13 para. 4 of the OECD MC). In this connection, the seller is generally not subject to the requirements of the anti-treaty-shopping rule of Sec. 50d(3) of the Income Tax Act.

bb) Intragroup Disposals

Another way of achieving tax-free repatriation by way of a gains-generating disposal of the shares is via Sec. 8b(2) of the Corporate Income Tax Act through an intragroup disposal. In this connection, care needs to be taken to ensure that legal and/or beneficial ownership (Sec. 39 of the General Tax Code) of the shares in the German corporation is actually transferred to the buyer.

It is possible that this result can also be achieved by having the German corporation acquire the foreign investor's shares ('acquisition of own shares').[16]

Finally, it needs to be borne in mind that the foreign investor may transfer its shares in a German corporation in a tax-neutral way and at book values to another (German) corporation (cf. Sec. 21 of the Reorganization Tax Act).[17] This option is available if shares in a corporation are contributed to the other corporation in exchange for new shares in the acquiring entity and, subsequently to the contribution, the transferee demonstrably has acquired, based on its stake including the contributed shares, a direct majority of the voting rights in the acquired entity ('qualified share exchange'). In this connection, an interesting option is for the contributing party to be allowed to receive, in addition to the

---

16 In this connection, cf. letter issued by the Federal Finance Ministry on 27 Nov. 2013, Federal Tax Gazette Part I, 2013, p. 1615.
17 For more details, cf. letter issued by the Federal Finance Ministry on 11 Nov. 2011, Federal Tax Gazette Part I, 2011, p. 1314.

shares, further assets up to a specific value in a tax-neutral way (Sec. 21(2) sentence 3 of the Reorganization Tax Act). Insofar, the foreign investor may for example be granted an (interest-bearing) shareholder loan which is capable of being used for tax-free repatriation.

2. Investment via a German Partnership

Investments by foreign corporations in German corporations are often structured not as direct investments but by way of an interposed German partnership carrying on a trade or business (co-entrepreneurship).[18] As a result, the foreign investor maintains a German trade or business, because the stake in the co-entrepreneurship leads to the partner having, by virtue of his being a co-entrepreneur and based on the transparency principle, a German PE.[19]

a) Current Taxation

In this case, a WHT burden on the repatriation of German profits can be avoided by ensuring that with regard to the profit distribution, a mandatory tax assessment in Germany is triggered, in the course of which the WHT deducted is credited against the tax liability (plus solidarity surcharge) of the investor who is subject to limited tax liability (Sec. 36(2) no. 2 of the Income Tax Act, Sec. 31 of the Corporate Income Tax Act) and for the most part refunded. The objective of such a structure is to prevent the WHT from having a definitive settling effect.

In this context, it needs to be observed that dividend income derived from a stake in a German corporation by a foreign investor who is subject to limited corporate income tax liability in Germany is in principle 100% tax-free in the context of an assessment (Sec. 8b(1) of the Corporate Income Tax Act). However, a fixed portion of 5% is treated as nondeductible business expenses (Sec. 8b(5) of the Corporate Income Tax Act). As a result, only 5% of the dividend income is subject to a corporate income tax charge at a rate of 15% (cf. Sec. 23(1) of the Corporate Income Tax Act). The effective corporate income tax burden amounts to 0.75%. While the tax exemption does not require a minimum participation period, it does require a minimum participation of 10% (cf. Sec. 8b(4) of the Corporate Income Tax Act).

If in addition one takes into account trade tax in the amount of e.g. a further approximately 0.75% (Sec. 7(1), and Sec. 8 no. 5 in conjunction with Sec. 9 no. 2a of the Trade Tax Act), one arrives at a tax burden of 1.5%, unless additional income is to be considered. In this respect, the WHT (plus solidarity surcharge) deducted is fully refunded in the context of an assessment.[20]

---

18 While conceivable, holding stakes via a German PE is significantly more difficult to defend in practice.
19 cf. Federal Tax Court of 17 Oct. 2007 – I R 5/06, Federal Tax Gazette Part II, 2009, p. 356.
20 Example: On dividend income in the amount of 100, corporate income tax and trade tax of 1.5 are assessed. Taking into account the 26.375 of WHT deducted, the tax assessment leads to a tax refund of approx. 24.87.

aa) Requirement for the Stake in the German Corporation to be Attributed to the German PE

The existence of a German PE as such does not lead to profit distributions of the German corporation constituting income of the German business. A domestic PE does not necessarily attract all domestic income, and thus also dividend income from the stake in the corporation, to the profit attributable to the PE.

Rather, a profit distribution by the affiliated entity forms part of the profit attributable to the domestic business only if the stake forms part of the business assets attributable to the PE. This question is subject to debate. In the view of the German tax authorities, stakes in corporations usually form part of the assets of the head office.[21] The tax authorities maintain that this also applies in the case of a PE attributable through a partnership, even if the legal ownership in the stake were transferred to the partnership.[22] The reason they give is the purported 'central function' of the head office.

It would seem rash to simply concur with this assumption by the German tax authorities regarding a central function of the head office as well as regarding the attribution of stakes to that head office. Rather, even in the case of a head office, the attribution of a stake to that head office needs to result from the criteria developed by case law. The criterion for their attribution is only a function attributed to the PE in the context of the overall enterprise, which is based on a functional attribution as determined by the entrepreneur or by specific circumstances and facts.

In practical terms, the attribution of a stake in a corporation to a German partnership's domestic PE requires that the partnership have a sufficient number of holding functions and that it effectively exercise them *vis-à-vis* the affiliated company. At the same time, it should be ensured that pertinent functions do not exist at all, or only to a minor degree, at the level of the partnership's foreign partner.

bb) Establishment of a Tax Group as an Additional Structural Optimization

By attributing the stake in a corporation to a German PE, the WHT situation can be improved in those cases in which there would be a risk of a definitive WHT burden because of the anti-treaty-shopping rule of Sec. 50d(3) of the Income Tax Act. The establishment of a tax group for income-tax purposes between the German partnership as the parent and the German corporation as the subsidiary would prevent WHT from arising in the first place. Given that a mandatory prerequisite for such a tax group is the existence of an effective

---

21 Letter issued by the Federal Finance Ministry on 24 Dec. 1999, Federal Tax Gazette Part I, 1999, p. 1076; letter issued by the Federal Finance Ministry on 25 Aug. 2009, Federal Tax Gazette Part I, 2009, p. 888, marginal no. 2.4.
22 Letter issued by the Federal Finance Ministry on 16 April 2010, Federal Tax Gazette Part I, 2010, p. 354, marginal no. 2.2.4.1. cf. also Federal Tax Court of 19 Dec. 2007 – I R 66/06, Federal Tax Gazette Part II, 2008, p. 510.

profit and loss transfer agreement between the parent and the subsidiary (cf. Sec. 14(1) sentence 1 of the Corporate Income Tax Act, and Sec. 2(2) sentence 2 of the Trade Tax Act), in the context of a tax group there are profit **transfers** rather than profit **distributions**, which would be subject to WHT. Accordingly, the tax group avoids not only WHT but also the 1.5% charge described above with regard to the taxation of the fixed portion of 5% of dividend income deemed to be nondeductible business expenses (cf. Sec. 8b(1) and (5) of the Corporate Income Tax Act).

The prerequisite for a partnership as the parent in a tax group is in particular that this partnership carry on its own trading or business activity within the meaning of Sec. 15(1) no. 1 of the Income Tax Act (cf. Sec. 14(1) sentence 1 no. 2 sentence 2 of the Corporate Income Tax Act); it is not sufficient for the partnership to be a 'deemed business partnership' (*gewerblich geprägte Personengesellschaft*, Sec. 15(3) no. 2 of the Income Tax Act).[23] In the view of the German tax authorities, a merely negligible trading or business activity is not sufficient.[24] A holding activity alone does not suffice either.[25] What is additionally required are services such as the provision of IT support or the preparation of accounting in exchange for separate remuneration.[26]

Furthermore it is crucial that the income from the tax-group subsidiary is solely taxable in Germany (Sec. 14 sentence 1 no. 2 sentence 7 of the Corporate Income Tax Act). Another advantage of group taxation is that the expenses at the level of the partnership in connection with the stake acquired, such as financing costs, can be set off against the profit from the tax-group subsidiary. That is because functionally, these expenses (given their nature as 'special business expenses' – *Sonderbetriebsausgaben* – of the foreign partner) should also be attributable to the partnership. This enables a debt push-down in the context of the tax group.

Caution should be exercised to the extent that this structure is envisaged also in order for financing costs to be taken into account twice ('double dip'), namely at the level of the foreign investor as well as with the domestic partnership. The legislature intends to put a stop to these structures and to this end might be able to draw on the provisions of Sec. 14(1) no. 5 of the Corporate Income Tax Act and Sec. 50d(10) of the Income Tax Act.

b) Tax Burden upon Exit

What would have an adverse effect in this structure is an exit by way of (a) the foreign investor selling its partnership interest or (b) the domestic partnership

---

23 cf. letter issued by the Federal Finance Ministry on 10 Nov. 2005, Federal Tax Gazette Part I, 2005, p. 1038, marginal no. 15.
24 Letter issued by the Federal Finance Ministry on 10 Nov. 2005, Federal Tax Gazette Part I, 2005, p. 1038, marginal no. 17.
25 Letter issued by the Federal Finance Ministry on 10 Nov. 2005, Federal Tax Gazette Part I, 2005, p. 1038, marginal no. 18.
26 Letter issued by the Federal Finance Ministry on 10 Nov. 2005, Federal Tax Gazette Part I, 2005, p. 1038, marginal no. 19.

selling its share in the corporation. In this regard, because of the existence of a German PE, in principle 5% of the capital gains would be taxed (cf. Sec. 8b(2) and (3) of the Corporate Income Tax Act). Because of the permanent-establishment reservation, this also applies for the purposes of DTTs (cf. Art. 13 para. 2 of the OECD MC).

IV. Conclusion

Tax-friendly profit-repatriation options require careful planning. Against the background of the BEPS project initiated by the OECD, sufficient substance in terms of physical and human resources should be ensured in particular at the level of the foreign investor. This helps notably in the context of an investment in a German corporation in order to meet the requirements of the anti-treaty-shopping rule of Sec. 50d(3) of the Income Tax Act. Unlike with an investment in a German PE or partnership, with an investment in a German corporation, the tax-free repatriation of *current profits* in Germany can be achieved only provided there is sufficient substance and activity of the foreign parent resident in an EU state or DTT state (cf. Sec. 50d(3) of the Income Tax Act).

In the context of a sale, tax-free repatriation can generally be achieved only via an investment in a German corporation. In principle, this already applies based on the unilateral exemption of capital gains pursuant to Sec. 8b(2) of the Corporate Income Tax Act (but 5% taxation).[27] In addition, tax-free repatriation can arise under an applicable DTT if the sole right to tax is assigned – as is usually the case – to the seller's state of residence (cf. Art. 13 para. 4 of the OECD MC). By contrast, a gain from the disposal of a German PE or of an interest in a German partnership is usually subject to taxation in Germany ('permanent-establishment principle') and thus tends to be unsuitable for repatriation purposes.

As a general rule, it would therefore seem fair to say that, with a view to tax-optimized repatriation, an investment in a German corporation (possibly by employing as an intermediary a German partnership carrying on a trade or business) is preferable. Ultimately, the optimum structure needs to be determined by weighing up all economic, legal and tax advantages and disadvantages of the particular case.

---

27 What remains to be seen is whether the German legislature will introduce – similarly to with the exemption of dividends (cf. Sec. 8b(4) of the Corporate Income Tax Act) – a minimum participation level (e.g. of 10%).

Dr. Jochen Bahns

Lawyer, Tax Advisor

Areas of Specialization

- Taxation of corporate groups
- Domestic and cross-border mergers & acquisitions and corporate reorganizations
- International tax law
- Tax audits and tax litigation
- Structuring of inbound and outbound investments

Telephone (ext.) +49 228/95 94-208

Email: jochen.bahns@fgs.de

Cross-Border Investments in German Private Equity Funds

by Helder Schnittker

Contents

I. Introduction
II. German Key Concepts of the Taxation of Funds
  1. Transparent Taxation of Partnerships
  2. Key Question: Private Asset Management Partnerships vs. Co-Entrepreneurships
    a) Classification of the Partnership
    b) Advantages of Private Asset Management Partnerships
    c) Legal Uncertainty
    d) Reasons for a Co-Entrepreneurship
III. Private Asset Management Partnerships
  1. Tax Consequences for Non-German Resident Investors
  2. Tax Consequences for Non-German Resident Sponsors
    a) Proportionate Profit Share
    b) Carried Interest
IV. Funds Organized as Co-entrepreneurships
  1. Tax Consequences for Non-German Resident Investors
    a) Personal/Corporate Income Tax
    b) Trade Tax
    c) Trade Tax Credit for Individual Investors
    d) Impact of Double Taxation Treaties
  2. Tax Consequences for Non-German Resident Sponsors
V. Conclusions

I. Introduction

Private equity funds are collective investment undertakings that mostly invest in equity securities of medium-sized entities. Private equity funds usually generate the return on the investments through a long-term investment strategy that aims at a sale or IPO of the portfolio companies after three to seven years.

As in the U.S. and the UK, private equity funds in Germany are usually organized as partnerships. German corporations are rarely used as fund vehicles.

The most common partnership structure is the *GmbH & Co. KG*, i.e. a German limited partnership (*KG*) with a German privately held corporation (*Gesellschaft mit beschränkter Haftung – GmbH*) as the sole general partner. The investors are admitted as limited partners of the *KG*. Furthermore, the sponsors receive an (indirect) interest in the fund. For this purpose, the sponsors usually become partners of another limited partnership ('carry vehicle'), and the carry vehicle is admitted to the fund as a limited partner.

The financial investment by the carry vehicle usually amounts to 1-3% of the overall committed capital and corresponds to a 1-3% proportionate share in profits and losses of the fund. In addition and in consideration for the contribution of intangibles such as knowhow, experience, networking etc., the sponsors receive a disproportionate profit share, which usually amounts to 20% of the fund's profits ('carried interest'). The carried interest applies if the fund has generated sufficient profit to repay the contributions of the investors plus a minimum rate of return (hurdle).

The participation of non-German residents as investors or sponsors in German private equity funds requires careful consideration of the German tax consequences in order to achieve a tax optimized structure and avoid double taxation. Against this background, this article describes the main German income tax concepts that are relevant for non-German resident investors and sponsors of German private equity funds organized as partnerships.

II. German Key Concepts of the Taxation of Funds

1. Transparent Taxation of Partnerships

Similar to the U.S. and the UK, partnerships are subject to a pass-through regime in Germany for personal and corporate income tax purposes, i.e. partnerships do not pay personal or corporate income tax on their income but the income flows through to the partners and is taxed at the level of the partners.[1] This also means that the partners are taxed on the income of the partnership irrespective of whether the partnership distributes its profits or not. Consequently, investors may have to pay German taxes on gains realized by the fund although they have not received any payments.

2. Key Question: Private Asset Management Partnerships vs. Co-Entrepreneurships

a) Classification of the Partnership

One of the key elements controlling the tax treatment of investors and sponsors is whether the fund is structured as a private asset management partnership (*vermögensverwaltende Personengesellschaft*) or as a partnership that is engaged or deemed to be engaged in a trade or business (*gewerbliche Personengesellschaft*) (hereinafter referred to as 'co-entrepreneurship').

The German tax administration released a revenue ruling in 2003[2] (the 'PE Ruling') that sets forth a test to classify a fund either as a private asset management partnership or as a co-entrepreneurship. As a general rule, the mere management of a portfolio of shares in corporations (i.e. acquiring, holding and selling shares) is not considered a trade or business activity. On the other hand, the fund will be considered to be engaged in a trade or business and is therefore a co-entrepreneurship if it carries out 'harmful' activities that (based on an assessment of all facts and circumstances) go beyond private asset management.

---

1 If partnerships are engaged or deemed to be engaged in a trade or business, they are, however, subject to trade tax and therefore not entirely transparent, see section IV 1. b).
2 Guidance issued by the German Federal Finance Ministry on 16 Dec. 2003, file no.: BMF IV A 6 –S 2240 – 153/03, Federal Tax Gazette Part I, 2004, 40, rev. 2006, p. 632.

Such harmful activities include debt financing of the portfolio, maintaining an extensive organization, short-term trading, substantial re-investment of sale proceeds and engagement in the active management of the portfolio companies. There is, however, no bright-line rule how many of these harmful activities can be pursued by the fund before it is considered to be engaged in a trade or business. Using the test laid out in the PE Ruling, it is relatively easy to structure a fund as a co-entrepreneurship whereas structuring a fund as private asset management partnership is subject to several restrictions.

Even if a fund is not considered to actually carry out trade or business activities according to the test in the PE Ruling, it may be deemed to be a co-entrepreneurship if (i) no limited partner is entitled to manage the fund or (ii) if the fund holds a (direct) interest in a partnership that is a co-entrepreneurship ('co-entrepreneurship by law').

b) Advantages of Private Asset Management Partnerships

Until 2009, private asset management partnerships offered a substantial tax advantage to German individual investors, as capital gains from the sale of portfolio companies after a holding period of one year were generally exempt from German personal income tax.[3]

For this reason, German private equity funds have in the past been carefully structured in order to avoid becoming a co-entrepreneurship. Consequently, the funds (to the extent possible) refrained from undertaking any 'harmful' activities listed in the PE Ruling. Furthermore, the funds usually admitted a managing limited partner (i.e. an individual or a corporate limited partner with the power to manage the fund)[4] and refrained from participating in other partnerships in order to prevent the fund from being treated as a co-entrepreneurship by law.

As of 2009, capital gains derived by a German individual investor from a fund organized as private asset management partnership are always taxable and the tax burden for the German individual investor is therefore not substantially lower when compared to funds organized as co-entrepreneurships.[5] As regards German corporate investors, the choice between a private asset management partnership and a co-entrepreneurship never affected the tax burden substantially.

---

3 Capital gains were only subject to German personal income tax if the investor held or had held in the preceding five years more than 1% in a portfolio company (based on a look-through approach).
4 Unlike in U.S. or UK law, a limited partner with managing powers will not incur the risk of personal liability.
5 Capital gains from the sale of shares derived from private asset management partnerships are generally subject to a flat income tax rate of 26.4%, whereas capital gains of co-entrepreneurships are subject to a progressive effective tax rate of up to 28.5%. The major portion of the trade tax that is levied at the level of a fund structured as a co-entrepreneurship is usually credited against the personal income tax of the investor so that the trade tax does not substantially add to the tax burden.

Non-German investors, however, are still reluctant to invest in a German fund that is organized as a co-entrepreneurship for the following reasons: (1) The foreign investor would become liable to tax in Germany, and the fund income would additionally incur a German trade tax burden. (2) The investor would be obliged to file tax returns in Germany. (3) There is a risk that a foreign investor could become liable to double taxation in Germany and its country of residence.

c) Legal Uncertainty

A major issue that is often not addressed in the discussion of whether a fund should be structured as a private asset management partnership or co-entrepreneurship is the legal uncertainty that goes along with the choice to structure the fund as a private asset management partnership. In its decision of 24 Aug. 2011, the German Federal Tax Court classified two UK private equity funds as co-entrepreneurships and expressed doubts on whether it would follow the tests contained in the PE Ruling for distinguishing private asset management partnerships from co-entrepreneurships.[6] There are rumors that the tax administration will adhere to the test of the PE Ruling despite the doubts expressed by the tax court. However, reports from recent tax audits show that the tax authorities use the decision by the tax court to classify funds as co-entrepreneurships. Therefore, it is not entirely clear whether a fund that is a private asset management partnership today under the test in the PE Ruling will be considered a co-entrepreneurship in the future. The tax court decision has also unsettled the German private equity industry, as can be easily noticed from the warning language of tax disclosures in recent private placement memorandums of German private equity funds.

d) Reasons for a Co-Entrepreneurship

Given this legal uncertainty, one might argue that it is better to structure a fund clearly as a co-entrepreneurship than having a fund with uncertain tax consequences for its investors as it cannot be clearly classified. In particular, many newly founded smaller private equity funds that only invest in portfolio companies directly and have many German investors have therefore decided to become a co-entrepreneurship. A significant advantage of a co-entrepreneurship is that the fund is not restricted in its activities by the test laid out in the PE Ruling. This is especially important for funds that act as company builders and therefore have to involve themselves in the management of the portfolio companies (which is a harmful activity according to the PE Ruling). Furthermore, a co-entrepreneurship opens up the opportunity for the management of the fund to use debt financing or to reinvest sale proceeds without restrictions.

---

6 Federal Tax Court of 24 Aug. 2011 – I R 46/10, BFH/NV 2011, p. 2165.

III. Private Asset Management Partnerships

1. Tax Consequences for Non-German Resident Investors

A non-German resident investor of a fund that is organized as a private asset management partnership will generally not become liable to German tax and will not be obliged to file tax returns in Germany. The income included in the distributive share of the foreign investor in the fund such as capital gains, dividends and interest derived by a non-German resident investor is usually considered to be income from sources outside Germany.

One exception is capital gains from the sale of shares in a German corporation if the foreign investor holds or has held in the preceding five years (based on a look-through approach) at least 1% in the share capital of the German corporation. Such capital gains are taxable under German domestic law, and the non-German resident investor will have to file a German tax return. However, if the foreign investor is entitled to double taxation treaty benefits, such capital gains are generally exempt from German tax (see Art. 13(5) of the OECD MC).

A further exception is dividends paid by German corporations. Such dividends are subject to a flat tax of approximately 26.4% which is usually withheld by the distributing corporation. The foreign investor does not have to file a tax return. If a treaty entitles the foreign investor to a reduced withholding tax rate, the foreign investor may, however, file a claim for a partial refund of the withholding tax with the German tax authorities.

2. Tax Consequences for Non-German Resident Sponsors

As described in the introduction in section I, the sponsors usually receive a profit and loss allocation in proportion of their financial investment of 1 to 3% ('proportionate profit share') and disproportionate profit share (carried interest) in consideration for their contribution of knowhow, networking etc., which usually amounts to 20%.

a) Proportionate Profit Share

The tax treatment of a non-German resident sponsor with respect to his proportionate profit share essentially corresponds to the tax treatment of non-German resident investors described under 1 above. In other words, the foreign sponsor is only liable in very limited circumstances to German tax on income derived from his proportionate profit share.

b) Carried Interest

aa) Introduction

The German tax treatment of carried interest differs significantly from the tax treatment in the UK or the U.S., where carried interest is considered to be a distributive share in the fund. Section 18(1) no. 4 of the German Income Tax

Act (*Einkommensteuergesetz*), which was introduced in 2004, explicitly classifies carried interest as compensation for the performance of independent personal services (*Einkünfte aus selbständiger Arbeit*) if the carried interest meets certain requirements. The main prerequisites of Sec. 18(1) no. 4 of the Income Tax Act are that (i) the fund is a mere private asset management partnership (and not a co-entrepreneurship) and (ii) the carried interest may only be paid after the investors have recovered their contributions. The tradeoff for compensation treatment is that 40% of the carried interest within the scope of Sec. 18(1) no. 4 of the Income Tax Act is exempt from personal income tax (Sec. 3 no. 40a of the Income Tax Act). Section 18(1) no. 4 of the Income Tax Act does not address the tax treatment of carried interest in funds organized as private asset management partnerships that do not meet the requirements of this provision. However, the German tax authorities will most likely treat carried interest outside the scope of Sec. 18(1) no. 4 of the Income Tax Act as fully taxable compensation since this approach was already pursued by the tax authorities in the PE Ruling before the introduction of Sec. 18(1) no. 4 of the Income Tax Act.

bb) Carried Interest in Cross-border Structures

The special tax treatment of carried interest in Germany does not affect a foreign sponsor if the carry vehicle does not have an office in Germany and all sponsors are non-German residents or if the foreign sponsor holds a direct interest in the fund.

If, however, the foreign sponsor is a partner of a carry vehicle that comprises German resident partners or if the carry vehicle has an office in Germany, the application of section 18(1) no. 4 of the Income Tax Act may raise double taxation issues.

As carried interest is viewed as compensation for independent professional services, the German tax authorities will probably apply the article on business profits (see Art. 7 of the OECD MC) or on independent personal services (see Art. 14 of the OECD MC [1992])) of the applicable treaty to determine whether Germany has the right to tax the carried interest. According to these articles, Germany would have the right to tax the carried interest of a foreign sponsor if and to the extent it is attributable to a German permanent establishment of the foreign sponsor.

As the carry vehicle is transparent, a permanent establishment of the partnership would be considered a permanent establishment of the foreign sponsor. The German tax authorities may therefore claim the right to tax a portion of the foreign sponsor's carried interest if the carry vehicle has a German office. But even if only a German resident sponsor but not the carry vehicle has a German office, the German tax authorities may tax the foreign sponsor on a portion of his carried interest based on the argument that the German permanent establishment of the German partner has to be attributed to the carry vehicle and is therefore also a permanent establishment of the foreign sponsor. The foreign sponsor's country of residence of the foreign sponsor, on the other hand, may claim the right to tax the carried interest entirely if such country treats carried interest as distributive share in the fund. The right to tax of the country of residence would then follow from the provisions of the applicable tax treaty that correspond to Art. 10(1) (dividends), 11(1) (interest), 13(5) (capital gains) and 21(1) (other income) of the OECD MC.

There are several arguments that a foreign sponsor may use to avoid the taxation of his carried interest in Germany. First, the foreign sponsor may argue that although carried interest is treated as compensation in Germany for domestic law purposes, the activities of the sponsors should not meet the definition of an enterprise within the meaning of Art. 7 of the OECD MC, or of an independent personal service provider within the meaning of Art. 14 of the OECD MC (1992).[7] This is because terms in double taxation treaties have to be construed in accordance with the common interpretation of both contracting states and not solely based on the respective domestic law. For this reason, a provision of domestic law such as Sec. 18(1) no. 4 of the Income Tax Act (which is often viewed as a mere legal fiction) cannot be decisive for the interpretation of a double taxation treaty. Second, the sponsor may argue that the office of another partner in the carry vehicle cannot be considered to be a permanent establishment of such sponsor as neither he nor the partnership can control the use of the German office. However, this discussion has apparently never been taken to or decided by the German tax courts.

IV. Funds Organized as Co-entrepreneurships

1. Tax Consequences for Non-German Resident Investors

A non-German resident investor who invests in a fund that is organized as a German co-entrepreneurship will usually become liable to German tax on his distributive share in the fund; he will also be obliged to file tax returns in Germany.

a) Personal/Corporate Income Tax

The foreign investor's distributive share in the fund as well as any capital gains upon the sale of the interest in the fund will be considered income from a German trade or business, which is income from sources within Germany and therefore subject to German personal or, as the case may be, corporate income tax.

aa) Individual Foreign Investors

The personal income tax rate for a foreign individual investor is progressive. The highest tax bracket which is applicable to income in excess of approximately EUR 250k[8] is approximately 47.5%.[9] The major portion of the investor's

---

[7] See *Fruechtl*, in: Internationales Steuerrecht 2009, p. 604.
[8] For married couples filing jointly: approximately EUR 500k.
[9] 45% personal income tax plus solidarity surcharge at a rate of 5.5% thereon.

distributive share will, however, be subject to a preferential effective tax rate of only up to 28.5% as capital gains from the sale of shares in corporations and dividends are generally 40% tax exempt. On the other hand, 40% of all capital losses from the sale of shares in corporations included in the distributive share are not tax deductible ('partial income taxation method' – *Teileinkünfteverfahren*).

The partial income taxation method also applies to capital gains or losses derived by the investor on the disposal of his interest in the fund to the extent the capital gains or losses relate to shares in corporations held by the fund.

bb) Corporate Foreign Investors

Corporate income tax is charged at a flat rate of approximately 15.8%.[10] Capital gains from the sale of shares in corporations that are included in the corporate investor's distributive share are, however, effectively 95% exempt from corporate income tax (participation exemption – *Schachtelprivileg*). Thus, the effective tax rate for the major portion of a corporate investor's distributive share in the fund only amounts to approximately 0.8%. On the other hand, capital losses from the sale of shares are not tax deductible. Corporate investors should note that the government plans to repeal the participation exemption for interests of less than 10% (determined at the level of the corporate investor on a look-through basis).

The participation exemption also applies to capital gains or losses derived by the investor on the disposal of its interest in the fund to the extent the capital gains or losses relate to shares in corporations held by the fund.

The effective 95% exemption from corporate income tax is also available for dividends included in the corporate investor's distributive share but only if the investor holds at least 10% in the corporation paying the dividend. As the 10% requirement is measured at the level of the corporate investor on a look-through basis, minor investors do usually not qualify for this tax exemption. If a private equity fund makes only direct investments, the 10% threshold for the participation exemption of dividends may not be an issue. However, if the acquisition structures of the fund are more complex (e.g. LuxCo acquisition vehicles), this may significantly affect the tax burden of a corporate investor.

cc) Special Rules for Short-Term Trading of the Fund

The 40% exemption of capital gains on the sale of shares and dividends from personal income tax (partial income taxation method) as well as the 95% exemption of capital gains on the sale of shares and certain dividends from corporate income tax (participation exemption) do not apply to shares held by 'financial institutions' within the meaning of the German Banking Act (*Kreditwesengesetz*) that have been acquired in order to realize 'short-term'

---

10 15% corporate income tax plus solidarity surcharge at a rate of 5.5% thereon.

gains. German tax courts and the tax administration have construed the term 'financial institution' broadly to include entities that only hold shares (such as funds). Consequently, if funds acquire shares in portfolio companies in order to realize a short-term gain, the partial income taxation method and the participation exemption may not be available to the investor. There is little guidance as to what is short-term but investors should be aware that disposals of shares within two years after the acquisition may be closely scrutinized by German tax auditors.

dd) Financing Costs

If the foreign investor takes out a loan to finance the acquisition of his interest in the fund, interest payments are generally (subject to certain restrictions) tax deductible for personal and corporate income tax purposes as 'special business expenses' (*Sonderbetriebsausgaben*) of the foreign investor with respect to the co-entrepreneurship.[11] The tax deductibility of financing costs is an advantage of a co-entrepreneurship when compared to a fund that is organized as a private asset management partnership, where investors usually cannot deduct financing costs.

b) Trade Tax

Co-entrepreneurships are (unlike private asset management partnerships) subject to trade tax. Trade tax is owed by the co-entrepreneurship so that funds organized as co-entrepreneurships are not entirely tax transparent. The trade tax rate is set by the municipalities in which the fund maintains offices and varies between 7 and 17%. Generally, the entire income of the fund is subject to trade tax.

However, the partial income taxation method for individual investors and the participation exemption for corporate investors also affect the calculation of the trade tax base. If and to the extent capital gains from the sale of shares are attributable to individual investors of the fund and the partial income taxation method applies at the level of the individual investors, 40% of such income is trade tax exempt at the level of the fund.[12] Conversely, if and to the extent capital gains from the sale of shares are attributable to corporate investors of the fund and eligible for the participation exemption at the level of the corporate investors, effectively 95% of such capital gains are exempt from trade tax.[13]

Dividends received by the fund are usually fully subject to trade tax unless the specific trade tax participation exemption (*gewerbesteuerliches Schachtelprivileg*) applies. The trade tax participation exemption generally requires that the fund held at (or, in the case of foreign corporations, has held since) the begin-

---

11 40% of the financing costs effectively connected with capital gains or dividends of an individual investor that are 40% tax exempt are, however, not deductible.
12 And 40% of capital losses are not tax deductible for trade tax purposes.
13 And capital losses are not tax deductible.

ning of the assessment period 15% of the shares in the corporation paying the dividend.[14] If the dividend qualifies for the trade tax participation exemption, the dividend is, in principle, fully exempt from trade tax.[15]

Special business expenses at the level of an investor (e.g. financing costs for the acquisition of the fund interest) are generally also deductible for trade tax purposes at the level of the fund and therefore decrease the trade tax liability of the fund.

As activities of investors and the status of an investor as an individual or corporation may affect the trade tax liability of the fund (e.g. through special business expenses or the application of the partial income taxation method vs. the participation exemption), the profit and loss allocation of the limited partnership agreement should provide for a compensation scheme that attributes trade tax increases and decreases to the respective investor.

c) Trade Tax Credit for Individual Investors

Trade tax levied at the level of the fund and attributable to the distributive share of an individual foreign investor can be credited against the personal income tax of such individual in accordance with a lump-sum method. Whether trade tax can be fully offset against personal income tax under the lump-sum method largely depends on the individual tax situation of the investor and the trade tax rate set by the municipality. Usually, if the fund maintains its offices in a major German city and the investor is in the highest tax bracket, the trade tax credit leaves the individual investor with an effective trade tax burden of 1 to 2% in addition to his income tax burden of up to 47.5%, provided the fund's investors are only individuals. If the fund admits also corporate investors the effective trade tax burden may increase slightly.

Corporate investors cannot credit the trade tax of the partnership against corporate income tax.

d) Impact of Double Taxation Treaties

The German tax consequences for foreign investors in a fund that is organized as a co-entrepreneurship do generally not depend on whether the foreign investor is entitled to double taxation treaty benefits or not.

---

14 If the EU Parent-Subsidiary Directive applies to such dividend, only a 10% threshold is required for the trade tax participation exemption. Other dividends of foreign corporations have to meet further requirements (active business test) in order to qualify for the trade tax exemption.

15 Expenses in connection with the trade tax exempt dividend are generally not deductible for trade tax purposes. An exception applies if and to the extent the dividend is included in the distributive share of a corporate investor and the requirements for the participation exemption at the level of such corporate partner are met. 5% of such portion of the dividend will be subject to trade tax at the level of the partnership, whereas actual expenses incurred in connection with such portion of the dividend will be fully trade tax deductible.

If a double taxation treaty applies, Germany will claim the right to tax the income of the fund under the business profits article of the treaty (see Art. 7 of the OECD MC). For German tax purposes, the co-entrepreneurship will be considered a German permanent establishment of the foreign investor. Double taxation issues arise if the investor's country of residence takes the view that the activities of the fund do not create a permanent establishment within the meaning of Art. 7 of the OECD MC. In this case, the foreign investor has to rely on a foreign tax credit for the German tax in his country of residence.

Until recently, the German tax administration also claimed a right to tax profits of a mere co-entrepreneurship by law (that did not actually carry out a trade or business) under Art. 7 of the OECD MC. Having been overruled by several decisions rendered by the Federal Tax Court, the German tax administration has released a new revenue ruling[16], according to which co-entrepreneurships by law are treated as private asset management partnerships for double taxation treaty purposes. Consequently, the description of the tax consequences for foreign investors in a co-entrepreneurship in this section IV should not apply if the fund is a co-entrepreneurship by law and the investor is entitled to treaty benefits. Such foreign investor should only be subject to tax in limited circumstances as described under section III for funds that are organized as private asset management partnerships.

2. Tax Consequences for Non-German Resident Sponsors

Unlike carried interest in a fund organized as a private asset management partnership (that is taxed as compensation), the German tax authorities can often be convinced that carried interest in a fund organized as a co-entrepreneurship should be considered a distributive share in the income of the fund. In this case, the description on the taxation of non-German investors also applies to the taxation of the proportionate interest and the carried interest of a non-German sponsor. Funds should, however, obtain a private letter ruling to this effect in order to obtain legal certainty.

V. Conclusions

- A German fund organized as a private asset management partnership is the only choice for foreign investors that wish to avoid tax filing and payment obligations in Germany. Those foreign investors should be aware, however, that there is a risk that the classification of the fund as a private asset management partnership will be challenged by the German tax authorities in the future (which would give rise to interest and penalty payments).
- For foreign corporate investors, a German fund organized as a co-entrepreneurship may still be a good choice if the income of the fund mainly comprises capital gains from the sale of shares. Due to the participation exemp-

---

16 Guidance issued by the German Federal Finance Ministry on 26 September 2014, file no: BMF IV B 5-S1300/09/10003, Federal Tax Gazette I 2014, 1258.

tion, the effective German tax burden would only amount to 1.5% (corporate income and trade tax).[17]

- However, if the participation exemption for capital gains becomes subject to a 10% holding requirement in the future or the fund mainly derives dividends, the aggregate German tax burden for corporate investors could be as high as 33%. This may still be acceptable for foreign investors that are (i) subject to a higher corporate tax rate and (ii) entitled to a tax exemption under a treaty or a foreign tax credit in their country of residence (possibly U.S. investors).

- For foreign individual investors, a German fund organized as a co-entrepreneurship[16] may increase the tax burden since the capital gains tax rate of his country of residence is often lower than the effective German tax rate of approximately 31% or higher (like for U.S. investors). If, however, the investor's country of residence has a higher capital gains tax rate than Germany and grants the investor a tax exemption under a treaty or a foreign tax credit, a co-entrepreneurship may still be an acceptable or even advantageous choice.

- Foreign sponsors of a German fund organized as private asset management partnership should consider a direct interest in the fund or the use of a carry vehicle that does not have a German office and does not comprise German-resident sponsors in order to avoid potential double taxation issues with respect to carried interest.

- Even if it is not possible to structure a carry vehicle without a German office and German-resident partners, the private asset management partnership may still be the preferred choice for foreign sponsors. In the case of a fund organized as a co-entrepreneurship[16], the entire carried interest derived from a fund organized as a co-entrepreneurship would be taxable in Germany. The major portion of the carried interest would be subject to German capital gains tax rates (approximately 31%) that are often higher than in his country of residence. By contrast, if the double taxation risk in a private asset management partnership scenario materializes, the carried interest would be subject to German tax at a rate of approximately 28% and the foreign sponsor may be able to successfully argue that only a portion of the carried interest is subject to German tax whereas the residual carried interest is attributable to a foreign permanent establishment.

---

17 Except for co-entrepreneurships by law, which are treated like private asset management partnerships if the investor/sponsor is entitled to treaty benefits.

Dr. Helder Schnittker LL.M.

Lawyer, Certified Tax Lawyer

Areas of Specialization

- Private equity and venture capital (fund formation and structuring of transactions)
- Structuring of cross-border investments (inbound and outbound)
- Real-estate transactions
- Taxation of corporations and partnerships
- Advice for professional partnerships

Telephone +49 30/21 00 20-20

Email: helder.schnittker@fgs.de

Typical Transaction Structures for Buyout Investments in Germany

by Martin Oltmanns

Contents

I. Introduction
  1. The Private Equity Industry in Germany
  2. Parameters for the Investment Structure
II. Acquisition and Holding Structure
  1. Fiscal Unity
  2. Downstream Merger
  3. Alternative Debt Pushdown Structures
  4. The Interest Barrier

III. Tax-Efficient Exit Structure
IV. Management Participations
  1. The Manager Limited Partnership
  2. Granting the Management Participation
  3. Beneficial Ownership by the Manager
V. Conclusion

I. Introduction

1. The Private Equity Industry in Germany

The private equity industry in Germany has grown immensely in the last 10 to 15 years. Private equity has become an important factor not only in the M&A market, but also in the modernization of the German economy. Private equity transactions have helped large German conglomerates to sell off noncore activities, and midsized companies to internationalize their activities and achieve a generational change. The venture capital industry, even though it has remained comparatively small by international standards, is nevertheless an important factor in bringing new business concepts and ideas to the market. Methods used in the private equity industry, such as for incentivizing management, financing acquisitions and valuing businesses, are today market standard and have been adopted in transactions outside the investment industry as well.

Between 200 and 250 private equity investment firms were active in Germany in 2013[1]. Apart from the internationally well-known large buyout funds, quite a number of midsize private equity funds with a focus on investing in the German *Mittelstand* exist.

At the end of 2013 the assets under management of private equity funds in Germany amounted to approximately EUR 40.26 billion. This sum is made up of the funds raised by German private equity funds, whether invested or not,

---

[1] This and the following figures are taken from the statistical data of the German Private Equity and Venture Capital Association (Bundesverband der Kapitalbeteiligungsgesellschaften) for 2013.

and the German investments of international funds and their German subsidiaries which do not manage Germany-specific funds. Of the EUR 40.26 billion, approximately EUR 22.74 billion can be attributed to the assets of German private equity funds and approximately EUR 17.52 billion are accounted for by the German investments of international private equity funds. Therefore, roughly 44% of the private equity investments in Germany are carried out by international funds. The remainder are the investments or not-yet-invested funds of Germany-based private equity funds.

About three-quarters of the investments of private equity funds can be attributed to buyout transactions. Venture capital investments account for a much smaller part. Buyout investments and venture capital investments have distinct characteristics and, even though they are similar in their aims, have very different transaction structures and mechanisms. The comments below focus on buyout transactions.

2. Parameters for the Investment Structure

The structures of buyout transactions are usually driven by three main factors:

- The acquisition and holding structure should minimize any tax leakage, so that the free cash flow is optimized;
- The structure needs to take into account that the acquired business is to be sold after a few years and needs to ensure a tax-efficient sale of the business;
- Practically all buyout transactions involve a management equity program, usually in the form that the management is granted a participation in the equity of the acquired business. The acquisition structure is designed to ensure that this management equity program is not subject to wage tax but receives beneficial capital gains taxation treatment.

These three structuring objectives are reviewed in turn below, followed by a discussion of how they affect the structures of buyout transactions in the German market.

II. Acquisition and Holding Structure

A key element of buyouts is the relatively high level of nonrecourse debt financing, so as to maximize the returns on the equity invested. Therefore, a standard structure provides for the use of a NewCo (the acquisition vehicle), which will take up the debt financing and receive equity financing from the private equity fund, and will, with these funds, acquire the target business.

This structure usually results in a NewCo with high interest expenses and a target company as the subsidiary of this NewCo. It is evident that the interest expenses of the NewCo should be used as a tax shelter for the operating profits of the target business. The means of achieving this, usually described as 'debt pushdown', are well-known and also well-established in the German market.

1. Fiscal Unity

The first approach is to create a fiscal unity between the acquisition vehicle and the target company. This fiscal unity will result in any interest payments of the acquisition vehicle being deductible from the earnings of the target, as these earnings will be taxed at the level of the acquisition vehicle. A further advantage is that the capital maintenance provisions of German corporate law are no longer applicable. This allows the target to grant security interests over its assets to the lenders of the acquisition vehicle (upstream securities). However, the fiscal unity may require a change in the business year of the target company and, more importantly, may mean that any tax loss carryforwards of the target that stem from before the fiscal unity are no longer usable. Such loss carryforwards can be used as a tax shelter only once the fiscal unity has been terminated and the target company is once again subject to corporate income tax itself.

2. Downstream Merger

The second instrument to achieve a debt pushdown is a downstream merger. The downstream merger results in the target company and the acquisition vehicle becoming one legal entity and the target assuming all debts of the acquisition vehicle. It may, however, require prior corporate measures, as it will usually result in a transfer of the liabilities of the acquisition vehicle only. The downstream merger will not lead to a transfer of assets since the only assets of the acquisition vehicle are normally the shares in the target. These shares are automatically transferred to the shareholders of the acquisition vehicle, who thereby become the direct shareholders of the target company. In order not to violate capital maintenance provisions of German corporate law, the net asset value of the target company must therefore exceed its stated capital by an amount at least equivalent to the amount of the debt financing transferred from the acquisition vehicle to the target. From an economic point of view, this requirement should always be fulfilled. The target is acquired in an arm's length transaction and the acquisition is financed by debt and equity. Therefore, the true economic value of the equity of the target company (as opposed to its book value) will exceed the amount of debt financing by the amount of the invested equity. Unless the invested equity is less than the stated capital of the target (which is very unlikely), the target should therefore always have a net asset value in excess of the debt financing and the stated capital. Since the capital maintenance provisions, however, are based on the book value of the equity and not on its economic value, it may be necessary to realize hidden reserves before the downstream merger can be carried out. Again, such a balance sheet step-up should of course be tax-neutral. As the fairly strict dependency of the tax accounts on the commercial balance sheet was relaxed in 2006, it is usually possible to achieve tax neutrality of step-ups in the commercial balance sheet.

It has to be noted that if the target is a German stock corporation (*Aktiengesellschaft*) such a downstream merger may not be possible, since the capital maintenance regime of a stock corporation is significantly stricter than that of a German privately held corporation (*GmbH*).

A further issue may be that the downstream merger may, for tax purposes, be treated as a disposal of the shares in the target. If these shares have been acquired not by means of a purchase transaction, but by means of a contribution in kind (which frequently happens when the management participation in a secondary buyout transaction is rolled over), this disposal may have a negative tax impact on the former tax neutrality of the contribution.

In spite of these complexities, a downstream merger is often the preferred route of a debt pushdown for the financing banks. It removes the structural subordination which the acquisition financing would otherwise be subject to.

3. Alternative Debt Pushdown Structures

A further method for a debt pushdown is an upstream merger of the target into the acquisition vehicle. However, in comparison to the downstream merger the upstream merger has the disadvantages of resulting in a forfeit of any tax loss carryforwards of the target and of potentially triggering real estate transfer tax.

A comparatively easy way of bringing about a debt pushdown, which is, however, used only in smaller transactions, is to transform the target into a limited partnership. Following the transformation, the target becomes tax-transparent for income tax purposes and the income of the limited partnership is directly attributed to its limited partner, the acquisition vehicle, where it can be offset against any interest payments. For trade tax purposes, a limited partnership is not transparent. However, the interest payments of the acquisition vehicle will be treated as expenses which may be deducted from the income of the limited partnership at the level of the limited partnership.

One other potential measure to achieve a debt pushdown is a credit-financed dividend payment from the target to the acquisition vehicle. The acquisition vehicle may use this dividend to repay the acquisition financing. To avoid any withholding taxes which the target may have to pay on such dividends, an upstream loan may be a viable option. Similarly, the target may redeem some of its shares held by the acquisition vehicle and finance the payment of the redemption amount through a bank loan. Again, the acquisition vehicle would use the redemption payment to repay the acquisition financing it had taken up.

4. The Interest Barrier

A specialty of German tax law is the interest barrier rule. According to this rule, which was introduced to German tax law in 2008, interest payments (net of any interest income) are deductible from the taxable earnings in an amount of no more than 30% of the 'tax EBITDA'. The intention of the interest barrier was to avoid any base erosion by international corporate groups, which could apply greater leverage to their German activities than to their activities in jurisdictions with a lower tax rate. The interest barrier rule does not apply if:

(i) the entity in question is not part of a corporate group;
(ii) the legal entity is part of a corporate group, and its equity as a percentage of its total assets is as high as or higher than the equity of the entire corporate group (the 'escape clause')[2];
(iii) the total amount of net interest expenses does not exceed EUR 3 million.

In smaller private equity transactions, the threshold of EUR 3 million may already solve the problem caused by the interest barrier rule. Given the current low interest rates, interest payments in an amount of EUR 3 million will allow for debt financing of between EUR 50 million and EUR 75 million. In larger private equity transactions, other measures will be required to avoid the tax leakage created by the interest barrier rule.

Some commentators have argued that private equity funds should always benefit from the escape clause, as each investment of the fund should be regarded as a separate corporate group. If this were the case, the financial sponsor could fairly easily structure the financing in such a way that the equity of the relevant entity is not lower than that of the entire group. However, this argument requires the private equity fund itself and its other investments to be disregarded for the equity comparison. Even though there is something to be said for the argument that a private equity fund does not qualify as the top entity of a corporate group, this argument has so far not been accepted by the tax authorities.

To some extent it may be possible to transfer the acquisition debt from the target (which, after the debt pushdown, has to bear the interest expenses) to its subsidiaries and thereby to reduce the interest payments of each entity. Again, this will in all likelihood work only in smaller transactions. In large transactions, it will be difficult to split the acquisition financing between the target group entities in such a way that each entity (which is not part of a fiscal unity) only has to bear interest payments of less than EUR 3 million. To the extent that the debt is pushed on to legal entities located outside of Germany, the threshold of EUR 3 million does not need to be observed. Depending on the size of the foreign activities of the target group, using the debt capacity of these foreign subsidiaries may present a way out of the interest barrier rule. A further means of using the debt capacity of foreign subsidiaries may be to establish additional acquisition entities in the foreign jurisdictions (as subsidiaries of the main acquisition vehicle) and for those foreign acquisition entities to acquire the foreign subsidiaries of the target group. The acquisitions carried out in the foreign jurisdictions can then be debt-financed. The proceeds received by the German target could be used to reduce the debt burden in Germany and thereby also the German interest payments.

---

2 A shortfall is disregarded if the equity ratio of the entity falls short of the equity ratio of the entire group by no more than 2 percentage points.

In summary, creating a tax-efficient holding structure presents a number of challenges under German tax and corporate law which can usually be resolved to the satisfaction of the private equity fund. However, they require a detailed analysis of the cash flows and the tax situation of the target group.

III.   Tax-Efficient Exit Structure

A further challenge for the acquisition structure is that it should allow for a tax-efficient exit of the private equity fund. In this context it should be noted that roughly 45% of the amounts invested in buyout transactions in Germany (as equity) come from private equity funds located outside Germany. In these cases, it usually makes sense for the private equity fund to sell its investment in the German target group by selling the top entity of the German acquisition structure (i.e. if there is only one acquisition vehicle in Germany which has acquired the target group, this acquisition vehicle should be sold). In this way, the private equity fund can avoid paying any withholding taxes which would otherwise have to be paid if the German entity which has sold the target group is paying out the sales proceeds as a dividend to the foreign private equity fund. By selling the German TopCo, the private equity fund can avoid withholding tax (since most double taxation treaties stipulate that no withholding tax can be levied on the sale of shares in a corporation unless it qualifies as a real estate corporation). In addition, issues relating to forum shopping and substance requirements can be mostly avoided. Of course, general provisions against tax abuse will nevertheless need to be observed. However, specific provisions against forum shopping generally apply only to dividend payments.

To ensure a tax-efficient sale of the German top holding company, Luxembourg holding companies are very often interposed between the German acquisition structure and the foreign private equity fund. The reasons for this are firstly that the capital gains achieved in the sale of the portfolio entity will under certain conditions remain tax-free in Luxembourg, and secondly that Luxembourg law allows the use of hybrid financing instruments which will be treated as debt financing by Luxembourg tax law and as equity financing by US tax law. Therefore, interest expenses on these hybrid instruments can be used to generate expenses in Luxembourg which may be used as a tax shelter for other income derived from the portfolio entity by the Luxembourg holding company. In addition, if the hybrid financing instruments are redeemed or repaid (at least if they qualify as convertible preferred equity certificates), Luxembourg tax law will treat this as a repayment of debt and will not levy any withholding taxes thereon.

As an alternative to using hybrid financing instruments, the Luxembourg holding company may issue different classes of stock, each class reflecting a specific investment of the holding company ('tracking stock'). The holding company can then use the proceeds obtained from the sale of a specific investment to redeem or repurchase the corresponding class of stock. By doing so, the shareholder of the relevant class of stock will achieve income from the sale of shares which is not subject to a withholding tax and which may be treated as capital gains in his jurisdiction.

It is for these reasons that foreign private equity funds very often go through Luxembourg when they invest in German targets. However, depending on the intended exit structure, other jurisdictions should be taken into consideration as well.

If the foreign private equity fund intends to carry out several investments in Germany or in Europe generally, it may make sense to work with at least two layers of holding companies in Luxembourg: on the lower layer a holding company for each investment and on the top layer a holding company for the lower-layer Luxembourg holding companies. By combining this structure with the use of convertible preferred equity certificates or tracking stock, a tax-efficient repatriation of the capital gains arising from the individual investments may be possible.

IV. Management Participations

There are of course many possibilities to structure a management participation in any increase in the value of the target. They range from a mere contractual arrangement entitling the management to additional compensation depending on the purchase price achieved in the exit process to making the managers true shareholders. The preferred method is generally a direct management participation in the equity of the acquisition vehicle. Firstly, such a direct participation usually has the strongest effect on the incentives of the managers and enhances their position as true co-owners of the target business. Secondly, only a true shareholder position will enable the managers to benefit from favorable capital gains tax treatment (in comparison to the otherwise applicable tax treatment as a wage component).

1. The Manager Limited Partnership

A management shareholding in the acquisition vehicle is sometimes structured as a direct shareholding in which each manager holds a certain percentage of the shares. Alternatively, a limited partnership that holds the shares for all managers may be set up; all managers then become limited partners in the limited partnership (the 'manager LP'). Such manager LPs have the obvious advantage of giving the sponsor greater control over the management participations. They are usually used where a large number of managers participate in the management equity program. With a manager LP, any changes in the managers participating in the program can be brought about simply by transferring limited partnership interests without having to transfer shares in the acquisition vehicle. The decision-making process in the acquisition vehicle is made easier by the fact that the general partner of the manager LP is usually an entity controlled by the financial sponsor. Finally, sometimes one of the limited partners is a warehouse that holds its limited partnership interest on behalf of future managers of the target who may wish to join the management equity program. If such a vehicle to bundle all management participation is used, it is important to ensure that the vehicle is tax-transparent.

2. Granting the Management Participation

The structure of the management participation should ensure that no wage tax is payable when the participation is granted. Therefore, each manager has to acquire his shares in the acquisition vehicle under the same conditions as the financial investor. If he were to receive beneficial treatment, the benefit could be attributed by the tax authorities to his services as a manager and could be made subject to wage tax. Charging the managers the same acquisition price per share will, however, usually mean that they hold very small participations in the acquisition vehicle only, since under normal circumstances they do not have sufficient funds available to finance a significant equity contribution to the acquisition vehicle out of their own means. A very small equity share of the managers will, however, not achieve the aims of making the managers co-owners of the business and giving them an incentive to increase the shareholder value. Therefore, financial sponsors usually aim to grant the management team between 5% and 15% (sometimes as much as 20%) of the common stock of the acquisition vehicle. The parameters conflict: On the one hand, the management team should receive a significant shareholding in the acquisition vehicle. On the other hand, the managers have limited funds available and should be protected against any downside risks. Usually, the top-level managers are expected to invest around the equivalent of one year's salary and should be protected from the risk of losing more than this investment. Various solutions are available to bridge these conflicts:

- The acquisition vehicle may issue different classes of shares. Ordinary shares, which entitle the holder to participate fully in any increase in value of the target business, are subscribed by the management team and the financial sponsor. Preferred shares are subscribed by the financial sponsor only. These preferred shares receive only a fixed share in the liquidation proceeds, usually expressed as their issue price plus a certain percentage per annum of that issue price. This share has priority over the common stock. In economic terms, the preferred shares can therefore be considered as a further layer of debt. The investment of the managers is effectively leveraged to a higher degree than the investment of the private equity fund. The managers have to invest less equity and have to accept that if the target group does not develop according to plan, the payments on the preferred shares may eat up all of the sales proceeds and result in the entire investment of the managers being lost. However, if the investment turns out well, the additional leverage will mean that the managers may earn significant rates of return.

- Comparable to the issuance of preferred stock is the granting of shareholder loans by the financial sponsor only. The management team would not participate in the granting of such shareholder loans, and would instead focus on acquiring common stock. The economic effect of such a structure is identical to a structure operating with preferred shares. Preferred stock may, however, have some advantages. Firstly, the liquidation preference to be paid on the preferred stock (in an exit event) should not be considered as interest expense of the acquisition vehicle and may therefore result in better key performance indicators for the entire target group. Secondly, shareholder loans may be harmful with regard to the interest barrier rule. Section 8a of the German Corporate Income Tax Act (*Körperschaftsteuergesetz*) stipulates that the interest barrier rule applies even though the entity in question is not part of the corporate group if the interest payments made to a shareholder who holds more than 25% of the shares in the entity exceed 10% of the net interest expenses. Similarly, the escape clause is applicable only as long as interest payments to a 25% or more shareholder do not exceed 10% of the net interest expenses.

In both cases, the consideration paid on the additional equity or the shareholder loan has to comply with arm's length conditions. As long as this is the case, it is unlikely that the financial authorities will be able to successfully argue that the beneficial treatment the managers receive by not having to contribute to the preferred equity or the shareholder loan amounts to a form of remuneration in kind and should be subject to wage tax.

- Finally, the financial sponsor may grant loans to the individual members of the management team so that they can acquire shares in the acquisition vehicle under the same conditions as the financial sponsor. However, such a loan would normally be structured as a 'nonrecourse' loan: The manager will have to repay this loan only out of the proceeds he receives from selling his shares upon an exit event. Otherwise, the manager would be exposed to an unreasonable downside risk. A nonrecourse structure has two disadvantages, however. Firstly, the financial authorities may argue that the manager has not become the beneficial owner of his shares in the acquisition vehicle as he is not exposed to any downside risk. Secondly, if the exit proceeds are insufficient to repay the entire loan granted by the financial sponsor, the financial sponsor will effectively waive the remaining amount. Such a waiver might be considered as income of the manager, which would then be fully subject to wage tax.

3. Beneficial Ownership by the Manager

A very important structuring issue is the question of beneficial ownership. For the managers to be entitled to capital gains taxation, it is important that they become not only the legal owners but also the beneficial owners of their shares in the acquisition vehicle. If they are not the beneficial owners of their shares, they will – from a tax perspective – receive part of the sales proceeds without giving up any asset in return. The profits from the sale can therefore not be subject to capital gains taxation, as there is no asset on which capital gains could have accrued. Therefore, the normal tax rate will apply. Only if the managers have obtained beneficial ownership in the shares *ab initio* will the entire increase in the value of these shares and the corresponding capital gains not be subject to wage tax. This is the very reason why vesting schemes are usually not used in buyout transactions, since they imply that the manager is not yet the owner of any nonvested shares.

The issue of beneficial ownership has an impact on the conditions of the management equity program. In particular, it has to be ensured that the manager fully participates in any increase or decrease in the value of the shares and that he has full control as to whether he receives the capital gains. Therefore, the 'bad leaver' cases in which the manager does not receive the full value of his shares, but is limited to the amount of his original capital contribution, have to be limited to cases of actual misconduct which are fully under the manager's control. Cases in which the manager is removed from office because his management has not achieved the desired results could be problematic if they are treated as 'bad leaver' cases.

V. Conclusion

Acquisition structures for buyout transactions tend to be fairly complex and have to take numerous aspects into account. From a tax perspective the most important aspects are the minimization of tax leakages during the period in which the investment is held, a tax-efficient exit structure, minimizing capital gains taxation and withholding taxes, and optimum management participation in the target. As shown above, German tax law provides a framework in which all of these aims can be achieved. However, careful tax planning and tax structuring is required. The potential pitfalls are numerous and the growing familiarity of the tax authorities with the functioning and concepts of leveraged buyouts has led to an increase in the number of cases where structuring mistakes have been identified.

Dr. Martin Oltmanns LL.M.

Lawyer, Tax Advisor, Attorney-at-Law

Areas of Specialization

- Mergers & acquisitions
- Corporate finance
- Capital markets law
- Private equity and venture capital

Telephone +49 30/21 00 20-20

Email: martin.oltmanns@fgs.de

Taxation of Partnership Income Under German International Law

by Franz Wassermeyer

Contents

I. Introduction
II. Treaty Entitlement and Taxable Entity
III. Provisions on Income Derived by Partnerships Contained in the Double Taxation Treaties Entered into by Germany
IV. German Tax-Treaty Treatment of Income Derived by a Partnership

1. Treaty Entitlement
2. Attribution to the Taxpayer of Taxation-Related Criteria
3. Taxation of a Personally Liable Shareholder of a *KGaA*
4. Methodological Classification

V. Conclusion

I. Introduction

While under German income tax and corporate income tax law, a partnership can derive income, it is not personally subject to tax on such income, and in this sense it is not itself a taxable entity. Rather, the income is attributed *pro rata* to the partners as their own income. The partners are liable for income tax or corporate income tax on such income. This also applies in the case of 'multi-tier' partnerships, provided that the income derived by a lower-tier partnership is attributed *pro rata* to the upper-tier partners if and to the extent that they are able to be a taxable entity under German tax law. Depending on the individual case, the income is calculated *pro rata* via several interposed partnerships. On an international level, many countries proceed in the same way, although differences may arise when it comes to the treatment of *Sondervergütungen* ('special business income'), which the partnership pays to its partners for services they render to it. The same applies to the tax treatment of *Sonderbetriebsvermögen* ('special business assets'), which partners hold in the interest of their partnership. Many countries, however, treat partnerships as separate taxable entities for corporate income tax purposes. US tax law even grants certain enterprises the right to choose how they wish to be classified ('check the box') and taxed: (a) as a corporation, or (b) as fiscally transparent, with their partners being taxed like co-entrepreneurs. This in turn can trigger differing classifications in the countries involved, resulting in differing interpretations of the applicable double taxation treaty (DTT).

For each case involving cross-border income, the general rule is that, on the first level, the following needs to be determined under the domestic law of the state applying the DTT: (i) the person taxable (the partnership or its partners), (ii) the nature of the income (e.g. trade or business income, or income from property administration), (iii) the amount in which the income is to be subjected to taxation, and (iv) in which amount statutory tax on income is assessable on the income in the applying state. The second level involves the application of the pertinent DTT in order to examine whether that DTT allows the applying state to tax the income without restrictions or provides for tax exemptions or tax credits. In this context, the question may arise of whether the partner of a partnership can invoke tax-treaty provisions realized by that partner's partnership and whose income is to be taxed, *pro rata*, at his level.

Based on German tax law, partnerships with their registered seat or place of management in Germany are covered – as *Personenvereinigungen* ('groups of individuals regarded as an entity') – by the term 'person' in Art. 3 para. 1(a) of the OECD Model Convention (OECD MC). They lack, however, the ability to be resident in Germany within the meaning of Art. 4 para. 1 of the OECD MC because they themselves are subject neither to income tax nor to corporate income tax. As a result, partnerships with their registered seat or place of management in Germany are usually – from the perspective of German tax law – not entitled to treaty benefits. Only the partners may be entitled to treaty benefits, to the extent that they may be a taxable entity within the meaning of Sec. 1 of the German Income Tax Act *(Einkommensteuergesetz)* or Sec. 1 of the German Corporate Income Tax Act *(Körperschaftsteuergesetz)*. It always has to be borne in mind in this connection that the partners of a partnership with its registered seat or place of management in Germany may be 'resident' in a third country. From a tax-treaty perspective this always raises the question as to what extent facts and circumstances that have been realized solely by the partnership may be attributed to its partners. This issue is frequently discussed under the heading of 'conflict of classification' *(Qualifikationskonflikt)*, and involves a broad range of aspects, only some of which can be covered in this article.

II. Treaty Entitlement and Taxable Entity

The question of treaty entitlement is, however, merely one side of the coin. The OECD MC employs the concept of 'residence' also in order to describe (i) the relevant taxable entity and (ii) its origin. In this connection, reference needs to be made to Art. 7 para. 1 of the OECD MC, which refers to the profits generated by an enterprise of a contracting state which carries on business in the other contracting state through a permanent establishment (PE) situated therein. This provision is supplemented by Art. 3 para. 1(d) of the OECD MC, which stipulates that the term 'enterprise of a contracting state' means an enterprise carried on by a resident of a contracting state. A partnership can naturally carry on an enterprise. However, if it lacks the ability to be resident in a contracting state, then the provision of Art. 7 para. 1 of the OECD MC appears to come to nothing, unless the partnership's PE can be attributed, from a tax-treaty perspective, to its partners who are resident in a contracting state. This is in line with the widely held legal opinion that the PEs of a partnership are 'simultaneously' treated as PEs of its partners.

However, reference also needs to be made to Arts. 10 and 11 of the OECD MC, which refer to dividends and interest 'paid' to a person resident in a contracting state. Without any doubt, dividends and interest can be 'paid' to a partnership if that partnership is a shareholder of the distributing corporation or the creditor of the loan receivable that triggered the interest. Even when interpreted in light of the wording of the rule, the term 'payment' does not shed any light on the level at which the payment is to be taxed as part of the income. The question therefore arises as to whether using the term 'payment' is appropriate in the circumstances. In practice, payment to a partnership is treated as a *pro-rata* payment to its partners. Also of relevance is the fact that only Art. 12 para. 1 (but not Arts. 10 and 11) of the OECD MC additionally use the term 'beneficial owner', which is why nothing can be deduced from that term for the purposes of interpreting Arts. 10 and 11 of the OECD MC.

Reference also needs to be made to Art. 15 para. 2(b) of the OECD MC. That provision concerns remuneration, derived in respect of an employment, which is paid by or on behalf of an employer who is resident in the contracting state in which the employment was exercised. In that respect, there is no doubt that a partnership can be an employer that pays the remuneration for employment, or on behalf of which such remuneration is paid. The partners of the partnership, by contrast, cannot usually be considered employers. Even based on German tax law, however, the partnership cannot be resident in any contracting state. Thus, if one sought to classify the partners of a partnership as fictitious employers and to proceed based on their residence, then one would encounter difficulties whenever a partnership consists of several partners who are resident in different states. This, of course, leads to the question of whether the OECD MC should not rather use the concept of residence solely to determine the treaty entitlement while describing both the taxable entity and the origin of income derived therefrom in a different way. Ultimately, payments made by, or for, a partnership are treated for tax-treaty purposes like payments made by, or for, its partners.

III. Provisions on Income Derived by Partnerships Contained in the Double Taxation Treaties Entered into by Germany

On 17 April 2013, the German Federal Finance Ministry published a basis for negotiations (GER-BN) with respect to entering into double taxation treaties. It was slightly amended on 22 Aug. 2013. Art. 11 para. 1 and Art. 12 para. 1 of the GER-BN refer to a person resident in a contracting state and deriving interest or royalties as beneficiary owner (*Nutzungsberechtigter*), which represents a departure from the OECD MC. The GER-BN does not contain any specific provisions regarding the taxation of income derived by partnerships. Reference should also be made to the letter issued by the Federal Finance Ministry on 16 April 2010[1], which specifically concerns the application of DTTs to partnerships. That letter is expected to be revised in 2014. A draft discussion paper was

---

1 Letter issued by the Federal Finance Ministry on 16 April 2010, Federal Tax Gazette Part I, 2010, p. 354.

issued in November 2013[2], the content of which is, however, expected to undergo further changes. The letters issued by the Federal Finance Ministry need to be viewed against the background of special provisions agreed in some of the DTTs entered into by Germany regarding the taxation of income derived by partnerships.

More specifically, the special provisions concern the following countries:

Albania/Algeria: Pursuant to Art. 4 para. 4 of the DTT-Albania and Art. 4 para. 4 of the DTT-Algeria, partnerships are deemed resident in the contracting state in which their place of actual management is situated. This applies irrespective of both (i) their personal liability to tax in one of the two contracting states and (ii) in which state the partners of the partnership are resident.

Belgium: Pursuant to Art. 3 para. 1 no. 4 of the DTT-Belgium, the German *OHG (Offene Handelsgesellschaft*, a 'general partnership'), *KG (Kommanditgesellschaft*, a 'limited partnership') and *Partenreederei* ('ship-owning partnership') within the meaning of the law prevailing in Germany are considered 'companies' and thus 'persons' within the meaning of Art. 3 para. 1 no. 2 of the DTT-Belgium, which pursuant to Art. 4 para. 1 of the DTT-Belgium are fictitiously considered resident in Germany. The same applies to partnerships under Belgian law which have opted in favor of their partners being liable to tax ('check the box').

Czech Republic/Slovakia: While the DTT-Czech Republic does not contain special provisions for partnerships, in the Czech Republic and in Slovakia certain partnerships are considered subject to corporate-income-tax liability on their entire income, which may trigger economic double taxation. The profit distributions made by such partnerships are taxed like dividends paid by a corporation.

Finland: Pursuant to Art. 4 para. 4 of the DTT-Finland, partnerships are considered resident in the contracting state under whose laws they were established. Pursuant to para. 1 of the Protocol to said DTT, however, the income must also be subject to taxation in that state (see also DTT-Iceland, DTT-Italy, DTT-Slovenia and DTT-Syria). Ultimately, para. 1 of the Protocol to the DTT limits the residence status of the partnership to its partners who are resident in that same state.

France: Under French tax law, French partnerships may opt to be taxed as corporations. Pursuant to Art. 2 para. 1 no. 4(c) of the DTT-France, a partnership is considered resident in France if its place of management is situated in France.

Greece: Greek partnerships are taxed as such in Greece. That is why they are also entitled to treaty benefits within the meaning of Art. 2 para. 1 no. 4(a) of the DTT-Greece. In certain circumstances, the tie-breaker rule of Art. 2 para. 1 no. 4(c) of the DTT-Greece is applicable.

Hungary: Under Hungarian tax law, certain partnerships are subject to Hungarian corporate income tax as legal entities. They thus fall within Art. 3 para. 1(b)

---

2 File ref. 2013/0950012.

and (c) of the DTT-Hungary, meaning that, pursuant to Art. 4 para. 1 of the DTT-Hungary, they can be resident in one of the two contracting states.

Iceland: Pursuant to Art. 4 para. 4 sentence 1 of the DTT-Iceland, partnerships are considered resident in the contracting state in which the place of their actual management is situated. As under the DTT-Finland, however, their income must also be subject to taxation in that state (see also DTT-Italy, DTT-Slovenia and DTT-Syria). Ultimately, Art. 4 para. 4 sentence 2 of the DTT-Iceland limits the residence status of the partnership to its partners who are resident in that same state.

Italy: Pursuant to para. 2 of the Protocol to the DTT-Italy, partnerships are considered resident in the contracting state under whose laws they were established or in which the primary subject of their activity is situated. As under the DTT-Finland and DTT-Iceland, however, their income must be subject to taxation in that state (see also DTT-Slovenia and DTT-Syria). Ultimately, the provision in the Protocol limits the residence status of the partnership to its partners who are resident in that same state.

Poland: While the DTT-Poland does not contain special provisions for partnerships, foreign partnerships have, since 2005, been subject to limited corporate income tax liability in Poland on their income derived from Poland, which may trigger economic double taxation.

Portugal: Pursuant to Art. 4 para. 4 of the DTT-Portugal, for purposes of Arts. 5–23 of the DTT-Portugal, partners are considered resident at their partnership's place of actual management. Commercial trading partnerships under Portuguese law are treated and taxed in Portugal like legal entities.

Romania: While the DTT-Romania does not contain special provisions for partnerships, in Romania certain partnerships are considered subject to corporate income tax liability with their entire income, which may trigger economic double taxation.

Slovenia: Under Slovenian tax law, certain partnerships are subject to Slovenian corporate income tax as legal entities. They thus fall within Art. 3 para. 1(c) of the DTT-Slovenia, meaning that, pursuant to Art. 4 para. 1 of the DTT-Slovenia, they can be resident in one of the two contracting states. Notwithstanding the above, pursuant to Art. 4 para. 4 of the DTT-Slovenia, partnerships are considered resident in the contracting state in which their place of management is situated. As in the DTT-Finland, DTT-Iceland and DTT-Italy, however, their income must also be subject to taxation in that state (see also DTT-Syria). Ultimately, this limits the residence status of the partnership to the income which is to be taxed in that same state.

Spain: Under Spanish tax law, certain partnerships are subject to Spanish corporate income tax as legal entities. They thus fall within Art. 3 para. 1(b) and (c) of the DTT-Spain, meaning that, pursuant to Art. 4 para. 1 of the DTT-Spain, they can be resident in one of the two contracting states.

Syria: Pursuant to Protocol No. 2 to the DTT-Syria, partnerships are considered resident in the contracting state in which the place of their actual management is situated. As under the DTT-Finland, DTT-Iceland, DTT-Italy and DTT-Slovenia, however, their income must also be subject to taxation in that state. Ultimately, this limits the residence status of the partnership to the income which is to be taxed in that same state.

Tunisia: Under Tunisian tax law, certain partnerships are subject to Tunisian corporate income tax as legal entities. They thus fall within Art. 3 para. 1(b) and (c) of the DTT-Tunisia, meaning that, pursuant to Art. 4 para. 1 of the DTT-Tunisia, they can be resident in one of the two contracting states.

US: In the US, there are corporate entities which are necessarily classified as corporate bodies and taxed as such ('*per-se* corporation'). Other corporate entities have an option, under the check-the-box regime, as to how they wish to be classified for tax purposes. In the event that they fail to exercise this option, their taxation follows certain standard classifications similar to those under German tax law (*Rechtstypenvergleich* or 'comparison of legal forms'). Eligible entities may diverge from this standard classification by choosing between being classified as a corporation or a partnership for tax purposes. Single-member business entities may also opt to be classified as a corporation.

IV. German Tax-Treaty Treatment of Income Derived by a Partnership

1. Treaty Entitlement

The fundamental problem as to the tax-treaty treatment of income actually derived by a partnership does not lie with treaty entitlement. In principle, the only persons who may be considered entitled to treaty benefits are persons who under the domestic tax law of the applying state are personally subject to tax with respect to the income concerned. That is why, in each case, what needs to be established in the first instance is which person is subject to tax on the respective income under the domestic tax law of the applying state. With respect to this person, it needs to be examined (i) whether it is a person within the meaning of Art. 3 para. 1(a) of the OECD MC and (ii) whether it is resident in one of the two contracting states within the meaning of Art. 4 of the OECD MC. If the answer to one of the questions is no, then the person that is subject to tax does not have treaty entitlement, meaning that it cannot claim any tax exemption/tax reduction under the DTT. This becomes evident if one considers the income derived by a partnership which is taxed as transparent in contracting state A, but as opaque in contracting state B. The opaque taxation in contracting state B leads to the partnership qualifying as a 'person' within the meaning of the DTT. It also follows from the relevant provision that it is conceivable for the partnership to be resident in contracting state B. This does not, however, affect the personal liability to tax of the partnership and its partners in contracting state A, which applies transparent taxation. From the perspective of contracting state A, tax exemptions and tax reductions can be claimed under the DTT only if the persons subject to tax in contracting state A are also entitled to treaty benefits.

2. Attribution to the Taxpayer of Taxation-Related Criteria

The problem in applying a DTT lies with the attribution of subject-matter taxation-related criteria, which in practical terms are solely realized by the partnership, to the respective person liable to tax. In many cases, such attribution does not cause any problems, i.e. it is self-evident. This is the case, for instance, with a partnership carrying on a trade or business *(gewerblich tätige Personengesellschaft)* which maintains a PE in another contracting state. A contracting state which applies transparent taxation already attributes the enterprise of the partnership to the partnership's partners pursuant to Art. 3 para. 1(d) of the OECD MC. Accordingly, that state assumes that each partner of the partnership carries on its own enterprise. As a result of this rule, the partnerships' PEs are also attributed *pro rata* to their partners.

The legal situation becomes complicated, however, if the DTT treats the partnership as a person resident in the source state, and opaque taxation is applied to its income in that state. The question then is whether the state of residence of the partners is not also bound to treat the enterprise within the meaning of Art. 3 para. 1(d) of the OECD MC as one of the partnership, meaning that it is only the partnership that maintains the PE, and that, when applying the method article, tax exemption/tax reduction is determined for tax-treaty purposes from the perspective of the resident partnership. The state of residence of the partner would be obliged to assume tax-free income of that partner because under the DTT and in view of the residence of the partnership in the source state, this contracting state does not have a right to tax. It would seem fair to say that the German tax authorities have been loath to implement this legal reasoning consistently. They treat as irrelevant for German tax purposes the partnership's residence in one of the two contracting states that is explicitly provided for in the DTT. This is evident when it comes to the taxation of the transfer of the interest in 'resident' partnerships. In the case of doubt, the partnership's state of residence applies Art. 13 para. 5 of the OECD MC, while Germany is likely to treat the same facts and circumstances as falling within Art. 13 para. 2 of the OECD MC. Put differently, with regard to their taxation of partners, the German tax authorities do not attach any importance to the partnership's residence in the source state that was explicitly agreed on in the DTT.

A conflict of attribution may also arise in another form. By way of illustration, let us imagine a German *GmbH* (*Gesellschaft mit beschränkter Haftung* or 'privately held corporation') with its registered seat and place of management in Germany and a PE in a foreign DTT state. The *GmbH*'s shareholders have to include German-resident taxpayers. In that foreign DTT state, the *GmbH* opts for transparent taxation, meaning that the tax levied in that state on the PE's profits is levied *pro rata* on the partners resident in Germany. The question now is whether the *GmbH*, which is subject to tax in Germany, is eligible for tax exemption or at least tax credit under the relevant method article – and, if so, whether the taxes paid by its shareholders may be credited at the level of the *GmbH* – or whether each contracting state interprets the DTT having regard to the person(s) involved. This also affects the application of certain tax-treaty fallback clauses, whose *raison d'être* consists in avoiding a situation where certain income ends up not being taxed at all. In this respect, however, Art. 22 no. 5(b) of the GER-BN solely focuses on whether the income is taxed at all rather than on whether it is taxed at the level of a particular person.

Another norm affected is Sec. 50d(9) no. 1 of the Income Tax Act, which, however, also solely focuses on the subject-matter taxation of the income rather than on whether it is taxed at the level of a particular person. Anybody who advocates that foreign tax should be credited for the benefit of the partners will need to take note of the fact that in the scenario set out above, these partners do not, under the tax law of their state of residence, derive any foreign income, which is why – for reasons of the calculation of the pertinent maximum amount – a tax credit is not available. It would therefore seem appropriate to grant the tax exemption/tax credit to the person that is subject to tax in each case, irrespective of the question at which level the source state levies the tax. The partnership's treaty entitlement expressly agreed on must extend to the persons which, under the domestic law of the contracting state, are subject to taxation of the income derived by the partnership.

3. Taxation of a Personally Liable Shareholder of a *KGaA*

The difficulty becomes even more evident if one includes in one's considerations the taxation of a personally liable shareholder of a *KGaA* (*Kommanditgesellschaft auf Aktien*, a 'partnership limited by shares') deriving foreign PE income. The *KGaA* is a company with its own legal personality (Sec. 278(1) of the German Stock Corporation Act *Aktiengesetz*). Pursuant to Sec. 1(1) no. 1 of the Corporate Income Tax Act, it is subject to unlimited corporate income tax liability to the extent that it has its registered seat or place of management in Germany. It may maintain a foreign PE and derive income from it which is tax-free under a DTT. The personally liable shareholder of the *KGaA* derives 'profit shares' and possibly *Sondervergütungen* ('special business income'), which are classified as income from trade or business *(Einkünfte aus Gewerbebetrieb)* by Sec. 15(1) sentence 1 no. 3 of the Income Tax Act. At least the profit share represents a part of the profit derived by the *KGaA*, which (pursuant to Sec. 9(1) sentence 1 no. 1 of the Corporate Income Tax Act) the *KGaA* may offset against its taxable profits like a fictitious business expense. The question is whether with imputed treaty entitlement on the part of the personally liable shareholder, the tax exemption agreed on in the applicable DTT does not also extend *pro rata* to the profit share within the meaning of Sec. 15(1) sentence 1 no. 3 of the Income Tax Act. Another question that may arise is whether any tax paid by the *KGaA* abroad has to be credited against the domestic (i.e. German) tax of the personally liable shareholder. According to the view advocated by this author, both questions should be answered in the affirmative because, in this respect, the DTT provides for subject-related rather than person-related tax exemption/tax credit. That is also a consequence of Sec. 50d(1) of the Income Tax Act. That provision solely deals with tax exemption for 'significant-holding' dividends *(Schachteldividenden)* but not with all tax exemptions agreed on in a DTT. Furthermore, reference should be made to Sec. 50d(1) sentence 11 of the Income Tax Act, which stipulates a partnership's eligibility for a refund of German taxes which were levied at the expense of its partners.

4. Methodological Classification

The legal question discussed here bears a factual relationship to experts' methodological understanding as to the interpretation of DTTs. In this connection, a position frequently encountered in the professional legal literature[3] is that the state of residence is bound, as a general rule, by the classification made by the source state. It need not be discussed here whether that position might perhaps be taking things too far. In any event, that position would seem to be right if and to the extent that a legal basis can be found for such a binding effect. Reasonably, such legal basis can only be contained in the applicable DTT. Accordingly, what is of key importance under the DTTs discussed above is that, therein, certain partnerships are expressly defined as a person resident in one of the two contracting states. This agreement must be observed in Germany even if a partnership is not classified as a taxable entity under domestic German tax law. The fact that Germany, as a contracting party, has contractually recognized a specific partnership as being a person resident within the meaning of the DTT can only mean that the application of the DTT – including that by the German contracting party – should be guided by that residence. However, if the partnership is liable for income tax and corporate income tax in Germany, then the tax exemption and tax credit agreed on under a tax treaty for the benefit of a partnership must be applied for the benefit of its partner who is subject to tax – at the very least if that partner is also personally entitled to treaty benefits.

V. Conclusion

In cross-border scenarios, one always has to examine very closely which legal entity to involve for the purposes of deriving foreign income. Said examination also extends to the personal liability to tax of the legal entity in question, which may be subject to different rules in the countries involved. In addition, possible option rights regarding classification have to be taken into account and exercised as appropriate. Next, note needs to be taken of the legal situation under the relevant DTT. More specifically, what matters is whether one of the contracting states recognizes the personal liability to tax of the entity in the other contracting state with all resulting consequences in terms of treaty law. A partnership's treaty entitlement, as contractually agreed, extends to its partners if and to the extent that at least one of the two contracting states taxes the partnership's income *pro rata* at the level of its partners and the partners themselves are also entitled to treaty benefits. Alternatively, many difficulties may be circumvented by reorganizing the chosen legal entity into one that does not give rise to such issues in the first place.

---

3 cf. in lieu of many: Vogel, in: Vogel/Lehner, DTTs, 5th edition, Introduction, marginal no. 176.

Prof. Dr. Dr. h.c. Franz Wassermeyer

Lawyer, Tax Advisor
Of Counsel

Areas of Specialization

- Corporate income tax law
- Taxation of international transactions
- Double taxation treaties
- Procedural law

Telephone (ext.) +49 228/95 94-311

Email: franz.wassermeyer@fgs.de

German Income Taxation of Foreign Partners in German Trading Partnership

by Klaus Sieker

Contents

I. Introduction
II. Basic Rules
  1. Qualification as a Partnership
  2. Allocation of Income to the Partners
  3. Additional Income Allocated to a Partnership as a Result of Dealings with Partners
  4. Taxation of Foreign Partners
III. Pitfalls
  1. Special Business Income
  2. Loss of Trading Status
  3. Trade Tax Consequences of the Acquisition of a Partnership Interest
  4. Conflicting Classification
IV. Structuring Considerations
  1. Avoiding Special Business Income/Asset Treatment
  2. Creating Special Business Expenses/Liabilities
  3. Avoiding German Dividend Withholding Tax
  4. Mitigating German Capital Gains Tax

I. Introduction

This article provides an overview of the most important German income tax issues faced by foreign partners in a German trading partnership. Foreign partners include for the purposes of this article individuals and corporations which maintain their tax residency in a country other than Germany.

A German partnership is a partnership established under the laws of Germany which maintains its place of management in Germany. Partnerships can be general partnerships (*offene Handelsgesellschaft – oHG*) or limited partnerships (*Kommanditgesellschaft – KG*). Most German partnerships are organized as a limited partnership with a German corporation (*GmbH*) as the sole general partner with an interest neither in the assets nor in the profits of the limited partnership. This structure is commonly known as a *GmbH & Co. KG*.

Trading partnerships are partnerships engaged in a trade of business giving rise to income from a trade (*Einkünfte aus Gewerbebetrieb*) within the meaning of Sec. 15(2) of the German Income Tax Act (*Einkommensteuergesetz*). Trading partnerships must be distinguished from 'deemed' trading partnerships (*gewerblich geprägte Personengesellschaft*), which (i) are not engaged in a trade or business (but rather earn income exclusively from investments) and (ii) have only corporations as general partners and (iii) are managed either only by general partners or by a person that is not a partner. Income earned by a trading (or deemed trading) partnership is subject to income tax and trade tax.

Operating a business in the form of a partnership is popular in Germany. It offers investors limited liability, a single level of income taxation and a high degree of flexibility in terms of structuring the relationship between the partnership and its partners and between the partners.

II. Basic Rules

1. Qualification as a Partnership

All German entities in the form of a partnership are treated as transparent for income tax purposes. Germany has no check-the-box type rules like those in the US Internal Revenue Code providing the partners with the option to have the partnership treated as a nontransparent (opaque) entity.

For purposes of trade tax, a partnership is a separate taxable entity and has to pay trade tax on its trade income. It is noted that individual, though not corporate, partners are entitled to a credit for the trade tax attributable to their share in the profits of the partnership against their personal income tax (Sec. 35 of the Income Tax Act). The amount of credit is capped, meaning that the credit reduces the income tax by the full amount of the trade tax only if the trade tax rate does not exceed 14%.

2. Allocation of Income to the Partners

For income tax purposes, the profits or losses of a partnership are attributed directly to the partners and taxed under the income tax rules in the case of individual partners and under the corporate income tax (*Körperschaftsteuer*) rules in the case of corporate partners. The partnership is, however, an accounting and reporting entity. Certain elections have to be exercised uniformly by all partners, and a partnership must maintain proper accounting records and file information returns with a tax local office where the partnership maintains its place of management. This tax office reviews the determination of profits (or losses) and their allocation among the partners, and its findings are binding for the income tax assessment of the partners (Secs. 180 and 181 of the General Tax Code).

Losses of limited partners are not deductible to the extent that the deduction results in a limited partner having a negative capital account (Sec. 15a of the Income Tax Act). The nondeductible portion is carried forward and set off against future profits from the same partnership, including profits realized on the disposition of the partnership interest or a portion of the partnership interest by the limited partner.

3. Additional Income Allocated to a Partnership as a Result of Dealings with Partners

A further peculiarity of German partnership taxation is that remuneration paid by a trading partnership to a partner for services rendered (e.g. management services), interest paid with respect to a partner's loan, or rentals paid for property let by a partner to the partnership, do not constitute business expenses for the partnership but increase the partners' distributive share in the partnership's profits (Sec. 15(1) sentence 1 no. 2 of the Income Tax Act). These payments from the partnership to a partner are known as special business income (*Sonderbetriebseinnahmen*). Expenses incurred by a partner in connection with earning special business income are deductible in computing the income of the partnership and the profit share attributable to the partner. Deductible expenses include depreciation in respect of a building owned by a partner and let to the partnership or interest expense suffered by a partner on a loan taken up for funding the purchase price of such a building. These expenses are known as special business expenses (*Sonderbetriebsausgaben*).

The relevant regulations cover not only the income from such dealings, but also the underlying assets. For example, if a partner rents property to a partnership, the property is allocated as a special business asset (*Sonderbetriebsvermögen I*) to the partnership and shown on a special balance sheet (*Sonderbetriebsbilanz*) of the partner that is part of the partnership declaration filed with the tax office. As a consequence, if a partner disposes of a special business asset, the profit or loss from the disposition is subject to trade tax (at the level of the partnership) and to income tax at the level of the disposing partner.

4. Taxation of Foreign Partners

A foreign partner is subject to German income tax/corporation tax with his share in the taxable profits of a German trading partnership to the extent that such profit share is attributable to a permanent establishment maintained in Germany (Sec. 49(1) no. 2(a) of the Income Tax Act). For this purpose, a permanent establishment maintained by the partnership in Germany is attributed to its partners. This further means that profits earned by the partnership which are derived from a permanent establishment maintained by the partnership outside Germany is not subject to German income tax as far as such profit is attributable to a foreign partner.

Taxable income of a foreign partner includes income derived from a disposition of his partnership interest, again as far as such income is attributable to the German permanent establishment.

German income tax arising on taxable income derived from an interest in a German trading partnership is collected by means of a tax assessment. The partners will be assessed with quarterly prepayments on their annual income tax/corporate tax charge. A partnership distributing funds to a partner is not under any obligation to withhold German income tax. Germany does not operate a branch profits tax or branch interest tax similar to a dividend withholding tax or interest withholding tax on payments made by a partnership to its partners.

A foreign individual partner is subject to German income tax with German source taxable income at progressive income tax rates. At present the marginal top income tax rate is set at 45%. Including the 5.5% solidarity surcharge, the top marginal rate comes to 47.475%. Upon application an individual partner is entitled to a preferential tax rate of 28.25% (29.80375% including solidarity surcharge) for that portion of his taxable profit share which is retained by the partnership (Sec. 34a of the Income Tax Act). If, in subsequent years, the partnership distributes some or all of the retained earnings that had been taxed at the preferential rate, the distributed retained earnings trigger a further income tax at a flat rate of 25%. In other words, the benefit of the preferential tax rate is granted only temporarily for as long as the profits are not distributed by the partnership to the partner.

For income tax purposes it makes essentially no difference whether the foreign partner resides in a treaty country or in an EU/EEA member state or anywhere else outside Germany. As an exception the country of residence of the foreign partner matters in the case of certain reorganizations such as the conversion or a merger of a trading partnership into a German (or EU/EEA) corporation. Rollover relief may be applied for only if certain conditions are met, including the requirement that the foreign partner is either resident in the EU/EEA or is not entitled to treaty protection against German capital gains tax arising on a disposition of shares in the German corporation resulting from the conversion.

III. Pitfalls

1. Special Business Income

Most other countries' tax systems do not operate a concept comparable to the German special business income and special business asset provisions. Foreign partners are therefore often surprised to learn that they are subject to German income tax with, for example, interest earned from a loan granted to the trading partnership. This is typically an expensive lesson for the foreign taxpayer since, as a rule, the foreign partner will also be subject to income tax in his country of residence with the interest earned.

One might expect this issue not to arise in cases where the foreign partner is resident in a country which has a tax treaty with Germany patterned against the OECD MC. Unfortunately, this is not the case. Germany's tax authorities have always insisted that the domestic rules concerning special business income are also applicable in a treaty context whether or not the treaty incorporates this concept (as a few treaties do, such as those with Austria and Switzerland). In contrast, Germany's highest tax court, the Federal Tax Court, has over the past 25 years rendered several decisions holding that interest earned by a foreign partner on a loan granted to a German trading partnership falls under article 11 (interest) rather than under article 7 (business income from a permanent establishment) of an applicable treaty conforming to the OECD MC.[1] Most of Germany's tax treaties provide that interest may be taxed only by the

---

[1] See Federal Tax Court of Oct. 17, 2007 – I R 5/06, Federal Tax Gazette Part II, 2009, p. 356; Federal Tax Court of Oct. 16, 2002 – I R 17/01, Federal Tax Gazette Part II, 2003, p. 631.

country of residence of the person earning the interest. Tax authorities and the legislator were not prepared to accept these decisions. Rather, treaty-overriding legislation was enacted in the German Annual Tax Act (*Jahressteuergesetz*) of 2009 allowing for the taxation of special business income as profits attributable to a permanent establishment on a retroactive basis in all open cases (Sec. 50d(10) of the Income Tax Act). Its original version was poorly drafted, rendering it virtually useless. A far more comprehensive version was enacted with the law of June 26, 2013, which again shall be applied on a retroactive basis in all open cases. The most recent version provides for relief against double taxation by granting the foreign partner a right to have any foreign tax credited against his German income tax attributable to the special business income being taxed in Germany.

2. Loss of Trading Status

If a German trading partnership discontinues a trade or business, foreign partners may be faced with quite dramatic German income tax charges. A typical situation giving rise to the question of whether the partnership is still engaged in a trade or business involves the carve-out of the partnership's business into a corporate subsidiary of the partnership. Arguably, if the partnership carves out its entire business and as a consequence limits its activities to holding the shares in the corporate subsidiary, the restructuring results in a cessation of the partnership's trade. A foreign partner of such nontrading partnership no longer earns income from a German trade or business but rather German source dividend income which is not subject to progressive German income taxation. In addition, and more importantly, the foreign partner residing in a treaty country will typically be protected against German income taxation on a profit derived from selling the interest in the nontrading partnership or on a profit derived by the nontrading partnership from selling the shares in the corporate subsidiary.

Against this background, it may not be surprising to learn that the change in status from trading to nontrading gives rise to a deemed disposition of the partnership interest in the hands of a foreign partner residing in a treaty country. Sec. 4(1) Sentence 3 of the Income Tax Act. Those partners who do not reside in a treaty country or are not entitled to treaty benefits should not be regarded as having disposed of their partnership interest if the partnership qualifies as a deemed trading partnership.

3. Trade Tax Consequences of the Acquisition of a Partnership Interest

A potential acquiror of an interest in a German trading partnership is typically pleased to learn that the acquisition of a partnership interest is treated for German tax purposes like an acquisition of the assets and liabilities of a partnership (asset deal). As a consequence, the tax basis of the partnership's assets and liabilities is stepped up to their fair market value as evidenced by the purchase price paid for the partnership interest. The step-up results in additional depreciation and amortization charges, and therefore provides future tax relief.

In contrast, a potential acquiror may be surprised to find out that the trade tax arising on the capital gain earned by the disposing partner is charged against the partnership (rather than against the disposing partner). This means that the acquiror indirectly bears the trade tax burden of the seller unless the acquiror protects himself in the sale and purchase agreement against such damage.

4. Conflicting Classification

As mentioned above, a German trading partnership is treated for German income tax purposes as a transparent entity. There is no exception to this rule. In particular, it is irrelevant whether the German partnership is classified as transparent entity under foreign tax laws applicable in the country of residence of a foreign partner.

Where a German trading partnership is treated as opaque under applicable foreign tax law, the foreign partner is regularly exposed to (unrelieved) double taxation. If, for instance, the foreign partner disposes of its partnership interest, the foreign partner is subject to German income tax with capital gain achieved on the disposition. Since the foreign tax laws treat the disposition as a disposition of shares in a German entity, the foreign seller is typically not entitled to any relief from double taxation in its country of residence. This is because from the perspective of the residence country, the seller is not disposing of a German permanent establishment precluding the application of tax treaty provisions which entitle the seller either to an exemption from tax in its country of residence or to a credit for the German tax against the seller's residence country tax.

IV. Structuring Considerations

1. Avoiding Special Business Income/Asset Treatment

In principle, special business income/asset treatment might be avoided quite easily because this concept applies only, as a rule, to income earned and assets held by the partner itself in a German trading partnership; in principle it does not apply to persons affiliated with the partners.

Let us suppose that a US resident corporation is a partner in a German trading partnership and further assume that the partnership requires funds for expanding its business operations. Such funds could be provided by the partner in the form of equity or as an interest-bearing loan resulting in the same German tax burden. Alternatively, the US parent corporation of the US corporation that is a partner in the German trading partnership may provide the required funds as an interest-bearing loan to the German partnership – in which case the interest expense should not be treated as special business income since the lender is not a partner itself.

2. Creating Special Business Expenses/Liabilities

Following up on the above example, a further alternative may be to have the US parent corporation grant an interest-bearing loan to its US subsidiary corporation that is a partner in the German trading partnership. Provided that the US subsidiary corporation is able to provide evidence that it has taken up the loan from its US parent in connection with its partnership interest in the German trading partnership, the interest expense arising on the loan from the US parent should be deductible in computing the trade tax income of the partnership and the taxable profit share of the US partner under the special business expense concept.[2] Whether the corresponding interest expense is subject to US income tax should be irrelevant in this regard.

3. Avoiding German Dividend Withholding Tax

Subject to treaty/EU directive relief, dividends distributed by a German corporation are subject to 26.375% dividend withholding tax. In contrast, a distribution by a German trading partnership to its foreign partner is not subject to withholding tax or a similar tax charge in Germany.

Multinationals headquartered outside the EU have frequently established European holding companies, often based in the Netherlands or Luxembourg, for holding their European subsidiaries including a German subsidiary. In principle, such a European holding company is entitled to full relief from German dividend withholding tax in respect of dividends received from a German corporate subsidiary. However, Germany operates a very strict anti-treaty-shopping provision (Sec. 50 d(3) of the Income Tax Act) that significantly restricts access to the zero dividend withholding tax rate.

In these circumstances it might be worth considering converting the legal form of the German subsidiary from a corporation to a trading partnership so that income earned following the conversion is not subject to dividend withholding tax. In principle, the conversion itself may be carried out on a rollover basis. As an exception, retained earnings are deemed distributed and will be subject to either dividend withholding tax or income tax on assessment basis. It should be noted that a foreign partner is subject to income tax with gain earned on disposing of a partnership interest, whereas a foreign shareholder disposing of shares in a German corporate subsidiary is typically protected by an applicable tax treaty against German capital gains taxation. Where such disposition is unlikely to occur, the partnership form is worth careful consideration.

4. Mitigating German Capital Gains Tax

Where a foreign partner disposes of an interest in a German trading partnership, the resulting gain is subject to trade tax at the level of the partnership and to

---

2 It should be noted that the current deductibility of the interest expense may be limited or excluded pursuant to rules against thin capitalization.

income tax/corporate tax at the level of the disposing partner. In addition, the foreign partner might be subject to capital gains tax in its country of residence.

In contrast, where a foreign partner disposes of shares in a German corporation, the foreign seller is typically protected against German capital gains tax. Against this background it might be beneficial for the foreign partner to transform the partnership interest into a stake in a corporation and then sell the latter. Obviously, this approach is beneficial only if the transformation itself may be carried out on a rollover basis. Rollover relief will often be available. However, rollover relief is denied retrospectively if the shares in the corporation are disposed within the first seven years following the effective date of the transformation. Rollover relief remains intact for each year which has elapsed since the effective transformation date. For example, only three-sevenths (five-sevenths) of the gain released from taxation is taxed retrospectively if at least four years (two years) have elapsed since the transformation date.

Foreign partners wishing to avoid German capital gains tax altogether must plan well ahead and take the necessary steps at least seven years in advance of any intended disposition.

Dr. Klaus Sieker

Tax Advisor

Areas of Specialization

- Taxation of corporate groups
- Structuring of German investments abroad
- Structuring of cross-border investments (inbound and outbound)
- Transfer pricing
- Mergers & acquisitions and corporate reorganizations
- Tax audits

Telephone +49 69/717 03-0

Email: klaus.sieker@fgs.de

German Tax Aspects in M&A Transactions

by Florian Kutt

Contents

I. Introduction
II. Sale of Interests in Commercial Partnerships
  1. General remarks
  2. From the Perspective of the Seller
    a) Corporations as Sellers
    b) Private Individuals as Sellers
  3. From the Buyer's Perspective
    a) Depreciation of acquired assets
    b) Deductibility of Interest Paid on the Acquisition Loan
  4. Other Implications for the Partnership: Trade-Tax Losses
III. Disposal of Corporate Shares
  1. From the Seller's Perspective
    a) Corporations as Sellers
    b) Private Individuals as Sellers
    c) VAT
  2. From the Perspective of the Buyer
    a) Depreciation of acquired assets
    b) Input VAT
    c) Deductibility of Interest Paid on the Acquisition Loan
    d) Debt Push-Down
  3. Other Implications for the Target: Loss Carryforwards and Interest Carryforwards

I. Introduction

The following sets out the material tax consequences of M&A transactions in which the target is a German corporation (share deal).

From a tax perspective, an important differentiation is whether a particular share deal involves (a) shares in a corporation (e.g. in a stock corporation – *Aktiengesellschaft* or *AG*, or a privately held corporation – *Gesellschaft mit beschränkter Haftung* or *GmbH*) or (b) interests in a partnership (e.g. a limited partner's stake in a *GmbH & Co. KG*, i.e. a limited partnership with a *GmbH* as the general partner). Both legal forms are very frequent in German M&A transactions because notably the German *Mittelstand*, i.e small and medium-sized enterprises, usually family-run businesses, are frequently organized as a *GmbH* or as a *GmbH & Co. KG*.

For each scenario, the most important tax consequences are described first from the perspective of the seller (in this respect, this article confines itself to corporations and private individuals as sellers) and then from that of the buyer (insofar confined to corporations as buyers).

II. Sale of Interests in Commercial Partnerships

1. General remarks

If interests in a German partnership are sold, then the first question is whether the partnership involved is (a) a partnership carrying on a trade or business *(gewerblich tätig)* or a 'deemed business partnership' *(gewerblich geprägt)* (these two types of partnership hereinafter collectively referred to as 'commercial partnerships') or (b) a partnership engaged in asset management *(vermögensverwaltend;* hereinafter 'asset-managing partnership'). As a rule, every operatively active partnership is also a commercial partnership, which is why only that type will be discussed in the following. By contrast, partnerships are frequently asset-managing if the partnership simply administers real estate or stakes; given the fact that many investment entities (private-equity, venture-capital and real-estate firms) are structured as partnerships, one frequently encounters asset-managing partnerships in this area as well, whose disposal in turn triggers other tax consequences. For reasons of simplification, asset-managing partnerships are not described in more detail here.

2. From the Perspective of the Seller

a) Corporations as Sellers

aa) Corporate Income Tax and Trade Tax

If the seller of the partnership interest is a corporation, then the resulting capital gains are subject to (i) corporate income tax (plus solidarity surcharge) and (ii) trade tax. Corporate income tax is due at the level of the selling partner and currently amounts to a uniform rate of 15% throughout Germany; the solidarity surcharge currently amounts to 5.5% on the 15% rate at which corporate income tax is charged, so that the seller's direct tax burden currently amounts to 15.825%.

This tax burden arises both at the level of German and of foreign sellers; for German sellers, in the context of their unlimited tax liability; for foreign sellers, in the context of their limited tax liability in Germany (and under most double taxation treaties ('DTTs'), the right to tax is also allocated to Germany, cf. Art. 7 of the OECD Model Convention (hereinafter 'OECD MC').

A tax that is highly unusual by international standards is German trade tax and in particular the person liable to that tax upon a corporation's disposal of partnership interests. Trade tax on the capital gains realized by the seller is due at the level of the partnership that has been disposed of (cf. Sec. 7 sentence 2 of the German Trade Tax Act – *Gewerbesteuergesetz*); in other words, the partnership itself owes the trade tax. The amount of trade tax due, in turn, depends on the *Hebesatz* (local rate of assessment or multiplier) applied by the municipality in which the partnership maintains its permanent establishment (hereinafter 'PE'). If the partnership maintains PEs in several German municipalities, then – put simply – the capital gains that have arisen are allocated among the municipalities involved (usually based on the *Lohnsumme*, i.e. the aggregate amount of wages and salaries paid out in the respective municipality by the enterprise concerned), with each municipality levying trade tax at its own individual local rate. In the major German municipalities and cities, these local rates usually range between 410% (e.g. Berlin) and 490% (e.g. Munich), thus resulting in a trade tax rate of approximately 14.35% to 17.15%. The only rule that applies uniformly throughout Germany is that each municipality must adopt a local rate of at least 200% (i.e. a trade tax rate of at least 7%).

bb) Determination of Capital Gains

The manner in which capital gains are determined when partnership interests are sold also constitutes a specifically German feature. First, the disposal costs and thereafter the tax book value of the stake have to be deducted from the sale price. The tax book value of the stake is considered to be the equity allocated to the seller, for tax purposes, by his partnership ('*Kapitalkonto der Gesamthandsbilanz*' or 'capital account of the partners' joint balance sheet') plus the purchase-price portion, if any, exceeding the partners' joint balance sheet and paid in the context of the acquisition (shown in an *Ergänzungsbilanz* or 'supplementary balance sheet'; see section II. 3. a) of this article). Because the tax book value of the stake is derived in particular from the capital account of the partners' joint balance sheet (albeit increased by the capital account of the supplementary balance sheet), this method of determination is also referred to as the *Spiegelbildmethode* or 'mirror-image method'. In determining the capital gains, the commercial-law book value of the stake as shown in the seller's balance sheet is irrelevant; that value usually exceeds the tax book value of the stake because only that value – or, more specifically, the assets represented in the tax book value of the stake – has been subject to regular depreciation. As a result, capital gains for tax purposes are often higher than capital gains for commercial-law purposes.

cc) Features Specific to Particular Assets

If a corporation disposes of partnership interests, there are only few assets which under German tax law are subject to a preferential tax rate. Such assets notably include shares in domestic or foreign corporations held by the partnership being disposed of; based on the transparency principle, there is a fiction for tax purposes that the seller is the corporation directly disposing of these corporate shares (even though this is only indirectly the case, of course). As set out in section III. 1. a) aa), 95% of the resulting capital gains are tax-free; only a fixed portion of 5% of the capital gains is subject to trade tax at the level of the partnership and to corporate income tax (plus solidarity surcharge) at the level of the seller.

dd) Taxation-Related Technique

When an interest in a German partnership is sold, yet another specific feature applies to the assessment procedure. Technically, the capital gains realized by the seller need to be included in the partnership's tax return (what is known as *'gesonderte und einheitliche Gewinnfeststellung'* or 'separate and uniform determination of profits') and are also assessed, with binding effect *vis-à-vis* the seller, by the tax office responsible for the partnership (namely with respect to both the corporate income tax payable by the seller – as stated earlier – and the trade tax payable by the partnership). Given that the seller is no longer a partner of the partnership when the tax return is being prepared, it is of particular importance to ensure that the SPA contains a provision on the seller's rights to be involved in preparing the tax return for the partnership.

The disposal is declared in the same tax return that also includes the regular profits or losses for the current fiscal year. If the closing of the M&A transaction (which should usually coincide with the date of transfer relevant for tax purposes) occurs at the end of the fiscal year (e.g. 31 Dec. of a given year), then no particular requirements apply. However, if the closing occurs during the fiscal year, then a distinction needs to be made between the profits and losses realized before and after the closing notably because the seller is also obliged to pay taxes *pro rata* on his portion of the regular profits generated up to the closing, and more specifically at a level corresponding to the amount of his interest. In principle, this also applies if a retroactive transfer date were agreed upon in the SPA; as a rule, such a retroactive effect is not recognized for tax purposes. For simplification purposes, the German tax authorities allow for an exception to that principle of non-retroactivity in cases where the closing takes place shortly after the start of the fiscal year; in this context, the tax authorities usually accept a time period of six weeks and, in some cases, even up to three months as an permissible period of retroactivity (on which the parties would, however, need to specifically agree).

b) Private Individuals as Sellers

aa) Income Tax

If the seller of the partnership interest is a private individual, then the resulting capital gains are exclusively subject to the seller's personal income tax but not to trade tax (provided it is the entire partnership interest held that is being sold rather than merely a part, cf. Sec. 16 of the German Income Tax Act (*Einkommensteuergesetz*). If the taxable income amounts to at least EUR 250,000 (in the case of a separate assessment) or at least EUR 500,000 (if the taxpayer is assessed together with his or her spouse), then the income-tax rate for the capital gains exceeding said amounts is 45% (plus 5.5% solidarity surcharge thereon and any applicable church tax), so that the tax rate then amounts to approx. 47.475% (while the amounts of taxable income below EUR 250,000 or EUR 500,000 are taxed at a lower rate).

If the seller meets certain personal prerequisites (at least 55 years of age or permanently unable to practice his or her profession), then capital gains of up to a maximum of EUR 5m are taxed at a preferential tax rate of between 14% and 25.2% ('56% of the average tax rate'), cf. Sec. 34(3) of the Income Tax Act. Any portion of the capital gains which exceeds EUR 5m is taxed at the standard rate. A seller may take advantage of this special tax rate only once in his lifetime, and needs to file a corresponding application in order to do so.

If the capital gains are merely low and the seller meets certain personal prerequisites, then the law provides for an exempt amount of up to EUR 45,000 (Sec. 16(4) of the Income Tax Act).

This tax burden arises both at the level of German and of foreign sellers; for German sellers, in the context of their unlimited tax liability, and for foreign sellers, in the context of their limited tax liability in Germany (and under most DTTs, the right to tax is also allocated to Germany, cf. Art. 7 of the OECD MC).

bb) Determination of Capital Gains

The comments in II. 2. a) bb) above apply to the manner in which capital gains are determined when partnership interests are sold.

cc) Features Specific to Particular Assets

When a private individual sells partnership interests, there are only few assets which under German tax law are subject to a preferential rate. Such assets notably include shares in domestic or foreign corporations held by the partnership being disposed of; based on the transparency principle, there is a fiction for tax purposes that the seller is the individual directly disposing of these corporate shares (even though this is only indirectly the case, of course). 40% of the resulting capital gains are tax-free, while the remaining 60% are subject to personal income tax (plus solidarity surcharge), cf. Sec. 3 no. 40(b) of the Income Tax Act. Accordingly, the resulting tax burden amounts to a maximum of approximately 27%.

dd) Taxation-Related Technique

If the interest in a German partnership is disposed of by a private individual, the comments in section II. 2. a) dd) above apply.

3. From the Buyer's Perspective

a) Depreciation of acquired assets

From a tax perspective, it is attractive for a buyer to acquire partnership interests. That is because the partnership interests acquired (or, more specifically, the assets contained therein) may usually be written down with an effect on tax. This depreciation of the assets decreases the partnership's tax base for trade-tax purposes and the buyer's tax base for corporate-income-tax purposes. Should the depreciation (or other transactions) lead to a loss, then such loss may be offset for corporate-income-tax purposes with other profits of the partner. A trade-tax loss, however, remains isolated within the partnership, where it may be offset against future profits only. By contrast, any offsetting against the buyer's trade-tax profits is not permissible.

The tax base for the depreciation depends on whether or not the purchase price paid by the buyer exceeded the partnership's *(pro-rata)* tax equity. If the purchase price did exceed the partnership's *(pro-rata)* tax equity (which should typically be the case), then a supplementary balance sheet reflecting this difference needs to be drawn up for the buyer. Technically, the assets side of a supplementary balance sheet shows the step-up of the hidden reserves contained in the individual assets. The liabilities side shows 'surplus capital' *(Mehrkapital)*. The tax-effective depreciation is now extended to (i) the assets shown in the partnership's joint balance sheet and (ii) the step-up volume of the supplementary balance sheet. By contrast, if the purchase price were equivalent to the partnership's *(pro-rata)* tax equity, then no supplementary balance sheet needs to be drawn up, and the depreciation is exclusively determined by the book value of the assets shown in the joint balance sheet.

There are a small number of assets that may not be written down with a tax effect. This involves land as well as stakes in corporations.

b) Deductibility of Interest Paid on the Acquisition Loan

If the buyer of partnership interests has taken out an interest-bearing acquisition loan, then several specific points apply to the tax deductibility of the interest payments. From a tax perspective, the acquisition loan and thus also the related interest expenses are attributable to the partnership (as *negatives Sonderbetriebsvermögen* / 'negative special business assets' or *negative Sonderbetriebsausgaben* / 'negative special business expenses'. In terms of trade tax, the interest expenses thus have an effect on the partnership rather than the buyer (= the debtor of the acquisition loan). If there are several partners in the partnership, then it is advisable to include in the partnership agreement a provision pursuant to which the buyer benefits proportionately, in terms of civil law, from the decrease in trade tax triggered by the buyer (which, initially, *de facto* benefits all partners) in the form of what is known as a *Gewinnvorab* or 'profit advance'. While, for corporate-income-tax purposes, interest expenses are technically included in the partnership's tax returns, the tax effects are realized exclusively by the buyer (= the debtor of the acquisition loan).

An important corporate-income-tax and trade-tax restriction applies to the deductibility of interest payments. For these tax purposes, interest payments may only be deducted within the limits of what is known as the *Zinsschranke* or 'interest barrier' (cf. Sec. 8a of the Corporate Income Tax Act and Sec. 4h of the Income Tax Act). This leads to restrictions in particular if the interest expenses per fiscal year reach or exceed an amount of EUR 3.0m. In addition, for trade-tax purposes, only 75% of interest expenses may be claimed, i.e. 25% of interest expenses are nondeductible for trade-tax purposes; this restriction on deductibility, however, only applies once interest expenses reach EUR 100,000 (while this exempt amount may well already have been used up by other effects).

4. Other Implications for the Partnership: Trade-Tax Losses

If, prior to the sale, the partnership possessed trade-tax loss carryforwards, then – to the extent that they could not be offset against trade-taxable capital gains in the context of the sale – these are forfeited (in full if the entire partnership interest were transferred, and *pro rata* if less than the entire interest were transferred). Timewise, the trade-tax loss carryforward is forfeited immediately upon closing. Accordingly, if closing takes place during the fiscal year, then any current profits that occur after the closing may not be offset against the loss carryforward.

The German 'minimum taxation' regime also needs to be taken into account with respect to the offsetting of the trade-tax loss carryforward against trade-tax capital gains. This means that the trade-tax loss carryforward may not be used in full in each case because this depends on the amount of the resulting gains. Gains of up to EUR 1.0m may be fully offset against a loss carryforward. Beyond that, 40% of the gains realized are subject to trade tax in any event, and only 60% of the gains may be offset against a loss carryforward.

III. Disposal of Corporate Shares

1. From the Seller's Perspective

a) Corporations as Sellers

aa) Corporate Income Tax and Trade Tax

If the seller of the corporate share is itself a German corporation, then as a general rule 95% of the resulting capital gains are free from corporate income tax and trade tax at the level of that seller (Sec. 8b(2) and (3) of the Corporate Income Tax Act). 5% of the capital gains are subject to corporate income tax and trade tax. Corporate income tax currently amounts to a uniform rate of 15% throughout Germany; the solidarity surcharge currently amounts to 5.5% on the 15% rate of corporate income tax. Again, the trade tax amount due depends on the local rate of the municipality in which the seller maintains its PE. The only rule that applies uniformly throughout Germany is that each municipality must adopt a rate of assessment of at least 200% (i.e. a trade tax rate of at least 7%). Accordingly, the overall tax burden on the German seller triggered by the capital gains is approximately 1.5%.

An exception to the principle of the 95% tax exemption applies if the seller is a credit institution, a financial-services institution or a financial firm within the meaning of the German Banking Act – *Kreditwesengesetz* (Sec. 8b(7) of the Corporate Income Tax Act). The courts, however, apply this provision also to certain holding companies, namely if at the time they acquired the shares they had already intended to resell those shares at the next opportunity (in this context, it is an important indicator if the shares acquired are shown in the buyer's balance sheet as part not of the noncurrent assets but of the current assets). In these cases, the resulting capital gains are fully subject to corporate income tax and trade tax (at an aggregate rate of approximately 29–32%).

As a general rule, a foreign seller is subject to limited corporate-income-tax liability on the resulting capital gains (while the 95% tax exemption would also be applicable in this case); most DTTs, however, allocate the taxation of capital gains from corporate shares to the state of the seller (cf. Art. 13 of the OECD MC), so that in these scenarios taxation arises only very rarely in Germany.

bb) Determination of Capital Gains

Capital gains are determined by deducting from the sale price (i) the disposal costs and (ii) the tax book value of the stake. Given that the disposal costs (especially costs for M&A advisors, for legal and tax advisors, notary's fees, etc.) decrease the tax-free gains, the disposal costs may not be claimed with full effect as expenses

cc) Taxation-Related Technique

In cases in which it is foreseeable during the SPA negotiations that closing will not take place until the subsequent fiscal year, the parties often agree on an 'economic reference date' (e.g. the beginning of the subsequent fiscal year). This is coupled with the instruction under civil law that, starting with the economic reference date, it is the buyer who will be entitled to the profits of the target; in exchange, the buyer will have to pay 'interest' on the purchase price. From a tax perspective, this usually constitutes a purchase price increase (given that this is not a case of remuneration for making capital available), so that the tax rules applicable to this 'interest' are those regarding the sale of corporate shares rather than those regarding 'genuine' interest. Given that – in terms of tax – this is advantageous from the seller's perspective and that this issue frequently leads to discussions with the tax authorities in the context of audits, one should avoid using the term 'interest' in SPAs; instead, one should include specific wording to the effect that the purchase price will increase accordingly.

b) Private Individuals as Sellers

If the seller of the corporate share, for his part, is a private individual resident in Germany (and if, from a tax perspective, this person holds this share – as is usually the case – as part of his private assets rather than his business assets), then the resulting capital gains are tax-privileged at the seller's level. As regards the tax exemption, there are minor differences depending on whether the seller holds a share of at least 1% or of less than 1% (and continuously for the past five years). If the seller holds at least 1% in the corporation, then 40% of the resulting capital gains are tax-free (Sec. 3 no. 40(c) of the Income Tax Act); 60% of the resulting capital gains are taxed at the taxpayer's personal income-tax rate (in the case of the maximum tax rate, this thus leads to a tax burden of approximately 28.5% including solidarity surcharge). If the seller holds less than 1% in the corporation, then the resulting capital gains are subject to a separate tax rate of 25% (Sec. 32d of the Income Tax Act), so that together with the solidarity surcharge, the resulting tax burden is 26.38% (exceptions apply, however, for certain scenarios which are rather rare, cf. Sec. 32d(4) and (6) of the Income Tax Act). Trade tax arises in neither case.

As a general rule, a foreign seller is subject to limited income tax liability on the resulting capital gains (while the 40% tax exemption would also be applicable here); however, most DTTs allocate the taxation of capital gains from corporate shares to the state of the seller (cf. Art. 13 of the OECD MC), so that in these scenarios taxation only very rarely arises in Germany.

c) VAT

As a general rule, the sale of corporate shares is VAT-free. Correspondingly, the seller may not deduct as 'input VAT' either the VAT contained in the transaction costs (fees of M&A advisors, legal and tax advisors, notary's fees, etc.). This disadvantage can be avoided by the seller taking advantage of the option, provided for in the German VAT Act, to treat the sale as subject to VAT ('option in favor of VAT'). The seller is only eligible for that option, however, if (i) he is himself an entrepreneur within the meaning of VAT law (which is frequently not the case with holding companies), (ii) the buyer is an entrepreneur within the meaning of VAT law, and (iii) the purchase is being effected for his enterprise within the meaning of VAT law (cf. Sec. 9(1) of the VAT Act); correspondingly, the buyer would then have a claim against the tax office to have the VAT reimbursed as input VAT. However, since this still leads to a certain interim financing of such VAT amount, this option in favor of VAT is only rarely used in practice.

2. From the Perspective of the Buyer

a) Despreciation of acquired assets

The buyer has to show the corporate share acquired at acquisition cost on the assets side of the balance sheet. The acquisition costs include in particular the transaction costs. Meanwhile, the courts are very restrictive on this point and classify even costs from an earlier planning stage (in particular due-diligence costs) as incidental acquisition costs. In audits, the German tax authorities frequently argue that internal costs (notably personnel costs of M&A and legal departments) should also be shown as incidental acquisition costs on the assets side of the balance sheet (rather than being deductible as personnel expenses); the latter has not, however, been decided by the courts to date, so that one should oppose this stance taken by the tax authorities.

The buyer of corporate shares is not entitled to write down the purchase price or the stake shown on the assets side of the balance sheet with an effect on tax; this corresponds with the right to dispose of the corporate share tax-free (or 95% tax-free at any rate) at a later stage. Even by way of reorganizational measures (such as by a change of legal form of the corporation into a partnership), acquisition costs cannot be converted into tax-effective depreciation potential. From the buyer's perspective, it is therefore more advantageous in terms of tax to acquire a partnership interest rather than a corporate share (even if the tax burden resulting for the seller in this context is likely to already have been reflected in an increased purchase price).

b) Input VAT

As a rule, the buyer may have the VAT contained in his transaction costs reimbursed as input VAT. This does not apply, however, if the buyer is a holding company that does not constitute an entrepreneur within the meaning of VAT law.

c) Deductibility of Interest Paid on the Acquisition Loan

If the buyer of corporate shares is, in turn, a German corporation, then this corporation may in principle fully deduct, as business expenses for tax purposes, the interest paid on the acquisition loan. This corresponds with the provision that future dividends – provided a minimum holding level of 10% is met – are free from corporate income tax, although not fully but only in an amount of 95%. Because of the fixed 5% taxation of dividends, interest expenses are also deductible. With respect to the deductibility of interest, there is an important corporate-income-tax and trade-tax restriction. For corporate-income-tax purposes, interest may only be deducted within the limits of what is known 'interest limitation barrier' (cf. Sec. 8a of the Corporate Income Tax Act and Sec. 4h of the Income Tax Act). This leads to restrictions in particular if the interest expenses per fiscal year reach or exceed an amount of EUR 3.0m. For trade-tax purposes, only 75% of the interest expenses may be taken into account, i.e. 25% of the interest expenses are nondeductible for trade-tax purposes; this restriction on deductibility, however, only applies once tax expenses reach EUR 100,000 (while this exempt amount may well already have been used up by other effects).

d) Debt Push-Down

If a German vehicle is used for the acquisition, then from a tax-planning perspective it is desirable for the interest expenses to be offsettable against other earnings (especially from the operating business) in the first place (because given that, for the remainder, there would only be tax-free dividend income, and the interest expenses would lead to a loss carryforward). There are two main structuring options that lend themselves to this situation: (1) merger of the operative company and the Acquico (upstream or downstream), or (2) entering into a profit-and-loss transfer agreement and thus establishing a tax group. In Germany, the second option (establishment of a tax group) is often used because it means less intensive interference in the enterprise (than would be the case with an upstream merger) and/or it would have less of a negative effect on equity (than would be the case with a downstream merger involving a high amount of liabilities on the part of Acquico). For details regarding the prerequisites and legal implications of the tax group, see section 'International and Domestic Aspects of German Group Taxation'.

3. Other Implications for the Target: Loss Carryforwards and Interest Carryforwards

If the buyer acquires more than 25% of a corporation's shares, then the question is in particular whether the corporation possesses any loss carryforwards or 'interest carryforwards'. This is because, as a general principle, these are either forfeited in part (if the buyer acquires more than 25% and a maximum of 50% of the shares) or forfeited in full (if the buyer acquires more than 50% of the shares, with respect to which all acquisitions of shares are aggregated within a five-year period). Such forfeiting of loss carryforwards does not occur, however, if either the 'group exception' or the 'hidden-reserves clause' applies. The group exception applies if the shares are transferred within a group (which, however, requires a holding in the hands of one owner throughout). Of greater significance for M&A transactions is the hidden-reserves clause; here, the agreed purchase price is compared with the tax equity of the corporation (subject to certain adjustments where the corporation either holds additional corporations or maintains foreign PEs). As a rule, this yields a positive difference, i.e. the purchase price exceeds the equity. In this situation, if the corporation possesses loss carryforwards or interest carryforwards, then these may remain in place up to the amount of that difference.

Dr. Florian Kutt

Lawyer, Tax Advisor

Areas of Specialization

- Taxation of corporations and partnerships
- Reorganization law and the taxation of reorganizations
- Corporate law
- Tax-law advice for tax-exempt organizations
- Mezzanine financing

Telephone (ext.) +49 30/21 00 20-20

Email: florian.kutt@fgs.de

Taxation of Real Estate Investments in Germany

by Torsten Engers

Contents

I. Taxation of Real Estate Investments: General Principles and Goals
 1. Taxes on Income
  a) (Individual) Income Tax
  b) Corporate Income Tax
  c) Trade Tax
  d) Double Taxation Treaties
 2. Other Taxes
  a) Real Estate Transfer Tax
  b) Value Added Tax (VAT)
  c) Land Tax *(Grundsteuer)*
II. General Goals of Tax-Optimized Real Estate Inbound Investments
 1. Trade Tax Structuring
  a) Planning Opportunities
  b) Non-PE Structure
  c) Trade Tax Real Estate Relief (Sec. 9 No. 1 Sentence 2 of the Trade Tax Act)
 2. Real Estate Transfer Tax Structuring
  a) Basics
  b) Schemes
III. Alternative Investment Structures
 1. Open Fund *(Sondervermögen)*
 2. Special Fund *(Spezial-Sondervermögen)*, Sec. 15 of the Investment Taxation Act
 3. G-REIT

I. Taxation of Real Estate Investments: General Principles and Goals

Investments in real estate situated in Germany may trigger various kinds of tax as a result of acquiring, holding, and disposing of real estate.

1. Taxes on Income

a) (Individual) Income Tax

Under the German Income Tax Act *(Einkommensteuergesetz)*, resident individuals or resident (transparent) partnerships are generally liable to income tax on their worldwide income. In contrast, nonresidents are liable to income tax only on their domestic source income, which can derive from real estate situated in Germany. Additionally, nonresident individuals carrying on a trade or business through a permanent establishment in Germany are subject to trade tax.

Gross income is limited to seven specified types of income. The following types of income are most likely to be applicable to real estate: (i) income from a trade or business, (ii) rental and leasing income, and (iii) income from other sources such as private capital gains. Classification of the type of income depends on the amount of real estate and frequency of transactions (as a rule of thumb: when three or more real estate properties (which are held for less than five years) are bought or sold within a five-year period, the investment will be regarded as a business investment). If real estate is held as a private asset for more than 10 years, capital gains are not subject to income tax.

In principle, recurring income deriving from leases and capital gains will be classed as taxable income. The standard depreciation method for buildings is straight-line depreciation, ranging between 2%–4% (depending on the age of the building and other factors). Land is not depreciable since it is considered not to decrease in value because of its use over the lifetime of the real estate.

Expenditures shortly after the acquisition of real estate have to be capitalized under certain circumstances. Other (business) expenses relating to German real estate are generally deductible immediately subject to general exceptions, e.g. cap on interest expenses on loans financing the acquisition termed the 'interest barrier rule', Sec. 4h of the Income Tax Act and Sec. 8a of the German Corporate Income Tax Act (*Körperschaftsteuergesetz*).

Income tax applies at a rate of up to 47.475% (including 5.5% solidarity surcharge).

b) Corporate Income Tax

Under the Corporate Income Tax Act, corporations (and other legal entities) with their place of management or their registered seat in Germany are liable to corporate income tax on their worldwide income as resident corporations. Nonresident corporations are only liable to tax on their domestic source income, e.g. income derived from real estate situated in Germany. The above-mentioned rules for individuals generally apply, subject to other more specific rules on computing income and determining the tax base. Capital gains of a corporation from the sale of German real estate are subject to German corporate income tax irrespective of a holding period.

A flat tax rate of 15.825% (including 5.5% solidarity surcharge) applies.

c) Trade Tax

German municipalities levy a trade tax in addition to income tax or corporate income tax under the German Trade Tax Act (*Gewerbesteuergesetz*). The rationale behind trade tax is that trade businesses with a permanent establishment in a particular municipality use its infrastructure more than other professions (such as doctors, dentists, engineers, lawyers, tax advisors, journalists etc.). Therefore, municipalities are entitled to compensation for providing trade businesses with the infrastructure they need to conduct their business.

Trade tax is levied when income qualifies as income derived from trade or business which is conducted through a permanent establishment. The tax base is basically the amount of profit derived from trade or business as determined for income tax purposes. However, the exact amount of trade tax is calculated on the basis of a complex formula subject to certain additions and reliefs multiplied by a trade tax coefficient that differs from municipality to municipality.

Items that are added back to the tax base insofar as they were deducted for income tax include e.g. one quarter of the total cost of debt financing (i.e. interest and/or discounts), insofar as this sum together with other add-backs exceeds EUR 100,000.

Trade tax is then computed in two steps: First, the trade or business profits are multiplied by a nationwide uniform factor of 3.5% ('tax measure'). The tax measure is then, as the second step, multiplied by the trade tax coefficient set by each municipality. The average coefficient in Germany is 387%, in cities 432%. Thus, the effective tax rate varies from municipality to municipality. The effective rate for trade tax can be calculated as the product of 3.5% and the trade tax coefficient. The effective rates in Germany vary between approximately 7% and 17%.

For additional information and structuring opportunities, see below (B. I. Trade Tax Structuring).

d) Double Taxation Treaties

Generally, double taxation treaties do not eliminate German taxation of the income from real estate located in Germany as the right to tax income from leasing activities such as the capital gains from the sale of real estate is allocated to Germany (Art. 6 and Art. 13(1) of the OECD MC).

2. Other Taxes

a) Real Estate Transfer Tax

As a general rule, real estate transfer tax is triggered upon the transfer of real estate located in Germany (Sec. 1(1) of the Real Estate Transfer Tax Act – *Grunderwerbsteuergesetz*) or several transactions that affect the title holder of real estate from a legal or even economic perspective. For the purposes of real estate transfer tax, the crucial factor is the form in which the real estate investment, thus the transfer of real estate, is to be conducted.

aa) Direct Transfer of Legal Title to Real Estate (Sec. 1(1) No. 1 *et seq.* of the Real Estate Transfer Tax Act)

The most straightforward transaction that imposes real estate transfer tax is the conclusion of a contract on the purchase of real estate or any other agreement that constitutes a right to claim legal title to such (Sec. 1(1) no. 1 *et seq.* of the Real Estate Transfer Tax Act). Other cases of direct investments include, for example, transactions that assign obligations and duties of a purchase contract to another person (Sec. 1(1) no. 6 of the Real Estate Transfer Tax Act), an acquisition of real estate through a foreclosure (Sec. 1(1) no. 1 of the Real Estate Transfer Tax Act), or the exchange of properties between two parties (Sec. 1(5) of the Real Estate Transfer Tax Act). What all these transactions have in common is that they are considered as asset deals since the asset itself, the real estate, or a share of it as joint tenants is the object of the investment.

bb) Direct or Indirect Transfer of Interest in a Partnership (Sec .1(2a) of the Real Estate Transfer Tax Act)

German legislators have enacted all kinds of tax-relevant transactions where taxpayers were using transfer vehicles to avoid real estate transfer tax such as a real estate holding partnership. Transferring only a share in a real estate holding partnership is legally not a transfer of the title to the real estate but has a similar economic result for the parties participating in the transaction. Therefore, this legal 'loophole' was closed for share deals in various ways.

If a partnership owns real estate situated in Germany, and within five years 95% or more of the interests in the partnership change directly or indirectly in such a way that they are acquired by one or more new owners, the transfers of interests accumulated will be deemed as a transfer of the real estate itself (Sec. 1(2a) sentence 1 of the Real Estate Transfer Tax Act). This legal assumption then triggers real estate transfer tax because the transfers are regarded as a substantial change in the interests of a partnership. For the computation of the 95% change of interests, all changes in owners at all levels must be taken into account. However, if such a partnership interest is inherited (through a will or intestate), it will not count as part of the relevant 95% change of ownership (Sec. 1(2a) sentence 2 of the Real Estate Transfer Tax Act).

cc) Direct or Indirect Transfer of Stake in a Partnership or Corporation to one Person (Sec. 1(3) No. 3 of the Real Estate Transfer Tax Act)

Furthermore, a single transaction imposing a duty to transfer (directly or indirectly) at least 95% of a real estate holding partnership or corporation will trigger real estate transfer tax as well (Sec. 1 (2a) sentence 2 of the Real Estate Transfer Tax Act). Further, the 95% or more shares must be transferred in only one single transaction (irrespective of the five-year time frame). This governs situations where a substantial 95% stake of a real estate holding corporation or partnership is transferred to one single person. Nonetheless, in the computation of the 95% of the ownership, all relevant stakes at all levels (regardless of whether the corporation or partnership owns the real estate directly or indirectly) must be taken into account.

dd) Direct or Indirect Unification of Stake in a Partnership or Corporation by one Person (Sec. 1(3) No. 1 of the Real Estate Transfer Tax Act)

A single transaction imposing a duty to transfer a single or multiple stakes of a real estate holding partnership or corporation will trigger real estate transfer tax if, due to this transfer, 95% of the stakes in the estate holding partnership or corporation are directly or indirectly unified in the person who acquires the holdings (Sec. 1(3) no. 1 of the Real Estate Transfer Tax Act). This person does not need to be a single person but can also be a group or a controlling corporation and one or more controlled corporations. Note that not necessarily 95% of stakes need to be transferred. It is sufficient that the direct or indirect 95% stake will result in the person or group receiving the stake after the transaction.

ee) Direct or Indirect Transfer of Economic Participation (Sec. 1(3a) no. 1 of the Real Estate Transfer Tax Act)

Finally, one of the most critical events that trigger real estate transfer tax exists when, from an economic point of view, one single person directly or indirectly holds 95% or more of the share in a corporation or interest in a partnership as a result of a transaction or measure, even if less than 95% is transferred within this transaction or measure. This rule has been in force since June 2013 and is relatively broad. This scenario may only be applicable if scenarios 2, 3, and 4 are not applicable.

ff) Tax Base for Real Estate Transfer Tax

The tax base is considered to be the face value of the transaction (Sec. 8(1) of the Real Estate Transfer Tax Act), i.e. the purchase price that is agreed on by the parties as the consideration for the transfer of the direct title in the real estate. In cases where the real estate or stakes in those corporations or partnerships are acquired by an operation of law (thus no consideration exists) or in case of a transfer of a real estate holding corporation or partnership, a fair value base in accordance with the German Valuation Act (*Bewertungsgesetz*) must be determined (which will usually result in a base below the fair market value).

gg) Applicable Tax Rates for Real Estate Transfer Tax

The real estate transfer tax rate depends on the state the respective real estate is located in. It ranges between 3.5% of the tax base in Bavaria and Saxony and 6.5% in Schleswig-Holstein (status 1 November 2014). Please note that both the buyer and seller of the real estate transfer tax triggering transaction are liable for the tax. However, as a matter of common practice, the purchaser is usually obliged to pay real estate transfer tax by contractual arrangement.

b) Value Added Tax (VAT)

aa) Leasing Activities

Individuals or corporations that carry on professional activities for consideration in Germany are generally subject to VAT. VAT is levied basically on the supply of goods and services supplied in Germany. Like sales tax, rationale behind VAT is to effectively burden only customers. However, for technical reasons, VAT has to be paid on taxable transactions between enterprises as well. The enterprise that is charged VAT will claim an 'input VAT deduction' in order to receive a refund for VAT paid. VAT is mostly harmonized within the EU in regard of its tax base and the technicalities of input VAT deductions. However, the VAT rate is still at the discretion of each member state. The standard VAT rate in Germany is 19%, and the reduced rate (e.g. for food and newspapers) is 7%.

The VAT regulations governing the leasing of German real estate apply regardless of whether the landlord is situated outside Germany. In principle, leasing real estate is exempt from VAT (Sec. 4 no. 12(a) of the German VAT Act – *Umsatzsteuergesetz*). However, the landlord may opt for VAT treatment (to claim input VAT deductions) if the tenant is a VAT taxpayer who uses the real estate for its business purposes and does not use more than 5 % of the leased premises for VAT-exempt services ('VAT lease').

If the landlord uses the real estate partly for VAT-exempt leases and partly for VAT leases, it is not entitled to input VAT deduction with regard to maintenance services that can be allocated to a VAT-exempt lease. Besides, the landlord is only entitled to a partial input VAT deduction for construction costs, for acquisition costs and for maintenance services which cannot be allocated directly to certain leased premises (Sec.(4) of the VAT Act). The *pro rata* key has to be based on a reasonable estimate. The *pro rata* key is calculated per property and is generally based on the leased premises. The portion of the input VAT deduction is reflected in the 'input VAT key'.

bb) Transfer of Real Estate

As a general rule, the transfer of untenanted real estate is exempt from VAT because the transfer is already subject to real estate transfer tax (Sec. 4 no. 9(a) of the VAT Act). However, sellers of real estate (similar to landlords) may opt for VAT treatment (to claim input VAT deductions) if the purchaser is an enterprise as well. The VAT option may only be declared in the notarized property purchase agreement. VAT will generally not burden the purchaser because it will only accept the option for VAT treatment if it may claim input VAT deductions on the purchase price. The purchaser will not have to adjust the deducted input VAT later when, for a period of ten years after the transfer, the tenants of the real estate are VAT payers who use the real estate for their business purposes and the real estate is not transferred exempt of VAT within this time. However, the transfer of leased real estate qualifies as a transfer of a going concern and thus does not fall within the scope of VAT (Sec. 1(1a) of the VAT Act). In this case, the purchaser steps into the position of the seller and has to continue the seller's potential input VAT adjustments.

c) Land Tax *(Grundsteuer)*

Real estate located in Germany is subject to land tax assessed by municipalities on an annual basis. Real estate includes land, buildings, fixtures, and condominiums. The tax base is the 'standard tax value' *(Einheitswert)* and was assessed by the tax authorities several decades ago (which is the reason for sharp criticism by practitioners and scholars in terms of its constitutionality). The standard tax value for real estate is generally much less than its actual fair market value (roughly 10%-20%). Each municipality levies land tax at its own tax rate, which varies according to the use of the real estate and the location, and ranges between an effective rate of 1.5%-3.5% on the standard tax value. Land tax is deductible for the computation of net taxable income from real estate for income tax and corporate income tax purposes.

II. General Goals of Tax-Optimized Real Estate Inbound Investments

When making inbound investments in German real estate, tax nonresidents should primarily aim at (i) a reduction or the avoidance of trade tax and (ii) real estate transfer tax. The principles of tax-optimized real estate investment are explained below.

1. Trade Tax Structuring

a) Planning Opportunities

All income of domestic entities is deemed to be income from trade or business. Thus, trade tax will generally apply if the entity holds a permanent establishment in Germany located in the respective municipality. This legal assumption does not exist for nondomestic entities. However, also a nondomestic entity will be held liable for trade tax if it creates a permanent establishment in Germany. Domestic and nondomestic real estate corporations may benefit from the trade tax relief for real estate corporations (*erweiterte Kürzung*). Hence, the well-considered planning of inbound investments can result in a very significant reduction of the trade tax burden for real estate investors. There are two schemes for avoiding trade tax: structuring the real estate investment without creating a German permanent establishment or complying with the requirements for trade tax relief.

b) Non-PE Structure

aa) Basics

For the purposes of trade tax, the German tax regime laid down in the German General Tax Code (*Abgabenordnung*) will apply in order to determine the existence of a permanent establishment. According to this, a permanent establishment is any fixed place of business or facility that serves the business of an enterprise (Sec. 12 of the General Tax Code). Mere leasing of real property does not create a permanent establishment when the foreign entity does not carry on a business through the real estate situated in Germany. However, *inter alia* offices of the foreign entity located in Germany and the place of business management are deemed to be permanent establishments.

bb) Pitfalls

Generally, it is not difficult to avoid establishing German offices of the foreign entity. The crucial aspect is to avoid business management being conducted in Germany. The relevant criterion is that day-to-day management is exercised in Germany. It is not relevant whether the decisions are made by the taxpayer, an affiliate or a third party. What qualifies as a management decision depends on the type and size of the entity's business. Generally, decisions on the sale and/or lease of units are management decisions. This can be different if the corporation holds a large number of units. In such case the management may give only guidelines for the leasing or even for the sale of units. Decisions on the refurbishment of units or the conclusion of long-term service contracts may also be regarded as management decisions. The scope of management decisions has to be determined on a case-by-case basis and naturally is a gray area.

cc) Schemes

In many cases foreign entities hire German asset managers and property managers for the administration of German properties. It is a crucial part of trade tax structuring to ensure that German service providers are not entitled to make or actually make management decisions under the asset management agreements or even the property management agreements concluded. Due to their knowledge of the German market, they may advise the foreign management. However, the contracts must explicitly state, and it should be well documented that, decisions are actually made abroad.

c) Trade Tax Real Estate Relief (Sec. 9 No. 1 Sentence 2 of the Trade Tax Act)

aa) Basics

For entities dealing predominantly in real estate, 'trade tax real estate relief' might be applicable even if one or more permanent establishments exist (Sec. 9 no. 1 sentence 2 of the Trade Tax Act). This rule states that entities may file an application for trade tax real estate relief if they manage and use exclusively real estate held by the entity itself. This also applies if, in additions to managing and using its own real estate, an entity performs certain permitted activities such as managing capital assets held by the entity for its own business purposes.

Trade tax real estate relief allows those qualified businesses to reduce all profits relating to the administration and use of their own real estate from the trade tax base. In a best case scenario, trade tax real estate relief could eliminate trade tax in total if the business makes profits only by managing and using its own real estate. Generally, the requirements for the business qualifying for trade tax relief must be satisfied throughout the whole taxable year. If the business fails to comply with these provisions even for a short period of time only, the business risks losing trade tax real estate reliefs, and in consequence a much lower general relief for real estate might apply.

bb) Pitfalls

The requirements for the application of trade tax relief are very strict. 'Exclusively managing properties' actually means exclusively. Any further business activity is detrimental. Short- term leasing is regarded as trading activity. Even leasing activities could be regarded as trading activities if they are accompanied by additional services such as cleaning of the leased premises, sale of electricity, advertising etc. Even the lease of other assets like business fixtures (which from a civil-law point of view may be regarded as an inseparable part of the real estate), goods, elevators, or ramps can be detrimental in this respect. Obviously, these limitations may conflict with business objectives. Moreover, careful drafting of the lease contracts is crucial.

cc) Schemes

If there are business fixtures to be leased and there are services to be rendered to the tenants, one option could be splitting the contract into two agreements with two separate legal entities – one for the pure real estate leasing and one for the detrimental activities. This, however, requires the legal or at least the economic/beneficial ownership of the 'detrimental' assets to be transferred to a separate taxpayer. Furthermore, the tenant has to agree to such structuring.

2. Real Estate Transfer Tax Structuring

a) Basics

German legislators developed an efficient real estate transfer tax regime. In particular, the latest introduction of Sec. 1(3a) of the Real Estate Transfer Tax Act targets the frequently used 'real estate transfer tax blocker' structuring according to which an investor could acquire 94.9% of the shares in a real estate corporation and 94.9% (more aggressive: 100%) via a partnership holding the residual 5.1% of the shares in a real estate corporation. However, there are ways of avoiding or reducing real estate transfer tax which will work under the current rules:

b) Schemes

aa) Real Estate Transfer Tax Planning via Partnerships

In a first step an investor could acquire 94.9% of the interest in a partnership holding real estate. More than five years thereafter the investor (on the basis of a call option) could acquire the residual 5.1%, triggering real estate transfer tax only upon the 5.1%. The sale of 94.9% of the interest in the partnership is below the relevant threshold of Sec. 1(2a) of the Real Estate Transfer Tax Act. The transfer of the residual stake is beyond the five-year period and thus not taken into account for the application of Sec. 1(2a) of the Real Estate Transfer Tax Act. The transfer of the residual interest, however, results in a unification of the stakes in a corporation or partnership holding German real estate. This is an event triggering real estate transfer tax pursuant to Sec. 1(3) no. 1 of the Real Estate Transfer Tax Act, but 94.9% exempt according to Sec. 6(2) of the Real Estate Transfer Tax Act since the investor has held the 94.9% for more than five years.

bb) Real Estate Transfer Tax Planning with Multiple Investors

The transfer of 100% of the shares in a corporation holding German real estate does not trigger real estate transfer tax if there are two or more acquirers, and none of them acquire 95% or more of the shares. Real estate transfer tax is triggered if 95% or more of the shares in a corporation are directly or indirectly acquired by one acquirer or related acquirers. It is crucial that the investors are actually not related and that one investor does not hold the shares in trust for the other investor. The structuring does not work with partnerships holding real estate since Sec. 1(2a) of the Real Estate Transfer Tax Act does require a transfer of 100% of the interest, but not a transfer of 100% of the interest to one acquirer.

cc) Reduction of Tax Base by Converting Asset Deal into Share Deal

The real estate transfer tax base in an asset deal is the purchase price. In the case of a share deal, the real estate transfer tax base is determined according to the rules of the German Valuation Act. According to the basic rule, the value is 12.5 times the annual rent reduced by up to 25% of such value, depending on the age of the building. Generally, the value according to the Valuation Act is lower than the fair market value.

The transfer of real estate into a subsidiary partnership is exempt from real estate transfer tax under Sec. 5(2) of the Real Estate Transfer Tax Act. Generally, the exemption is revoked if and to the extent the former owner of the real estate reduces its interest in this partnership within a five-year period. However, the exemption is not revoked if the transfer of the interest in the partnership is subject to real estate transfer tax, e.g. since the requirements of Sec. 1(2a) of the Real Estate Transfer Tax Act are met. Hence, in this structuring, real estate transfer tax is triggered according to Sec. 1(2a) of the Real Estate Transfer Tax Act on the basis of the value as determined under the Valuation Act, and not on the basis of the purchase price. The transfer of real estate to a partnership and subsequent sale is a taxable event for income tax purposes. However, an asset deal will also trigger (corporate) income tax.

III. Alternative Investment Structures

Among the obvious options of making a real estate investment in Germany through an individual person or an ordinary entity (corporation or partnership), several investment vehicles can be used to invest in real estate to meet the needs of the investor's investment plans and investment structure.

1. Open Fund (*Sondervermögen*)

Open funds are separate investment assets held by a special type of an investment entity (*Kapitalanlagegesellschaft*) on behalf and on account for its unit holders. Technically, the investment entity, as a corporation, is subject to corporate income tax. However, it is tax-exempted and will be treated as transparent for tax purposes. Thus, the investment entity itself is not subject to income tax (neither corporate income tax nor trade tax). Profits and capital gains then will be taxed at the level of the foreign investor as they are deemed to be taxable domestic income. Generally, distributions from an open fund investing in German real estate to a foreign investor will be subject to withholding tax at a rate of 26.375%. Final tax rates depend on the form of the legal entity of the investor and applicable double taxation treaties. Generally, Art. 10 of the OECD MC applies and reduces the German tax exposure.

2. Special Fund (*Spezial-Sondervermögen*), Sec. 15 of the Investment Taxation Act

A special fund is a particular open fund (also referred to as 'nonpublic fund') with not more than 100 (non-individual) investors. The principle of transparency also applies to special funds. The income of these funds is also exempt from corporate income tax and trade tax. In contrast to the open fund, the special fund enjoys certain reliefs on compliance rules that are mandatory for open funds, e.g. reporting obligations for foreign and domestic nonpublic investment funds are less rigorous and not all information has to be published. Furthermore, in contrast to open funds, the investors are treated as directly investing in German real estate (Sec. 15(2) of the German Investment Taxation Act – *Investmentsteuergesetz*). Generally, Art. 6 of the OECD MC applies and assigns the right to tax income deriving from real estate to Germany, where the real estate is situated.

3. G-REIT

G-REIT (abbreviation for 'German Real Estate Investment Trust') is a rather new investment vehicle for investors in German real estate (available since 2007) incorporated as a stock listed corporation. Nonetheless, the amount of G-REITs is still limited. A G-REIT must comply with several regulatory requirements. For example, at least 75% of the investments by the G-REIT have to be made in real estate or real estate holding partnerships, the G-REIT's minimum capital must not be less than 15 million euros, at least 15% of the shares must not be held by shareholders with more than 3% of the shares, a single direct investor must not hold more than 10% of the shares, and the G-REIT is obligated to distribute at least 90% of its profits as dividends on an annual basis (and must not plough back profits). A G-REIT must not generally trade in its real estate (Sec. 15 of the G-REIT Act). Noncompliance with these requirements will result in penalty charges. The G-REIT itself is, however, exempted from corporate income tax and trade tax. In general, a withholding tax of 26.375% will apply to distributed dividends. Treaty benefits under Art. 10 of the OECD MC apply as if the shareholder holds less than 10% of the shares in the G-REIT, irrespective of percentage of shares actually held.

Dr. Torsten Engers

Lawyer, Tax Advisor, Expert Advisor on International Tax Law
Areas of Specialization
- Taxation of real-estate transactions
- International tax law
- Structuring of cross-border investments (inbound and outbound)
- Mergers & acquisitions and corporate reorganizations
- Business taxation

Telephone +49 69/717 03-0
Email: torsten.engers@fgs.de

Tax Aspects of Corporate Financing

by Matthias Rogall

Contents

I. Overview
II. General Tax Aspects on External Financing
  1. Basics
  2. Pitfalls
  3. Schemes
III. Shareholder Financing
  1. Basics
  2. Pitfalls
  3. Schemes
IV. Inbound Investments
  1. Basics
  2. Pitfalls
  3. Schemes
V. Special Aspects in the Face of a Crisis

I. Overview

This chapter provides insights into tax aspects of corporate financing with regard to German tax law. In doing so, it aims at a sound balance between presenting a general overview and going into key tax details.

The four parts of this section share a common inner structure, leading from basics to specific pitfalls to tax schemes. The chapter starts with general aspects on external financing (II.), followed by a discussion of shareholder financing (III.), financing of inbound investments (IV) and special aspects of financing in the face of a crisis (V.).

II. General Tax Aspects on External Financing

1. Basics

Debt vs. Equity

We start with the cornerstones of financing relevant to German taxation. Financing means can generally be provided either in the form of debt or in the form of equity. The interest to be paid on debt is generally tax-deductible, whereas the dividends derived from equity are not. Purely from a tax point of view, debt financing is preferable to equity financing.

Limited Interest Deductibility

The deductibility of interest is limited to the extent that the interest paid is in line with the arm's length principle. To further prevent excessive debt financing – especially in cross-border settings – the German legislature established and modified a thin capitalization rule called the 'interest barrier'. Building on a comparison between interest paid and interest received rather than on the debt/equity ratio, the interest barrier prevents the tax deductibility of interest if certain limits are exceeded. The details and pitfalls of the interest barrier, along with schemes to approach it, are discussed below.

With regard to the trade tax, it has to be noted that, based on Sec. 8 no. 1(a) of the German Trade Tax Act (*Gewerbesteuergesetz*), a part of the interest paid may be considered nondeductible. If the sum of potential additions, including one quarter of interest paid, exceeds the threshold of EUR 100,000, then one quarter of the interest paid is effectively considered nondeductible for trade tax purposes. Technically, this one quarter is added back to the net amount of the business profit that was previously reduced by the full interest.

Value of the Debt Tax Shield

The value of interest deductibility depends on the tax rate on profits. In Germany, different tax schemes apply depending on whether a tax-transparent entity or a corporation is taxed. Tax-transparent entities are sole proprietorships and partnerships. Profit originating from such entities is subject to personal income tax (provided the partners are individuals), whose progressive rate runs up to 45% plus an extra 5.5% solidarity surcharge on the tax, i.e. 47.475% in total (Sec. 32a(1) of the German Income Tax Act – *Einkommensteuergesetz*, Secs. 3 and 4 of the German Solidarity Surcharge Act – *Solidaritätszuschlaggesetz*). Sole proprietorships and partnerships are also required to pay a trade tax. Given that this trade tax is, however, credited across the board against the personal income tax (Sec. 35 of the Income Tax Act), materially it is only of limited importance.

Sec. 34a of the Income Tax Act provides for a retained earnings privilege concerning transparent entities such as partnerships and sole proprietorships. Income from trade and businesses which is retained in the business of such a transparent entity can be taxed at a rate of only 28.5%. However, later drawings of such income are taxed at an additional 25%. The two charges together amount to 46.375% (28.5% + 25% of 71.5%), which exceeds the top income tax rate of 45%.

Corporations are required to pay both a corporate income tax and a trade tax. In total, these two taxes yield a tax rate of about 30%. The corporate income tax amounts to 15% (Sec. 23 of the German Corporate Income Tax Act [*Körperschaftsteuergesetz*]) and is grossed up by an additional 5.5% solidarity surcharge on the tax, resulting in 15.825% in total. The trade tax, which needs to be paid in addition, can generally not be credited against another tax. The trade tax rate is calculated by multiplying an index of 3.5% by a specific municipal rate. This municipal rate has a lower bound of 200%. As of 2014, the city of Munich levies one of the highest municipal rates, amounting to 490%. Therefore, the trade tax ranges from 7% at minimum to about 17.15% at maximum.

2. Pitfalls

Interest Barrier: General Setup

Most countries apply thin capitalization rules based on a certain debt/equity ratio. Once this defined debt/equity ratio is exceeded, interest is partly or fully defined as nondeductible. In Germany, such a form of thin capitalization rule was in place until 2007. Before 2008, the interest on internal debt exceeding 1.5 times the equity of the shareholder in question was not deductible.

As of 2008, the deductibility of interest depends on interest payments instead of the debt/equity ratio. The interest barrier applies to incorporated and unincorporated businesses that are part of a group. It considers all interest, without distinguishing between loans from related parties and from third parties such as banks. The interest expenditure of a business entity is generally deductible up to the amount of the interest income, and thereafter only up to the level of creditable EBITDA. The creditable EBITDA is 30 percent of the relevant profit after adding back the interest expense and the amounts deducted under Sec. 6(2) sentence 1 of the Income Tax Act, Sec. 6(2a) sentence 2 of the Income Tax Act and Sec. 7 of the Income Tax Act (depreciations) and after deducting the interest income. If, however, certain exception criteria are met, the exceeding net amount of interest is fully deductible.

Interest Barrier: The Three Exceptions

There are three general exceptions, codified in Sec. 4h(2)(a–c) of the Income Tax Act. If any of these three exceptions applies, interest deductibility is not precluded by the interest barrier. For corporations, the second and third exceptions apply only under the additional requirements of Sec. 8a(2 and 3) of the Corporate Income Tax Act.

The first exception is the one most relevant to small and medium enterprises. It states that the limitation of deductible interest does not apply if the amount of interest expenditure in excess of interest income is less than EUR 3 million. Once this exemption limit of EUR 3 million is exceeded, the general limitation described above applies to all interest expenses going beyond interest earnings, without previously deducting the EUR 3 million. The exemption limit was retroactively increased in 2009. In its initial form, the exemption limit amounted to only EUR 1 million.

The second exception excludes those businesses from the interest barrier which do not or only partly belong to a group. If the business entity concerned is a corporation, Sec. 8a(2) of the Corporate Income Tax Act states an additional requirement: The exception can apply only if the interest paid to a shareholder holding more than one quarter of the ordinary share capital, his related party or to a third party which is able to recourse to either of the aforementioned two, is no more than 10% of the amount by which the interest expense of the entity exceeds its income as defined in Sec. 4h(3) of the Income Tax Act.

The third exception provides for an equity test. The limited interest deductibility does not apply if the business belongs to a group and its equity ratio as of the preceding balance sheet date is equal to or more than that of the entire group. Underscoring the group's equity ratio by no more than two percentage points is harmless. As with the second exception, based on Sec. 8a(3) of the Corporate Income Tax Act, corporations need to fulfill the additional requirement as described above. The equity test therefore applies only if there is no harmful debt financing by an at least 25% shareholder or his related parties.

Interest Barrier: Carry-Forwards

An excess of the business's EBITDA over its interest expense net of the interest income is to be carried forward to the following five business years (EBITDA carry-forward). The remaining nondeductible interest expense is to be carried forward to the following years (interest carry-forward). This increases the interest expenditure of those years, but not the relevant profit.

Interest Barrier: Evaluation

The German interest barrier provides for fairly generous exceptions. Most of the small and medium-sized enterprises are supposed to fall under the EUR 3 million exemption limit. The bigger the business unit, the harder is it to avoid the detrimental consequences of the interest barrier. Firstly, the additional requirements stated in Sec. 8a of the Corporate Income Tax Act are difficult to monitor in big multinational groups and secondly, the so-far disregarded interest from external debt such as bank loans is now just as harmful as that originating from internal debt. Furthermore, the interest barrier discriminates against certain types of businesses, namely those shouldering considerable debt financing and long amortization spans. Real estate companies and private equity firms are just two examples of businesses frequently falling into this category. Given that some specifics of the rule are still ambiguous, some aspects show inconsistencies and given that parts tie in with accounting based on IFRS or US-GAAP, the existence and magnitude of an interest barrier effect are at times hard to foresee. If, for example, the equity test is required to be IFRS-based, assumptions need to be made regarding the goodwill assignment and regarding cash flows from pools. Further inconsistencies relate to the cutback of investment book values and to the combination of financial instruments (International Accounting Standard 32) and partnerships.

If the interest barrier actually defines a part of the interest expenses as nondeductible for tax purposes, the liquidity effects are detrimental. A business unit might even be forced to pay taxes in one period which exceed its taxable profit before considering the interest barrier. Due to the interest carry-forward, this disadvantage might possibly iron out over time; however, the current disadvantage in terms of liquidity might mean a considerable threat to an entity's going concern. After all, it is highly indebted entities (high interest expenses) with low profitability (small EBITDA and small interest earnings) that are likely to be hit by the interest barrier. The detrimental interest barrier effects might be the final nail in the coffin of insolvency. Therefore, measures should be taken to keep the interest barrier from actually becoming relevant in the individual case. Some approaches for how to achieve this are described below.

3. Schemes

It can be considered a general motivation of an entity to keep all of its interest tax-deductible. In considering whether measures should be taken to avoid the interest barrier from affecting the entity, first of all its general profitability needs to be analyzed. The higher the EBITDA, as defined in Sec. 4h(3) of the Income Tax Act, the larger the buffer of deductible interest. This holds regardless of the fulfillment of any of the above-mentioned three exceptions and of the interest revenue.

Adjusting the financing mix and the financing conditions is another approach to avoid negative interest barrier effects. As described, interest expenses are always deductible to the extent of interest revenue. Therefore, internal loans might be provided by a firm in order to generate interest revenue and in doing so bridge a gap of otherwise temporarily nondeductible interest expenses. One might consider cancelling internal or external loans which are no longer required or to carry out a debt-to-equity swap. Furthermore, the conditions of the existing taken and provided loans might be scrutinized for adjustments or might be set up with floating rates right from the start. Loans could be provided in foreign currencies from external or internal lenders situated in countries such as Switzerland or Japan, where the interest rates are traditionally relatively low. With all of these measures, entities must adhere to the arm's length principle when setting the (internal) interest rates. Changed market conditions might allow for justified adjustments leading to higher interest revenue and lower interest expenses for a firm.

Another approach to avoid detrimental interest barrier effects is trying to benefit from the EUR 3 million exemption limit. To do so, a firm might consider splitting up into separate units in such a way that in none of them do the interest expenses exceed the interest revenue by more than EUR 3 million. Subject to specific requirements outlined *inter alia* in Sec. 15 of the German Reorganization Tax Act (*Umwandlungssteuergesetz*), such restructuring can in many cases be carried out in a tax-neutral way.

A further approach to avoid harmful interest barrier effects builds on consolidation for tax purposes. Based on Sec. 15 sentence 3 no. 3 of the Corporate Income Tax Act, Sec. 4h of the Income Tax Act is not to be applied by the subsidiary which is part of a tax group. The tax consolidated parent and subsidiary are considered a single business within the meaning of Sec. 4h of the Income Tax Act. If the income attributed to the parent by the subsidiary includes interest income and expense within the meaning of Sec. 4h(3) of the Income Tax Act, the amounts shall be taken into account in the application of Sec. 4h(1) of the Income Tax Act to the parent. Therefore, if there is a subsidiary potentially yielding nondeductible interest and this subsidiary is so far not part of a tax consolidated group, one might consider establishing or extending the tax consolidation. In a way, this approach reverses the logic of the escape clause, which deals with the equity percentage comparison. The escape clause can be used if the equity ratio of a single subsidiary does not exceed that of the entire group by more than two percentage points. Embedding a highly indebted subsidiary into a tax group with the aim of avoiding the interest barrier, however, is sensible only if the rest of the group has higher equity ratios and therefore an excess of deductible interest over its own actually deducted interest. The effects brought about by tax consolidation can, of course, also be achieved by mergers following the Reorganization Tax Act.

The interest barrier considers compensations for provided loans, but generally not compensations for provided real assets. Therefore, in order to avoid detrimental interest barrier effects, one might consider leasing certain assets instead of using debt to finance them. In the course of leasing, it is important that the beneficial ownership remains with the lessor (operating lease). The opposite form, a financing lease, does not provide any advantages because it is treated just like a debt-financed buy. With a financing lease, the lessee has to show the asset in his accounts and the lease payments are considered like interest expenses. It should be noted that even though the operating lease can reduce the net interest expense, it comes at a cost in the form of a grossed up tax base of the trade tax (Sec. 8 no. 1(d and e) of the Trade Tax Act). While the nominal rates of these additions appear to be only half or even a fifth of the rate applicable to additions of regular interest payments, the effective rate embracing the amortization of the leased object could actually exceed it.

III. Shareholder Financing

1. Basics

Shareholders of a corporation may finance their business operations in Germany by way of equity capital or by way of shareholder loans.

Generally speaking, there are two ways how a shareholder can transfer equity capital into the corporation. In the case of a formal contribution, the shareholder transfers capital in exchange for new shares. Hence, the registered equity capital of the corporation is increased. The formal contribution therefore requires an amendment of the company's articles of association and has to be registered in the commercial register. Alternatively, a shareholder may transfer equity capital informally, which does not lead to an increase of the registered capital, but only increases the company's capital reserve (cf. Sec. 272(2) no. 4 of the German Commercial Code – *Handelsgesetzbuch*).

As opposed to financing the corporation with equity capital, a shareholder may also grant a shareholder loan. Although both forms finance the corporation's business, different tax consequences apply.

As the corporation is treated as an independent legal subject, its taxable income is economically taxed not only at the company level, but also at the level of the shareholders by way of dividend taxation. The taxation of any profit distribution depends on who the shareholder is.

If another corporation is a shareholder, profit distributions are generally 95% tax-exempt due to the participation exemption (Sec. 8b(1) of the Corporate Income Tax Act). However, the corporation paying the dividend must deduct withholding tax (*Kapitalertragsteuer*) on the dividend (generally 25%). The shareholder can offset the amount withheld against his own tax liability.

The recently amended Sec. 8b(4) of the Corporate Income Tax Act now excludes the application of the participation exemption for a corporate shareholder who directly holds less than 10% of the share capital of the corporation. Such dividends are now fully taxable. Stakes in corporations held through a partnership are attributed to the partners in proportion to their participation ratio. This change of law applies to all dividends received after 28 Feb. 2013.

For purposes of trade tax, *inter alia* a threshold of 15% has to be met in order for dividends to fall under the trade tax exemption (Sec. 9 no. 2(a) and no. 7 of the Trade Tax Act).

These thresholds apply to dividends only. For the time being, 95% of capital gains derived from the sale of shares of another corporation remain tax-exempt, irrespective of minimum shareholdings.

Dividends received by an individual are partially (40%) tax-exempt (Sec. 3 no. 40 of the Income Tax Act). Accordingly, business expenses related to such income are deductible at a rate of 60% (Sec. 3c(2) of the Income Tax Act). The taxation of profit distributions received by a partnership depends on whether the partner in question is a corporation or an individual.

As a corporation is itself a tax subject, the company can contract with its shareholders. Hence, it is possible to transfer funds into the corporation by way of a shareholder loan. Such agreements are given full tax effect, provided the terms of the agreement are at arm's length. Therefore, arm's length interest is deductible as a business expense. The aforementioned caveats, i.e. the interest barrier, apply.

Hybrid Financial Instruments

As stated above, financing means can generally be provided either in the form of debt or in the form of equity. The main difference between the two forms is the rights they adhere to. Whereas debt is based on contractual rights, equity is based on corporation rights. There are, however, in-between forms of these two categories, namely hybrid financial instruments.

Financial instruments can be considered as hybrids in two respects. In the first respect, their classification following German tax law differs from that following German corporate and/or commercial law. Based on Sec. 8(3) sentence 2 of the Corporate Income Tax Act, all types of participating rights combining rights to a share in the current profits with a share in the liquidation proceeds are considered equity. Therefore, distributions resulting from such rights do not reduce the income for tax purposes. In German corporate and/or commercial law, such participating rights may well be considered as debt rather than as equity. In the second respect, the classification following German tax law differs from that following the tax laws of other countries.

From a German national perspective, financial instruments might embrace some features of both debt and equity. Ultimately, however, German tax law will classify a financial instrument either as debt or as equity. Widening the perspective to a multinational setup reveals the opportunity and the threat of hybrid financial instruments concerning taxation. A differing classification of the same financial instrument in two countries can result at best in double tax deductibility and at worst in double taxation. Therefore, when analyzing a financial instrument based on German tax law, one might also want to consider how tax legislation of other countries assesses the instrument in question and the cash flows generated from it.

When it comes to determining a financial instrument's tax classification, the German approach differs in some respects from that of most other countries. Germany assigns relevance not only to the instrument's economic meaning, but equally to its legal form. As a consequence, shares of any kind always classify as dividend-generating equity for German tax purposes. Both the repayment and the remuneration matter in assessing whether the debt or equity elements predominate for German tax purposes.

2. Pitfalls

Shareholder Loans

If a shareholder chooses to grant a shareholder loan, the primary focus is to prevent hidden profit distributions (Sec. 8(3) of the Corporate Income Tax Act). In a multinational setting, the rules regarding transfer pricing also have to be obeyed (Sec. 1 of the German Foreign Tax Act – *Außensteuergesetz*). Under German law, a hidden profit distribution is a decrease in corporate property or a prevented increase in corporate property that is caused by the shareholder relationship and has an impact on the business profits, and is not based on a regular profit distribution (arm's length principle). Such a hidden profit distribution can also occur in favor of a related party such as a subsidiary. In this case, the distribution is deemed to be made to the parent company, which, in turn, is deemed to have made a hidden capital contribution to the subsidiary that is receiving the loan.

The consequences of a hidden profit distribution are twofold. The income of the subsidiary is adjusted to be in order with the arm's length principle. Hence, the taxable business profits are increased (i.e. reversing of interest deduction) and subject to tax (jointly approximately 30% effective tax rate for corporations). The parent corporation is deemed to have received a dividend, which is taxable at the level of the parent (approximately 1.5% effective tax rate for corporations).

Shareholder loans could for instance give rise to hidden profit distributions if the receiving subsidiary pays interest that exceeds the reasonable charge. Furthermore, in the case of a controlling shareholder, certain formal requirements have to be met. In this case, a hidden profit distribution is deemed to have taken place where no clear and legally valid agreement was entered into before the loan was granted.

In the case of upstream loans (loans granted from the subsidiary to the parent), hidden profit distributions may occur if the loan is granted interest-free or the interest falls short of the reasonable charge.

Generally, under German tax law, interest-free loans should be avoided if possible because from the borrower's point of view, the interest-free liability generally has to be devalued (cf. Sec. 6(1) no. 3 of the Income Tax Act). Hence, the interest-free loan may lead to a taxable profit at the level of the borrower (decline of a liability). On the other hand, German tax authorities apply a comparatively formal view and treat any loan with a positive nominal interest rate (e.g. 0.5%) as not interest-free.

Other examples of where hidden profit distributions may have taken place are write-downs of the relevant receivables, provided it could have been anticipated that the parent entity is not able to repay the loan and the subsidiary granted the loan without collateral.

Cross-Border Shareholder Loans

As outlined above, a divergent classification of the same financial instrument in two countries can at worst result in double taxation. This is the case if the country of the firm receiving the financial means classifies them as interest, whereas the country of the firm providing them classifies them as dividends. If there is no double taxation treaty effectively preventing the double taxation, these financial means will be taxed twice, namely in both countries. On the other hand, it is also possible that income is treated by both countries as non-taxable. In this case, unilateral switchover clauses may apply (in Germany Sec. 50d(9) of the Income Tax Act).

3. Schemes

Sec. 90(3) of the German General Tax Code (*Abgabenordnung*) requires taxpayers to keep records of the nature and scope of their business affairs involving foreign jurisdictions. For substantial intercompany loans, it may be advisable to follow the principles that apply for general transfer pricing, even if the formal prerequisites of Sec. 90(3) of the General Tax Code are not met (e.g. no foreign jurisdictions). The German tax authorities specified the details regarding the necessary documentation. These decrees can serve as guiding principles in order to prove that the interest rate is reasonable and therefore no hidden profit distribution took place.

Concerning hybrid financial instruments, taxpayers should be aware of the risk of double taxation. When anticipating that a different assessment of the financial instrument might lead to double taxation, they might consider either obtaining an agreement with the fiscal authorities or adjusting their financing mix so that the detrimental hybrids are avoided.

Section 8(3) sentence 2 of the Corporate Income Tax Act distinguishes between equity and debt characterization based on the existence or nonexistence of participating rights in the profits and liquidation proceeds. In aiming for an equity classification, it is recommended to set up the compensation in such a way that it largely depends on and scales with the profit. In this way, it fulfills the requirement of a participating right in the profit both from a jurisdictional and an economic perspective. In order to prove the participating right in the liquidation proceeds, one should set up a written agreement that there is a participation in the hidden reserves not only in the case of liquidation, but also in the event of premature back payment. This written agreement serves as the decisive proof of a participating right in the liquidation proceeds. The consent to also share in potential losses additionally emphasizes the character of equity.

In aiming for a debt classification, the compensation does not serve as the decisive instrument for tax structuring. A debt classification can exist regardless of how profit-related the compensation actually is. It is, however, essential that a participation in the liquidation proceeds is ruled out. Therefore, one has to set up an agreement for documentation purposes that the amount which will be paid back is the nominal value, i.e. that there is no participation in hidden reserves. Generally, the agreed-upon term of a financial instrument to be characterized as equity should not exceed 30 years. For longer terms, an advance ruling is advisable.

IV. Inbound Investments

1. Basics

Different Forms of Inbound Investments

A foreign investor wanting to conduct business in Germany can do so via several vehicles. Active business goals can be pursued in the form of direct selling, operations through a branch, forming or acquiring an incorporated subsidiary or acquiring an interest in a partnership. The tax consequences regarding financing vary in some respects between these options.

Taxation of Profit and Interest for Each Investment Form

In the case of direct selling, the method of taxation, i.e. whether the tax is assessed or withheld, depends on the type of income. If interest income related to direct selling is taxed at all, it is generally withheld. Such interest is taxable in Germany only if it is based on a profit sharing loan to a German borrower, on loans secured by mortgage on a German property or ship, or on a hybrid financing instrument with predominantly equity characteristics. Interest on a German mortgage is taxed by assessment as income from property.

If the German business operation meets the definition of a permanent establishment or permanent representative, as codified in Sec. 49(1) no. 2a of the

Income Tax Act, a foreign investor becomes subject to restricted liability to German income tax or corporation tax. The national rights of taxation can be reduced or even eliminated by double taxation treaties. The definition of a permanent establishment in such a double taxation treaty might differ from the national definition, so the taxation rights may be assigned differently. Most of the German double taxation treaties follow the definition of a permanent establishment as stated in Art. 5 of the OECD Model Convention. The basic considerations outlined above for direct selling also apply to the taxation of interest. There are, however, two additional exceptions. Distributed profits and comparable transactions within the EU are exempt from withholding tax if they are subject to the Parent-Subsidiary Directive, i.e. show a minimum shareholding of 10% by an EU company. The same applies to interest and royalties falling under the Interest and Royalties Directive, i.e. of a 25% minimum shareholding by an EU company.

Regarding inbound investments in the form of partnership interests, conceivable forms include the limited partnership (KG), the general partnership (OHG), the silent partnership and the partnership constituted under civil law (GbR). The KG and OHG are the most common forms. Given that they have a limited legal personality, they can also contract with their own partners. The partners are liable for the debts of a partnership. If a partner provides a loan to his partnership, his claim is considered an assigned business asset. The income and expense items resulting from this loan are included in the results of the partnership, but are then allocated to the donating partner as prior profit shares or charges. Put differently, special partner remuneration, such as interest paid to a partner, is deducted at the level of the partnership, but then added back to the partner's profit share when determining the income from the partnership. In contrast, business expenses paid by the partner in connection with the partnership, e.g. re-financing costs, will be deductible for German tax purposes at the level of the partnership. The profit allocated to a foreign member of a partnership falls under his restricted liability to taxation to the extent that the partnership income was earned through a German permanent establishment. His tax consequences, also regarding interest taxation, are similar to those of a permanent establishment.

Investing in a corporation means investing in a tax subject of its own. The combined tax burden at the level of the company in the form of a corporate tax including a solidarity surcharge (in total 15.825%) and a trade tax of about 15% has been outlined above. At the level of the foreign shareholder, tax consequences tie in with the distributions in the form of dividends or interest. The aforementioned Parent-Subsidiary Directive and Interest and Royalties Directive, just like provisions in double taxation treaties, are applicable and may significantly reduce these tax burdens.

Withholding Tax

As indicated, Germany charges withholding taxes on various forms of earnings paid from a German source to taxpayers residing abroad. Based on Sec. 43 of the Income Tax Act, dividends paid and other forms of distributed capital gains are generally subject to a withholding tax of 25% plus a 5.5% solidarity surcharge, resulting in 26.375%. Most double taxation treaties, however, reduce this rate and the multilateral EU Parent-Subsidiary Directive eliminates it entirely for qualifying dividends stemming from at least 10% shareholdings. However, the following section on pitfalls illustrates that the withholding tax can actually result in double taxation.

2. Pitfalls

Withholding Tax

In the case that a part of the outflowing dividends or the outflowing interest is withheld in Germany, this withheld amount is not automatically credited abroad. If dividends are exempt abroad, no extra credit is provided for taxes already withheld by the country of the distributing unit. Furthermore, even if the foreign country usually applies a credit system, the specific situation of the foreign entity might in effect prevent its application. The entity abroad might, for example, show tax losses in the year in question. Therefore, it does not benefit from a tax credit of the tax withheld in Germany. In the reverse case of outbound investments, Sec. 34c(2) of the Income Tax Act provides the option to switch from crediting to deducting the taxes paid abroad. Such an option might, however, not be provided by the foreign country, which would be relevant in the case of inbound investments into Germany.

Anti-Treaty-Shopping Rule

Double taxation treaties can considerably reduce the tax burden on distributed dividends and on distributed interest. However, the foreign business entity must meet specific requirements in order to benefit from the reduction or elimination of the German withholding tax. Section 50d(3) of the Income Tax Act, which lists these requirements, exerts a 'treaty override'. This means that, regardless of what is defined in the tax treaty, the national law is not superseded. All in all, the anti-treaty-shopping regulation aims to prohibit the application of artificial, purely tax-motivated structures which solely aim to claim benefits brought about by the combination of specific double taxation treaties.

In the recently revised version of Sec. 50d(3) of the Income Tax Act, a foreign entity cannot claim whole or partial relief from withholding taxes under a double taxation treaty or applicable EU directive in so far as (1) its shareholders would not have been entitled to the relief had they received the income directly, (2) the gross earnings of the foreign entity in the year in question did not stem from its own business activity and (3) in respect of these earnings there were no business or other good reasons for involving the foreign entity, or that entity did not take part in active business activity with a business establishment suitably equipped for its business purposes. The foreign entity is obliged to demonstrate business or other good reasons as well as the business operation.

If Sec. 50d(3) of the Income Tax Act applies, despite the existence of a favorable double taxation treaty, the full withholding tax on a dividend amounting to 26.375% will be levied. This threat needs to be seen in combination with the one described above, i.e. that there is no automatism ensuring that the tax withheld would be credited against the tax to be paid abroad.

3. Schemes

A foreign entity planning an investment in a German corporation faces multiple issues from a tax and finance point of view. As mentioned above, one problem is that withholding taxes on dividends can often not be credited abroad if the state of residence exempts dividends paid between corporations from corporate income tax (similar to Sec. 8b(1) of the Corporate Income Tax Act).

One way to address this issue could be to implement a German partnership between the foreign and the German corporation and then establish a tax group (*Organschaft*) between the German partnership and the corporation, with the partnership being the controlling company.

The tax group allows for a tax consolidation between the corporation and the controlling partnership. However, certain prerequisites have to be met. Firstly, the partnership has to carry out a genuine commercial activity. It is therefore not possible to simply use a shell company as a partnership. Moreover, the shares in the subsidiary corporation have to be functionally assigned to the partnership's business. This is the case if the corporation is economically connected to the business of the controlling company. It is unclear whether the partnership could also meet this requirement by acting as a 'functional holding'.

Generally, to achieve and secure this assignment, it is advisable to pay close attention to all aspects of the case at hand and to apply for a binding advanced ruling from the German tax authorities.

The reason why it is often beneficial to have a partnership as an intermediary is that a partnership is treated as transparent for tax purposes. The profits of the partnership are attributed to the partners and generally not taxed at the level of the partnership (trade tax being the exception). When a tax group with a corporation is in place, the same holds true as regards the profits of the corporation (no dividend taxation). These profits are attributed to the partnership by way of the tax group and then attributed to the partners by way of transparency.

For purposes of the relevant double taxation treaty between the investor's state of residence and Germany, the profits of the partnership qualify as business profits that are attributed to the German permanent establishment. The profits are taxable in Germany only, provided the double taxation treaty follows the principles of the OECD Model Convention, which is usually the case. As a consequence, no withholding taxes apply.

The aforementioned structure with an intermediary partnership is also beneficial from a finance point of view. Assuming the foreign entity took out a loan either to buy or to finance the partnership or the German corporation, it is possible that interest expenses can be deducted both at the level of the foreign entity and at the level of the partnership (double dip). In the state of residence, interest expenses are usually deductible as regular business expenses. Of course, these consequences would have to be ascertained before implementing the structure. From a German tax law point of view, the loan is assigned to the partnership. Expenses are treated as special business expenses. These consequences have the provision that the loan must not be attributed to a permanent establishment of the foreign company in Germany. Moreover, the provisions of the interest barrier (outlined above) apply.

V. Special Aspects in the Face of a Crisis

In the face of a financial crisis, typical financial decisions regarding balance sheet reconstruction have to be made after careful consideration of the tax consequences of the intended measures.

To give an example, if a subsidiary is over-indebted in accountancy terms, the parent company may consider a waiver of debts. In so doing, the parent company reduces its receivables against the subsidiary, which leads to expenses of the parent company that are usually not tax-deductible (Sec. 8b(3) of the Corporate Income Tax Act). On the other hand, the subsidiary has to remove the liability in question from its balance sheet, which leads to a profit. Insofar as this profit is not matched by a hidden equity contribution (if the liability would be partially of value) the profit is generally fully taxable at the level of the subsidiary. However, the profit could at least partly be offset against tax-loss carry-forwards. Furthermore, it is possible to apply for a ruling of the German tax authorities that they waive their rights to tax the profit. Such an application has to be filled before the waiver of debts is concluded.

If the borrower agrees upon the waiver subject to restoration (*Forderungsverzicht mit Besserungsschein*), the same principles apply. When the restoration takes place, the consequences of the waiver of debts are reversed. Insofar as the company has removed the liability and incurred a taxable profit, the restoration leads to a deductible expense.

Another measure to reduce the struggling company's liabilities is for the lender to agree on a subordination of the claim to repay the loan. In this case, the liability in question is not considered for determining whether the company is over-indebted. The subordination agreement does not trigger any taxes provided the agreement does not fall under Sec. 5(2a) of the Income Tax Act.

Lastly, lenders often try to reduce the company's financial burdens by reducing the interest rates. As stated above, the loan should not be granted interest-free as this would lead to a profit at the level of the borrower due to devaluation of the liability in question. To prevent this, the lenders therefore often agree on a marginal interest rate. Reducing interest rates can result in adjusting both the lender's and the borrower's profits for tax purposes. For instance, such a measure could lead to hidden profit distributions if the borrower is the parent entity of the lender (upstream loan). However, in the usual case of the parent being the lender, no hidden equity contribution takes place.

This overview shows that financing decisions always need to take accompanying tax consequences into consideration. In the face of a financial crisis, taxes inadvertently triggered could foil the reconstruction of the struggling entity.

Prof. Dr. Matthias Rogall

Tax Advisor, Diplom-Ökonom

Areas of Specialization

- Business taxation
- Mergers & acquisitions and corporate reorganizations
- Taxation of partnerships
- Tax accounting

Telephone (ext.) +49 228/95 94-637

Email: matthias.rogall@fgs.de

The German Investment Tax Act

by Marcus Mick

Contents

I. Introduction
II. The New Legislation
III. Taxation of Investment Funds
   1. Prerequisites of an Investment Fund under the Investment Tax Act
   2. Tax Regime for Investment Funds
IV. Tax Regime for Investment Companies
V. Change in Tax Status
VI. Transitional Period

I. Introduction

The German Investment Tax Act (*Investmentsteuergesetz*) regulates the tax regime applicable to investment asset pools (*Investmentvermögen*) and their investors. The Investment Tax Act was amended in November 2013 in response to the introduction of the Act on the Adjustment of the German Investment Tax Act and Other Acts to the AIFM Implementation Act (*AIFM-Steuer-Anpassungsgesetz*). The amended Investment Tax Act took effect on 24 December 2013 and contains the relevant tax provisions corresponding to the German Capital Investment Code (*Kapitalanlagegesetzbuch*). This Code was introduced in July 2013 and provides for the regulatory and legal framework of investment asset pools and their management companies.[1] Apart from UCITS funds, all domestic and foreign alternative investment funds (AIFs) fall within the personal scope of the Capital Investment Code. Correspondingly, the Investment Tax Act now covers the tax provisions for both types of investment entities. The introduction of the new legislation was long-awaited by tax practitioners who were keen to eliminate the taxation uncertainties connected to the new legal framework of the Capital Investment Code.

II. The New Legislation

According to Sec. 1(1 and 2) of the Investment Tax Act the new law applies to all domestic and foreign UCITS funds and AIFs and their units, except for (typical) holding companies, company pension schemes, central banks, employee profit-sharing schemes and securitization companies. An AIF is defined as a collective investment undertaking to raise capital from a number of investors governed by a statutory investment policy and which is not an operative business outside the finance sector and not a UCITS. This very broad definition

---

1 The European Alternative Investment Fund Manager Directive 2011/61/EU had to be transposed into domestic legislation by 22 July 2013.

expands the personal scope of the new Investment Tax Act compared to the former law. Additionally, investments in risk-diversified assets are no longer mandatory to apply the Investment Tax Act.

Historically, the Investment Tax Act always provided a special tax regime for investment asset pools and their investors and partly privileged those investments for German tax purposes. The characteristic of the tax regime for investment asset pools is that an investor is principally treated as if he invested directly in the underlying assets. The intermediate fund level is almost ignored for tax purposes. This principle still applies under the amended Investment Tax Act, but only for investment funds that fulfill further requirements.

However, because of the widened personal scope of the Investment Tax Act, the legislator has also introduced a second class of investment entities that follow a different tax treatment. An investment company (*Investitionsgesellschaft*) can now qualify as a partnership-type or a corporate-type entity. When taxing investments in investment companies the existence of an investment entity is not ignored; instead, general taxation rules apply. Under the general rules, a corporate-type investment company is opaque for German tax purposes and fully subject to corporate tax and trade tax. Depending on the type of investor, the distributions benefit from the domestic participation exemption or the partial income taxation, provided that the company resides within the EU or the EEA or is subject to a (corporate) income tax of 15% or more. Otherwise dividend relief is not granted to the investors. A domestic partnership-type investment company engaged in trade or business with a German permanent establishment is subject to trade tax, but is transparent for (corporate) income tax purposes.

This dual approach to the taxation of investment funds and investment companies is critical because of fundamental differences between the two tax regimes for the entity and its investors. The investment entity must be characterized as either one or the other – not only when the investment is set up, but also during the lifetime of the investing entity. A qualifying fund can at any time change into a non-qualifying fund, resulting in a change of the applicable tax regime and an exit tax upon requalification (see below).

III. Taxation of Investment Funds

1. Prerequisites of an Investment Fund under the Investment Tax Act

Only investment funds and their unit holders are subject to the special investment fund tax regime. For the purposes of the Investment Tax Act an investment fund is defined as a UCITS fund or an AIF provided further requirements are fulfilled, such as

- investment supervision of the fund exists in its resident country;
- the right to annually redeem the units (unless the units are traded on an exchange);

- the business purpose must be limited to the investment and administration of the investments for the account of the investors and an active asset management must be excluded. The latter does not apply to real estate companies as defined in the Capital Investment Code;
- investments must be made in a risk-diversified investment portfolio, i.e. at least three assets with different investment risks;
- at least 90% of the investments must be made in certain eligible assets (i.e. securities, money market instruments, derivatives, bank accounts, real estate and comparable rights, participations in real estate companies, business fixtures, units and shares in investment funds, participations in public-private partnerships, precious metal, non-securitized loan receivables and shares in corporations). The legislator is of the opinion that an asset managing partnership that is not engaged or deemed to be engaged in trade or business also qualifies as an eligible asset insofar as its assets comply with this test;
- a 20% barrier for investments in non-listed corporations must not be exceeded. This investment barrier does not apply to real estate companies;
- less than 10% of the (share) capital in a corporation must be acquired (unless the investment is made in a real estate, public-private or renewable energy company);
- in general only short term and limited amount of leverage;
- investment limitations must be included in the fund documentation.

Only a UCITS fund or AIF that meets all criteria of this qualification test shall fall under the investment fund tax regime of the Investment Tax Act. In addition, domestic investment funds must be established as separate assets (*Sondervermögen*), an investment stock company (*Investmentaktiengesellschaft*), or an investment limited partnership (*Investmentkommanditgesellschaft*).

2. Tax Regime for Investment Funds

For investment funds the Investment Tax Act still pursues the principle of (limited) tax transparency: The proceeds are determined at the level of the fund and attributed to the investors irrespective of their actual distribution. Only the investor is subject to tax on the earnings, whether distributed or not.

A domestic investment fund and an investment stock corporation (with variable capital) are subject to unlimited tax liability but exempt from corporate and trade tax.

The tax consequences for the investors in investment funds, however, depend on the fulfillment of a number of reporting and disclosure requirements by such funds. The Investment Tax Act still provides for three principles of taxation for investments in investment funds:

- transparent taxation for investments in (white) investment funds: most beneficial tax treatment for investors; or

- semi-transparent taxation for investments in (gray) investment funds: non-privileged tax treatment for investors; or
- non-transparent taxation in (black) investment funds: penalty taxation for investors.

(1) Under the general principles of the (white) investment fund taxation, investors are taxed on the investment fund's 'distributed earnings', 'deemed distributed earnings' and 'interim profits'. 'Distributed earnings' derive from all kinds of capital investments, ordinary and usufruct letting of real estate and similar rights and other income and gains from disposals. The 'deemed distributed earnings' include the following earnings after deduction of income-related expenses that have been appropriated by an investment asset pool for distributions: interest, dividends, income from lease of real estate and similar rights, and other income and gains from disposals. Because of the taxation of the 'deemed distributed earnings' a tax deferral for retained earnings cannot be achieved. However, some items of income are excluded from taxation as 'deemed distributed earnings' and will be taxed only at the time when an actual distribution is made. They comprise capital gains realized from the disposal of securities, income from cash-settled forward transactions, and short sales of securities. Thus, for this item of income the investor achieves a tax deferral by investing through an investment fund. 'Interim profits' refers to the consideration for certain investment income of the investment fund that belongs to the earnings deemed to have been distributed and accrued claims of the investment fund.

Generally, distributed earnings and deemed-to-be-distributed earnings as well as the interim profits constitute investment (dividend) income. This income is subject to the normal tax rates. Individuals are generally subject to a flat tax rate of 26.38%. Progressive income tax rates up to 47.48% apply to business investors. Corporations are subject to corporate tax of 15.83% and generally also to trade tax. The dividend tax privilege for business investors (i.e. only 60% of the dividends are subject to tax) applies with respect to genuine dividends or capital gains from the disposal of shares held by the fund. For incorporated investors the domestic participation exemption (i.e. 95% of the income is exempt from tax) is provided with regard to capital gains from the disposal of shares by the fund but shall not apply to dividend income from the fund's investments. Thus, for domestic corporate investors dividend income is always subject to corporate (and trade) tax irrespective of the percentage of the shares held by the fund.[2] In principle, tax treaty benefits are granted to German investors as if the investor held the

---

[2] According to the generally applicable Sec. 8b(4) of the Corporate Income Tax Act, dividends are exempt from tax if the corporation holds 10% or more in another corporation. Since the qualification of an investment fund generally requires that the fund must not hold 10% or more in a company's equity (Sec. 1(1b) no.7 of the Investment Tax Act) the exclusion of the tax exemption does no harm. However, the exclusion of the participation exemption is a disadvantage for certain companies that are exempt from the 10% test and participations in companies during the grandfathering period of Sec. 22(2) of the Investment Tax Act (see below).

foreign assets directly, i.e. the foreign source income is either exempt from German tax or foreign tax can be credited against the investors' tax liability. If an item of income has already been subject to tax as a deemed distribution, the actual distribution will not be taxed again.

The described tax principles apply only for white funds, i.e. investment funds that fully disclose and report their bases of taxation to the investors and the Federal Gazette. The Investment Tax Act provides a list of reporting details that must be disclosed (in relation to a single investment unit *inter alia* the amount of distributions and deemed distributions, capital amounts, capital gains, and foreign taxes). This is a major hurdle to overcome since for certain types of funds the requirements are quite extensive and difficult to fulfill. Difficulties arise for funds with a large number of assets and asset transactions. Only for (foreign or domestic) special investment funds are the disclosure requirements less rigorous.

Under the Investment Tax Act the amount of the investor's taxable income is determined in two steps. First, the income is determined by deducting the costs of the fund. Second, the expenses of the investor that relate to the investment are deducted. The determination of the investment fund's income follows the principles of a non-business taxpayer and is calculated on a cash-accounting basis, i.e. income or expenses are regarded in principle on an inflow and outflow basis. Certain restrictions that apply to business taxpayers do not apply to the determination of the fund's income, such as the limitations under the interest barrier rule. Special rules apply to the tax deductibility of costs that are not directly connected to a specific item of income generated by the fund.

The taxation of the capital gain or loss from the disposal or redemption of an investment fund unit follows the general tax principles. However, to avoid double taxation the proceeds will be adjusted downwards by the pre-taxed 'deemed distributed earnings'. Business investors are fully subject to tax on any capital gain and private investors are subject to a tax flat rate of 26.38% on the realized gain. However, investors will benefit from tax relief to the extent that the underlying assets are subject to such favored taxation. Therefore, business investors are subject to the partial income taxation to the extent the underlying assets and income qualify for such taxation (capital gains from shares, dividend income). The participation exemption applies to corporate investors for any capital gain from a share disposal held by the fund (but not dividend income). Also any treaty tax exemption will apply to the extent attributable to such income.

(2) Non-compliance with specific reporting requirements, i.e. the reporting and disclosure of details and amounts included in the distribution (e.g. deemed distributions of prior years; capital gains from shares and derivatives; dividends and similar income) and the amount of foreign taxes related to foreign source income, results in a semi-transparent (gray) tax regime. The taxation of the investors in such a (gray) investment fund follows the same principles as described above, but the investor is taxed on all income realized by the fund whether distributed or not.

(3) Should an investment fund not fulfill the reporting and disclosure requirements under the Investment Tax Act, the investor is faced with penalty taxation. This means that in addition to the taxation of the distribution and the interim profits the investor is subject to tax on 70% of the difference between the first assessed redemption price of the investment unit and its last assessed redemption price of the year; at least 6% of the last redemption price will be assessed. Investors in such a 'black' fund are also excluded from other tax benefits, e.g. foreign tax credits. In addition, the taxation on the deemed distributed proceeds is not taken into consideration when assessing the taxation on the actual distribution. This provision clearly results in an overtaxation of the investor because of the violation of the reporting and disclosure requirements.

The taxation of capital gains realized from a disposal of black fund units follows the same principles as described above (see (1)).

IV. Tax Regime for Investment Companies

Investment companies are UCITS or AIF that do not comply with the qualification test of Sec. 1(1b) of the Investment Tax Act (see II.1. above). Investment companies are, for example, closed-end funds that do not guarantee a redemption of the fund units or other investment entities that do not invest in the eligible asset classes.

(1) Income from a partnership-type investment company is subject to taxation at the level of the investors and subject to the general tax principles. A partnership-type investment can be a domestic investment limited partnership (*Investmentkommanditgesellschaft*) or an equivalent foreign entity. Such an entity can be any foreign company with at least two partners of whom at least one is liable with no limitation. The characterization of an entity under the foreign fund supervision rules is irrelevant. From a German tax perspective partnerships are transparent for corporate (income) tax purposes but are subject to German trade tax provided they carry out a trade or business through a domestic permanent establishment. The same principles apply to investment companies at hand. Partnership-type investment companies are not exempt from trade tax.

(2) An investment company that is not partnership-type qualifies as a corporate-type investment company. Corporate-type investment companies can be domestic or foreign open-end funds that, for example, do not invest in the eligible asset classes. They can also be domestic closed-end funds legally formed as a limited liability corporation (GmbH), stock corporation (AG) or investment stock corporation with fixed capital or any foreign corporation equivalent to the respective domestic companies (e.g. S.à.r.l.; Ltd., FCP).

Under the former Investment Tax Act any legal entity that could not be classified as a corporation (according to a German comparison test) was automatically treated as tax-transparent and, thus, not subject to limited taxation in Germany. Since the new Investment Tax Act does not require an incorporated investment body to qualify for a corporate-type investment company, even non-corporates can qualify and be subject to limited tax liability.

The corporate-type investment company is opaque for German tax purposes and, thus, its income is subject to corporate tax (and trade tax if it provides for a German permanent establishment). The German investor is generally taxed on the distributed income pursuant to the generally applicable principles, i.e. distributions received by a private investor are subject to a 26.38% flat tax rate. Corporate shareholders are subject to the participation exemption (95% tax-exempt), unless the shareholding interest falls below 10%, in which case full taxation applies. Non-incorporated business investors are subject to privileged taxation on the basis of 60% of the distributed amount at ordinary tax rates. In addition, a German paying agent must withhold 26.38% tax on the distributions that are credited or refunded.

The (partial) tax exemptions apply only to tax-resident investment companies in the EU or EEA or in a country with a (nominal) business tax rate of at least 15%. In the case of indirect investments in corporations the result may be a requalification from privileged participating income at the level of the investment company to fully taxable earnings for the investor. This constitutes a significant negative development for German residents. The negative effect can be avoided by, for example, using partnership-type investment companies.

A foreign corporate-type investment company can also become subject to German CFC legislation (*Außensteuergesetz*) if it is subject to an (effective) foreign tax rate of less than 25% provided it generates passive (investment) income (dividends, interest, proceeds from forward transactions, options etc.). German tax residents that derive income from CFC (investment) companies are taxed on any retained earnings subject to the ordinary tax rates. The participation exemption or partial-income taxation does not apply to these deemed distributions. The CFC legislation applies to all foreign corporations within or outside the EU/EEA.

V. Change in Tax Status

The introduction of the new tax regime for investment companies also requires entities to deal with the change in their tax status from an investment fund into an investment company and *vice versa*.

In the case that an investment fund changes its investment conditions (to the extent that it does not comply with the requirements under the qualification test), or in the case that the investments of the fund fundamentally violate the list of the eligible assets, the investment fund will be treated as an investment company. A 'fundamental' violation of the permitted assets is not assumed if the violation is only for a short period, the management does not act with negligence or the violation is small compared to the overall investment. Denial of the status of an investment fund is the *ultima ratio* of possible sanctions.

An investment fund that violates the list of eligible assets will be assessed by the representative tax authority (for a domestic investment fund) or the Federal Central Tax Office (for a foreign investment fund) by way of an assessment notice. The investment fund will be treated as an investment company for at least three years starting after the year in which the assessment notice has become final (*unanfechtbar*). With the expiration of the business year of the investment fund in which the assessment notice becomes final, the investor will be treated as if he had disposed of his investment fund's unit and had acquired a new share in the newly established investment company. The sales price equals the redemption price or the market or stock price, as the case may be, at the end of the fund's business year. The assessed tax on any capital gain (minus certain adjustments for pretaxed undistributed earnings and other adjustments) will be deferred until the actual sale of the new share in the investment company occurs. The tax deferral is free of interest. For special investment companies a deemed disposal of the investment unit will be assumed. However, the disposal is assessed already at the end of the investment fund's business year. Any capital gains will be immediately subject to tax; deferred taxation is not applicable in this case.

The Investment Tax Act does not provide for any regulations for the change in status at the level of the investment fund. If an investment fund changes into a partnership-type investment company, the step-up that results from the deemed acquisition of the new interest in the investment company should also result in a step-up of the underlying assets in the tax-transparent investment company. For a corporate-type investment company the same result should be arguable because of the (limited) tax transparency of the fund.

If the status of an investment company is changed into an investment fund (e.g. because of compliance with the eligible assets list) the representative tax authority or the Federal Central Tax Office has to assess this new status (similar procedure to that described above). The tax consequences for the investor are also similar to those discussed above, i.e. any taxes assessed on the deemed disposal of the share in the investment company will be deferred until the actual sale of the investment fund unit. At the level of the company the change in status results either in a step-up of the underlying assets (like a sale of an ordinary partnership interest) or a deemed liquidation of the corporate-type investment company subject to capital gains tax at the level of the company.

VI. Transitional Period

The new Investment Tax Act is effective as of 24 December 2013 unless special grandfathering provisions apply. A special grandfathering takes place for 'former' investment funds, i.e. for funds that qualified as funds under the former rules but do not comply with the new requirements under the Investment Tax Act. Such investment entities shall benefit from the new legislation for investment funds, irrespective of whether they comply with the eligible asset investment list. The grandfathering is provided until the end of the fund's business year that ends after 22 July 2016, provided that the fund fulfills the requirements under the former Investment Tax Act in the interim period. The grandfather period enables the fund managers to comply with the new rules and to arrange for necessary adjustments without immediately changing the investment policy.

Dr. Marcus Oliver Mick LL.M.

Lawyer, Tax Advisor

Areas of Specialization

- Structuring of German investments abroad
- Structuring of foreign investments in Germany
- Taxation of capital investments
- Value-added tax law

Telephone +49 69/717 03-0

Email: marcus.mick@fgs.de

2. Transfer Pricing

Taxation of Royalties Between Affiliated Companies

by Hubertus Baumhoff

Contents

I. Basics
II. Pitfalls
  1. Existing Court Case
  2. Arm's Length Character of Licensing
    a) Appropriateness of Royalties on the Merits
    b) Appropriateness of Royalties in Terms of the Amount
  3. Addition of Licensing Expenses for Trade Tax Purposes
  4. Withholding Taxes
III. Schemes
  1. Avoidance of Licensing Transactions Where Possible
  2. Clearly Worded Agreements and Transfer Pricing Documentation
  3. Benchmarking Analysis, Value Chain Analysis and Rules of Thumb
  4. Application for Exemption Certificates

I. Basics

The determination of prices for the transfer or licensing of intangible assets is one of the most complex valuation issues of relevance to taxation.[1]

From FY 2008 onwards, Germany introduced special rules for the profit-oriented valuation of a bundle of assets, intangibles, chances and risks related to a 'business function' (termed 'transfer package'). These unique German valuation rules are the subject of Sec. I.13. Therefore, this article will only focus on licensing issues arising for separate intangible assets such as patents, brands, trademarks and know-how.

Apart from the transfer pricing of intangibles related to business functions, the German tax authorities normally apply the OECD Transfer Pricing Guidelines for Multinational Enterprises and Tax Administrations 2010 (hereinafter 'OECD TPGL 2010') and the arm's length principle for the transfer pricing of licensing transactions with only a few exceptions.

---

[1] The significance of transfer pricing related to intangibles becomes evident when considering the extent of the responses to the OECD on the Discussion Draft on the Transfer Pricing Aspects of Intangibles. These comments comprised more than 1,000 and over 600 pages for the first and second drafts, respectively, which were issued by the OECD on the topic.

II. Pitfalls

1. Existing Court Case

As is typically the case for German transfer pricing issues, only a few tax court cases exist. In particular, there is only one tax court decision available for transfer pricing related to the licensing of intangibles. On 9 Aug. 2000, the German Federal Tax Court ruled[2] on a case where the name of a firm was similar to a registered brand/trademark of a related company.

Facts of the case: The purpose of the enterprise which sued was the production, distribution, import and export of automotive components. The German entity acted as a fully-fledged manufacturer and distributor. The firm's name was combined with a logo. Both the name and logo were registered trademarks of a related company in the UK. On the basis of a written license agreement, the German party was entitled to use the name and logo for the production and distribution of products within the (German) distribution territory and was, therefore, obliged to pay a royalty of 1.5% of the turnover generated by marked products. The German tax authorities did not accept the royalty and reclassified the royalty expenses as a (non-deductible) constructive dividend ('hidden profit distribution') paid to the (foreign) shareholder. The German tax authorities argued that the naming of a firm is an obligation under corporate law and that costs related to the fulfilment of such obligations are (correctly) not deductible for tax purposes.

Opinion of the Federal Tax Court: The Federal Tax Court held that the naming of a firm may, in general, be compensated (*entgeltfähig*) and netted (*verrechenbar*). However, the naming of a firm is an obligation under corporate law and subject to what is termed 'support by the corporate group' (*Rückhalt im Konzern*). Therefore, under arm's length circumstances, license payments for the mere use of a firm's name would, in general, not be deductible for tax purposes.

However, the court ruled that the mere use of a firm's name has to be distinguished from the use of a brand or trademark (logo). In general, the use of a brand or trademark under a licensing agreement may also be compensated and netted. Further, related expenses should be deductible for tax purposes if the use of the brand/trademark might provide a benefit for the licensee. Therefore, the tax court was required to decide on the relationship between corporate law (i.e. the shareholder's obligation to name a firm) and the German Trademark Act (*Markengesetz*) in terms of taxation issues. The court distinguished between the firm's name as a term for an enterprise from a corporate law perspective on the one hand and the brands/trademarks as labelling/marking products under the Trademark Act on the other hand. It decided that if the firm's name and the brand/trademark are similar, corporate law is (partially) subordinated to the Trademark Act for tax purposes.

---

2 Federal Tax Court of August 9, 2000 – I R 12/99, Federal Tax Gazette Part II, 2001, p. 140.

Therefore, if the firm's name and brand/trademark are similar, the facts of the case have to be established for tax purposes. The key question is whether a license payment is made for the firm's name or for the use of a similar brand/trademark. If the license payment is made for the use of a brand/trademark, relevant expenses have, in general, to be considered tax deductible if the brand/trademark is of value.

Whether a brand/trademark is of value for the licensee does not have to be determined only on the criteria as to whether the licensee could increase the market share and/or could increase the turnover. In fact, the court decided that such value has to be assumed if the use of the brand/trademark might contribute to the promotion of sales. Such contribution to sales promotion does not depend on the existing reputation of the licensee. Even licensees with a good reputation might license brands/trademarks for sales promotion purposes. Whether the licensing of brands/trademarks should be accepted for tax purposes on the merits is, therefore, not linked to the fact that such brand/trademark is similarly used by the licensee as the name of a firm. To determine the appropriateness of the royalty rate for such licensing, it is only necessary to evaluate whether third parties purchase products from a licensee either by using the brand/trademark or the firm's name.

2. Arm's Length Character of Licensing

a) Appropriateness of Royalties on the Merits

If intangible assets are licensed to related parties, an arm's length payment should be made by the licensee. According to the 'benefit test' stipulated in Sec. 6.14 of the OECD TPGL 2010, *"the licensee will generally be prepared to pay this licence fee if the benefit it reasonably expects to secure from the use of the intangibles is satisfactory having regard to other options realistically available. Given that the licensee will have to undertake investments or otherwise incur expenditures to use the licence it has to be determined whether an independent enterprise would be prepared to pay a licence fee of the given amount considering the expected benefits from the additional investments and other expenditures likely to be incurred".*

The German tax authorities require the benefit test to be conducted on an *ex-ante* basis, i.e. a royalty should be paid if the licensing of an intangible is expected to provide a benefit irrespectively of whether such benefit can be realized.[3] Consequently, the German tax authorities accept the payment of a royalty even if the intangible is not directly used, but a benefit is expected for other reasons, e.g. defense against competitors by the licensing of blocking patents. Royalties are, therefore, tax deductible even if the licensed intangible is not employed.

---

3 cf. Administrative Principles of 23 Feb., 1983, Federal Tax Gazette Part I, 1983, p. 218, Sec. 5.1.1.

However, payments for royalties are not tax deductible if such payments are deemed to be duplicated. Such duplication would be assumed if a distribution company paid a license for a brand/trademark which is used for marking products supplied by the licensor as a fully-fledged manufacturer. If the licensor manufactures branded/trademarked products which are subsequently sold to a related distribution company for distribution purposes, the German tax authorities would assume that the royalty is already included in the transfer price to be paid for the supply of the products. Such (deemed) duplication would not be tax deductible.[4]

b) Appropriateness of Royalties in Terms of the Amount

aa) General

In line with the view of the OECD,[5] the German tax authorities[6] require any royalty to comply with the arm's length principle. In particular, an arm's length royalty should consider the following points:

- the territory of the license,
- the specification of the licensing (e.g. exclusive vs. non-exclusive license),
- the investments required to exploit the intangible assets (e.g. investments in manufacturing facilities),
- the marketing and sales expenses required to exploit the intangible assets (e.g. promotion costs to build a customer base),
- the option to grant sublicenses,
- the option to register further developments based on the licensed intangible,
- the kind of license (e.g. patents, brands/trademarks or other sales related license),
- the extent and duration of protection (e.g. duration of remaining patent protection),
- obligation to bear (legal) costs of actions to be taken to retain the value (e.g. enforcement of patent infringement claims),
- bearing of risks of substitution of the intangible (e.g. risk of substitution by a new technology),
- bearing of risks related to the exploitation of the intangible (e.g. product liability risks),
- ordinary and/or extraordinary rights of termination and
- purchase options by the licensee and/or put option by the licensor.

---

4 cf. Administrative Principles of 23 Feb., 1983, Federal Tax Gazette Part I 1983, p. 218, Secs. 3.1.2.3 and 5.1.2.
5 cf. OECD TPGL 2010, Sec. 6.13.
6 cf. Administrative Principles of 23 Feb., 1983, Federal Tax Gazette Part I 1983, p. 218, Sec. 5.1.1.

To determine an arm's length royalty, it is necessary to consider any realistic options available to both the licensor and the licensee as well as their decision-making behaviour. Normally, on the one hand, one would expect the licensor to charge – at least – the net present value of any costs incurred that are related to the intangible. Therefore, the net present value of the costs incurred by the licensor might be considered as a lower boundary (except for cases of failed R&D). On the other hand, the potential benefit to the licensee has to be taken into account. The upper boundary of any royalty to be paid under arm's length circumstances should not exceed the total (net present) value/benefit a licensee might expect to generate by using the intangible. Therefore, the lower boundary from the perspective of the licensor and the upper boundary from the perspective of the licensee would form a range of mutual consent between which an arm's length royalty would be expected to lie under normal circumstances.

Such principles are explicitly stipulated in German tax law. Sec. 1(3) sentence 5 of the Foreign Tax Act (Außensteuergesetz) which provide for the "hypothetical arm's length test" if no comparable values can be determined to apply another transfer pricing method more precisely. Prior to the enactment of this legislation, such principles were already developed under German case law into what is termed the 'double diligent and prudent business manager'[7].

bb) Application of the Traditional Transfer Pricing Methods

(1) Application of the Comparable Uncontrolled Price Method

German tax law stipulates in Sec. 1(3) sentences 1 and 2 of the Foreign Tax Act that an actual arm's length test is preferable. Therefore, the comparable uncontrolled price method would be preferred if respective comparables can be found which are comparable at least to a limited extent.

According to Sec. 2.13 of the OECD TPGL 2010, the comparable uncontrolled price method *"compares the price charged for property or services transferred in a controlled transaction to the price charged for property or services transferred in a comparable uncontrolled transaction in comparable circumstances."* The application of the comparable uncontrolled price method to licensing transactions would require the royalty charged for a controlled licensing transaction to be comparable to the royalty charged for an uncontrolled transaction in comparable circumstances. However, the application of the comparable uncontrolled price method is a challenge for taxpayers because such comparables for the licensing of intangibles are often not available due to the unique character of the intangible.

The application of the comparable uncontrolled price method might sometimes be practicable if intangibles are licensed to both related and unrelated parties, meaning that internal comparable values can be determined.

---

7 cf. Federal Tax Court of 17 May, 1995 – I R 147/93, Federal Tax Gazette Part II, 1996, p. 204, and of 6 April, 2005 – I R 22/04, Federal Tax Gazette Part II, 2006, p. 196.

External comparables would have to be derived from licensing transactions between unrelated third parties. The German tax authorities therefore have established their own database, which contains royalty rates for intangibles that they have obtained during recent tax audits (*Lizenzkartei*). However, German taxpayers do not have access to this database because of the German principle of secrecy in tax matters (cf. Sec. 30 of the General Tax Code - *Abgabenordnung*). Comparable royalty rates are only communicated to tax auditors on specific request.

As German taxpayers do not have access to such database, the application of the database information for an arm's length test within tax audits is controversial in Germany. Nevertheless, in its decision of October 17, 2001[8], the Federal Tax Court held that the application of such secret comparables is permitted. During tax audits, however, the application of such secret comparables for an arm's length test, as a rule, only serves as an indication.

(2) Application of the Resale Price Method

According to Sec. 2.21 of the OECD TPGL 2010, the resale price is *"the price at which a product that has been purchased from an associated enterprise is resold to an independent enterprise. This price (the resale price) is then reduced by an appropriate gross margin on this price (the 'resale price margin') representing the amount out of which the reseller would seek to cover its selling and other operating expenses and, in light of the functions performed (taking into account assets used and risks assumed), make an appropriate profit."* However, this method is probably most useful where it is applied to marketing operations.

For this reason, the application of the resale price method is only quite useful in the case of sublicensing transactions. Such sublicensing transactions occur within corporate groups if a central IP utilization company is established to be responsible for the (intragroup and external) utilization of the total group intangibles. Often such IP utilization companies license the intangibles from all intangible owning group companies and sublicense these intangibles to third companies. If such sublicensing transactions with third parties are available, the royalty for the controlled licensing transaction can be determined by applying the resale price method.

The resale price method is applied by subtracting from the sublicensing fee agreed with the third party an appropriate gross margin to determine the licensing fee:

	Sublicensing fee with third parties
./.	appropriate gross margin (= appropriate profit margin + budgeted costs)
=	arm's length royalty by applying the resale minus method

---

[8] Federal Tax Court of 17 Oct., 2001 – I R 103/00, Federal Tax Gazette Part II, 2004, p. 171.

However, the resale price method requires sublicensing transactions with third parties to occur. Therefore, the scope of application of this method is also rather limited.

(3) Application of the Cost Plus Method

The OECD describes the cost plus method in Sec. 2.39 of the OECD TPGL 2010. It *"begins with the costs incurred by the supplier of property (or services) in a controlled transaction for property transferred or services provided to an associated purchaser. An appropriate cost plus mark up is then added to this cost, to make an appropriate profit in light of the functions performed and the market conditions. What is arrived at after adding the cost plus mark up to the above costs may be regarded as an arm's length price of the original controlled transaction."*

However, this method is probably most useful where semi-finished goods are sold between associated parties, where associated parties have concluded joint facility agreements or long-term buy-and-supply arrangements, or where the controlled transaction is the provision of services.

Also, the German tax authorities accept the cost plus method only in exceptional cases, e.g. for rough validation or estimation purposes.[9] In line with the OECD, they assume that costs related to research and development measures are not directly linked to the value of intangibles resulting from such measures.[10] Therefore, the application of the cost plus method for determining arm's length royalty rates is also limited to exceptional cases.

cc) Application of the Transactional Profits Method

As traditional transfer pricing methods might only be applied in limited cases due to the lack of reliable comparables, transactional profit methods need to be considered to determine arm's length royalty rates. The German tax authorities already specified in 1983 that the operating profit of the licensee is decisive for determining an arm's length royalty rate.[11] They argue that a prudent and diligent business manager of the licensee would only be prepared to pay a royalty in an amount that would allow the licensee still to earn an arm's length operating profit from using the licensed intangibles.

Consequently, the German tax authorities would accept the application of the (residual) profit split method in line with Sec. 2.108 of the OECD TPGL 2010. Of course, it has to be ensured that the profit split method is applied on a transactional basis because the application of the comparable profit method would not be sufficient.

---

9 cf. Administrative Principles of 23 Feb., 1983, Federal Tax Gazette Part I, 1983, p. 218, Sec. 5.2.4.
10 cf. Sec. 6.27 of the OECD TPGL 2010.
11 cf. Administrative Principles of 23 Feb., 1983, Federal Tax Gazette Part I, 1983, p. 218, Sec. 5.2.3.

Under the profit split method, the profit has to be split in line with the functions performed and risks assumed by the licensor and licensee. In general, a contribution analysis / residual analysis is, therefore, required (cf. Secs. 2.119 and 2.121 of the OECD TPLG 2010) to determine an arm's length split of the profit caused by the use of the intangibles. The German tax authorities support such approach. Even within the administrative principles on transfer pricing documentation requirements[12] they stipulate that an analysis of the total value chain of the group companies is required[13] to determine the (arm's length) value contribution of each company within the supply chain. Such value contribution would have to be considered for the determination of the royalty rate.

dd) Application of Rules of Thumb

In addition to the traditional and profit-oriented transfer pricing methods, the German tax authorities regularly apply a rule of thumb for validation purposes within tax audits. A very common rule of thumb is the 'Knoppe formula', which is based on an empirical analysis performed by Mr. *Knoppe*[14]. This empirical analysis concluded that normally about 25% to 33% of the operating profit (prior royalty) earned by using the licensed intangible is paid as a royalty.

However, the application of this rule of thumb entails certain drawbacks. First of all, the method is not based on current financial data. The analysis was performed more than 40 years ago. Therefore, any changes in the economic environment are not considered. Second, the analysis did not consider details of the functions and risks of the licensor and licensee. Therefore, the rule only provides an indication for arm's length royalties.

A more up-to-date analysis is contained in a study by *Goldscheider*, who determined that about 25% of the operating profit (prior royalty) earned by using the licensed intangible is paid as a royalty.[15] Nevertheless, this study does not consider details of the functional and risk profile of the licensor and licensee, either, and therefore provides only an indication.

3. Addition of Licensing Expenses for Trade Tax Purposes

Any business operations performed in Germany (irrespective of whether a corporation, partnership or permanent establishment does so) are subject to trade taxes there (in addition to corporate income taxes or partially offset against personal income taxes). The effective trade tax rate depends on the location of the business. Therefore, the trade tax rate ranges from about 7% (only in geo-

---

12 cf. Administrative Principles – Procedures of 12 April, 2005, Federal Tax Gazette Part I, 2005, p. 570.
13 cf. Administrative Principles – Procedures of 12 April, 2005, Federal Tax Gazette Part I, 2005, p. 570, Sec. 3.4.11.5.
14 cf. *Knoppe*, Die Besteuerung der Lizenz- und Know-how-Verträge, 2nd ed., Cologne 1972.
15 cf. *Goldscheider/Jarosz/Mulhern*, in: Parr, Royalty Rates for Licensing Intellectual Property, Hoboken 2007.

graphically quite unfavorable towns) to about 17%, the average being about 15% in geographically favorable towns.

Normally, any expenses for royalties are tax deductible for trade tax, corporate income and personal income tax purposes in Germany. However, according to Sec. 8 no. 1(f) of the Trade Tax Act (*Gerwerbesteuergesetz*), 6.25% of the royalty expenses are, in general, added back for trade tax purposes insofar as the total amount of (also other) additions exceeds EUR 100,000. Therefore, if significant royalty payments are made by a German licensee, *de facto* double taxation will occur as a result of these additions for trade tax purposes because two affiliated corporations will each be taxed for the same taxable event.

4. Withholding Taxes

According to Sec. 49(2) no. 2(f) of the Income Tax Act (*Einkommensteuergesetz*, alternatively Sec. 49(2) nos. 6 and 9 of the Income Tax Act), royalties paid by a German licensee can pose a threat for a foreign licensor as a non-resident taxpayer in Germany. The royalties are subject to a 15% withholding tax (cf. Sec. 50a(1) no. 3 of the Income Tax Act and Sec. 50a(2) sentence 1 of the Income Tax Act). In general, the licensee is obliged to retain this withholding tax and to pay it quarterly to the German tax authorities for the account of the licensor. The payment of this withholding tax from licensee to the German tax authorities discharges all tax claims of the German tax authorities against the licensor.

However, applicable tax treaties might provide for a reduction of this withholding tax. In particular, if the licensor is located in a European Union country, the EC Interest and Royalty Directive provides for a limitation of any withholding taxes on royalties to 0%. However, even in such case, the licensee generally has to retain the withholding taxes and the licensor is able to apply (using standardized forms) for a refund (cf. Sec. 50d(1) of the Income Tax Act). However, if a reduction of the withholding tax is stipulated by a tax treaty or the EC Interest and Royalty Directive, withholding is not required if the licensor has obtained an exemption certificate from the Federal Central Tax Office in advance (cf. Sec. 50d(2) of Income Tax Act) after a detailed application and the fulfilment of certain circumstances.

III. Schemes

1. Avoidance of Licensing Transactions Where Possible

The determination of arm's length royalty rates is the most complex transfer pricing issue facing taxpayers. Furthermore, German licensees cannot avoid *de facto* double taxation because any royalty payments are added back proportionally to the operating profit for trade tax purposes.

Therefore, taxpayers are strongly recommended to avoid licensing transactions where possible. This can be achieved, in general, through supply chain management. If feasible from an operational perspective, the transfer of intangibles should be included in the sale of (semi-finished or finished) goods instead of taking the form of a separate licensing transaction.

In general, the whole supply chain should be arranged so that the owner of the intangible assets manufactures the products by itself (or engages contract or toll manufacturers) and sells these products to the distribution companies. In such supply chain, the owner of the intangibles (principal) does not have to charge the contract or toll manufacturers for using the intangibles because, as the principal, it purchases the total production volumes from these manufacturers, while the intangibles can be made available free of charge. Further, the distribution companies do not have to pay separate royalties (e.g. for using brands and trademarks) because the products are branded by the principal and the distribution companies use the brands/trademarks for the benefit of the principal.

Such supply chain management avoids the complex valuation of intangibles in favour of the quite simple determination of arm's length transfer pricing for the purchase and sale of (semi-finished/finished) goods. Further, as separate expenses for royalties do not have to be borne by a German company, *de facto* double taxation can be avoided because of the limitation of such expenses for trade tax purposes.

2. Clearly Worded Agreements and Transfer Pricing Documentation

If licensing transactions cannot be avoided by the use of supply chain management (e.g. because of 'co-entrepreneur' structures where different entrepreneurs use the intangibles), it is recommended to document all the terms of the licensing transaction meticulously in written licensing agreements and to prepare sufficient transfer pricing documentation (including a transfer pricing analysis of the arm's length character of the royalty).

This recommendation is particularly important because the burden of proof for any non-compliance with the arm's length principle normally lies with the German tax authorities (cf. Sec. 88 of the General Tax Code). However, the German taxpayer has to provide transfer pricing documentation to the tax auditor (on specific request for ordinary transactions and to be prepared simultaneously for extraordinary transactions). Otherwise, the burden of proof is reduced for the tax authorities or even shifted to the taxpayer.

To avoid any shifting of the burden of proof to the taxpayer, written licensing agreements and transfer pricing documentation should carefully describe the functions and risks of licensor and licensee, as well as provide details on the determination of the royalty and for documentation of its arm's length character (see below).

3. Benchmarking Analysis, Value Chain Analysis and Rules of Thumb

To fulfil German transfer pricing documentation requirements and avoid shifting the burden of proof to the taxpayer, the taxpayer is obliged to demonstrate that it has made all reasonable efforts to comply with the arm's length principle (cf. Sec. 1(1) sentence 2 of the Profit Allocation Documentation Regulation – *Gewinnabgrenzungsaufzeichnungsverordnung*). Even if comparables for royalties do not exist within the documentation, it has to be demonstrated that all reasonable efforts have been undertaken to find such comparables. Therefore, even in such case, the documentation normally should demonstrate that databases have been searched to determine comparables.

If comparables do not exist, a thorough value chain analysis should be performed and documented to determine the value-added contribution of each group company within the supply chain, especially the value-added contribution of the owner of any intangibles. Such analysis should be used to determine a royalty which would be deemed to be at arm's length.

However, even if such value chain analysis is diligently performed, tax auditors still often apply the Knoppe formula/Goldscheider rule for validation purposes. To minimize discussions on the arm's length character of royalties during tax audits, the taxpayer should normally perform such validation in advance itself. If the royalties applied are not within the range suggested by these rules of thumb, it is recommendable the transfer pricing documentation should directly include a section which demonstrates specification of the transaction at hand and its arm's length character.

4. Application for Exemption Certificates

If a licensor is entitled to a reduction of withholding taxes under a tax treaty or the EC Interest and Royalty Directive, the licensor should apply to the Federal Central Tax Office in Bonn for an exemption certificate. The relevant forms can be downloaded at the following URL: http://www.bzst.de/EN/Steuern_International/Abzugsteuerentlastung/Freistellung_Erstattung/Formulare/formulare_node.html.

Prof. Dr. Hubertus Baumhoff

Public Auditor, Tax Advisor

Areas of Specialization
- Taxation of corporate groups
- Transfer pricing
- Structuring of German investments abroad
- Tax audits
- Auditing

Telephone (ext.) +49 228/95 94-218

Email: hubertus.baumhoff@fgs.de

German Transfer Pricing Documentation Requirements

by Xaver Ditz

Contents

I. Introduction
II. Transfer Pricing Documentation Requirements Pursuant to Sec. 90(3) of the General Tax Code
III. Form and Content of Transfer Pricing Documentation
   1. General Information on Shareholder Structure, Business Operations and Organizational Structure
   2. Business Conducted with Related Parties
   3. Functional and Risk Analysis
   4. Transfer Pricing Analysis
   5. Complementary Information in Special Cases
IV. Penalties for Documentation-Related Noncompliance
V. Conclusion

I. Introduction

Transfer pricing has recently become one of the most topical issues of international tax law, not least because of the increasing scrutiny of cross-border transfer prices by tax authorities. The driving force behind this development is tax authorities' fear that corporate profits will be shifted to countries with low tax rates, thereby reducing their domestic tax bases to an unacceptable degree. This development has also been reinforced by the financial and economic crisis, for national tax authorities are prone to want to compensate for revenue shortfalls by, among other things, seeking downward revision of transfer prices at the expense of other states. In turn, this means that multinational companies are now finding that they have to defend their transfer pricing systems in the context of tax audits more than ever before.

In order to assess the appropriateness of transfer prices, the tax authorities require a certain information base. Germany, like many other industrialized countries, addresses this need by requiring multinational organizations to document the reasoning and calculations underlying their transfer prices. The obligations are presented in detail below.

II. Transfer Pricing Documentation Requirements Pursuant to Sec. 90(3) of the General Tax Code

In its leading judgment of 17 Oct. 2001[1], Germany's Federal Tax Court addressed in detail the duties of companies to provide documentation and cooperate with tax authorities in connection with audits of cross-border transfer prices. The court concluded that there were no specific documentation require-

---

1 Federal Tax Court of 17 Oct. 2001 – I R 103/00, Federal Tax Gazette Part II, 2004, p. 171.

ments for transfer prices under then-current law apart from the provisions contained in Secs. 238 *et seq.* of the German Commercial Code (*Handelsgesetzbuch*) and Secs. 140 *et seq.* of the German General Tax Code (*Abgabenordnung*).

The German legislature reacted to the decision of the Federal Tax Court in 2003 by incorporating documentation requirements into Sec. 90(3) of the General Tax Code. The provision requires companies to keep records of the nature of cross-border transactions with related parties within the meaning of Sec. 1(2) of the German Foreign Tax Act (*Außensteuergesetz*). The duty to keep records also pertains to the economic and legal bases for agreements on prices and other business conditions among related parties, which must be at arm's length. More concrete regulation of documentation requirements can be found in the Profit Allocation Documentation Regulation (*Gewinnabgrenzungsaufzeichnungsverordnung*)[2] of 13 Nov. 2003 and the circular of 12 April 2005 issued by the Federal Finance Ministry (Principles of Administrative Practice – *VWG-Verfahren*)[3].

Some ten years after the initial implementation of these documentation requirements, the Federal Tax Court decided that the regulations anchored in Sec. 90(3) of the General Tax Code did not violate European law. The court found that requiring transfer pricing documentation from companies constituted interference with the freedom to provide services. However, the court argued that this was warranted since the purpose of the requirement (that records have to be kept contained in Sec. 90(3) of the General Tax Code) was to facilitate fiscal oversight.[4]

According to Sec. 90(3) sentence 6 of the General Tax Code, transfer pricing documentation must be disclosed only in connection with tax audits. When requesting records, the tax authorities have to identify relevant business areas and relationships of the taxpayer that are covered by the tax audit and specify the nature and scope of the records requested. As a result, it is not necessary to disclose a company's entire documentation; only that for areas specifically covered by the tax audit. Nevertheless, experience has shown that tax auditors will regularly attempt to obtain as much information as possible from the taxpayer and therefore request all records. The tax administration gives companies 60 days to comply with such requests (Sec. 90(3) sentence 8 of the General Tax Code). In the case of extraordinary business transactions, which according to Sec. 3(2) of the Profit Allocation Documentation Regulation include base shifting, restructuring measures or the conclusion of especially important long-term agreements, the requested records must be submitted within 30 days (Sec. 90(3) sentence 9 of the General Tax Code). Sec. 90(3) sentence 3 of the General Tax Code stipulates that the records requested must be submitted in a timely

---

[2] Federal Law Gazette Part I, 2003, p. 2296.
[3] Federal Finance Ministry of 12 April 2005, Federal Tax Gazette Part I, 2005, p. 570.
[4] Federal Tax Court of 10 April 2013 – I R 45/11, Federal Tax Gazette Part II, 2013, p. 771.

manner, i.e. within six months of the end of the financial year in which the relevant transaction takes place (Sec. 147(3) and (4) of the General Tax Code).[5]

III. Form and Content of Transfer Pricing Documentation

German transfer pricing documentation does not need to comply with any specific form requirements and may therefore in principle consist of various records pertaining to business conducted with foreign related parties. Such records, which may be prepared in written or digital form, have to be properly organized and kept for at least ten years (Sec. 147(3) and (4) of the General Tax Code).[6] Sec. 2(1) of the Profit Allocation Documentation Regulation requires that the records be such that a qualified third party can within a reasonable period of time ascertain what business the taxpayer has transacted with related parties. Moreover, the qualified third party ought to be able to ascertain whether and to what extent the business was transacted on an arm's length basis. Additionally, the taxpayer must make a 'serious effort' to transact business with related parties on an arm's length basis (Sec. 1(1) sentence 2 of the Profit Allocation Documentation Regulation).

In general, it is advisable to align transfer pricing documentation with the requirements contained in Secs. 4 and 5 of the Profit Allocation Documentation Regulation. That means – depending on the circumstances of the individual case (Sec. 2(2) of the Profit Allocation Documentation Regulation] – providing the following information:

1. General Information on Shareholder Structure, Business Operations and Organizational Structure

- Presentation of the ownership interests of the taxpayer and related parties within the meaning of Sec. 1(2) of the Foreign Tax Act with which the taxpayer has transacted business (including changes in such interests);
- Presentation of other circumstances that could contribute to "related party" status within the meaning of Sec. 1(2) no. 3 of the Foreign Tax Act;
- Presentation of the organizational and operational structure of the group as well as changes in that structure (including permanent establishments and partnership interests);
- Description of the activities of the taxpayer (e.g. functions exercised in the areas of services, production, research and development).[7]

These records serve primarily to give the auditor an overview of the group of companies and enable the identification of the main audit issues. The corpo-

---

[5] Federal Finance Ministry of 12 April 2005, Federal Tax Gazette Part I, 2005, p. 570, para. 3.2.3.
[6] Federal Finance Ministry of 12 April 2005, Federal Tax Gazette Part I, 2005, p. 570, para. 3.2.3.
[7] Sec. 4 no. 1 of the Profit Allocation Documentation Regulation; Federal Finance Ministry of 12 April 2005, Federal Tax Gazette Part I, 2005, p. 570, para. 3.4.11.2.

rate records mentioned above will regularly relate to information of a general nature concerning the determination of transfer prices that changes only very little (if at all) over time and need therefore not be produced anew each year.

2. Business Conducted with Related Parties

- Presentation of business transacted with related parties, showing in particular the nature and scope of the business conducted and the underlying contractual arrangements (e.g. for procurement, services, assignment of rights, allocation of costs);
- List of material intangible assets that the taxpayer uses in connection with the transaction of business or makes available for use by related parties (Sec. 4 no. 2 of the Profit Allocation Documentation Regulation).[8]

Records on related-party transactions relate largely to issues that exhibit a certain stability over time. As a result, they do not need to be produced anew each year but must simply be updated at regular intervals. This does not, however, apply in cases of extraordinary business transactions[9], which must be recorded on a timely basis according to Sec. 90(3) sentence 3 of the General Tax Code and will regularly refer only to a specific financial year.

3. Functional and Risk Analysis

- Information on the functions exercised by the company and related parties respectively, risks assumed and significant assets deployed;
- Information on contractual agreements, major markets and competition;
- Description of the value chain and presentation of the company's contribution to added value of related parties with which cross-border business is transacted (Sec. 4(3) of the Profit Allocation Documentation Regulation).[10]

The above information requirements can be satisfied by adequate documentation of the functional analysis of the individual undertakings involved in the transactions, taking care in particular to include mention of factors affecting transfer prices (functions exercised, risks assumed and assets deployed for production purposes). This information can also be retained from one year to the next and updated only if necessary to reflect significant changes in the situation.

---

[8] Federal Finance Ministry of 12 April 2005, Federal Tax Gazette I 2005, p. 570, para. 3.4.11.3.

[9] According to Sec. 3(2) of the Profit Allocation Documentation Regulation, these include in particular transfers of assets in connection with restructuring measures, significant changes in functions or risks, business transactions following a significant change in business strategy, and the execution of and changes in long-term agreements (long-term obligation) of significant importance. Federal Finance Ministry of 12 April 2005, Federal Tax Gazette I 2005, p. 570, para. 3.4.8.2.

[10] Federal Finance Ministry of 12 April 2005, Federal Tax Gazette I 2005, p. 570, para. 3.4.11.4.

4. Transfer Pricing Analysis

- Presentation and application of transfer pricing methodology;
- Presentation of the transfer pricing methodology adopted;
- Records of calculations involved in the use of the transfer pricing methodology adopted;
- Presentation of prices or financial data from unrelated companies for the purposes of comparison, and documentation of calculations made for adjustment purposes (Sec. 4(4) of the Profit Allocation Documentation Regulation).[11]

In addition to general information on the transfer pricing methodology employed, the analysis of transfer prices must document the determination of transfer prices for specific types of business or business areas. In that regard, the analysis of transfer prices is based on a documentation of intragroup business relationships. This can involve the presentation of calculation templates showing the transfer pricing methodology employed, margins or markups and basic information used to determine margins or markups. Records should also be kept that show how calculation templates are used to determine transfer prices in the individual case. They can include, for example, identification of specific reference prices used for the comparable uncontrolled price method or determination of planned costs for a specific financial year and allocation of such costs as well as determination of the gross profit markup (e.g. by means of database analysis) for using the cost plus method.

In addition to documenting the actual determination of transfer prices, the records must satisfactorily affirm that an organization is making a "serious effort" to align transfer prices with the arm's length principle (Sec. 1(1) sentence 2 of the Profit Allocation Documentation Regulation), and necessarily also show why the corresponding transfer pricing methodology was considered appropriate for the business relationship mentioned (Sec. 4 no. 4 of the Profit Allocation Documentation Regulation).

5. Complementary Information in Special Cases

- Information on business strategies (e.g. marketing strategies, expansion of market share);
- Information on intentional setoffs;
- Information on pool members, breakdown and benefits anticipated from cost-sharing arrangements[12];
- Information on transfer pricing understandings or agreements with foreign tax authorities and information on mediation and arbitration proceedings;

---

[11] Federal Finance Ministry of 12 April 2005, Federal Tax Gazette Part I, 2005, p. 570, para. 3.4.12.
[12] Federal Finance Ministry of 30 Dec. 1999, Federal Tax Gazette Part I, 1999, p. 1122, para. 5.

- Records on price adjustments made by the company, in particular if made as a result of adjustments in transfer prices or advance rulings issued by foreign tax authorities regarding related parties;
- Records on the causes of losses and measures taken to remedy the situation if statutory accounts show losses from business relationships with related parties for over three consecutive financial years (Sec. 5 of the Profit Allocation Documentation Regulation).[13]

IV. Penalties for Documentation-Related Noncompliance

Pursuant to Sec. 162(3) sentence 1 of the General Tax Code, it will be assumed, until demonstrated otherwise, that the domestic income from cross-border business relationships is higher than that declared if the taxpayer fails to comply with the transfer pricing documentation requirements contained in Sec. 90(3) in the following cases:

- Failure to submit documentation pursuant to Sec. 90(3) of the General Tax Code or the Profit Allocation Documentation Regulation;
- Submission of documentation that cannot be used; or
- Failure to prepare documentation on unusual business transactions within the meaning of Sec. 90(3) sentence 3 of the General Tax Code on a timely basis.

Ultimately, it is assumed that the income reported was not determined on an arm's length basis. Therefore, since the above provision applies until the taxpayer "demonstrates otherwise", the taxpayer must prove that the transfer prices used were appropriate. This will, however, regularly be possible only if the taxpayer can present the tax authorities with a credible case for the underlying business relationships and determination of the corresponding transfer prices, much as the taxpayer would have been required to show in proper documentation pursuant to Sec. 90(3) of the General Tax Code.

The provision contained in Sec. 162(3) of the General Tax Code ultimately reverses the burden of proof to the detriment of the taxpayer. Consequently, it is at odds with conventional procedural rules governing the burden of proof on the one hand and the principle under German law requiring investigations to be initiated and led by the respective jurisdictional authorities on the other hand. Sec. 88(1) of the General Tax Code requires the tax authorities to initiate an investigation. In addition, companies have certain duties to cooperate with the tax authorities, in particular pursuant to Sec. 90(1) and (2) of the General Tax Code. If a company fails to comply with these duties and the matter cannot be resolved otherwise, it is then theoretically possible to assume – to the disadvantage of the taxpayer – that the factual background is that which appears most probable.

---

[13] Federal Finance Ministry of 12 April 2005, Federal Tax Gazette I 2005, p. 570, para. 3.4.15.

Despite the existence of these general principles of procedural law, it is no longer important under Sec. 162(3) in conjunction with Sec. 90(3) of the General Tax Code whether the factual background can be otherwise ascertained or if is probable that the transfer prices reflect application of the arm's length principle. In fact, the law assumes the existence of a violation of the arm's length principle, albeit one that the taxpayer may refute[14]. This approach may in the individual case result in a violation of the double taxation treaty clause based on Art. 9(1) of the OECD MC since the appropriate adjustment of income is possible under treaty law only in the case of transfer prices that are actually inappropriate.[15]

If a company is not able to refute the assumption that its transfer prices are inappropriate due to the fact that the transfer pricing documentation is unreliable or nonexistent, the tax authorities may estimate the income on the basis of the corresponding business transactions. If it is possible to obtain only a rough estimate of income, for example in the form of range of transfer prices, the tax authorities may – despite previous legal opinion[16] – adopt the upper limit to that range to the detriment of the taxpayer (Sec. 162(3) sentence 2 of the General Tax Code). The tax authorities are, however, under no obligation to do so; as long as they remain in that range, their decision is ultimately a matter of administrative discretion.

In addition, Sec. 162(4) of the General Tax Code calls for application of a penalty in the case of nonexistent or unreliable transfer pricing documentation. This penalty prescribed by law for failure to fulfill the duty to keep records is 5% to 10% of the increase in taxable increase resulting from the adjustment of transfer prices pursuant to Sec. 162(3) but no less than EUR 5,000. Sec. 162(4) sentence 3 of the General Tax Code calls for a penalty of up to EUR 1,000,000 and at least EUR 100 for each full day beyond the official deadline.

The amount of the penalties pursuant to Sec. 162(4) of the General Tax Code is in any case not completely left to the discretion of the tax authorities. On the other hand, no penalties may be imposed in cases in which failure to comply with the duty to cooperate with the authorities as required by Sec. 90(3) of the General Tax Code is 'excusable or culpability only slight' (Sec. 162(4) sentence 5 of the General Tax Code). As a result, there must be no evidence of willful misconduct or gross negligence on the part of the taxpayer, and the taxpayer will also be held accountable for any misconduct on the part of a legal representa-

---

14 Federal Finance Ministry of 12 April 2005, Federal Tax Gazette Part I, 2005, p. 570, para. 4.6.1; dis. opin. rul. of the Federal Tax Court of 10 May 2001 – I S 3/01, DStR 2001, p. 985, according to which the absence of transfer pricing documentation may not be automatically taken to meant that transfer prices will not withstand arm's length scrutiny.
15 Federal Tax Court of 11 Oct. 2012 – I R 75/11, Federal Tax Gazette Part I, 2012, p. 1046.
16 Federal Tax Court of 17 Oct. 2001 – I R 103/00, Federal Tax Gazette Part II, 2004, p. 171, according to which the tax administration must regularly align its decisions with the upper or lower limit of the range of transfer prices as a function of what is more advantageous to the taxpayer.

tive or agent. In exercising their discretion as regards the amount of the penalty, the tax authorities are required by Sec. 162(4) of the General Tax Code to take into account not only the fact that the purpose of the penalty is to ensure compliance with the duty to prepare and submit transfer pricing documentation on a timely basis. In fact, the authorities also have to consider any benefits that may have accrued to the taxpayer as well as the degree of lateness in the case of failure to comply with deadlines (Sec. 162(4) sentence 4 of the General Tax Code). In the event the minimum of EUR 5,000 or EUR 100 per day is prescribed by law, the tax administration has no room for the exercise of any discretionary judgment.

The question as to when records are to be considered "usable" or "essentially unusable" arises in connection with penalties called for under Sec. 162(3) and (4) of the General Tax Code. Records can be qualified as usable if they enable a competent third party to identify the taxpayer's transactions with related parties and verify compliance with the arm's length principle within a reasonable period of time[17]. On the other hand, whether or not records are to be considered "essentially usable" (Sec. 162(3) of the General Tax Code) can be determined only in the specific case. However, according to the tax administration[18], deficiencies in terms of completeness or inaccuracy in a company's records do not lead to an organization's entire transfer pricing documentation being classified as essentially unusable. The tax administration will regularly assume that records are "essentially unusable" in the following cases[19]:

– Submission of records to document appropriateness of transfer prices in a foreign language[20] (see on this Sec. 2(5) of the Profit Allocation Documentation Regulation) if not translated despite a request to do so.
– Submission of records to document appropriateness of transfer prices that show only that the transfer prices were dictated by a related party or justify transfer prices by providing only the transfer pricing method and its suitability for a concrete case without alignment with arm's length data or adequate forecasts.
– Submission of records to document appropriateness of transfer prices that are based exclusively on data that do not withstand arm's length scrutiny.

V. Conclusion

Practical experience shows that the tax authorities request transfer pricing documentation in almost all tax audits of German companies that are engaged in business transactions with foreign related parties. Since the documentation re-

---

17 Federal Finance Ministry of 12 April 2005, Federal Tax Gazette Part I, 2005, p. 570, para. 3.4.19.a.
18 Federal Finance Ministry of 12 April 2005, Federal Tax Gazette Part I, 2005, p. 570, para. 3.4.19.a.
19 Federal Finance Ministry of 12 April 2005, Federal Tax Gazette Part I, 2005, p. 570, para. 3.4.19.c.
20 Federal Finance Ministry of 12 April 2005, Federal Tax Gazette Part I, 2005, p. 570, para. 3.4.16.

quirements were enacted more than ten years ago, the majority of taxpayers are accustomed to providing the information requested by the tax authorities. In some cases however, tax authorities are trying to enforce income estimates to the detriment of the taxpayer on the ground that records are qualified as being 'essentially unusable'. Such qualifications are regularly based on insufficient and unreliable content of the records provided concerning transfer prices. However, taxpayers are mostly given the opportunity to refute the assumption of inappropriateness by providing the requested information.

Dr. Xaver Ditz

Tax Advisor

Areas of Specialization
- Taxation of corporate groups
- International tax law
- Transfer pricing
- Tax audits
- Mutual Agreement Procedures

Telephone (ext.) +49 228/95 94-226
Email: xaver.ditz@fgs.de

Business Restructurings

by Markus Greinert

Contents

I. Introduction
II. Basics
   1. The Transfer of a Function to Another Country as a Taxable Event
      a) Basic Characteristics of a Transfer of a Function
      b) The Transfer of a Function in Typical Situations
      c) The OECD Concept of a 'Transfer of Activity'
   2. General Principles for Evaluating a Transfer Package
      a) Normal Case: Aggregate Evaluation
      b) Individual Evaluation in Exceptional Cases
      c) The 'Aggregate Evaluation' of the OECD
III. Pitfalls
IV. Schemes

I. Introduction

The process of economic globalization means that multinational enterprises constantly have to assess their business structures and adapt them to current developments. This often leads to cross-border business restructurings that may result in a transfer of functions, assets or risks between affiliated companies. The reasons for such business restructurings are plenty. Examples include better marketability, cost advantages, synergy effects, risk reduction, and tax advantages.

In 2008, Germany introduced a new Sec. 1(3) sentence 9 and 10 of the German Foreign Tax Act (*Außensteuergesetz*) which for the first time explicitly focuses on cross-border business restructurings. The provision relates to cases in which a whole business function is transferred from Germany to another country and requires the evaluation of a 'transfer package' on an aggregate basis that might have considerable tax effects. Determining individual transfer prices for the elements of the transfer package is permitted in exceptional cases only.

The importance of cross-border business restructurings is recognized by the OECD as well. In 2010, the OECD published a new Chapter IX of its Transfer Pricing Guidelines (hereinafter 'OECD TPGL 2010') dealing with the transfer pricing aspects of business restructurings. Similar to Germany, the OECD discusses the transfer of a whole business activity and the concept of aggregate evaluation. However, the OECD approach is not as rigorous as the new German rules and gives greater flexibility to the taxpayer.

The first cases have occurred in which the German tax authorities aim to tax cross-border business restructurings pursuant to Sec. 1(3) sentence 9 and 10 of the Foreign Tax Act. In the light of these developments, the following article provides an overview of the new Sec. 1(3) sentence 9 and 10 of the Foreign Tax Act and identifies similarities with and differences to the new Chapter IX of the OECD TPGL 2010.

II. Basics

Section 1(3) sentence 9 and 10 of the Foreign Tax Act contains the central provisions with regard to the evaluation and taxation of a transfer package. Section 1(3) sentence 9 of the Foreign Tax Act states: "Where a function is transferred including the corresponding opportunities and risks and including the assets and other advantages transferred or otherwise provided (transfer of a function) and shall sentence 5 apply to the transferred function as at least restrictedly comparable arm's length prices are not available for the transfer package as a whole, the taxpayer shall determine the range of mutual consent based on the transfer package." Sec. 1(3) sentence 10 of the Foreign Tax Act expands this provision as follows: "After having made appropriate adjustments, the determination of individual transfer prices for all assets and services affected shall be accepted for cases covered by sentence 9 if the taxpayer shows credibly that no essential intangible assets and advantages were subject to the transfer of the function or that the sum of the applied individual transfer prices measured by the evaluation of the transfer package as a whole complies with the arm's length principle; if the taxpayer shows credibly that at least one essential intangible asset was subject of the transfer of a function and if he specifies it exactly, individual transfer prices shall be acknowledged for the elements of the transfer package." Section 1(3) sentence 9 and 10 of the Foreign Tax Act constitutes a rather abstract provision. In order to substantiate the new rules, a Transfer of Function Regulation (*Funktionsverlagerungsverordnung*) was adopted in 2008.[1] In addition, the German tax authorities published a detailed Administrative Circular on the Relocation of Functions (*Verwaltungsgrundsätze Funktionsverlagerung*) in 2010.[2]

1. The Transfer of a Function to Another Country as a Taxable Event

a) Basic Characteristics of a Transfer of a Function

Sec. 1(3) sentence 9 of the Foreign Tax Act requires a 'transfer of a function'. According to Sec. 1(2) sentence 1 of the Transfer of Function Regulation, a transfer of a function is given if an enterprise transfers or concedes the right to use of assets and other advantages including the corresponding opportunities and risks to another affiliated enterprise, thereby enabling the acquiring enterprise to perform a function that has thus far been performed by the transferring enterprise and limiting the transferring enterprise in exercising the function. A transfer of a function within the meaning of Sec. 1(3) sentence 9 of the Foreign

---

[1] Transfer of Function Regulation of 12 August 2008, Federal Law Gazette Part I, 2008, p. 1680.
[2] Federal Finance Ministry of 13 October 2010, Federal Tax Gazette Part I, 2010, p. 774.

Tax Act thus requires the existence of a function, its transfer to an affiliated enterprise, and the passage of assets or other advantages.

Section 1(1) sentence 1 of the Transfer of Function Regulation defines a 'function' as a business activity consisting of an aggregation of similar operational tasks that are performed by certain centers or departments of an enterprise. A function is thus an organic part of an enterprise without having to form a part of a business unit. According to the German tax authorities, company management, research and development, material procurement, warehousing, production, packaging, distribution, assembly, processing or refinement of products, quality control, financing, transport, organization, administration, marketing and after-sales services as well as parts of these activities, such as the manufacturing or the distribution of a single product, may be considered as a function.

In addition to the existence of a function, Sec. 1(3) sentence 9 of the Foreign Tax Act requires its 'transfer' to an affiliated enterprise. According to the German tax authorities, a transfer is given only if the transferring enterprise either terminates or restricts the performance of the function. From a qualitative point of view, it is not necessary that the acquiring enterprise perform the function in the same way as the transferring enterprise. In addition, in quantitative terms, a transfer is not assumed if the annual turnover of the transferring enterprise drops by less than EUR 1 million within a five-year period following the transfer. However, according to the German tax authorities, a transfer might be given if a function is replaced by another function, for example if product B takes the place of product A, whose production is relocated to another country. This is rather surprising, as the turnover, the profits, and the employees might be unaffected by the product replacement.

A further condition for a transfer of a function within the meaning of Sec. 1(3) sentence 9 of the Foreign Tax Act is the transfer of the opportunities and risks as well as the assets and other advantages related to the function. The term 'asset' includes not only goods and rights but also actual conditions and concrete possibilities; in other words, all advantages for which an enterprise would pay remuneration. Advantages that do not meet these requirements might qualify as 'other advantages'. These include, for example, good customer relationships and well-trained employees. Together with the assets and other advantages, the corresponding 'opportunities and risks' have to be transferred to the acquiring enterprise. An isolated transfer of opportunities and risks cannot be considered as a transfer of a function and should therefore not give rise to any tax issues.

b) The Transfer of a Function in Typical Situations

Based on the principles set out above, a transfer of a function within the meaning of Sec. 1(3) sentence 9 of the Foreign Tax Act can appear in different forms. The basic form would be the outsourcing of a function (*Funktionsausgliederung*). In such a case a function is entirely relocated to an affiliated enterprise in another country and terminated in Germany. All assets and advantages related to the function are transferred to the acquiring enterprise or a right to use them is granted. As a consequence, the transferring enterprise is no longer able to use the assets and advantages or to perform the function in question. An example of outsourcing a function would be the complete relocation of the production of a product from Germany to another country. According to the German tax authorities, this includes cases in which the production of one product is replaced by the production of another.

An application of Sec. 1(3) sentence 9 of the Foreign Tax Act also has to be considered in cases in which a function is downsized (*Funktionsabschmelzung*). In such cases only a part of a function is transferred to an affiliated enterprise. The transferring enterprise thus does not end the function completely but continues to perform it on a lower level. The German tax authorities tend to assume a transfer of a function in such cases as, according to them, a function has to be defined taking into account single objects as well as specific activities. Therefore parts of a function might themselves constitute a function. The conversion of a fully-fledged manufacturer into a contract manufacturer or of a fully-fledged distributor into a low risk distributor would serve as good examples of the downsizing of a function.

Taxation on the basis of Sec. 1(3) sentence 9 of the Foreign Tax Act might, however, be excluded if a function is separated (*Funktionsabspaltung*). Although in such cases a function is transferred from Germany to an affiliated company in another country, the essential intangible assets related to the function remain in Germany. As a consequence, the opportunities and risks resulting from the function are still attributable to the transferring enterprise. Therefore, the relocation of the function does not constitute a taxable event under Sec. 1(3) sentence 9 of the Foreign Tax Act. An example of a separation of a function would be the transfer of a routine function to an affiliated company and its subsequent remuneration by the transferring enterprise on the basis of the cost plus method or the transactional net margin method. In such a case only the disposition or transfer for use of single assets might be taxed.

Another situation in which Sec. 1(3) sentence 9 of the Foreign Tax Act might not apply is when a function is duplicated (*Funktionsverdoppelung*). In such cases a function is established in another country while also being maintained in Germany. If there is no restriction in the exercise of the function by the transferring enterprise within five years after the function has been acquired by the affiliated enterprise, the relocation of the function will not be taxed under Sec. 1(3) sentence 9 of the Foreign Tax Act, according to Sec. 1(6) sentence 1 of the Transfer of Function Regulation. Establishing the manufacture of a product in another country while the same product is still produced in Germany without restrictions would constitute a good example of a duplication of a function. In such a situation only the disposition or transfer for use of single assets might constitute a taxable event.

c) The OECD Concept of a 'Transfer of Activity'

At first glance, the OECD concept with respect to the taxation of business restructurings in the new Chapter IX of the OECD TPGL 2010 looks very similar to the German approach. However, a closer look reveals substantial differences. Contrary to Sec. 1(3) sentence 9 of the Foreign Tax Act, the new Chapter IX of the OECD TPGL 2010 refers not to a 'transfer of a function' but to a 'transfer of activity'. The OECD considers this term as synonymous with 'ongoing concern', which means a 'functioning, economically integrated business unit'. As an ongoing concern regularly comprises several functions, the concept of a transfer of activity in the OECD TPGL 2010 has a much more limited scope than the transfer of a function in Sec. 1(3) sentence 9 of the Foreign Tax Act. The German approach thus proves to be much stricter than the proposal of the OECD.

2. General Principles for Evaluating a Transfer Package

a) Normal Case: Aggregate Evaluation

When a function is transferred, a transfer package must be evaluated on an aggregate basis according to Sec. 1(3) sentence 9 of the Foreign Tax Act. Pursuant to Sec. 2(2) sentence 1 of the Transfer of Function Regulation, the aggregate evaluation has to be conducted in accordance with the general rules set out in Sec. 1(3) sentence 1 to 8 of the Foreign Tax Act. Thus, if it is possible to identify unrestrictedly or restrictedly comparable prices for the transfer package, a factual arm's length test according to Sec. 1(3) sentence 1 to 4 of the Foreign Tax Act has to be performed. In all other cases the transfer price for the transfer package has to be determined on the basis of a hypothetical arm's length test pursuant to Sec. 1(3) sentence 5 to 8 of the Foreign Tax Act.

The factual arm's length test according to Sec. 1(3) sentence 1 to 4 of the Foreign Tax Act refers to actually identifiable prices, gross margins, net margins, markups, and similar data agreed between unrelated third parties. In the case of a transfer of a function the factual arm's length test will be the exception, as intangible assets play a key role in cross-border business restructurings and arm's length data is difficult to obtain for these. If, nonetheless, arm's length prices have been identified, these will form a range. In the case of unrestrictedly comparable prices, every price within the range may be chosen as a transfer price for the transfer package. In the case of restricted comparability, the price range has to be narrowed, for example by using the method of interquartile range. Subsequently, every price from the narrowed range is acceptable as a transfer price for the transfer package. If a transfer price outside the narrowed range has been chosen, the German tax authorities are entitled to effectuate an adjustment based on the median.

In contrast to the factual arm's length test, the hypothetical arm's length test pursuant to Sec. 1(3) sentence 5 to 8 of the Foreign Tax Act refers to a functional analysis and internal planning data in order to determine a transfer price. With respect to a transfer of a function, the hypothetical arm's length test will constitute the normal case due to the importance of intangible assets in cross-border business restructurings and the problems arising from their evaluation. In order to determine a transfer price on the basis of the hypothetical arm's length test, a range of mutual consent first has to be worked out. For this purpose, the taxpayer is obliged to identify the minimum price of the transferring enterprise and the maximum price of the acquiring enterprise with respect to the transfer package. The range of mutual consent is then formed by the respective profit expectations, which have to be identified by means of the discounted cash flow method.

In the second step, the hypothetical arm's length test requires a transfer price to be chosen from the range of mutual consent. Pursuant to Sec. 1(3) sentence 8 of the Foreign Tax Act the price that, with utmost probability, complies best with the arm's length principle has to be selected. Unless another price is credibly shown, the mean value of the range of mutual consent has to be taken as a transfer price. In order to show another price in a credible way, the taxpayer has to provide sound reasons indicating that a certain price within the range of mutual consent complies better with the arm's length principle than another price. If the range of mutual consent proves to be incorrect, the German tax authorities are entitled to effectuate an adjustment of the transfer price. They may, however, refrain from a correction if the transfer price chosen is within the correct range.

The concept of aggregate evaluation in the case of a transfer of a function according to Sec. 1(3) sentence 9 of the Foreign Tax Act does not have precedents in German tax law. According to the German legislature, the necessity of an aggregate evaluation is justified by the fact that individual transfer prices would not accurately reflect the value of the function. Advantages that are difficult to detect with an evaluation of the individual assets forming the transfer package might be identified by recourse to an aggregate evaluation. When a function is transferred, the German legislature thus aims to tax an additional value which might remain untaxed in the case of an individual evaluation. This might result in a considerable tax burden for the transferring enterprise.

The reasons given by the German legislature for the necessity of an aggregate evaluation are hardly convincing. In the past, the taxation of an additional value was discussed only in connection with the transfer of a whole business unit or a part thereof. In this case it was accepted that a transfer of goodwill might take place if goodwill-forming factors such as good customer relationships or well-trained employees were transferred. In the case of a transfer of a function these considerations cannot, however, apply because goodwill-forming factors are generally not relocated. Only the transferring enterprise has good customer relationships or well-trained employees; the acquiring enterprise needs to newly establish them. Consequently, a transfer of goodwill does not take place. An aggregate evaluation and the taxation of an additional value in the case of a transfer of a function are therefore not justified.

b) Individual Evaluation in Exceptional Cases

An individual evaluation of the assets and advantages forming the transfer package is permitted in exceptional cases, according to Sec. 1(3) sentence 10 of the Foreign Tax Act. According to the German tax authorities, the individual evaluation of the assets and advantages has to be based on the general rules set out in Sec. 1(3) sentence 1 to 8 of the Foreign Tax Act. Thus, if it is possible to identify unrestrictedly or restrictedly comparable prices for the assets and advantages transferred, a factual arm's length test according to Sec. 1(3) sentences 1 to 4 of the Foreign Tax Act is necessary. In all other cases the price for the assets and advantages has to be determined on the basis of a hypothetical arm's length test pursuant to Sec. 1(3) sentence 5 to 8 of the Foreign Tax Act.

Section 1(3) sentence 10 of the Foreign Tax Act distinguishes three cases in which an individual evaluation is permitted. The first relates to situations in which the taxpayer shows credibly that no essential intangible assets and advantages were subject of the transfer of the function, as set out in Sec. 1(3) sentence 10 alt. 1 of the Foreign Tax Act ('first escape clause'). Intangible assets and advantages are essential if they are required for the transferred function and if their transfer price amounts to more than 25% of the total of all individual prices of all assets and advantages of the transfer package, according to Sec. 1(5) of the Transfer of Function Regulation. Given the importance of intangible assets in the context of cross-border business restructurings, the provision has only a limited scope and solely applies if support functions such as accounting or administration are relocated or if a function is separated.

Another case in which an individual evaluation of the assets and advantages transferred is permitted can be found in Sec. 1(3) sentence 10 alt. 2 of the Foreign Tax Act ('second escape clause'). This provision covers cases in which the taxpayer demonstrates credibly that the sum of the applied individual transfer prices measured by the evaluation of the transfer package as a whole complies with the arm's length principle. In these cases both the range of mutual consent and the value of the transfer package must be determined, as set out in Sec. 2(3) sentence 1 of the Transfer of Function Regulation. Thus, the taxpayer has to determine not only the value of the individual assets and advantages but also the value of the transfer package as a whole, which represents a substantial effort. Therefore, this provision has only a limited scope.

An individual evaluation of the assets and advantages transferred is also permitted if the taxpayer shows credibly that at least one essential intangible asset was subject to the function transferred and if he specifies it exactly, pursuant to Sec. 1(3) sentence 10 alt. 3 of the Foreign Tax Act ('third escape clause'). Due to the importance of intangible assets in the context of cross-border business restructurings, Sec. 1(3) sentence 10 alt. 3 of the Foreign Tax Act should apply in most cases in which a function is transferred to another country. The individual evaluation according to Sec. 1(3) sentence 10 alt. 3 of the Foreign Tax Act thus becomes the normal case, whereas the aggregate evaluation pursuant to Sec. 1(3) sentence 9 of the Foreign Tax Act should apply only in a limited number of situations. Section 1(3) sentence 10 alt. 3 of the Foreign Tax Act therefore has considerable significance for the taxpayer.

c) The 'Aggregate Evaluation' of the OECD

The OECD discusses the evaluation of a 'transfer of activity' in the case of a cross-border business restructuring as well. Like Germany, the OECD proposes the application of an 'aggregate evaluation' and makes reference to evaluation methods known from acquisition deals between independent enterprises. However, unlike Germany, the OECD does not consider the application of an aggregate evaluation as obligatory. It states only that an aggregate evaluation 'may be necessary' to achieve the most reliable arm's length price. An individual evaluation of the assets and advantages transferred in the course of the transfer of an activity is therefore not excluded. In addition, the OECD maintains the factual arm's length test in order to identify a transfer price for the transferred activity. It does not discuss a hypothetical arm's length test which requires the identification of a range of mutual consent and the application of the mean value unless another value is credibly shown. The German provisions thus prove, once more, to be much stricter than the proposal of the OECD.

III. Pitfalls

The pitfalls of the new Sec. 1(3) sentence 9 of the Foreign Tax Act are best shown by a typical example of a cross-border business restructuring. For that purpose reference is made to a German privately held corporation ('*GmbH*') with its registered seat and central administration in Germany having its main activity in the development, production and distribution of refrigerators. Due to the current economic situation, the *GmbH* has lost a considerable market share, in particular in eastern Europe. It therefore assumes that in the future it will generate profits only to the amount of EUR 1,000,000 per year. The *GmbH* therefore decides to transfer its distribution to Hungary. It hopes that its proximity to the eastern European market will lead to an increase in profits. To achieve this goal, it establishes a Hungarian privately held corporation *kft* to which it transfers the customer base necessary to perform the distribution function. The value of the customer base is EUR 1,100,000. The *kft* plans to make profits to the amount of EUR 2,000,000 per year.

The relocation of the distribution from Germany to Hungary constitutes a transfer of a function within the meaning of Sec. 1(3) sentence 9 of the Foreign Tax Act. As it is not possible to identify unrestrictedly or restrictedly comparable prices for the transfer package, a hypothetical arm's length test pursuant to Sec. 1(3) sentence 5 to 8 of the Foreign Tax Act is necessary. Therefore, a range of mutual consent formed by the respective profit expectations of the transferring and the acquiring enterprise has to be worked out. In the case at hand, this range is from EUR 1,000,000 (transferring enterprise) to EUR 2,000,000 (acquiring enterprise). Unless another price is credibly shown, the mean value of the range of mutual consent to the amount of EUR 1,500,000 has to be taken as a transfer price for the distribution function. This shows the considerable tax effect of the new Sec. 1(3) sentence 9 of the Foreign Tax Act. Even though the value of the transferred customer base is only EUR 1,100,000, the amount of EUR 1,500,000 has to be chosen as a transfer price. This leads to a taxation of goodwill with a value of EUR 400,000, although it is highly questionable and not proven whether such goodwill is transferred.

IV. Schemes

In the case at hand, several options are available to avoid the taxation of a transfer package according to Sec. 1(3) sentence 9 of the Foreign Tax Act. The first would be to organize the acquiring enterprise as a low risk distributor of the transferring enterprise. This means that the *kft* would have to act as a low risk distributor for the *GmbH* with respect to the eastern European market. In this context, it would be important for the acquiring enterprise to assume routine functions only. Transferring a customer base or other essential intangible assets to the *kft* should be avoided. In addition, the acquiring enterprise should not carry any risks associated with the distribution of the refrigerators. The *GmbH* should thus pay a low but stable provision to the *kft* based on the cost plus method or a commission considering the minor risk of the *kft*.

If the aforementioned conditions are met, the taxation of a transfer package should be excluded by recourse to the first escape clause set out in Sec. 1(3) sentence 10 alt. 1 of the Foreign Tax Act. This rule allows the determination of individual transfer prices for all assets and services affected if the taxpayer shows credibly that no essential intangible assets and advantages were subject to the transfer of the function. According to Sec. 2(2) sentence 1 of the Transfer of Function Regulation, these requirements are met if the acquiring enterprise performs the transferred function exclusively for the transferring enterprise and if the compensation paid for performing the function is determined using the cost plus method or considering the minor risk of the acquiring enterprise. The application of the first escape clause set out in Sec. 1(3) sentence 10 alt. 1 of the Foreign Tax Act thus proves to be a reasonable solution in the example above.

A second option to avoid the taxation of a transfer package is to transfer the customer base from the transferring to the acquiring enterprise. In the example above, this would mean that the *GmbH* sells its customer base for eastern Europe to the *kft*. In this way, taxation of a transfer package could be prevented by applying the second escape clause set out in Sec. 1(3) sentence 10 alt. 2 of the Foreign Tax Act. According to this provision, the determination of individual transfer prices for all assets and services affected is acceptable if the taxpayer shows credibly that the sum of the applied individual transfer prices measured by the evaluation of the transfer package as a whole complies with the arm's length principle.

However, pursuant to Sec. 2(3) sentence 2 of the Transfer of Function Regulation, individual transfer prices for all assets and services affected are acceptable only if the sum of the individual transfer prices is within the range of mutual consent. In the case at hand, the individual transfer prices for all assets and services affected amount to EUR 1,100,000. This amount is within the range of mutual consent from EUR 1,000,000 to EUR 2,000,000. As a consequence, the value of the customer base to the amount of EUR 1,100,000 might be chosen as a transfer price. Hence, in the example above, recourse to the second escape clause set out in Sec. 1(3) sentence 10 alt. 2 of the Foreign Tax Act would be another reasonable solution.

A third way of avoiding the taxation of a transfer package would be to transfer the customer base from the transferring to the acquiring enterprise and specify its transfer to the German tax authorities. In the present case, this would mean that the *GmbH* sells its customer base for eastern Europe to the *kft* and makes the existence of the customer base known to the German tax authorities. With this approach, taxation of a transfer package could be prevented by applying the third escape clause set out in Sec. 1(3) sentence 10 alt. 3 of the Foreign Tax Act. According to this provision, individual transfer prices are acknowledged for the elements of the transfer package if the taxpayer shows credibly that at least one essential intangible asset was subject of the transfer of the function and if he specifies it exactly. These conditions should be met by proceeding as described above. As a consequence, the value of the customer base to the amount of EUR 1,100,000 might be chosen as a transfer price. Applying the third escape clause set out in Sec. 1(3) sentence 10 alt. 3 of the Foreign Tax Act thus proves to be another reasonable solution in the example above.

A fourth option to avoid the taxation of a transfer package might be to recur to legal or contractual claims for damages, reimbursement or compensation. According to Sec. 1(7) sentence 2 alt. 2 of the Transfer of Function Regulation, a transfer of a function is not given if a transaction is not viewed as a disposal or acquisition of a function by unrelated third parties. Pursuant to the German tax authorities, these conditions are met if an existing contractual relationship is terminated by the parties. In a situation where this gives rise to claims for damages, reimbursement or compensation, these claims might be accepted as a transfer price. A prominent example of such a claim would be the claim of a sales agent for compensation according to Sec. 89b of the German Commercial Code (*Handelsgesetzbuch*). In the case at hand, however, no legal or contractual claims for damages, reimbursement or compensation exist. The relocation of the distribution from the *GmbH* to the *kft* arises not from the termination of an existing contractual relationship, but from the founding of a new subsidiary by the *GmbH*. Therefore, in the present case, recourse to Sec. 1(7) sentence 2 alt. 2 of the Transfer of Function Regulation is not possible.

Dr. Markus Greinert

Tax Advisor, Diplom-Kaufmann

Areas of Specialization

- Transfer pricing and business restructurings
- Taxation and valuation of intangible assets
- International tax law
- Taxation of corporate groups and tax accounting

Telephone (ext.) +49 89/80 00 16-51

Email: markus.greinert@fgs.de

3. Reorganization Tax

An Overview of Reorganizations Under German Tax Law

by Ingo Stangl

Contents

I. Treatment of Reorganizations as Taxable Realization Events

II. Provisions of Law Governing Basis Rollover in the Case of Reorganizations

III. Types of Reorganization Governed by the Reorganization Act

IV. Structure of the Reorganization Tax Act

V. Reorganizations Involving Conversion of Corporations to Partnerships
 1. Merger of Corporations with Partnerships
 2. Division of Corporations to Partnerships
 3. Change of Form from Corporations to Partnerships

VI. Reorganizations Involving Only Corporations
 1. Corporate Mergers
 2. Corporate Divisions
 3. Changes of Form from One Type of Corporation to Another

VII. Contributions to Equity
 1. Contributions to Equity in the Case of Corporations
 2. Contributions to Equity in the Case of Partnerships

I. Treatment of Reorganizations as Taxable Realization Events

Reorganizations can in a broad sense be understood to mean transfers of assets between legal entities. Such legal entities may be natural persons (individuals), legal persons (e.g. corporations) or partnerships. Transfers can in such cases be classified according to the nature of the consideration given. A transfer may or may not involve consideration. When consideration is involved, it can take various forms such as a purchase price (disposal) or other assets (exchange). A transfer of assets in exchange for shareholder rights also qualifies as a transfer in exchange for consideration. Transfers made in exchange for consideration regularly result in taxation of hidden reserves, i.e. the difference between the market value of the assets transferred and their book values for tax purposes[1]. As a result, the tax authorities[2] consistently view reorganizations as disposals and therefore classify them as transfers in exchange for consideration. The basic treatment of transfers that do not involve consideration entails various distinctions. There are many special provisions of law that also require hidden

---

1 The book value for tax purposes in such cases will as a rule be based on historical acquisition or manufacturing costs less any depreciation taken for tax purposes.
2 See Federal Finance Ministry of 11 Nov. 2011, Federal Tax Gazette Part I, 2011, 1314 marginal no. 00.02 *et seqq.*

reserves to be unlocked when assets are transferred even if no consideration is received. One major example can be found in the case of gratuitous transfers of assets by corporations to their shareholders or the other way around, in which transfers qualify as hidden profit distributions and constructive contributions to equity and require that hidden reserves be unlocked even if no consideration is involved.

II. Provisions of Law Governing Basis Rollover in the Case of Reorganizations

In the case of transfers that fulfill the conditions mentioned above (i.e. that are qualified as a taxable realization event), it is possible to avoid unlocking hidden reserves only if the law makes provision for an exception and the taxpayer is eligible for such treatment. In practice, such exceptions regularly mean that hidden reserves contained in assets that are transferred to another legal entity will not be unlocked by the transferor entity and that the assets will be recognized at book value by the transferee entity ('basis rollover'). In such cases, the hidden reserves are transferred from one legal entity to another.

The provisions governing the basis rollover are not uniformly bundled, but found in various tax acts. Those contained in the German Reorganization Tax Act (*Umwandlungssteuergesetz*) represent a certain core body of law and proceed primarily from the provisions of corporate law pertaining to reorganizations contained in the German Reorganization Act (*Umwandlungsgesetz*). The tax implications of many reorganizations that fall under the Reorganization Act are governed by the Reorganization Tax Act, which – under certain restrictive conditions – makes provision for the possibility of a basis rollover. Reorganizations pursuant to the Reorganization Act that are not covered by the Reorganization Tax Act are either not addressed by any special provision or may fall under other tax regulations governing reorganization. The latter case will as a rule involve specific provisions of the German Income Tax Act (*Einkommensteuergesetz*) and the German Corporate Income Tax Act (*Körperschaftsteuergesetz*) or a construction of the general provisions of the Income Tax Act found for specific types of reorganization.

The chart below shows firstly the interrelationship between the Reorganization Act and the Reorganization Tax Act and secondly the general provisions of tax law governing restructuring that exist outside the scope of the Reorganization Tax Act.

An Overview of Reorganizations Under German Tax Law

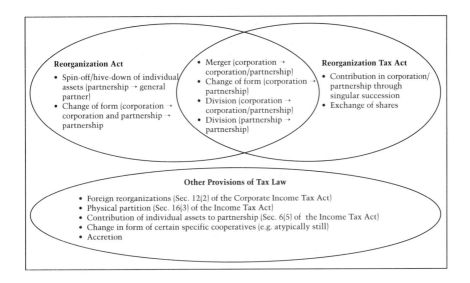

This article focuses on the provisions of the Reorganization Tax Act.[3]

III. Types of Reorganization Governed by the Reorganization Act

As mentioned above, the Reorganization Tax Act is based primarily on the types of reorganization that fall under the Reorganization Act. An understanding of the aspects of corporate law contained in the Reorganization Act is therefore needed to acquire a basic understanding of the tax aspects governed by the Reorganization Tax Act.

The provisions of corporate law contained in the Reorganization Act make a distinction between the types of reorganization shown below:

---

3 See the chapter titled "Foreign Reorganizations with a Connection to the German Tax Net" on the special treatment of foreign reorganizations not covered by the Reorganization Tax Act.

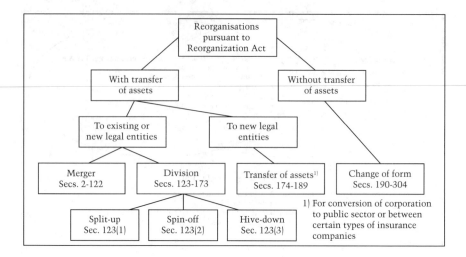

In a merger (Secs. 2-122), two or more legal entities unite to form a single entity (the transferor entity/entities cease/s to exist).

A division (Secs. 123-173) can be of one of the following three types:

- Split-up: A legal entity transfers its entire assets to two or more transferee entities and ceases to exist.
- Spin-off: A legal entity transfers part of its assets to one or more transferee entities such that the transferor entity continues to exist and receives no shares in the transferee entity or entities as consideration.
- Hive-down: A legal entity transfers part of its assets to one or more transferee entities such that the transferor entity continues to exist and receives shares in the transferee entity or entities as consideration.

The transfer of assets (Secs. 174-189) in this context refers to transfers of any or all of the assets between entities with special legal forms. The transferor entities in such cases will usually be stock or mutual insurance companies. The transferee entities will often be the federal government, a federal state, a local authority or a group of local authorities. This particular type of reorganization is thus as a rule not of any great importance as regards the legal forms found in the private sector.

A change of form (Secs. 190-304) simply involves a change in the form of a legal entity: for example, when a German privately held corporation (*GmbH*) becomes a limited partnership. No transfer of assets takes place; the legal entity changes its legal form, but retains its legal identity.

IV. Structure of the Reorganization Tax Act

The Reorganization Tax Act basically covers the types of reorganization discussed in the previous section. It distinguishes primarily between those legal entities that enjoy tax transparency for the purposes of taxation under German personal and corporate income tax law (essentially individuals and partnerships) and those that are considered opaque for the same purposes (essentially corporations).

Based on this conceptual classification, the Reorganization Tax Act is structured as shown below:

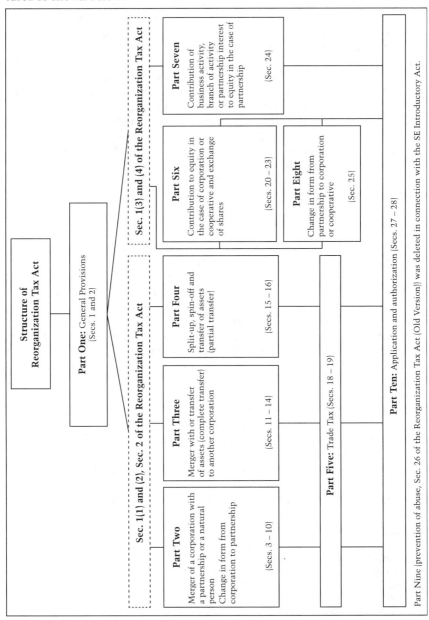

Parts Two through Five address reorganizations covered by the Reorganization Act and make a distinction based on whether they involve a transfer from a legal entity that is opaque for tax purposes to one that is transparent for tax purposes (Part Two and Sec. 16 of the Reorganization Tax Act in Part Four) or whether they take place between legal entities that are opaque for tax purposes (Part Three and Sec. 15 of the Reorganization Tax Act in Part Four). Parts Two through Four are preceded by Sec. 1(1) and (2), which stipulate the basic conditions for application of Parts Two through Four. This is where, for example, the provision of law is found that limits application of the Reorganization Tax Act to reorganizations that take place within the EU and the EEA (see the chapter titled "Foreign Reorganizations with a Connection to the German Tax Net" for more details). The scope of application encompasses primarily reorganizations that fall under the Reorganization Act and comparable reorganizational measures taken under the provisions of foreign law[4]. In addition, application is limited to individuals who maintain their residence or habitual place of abode in the EU and the EEA and legal entities (e.g. corporations) that maintain their registered offices or places of effective management in the EU and the EEA.[5] Sec. 2 of the Reorganization Tax Act governs the possibility (along with exceptions) of retroactive application for up to eight months for tax purposes of all of Parts Two through Five.

Parts Six through Eight of the Reorganization Tax Act do not deal with reorganizations pursuant to the Reorganization Act, but rather with a type of reorganization that is defined separately for tax purposes: equity contributions. Such contributions involve transfers of assets from one legal entity to another such that the transferor entities continue to exist and receive as consideration for such transfers of assets – at least in part – shares in the transferee entity. In such cases, the contributions may be made in various ways for the purposes of application of corporate law (e.g. as a hive-down within the meaning of the Reorganization Act, as an increase in capital by way of in-kind contribution or through the change of form from a partnership to a corporation within the meaning of the Reorganization Act that is treated as a contribution for tax purposes pursuant to Sec. 25 of the Reorganization Tax Act). The Reorganization Tax Act also makes a distinction based on whether the contributions are made to legal entities that are opaque for tax purposes (i.e. primarily corporations, Parts Six and Eight) or to legal entities that are transparent for tax purposes (i.e. primarily partnerships, Part Seven). Parts Six through Eight are preceded by Sec. 1(3) and (4), which describe the basic scope of application of Parts Six through Eight. Here too, application is essentially limited to 'European' contributions, i.e. the transferor entities and the transferee entities must maintain their places of residence or habitual places of abode or their statutory registered offices and

---

4 The tax authorities have developed extensive criteria for whether a foreign reorganization involves a procedure that can be compared with a domestic reorganization, which is in practice often difficult to determine; see Federal Finance Ministry of 11 Nov. 2011, Federal Tax Gazette Part I, 2011, p. 1314 marginal no. 1.20 *et seqq*.
5 See also on this aspect the chapter titled "Foreign Reorganizations with a Connection to the German Tax Net".

places of effective management within the EU or the EEA.[6] However, Parts Six through Eight also contain major exceptions to this strict EU/EEA rule (e.g. a certain degree of globalization as regards the exchange of shares and contributions to partnerships). There is also the possibility of retroactive application for up to eight months for tax purposes.

V. Reorganizations Involving Conversion of Corporations to Partnerships

Reorganizations involving the conversion of corporations to partnerships through merger are governed by Secs. 3 to 7 of the Reorganization Tax Act, reorganizations involving change of corporate form by Sec. 9 of the Reorganization Tax Act, and reorganizations involving split-up and spin-off by Sec. 16 of the Reorganization Tax Act. A hive-down to a partnership qualifies as a contribution to equity for tax purposes and is therefore treated separately in Sec. 24 of the Reorganization Tax Act; see on this 7.2 below.

All reorganizations involving the conversion of corporations to partnerships pursuant to Secs. 3 to 7, 9 and 16 of the Reorganization Tax Act must be accompanied by a change from opaque tax treatment to tax transparency. This in effect eliminates a taxation tier, which requires special taxation measures.

1. Merger of Corporations with Partnerships

In practice, the law calls for the following sequence of measures for the purposes of taxation when a corporation merges with a partnership:

a) **Taxation of Transferor Corporation:** The transferor corporation must prepare a balance sheet as of the effective date of reorganization for tax purposes. In principle the valuation of assets shown in this balance sheet must be based on fair value, i.e. any hidden reserves contained in the assets of the transferor corporation must be disclosed and taxed ('transfer gain'). Alternatively, a transferor corporation may apply for permission for a basis rollover in order to obtain tax-neutral treatment of the balance sheet prepared for the purposes of reorganization if all three of the following conditions are met:

- It must be certain that the transferred assets will remain subject to payment of income tax or corporate income tax by the transferee.

- The right of the Federal Republic of Germany to tax any gain on the disposal of the transferred assets realized by the transferee must not be excluded or restricted. In cross-border reorganizations, this condition regularly proves to be of crucial importance. See the chapter titled "Foreign Reorganizations with a Connection to the German Tax Net" for more details on this aspect.

---

6 See the chapter titled "Tax-Neutral Contributions in Kind of Business Units" for more on this aspect.

- No consideration may be given or exist in the form of shareholder rights. If the assets received include an EU/EEA permanent establishment and a transfer gain results, Sec. 3(3) of the Reorganization Tax Act takes into account the requirements of Art. 10 of the Merger Directive. Undercertain preconditions fictitious foreign tax can then be credited towards the German tax on the transfer gain.

b) **Taxation of the Transferee:** The transferee must recognize the values shown in the closing balance of the transferor entity prepared for tax purposes. Furthermore, a fictitious contribution is assumed according to which the shares in the transferor corporation prior to reorganization are considered to be held by the transferee entity (if not actually already held by the latter). This contribution is tax-neutral. As a result, the shares in the transferor entity are initially treated as operating assets of the transferee entity. As regards accounting treatment, the transferee entity then receives the assets of the transferor entity through the merger and the shares in the transferor entity held by the transferee entity – which may have been contributed shortly prior to that point – ceases to exist. Any difference between the book value of the transferor entity's shares that thereby ceases to exist and the value of the assets transferred by the transferor entity pursuant to the closing balance sheet prepared by the transferor entity for tax purposes immediately prior to reorganization[7] is included in the taxable 'transfer gain' realized by the transferee entity. This gain is essentially subject to the regulations that also govern disposals of shares in corporations (therefore as a rule 40% tax-exempt for taxpayers subject to income tax or 95% tax-exempt for taxpayers subject to corporate income tax).

In addition, a 'dividend share' fictitiously accrues to the transferee through the restructuring measure. This is essentially the profit of the transferor entity available for distribution that is fictitiously distributed to the transferee shareholder in connection with the reorganization. This dividend share is treated as a usual distribution for the purposes of taxation and is therefore not included in the transfer gain. As a result, the dividend share is subject to withholding tax, which is particularly important in the case of foreign transferee entities. It should be kept in mind that the German tax authorities will not apply the Parent-Subsidiary Directives to the dividend share.[8]

In addition to the transfer gain and the dividend share, various special circumstances exist that can also result in partial realization of gains.

---

[7] Assets of transferor entities that were not subject to taxation of gains realized upon disposal by Germany prior to reorganization are accorded special treatment. These assets are also recognized at fair market value for the purposes of determining gains upon acquisition if the transferor entity had opted for rollover in the balance sheet prepared for the purposes of reorganization (Sec. 4(4) sentence 2 of the Reorganization Tax Act).

[8] See Federal Finance Ministry of 11 Nov. 2013, Federal Tax Gazette Part I, 2013, p. 1314 marginal no. 07.09. See also on this aspect the chapter titled "Foreign Reorganizations with a Connection to the German Tax Net".

2. Division of Corporations to Partnerships

Split-ups and spin-offs[9] from corporations to partnerships are governed by Sec. 16 of the Reorganization Tax Act. This provision essentially involves application of the relevant provisions of Secs. 3 to 7 of the Reorganization Tax Act governing mergers of corporations with partnerships. However, these provisions apply only to the assets transferred through the reorganization measure. In that respect, such reorganizations are treated as partial mergers for tax purposes.

In addition, a rollover at the level of the transferor corporation presupposes that a branch of activity will be transferred and that a branch of activity will also be retained. This reflects the requirements of Sec. 15 of the Reorganization Tax Act as regards the division of corporations. It is possible to refer to the content of 6.2 below by analogy in this connection.

3. Change of Form from Corporations to Partnerships

According to Sec. 9 of the Reorganization Tax Act, the changes of Form from corporations to partnerships are treated as mergers with partnerships for tax purposes. The comments on Secs. 3 to 7 of the Reorganization Tax Act contained in V.1 above concerning mergers of corporations with partnerships apply accordingly to the changes of Form from corporations to partnerships.

VI. Reorganizations Involving Only Corporations

1. Corporate Mergers

Mergers of corporations are governed by Secs. 11 to 13 of the Reorganization Tax Act. In practice, the law views such reorganizations as the following sequence of measures for the purposes of taxation:

a) **Taxation of the Transferor Corporation:** Taxation of the transferor corporation can be compared with the corresponding procedure involved in the reorganization of corporations to form partnerships (see V.1 above). As a result, the transferor corporation must prepare a balance sheet for tax purposes as of the tax-transfer date of the reorganization that can be used to avoid unlocking gains (transfer gain) based on valuation at fair market value upon application if the conditions corresponding to those contained in the three bullet points under a) in V.1. are met.

b) **Taxation of the Transferee Corporation:** The transferee corporation must recognize the assets at the book values shown in the balance sheet prepared by the transferor corporation for tax purposes prior to the transfer. The transferee corporation receives a transfer gain or a transfer loss in the amount of any difference between the value of the transferred assets according to the balance sheet prepared for tax purposes prior to the transfer and the book

---

9 Hive-downs to partnerships will be treated as contributions to a partnership for tax purposes, in which case Sec. 24 of the Reorganization Tax Act is applicable.

values of the transferee entity's shares in the transferor entity. This amount is tax-exempt (gain) and nondeductible (loss). However, insofar as the transferee entity holds a stake in the transferor entity, 5% of the transfer gain is taxable.

c) **Taxation of the Shareholder of the Transferor Corporation:** If the shareholder of the transferor corporation is not at the same time the transferee, the shareholder receives shares in the transferee corporation in exchange for the shares in the transferor corporation that cease to exist due to the merger. This exchange of shares is taxable, i.e. the hidden reserves associated with the shares in the transferor entity are subject to the regulations applicable to capital gains realized on the disposal of shares (therefore generally 40% tax-exempt for taxpayers subject to income tax or 95% tax-exempt for taxpayers subject to corporate income tax). It is possible to apply to have this taxation waived (i.e. possibility of a basis rollover) only if Germany's right to tax the shares in the transferee corporation is not excluded or restricted.

Under special circumstances, a basis rollover is possible even if Germany's right to tax the shares in the transferee corporation is excluded or restricted. If the reorganization at issue falls under Art. 8 of the Merger Directive, then Sec. 13(2) sentence 1 no. 2 of the Reorganization Tax Act permits such a rollover even in the case of loss or restriction of Germany's right to tax the transaction. If the shares in the transferee entity are subsequently sold, Germany will then proceed to tax the transaction as though its rights had never been relinquished or restricted. That means that it may not be possible to rely on a double taxation treaty in the case of disposal of the shares (i.e. execution of a treaty override) or that it may also be possible to claim a right to constructive nonresident taxation in Germany.

2. Corporate Divisions

Corporate split-ups and spin-offs[10] are governed by the provisions of Sec. 15 of the Reorganization Tax Act. The provisions contained in Secs. 11 to 13 of the Reorganization Tax Act apply accordingly. As a result it is possible to refer here to the corresponding comments in 5.1 above. So split-ups are treated as partial mergers for tax purposes.

There are, however, two restrictive conditions that must be met at the level of the transferor corporation and its shareholders to permit rollover:

- 'Double branch of activity rule': The transferred assets must constitute one or more branches of activity and the same applies to the assets retained by the transferor entity. Shares in partnerships and corporations may under certain conditions be considered as constructive branches of activity.

---

10 Reorganizations that fall under the third type of divisions under corporate law (hive-downs) are considered as contributions for tax purposes and are as a result governed by the provisions of tax law presented in 7.1 below on hive-downs involving corporations as transferees.

The tax authorities[11] base their understanding of the term 'branch of activity' on the definition found in the Merger Directive.[12] No reliable case law exists for the construction of this term in Germany, which results in considerable legal uncertainty.

- It is not only necessary that branches of activity exist, but the transferred assets and the assets retained must also be attributable exclusively to specific branches of activity ('exclusive-use rule'). Expressed in simple terms, tax-neutral treatment will be denied if "too little" or "too much" is transferred.[13]

In this context, the tax authorities[14] distinguish between three categories of assets:

(1) Functionally material business assets of a branch of activity;

(2) Assets that can be attributed to a branch of activity on the basis of economic criteria; and

(3) Neutral assets (assets that cannot be assigned to either category (1) or category (2)).

Assets in categories (1) and (2) are subject to the exclusive-use rule, which means that it must be possible to assign them either to a branch of activity that is retained or to one that is transferred. Although it is possible to rely to some extent on interpretations found in the case law for the purposes of assignment of assets to category (1), the precise definition of category (2) has essentially not yet been clarified (i.e. no more precise information has been forthcoming from the tax authorities and no relevant decisions have been handed down by the highest courts). As a result, the legal uncertainty is significant.

It also follows from the exclusive-use rule that at least assets of category (1), which can be used by the branches of activity that are retained as well as by those that are transferred ('mixed-use functionally material business assets'), stand in the opinion of the authorities[15] in the way of tax-neutral reorganization by division ('impediment to division')[16]. Various possible solutions have

---

11 See Federal Finance Ministry of 11 Nov. 2011, Federal Tax Gazette Part I, 2011, p. 1314 marginal no. 15.02.
12 See also the chapter titled "Tax-Neutral Contributions in Kind of Business Units".
13 If "too little", no branch of activity will be transferred; if "too much", no branch of activity will remain.
14 See Federal Finance Ministry of 11 Nov. 2011, Federal Tax Gazette Part I, 2011, p. 1314 marginal no. 15.07 *et seqq.*
15 See Federal Finance Ministry of 11 Nov. 2011, Federal Tax Gazette Part I, 2011, p. 1314 marginal no. 15.08.
16 No comparable legal consequences are imposed by the tax administration as regards assets belonging to category (2). According to what is most likely the prevailing opinion in the scholarly literature, this means that mixed-use assets belonging to category (2) do not stand in the way of reorganization by division, but must be assigned to the unit that uses them most. They must then either be transferred with this branch of activity or be retained together with it. In the case of assets belonging to category (3) that are used by several branches of activity, the assets may be assigned to any of the

been devised for such situations, but it would be advisable to consult the tax authorities and obtain an advance ruling before adopting any of them.

In practice, the double branch of activity rule and exclusive-use rule discussed above frequently constitute the biggest pitfalls when seeking tax-neutral treatment of a corporate division. Legal certainty can in such cases regularly be obtained only by requesting an advance ruling (subject to payment of a user fee). In such cases, the issues to be clarified with the tax authorities would include both compliance with the rule regarding the existence of branches of activity in respect of the principle involved and concrete assignment of assets. The latter point is often responsible for the fact that consultation with the tax authorities requires considerable time and effort for asset-intensive entities. In this context, it is important to keep in mind that as many issues as possible should be clarified since the binding effect of advance rulings applies only in respect of those issues that are expressly agreed on by the tax authorities for the purposes of issuing the advance ruling.

3. Changes of Form from One Type of Corporation to Another

Changes in form from one type of corporation to another (e.g. from a privately held corporation to a stock corporation) are covered by the Reorganization Act, but not by the Reorganization Tax Act. By far the most prevalent opinion is that such changes in form are without tax effect as regards corporations and their shareholders in such situations and are therefore (necessarily) tax-neutral.

VII. Contributions to Equity

1. Contributions to Equity in the Case of Corporations

Equity contributions to corporations fall under the concept contained in the provisions of Secs. 20 to 23 of the Reorganization Tax Act, which by virtue of Sec. 25 of the Reorganization Tax Act also applies to the change in form from a partnership to a corporation.

a) **Transferor Entity:** Contributions consistently result in the taxation of hidden reserves unlocked when assets are transferred. This can be avoided only under the following conditions:

- The transferred assets must represent a business activity, a branch of activity or a partnership interest.

    Regarding the term 'branch of activity', reference can be made to VI.2 above, which applies accordingly as regards the definition of branches of activity for the purposes of Sec. 20 of the Reorganization Tax Act. The branch of activity rule applies only in respect of transferred assets. Whether a branch of activity is retained is – unlike in the case of Sec. 15 of the Reorganization Tax Act (see VI.2 above) – immaterial concerning

---

branches of activity; see Federal Finance Ministry of 11 Nov. 2011, Federal Tax Gazette Part I, 2011, p. 1314 marginal no. 15.09.

tax-neutral treatment of contributions to equity. Any such branch of activity transferred as a contribution to equity must at the very least include those assets belonging to categories (1) and (2) discussed in greater detail in VI.2 above that can be assigned to it. If these assets are not completely transferred at the same time (transfer of "too little"), then the contribution to equity will not qualify for tax-neutral treatment (a transfer of "too much" on the other hand does not – unlike for the purposes of application of Sec. 15 of the Reorganization Tax Act (see VI.2 above) – preclude tax-neutral treatment for the purposes of application of Sec. 20 of the Reorganization Tax Act). As in the case of division (see VI.2 above), it is also recommended that advance rulings be sought from the tax authorities in practice before any contribution to equity is effected.

- Contributions must – at least in part – result in the issuance of new shares in the transferee entity.
- It must be certain that the assets transferred will in the future be subject to payment of corporate income tax by the transferee corporation.
- Transferred liabilities may not exceed the assets transferred (ignoring shareholders' equity).
- The right of the Federal Republic of Germany to tax any gain on the disposal of the contributed assets must not be excluded or restricted.
- The transferee corporation must apply for permission to recognize the assets received at the book values carried by the transferor corporation.
- The transferor corporation must not violate a blocking period of seven years from the date of the contribution, during which time the shares given as consideration for the contribution to equity may essentially not be disposed of by the transferor corporation.

b) **Transferee Entity:** The transferee entity must recognize the assets at the book values of the transferor entity if the contribution should be tax-neutral for the transferor entity (see above under a) for the conditions for this).

In practice, the most frequent pitfalls encountered in connection with tax-neutral treatment are to do with the conditions to be met by the transferred assets (business activity, branch of activity, partnership interest) and the subsequent seven-year blocking period. The chapter titled "Tax-Neutral Contributions in Kind of Business Units" contains more on this aspect.

Special rules apply in cases in which contributions to equity consist of shares in corporations. Such cases are dealt with in greater detail in the chapter titled "Share-for-Share Transactions".

2. Contributions to Equity in the Case of Partnerships

Contributions to partnerships are governed by Sec. 24 of the Reorganization Tax Act. In general, the rules presented in VII.1 above for equity contributions to corporations also apply in the case of contributions to partnerships. That means that the hidden reserves of assets to be transferred will also consistently be unlocked. This can be avoided only by applying for permission for a basis rollover, in which case conditions similar to those discussed in VII.1 above are in place. However, unlike Sec. 20 of the Reorganization Tax Act (see VII.1 above), Sec. 24 of the Reorganization Tax Act does not require the balance of book values of the transferred assets to be positive.

Prof. Dr. Ingo Stangl

Tax Advisor

Areas of Specialization

- Business and corporate taxation
- Mergers & acquisitions and corporate reorganizations
- Tax-orientated corporate financing
- International tax law

Telephone (ext.) +49 89/80 00 16-0

Email: ingo.stangl@fgs.de

Tax-Neutral Contributions in Kind of Business Units

by Holger Dietrich

Contents

I. Overview
II. Basics
  1. Business Units
    a) Entire Business (*Betrieb*)
    b) Branch of Activity (*Teilbetrieb*)
    c) Interest in a Partnership (*Mitunternehmeranteil*)
  2. Transfers
  3. Transferors
  4. Transferees
  5. Profits from Disposal Remain Subject to German Taxation and are Subject to German (Corporate) Income Tax
  6. Retroaction
  7. Application
  8. Tainted Shares as a Result of a Tax-Neutral Transfer to a Corporation
III. Pitfalls
  1. Partnership with Partners Being Resident in Third Countries as the Transferor
  2. Contribution of Business Units into a Corporation Resident in an EU Member State
IV. Final Remarks

I. Overview

Business entities that are engaged in cross-border operations (like entities that are engaged in domestic business only) may find it necessary to transfer business units from one legal entity to another. Under German tax law, such transfers in principle trigger the taxation of unrealized capital gains in the business unit that is subject to the transfer. Business units normally include not only employees or machinery for which unrealized capital gains might be negligible, but often also property, buildings and intellectual property rights or goodwill for which unrealized capital gains might be substantial. If the business unit to be transferred has substantial unrealized capital gains, the taxation may be prohibitive to a transfer.

Businesses and their advisors therefore usually seek possibilities to transfer business units tax-neutrally at book values. If the transferor has previously encountered tax losses that have been carried forward and are still available for offsetting taxable profits, a transfer at an intermediate value (i.e. a chosen value between book and market value) or even a transfer at market value might be preferable from a tax perspective to allow utilization of the tax losses and depreciation of the stepped-up values in the future.

The German Reorganization Tax Act (*Umwandlungssteuergesetz*) contains rules allowing transfers of business units to corporations and partnerships by contributions in kind at book values (or intermediate values or market values) if certain conditions are fulfilled. The rules for such "tax-neutral" transfers of business units apply not only to domestic transfers, but also to transfers that involve entities within the European Union and to some transfers that involve entities in third countries.

II. Basics

1. Business Units

According to the Reorganization Tax Act, the preferential tax regime for tax-neutral transfers of business units is applicable only to certain types of business units.

a) Entire Business (*Betrieb*)

A tax-neutral transfer is possible for the entire business of a corporation, a partnership or a sole proprietor. The transfer of an entire business requires all assets and liabilities that are essential for the entire business from a functional point of view to be effectively transferred.

b) Branch of Activity (*Teilbetrieb*)

Likewise, a branch of activity may be transferred tax-neutrally from one legal entity to another. Under the Reorganization Tax Act, "branch of activity" has the same meaning as in Art. 2(j) of the EU Merger Directive (Directive 2009/133/EC), i.e. branch of activity "… means all the assets and liabilities of a division of a company which from an organizational point of view constitute an independent business, that is to say an entity capable of functioning by its own means." As a consequence, the branch of activity must have a certain degree of independence within an entire business and it must to a certain degree be capable of functioning as an independent business. Furthermore, the German tax authorities ask that (i) all assets and liabilities that are essential for the branch of activity from a functional point of view and (ii) all assets and liabilities that are allocable to the branch of activity from an economic point of view are effectively transferred. The latter requirement is often difficult to meet as it is unclear in how much detail the allocation needs to be conducted. As, *inter alia*, the allocation of assets and liabilities from an economic point of view is decisive for whether a business unit qualifies as a branch of activity under the Reorganization Tax Act, a binding ruling of the tax authorities is frequently recommended to ascertain classification of a business unit as a branch of activity under the Reorganization Tax Act.

c) Interest in a Partnership (*Mitunternehmeranteil*)

Finally, an interest, or a part of an interest, in a partnership that is engaged in a commercial, professional or agricultural business may be transferred tax-neutrally from one legal entity to another. A tax-neutral transfer of a partnership interest may also require business assets owned by the partner (*Sonderbetriebsvermögen*) to be transferred with the partnership interest. This applies especially where such assets are essential for the business of the partnership from a functional point of view.

2. Transfers

A tax-neutral transfer of the aforementioned business units is possible only if the transfer is structured as a contribution in kind against issuance to the transferor of new shares in the transferee corporation or new interests in the transferee partnership. The share capital of the corporation or the fixed capital of the partnership must be increased by at least EUR 1. The remaining (book, intermediate or market) value of the assets and liabilities may be allocated to the capital reserve of the corporation or partnership for German GAAP and tax purposes.

A contribution in kind may be structured as a singular succession (i.e. a deed of contribution against issuing new shares or interests where the transfer is effected by signing such a deed) or as a (partial) universal succession under the German Reorganization Act (i.e. a deed of hive-down where the transfer is effected by registration of the hive-down with the commercial register of the transferor and the transferee). Especially for business units that have numerous legal relationships with third parties (e.g. companies with a number of clients for long-term services) a transfer by universal succession may be advantageous as it normally avoids the necessity of consent from third parties to the transfer of the contractual relationships.

As a result of the contribution, at least the beneficial ownership of the assets and liabilities must be transferred to the transferee corporation or partnership. If, for example, the ownership in a certain asset must not be transferred due to legal or contractual restrictions, the asset may be transferred economically. Again, a binding ruling of the tax authorities is recommendable in this situation.

3. Transferors

The rules of the Reorganization Tax Act on tax-neutral transfers of business units apply only to certain transferors. As a basic rule, (i) any entity (i.e. corporation or partnership) that is established under the law of a member country of the EU or the EEA and has its seat and place of effective management within that country and (ii) any individual that is domiciled or has his habitual abode in a member state of the EU or the EEA may be a transferor of a tax-neutral transfer under the Reorganization Tax Act. If an individual is double resident in a member state of the EU and in a third country, the double taxation treaty between the EU member state and the third country must allocate tax residency to the EU member state. Therefore, as a basic rule an individual needs to be subject to resident taxation in a member state of the EU or the EEA.

For example, a French *société anonyme* may transfer its German branch to a German corporation under the rules of the Reorganization Tax Act for tax-neutral transfers of business units if the other requirements for those transfers are met.

If the transferor of the business unit is a partnership, the direct or (in the case of multi-level partnerships) indirect partners must be eligible as a transferor in accordance with the Reorganization Tax Act.

For instance, a German *Kommanditgesellschaft* (limited partnership, abbreviated as KG) with solely US residents as partners is, in principle, not eligible for a tax-neutral transfer of a branch of activities to a German corporation under the Reorganization Tax Act. If only one partner holding an interest of, for example, 10% is a US resident and the other partners are EU residents, the KG is eligible to the extent of the EU resident partners' interests in the KG (in this case 90%).

However, even individuals that are resident or companies that are established in third countries may qualify for a tax-neutral transfer of business units under the Reorganization Tax Act if the shares or interests being granted as a consideration for the transfer as part of the contribution in kind are subject to unlimited German (corporate) income taxation.

For example, a sole proprietor that is a tax resident in Switzerland but engaged in business in Germany with a permanent establishment may contribute a branch of activity of his permanent establishment to a German corporation in a tax-neutral way if the resulting shares in the transferee corporation are allocable to his remaining German permanent establishment and are therefore subject to income taxation in Germany under the double taxation treaty between Switzerland and Germany.

4. Transferees

Likewise, the rules of the Reorganization Tax Act on tax-neutral transfers of business units apply only to certain transferees. If the transferee is a corporation, it needs to be established under the laws of a member country of the EU or the EEA and needs to have its seat and place of effective management within that country. If the transferee is a partnership, the aforementioned restrictions do not apply, i.e. any partnership may be a transferee of a tax-neutral transfer according to the Reorganization Tax Act.

5. Profits from Disposal Remain Subject to German Taxation and are Subject to German (Corporate) Income Tax

All tax-neutral transfers of business units require that profits from a disposal of the business assets belonging to the transferred business unit remain subject to German taxation and are effectively subject to corporate income tax (transfer to a corporation) or German (corporate) income tax (transfer to a partnership) upon realization. If the transferred business units are not subject to German taxation after the transfer, the contribution will mandatorily trigger taxation of unrealized capital gains in the business unit.

However, this condition is relevant only if profits from a disposal of the transferred business unit were subject to German taxation before the transfer. If, for example, a German corporation transfers its entire business to a subsidiary and the entire business includes a foreign branch whose profits were exempt from German taxation before the transfer and will be exempt afterwards, this exemption is not detrimental for the tax-neutral transfer. On the other hand, if a German corporation contributes a foreign branch whose profits were taxable in Germany according to the credit method of the relevant double taxation treaty before the transfer into a foreign corporation, the transfer will most likely exclude German taxation of profits from that branch, so a tax-neutral transfer will not be possible.

6. Retroaction

Some kinds of contributions of business units into corporations or partnerships may be performed retroactively. The rationale is that business units may include a large amount of assets and liabilities as well as legal and factual relationships. Determining the assets and liabilities and relationships to be transferred may therefore be time-consuming and require some discussion within a company. For transfers of business units by (partial) universal succession under the Reorganization Act a balance sheet of the transferor is required to determine the assets and liabilities to transfer. A retroactive transfer is in principle possible for up to eight months. This means that the contracts to be concluded for the contribution need to be signed (and, for transfers including a (partial) universal succession, filed with the commercial register) by 31 August if the parties aim for a retroaction as of 31 December of the preceding year (tax transfer date). As of the tax transfer date all assets and liabilities of the business unit that is subject to the contribution will be deemed transferred from the transferor to the transferee. The retroaction applies only for income tax purposes, not for other taxes such as VAT and real estate transfer tax. The business unit to be transferred must already exist and meet the criteria for qualifying as a business unit under the Reorganization Tax Act on the tax transfer date.

The retroaction rule does not apply for transfers of business units to partnerships by singular succession (i.e. a deed of contribution with individual transfer of each single asset and liability by that deed).

7. Application

A tax-neutral contribution of a business unit at book values (or intermediate values) requires an application to the competent tax authorities. According to the Reorganization Tax Act, solely the transferee is entitled to decide at which values (book values, intermediate values or market values) the business unit is transferred. The value recognized for the transferred business unit in the tax balance sheet of the transferee is mandatorily equal to the value recognized for the new shares in the transferee in the balance sheet of the transferor. As a consequence, solely the transferee is entitled to file the application for a transfer below market value to the tax authorities. If the transferee does not file such an application, the transferor has no immediate right to file one on its own. In the worst case, the transferee simply does not file an application for a transfer at book values and, consequently, the contribution of the business unit will be at market value. The transferor might in that case suffer a tax burden because the transferee did not file the application for a transfer at book values. Especially in cases where the transferor and the transferee are third parties, the underlying agreements must be carefully drafted.

8. Tainted Shares as a Result of a Tax-Neutral Transfer to a Corporation

Whereas profits resulting from the sale of a business unit are regularly subject to normal (corporate) income and trade tax in Germany, profits from the sale of shares in a corporation are 40% exempt (individuals) or 95% exempt (corporations). The tax-neutral transfer of a business unit into a corporation and a subsequent sale of the shares in the transferee corporation would therefore allow for a partial or nearly full exemption of the profits.

The Reorganization Tax Act prevents such tax avoidance structures by classifying the shares in corporations resulting from a tax-neutral transfer as 'tainted' (*sperrfristbehaftete Anteile*) for seven years from the transfer date. Any sale of the tainted shares during the lock-up period triggers retroactive taxation of the transfer of the business unit. For each year that has passed since the transfer date, one-seventh of the profit is exempt. For example, if a German corporation transfers a branch of activities to a subsidiary in June 2014 and elects for the transfer to become tax-neutral and effective as of 31 December 2013, any sale of the shares in the subsidiary before 31 December 2020 will trigger retroactive taxation of the transfer (i.e. the transfer will be taxable in the business year 2013 and the tax assessment for the business year 2013 will be re-opened). If the shares are sold in 2016, two-sevenths of the profit from the transfer will be exempt. The profits that were subject to retroactive taxation increase the acquisition cost of the shares in the subsidiary, i.e. the profit from the sale of the shares (95% tax-exempt) will decrease.

III. Pitfalls

Of course, the rules for tax-neutral contributions open up several pitfalls that taxpayers and their advisors seek to avoid. In cross-border transactions, especially the following pitfalls may be of relevance:

1. Partnership with Partners Being Resident in Third Countries as the Transferor

As mentioned above, a partnership qualifies as a transferor in a tax-neutral contribution of business units only to the extent that its partners would qualify as transferors. This is because under German tax law a partnership is transparent for (corporate) income tax purposes, i.e. the partnership income is subject to (corporate) income tax at the level of the partners.

Therefore, a German *Kommanditgesellschaft* with partners that are tax residents in third countries is, to the extent of the partnership interests held by partners in third countries, in principle not eligible for a tax-neutral contribution of business units to a German corporation. However, if the shares resulting from the contribution remain entirely subject to German tax as business assets of the *Kommanditgesellschaft*, the transfer of the business unit may be tax-neutral regardless of the third-country partners. This requires that the shares resulting from the contribution remain business assets of the partnership and allocable to a German commercial activity of the partnership. It has become more difficult to meet this requirement due to developments in the jurisdiction of the Federal Tax Court that have been adopted by the tax authorities.

Under German domestic tax law, a German *Kommanditgesellschaft* in which only corporations are general partners (i.e. a GmbH & Co. KG) automatically and irrespective of the extent and nature of its German business is deemed to be engaged in a German commercial activity. The profits of the KG are subject to German (corporate) income tax at the level of its limited or general partners and subject to trade tax at KG level. For many years, the German tax authorities held the view that under double taxation treaties such a partnership – again irrespective of the extent and nature of its German business – was deemed to be engaged in a commercial activity in Germany and, hence, constituted a German permanent establishment of its domestic or foreign partners. However, the Federal Tax Court has since ruled that the domestic law fiction for a commercial activity does not apply for double taxation treaty purposes. Taxation of the partnership as a permanent establishment of its foreign partners therefore requires that the partnership is in fact engaged in a German commercial activity. The German tax authorities have decided to follow these guidelines of the Federal Tax Court (cf. decree of the Federal Ministry of Finance dated 26 September 2014, no. 2.2.1).

In the past, a partnership with third-country partners in which only corporations were general partners could therefore successfully argue that following a contribution of its entire business into a corporation the shares in the corporation remained taxable in Germany irrespective of the extent and nature of the partnership's German business.

Today this argument is valid only if (i) the partnership is still in fact engaged in a German commercial activity after the contribution of its business and (ii) the shares granted as a consideration for the contribution will be allocable to the commercial activity after the contribution. If the entire business of the partnership is to be contributed, the first requirement will most likely not be met and the transfer will trigger taxation of unrealized capital gains to the extent of the interests held by third-country partners in the partnership. Even if the partnership decides to transfer only a branch of activity, the shares must be allocable to the remaining commercial activity under the allocation rules of the applicable double taxation treaty and domestic tax law after the transfer to allow a tax-neutral contribution. In essence, such an allocation requires a functional link between the remaining business of the partnership and the shares in the transferee corporation.

If, for example, a German KG with US-resident limited partners contributes its "automotive supplies" branch of activity to a German GmbH and keeps its "wholegrain bread production" branch, it seems quite difficult to argue that the shares in the GmbH have a functional link to the remaining production of wholegrain bread.

2. Contribution of Business Units into a Corporation Resident in an EU Member State

As stated above, all tax-neutral transfers of business units require that profits from a disposal of the business assets belonging to the transferred business unit remain subject to German taxation. For outbound cross-border contributions this normally requires the business assets to be allocable to a German permanent establishment of the foreign transferee corporation or partnership under the rules of the applicable double taxation treaty.

If, for example, a German corporation contributes a branch of activity to a Spanish corporation, the assets and liabilities that are part of the business unit must remain taxable in Germany regardless of the new Spanish owner.

The "allocable to a German permanent establishment" requirement of the transferee is normally easy to fulfill for property, buildings, plants and machinery that are immobile or nearly immobile. It can, however, be hard to fulfill for financial investments, intellectual property or shares in other corporations in particular. The German tax authorities (still) hold the view that a company's head office normally "attracts" all financial investments, intellectual property or shares held by a company. An allocation to a permanent establishment is possible only for such assets that solely (or at least predominantly) serve the business of the permanent establishment. It would therefore not be possible for assets serving the business of the entire company.

It is currently unclear whether the German tax authorities are likely to change this view as a result of the implementation of the Authorized OECD Approach into German tax law. However, until further guidance is available there is a strong risk that the German tax authorities would allocate financial investments, intellectual property and shares to the foreign head office and not to a German permanent establishment of the foreign transferee corporation. This would result in a taxation of unrealized capital gains in such assets upon the contribution.

IV. Final Remarks

Avoiding the above-mentioned pitfalls requires a thorough analysis of the underlying facts and of the applicable legal and tax rules of the jurisdictions involved.

Partnerships with third-country partners aiming at contributing a business unit to a corporation might consider creating a 'management business' within the partnership to deal with the management of the subsidiary corporation. The partnership might then argue that the shares in the corporation are allocable to the management business and, as a consequence, allocable to a German permanent establishment.

Likewise, if there is a risk that the German tax authorities would not accept allocation of assets to a German permanent establishment after the assets are contributed to a foreign corporation, the functional link between the assets and the business of the remaining permanent establishment might be strengthened by creating additional business in the German permanent establishment that is dependent on or at least engaged in administrating the financial assets, intellectual property or shares.

However, any of these alternatives requires "a diligent review of the facts and circumstances and usually a binding ruling of at least the German or also the third-country tax authorities. Finally, if a structure has been accepted by the tax authorities involved, the resulting constraints need to be obeyed in day-to-day business – which often creates a challenge for the companies involved and their tax advisors.

Dr. Holger Dietrich

Lawyer, Tax Advisor

Areas of Specialization

- Business taxation
- Mergers & acquisitions and corporate reorganizations
- Taxation of financial institutions

Telephone (ext.) +49 228/95 94-266 /-383
Email: holger.dietrich@fgs.de

Share-for-Share Transactions

by Jens Hageböke

Contents

I. Introduction
II. Scope of Sec. 21 of the Reorganization Tax Act
  1. Contribution
  2. Contributor
  3. Acquiring Entity
  4. Contributed Shares
  5. Contribution in Kind Against 'New Shares'
III. Qualified Share-for-Share Transactions
  1. Direct Majority of Voting Rights to the Contributed Shares
  2. Application for Book Value or Interim Value Recognition in the Tax Accounting
IV. Pitfalls

I. Introduction

In the context of business reorganizations, shares of a German or foreign corporation or cooperative are often contributed in exchange for new shares in the acquiring domestic or foreign corporation or cooperative. This arrangement is considered to be a share-for-share transaction (*Anteilsaustausch*) and can be structured in a tax-neutral way under the requirements of the German Reorganization Tax Act (*Umwandlungssteuergesetz*). A stake in a business, a business unit or what is termed a *Mitunternehmerschaft* ('partnership for tax purposes') may be contributed retroactively in accordance with Sec. 20 of the Reorganization Tax Act. This retroactive effect does not take place under Sec. 21 of the Reorganization Tax Act in the case of share-for-share transactions.

The provisions are applicable only to shares which are 'taxable' in Germany. The main applications are shares in business property and shares within the meaning of Sec. 17 of the German Income Tax Act (*Einkommensteuergesetz*) (shares >1%). In contrast, 'small shareholdings' (<1%) are governed by Sec. 20(4a) sentences 1 and 2 of the Income Tax Act. Thus, for example, in a share-for-share transaction in a listed corporation, the shares received must be recognized at their book value. In this respect, the discretionary valuation provided for in Sec. 21 of the Reorganization Tax Act is not applicable.

Sec. 21(1) sentence 1 of the Reorganization Tax Act contains a legal definition of the concept of share-for-share transactions and the underlying valuation rule. According to this provision, the acquiring entity must, in principle, recognize the contributed shares at their fair market value. Thus, unless Sec. 20(4a) of the Income Tax Act (for small shareholdings) is applicable, share-for-share transactions lead to the disclosure (realization) of hidden reserves of the contributing shareholder (gain on the exchange). The receiving entity then recognizes the received shares at fair market value in its tax accounting, and for the contributor (*Einbringenden*) this valuation applies both as the sales price of the contributed shares and as the historical acquisition costs for the (new) shares in the receiving entity received during the course of the share-for-share transaction.

Notwithstanding this principle, according to Sec. 21(1) sentence 2 of the Reorganization Tax Act, a share-for-share transaction can, under certain conditions, be carried out at a lower than fair market value (i.e. at the book value or interim value), provided it is a 'qualified share-for-share transaction'. In practice, the qualified share-for-share transaction is the primary case that arises under Sec. 21 of the Reorganization Tax Act. This provision is equivalent to Art. 2(e) of the EC Merger Directive2009/133/EC.

II. Scope of Sec. 21 of the Reorganization Tax Act

1. Contribution

The concept of 'contribution' is not defined in the statute. As in Sec. 20 of the Reorganization Tax Act, it is a creature of tax law. The way in which a share-for-share transaction is consummated is not defined in the law and is also not limited to any specific transactions. According to Sec. 1(3) no. 5 of the Reorganization Tax Act, the scope of Sec. 21 of the Reorganization Tax Act is broadly defined, and thereby includes all transactions which lead to an attribution (at least) of the beneficial ownership of the contributed shares to the acquiring legal entity in return for the grant of at least one new share. The transfer may occur by way of singular or universal succession (e.g. by way of a hive-down within the meaning of Sec. 123(3) of the German Reorganization Act – *Umwandlungsgesetz*).

2. Contributor

With respect to the identity of the contributor, there are no further restrictions (other than the requirement that the shares contributed by the contributor are used to generate taxable income in Germany (*Steuerverhaftung*)). Thus, any private individual, legal entity or partnership can be a 'contributor.' This applies also, for example, to contributors resident in a third country. The contributor's domicile, usual abode, registered seat or place of management is irrelevant.

3. Acquiring Entity

The acquiring entity can be any EU/EEA corporation or cooperative which meets the requirements of Sec. 1(4) sentence 1 no. 1, and (2) sentence 1 no. 2 of the Reorganization Tax Act, i.e. the receiving corporation or cooperative must have been formed under the legal provisions of a member state of the EU or EEA within the meaning of Art. 54 of the Treaty on the Functioning of the European Union (formerly Art. 48 of the Treaty Establishing the European Community) or Art. 34 of the EEA Agreement, and the registered seat and place of management must be within the territory of these countries (does not have to be the same country). Its unlimited or limited tax liability is irrelevant here. In other words, the provision covers purely domestic share-for-share transactions as well as cross-border share-for-share transactions.

> Example 1: German X GmbH contributes its 100% stake in German Y GmbH to German Z HoldCo. GmbH in exchange for new shares.

> Example 2: German X GmbH contributes its 100% stake in French Y SA to UK HoldCo. Ltd in exchange for new shares in UK HoldCo. Ltd.

> Example 3: US X Co. holds its 100% stake in German Y GmbH in its German branch. US X Co. contributes its 100% stake in German Y GmbH to UK HoldCo. Ltd against new shares in UK HoldCo.

Nevertheless, with a cross-border qualified share-for-share transaction, the right to tax the received shares prescribed in the relevant double taxation treaty (DTT) must not be excluded. In examples 2 and 3 (UK HoldCo. Ltd), Germany is entitled under the UK Taxation Treaty to tax the received, new shares of UK HoldCo. Ltd. However, the following example is different 4:[1]

> Example 4: German B GmbH contributes its 100% stake in A GmbH against new shares into Czech X s.r.o.

In this case, the right to tax the contributed shares is neither excluded nor limited, since according to the Czech DTT, it is the country of residence – in this case Germany – that remains entitled to tax the gain from the sale of the contributed shares. However, the Czech DTT contains a restriction in terms of the gain from the sale of the received shares, since the country of residence of X s.r.o. – here the Czech Republic – also has the right of taxation. Thus, book valuation is basically excluded in accordance with Sec. 21(2) sentence 2, second half-sentence, of the Reorganization Tax Act.

The restriction of the statute to EU/EEA corporations and cooperatives is problematic. Here, under Art. 24 of the OECD MC (non discrimination), the general question can be posed as to whether, for example, third country corporations relocating to, and establishing a place of management in, an EU/EEA country (e.g. a US Inc. relocating to, and establishing its place of management in, Germany; it has US shareholders) should also gain the benefits of the automatically extended scope of Sec. 21(1) sentence 2 of the Reorganization Tax Act as an acquiring legal entity of a qualified share-for-share transaction. Otherwise if the book value or interim value recognition is rejected, there would be another invalid 'other taxation'. From the perspective of the receiving entity, the scope of Secs. 1(4) and 21(1) of the Reorganization Tax Act is therefore 'too narrow' in certain situations. The ban on discrimination in the treaty is absolute in its effect, and no justification is possible; the discriminating rule remains inapplicable in this respect.

---

1 The example is based on the decree issued by the German Finance Ministry on 11 Nov. 2011 on the Tax Reorganization Act, Federal Tax Gazette Part I, 2011, p. 1314.

From the perspective of the contributor (which is not protected by Art. 24(5) of the OECD MC), the question also arises as to whether such inequality is in accordance with Art. 3 of the German Constitution (*Grundgesetz*), since, for example, in the case of a cross-border qualified share-for-share transaction with a third country corporation (e.g. contribution to a US subsidiary), Sec. 21(2) sentence 3 of the Reorganization Tax Act (2006) would also become applicable without any problems once the hidden reserves are caught up in the German tax net (only) at the shareholder level, so that the nondiscriminatory *mutatis mutandis* application of sentence 3 would appear possible. In this respect, the 'EU-EEA focus' of the Reorganization Tax Act 2006 is 'too narrow' and breaches the principle of equality. It may constitute a breach of the freedom of movement of capital (Art. 63 of the Treaty on the Functioning of the European Union, formerly Art. 56 of the Treaty Establishing the European Community), the scope of which also protects shares from third countries, since the qualified share-for-share transaction (contribution to third country entities) is less attractive from the perspective of the contributor due to the lack of tax-neutrality. The object of protection here would be the receiving third country entity (and not the contributor). However, this would have to be enforced by way of legal action.

4. Contributed Shares

Contributed shares are the shares which are contributed by the contributor to the receiving entity in exchange for new shares. The entity can be German or European, or from a third country (non-EU/EEA, e.g. Switzerland, US), provided that these entities qualify as a corporation or cooperative according to an evaluation under German tax law. To this end, a comparative type analysis is required. The concept of an 'acquired entity' is taken from Art. 2(h) of the EC Merger Directive 2009. The shares must be attributable for tax purposes to the contributor prior to execution of the share-for-share transaction. For this, it suffices if the contributor possesses beneficial ownership of the contributed shares at the time of the contribution (Sec. 39(2) no. 1 of the German General Tax Code – *Abgabenordnung*).

5. Contribution in Kind Against 'New Shares'

In the course of the contribution, at least **one new** share must be granted to the receiving entity (capital increase in return for a contribution in kind). Granting only treasury stock in exchange will not suffice.

If, in addition to the shares, the contributor also receives other assets (e.g. an interest-bearing loan), the fair market value of which exceeds the book value of the contributed shares, then the acquiring entity must recognize the contributed shares at least at the fair market value of the other assets. Up to the amount of the book value, however, the tax-neutral grant of another form of consideration is possible.

Example: A contributes his 100% stake in X GmbH (tax book value of EUR 1,000,000) to Y GmbH in exchange for a new share in Y GmbH (nominal value of EUR 100,000) plus a debt instrument (fair market value of EUR 900,000). The contribution can be made in a tax neutral way because the total of the new share (EUR 100,000) and the debt instrument (EUR 900,000) does not exceed the tax book value of EUR 1,000,000.

III. Qualified Share-for-Share Transactions

The requirement for a qualified share-for-share transaction is that after the contribution, the acquiring entity, based on its investment including the contributed shares, directly holds the majority of the voting rights in the acquired entity and this fact can be verified. In this case, the acquiring entity can recognize the contributed shares at book value or at an interim value below the fair market value instead of at the fair market value if Germany's rights to tax the gain from the sale of the received shares are not excluded or limited.

1. Direct Majority of Voting Rights to the Contributed Shares

The 'majority of voting rights' attached to the contributed shares must exist 'directly'; indirect investments are insufficient according to the wording of the statute. Mere equity capital-based majorities are equally insufficient (e.g. in the form of nonvoting preferred stock); nevertheless, nonvoting preferred stock can be contributed without triggering tax if the acquirer (transferee) already has the majority voting interest or will obtain it through the contribution. According to Sec. 21(1) sentence 2 of the Reorganization Tax Act, the majority voting interest must be 'based on its shareholdings, meaning that the only relevant factor is a participation-based majority of the voting rights (e.g. also in the case of multiple voting rights), not, in contrast, contractual arrangements (e.g. voting trust agreements or pooling agreements); majority requirements under the bylaws for adopting certain resolutions (e.g. ¾ majority vote), veto rights or reservations of consent are irrelevant here.

It is not a requirement for the contributor to have the majority interest in the receiving company only after the contribution. The first case is where a majority holding is obtained by way of the contribution, and the second is where a majority holding, which previously existed on the transfer date, is stepped up even more. It suffices if several persons contribute shares which do not individually meet the requirements contained in Sec. 21(1) sentence 2 of the Reorganization Tax Act but instead only collectively meet the requirements of Sec. 21(1) sentence 2, provided the contributions are based on a single transaction.[2]

Example: Y AG acquires from A 51% of the shares in X GmbH, in which Y AG had not previously held a share.

---

[2] The following examples 1-3 are based on the decree issued by the German Finance Ministry on 11 Nov. 2011 on the German Tax Reorganization Act, Federal Tax Gazette Part I, 2011, p. 1314.

Example 2: Y AG acquires from B 10% of the shares in X GmbH, in which Y AG had previously held a 51% share.

Example 3: Y AG already holds 40% of the shares in X GmbH. In connection with a single capital increase transaction, C and D each contribute an additional 6% of the shares in X GmbH.

The law in Sec. 21 of the Reorganization Tax Act otherwise stipulates no prior or subsequent holding periods or any other 'blocking periods' (unlike, for example, Sec. 6a of the German Real Estate Transfer Tax Act – *Grunderwerbsteuergesetz*), such that, in particular, the majority of the shares can also be surrendered again shortly after the share-for-share transaction (e.g. through a sale). However, the seven-year blocking period under Sec. 22(2) of the Reorganization Tax Act, which is a special anti-abuse statutory provision, must be observed here if applicable: If a sale of the contributed shares did not create an advantage for the contributor under Sec. 8b(2) of the German Corporate Income Tax Act (*Körperschaftsteuergesetz*), i.e. were up to 95% tax-exempt, then a sale of the contributed shares (by the receiving entity) would be subject to retroactive taxation as of the date of the contribution based on the fair market value (Sec. 22(2) of the Reorganization Tax Act).

'Sale', within the meaning of Sec. 22(2) of the Reorganization Tax Act, can basically also mean a subsequent reorganization (e.g. a merger, division or re-contribution to a partnership) by the receiving company, regardless of whether this reorganization is carried out on a tax-neutral basis at book value. The tax administration is very restrictive here according to the decree issued by the German Finance Ministry on 11 Nov. 2011, so the greatest caution is required for subsequent reorganizations in order to avoid exposing the contributor to the retroactive taxation of hidden reserves in the contributed shares within the seven-year blocking period.

Example 4: German resident A contributes his 100% stake in German X GmbH to German Y HoldCo GmbH in exchange for new shares in 2014. The transaction is a qualified share-for-share transaction and can be made without triggering tax at the request of Y GmbH at the historical tax book value (in the hands of A) of the contributed shares in X GmbH. In this case, the disposal price of the contributed shares is equal to the tax book value at the level of A, and the acquisition costs of the new shares in Y GmbH are equal to the former tax book value (the end result being that it is a qualified share-for-share transaction at book value).

A is a German resident and subject to German income tax, not to German corporate income tax. Therefore, the 95% participation exemption of capital gains derived from selling shares in a corporation according to Sec. 8 (2) of the Corporate Income Tax Act is not applicable (being applicable to German corporations only). A disposal of the (contributed) shares in X GmbH by A would have been subject to income tax according to Sec. 3 no. 40 of the Income Tax Act (60% of a gain would have been subject to income tax at the level of A).

Therefore, the shares in Y GmbH are 'tainted shares' within the meaning of Sec. 22(2) of the Reorganization Tax Act. In the event that Y HoldCo. GmbH disposes of the contributed shares in X GmbH within seven years after contribution or the shares in X GmbH are subject to a subsequent reorganization within seven years (e.g. a tax-neutral merger of X GmbH and Z GmbH), the contribution is made at fair market value with retroactive effect at the level of A (a taxable gain occurs at the level of A with retroactive effect in 2014).

With a qualified share-for-share transaction within the meaning of Sec. 21(1) sentence 2 of the Reorganization Tax Act, a distinction must be made between domestic and cross-border share-for-share transactions: (i) In domestic share-for-share transactions, the receiving company is entitled to choose a book value or interim value (Sec. 21(2) sentences 3 and 4 of the Reorganization Tax Act); (ii) in cross-border qualified share-for-share transactions, the contributor is, in principle, the party entitled to choose pursuant to Sec. 21(2) sentence 3 of the Reorganization Tax Act (in Germany).

2. Application for Book Value or Interim Value Recognition in the Tax Accounting

Furthermore, it is vital for the book value or interim value that a timely application is filed by the correct applicant (Sec. 21(1) sentence 2, and (2) sentences 3 and 4 of the Reorganization Tax Act). The applicant in domestic qualified share-for-share transactions is the receiving legal entity, not the contributor, while in cross-border qualified share-for-share transactions it is the (domestic) contributor. The application must be filed no later than when the initial tax return is filed with the tax office responsible for the taxation. Any filed application is final and may not be revoked or amended.

The commercial value recognition of a share does not affect the tax accounting, i.e. the option to choose between the tax book value or the interim value can be exercised independently of the accounting both at the level of the contributor and at the level of the receiving company. Thus, it is irrelevant, for example, if the contributor recognizes on its balance sheet a gain from the exchange due to the contribution in the share-for-share transaction. When using book value recognition in the tax accounting, the book value will be deemed the contributor's sale price for tax purposes and as the acquisition costs of the received shares. In cross-border share-for-share transactions, the contributor exercises the right to choose to recognize book value or interim value in the tax accounting. The contributor may, for example, request roll-over of the book value for tax purposes, but elect to report a contribution gain on its balance sheet. Thus, in a cross-border qualified share-for-share transaction, the value recognition of the contributed shares on the balance sheet and in the tax accounts of the receiving, foreign entity is irrelevant for taxation in Germany at the level of the contributor.

Example 5: German X GmbH contributes its 100% stake in German Y GmbH to German Z HoldCo. GmbH in exchange for new shares. The tax book value and book value of the contributed shares in the statutory accounts at the level of X GmbH is EUR 100,000, and the fair market value is EUR 1,000,000. Z HoldCo. GmbH requests the contributed shares to be recognized at tax book value. Therefore, there is no taxable gain at the level of X GmbH (the sale price of EUR 100,000 is equal to the tax book value; the acquisition costs of the newly issued shares in Z HoldCo. GmbH are EUR 100,000). In the statutory accounts, X GmbH can realize a capital gain of 900,000. Z HoldCo. GmbH can recognize the contributed shares at book value (EUR 100,000) or at fair market value (EUR 1,000,000).

IV. Pitfalls

It is procedurally problematic in domestic qualified share-for-share transactions that the request or application (usually for rolling over book values) has to be filed by the receiving entity, while this has no direct tax effects for that party, but rather only for the contributor. The value at which the receiving entity recognizes the contributed shares in its tax accounts is deemed the sale price of the contributed shares for the contributor and the acquisition costs for the received new shares. Here, the contributor should generally ensure in the contribution and subscription agreement (*Einbringungsvertrag*) that the receiving entity is obligated to use book valuation and to file an application in a timely manner. The contribution and subscription agreement should also contain provisions on compensatory damages in case, for example, the receiving entity does not file the application in a timely manner or files it incorrectly, resulting in an unwanted disclosure and taxation of the hidden reserves in the contributed shares at the level of the contributor.

Likewise, the contribution and subscription agreement should, in the case of a contributor that does not enjoy the advantages under Sec. 8b(2) of the Corporate Income Tax Act, provide for compensatory damages for the unwanted retroactive taxation of hidden reserves in the event that the receiving legal entity triggers the (unwanted) retroactive taxation of a sales gain within the seven-year blocking period under Sec. 22(2) of the Reorganization Tax Act where there is a resale or a reorganization. Caution is warranted here also with respect to subsequent reorganizations within the seven-year blocking period in terms of the contractual requirements of the receiving entity, as described above. In view of the many pitfalls, best practice is generally to obtain a binding ruling on reorganization measures, even though charges are applicable.

In this context, it can be a challenge to determine who can be the applicant in a request for recognition of tax book value in a share-for-share transaction. Is it the contributor and/or the receiving entity? In a cross-border qualified share-for-share transaction, the applicant is the contributor. In a German-only contribution, it is still not entirely clear. In practice, it is recommended as a precautionary measure that both the contributor and the receiving entity file a joint application for a binding ruling.

The right to sue is also problematic. According to the case law of the Federal Tax Court on the contributor's right to sue (e.g. Federal Tax Court decision of 8 June 8 2011, I R 79/10), the receiving entity cannot assert – either by way of an action for annulment (*Anfechtungsklage*) or by way of an action for a declaratory judgment (*Feststellungsklage*) – that the value of the contributed assets, on which the tax assessment is based, is too high. Such a request can be made only by the contributor pursuant to a third-party action for annulment (*Drittanfechtung*). Accordingly, the contributor would probably be required to contest the corporate tax assessment of the receiving entity (!) by way of a third-party action for annulment, yet generally the contributor is unaware of this tax assessment since it is not the addressee on the notification of this tax assessment. In practice, this results in numerous (sometimes unresolved) problems.

Dr. Jens Hageböke

Public Auditor, Tax Advisor, Diplom-Finanzwirt, Diplom-Kaufmann

Areas of Specialization

- Business taxation
- Mergers & acquisitions and corporate reorganizations
- Structuring of German investments abroad
- Tax accounting

Telephone (ext.) +49 228/95 94-199

Email: jens.hageboeke@fgs.de

Foreign Reorganizations with a Connection to the German Tax Net

by Andreas Schumacher

Contents

I. Introduction
II. The Scope of Application for the German Reorganization Tax Act
III. Direct Tax Consequences of Foreign Reorganizations
   1. Reorganizations of Foreign EU/EEA Companies
      a) Domestic Shareholders and Partners
      b) Domestic Assets
   2. Reorganizations of Companies Located in Third Countries
      a) Domestic Shareholders
      b) Domestic Assets
IV. Indirect Tax Consequences of Foreign Reorganizations
   1. Real Estate Transfer Tax
   2. Forfeiture of Domestic Losses
   3. Add-Back Taxation Under the German CFC Rules

I. Introduction

Foreign reorganizations have German tax ramifications if they have a direct or indirect connection to Germany. This applies to reorganizations of foreign companies[1] with domestic owners and/or with assets located in Germany. Under general principles, the immediate effect of such reorganizations is the realization of capital gains at the level of the shareholders or partners or with regard to the assets located in Germany, unless special rules exist. Foreign reorganizations could also have indirect consequences with regard to German real estate and unused losses of domestic companies and could trigger 'add-back taxation' (*Hinzurechnungsbesteuerung*) under the German controlled foreign corporation ('CFC') rules.

In addition to the foreign reorganization's effects under German tax law, its effects under foreign tax law must always be examined as well.

II. The Scope of Application for the German Reorganization Tax Act

The German Reorganization Tax Act (*Umwandlungssteuergesetz*) applies to foreign reorganizations if the only parties to the reorganization are legal entities which have been founded in EU or EEA countries and which have their registered seat and place of management in one of those countries (Sec. 1(2) and (4) of the Reorganization Tax Act). Where partnerships are reorganized into

---

[1] For the purposes of this article, corporations or partnerships with a registered seat or place of management outside Germany. This article does not address reorganizations involving dual-resident companies.

corporations, the partners of the transferring partnership must generally reside within the EU/EEA (Sec. 1 (4) sentence 1 no. 2(a)(aa) of the Reorganization Tax Act). By contrast, reorganizations between partnerships also fall under the Reorganization Tax Act if they are resident in a third country (Sec. 1(4) sentence 2 of the Reorganization Tax Act).

The German-tax classification of participating foreign companies as either a corporation or a partnership and hence the application of the corresponding rules under the Reorganization Tax Act are based on a comparative analysis between the type of foreign company and the type of corresponding German legal form. Furthermore, the Reorganization Tax Act should be applied only if the foreign reorganization is comparable to a reorganization recognized under the German Reorganization Act (*Umwandlungsgesetz*). In the opinion of the German tax administration, the focus of the comparative analysis is on, above all, the structural features of the reorganization; e.g. with respect to a merger, on the transfer of the assets in their entirety by operation of the law, the issue of shares as consideration and the dissolution of the transferring entity without winding it up.

In addition to comparable foreign reorganizations, contributions made by way of singular legal succession in EU/EEA partnerships and corporations are also covered by the Reorganization Tax Act (Sec. 1(3) nos. 4 and 5 of the Reorganization Tax Act).

If the Reorganization Tax Act applies, the foreign EU/EEA reorganization is subject to the same rules as a domestic reorganization. Thus, the following discussion will focus only on the specific features arising from the international dimension. Cross-border reorganizations involving the participation of domestic companies will not be considered in the discussion.

III. Direct Tax Consequences of Foreign Reorganizations

1. Reorganizations of Foreign EU/EEA Companies

a) Domestic Shareholders and Partners

Where there is a merger of corporations, the shareholders may regularly avoid the recognition of a gain with respect to the shares in the transferring corporation by applying to have the shares recognized at book value or historical acquisition cost in accordance with Sec. 13(2) of the Reorganization Tax Act, provided no consideration other than shares is granted. In the case of a split-up or spin-off, the partial business unit qualification requirement (*Teilbetriebsvoraussetzung*) under Sec. 15(1) sentence 2 of the Reorganization Act must also be satisfied. Thus, one must review whether the allocation of assets and liabilities in the foreign reorganization satisfies the restrictive criteria which the German tax administration has established.

In order to avoid the recognition of a gain at the shareholder level, Section 13(2) sentence 1 no. 1 of the Reorganization Tax Act generally requires that a previously existing German right to tax a gain from the sale of shares is not precluded or restricted. Under the double taxation treaties (DTTs) routinely entered into by Germany, this is typically not the case (cf. Art. 13(5) of the OECD MC). If, as an exception, the country where the transferring company's registered seat is located, (also) has a right to tax (e.g. DTT Czech Republic), then the German right to tax could be restricted in the event that there is a cross-border merger (e.g. an Austrian corporation merged into a Czech corporation). In that case, however, Art. 8 of the Merger Directive would have to be applied, and it might be possible to recognize book value pursuant to Sec. 13(2) sentence 1 no. 2 of the German Reorganization Tax Act. As a consequence and regardless of the DTT, Germany would tax a subsequent capital gain just as it would tax the sale of shares in the transferring company (i.e. without crediting any foreign taxes owed). For any shareholders who hold less than 1% as private assets and are therefore liable to final withholding tax (*Abgeltungsteuer*), the shares in the acquiring company will, automatically and without the need for an application, replace the shares in the transferring company pursuant to Sec. 20(4a) sentence 1 of the German Income Tax Act (*Einkommensteuergesetz*), provided that one of the conditions under Sec. 13(2) sentence 1 of the Reorganization Tax Act is satisfied. The foregoing rule also applies to split-ups and spin-offs.

Corresponding rules apply to the exchange of shares (Sec. 21(2) sentence 3 of the Reorganization Tax Act).

If a corporation is reorganized into a partnership either through a change of legal form (*Formwechsel*) or a merger, taxes will be imposed on the domestic shareholders according to Secs. 4 and 7 of the Reorganization Tax Act, just as they would be imposed in a domestic case. The calculation of the book value under German tax law and the tax reserve account (*steuerliche Einlagekonto*) relevant for Sec. 7 of the Reorganization Tax Act will lead to considerable practical problems here.

Since the deemed (fictitious) dividend income under Sec. 7 of the Reorganization Tax Act will be increased through the recognition of the fair market value on the closing balance sheet of the foreign company, an application under Sec. 3(2) sentence 2 of the Reorganization Tax Act to obtain recognition at book value makes sense even if the assets of the company all belong to a foreign permanent establishment. It should be noted, however, that the reorganization could result in the first-time establishment of a German right to tax the foreign assets (*Verstrickung*). It is not clear here whether – regardless of the recognition approach applied to the transferring corporation – a valuation method using the fair market value of the entity in accordance with Sec. 4(1) sentence 8 in combination of Sec. 6(1) no. 5a of the Income Tax Act is applied to the acquiring partnership.

Regardless of whether or not the assets are recognized at book value, the transferred assets must still be recognized at fair market value when calculating the acquisition profit or loss (*Übernahmeergebnis*), to the extent that there was no German right to tax the capital gains realized from the sale of such assets (Sec. 4(4) sentence 2 of the Reorganization Tax Act). This relates in particular to assets that are attributable to a foreign permanent establishment when capital gains are subject to the exemption method under the applicable tax treaties. As a result of recognition at fair market value, an acquisition gain is increased or an acquisition loss is decreased. This rule avoids the German right to tax such hidden reserves (built-in gains), which exist prior to the merger in the case of a sale of shares in the transferring corporation, from being lost due to the disappearance of this taxation level. Indeed, after the merger, neither domestic nor foreign partners will be taxed in Germany on a gain from the sale of such assets. Under the various treaties, the acquisition gain will be classified as a capital gain within the meaning of Art. 13 of the OECD MC. If shares in the transferring corporation cannot be attributed functionally to a permanent establishment (in that case, Art. 13(2) of the OECD MC is applied), then – subject to a special rule for real estate companies (Art. 13(4) of the OECD MC) – Art. 13(5) of the OECD MC must be applied, according to which only the shareholder's country of residence will have the right to tax the gain.

If **a foreign partnership is reorganized into a corporation**, then for the domestic owners, the fair market value of the business assets will be considered the historical acquisition cost of the acquired ownership interest, regardless of which valuation approach the acquiring corporation uses, to the extent that Germany does not have the right to tax either before or after the merger (Sec. 20(3) sentence 2 of the Reorganization Tax Act). This applies in particular to assets that are functionally attributable to a foreign permanent establishment which falls under the exemption method of a DTT. By virtue of this special rule, it is avoided that previously tax-exempt hidden reserves become subject to German taxation at the shareholder level.

In any such reorganization of a partnership, a right to tax, which exists at the partner level with regard to **foreign assets,** can be eliminated or restricted, so that the fair market value would need to be recognized and a capital gain will arise. This requires that such a right to tax existed before the reorganization because, in the absence of a DTT, or due to specific treaty provisions or special national rules (Secs. 50d(9) of the German Income Tax Act, and 20(2) of the Foreign Tax Act – *Außensteuergesetz*), no exemption would be available in Germany. Another issue requiring careful review is whether the absence of any taxation on the foreign reorganization (particularly where book values are rolled over under foreign rules) could trigger taxation of the transfer gain in Germany.

b) Domestic Assets

To the extent that the reorganizing foreign entity holds domestic assets, the taxation of the transfer gain can be avoided subject to the general requirements by filing a request for a book-value rollover (e.g. pursuant to Sec. 11(2) of the Reorganization Tax Act for reorganizations between corporations). A preclusion or restriction of the German right to tax with regard to the transferred domestic assets does not typically arise only because of a foreign reorganization as the functional attribution of the assets does not change as a result thereof.

2. Reorganizations of Companies Located in Third Countries

a) Domestic Shareholders

Reorganizations, in which one of the participants is a company located in a country outside the EU/EEA, will not be governed by the Reorganization Tax Act (unless the reorganization is between partnerships). However, **mergers** of corporations which are subject to limited tax liability and have their corporate domicile in the same third country are subject to a provision under Sec. 12(2) of the Corporate Income Tax Act (*Körperschaftsteuergesetz*). At **the shareholder level**, Section 13 of the Reorganization Tax Act applies *mutatis mutandis* if the assets are transferred to an entity pursuant to a transaction as defined in Sec. 12(2) sentence 1 of the Corporate Income Tax Act (Sec. 12(2) sentence 2 of the Corporate Income Tax Act). Accordingly, domestic shareholders can, upon application made, avoid the recognition of a gain (as with a merger of EU/EEA corporations). The correct view is that the rule is applicable if the merger consummated pursuant to foreign law is comparable to a domestic merger. The foreign transferring corporation does not have to be subject to actual limited tax liability. The German tax administration does not share this view, however.

Under general principles, other reorganizations will result in domestic partners or shareholders having to recognize a gain. What is unclear is how the tax treatment applies to a domestic shareholder where there is a **split-up** or **spin-off** of a corporation located in a third country. Since Sec. 12(2) sentence 2 of the Corporate Income Tax Act governs only the third country merger, the division should be analyzed under general recognition of gain principles. The split-up or spin-off could be treated as a (partial) sale of shares, but it could also be viewed as the liquidation or the distribution in kind of the transferred assets by the transferring corporation. In the event that the transaction is classified as a distribution in kind, the question arises – where a tax basis (book value) rollover has been recognized in the foreign state – whether such a distribution could trigger full tax liability for a domestic shareholder. This is because a distribution will be exempted only to the extent that it has not decreased the income of the paying entity (Secs. 3 no. 40(d) of the German Income Tax Act, and 8b(1) sentence 2 of the Corporate Income Tax Act). Based on the questionable view taken by the tax administration, this requirement is not met to the extent that assets are transferred at book value in the course of a split-up or spin-off.

The **change of the legal form** of a partnership which is located in a third country into a corporation (and *vice versa*), is presumably treated for tax purposes – contrary to the rules under civil law – as an exchange that triggers the recognition of a gain. The reason for such treatment is that the change also transforms the tax concept from a German point of view, according to which a corporation is treated as nontransparent and the partnership is treated as transparent.

b) Domestic Assets

In mergers of corporations which are subject to limited tax liability and which are all located in the same third country, the domestic assets being transferred will be recognized at book value pursuant to Sec. 12(2) sentence 1 of the Corporate Income Tax Act under the same conditions which also apply under Sec. 11(2) of the Reorganization Tax Act. The same results apply to a merger of foreign partnerships or to a contribution into a foreign partnership to which Sec. 24 of the Reorganization Tax Act applies.

A preclusion or restriction of the German right to tax with regard the transferred domestic assets does not typically arise only because of a foreign reorganization as the functional attribution of the assets does not change as a result thereof.

In the absence of rules for the other types of reorganization, such reorganizations will necessarily trigger the recognition of gain with respect to domestic assets. This would also seem to apply to any change of legal form where the identity of the entity is preserved.

IV. Indirect Tax Consequences of Foreign Reorganizations

1. Real Estate Transfer Tax

Even if no domestic real estate is transferred directly through a foreign reorganization, such reorganization could still have real estate transfer tax ramifications. This can happen when there is a direct or indirect transfer of shares in corporations or partnerships which have real estate assets located in Germany; that transfer transaction could satisfy the prerequisites of Sec. 1(2a), (3) or (3a) of the Real Estate Transfer Tax Act (*Grunderwerbsteuergesetz*). Even an intragroup reorganization at numerous holding levels above a company which holds German real estate can therefore trigger real estate transfer tax.

For mergers and divisions based on the laws of an EU/EEA member state, real estate transfer tax will not be levied under certain conditions set forth in Sec. 6a of the Real Estate Transfer Tax Act. Section 6a of the Real Estate Transfer Tax Act requires that only a controlling company and/or one or more companies dependent on such a controlling company participate in the reorganization. A company is deemed dependent if at least 95% of its capital or assets are held directly and/or indirectly by the controlling company within five years before the legal transaction and for five years following the legal transaction. In the opinion of the tax administration, the features of the controlling company must be examined using value added tax criteria.

2. Forfeiture of Domestic Losses

According to the provisions of the Reorganization Tax Act (specifically Sec. 4(2) sentence 2), any unused losses of the transferring company will not pass to the acquiring company. This also applies to losses of a foreign company, which were generated from domestic activities as part of the limited tax obligation.

If the foreign reorganization leads to a direct or indirect transfer of shares in a corporation which has not used its German losses and specifically its loss carryforwards, then these losses could be disallowed (forfeited) under Sec. 8c of the Corporate Income Tax Act. Under Sec. 8c of the German Corporate Income Tax Act, the unused losses can no longer be deducted *pro rata* if within five years more than 25% of the shares or voting rights are transferred either directly or indirectly to a purchaser or certain groups of purchasers. If more than 50% are transferred within five years, then none of the unused losses will be available for deduction. A capital increase will be treated the same as a transfer, to the extent that it leads to a change in the ownership percentages.

In general, the transfer of shares between companies affiliated within a group will also trigger loss forfeiture if the seller and purchaser are not wholly owned (100%) by one and the same person. Even if a share acquisition occurs that in principle triggers a forfeiture, the losses will still not lapse to the extent that they do not exceed the hidden reserves in the corporation's business assets.

3. Add-Back Taxation Under the German CFC Rules

In addition to the direct consequences of a foreign reorganization, one should also consider that a reorganization, which may have tax benefits outside Germany, could lead to the taxation of the domestic shareholders pursuant to the German CFC rules on add-back taxation. In accordance with Secs. 7 *et seqq.* of the Foreign Tax Act, this scenario arises when there is certain 'passive' income of foreign corporations (e.g. income derived from capital investments or from intangible assets that were not developed by the foreign corporation) which is subject to low tax rates (less than 25%; Sec. 8(3) of the Foreign Tax Act). Under Sec. 7(1) of the Foreign Tax Act, add-back taxation generally requires German tax residents to hold more than 50% of the shares in the foreign corporation. If the EU/EEA corporation actually pursues a business activity, then there will be no add-back taxation (Sec. 8(2) of the Foreign Tax Act).

Because reorganizations typically entail a sale of the transferred assets, a foreign reorganization which is conducted at book values according to the tax laws in that foreign country will generate capital gains that are taxed at low rates. Pursuant to Sec. 8(1) no. 10 of the Foreign Tax Act, such capital gains are classified as active income; however, if they originate from reorganizations which, notwithstanding Sec. 1(2) and (4) of the Reorganization Tax Act (i.e. independently of where the enterprises are considered resident), they could be made at book value. Accordingly, it must be determined whether the reorganization could have occurred in Germany at book values if the participating legal entities satisfied the residency requirements of Sec. 1(2) and (4) of the Reorganization Tax Act, and the Reorganization Tax Act would therefore apply. This does not apply to the extent that the reorganization includes shares of a corporation whose sale would not meet the requirements of Sec. 8(1) no. 9 of the Foreign Tax Act. This will be the case to the extent that the taxpayer cannot prove that the gain from the sale of the share is not attributable to the assets of the company which are used for 'investment income activities'.

Section 8(1) no. 10 of the Foreign Tax Act also does not contradict or preclude the other income categories of Sec. 8(1) of the Foreign Tax Act, so that that a reorganization which does not meet the requirements of Sec. 8(1) no. 10 of the Foreign Tax Act could nevertheless generate active income. This is because a capital gain is classified as active income if the activity for which the asset was used was active (e.g. production of goods, etc.; Sec. 8(1) no. 2 of the Foreign Tax Act). Furthermore, under Sec. 10(3) sentence 4 of the Foreign Tax Act, the provisions of the Reorganization Tax Act could generally be taken into account when calculating any added-back tax amount, provided that there is no passive income based on the above-mentioned exception stipulated in Sec. 8(1) no. 10 of the Foreign Tax Act. This is of particular relevance when valuing passive assets which are transferred by virtue of the reorganization and when the increase in the book value of such assets – which under the conditions set forth Sec. 8(1) no. 10 of the Foreign Tax Act leads to active income – will result in a decrease in future passive income.

Prof. Dr. Andreas Schumacher

Tax Advisor

Areas of Specialization

- Taxation of corporate groups
- Domestic and cross-border mergers & acquisitions and corporate reorganizations
- Structuring of real-estate transactions
- Structuring of cross-border investments (inbound and outbound)

Telephone (ext.) +49 228/95 94-637

Email: andreas.schumacher@fgs.de

4. Tax Accounting

Provisions in German Income Tax Law

by Joachim Hennrichs

Contents

I. Introduction
II. Legal Framework and Basics
III. Cases, Pitfalls, and Solutions
  1. Present legal obligation vs. future obligation that can be attributed economically to a preceding period
    a) Provision for future obligation to modify technical equipment to meet environmental standards (*TA Luft II*)?
    b) Provision for costs incurred for the authorization of plant protection products
    c) Provisions for refunds of excess fees charged by network operators (*Rückstellungen für Mehrerlösabschöpfungen*)
  2. Provisions and assumption of obligations, collateral promise, and similar transactions (assumed provisions) – Sec. 4f and Sec. 5(7) of the Income Tax Act (new version)
IV. Summary

I. Introduction

Provisions are frequently a cause of disputes in tax proceedings. Provisions for uncertain obligations are recognized on the liabilities side of the balance sheet. In tax accounting, recognizing them reduces taxable income, thereby strengthening the business's internal sources of finance. For taxpayers, provisions in the tax accounts are therefore a welcome relief. The tax authorities take precisely the opposite view: Provisions in tax accounting reduce tax revenue. That is why both tax legislators and tax authorities tend to look critically at provisions, with the former increasingly curtailing the opportunities for recognizing and measuring tax provisions in the tax accounts (see Sec. 5(3) to (4b), Sec. 6(1) no. 3a, and Sec. 6a of the German Income Tax Act (*Einkommensteuergesetz*); most recently also Secs. 4f and 5(7) of the Income Tax Act – see also III. 2. below). Provisions are also coming under particularly intense scrutiny in tax audits and are being challenged by the tax authorities. This is leading to a growing number of disputes about provisions being heard before the tax courts (see III. 1. below).

This article outlines the fundamental principles governing the recognition and measurement of provisions under German financial and tax accounting law (see II. below) and then presents a selection of current disputes involving provisions and their solutions (III. below).

II. Legal Framework and Basics

Liabilities must be reported on the equity and liabilities side of the balance sheet. Together with equity, they represent the source of the funding for the assets that the entity uses to generate its income. Provisions are also a category of liabilities.

As a general rule, recognizing provisions in the tax accounts follows the German accepted accounting principles that generally apply to financial accounting (normally abbreviated to 'German GAAP'; see Sec. 5(1) sentence 1 of the Income Tax Act). Provisions are therefore governed in this respect by Sec. 249 of the German Commercial Code (*Handelsgesetzbuch*). However, the German GAAP principle that 'financial accounting leads tax' is breached by a significant number of special rules governing tax accounting. Not all provisions that are required to be recognized in the financial statements are also recognized for tax accounting purposes. For example, provisions for expected losses from executory contracts (i.e. onerous contracts) must be recognized in the financial statements (Sec. 249(1) sentence 1 alternative 2 of the Commercial Code), whereas they are not permitted in the tax accounts (see Sec. 5(4a) of the Income Tax Act). Additionally, the measurement of provisions for tax accounting purposes is extensively addressed by special rules in tax law (Sec. 6(1) no. 3a of the Income Tax Act). As a result, there may well be differences between the amounts recognized in the financial statements and the tax accounts.

Provisions must be recognized for liabilities for which settlement is more likely than not. Because of the probability of settlement, provisions rank equally with liabilities when it comes to assessing the business's financial position. Provisions therefore represent outflows of resources that the business cannot avoid. The assets needed to cover these liabilities are not unrestricted under either financial or tax accounting law, and must therefore be eliminated from profit so that they are neither distributed nor taxed.

The criteria for recognizing provisions are:

(1) There must be a liability to a third party, meaning that liabilities may not be recognized for purely internal 'obligations of the business to itself'. The reason for the liability is not relevant. Provisions can be recognized for both private contractual obligations and obligations under public law (e.g. for obligations to modify technical equipment to meet environmental standards). Prevailing opinion holds that provisions can even be recognized for unavoidable 'constructive obligations' if the business has no realistic alternative to settling the obligation.

(2) The liability must be uncertain (otherwise it must be recognized as a liability in the appropriate balance sheet heading under Sec. 266(3) C. of the Commercial Code).

    a. This uncertainty can relate to either only the amount of the liability (e.g. there is no doubt about the business's product liability, but the actual amount of its liability is still unclear) or

    b. to the grounds for the liability as well (e.g. the business's product liability is disputed). In the latter case, however, the liability must be more likely than not.

    c. Finally, under German law (and in contrast to International Accounting Standard 37), provisions can also be recognized for a number of uncertain liabilities that will only arise legally at some point in the future (e.g. for an obligation to modify or adapt that, under the applicable statutory regulations, will only arise after the balance sheet date). Admittedly, provisions may be recognized for such (probable) future liabilities only if they can already be attributed economically to a preceding period at the balance sheet date and there is a present obligation in this respect. This is frequently a cause of disputes between taxpayers and the tax authorities (see III. 1. below).

(3) Settlement of the liability must be more likely than not. This may be doubtful if the other side is not even aware of their rights.

(4) Provisions may be recognized only for future expenses that are immediately deductible if they occur; they may not therefore be recognized for future components of the cost of an asset (Sec. 5(4b) of the Income Tax Act).

The rules for measuring provisions are as follows: In the financial statements, provisions are recognized at the settlement amount dictated by prudent business judgment (Sec. 253(1) sentence 2 with Sec. 252(1) no. 4 of the Commercial Code). Expected future price inflation must be reflected in the carrying amount. If they have a term of more than one year, the provisions must be discounted, whereby financial accounting law requires the application of an average market interest rate (Sec. 253(2) of the Commercial Code).

By contrast, the measurement rules applicable to tax accounting are very restrictive. For example, future cost increases may not be reflected in the tax accounts (strict closing date principle, Sec. 6(1) no. 3a(f) of the Income Tax Act). Nevertheless, provisions must also be discounted for tax accounting purposes – currently at a rate of 5.5% (Sec. 6(1) no. 3a(e) of the Income Tax Act), which is extremely unrealistic in the present low interest-rate environment. In addition, future benefits that are expected to be associated with the settlement of the obligation have the effect of reducing the tax carrying amount (Sec. 6(1) no. 3a(c) of the Income Tax Act). Finally, special tax rules pursuant to Sec. 6a of the Income Tax Act apply to pension obligations. As a result, pension liabilities are not reflected realistically in the tax accounts. In other words, German entities are carrying considerable hidden liabilities in their tax accounts.

III. Cases, Pitfalls, and Solutions

1. Present legal obligation vs. future obligation that can be attributed economically to a preceding period

a) Provision for future obligation to modify technical equipment to meet environmental standards (*TA Luft II*)?

As mentioned above, it is necessary to make a distinction between liabilities that already exist legally at the balance sheet date and liabilities that will only (probably) arise in the future. Irrespective of the period to which they can be attributed economically, obligations that already exist at the balance sheet date (present obligations) must be recognized if the other criteria for recognizing a provision have been met.[1] By contrast, the recognition of provisions for future obligations additionally requires (a) that it is more likely than not that the obligation will arise in the future, and (b) that the future obligation can be attributed economically to a preceding period.

It is not always a simple matter to identify the precise dividing line as to when a legal obligation has arisen. This can be seen from two recent judgments by the Federal Tax Court, namely one dated 6 Feb. 2013 and one dated 17 Oct. 2013.[2]

The first of these judgments by the First Senate addressed whether a provision may be recognized for an obligation under public law to modify technical equipment because of an official instruction pursuant to the 2002 Technical Instructions on Air Quality Control (*TA Luft 2002*). The taxpayer manufactures wooden boards and operates a combustion installation fired by surplus wood and heating oil. In an official decree dated 1 July 2005, the responsible environmental protection authority directed that the existing installations had to meet a defined emission standard 'effective by no later than 1 Oct. 2010'. In its balance sheet for the year ending 31 Dec. 2005, the taxpayer recognized a provision for the costs of converting the existing installations. The tax authorities refused to recognize this provision.

The tax court (Münster) allowed the appeal.[3] It ruled that the obligation had already arisen; the time limit merely related to the date by which this obligation had to be discharged. It argued that a provision must also be recognized for such present legal obligations even if they cannot yet be attributed economically at the balance sheet date. The ruling by the Finance Court of Münster was

---

[1] Federal Tax Court of 17 June 2001 – I R 45/97, Federal Tax Gazette Part II, 2003, p. 121; Federal Tax Court of 6 Feb. 2013 – I R 8/12, Federal Tax Gazette Part II, 2013, p. 686; Federal Tax Court of 6 Feb. 2013 – I R 62/11, Federal Tax Gazette Part II, 2013, p. 954; Federal Tax Court of 17 Oct. 2013 – IV R 7/11, Federal Tax Court Official Collection pp. 243, 256.

[2] Federal Tax Court of 6 Feb. 2013 – I R 8/12, Federal Tax Gazette Part II, 2013, p. 686 –'TA Luft II'; Federal Tax Court of 17 Oct. 2013 – IV R 7/11, Federal Tax Court Official Collection pp. 243, 256.

[3] Tax Court of Münster of 14 Dec. 2011 – 10 K 1471/09 K, G, Decisions of the Tax Courts 2012, p. 944.

therefore in line with an earlier ruling by the First Senate of the Federal Tax Court dated 27 June 2001[4], in which the First Senate also held that the time limit stipulated in the official decree related merely to the date by which the obligation had to be discharged, which was not decisive for tax accounting purposes.

However – following the decision by the Fourth Senate dated 13 Dec. 2007 and in contrast to its own earlier judgment dated 27 June 2001 – in its new decision dated 6 Feb. 2013 the First Senate of the Federal Tax Court revised its interpretation of the official decree and ruled that the obligation to meet the emission standard at the balance sheet date had not yet arisen.[5] Under the general principles, liabilities would arise at the time when they have satisfied the various criteria that apply to their recognition. In the case of obligations under public law that are based on an administrative act, recognition is based on the time when the substantive legal consequences contained in the administrative act are triggered. If an administrative act contains a condition precedent or stipulates a time limit, the obligation only arises legally at the time when the condition is fulfilled or the time limit expires.

Hence, in the case at issue, it would have been legitimate to recognize a provision only if it had been possible to attribute the future obligation to a preceding period at the balance sheet date. However, the First Senate also ruled that this was not the case. It noted that the obligation to modify the technical equipment was designed to address the use of the assets in the future. It thus did not result from a past event and could not therefore be attributed economically to a preceding period.

The decision by the Fourth Senate of the Federal Tax Court dated 17 Oct. 2013[6] adopted the same line. This case involved provisions for the obligation under aviation engineering law to modify aircraft systems to comply with the state of the art. In this case, too, the provision was ultimately not recognized. The court ruled that the obligation to modify the technical equipment contained a (suspensive) time limit, so the obligation had not yet arisen legally at the balance sheet date. Nor was it attributable economically to a previous period because the obligation to modify the aircraft related purely to their future use.

Under these decisions, obligations under public law to modify technical equipment that are based on an administrative act that contains a condition precedent or stipulates a time limit arise legally only at the time when the condition is fulfilled or the time limit expires. Prior to that time, no provision may be recognized for the obligation (for example to meet defined emission standards after a certain date) even though it has been specified in detail in an administrative act.

---

4 Federal Tax Court of 17 June 2001 – I R 45/97, Federal Tax Gazette Part II, 2003, p. 121
5 Federal Tax Court, IV R 85/05, Federal Tax Gazette Part II, 2008, p. 516; Federal Tax Court, I R 45/97, Federal Tax Gazette Part II, 2003, p. 121.
6 Federal Tax Court of 17 Oct. 2013 – IV R 7/11, Federal Tax Court Official Collection pp. 243, 256.

b) **Provision for costs incurred for the authorization of plant protection products**

The decision by the Federal Tax Court dated 8 Sept. 2011[7] also addresses the problem surrounding the distinction between present legal obligations and future obligations that can be attributed economically to a preceding period. This dispute related to a provision for costs incurred for the authorization of a plant protection product. The taxpayer operates a business that manufactures and distributes plant protection products. It applied to the responsible authority for authorization for two active substances in accordance with the German Plant Protection Act (*Pflanzenschutzgesetz*). Based on the fee schedule, it estimated the costs of authorization by the authority to be around EUR 110,000 and recognized a provision for this amount. The tax authorities did not recognize the provision, arguing that the obligation was not attributable economically to a preceding period; rather, the future authorization costs were incurred in connection with future income that the taxpayer intended to generate using the active substances (matching principle).

By contrast, the Fourth Senate of the Federal Tax Court allowed the provision. According to this decision, a liability is always a result of a past event and thus attributable economically to a preceding period at the balance sheet date if the obligation must be discharged irrespective of whether the business continues to operate in the future or is discontinued as of the balance sheet date in question. This was the case in this particular dispute. Under the applicable fee rules, the liability to pay the fee arose on receipt of the application for authorization and was not tied to the outcome of the procedure. The applicant would have had to pay the costs of the authorization procedure even if the application had been denied and authorization to use the plant protection products had been refused. In such a situation, it cannot be argued that the obligation does not result from a past event because the expenses will be used only to generate income in the future. What matters here is that the liability has to be settled regardless of the outcome of the application. This unavoidability of the obligation justifies the recognition of a provision.

By contrast, if it involves an obligation that will only take effect if the business is continued beyond the balance sheet date, the effect of this ruling is that it cannot be attributed economically to a preceding period.

c) **Provisions for refunds of excess fees charged by network operators (*Rückstellungen für Mehrerlösabschöpfungen*)**

Provisions for compensation obligations in the case of amounts charged in excess of cost under public law rules (special-purpose associations of local authorities) and for refunds of excess fees charged by energy utilities must also correctly be allowed.[8] These involve cases in which enterprises operating in regulated markets (e.g. power suppliers in the energy sector) charged fees in

---

7 Federal Tax Court of 8 Sept. 2011 – IV R 5/09, Federal Tax Gazette Part II, 2012, p. 122.
8 Federal Tax Court of 6 Feb. 2013 – I R 62/11, Federal Tax Gazette Part II, 2013, p. 954.

previous years that were subsequently deemed by the regulator to be excessive (excess fees). Under the relevant legislation, such excess fees have to be compensated by offsetting them against future fees across multiple periods. Substantively, this involves the repayment of wrongfully charged fees. Technically, however, there is no obligation to repay the fees, but rather to offset them against future fees. The question is whether provisions should be recognized for these compensation obligations.

In these cases, the obligation to compensate the excess fees from previous years by offsetting them against future income arises legally when the excess fees are received. Under the principles outlined above, a provision must therefore be recognized for these compensation obligations irrespective of the controversial question of whether they can be attributed economically to a preceding period.

It should be noted, however, that the compensation obligations can indeed be attributed economically to a preceding period. This is because the excess fees to be compensated are based on past income for services provided at that time. The excess fees are attributable to the previous calculation periods for which they were charged. The obligation to refund excess fees therefore results from and compensates for a past event (excess fees charged). The requirement to settle the obligation over multiple periods is merely a technique for compensating the excess fees charged without any basis in law that is permitted for reasons of procedural economy.

If the provision for the obligation to refund excess fees were not to be recognized in such cases, the network operators would have to recognize the excess fees as income, without paying any compensation, even though it is clear that they are not legally entitled to the excess fees and they may not keep the amounts, but must offset them. This would result in an increase in net worth being reported that does not actually exist, either legally or constructively.

2. Provisions and assumption of obligations, collateral promise, and similar transactions (assumed provisions) – Sec. 4f and Sec. 5(7) of the Income Tax Act (new version)

One consequence of the special tax rules applying to provisions, specifically the requirements of Sec. 6a of the Income Tax Act governing pension provisions, may be that the taxpayer's expected outflows of resources are not reflected realistically in the tax accounts, and that there are hidden liabilities. If these liabilities are outsourced to an acquirer or transferred in the course of an M&A transaction, the acquirer will seek to obtain plan assets in an amount that offsets the true economic value of the liability (not its tax value) as compensation for the obligations it has assumed.

> *Example:* Seller (S) recognizes pension provisions with a tax value of EUR 700,000 pursuant to Sec. 6a of the Income Tax Act in its tax accounts. The obligations have a fair value of EUR 1 million. Acquirer (A) acquires the pension obligations by way of an indemnifying collateral promise. In

return, S grants A plan assets amounting to EUR 1 million. The question is what accounting consequences this transaction triggers for S and A.

Under the (in our opinion correct) rulings by the Federal Tax Court, the transaction results in S realizing the hidden liability – S must derecognize the provision and the plan assets, and the difference between the carrying amount of the derecognized provision (EUR 700,000) and the value of the derecognized plan assets (EUR 1 million) is an expense.

Under the (in our opinion equally correct) rulings of the Federal Tax Court, A is involved in an acquisition transaction with no effect on profit or loss: A acquires the plan assets against assumption of the obligations. Sec. 6a of the Income Tax Act does not apply to the indemnity assumed by E.[9]

Lawmakers used the German AIFM Tax Act (*AIFM-Steuer-Anpassungsgesetz*) of 18 Dec. 2013[10] to (retrospectively) reverse this ruling because they feared a shortfall in tax revenue. The rule that now applies under Sec. 5(7) sentence 1 of the Income Tax Act is that assumed obligations which, at the party originally subject to the obligation, were covered by prohibitions or restrictions on recognition, or for which measurement under tax accounting rules took precedence over financial accounting rules, must be accounted for by the acquirer at the balance sheet dates following the acquisition in the same way as they would have had to have been accounted for at the party originally subject to the obligation if no acquisition had occurred. This change in the law perpetuates the fiscal policy-motivated exceptions where tax recognition or measurement rules take precedence over the financial accounting rules (specifically Sec. 6a of the Income Tax Act). These continue to apply irrespective of the acquisition transaction and irrespective of the civil law structures governing the acquirer. In the first closing balance following the acquisition, the acquirer must therefore recognize a gain (acquisition gain).

> In the example given above, A must therefore initially record the plan assets it has acquired and the indemnity it has assumed in its accounts at cost (EUR 1 million). However, in the first closing balance sheet following the acquisition, pursuant to Sec. 5(7) sentences 1 and 2 of the Income Tax Act the obligation constructively assumed by A must be adjusted down to the value in accordance with Sec. 6a of the Income Tax Act (EUR 700,000). The difference is recognized as income. Pursuant to Sec. 5(7) sentence 5 of the Income Tax Act, recognition of the gain that results from application of Sec. 5(7) sentence 1 of the Income Tax Act can be spread over 15 years.

---

9 For the details of the entire case, see Federal Tax Court of 16 Dec. 2009 – I R 102/08, Federal Tax Gazette Part II, 2011, p. 566; Federal Tax Court of 14 Dec. 2011 – I R 72/10, Federal Tax Court Official Collection p. 236, p. 101; Federal Tax Court of 12 Dec. 2012 – I R 69/11, Federal Tax Court Official Collection p. 240, p. 34; Federal Tax Court of 12 Dec. 2012 – I R 28/11, Federal Tax Court Official Collection p. 240, p. 22; Federal Tax Court of 26 April 2012 – IV R 43/09, Federal Tax Court Official Collection 237, p. 215.
10 Federal Law Gazette Part I, 2013, p. 4318.

The revised rule does not contain any group exemption or similar relief for the acquirer (Sec. 5(7) of the Income Tax Act). It therefore applies for example not only to intercompany transactions within groups, but also to third-party transactions at arm's length terms. In addition, under Sec. 52(14) sentence 1 of the Income Tax Act, it applies retrospectively for tax years ending after 28 Nov. 2013. It is irrelevant in this respect when the transaction occurred, so transfers made at some point in the past will also be affected.

In addition, the AIFM Tax Act revised the tax consequences for sellers in cases where the obligations are assumed. The new rule in Sec. 4f(1) sentence 1 of the Income Tax Act now requires the expense to be amortized: As a general principle, the realized hidden liability is no longer immediately deductible as a business expense by the party originally subject to the obligation, but must be amortized over 15 years. The expense arising when calculating taxable income must be accounted for as an off-balance-sheet adjustment. However, the law offers generous exemptions for sellers (Sec. 4f(1) sentence 3 of the Income Tax Act). In contrast to acquirers, for which Sec. 5(7) of the Income Tax Act does not contain any corresponding exemptions, sellers in M&A transactions involving small and medium-sized enterprises are therefore ultimately not affected.

The new rules contained in Secs. 4f and 5(7) of the Income Tax Act run counter to established practice and are questionable in terms of constitutional law. Sec. 5(7) of the Income Tax Act poses a particular problem. This rule is yet another example of fundamental principles of tax accounting (in this case the realization principle) being breached for fiscal policy considerations only. The gain resulting from the application of Sec. 5(7) of the Income Tax Act is purely fictitious and is not based on any event that triggers realization. The new special rules are an example of the old saying that "evil begets evil" (Schiller), namely an outcome of special rules such as Sec. 5(4a) and Sec. 6a of the Income Tax Act, which are in turn the consequence of misguided legal policy and result in hidden liabilities being created in the tax accounts. One can certainly take the view that it is acceptable to wish to safeguard the applicability of the precedence of tax recognition and measurement rules over the financial accounting rules in the case of transactions between companies in the same group if it is assumed that these might result in abusive tax avoidance transactions. However, as described above, Sec. 5(7) of the Income Tax Act is not limited to intercompany transactions within groups, but also applies to normal third-party transactions at arm's length terms. At any rate, in the case of third-party transactions at arm's length terms, the fiction that there is an acquisition gain conflicts with the 'ability to pay' principle. Finally, the retrospective application of Sec. 5(7) of the Income Tax Act pursuant to Sec. 52(1)4 of the Income Tax Act is also problematic, as it means that the lawmakers may also be encroaching on transactions that may well have been completed in the distant past.

IV. Summary

Provisions are often a cause of disputes between the tax authorities and taxpayers. In principal, tax law follows the German accepted accounting principles that generally apply to financial accounting. The recognition of provisions is governed by Sec. 249 of the Commercial Code. However, these rules require interpretation in many respects. Provisions frequently give rise to questions in practice, especially in cases involving (uncertain) liabilities where it is unclear when they have arisen legally and whether they can be attributed economically to a preceding period. Recent decisions by the Federal Tax Court have now provided some guidance covering provisions for obligations under public law to modify technical equipment, for the costs incurred for the authorization of products subject to authorization, and for refunds of excess fees charged in regulated (energy) markets.

Despite the basic principle that tax accounting should be based on financial accounting, the recognition and measurement of provisions in tax accounts is largely governed by separate tax rules. Under current German tax law, pension provisions in particular are not measured realistically in the tax accounts, with the result that hidden liabilities are created. If such pension obligations (and similar liabilities) are transferred to other legal entities (e.g. in cases where pension provisions are spun off or in the course of M&A transactions), under previous Federal Tax Court rulings the hidden liability was realized by the party originally subject to the obligation and the acquirer assumed the obligation with no effect on profit or loss. The lawmakers recently reversed this advantageous ruling for taxpayers in Sec. 4f and Sec. 5(7) of the Income Tax Act. Under these new special tax rules, sellers generally cannot recognize the realized hidden liability immediately as a business expense in their tax accounts, but rather have to amortize it over 15 years. Acquirers must recognize the obligation assumed at the amount at which it would have had to be measured and subsequently adjusted by the seller. This means that a fictitious gain arises for the acquirer from the transaction. The tax due on this gain can be spread over a period of 15 years by establishing a reserve. The divergence of the new rules from German GAAP can be attributed to purely fiscal policy considerations and is open to criticism on both legal policy and constitutional grounds.

Prof. Dr. Joachim Hennrichs

Professor of Civil Law
Of Counsel

Areas of Specialization

- Accounting law
- Tax accounting
- Corporate law

Telephone (ext.) +49 228/95 94-226

Email: joachim.hennrichs@fgs.de

Specific Features of Tax Accounting in Germany

by Norbert Herzig

Contents

I. Fundamentals
  1. Starting Point
  2. Classification System
    a) Accrual Accounting
    b) Financial Accounting Leads Tax (*Maßgeblichkeitsgrundsatz*)
    c) Beneficial Ownership
  3. Principles
    a) Realization
    b) Imparity
    c) Itemized Measurement
    d) Closing Date Principle, Principle of Consistency

II. Characteristics of Specific Legal Forms
  1. Sole Traders
  2. Partnerships
  3. Corporations
  4. Groups

III. Specific Aspects
  1. Intangible Assets
  2. Provisions
  3. Digitization
  4. European Harmonization
  5. Outlook

I. Fundamentals

1. Starting Point

The process of determining taxable income in Germany starts with the various categories of income that may be generated by the taxpayer. For income from agriculture and forestry, trade or business, and self-employment, the level of income is determined by the business profit. This must be calculated using accrual accounting pursuant to Secs. 4 and 5 of the German Income Tax Act (*Einkommensteuergesetz*) if the taxpayer is required by law to apply double-entry bookkeeping, or does so voluntarily. If this is not the case, the business profit is determined using cash basis accounting, which is driven by the cash inflows and outflows. By contrast, accrual accounting is based on the accounting profit reported in financial statements, which requires expenses to be matched to the related revenues, regardless of when the cash transactions occur ('matching principle'). This article focuses on determining profit using the accrual method of accounting. These rules are relevant for income tax (*Einkommensteuer*), corporate income tax (*Körperschaftsteuer*), and trade tax (*Gewerbesteuer*) in Germany.

2. Classification System

a) Accrual Accounting

The process of determining taxable income using accrual accounting focuses primarily on the balance sheet, rather than the income statement (although the latter does provide supporting information). The process starts with the 'business assets', which are defined as 'net business assets' – i.e. assets minus liabilities – and thus correspond to owners' equity. Profit for a period is calculated by comparing the business assets at the end of the period with the business assets at the end of the preceding period, after adjustments for withdrawals and contributions by the owners. An increase in business assets represents a profit, and a reduction results in a loss. The profit determination period is the tax year (business year), which may differ from the calendar year and normally comprises 12 months.

b) Financial Accounting Leads Tax (*Maßgeblichkeitsgrundsatz*)

The principle that financial accounting leads tax (Sec. 5(1) of the Income Tax Act), which is codified in German accepted accounting principles, has a long tradition in tax accounting in Germany. Because German law generally requires a 'merchant' (*Kaufmann*) to prepare a balance sheet for the purposes of financial accounting and company law as well, it was a logical step to base the tax rules on this financial accounting policy for reasons of simplification. The objective behind the notion of simplification was to create a 'unitary' (or 'single') balance sheet that could be used for both financial and tax accounting purposes.

This concept of a unitary balance sheet, which held sway for a very long time, has lost a lot of its persuasive power in recent years because financial and tax accounting have been following diverging paths. German financial accounting law, which was formerly heavily influenced by tax law, is increasingly converging with the International Financial Reporting Standards (IFRSs), with the goal of enhancing the decision-usefulness of German GAAP financial statements. By contrast, the evolution of tax accounting is being driven by the budgetary interests of the tax authorities, and by the goal of creating objectifiable, practicable rules for mass processes. A not uncommon consequence of this gradual divergence of financial and tax accounting is that the affected businesses have to prepare multiple sets of accounts as of the end of each fiscal and/or tax year, namely German GAAP financial statements plus their tax accounts, as well as possibly IFRS or US GAAP financial statements if they have to prepare IFRS or US GAAP consolidated financial statements, or do so voluntarily.

c) Beneficial Ownership

One of the core questions in accounting revolves around the issue of who is going to carry assets and liabilities on their books. In line with financial accounting law, tax accounting in Germany is also based on the principle of 'substance over form'. Legal ownership is always the starting point for these considerations. However, legal ownership is supplanted by beneficial ownership if the beneficial owner actually controls an asset in such a way that he can constructively stop the legal owner from exercising any influence over it, as a rule for the duration of its standard useful life (Sec. 39 of the German General Tax Code – *Abgabenordnung*). This difference is the subject of substantial debate when it comes to accounting for leases, with a distinction being made between different types of lease (e.g. operating and finance leases).

3. Principles

a) Realization

Tax accounting follows the 'nominal value principle' (i.e. the actual value of money is ignored). At most, inflation can be reflected only in inventories, by applying the last-in, first-out method. Because only profit that has actually arisen is supposed to be taxed, the realization principle is particularly important in tax accounting. This principle is understood to mean that profits may be recognized only as a result of revenue-generating market transactions, but not for example because of 'holding gains' on assets. It follows necessarily from the realization principle that cost represents the upper limit for measuring fixed and current assets. In addition to generating profits on the market, taxable income may also arise if business assets are transferred to an owner's private assets (withdrawals) or if business assets leave the German tax jurisdiction (taxable outbound transfers). This narrow interpretation of the realization principle also means that profit from construction contracts cannot be recognized for tax accounting purposes using the percentage of completion method. Profit can be recognized based on the stage of completion only if there has been partial acceptance by the client that has reduced the risks associated with this transaction, and if the only remaining risk is a credit risk that can be taken into account by adjusting the carrying amount of the receivable.

b) Imparity

A conservative approach to determining profit means that it is not necessary to wait for losses to materialize before they are recognized for tax accounting purposes. On the contrary, tax law allows losses associated with items of fixed assets to be recognized if those assets have become permanently impaired. There is no obligation to write down the assets to the lower value, but there is an option under tax law.

The tax rules for recognizing losses associated with liabilities are much more restrictive. In contrast to the previous practice, provisions for expected losses from executory contracts can no longer be recognized for tax accounting purposes (Sec. 5(4a) of the Income Tax Act). Such losses may be recognized only if they involve an uncertain liability for which a provision may be recognized. This uncertain liability may be attributable both to contractual obligations and

259

to obligations under public law, whereby it must be probable that the taxpayer will be required to settle the obligation.

However, measurement of the provisions for tax accounting purposes does not adequately reflect the actual outflow of resources. This is because – in contrast to financial accounting law – tax law does not assume a future settlement amount that reflects price and cost inflation, but rather bases measurement on the carrying amounts as they stand at the balance sheet date, and additionally discounts them using a discount rate that is fixed by law at 5.5% or 6%.

c) Itemized Measurement

The realization and imparity principles can take full effect only if they are rooted in the principle of itemized measurement, which dominates tax accounting and prohibits collective measurement. Increases in the value of an asset cannot be offset against decreases in the value of another asset. Likewise, assets and liabilities may not be offset. Each individual asset and liability must be recognized and measured in accordance with the relevant legal requirement, although considerations of practicability mean that simplified measurement options are available – for example measuring inventories using the weighted average method – provided that certain conditions are met. To clarify the often difficult question of whether a complex asset is a single recognizable asset or comprises several assets, the approach in Germany is to base the assessment on whether the asset meets the criterion of uniform usage and function that defines the concept of an asset. The principle of itemized measurement has been modified to accommodate the requirements of hedge accounting (Sec. 5(1a) of the Income Tax Act), in that recognized hedges of financial risks are also allowed for tax accounting purposes.

d) Closing Date Principle, Principle of Consistency

Recognition and measurement in tax accounting are always based on the circumstances prevailing at the balance sheet date. Events after the balance sheet date may be recognized up to the preparation date of the financial statements if they provide evidence of conditions that existed at the balance sheet date (adjusting events). New facts that arise after the balance sheet date (nonadjusting events) cannot be recognized. It is only very recently that the supreme courts in Germany have ruled on how changes in court rulings or initial rulings on a new problem area are to be accounted for. In contrast to the previously valid concept of the subjective accuracy of financial statements, the courts have come down in favor of the objective accuracy of the tax accounts, at least where issues of law are concerned. Consequently, changes in court rulings result in the retrospective adjustment of those tax accounts that may still be modified.

The aspect of consistency addresses whether tax accounting options must be exercised in the same way in consecutive annual tax accounts. The general principle is that the requirement for consistency of recognition and measurement in the financial statements must also be complied with in the tax accounts because of the applicability of German accepted accounting principles. However, this restriction does not apply to standalone tax options, although there are limits on these because of the prohibition on arbitrariness in tax law.

II. Characteristics of Specific Legal Forms

1. Sole Traders

From a tax accounting perspective, the main focus of interest in the case of sole traders is on the dividing line between business and personal affairs. Assets are transferred from personal assets to business assets at their market value (contributions) in order to avoid transporting hidden reserves between the two spheres. For the same reason, market value must also be applied when transferring assets from business assets to personal assets (withdrawals). As a rule, an asset may be allocated to either personal or business assets in its entirety only. If an asset cannot be attributed to only business or personal assets by reason of its purpose, its allocation depends on a decision on its allocation by the taxpayer, which generally results from the asset being included in the balance sheet (or not). Private use of a business asset is classified as a withdrawal, and the reverse case is classified as a contribution.

2. Partnerships

Business activities in Germany are frequently organized in the legal form of a partnership, with the 'GmbH & Co. KG' (a limited partnership that has a limited liability company as its general partner) being particularly popular because it allows the personal liability of the partners to be limited. A characteristic of partnerships is that they are not structured as legal persons. They are treated as fiscally transparent entities (also known as 'flow-through entities') and do not function as independent taxable entities for income and corporate income tax purposes. Rather, it is the partners behind the partnership who are taxable. Despite the fact that they are not fiscally opaque, partnerships are important when it comes to classifying and determining income. More specifically, the income of a partnership is determined in several stages. In the first step, the partnership's financial statements are used to derive first-level taxable income, which is then modified in two ways. Any premium paid by a partner to acquire an interest in the partnership, i.e. the amount in excess of the capital account maintained at the partnership, is recognized in a 'supplementary partner tax account', allocated to the individual assets, and adjusted in future periods. Finally, German tax law classifies assets that do not form part of a partnership's assets, but are the personal property of a partner, as belonging to the partnership's business assets for tax purposes if they have been made available for use by the partnership or at least serve the equity interest in the partnership. Such assets are classified as 'separate business assets' and captured in 'special partner balance sheets'. As a result, the complete tax accounts of a partnership also include the supplementary partner tax accounts and special partner balance sheets. The German system for taxing partnerships is difficult to communicate to an international readership, which is why tax conflicts frequently arise, especially in cross-border scenarios.

3. Corporations

In contrast to partnerships, corporations are classified by German tax law as fiscally opaque entities that are subject to corporate income and trade taxes. The tax base is established by determining taxable income in two stages. According to court rulings, corporations have only a business sphere, not a private sphere. The first stage in determining taxable income focuses on the comparison of business assets at the end of the period with the balance at the end of the preceding period, as described above. In the second stage, the adjustments resulting from the relationship between the company and its shareholders, which are generally guided by the arm's length principle, are particularly important. However, court rulings have resulted in the application of – debatable – special rules to controlling shareholders. Because benefits cannot be contributed, there is no symmetry between diminutions in the value of the company's net assets classified as constructive dividends on the one hand, and increases in the value of its net assets classified as constructive contributions on the other.

4. Groups

Groups are not taxed separately in Germany. Rather, in principle the individual legal entities are taxed in accordance with the general principles. Consolidated financial statements prepared in accordance with German GAAP, IFRSs, or US GAAP are therefore generally irrelevant for tax purposes, and are of interest at most in connection with special tax rules such as the German earnings stripping rule (*Zinsschranke*). German tax law has created the institution of the (consolidated) tax group (*Organschaft*) to reflect group-related tax issues. A tax group subsidiary's income is attributable to the tax group parent, which must then tax that income. The conditions for including a subsidiary in a tax group are that the parent holds a majority of the voting rights and a profit transfer agreement is in place and can be enforced. In particular this linking of the tax group with the company law instrument of a profit transfer agreement has been the subject of heated debate for some time now because it is very difficult to justify objectively and difficult to communicate internationally, and additionally causes considerable problems in practice. Despite these concerns, lawmakers have not been prepared to implement a fundamental reform of the group taxation rules, with the only movement so far being limited to a minor reform of tax group accounting involving some marginal changes.

III. Specific Aspects

1. Intangible Assets

Despite the steadily growing importance of intangible assets, German tax accounting continues to prohibit the recognition of internally generated intangible assets (Sec. 5(2) of the Income Tax Act), although a recognition option was introduced for these assets when German financial accounting law was modernized (Sec. 248(2) of the German Commercial Code – *Handelsgesetzbuch*).

2. Provisions

The issue of provisions is of central importance in German tax accounts because of their significance and tendency to result in disputes. Although they generally do no more than postpone the timing of profit recognition, their relevance is attributable to their not inconsiderable interest effects together with the prohibition on the deductibility of interest on arrears of tax (Sec. 12(3) of the Income Tax Act). Because provisions for expected losses from executory contracts are not recognized for tax purposes (Sec. 5(4a) of the Income Tax Act), tax accounting concentrates on provisions for uncertain liabilities, which can result from both private contractual obligations and obligations under public law. In addition to pension provisions, the debate focuses in particular on provisions for decommissioning, removal, and restoration obligations, as well as more recently on refunds of excess fees charged by network operators (*Mehrerlösabschöpfungen*).

3. Digitization

Since 2013, German companies have been subject to a constructive obligation (Sec. 5b of the Income Tax Act) to upload their balance sheet and income statement data to the responsible tax office electronically using an officially prescribed data format. This obligation is designed to avoid data being lost or corrupted due to data format and interface problems and thus to enhance the efficiency of the taxation process. By standardizing the data to be transmitted, the '*E-Bilanz*' is allowing the tax authorities to develop a risk management system that will simplify comparisons over time and across businesses. In addition, because it requires data to be entered into mandatory fields, the highly elaborate tax accounting taxonomy has consequences for the design and structure of business accounting systems.

4. European Harmonization

As part of its project to harmonize tax accounting in the European Union, the European Commission published a draft directive on a 'Common Consolidated Corporate Tax Base' on 16 March 2011. In addition to harmonizing the way taxable income is computed, the Commission's proposal would consolidate all profits and losses across the EU, and is backed by a formula for subsequently apportioning the consolidated tax base. Although a consensus about consolidation and a formula for apportionment is currently a long way in the future, the proposals on computing taxable income send a strong signal to the member states that should not be underestimated and that can promote behind-the-scenes harmonization, as the example of depreciation pooling in Germany shows (Sec. 6(2a) of the Income Tax Act). However, the cross-border allocation effects of the profit apportionment rule should not be neglected, for example because they may result from differences in national environmental protection standards that are reflected in differences in tax provisions.

5. Outlook

It is not easy to forecast how tax accounting will evolve in Germany. Together with a trend toward the further divergence of tax and financial accounting and moves in the direction of closer European harmonization, there is also pressure in the opposite direction, with calls for tax and financial accounting to start converging again. However, the fiscal consequences mean that it is doubtful whether tax legislators will follow such a path. Advancing globalization and greater European harmonization are likely to dominate the future development of tax accounting and to encourage its evolution as a separate discipline.

Prof. Dr. Dr. h.c. Norbert Herzig

Public Auditor, Tax Advisor
Of Counsel

Areas of Specialization

- Business taxation
- Issues relating to the commercial balance sheet and the tax balance sheet
- Deferred taxes and tax accounting

Telephone (ext.) +49 228/95 94-227

Email: norbert.herzig@fgs.de

5. VAT, Trade and Real Estate Transfer Tax

Subordination or Close Links

by Ulrich Grünwald

Contents

I. Contours of VAT Group Taxation Consistent with EU Directives
II. Historical Development
III. Key Aspects of the German Concept of Fiscal Unity
IV. Key Elements of the European Concept of Fiscal Unity
   1. Wording of the Provision
   2. Specific Statements by the European Court of Justice
      a) Requirements for Fiscal Unity
      b) Legal Consequences of Fiscal Unity
V. Practical Relevance of Discrepancy
VI. Consequences
   1. Positions no Longer Consistent
      a) No General Discretion
      b) Special Discretion
      c) Partnerships
      d) Non-Taxable Persons
      e) Superordinate and Subordinate Relationship
   2. Contours of a Tax Group Conforming to Community Law
      a) Superordinate and Subordinate Relationship
      b) The Prerequisites of Art. 11 of the Directive on the VAT System
      c) Procedural Law
VII. Conclusion

I. Contours of VAT Group Taxation Consistent with EU Directives

German VAT fiscal unity, once a model for EU legislation governing group taxation, now itself has to be measured against it. Some key elements of the German concept of fiscal unity appear to be either inconsistent, or at least difficult to reconcile, with the European Court of Justice understanding of the tax group under European Union law.

Along with the individual questions of whether a partnership is excluded from a tax group by virtue of its legal form and whether a non-taxable person can also be part of a tax group, the fundamental issue arises as to the legal nature of the elements that link several independent persons to form one taxable person for the purposes of VAT law.

Does the Council Directive on the Common VAT System, as interpreted by the European Court of Justice, permit a VAT tax group to be based solely upon the common intention of the parties, or is a superordinate and subordinate relationship needed to enable the majority shareholder to impose its will upon the tax group?

II. Historical Development

The VAT Act 1934 (*Umsatzsteuergesetz*) codified the concepts of VAT fiscal unity and entrepreneur.[1] However, this was not a creation of the legislature at the time, but the statutory wording of a legal precept applied by the established case law of the German Imperial Court of Justice.[2]

Since then VAT fiscal unity – with brief interruptions and minor modifications – has been a component of no little importance for the concept of entrepreneur under German VAT law.[3]

As long as VAT was levied in the form of all-phase, gross VAT on every stage of production or trading, fiscal unity served the purpose of reducing this cumulative taxation depending on the number of production and/or trading stages. The introduction of all-phase, net VAT and input VAT eliminated the need for such. Fiscal unity could have dispensed with entirely. Nonetheless, it was retained since it simplified tax assessment. With this legislative intention it was adopted as an option for the member states firstly in the Second Directive on the VAT System in 1967, then in the Sixth Directive on the VAT System in 1977, and finally as Art. 11 of the Directive on the VAT System in 2006. As a provision in an EU directive, it served as a blueprint for the VAT laws of the member states and has meanwhile become an element of national VAT law in 15 member states.[4]

Art. 11 of the Directive on the VAT System constitutes an autonomous provision of EU law and may be interpreted by the European Court of Justice only. The European Court of Justiceis not bound in its interpretation by legislative history and hence not by the German understanding of fiscal unity.

Germany thus finds itself confronted with an interpretation of this legal principle that is completely different from the German understanding of the concept.

III. Key Aspects of the German Concept of Fiscal Unity

The German understanding of fiscal unity is characterized by autonomy as a necessary prerequisite for entrepreneurial status. In principle, an entrepreneur can be any business person who receives payment for rendering independent services on a permanent basis. In the terminology of the Directive on the VAT System, this is a taxable person who is subject to the legal principles of VAT law. If the economic cooperation of a legal entity with its majority shareholder

---

1 *Reiß* in Reiß/Kraeusel/Langer Value Added Tax Act Sec. 2, marginal no. 4.
2 *Reich* Tax Court of 26 Sep. 1927, V A 417/27, *RFHE* Vol. 22, p. 69; of 11 Nov. 1932, V A 948/31, *Reich* Tax Gazette, 1933, p. 295; cf. also the comprehensive remarks and citations on the inception of fiscal unity in Federal Tax Court of 17 July 1952 – V 17/52, Federal Tax Gazette Part III, 1952, p. 234.
3 *Reiß* with further citations, in Reiß/Kraeusel/Langer, Sec. 2, marginal no. 4.
4 Cf. *Stadie*, in Rau/Dürrwächter/Wäger, Sec. 2, marginal no. 816 with reference to the Pronouncement of the EU Commission of 2 July 2009, KOM(2009) 325.

reaches a level such that its business activities can appear to be governed by a third party and seem to be part of that shareholder's business activities, then the entity loses its autonomy for VAT purposes and hence its status as an entrepreneur.

The legal element of this concept is found in the prerequisites of 'integration' in Sec. 2(2) no. 2 sentence 1 of the German VAT Act and 'autonomy' or loss thereof in Sec. 2(2) no. 2 of the VAT Act. The judgments of the German Federal Tax Court, which had to decide on the existence of fiscal unity, addressed the question of whether the degree of entrepreneurial autonomy was insufficient and therefore the scope of integration sufficient to trigger the legal consequence of loss of entrepreneurial status.[5]

Thus financial integration requires the majority of shares to be linked to the majority of voting rights, ensuring that the majority shareholder can impose its will on the tax group.[6] Organizational integration requires the majority shareholder not only to ensure, through organizational measures, that no decisions are taken contrary to its own; it must also ensure that it can actually impose its will.[7] The superordinate (control) and subordinate relationship is therefore an essential characteristic of the German understanding of fiscal unity.[8]

The class of potential controlled corporations is limited to legal entities since the principle of self-governance (Selbstorganschaft) in particular makes integration in another entity irreconcilable with the legal concept of a partnership. It is argued that the nature of a partnership, unlike that of the corporation, is unsuitable for financial and organizational integration in another enterprise, i.e. for control by it, as required by fiscal unity under Sec. 2(2) no. 2 of the VAT Act.[9]

Even if the wording of Art. 11 of the Directive on the VAT System is broader than that of Sec. 2(2) no. 2 of the VAT Act, the legal opinion on EU law currently prevailing in Germany accepts the above-mentioned view since – so the thinking goes – the European directive has granted the German legislature a certain level of discretion which the German Parliament has not exceeded.[10]

The subordination of a controlled corporation is a characteristic element of German VAT fiscal unity. The Federal Tax Court explicitly pointed this out only recently, in cognizance of the European Court of Justice decisions in the *Commission v. Ireland* and *Commission v. Sweden* cases.

---

5 Federal Tax Court of 3 April 2008 – V R 76/05; Federal Tax Court of 19 May 2005 – V R 31/03; Federal Tax Court of 18 Dec. 1996, XI R 25/94.
6 Federal Tax Court of 29 Oct. 2008 – XI R 74/07; Federal Tax Court of 19 May 2005 – V R 31/03, Federal Tax Gazette Part II, 2005, p. 671.
7 Federal Tax Court of 8 Aug. 2013 – V R 18/13, MwStR 2013, 668 (m. Anm. *Erdbrügger*).
8 Cf. *Reiß*, in Reiß/Kraeusel/Langer Sec. 2 marginal nos. 107 and 107.1.
9 *Stadie*, in Reiß/Kraeusel/Langer Sec. 2 marginal no. 839.
10 *Wäger*, Festschrift für Schaumburg, pp. 1189 (1195).

"When interpretation is consistent with Art. 4(4)(2) no. 2 of Directive 77/388/EEC[11], fiscal unity pursuant Sec. 2(2) no. 2 of the VAT Act leads to a "merger into a single taxable person (...), for which, under the established case law of the Federal Tax Court, there must be a superordinate and subordinate relationship between a controlled corporation as the "subordinated person" and the controlling entity (...)."[12]

It explicitly cites the judgments in the cases *Commission v. Ireland* and *Commission v. Sweden*, without addressing the questions raised in tax literature as to whether the established Federal Tax Court case law cited is consistent with the European Court of Justice case law cited.[13] It is difficult to imagine that the Federal Tax Court will not return to this in its proceedings pending under VR 25/13, in which it has to rule on a judgment rendered by the Tax Court of Munich, which held Sec. 2(2) no. 2 sentence 1 of the VAT Act to be inconsistent with the principle of legal form neutrality by limiting potential controlled corporations to legal entities. The Tax Court of Munich expanded the principle to conform to EU law so that limited partnerships in the legal form of a *GmbH & Co. KG* can also be integrated into the controlling entity's enterprise, and will not refer this legal issue to the European Court of Justice.[14]

IV. Key Elements of the European Concept of Fiscal Unity

1. Wording of the Provision

When interpreting Art. 11 of the Directive on the VAT System, the European Court of Justice assumes at least partially different criteria. This does not come as a surprise because Art. 11 of the Directive on the VAT System defines neither the concept of (insufficient) autonomy nor that of integration. The directive refers to persons being "bound to one another" by "close links", suggesting a relationship in the sense of willing cooperation and pursuit of a common economic purpose by means of a division of labor. The wording of Art. 11 of the Directive on the VAT System would also allow a voluntary amalgamation of autonomous persons to be recognized as a VAT group without a controlling entity that is actually and legally in the position to impose its will on the other parties.

2. Specific Statements by the European Court of Justice

However, specific European Court of Justice statements on the requirements for fiscal unity are rare.

---

11 Corresponds to Art. 11 of the Directive on the VAT System. [Author's note]
12 Federal Tax Court of 8 Aug. 2013 – V R 18/13, MwStR 2013, 668 (m. Anm. *Erdbrügger*).
13 *Birkenfeld* UR, 2014, p.120; Erdbrügger, *DStR* 2013, p. 1573; *Grünwald*, Directive on the VAT System, 2013, p. 328; *Küffner/v. Streit*, UR 2013, p. 401, *Slapio*, UR 2013, p. 407.
14 Also *Birkenfeld*, UR 2014, p. 120.

a) Requirements for Fiscal Unity

aa) Consultation of the Advisory Committee

The European Court of Justice decided that, among the requirements for fiscal unity, the option, granted in Art. 11 of the Directive on the VAT System, to permit the VAT group in the respective member state can be exercised "only after the Advisory Committee on VAT has been consulted."[15]

bb) No Requirement for Being a Taxable Person

According to the view taken by the European Court of Justice, the legislative body which drafted Art. 11 of the Directive on the VAT System deliberately used the more general term 'person' and not the narrower 'taxable person'. "The application of that article is not, according to its wording, made subject to other conditions, in particular to the condition that those persons could themselves, individually, have had the status of a taxable person within the meaning of Article 9(1) of the Directive on the VAT System. As it uses the word 'persons' and not the words 'taxable persons', the first paragraph of Article 11 of the Directive on the VAT System does not make a distinction between taxable persons and non-taxable persons."[16] In the opinion of the European Court of Justice, the wording of Art. 11 of the Directive on the VAT System therefore opens up the possibility of including non-taxable persons in a VAT group.

cc) Same Prerequisites in All Member States

Both the requirements for the uniform application of EU law and the principle of equality dictate "that the terms of a provision of European Union law which makes no express reference to the law of the Member States for the purpose of determining its meaning and scope must normally be given an autonomous and uniform interpretation throughout the European Union."[17]

"It is especially important for the uniform application of the Directive on the VAT System that the notion of 'taxable person', defined in Title III thereof, is given an autonomous and uniform interpretation. In that context, such an interpretation is necessary for Article 11 of the Directive on the VAT System, despite the optional nature, as regards the Member States, of the scheme for which it provides, in order to avoid differences in application of that scheme between one Member State and another when it is implemented."[18]

---

15 European Court of Justice of 22 May 2008 – C-162/07 – Ampliscientifica Amplifin, DStRE 2008, 902, marginal no. 18.
16 European Court of Justice of 9 April 2013 – C-85/11 – Kommission/Irland, MwStR 2013, 238 (m. Anm. *Grünwald*), marginal no. 36.
17 European Court of Justice of 25 April 2013 – C-480/10 – Kommission/Schweden, MwStR 2013, 276 (m. Anm. *Grube*), marginal no. 33.
18 European Court of Justice of 25 April 2013 – C-480/10 – Kommission/Schweden, MwStR 2013, 276 (m. Anm. *Grube*), marginal no. 33, marginal no. 30.

dd) No Need for a Superordinate and Subordinate Relationship

In the case of *Ampliscientifica*, the European Court of Justice repeatedly uses the term 'subordinated person' to designate the subsidiary defined as the controlled corporation (*Organgesellschaft*) in German. However, it uses this term solely to describe the legal consequences of the merger into one taxable person. Thus these 'subordinated persons' can no longer be deemed taxable persons. Moreover, it is impossible for the 'subordinated persons' to continue filing separate tax returns since there is only one taxable person – the controlling corporation in German terminology – that is entitled to file a return.[19] No statement made by the European Court of Justice indicates that it takes the view that a superordinate and subordinate relationship is a requirement for fiscal unity. Probably the European Court of Justice has to decide whether the existence of a VAT group depends on such a relationship.[20]

b) Legal Consequences of Fiscal Unity

The persons amalgamated into a tax group constitute one single taxable person.

With respect to the legal consequences of fiscal unity, the European Court of Justice explains that it allows member states to draft a provision of national law on the basis of Art. 11 of the Directive on the VAT System and to stop treating persons who satisfy the legal requirements of the member state's relevant provision "as separate taxable persons for the purposes of VAT but (…) as a single taxable person." In this connection the European Court of Justice refers to the "treatment as a single taxable person".[21]

Such treatment precludes "persons who are thus closely linked from continuing to submit VAT returns separately and from continuing to be identified, within and outside their group, as individual taxable persons, since the individual taxable person alone is authorized to submit such returns."[22]

V. Practical Relevance of Discrepancy

Until now, this discrepancy between the narrower German view and the broader European Court of Justice view has not been very important,[23] since the German legislature assumed that it had leeway to formulate the particular requirements for fiscal unity and that it had the discretion to exploit this leeway.

Given the court's extensive remarks in the *Commission v. Sweden* case, this position can no longer be maintained without qualification. The court explicit-

---

19 European Court of Justice of 22 May 2008 – C-162/07 – Ampliscientifica Amplifin, DStRE 2008, 902, marginal no. 19.
20 Federal Tax Court of 11 Dec. 2013 – XI R 38/12 , BStBl. II 2014, 428.
21 European Court of Justice of 22 May 2008 – C-162/07 – Ampliscientifica Amplifin, DStRE 2008, 902, marginal no. 19.
22 European Court of Justice of 22 May 2008 – C-162/07 – Ampliscientifica Amplifin, DStRE 2008, 902, marginal no. 19.
23 *Wäger*, Festschrift für Schaumburg, p. 1195.

ly refers to the special significance of uniform interpretation and the objective to avoid variations in the interpretations of member states.[24] It may thus be concluded that a member state which decides to transpose fiscal unity into its VAT law has to comply with the European Court of Justice understanding of such in its interpretation of Art. 11 of the Directive on the VAT System.

Hence the discrepancy between Art. 11 of the Directive on the VAT System and Sec. 2(2) no. 2 of the VAT Act has become considerably more relevant in practice.

VI. Consequences

As a result, both the regulation in Sec. 2(2) no. 2 of the VAT Act and the Federal Tax Court's established case law on this provision have to be reviewed for consistency with Community law.

1. Positions no Longer Consistent

a) No General Discretion

The assumption that there is leeway within which each member state may formulate the legal principle of fiscal unity as it sees fit contradicts the statement that, although the application of Art. 11 of the Directive on the VAT System is in fact optional for the member states, a single European Court of Justice interpretation is designed to prevent substantive variations in the provisions drafted by the member states that exercise this option. Therefore, to the extent that the Federal Tax Court deems the wording of German VAT law, which is narrower than that of Art. 11 of the Directive on the VAT System, to be compliant with such, on the assumption that the national legislature is granted leeway, a reassessment seems to be necessary.

b) Special Discretion

aa) Option at the Level of the Taxable Person

According to the European Court of Justice established case law, it appears that there is also an option for the application of the fiscal unity rule at the level of the taxable person. However, there is no obligation for the member state to grant the *taxable* person such an option. To this extent, the member state is entitled to leeway.[25]

---

[24] European Court of Justice of 25 May 2013 – C-480/10 – Kommission/Schweden, MwStR 2013, 276 (m. Anm. *Grube*), marginal no. 30.
[25] *Reiß* in Reiß/Kraeusel/Langer, VAT Act, Sec. 2, marginal nos. 98.9 and 98.10.

bb) Measures to Prevent Tax Evasion or Avoidance

However, the European Court of Justice recognizes a member state's discretion in applying this provision to measures that it deems necessary so as to prevent tax evasion and avoidance. To the extent that such measures are taken in compliance with EU law, the member states retain the right to restrict the application of the provisions contained in Art. 11 of the Directive on the VAT System in order to counter tax evasion or avoidance.[26]

c) Partnerships

It appears that the exclusion of partnerships as possible members of a tax group is also no longer consistent with EU law. Meanwhile this is likely to be considered the prevailing legal opinion.[27]

d) Non-Taxable Persons

According to the detailed explanations rendered in the *Commission v. Ireland* case and the unambiguous analysis of the wording of the provision, it must be assumed that the legal opinion prevailing in Germany that membership in a tax group presupposes the entrepreneurial status of all parties is no longer sustainable.[28]

e) Superordinate and Subordinate Relationship

Even if the Federal Tax Court again affirmed the requirement of a superordinate and subordinate relationship in its decision of 8 Aug. 2013, it is doubtful whether this legal position conforms to Community law in the form interpreted by the European Court of Justice.[29]

The Federal Tax Court may itself have been in doubt. Hence it does not cite the European Court of Justice rulings to support the argument that a superordinate and subordinate relationship is a requirement for a tax group. Instead, it only derives from the European Court of Justice the position that this would lead to merger into a single taxable person.

> "When interpretation is consistent with Art. 4(4)(2) no. 2 of Directive 77/388/EEC[30], fiscal unity pursuant Sec. 2(2) no. 2 of the VAT Act leads to a "merger into a single taxable person (…),

---

26 European Court of Justice of 25 April 2013 – C-480/10 – Kommission/Schweden, MwStR 2013, 276 (m. Anm. *Grube*), marginal no. 38.
27 *Birkenfeld*, UR 2014, p. 120; *Erdbrügger*, DStR 2013, p. 1573; *Grünwald*, Directive on the VAT System, 2013, p. 328; *Küffner/Streit*, UR 2013, p. 401; *Slapio*, UR 2013, p. 407.
28 cf. footnote 26; contra *Sterzinger*, UR 2014, p. 133.
29 Also *Erdbrügger*, DStR 2013, p. 1573.
30 Corresponds to Art. 11 of the Directive on the VAT System. [Author's note]

the Federal Court of Justice supports the existence of a superordinate and subordinate relationship solely with its own established case law:

> ... for which, under established Federal Tax Court case law, there must be a superordinate and subordinate relationship between a controlled corporation as 'the subordinated person' and the controlling entity (...)."[31]

One could continue

> ..., which, however, has not yet been affirmed by the European Court of Justice.

The linking of both statements in one sentence suggests, however, that the Federal Tax Court sees its established case law as being compliant with the directive and consistent with the interpretation of Art. 4(4)(2) of the Sixth Directive or Art. 11 of the Directive on the VAT System.

2. Contours of a Tax Group Conforming to Community Law

As easy as it may be to enumerate the aspects of the German understanding of fiscal unity that are not in line with European Court of Justice case law, it is difficult to specify positively, on the basis of the statements made by the European Court of Justice, the requirements for a VAT group under Community law.

In light of the few judgments available to date, the contours of group taxation under Art. 11 of the Directive on the VAT System as interpreted by the European Court of Justice are rather blurred. However, the European Court of Justice makes clear that it primarily relies on the wording of the provision, its context and objectives.[32] The European Court of Justice names the simplifying of administration and the prevention of abuses as the objectives being pursued.[33]

What requirements need to be satisfied to fulfil the conditions of group taxation within the meaning of Art. 11 of the Directive on the VAT System?

a) Superordinate and Subordinate Relationship

A superordinate and subordinate relationship is not a prerequisite for group taxation within the meaning of Art. 11 of the Directive on the VAT System. Group taxation does not require that any member of the group of persons amalgamated into one taxable person has to be deemed the superordinate controlling entity while the other members of the group are integrated into this entity as subordinate enterprises (or parts of such enterprises). Instead, Art. 11 of the Directive on the VAT System allows a group of several enterprises of equal

---

31 Federal Tax Court of 8 Aug. 2013 – V R 18/13, MwStR 2013, 668 (m. Anm. *Erdbrügger*).
32 European Court of Justice of 9 April 2013 – C-85/11 – Kommission/Irland, MwStR 2013, 238 (m. Anm. *Grünwald*), marginal no. 35 *et seqq.*
33 European Court of Justice of 9 April 2013 – C-85/11 – Kommission/Irland, MwStR 2013, 238 (m. Anm. *Grünwald*), marginal no. 47.

standing and rank to be treated by the member states as one single taxable person only, provided that they are closely linked to one another. Art. 11 of the Directive on the VAT System thus also permits a group of enterprises of equal standing to be treated as one single taxable person.[34]

b) The Prerequisites of Art. 11 of the Directive on the VAT System

aa) Financial Links

Art. 11 of the Directive on the VAT System states that mutual financial links lead to the persons involved being closely bound to one another.

It is the general view that such a financial link is created by the contribution of equity capital. The shareholder provides the corporation with equity and receives shareholder's rights in return. Mutual financial links are deemed to exist regardless of the amount invested. The higher the contribution, the closer the link thereby established between the shareholder and the corporation becomes. The use of the prerequisite 'close' makes clear that – from the perspective of the Community legislature – there may be financial links that are not 'close' within the meaning of this provision. Such financial links need to have additional features to be considered as close.

Any understanding suggesting that the prerequisite 'close' has to be interpreted to mean that the investment must exceed a certain minimum amount would be compatible with the wording. The same would be true if the said prerequisite were combined with the requirement of majority holding because the latter is different in quality from any minor holding in that it creates, for the first time, a position in the shareholders' meeting which enables the majority shareholder to assert its will without restriction. However, the wording of the provision does not preclude financial links being established by a holding of less than 50% plus x, which would lead to the parties being closely bound to one another.

The meaning of 'financial link' is much broader than the definition of a shareholder's position and, in particular, covers debt financing as well.

If a person provides a corporation with capital by granting loans, such funding is deemed to establish a financial link. If the economic relevance of the loan granted is not insignificant for the borrower, the financial link established thereby can be referred to as a 'close' one. If the situation is of the kind that the borrower is economically dependent on the funds granted by such person because the borrower is unable to raise alternative funds in the market or only on terms that cannot be compared to those granted by the person in question, the link established by the financial relationship must certainly be designated as close.

Finally, clarification is necessary to determine which additional requirements need to be fulfilled in terms of the prerequisite of being bound 'to one another',

---

[34] *Reiß*, in Reiß/Kraeusel/Langer, VAT Act, Sec. 2, marginal no. 98.11.

i.e. of 'mutual' links. This might refer to the mutual grant of rights of the same kind such as cross-holdings.[35] However, entering into a legal relationship that leads to the inception of mutually related rights and duties should also establish mutual links, meaning that any legal relationship imposing on the parties reciprocal obligations in terms of *do ut des* (*Synallagma*), in particular a loan agreement, would create mutual links within the meaning of Art. 11 of the Directive on the VAT System.

bb) Economic Links

As to economic integration, the element of the superordinate and subordinate relationship is the least emphasized aspect in the case law of the Federal Tax Court. The Federal Tax Court, for instance, makes clear that the controlled corporation does not have to provide auxiliary services for a group to qualify for economic integration.[36] Economic integration may thus exist if, due to mutual promotion, assistance and complementary functions, the economic links between the controlling corporation and the controlled corporation are not insignificant. A reasonable economic connection in terms of economic unity, cooperation and integration is sufficient.[37] The controlled corporation need not be dependent on the controlling entity.[38] Economic integration may arise from cooperation between controlled corporations.[39] If economic integration is based on the provision of services to the controlled corporation by the controlling corporation, this must pertain to services which can be compensated and are not of mere minor importance for the economic activity of the controlled corporation.[40]

All of these requirements can be fulfilled if several persons cooperate to achieve a common economic purpose by the division of labor without a superordinate and subordinate relationship being required. Thus it cannot be seen from the Federal Tax Court rulings on the issue of economic integration that, as far as the superordinate and subordinate relationship is concerned, the court would define requirements going beyond the concept of mutual relations that establish 'close links'.

In this respect, there is no recognizable discrepancy between the wording of Art. 11 of the Directive on the VAT System and the criteria developed by the Federal Tax Court in its case law on the prerequisite of economic integration.

cc) Organizational Links

As to organizational integration, the Federal Tax Court does attach much importance to the element of a superordinate and subordinate relationship in its

---

35 Cf. *Wäger*, Festschrift für Schaumburg, p. 1195.
36 *Korn* in Bunjes, Sec. 2, marginal no. 123 with further citations.
37 Federal Tax Court of 29 Oct. 2008 – XI R 74/07, BStBl. II 2009, 256.
38 Federal Tax Court of 3 April 2003 – V R 63/01 , BStBl. II 2004, 434.
39 Federal Tax Court of 20 Aug. 2009 – V R 30/06, BStBl. II 2010, 863.
40 Federal Tax Court of 18 June 2009 – V R 4/08, BStBl. II 2010, 310.

rulings. If one leaves this aside and relies exclusively on the wording of Art. 11 of the Directive on the VAT System, there are further scenarios imaginable – besides appointing identical directors on executive bodies in some cases and executive employees of the majority shareholder as chief executive officers of the controlled corporation, and concluding control agreements – where close mutual organizational relations create a close link. One option would be a supervisory or advisory board that is controlled by the majority shareholder or joint corporation management by a CEO appointed by the majority shareholder and an external CEO. Also, the rules of procedure referred to by the Federal Tax Court and 'group guidelines' can create close links between the parties involved which fulfil the prerequisites of Art. 11 of the Directive on the VAT System and thus – not only in exceptional cases[41] but as a rule – constitute the organizational element of fiscal unity.

c) Procedural Law

The VAT group can but need not necessarily be structured as an option for (a) taxable person(s). The introduction of any procedure which is binding on the parties involved as to whether or not the prerequisites of VAT fiscal unity are fulfilled would be welcome for the sake of legal certainty.[42]

VII. Conclusion

The general exclusion of certain persons (non-taxable persons and partnerships) from the class of potential tax group members is contrary to Community law. National legislatures are free to introduce the concept of fiscal unity or not. If they decide to, the leeway granted in terms of the legal concept of fiscal unity is limited to the grant of an option to the taxable person and the prevention of tax evasion or avoidance.

The details of fiscal unity conforming to Community law have not been defined yet. However, the decisive feature appears to be deliberate cooperation of group members instead of integration based on a superordinate and subordinate relationship and the loss of independency.

The limitation of financial links to holdings in terms of corporate law does not appear to be mandatory. Also, financing by granting loans might create financial links within the meaning of Art. 11 of the Directive of the VAT System.

Pursuant to the wording of the directive, organizational links do not require the majority shareholder to hold a controlling position, but measures to assure cooperation aimed at concerted economic action seem to be sufficient.

---

41 Cf. Sec. 2.8(10) of the Rules for the Application of the German VAT Act (*Umsatzsteueranwendungserlass*).
42 Also *Birkenfeld* UR 2014, pp. 120 (127).

Dr. Ulrich Grünwald

Lawyer, Tax Advisor

Areas of Specialization

- German value-added tax law
- European value-added tax law
- Insurance tax
- Excise tax
- Tax audits
- Tax litigation

Telephone (ext.) +49 228/95 94-524

Email: ulrich.gruenwald@fgs.de

International Aspects of German Trade Tax

by Arne von Freeden

Contents

I. Introduction
II. Basics
III. Pitfalls
IV. Schemes
  1. Inbound Structure
    a) Existence of a Domestic Business of a Foreign Entity
    b) Renting-out of Real Estate via Interposition of a Domestic Real-Estate Entity
    c) Foreign Entity with Management in a Treaty State
    d) Group Taxation for Trade-Tax Purposes with Foreign Controlling Entity and/or Foreign Controlled Entity
  2. Outbound Structure
    a) Domestic Business with Foreign Permanent Establishment
    b) Domestic Business with Stake in Foreign Partnership
    c) Domestic Business with Stake in Foreign Corporation
    d) Application of a Double Taxation Treaty
    e) Taking Account of a Final Loss of a Foreign Permanent Establishment
    f) Implications from Application of the Foreign Tax Act
V. Summary

I. Introduction

Alongside income tax and corporate income tax, trade tax represents one of the pillars of German business-taxation law. Indeed, the trade-tax burden of an entity may exceed its income-tax or corporate-income-tax burden. Trade tax is a (purely) domestic tax; profits earned by foreign permanent establishments (hereinafter 'PEs') of the *Gewerbebetrieb* (hereinafter 'business') are not subject to trade tax. Accordingly, there can be no double taxation of trade tax at an international level. Nevertheless, matters with a foreign component may also have implications for the trade-tax assessment (e.g. cross-border *Betriebsaufspaltung* ('operational split').[1] For this reason, considerations in the context of inbound or outbound structuring must always include trade-tax aspects. Some aspects of particular relevance in practice are outlined below.

II. Basics

The object of taxation in the context of trade tax is the domestic (i.e. German) business. The existence of a business must be determined on the basis of income-tax-law principles. The activity of a corporation is always deemed to be a

---

[1] see Tax Court of Baden-Württemberg of 21 April 2004 – 12 K 252/00, IStR 2005, p. 172, with a commentary by *Piltz*.

business (Sec. 2(2) sentence 1 of the German Trade Tax Act – *Gewerbesteuergesetz*). A business carries on domestic operations if a PE is maintained for it in Germany (Sec. 2(1) sentence 3 of the Trade Tax Act). The share of profits attributable to foreign PEs of the business is not subject to trade tax.

The basis for determination of trade tax is the trading profit. Pursuant to Sec. 7(1) of the Trade Tax Act, the trading profit is the profit of the taxable entity, to be calculated in accordance with the provisions of the German Income Tax Act *(Einkommensteuergesetz)* or German Corporate Income Tax Act *(Körperschaftsteuergesetz)*. In the case of partnerships, special balance sheets *(Sonderbilanzen)* and supplementary balance sheets *(Ergänzungsbilanzen)* as well as special business income *(Sondervergütungen)* must also be included. In determining the profit, account must also be taken – if express reference is made to the same in the individual statute – of provisions in other statutes in addition to those of the Income Tax Act and Corporate Income Tax Act (e.g. the German Foreign Tax Act – *Außensteuergesetz* – and German Investment Tax Act – *Investmentsteuergesetz)*.

The profit determined by applying the provisions of the Income Tax Act or Corporate Income Tax Act must be modified for trade-tax purposes. Certain expenses deducted in the context of profit determination must be added back *(pro rata)* to the profit to determine the trading profit (Sec. 8 of the Trade Tax Act), while, conversely, certain other earnings added in the context of profit determination must be deducted from the profit again (Sec. 9 of the Trade Tax Act).

Applying the statutory base rate *(Steuermesszahl)* of 3.5% to the trading profit produces the tax base *(Steuermessbetrag)* (Sec. 11(1) of the Trade Tax Act). The amount of trade tax is determined by applying, to that tax base, the *Hebesatz* set by the pertinent municipality (local rate of assessment or multiplier; e.g. Munich 490%) (Sec. 16(1) of the Trade Tax Act).

Example 1

A German corporation maintains a PE in Munich; it has no other PEs. The corporation has a trading profit of EUR 1m. Trade tax is EUR 171,500 (EUR 1m × base rate of 3.5% × local rate of assessment for Munich of 490%).

Private individuals may have the trade tax credited *(pro rata)* against their income tax; corporations do not have this option.

III. Pitfalls

Whether trade tax will be levied on the German activities of a domestic or foreign entity mainly depends on whether there is a German business and whether the requirements for a trade-tax deduction to be applied to the trading profit are met. When structuring inbound or outbound investments, trade-tax pitfalls may arise that can be divided up into the following groups:

Inbound Structure

- Existence of a domestic (German) business of a foreign entity
- Renting-out of real estate by interposition of a domestic real-estate entity
- Foreign entity with management in a treaty state (i.e. a state that is a contracting party to a double taxation treaty [hereinafter 'DTT'])
- Group taxation *(Organschaft)* for trade-tax purposes with foreign controlling entity and/or controlled foreign entity

Outbound Structure

- Domestic (German) business with foreign PE
- Domestic business with stake in foreign partnership
- Domestic business with stake in foreign corporation
- Application of a DTT
- Taking account of a final loss of a foreign PE
- Implications arising from the application of the Foreign Tax Act

IV. Schemes

1. Inbound Structure

a) Existence of a Domestic Business of a Foreign Entity

The levying of trade tax requires the existence a domestic business. A business carries on operations in Germany if a domestic PE is maintained for it (Sec. 2(2) sentence 2 of the Trade Tax Act).

> **Example 2**
>
> A corporation with its registered seat and place of management in the United States operates, *inter alia*, a production plant in Germany. The production plant constitutes a (German) PE of the corporation. The profit of the PE is subject to trade tax.

Answering the question whether specific domestic activities of a foreign entity constitute a PE is frequently fraught with legal uncertainties. If an investor wishes to avoid trade tax arising as part of an inbound structure, then the basic rule is to avoid the existence of a PE. In practice, this can normally only be achieved by investing in 'passive' assets (e.g. real estate).

> **Example 3**
>
> A corporation with its registered seat and place of management in the United States acquires real estate in Germany in order to rent it out. The rented-out real estate does not constitute a (German) PE of the corporation. There is no domestic business; the rental income is not subject to trade tax.

b) Renting-out of Real Estate via Interposition of a Domestic Real-Estate Entity

The acquisition of real estate situated in Germany may require an acquisition via a German partnership or corporation (real-estate entity) for reasons unrelated to tax considerations. In this case, there is a business of the real-estate entity; its management establishes a 'management PE' *(Geschäftsleitungsbetriebsstätte)* in Germany. In principle, the rental income is subject to trade tax.

Example 4

A corporation with its registered seat and place of management in the United States establishes a *GmbH (Gesellschaft mit beschränkter Haftung* – privately held corporation) in Germany. The *GmbH* acquires real estate in Munich and rents it out. The rental income derived by the *GmbH* increases the trading profit (which is subject to trade tax) of the *GmbH*.

Nevertheless, a trade-tax peculiarity applies with regard to a real-estate entity: An entity that solely manages and uses its own real estate is entitled, for purposes of determining its trading profit, to have its profit attributable to management and use deducted (Sec. 9 no. 1 sentences 2 to 6 of the Trade Tax Act). Provided the statutory requirements are satisfied, the taxation of such entity's profit is avoided. It is a prerequisite for such 'extended trade-tax deduction' *(erweiterte Gewerbesteuer-Kürzung)* that the entity manage and use only real estate it owns); the ancillary management and use of its own capital resources is not harmful in this context. If the *GmbH* in Example 4 meets the statutory requirements, then any levying of trade tax on the rental income is avoided.

c) Foreign Entity with Management in a Treaty State

If the management of a foreign entity is located in a country with which Germany has entered into a DTT, then Germany's right to tax may be excluded or limited under the treaty. As a general rule, the topic of trade tax falls within the scope of application of the DTTs entered into by Germany. No express provision for trade tax is made in the German treaties. If Germany has a right to tax under the relevant treaty, it may be possible to levy trade tax if the statutory trade-tax prerequisites are met.

If the foreign entity whose management and registered seat are located in a different contracting state maintains a PE in Germany, then Germany has a right to tax. This right to tax also extends to trade tax. If the PE under treaty law is also a PE under national tax law (cf. Sec. 12 of the German General Tax Code – *Abgabenordnung)*, then this constitutes a German business within the meaning of the Trade Tax Act (Sec. 2(1) sentences 1 and 3 of the Trade Tax Act). The profit of the PE is subject to trade tax. In that context, any adding-back for trade-tax purposes under Sec. 8 of the Trade Tax Act is not restricted by DTTs. The foreign state normally credits German trade tax against tax liability arising under its own national tax law. Thus, a double tax burden on the foreign entity (and/or its shareholders) should be (largely) avoidable.

If a foreign entity with management in a non-treaty state maintains a domestic (i.e. German) PE, then the right of Germany to levy trade tax on the profit from the PE is not limited under treaty law. As an exception, the taxation of income derived by the PE from the operation of its own or of chartered ships or aircraft is excluded if the requirements of Sec. 2(6) of the Trade Tax Act in conjunction with Sec. 49(4) of the Income Tax Act are met.

d) Group Taxation for Trade-Tax Purposes with Foreign Controlling Entity and/or Foreign Controlled Entity

If there is group taxation for trade-tax purposes between a controlling entity (e.g. a German stock corporation – *Aktiengesellschaft* or *AG*) and a controlled entity (e.g. a *GmbH*), then the controlled entity is deemed to be the PE – for trade-tax purposes, of the controlling entity. Profits and losses are set off mutually within the tax group *(Organkreis)*. The tax base for trade-tax purposes of the tax group is attributed to the different PEs in relation to the wages of the employees employed in these PEs and taxed by applying the relevant municipality's local rate of assessment.

Example 5

Parent *AG* (5 employees) is the 100% owner of Subsidiary 1 *GmbH* (1,000 employees) and Subsidiary 2 *GmbH* (300 employees). There is a tax group for trade-tax purposes. The trading profit of the tax group amounts to 1,000 (Parent *AG*: 100; Subsidiary 1 *GmbH*: 1,500; Subsidiary 2 *GmbH*: –600). The trading profit must be divided in relation to the wages. Trade tax is levied *pro rata* by the municipalities in which the companies have their registered seats. The percentage tax burden depends on the amount of the applicable municipality's local rate of assessment.

The controlling entity of the tax group may also be an entity with its registered seat and/or place of management outside Germany. This requires that the entity maintain a PE in Germany and that the stakes in the controlled entities be functionally attributable to this PE.

Example 6

A corporation with its registered seat and place of management in the Netherlands maintains a (distribution) PE in Germany. Subsidiary 1 *GmbH* and Subsidiary 2 *GmbH* are both wholly owned by the corporation. The stakes are functionally attributable to the German PE. The Dutch corporation is able (via its PE) to be a controlling entity.

A controlled entity in a tax group may also be a corporation with its registered seat in an EU member state or a member state of the European Economic Area (EEA). This requires the place of management to be located in Germany. In the opinion of the German tax authorities, another requirement is for the profit-and-loss transfer agreement to be entered in the foreign commercial register of the controlled entity. This entry is problematic because foreign commercial registers are not familiar with a German profit-and-loss transfer agreement (and thus tend to refuse such entry).

Example 7

Parent *AG* is the 100% owner of a Dutch *B.V.* The place of management of the *B.V.* is in Germany. The Dutch *B.V.* is able (via its German PE) to be a controlled entity. Entry of the profit-and-loss transfer agreement in a Dutch commercial register is a requirement for the validity (in Germany) of the tax group.

2. Outbound Structure

a) Domestic Business with Foreign Permanent Establishment

The German business of a (domestic) partnership or corporation is subject to trade tax if it maintains a PE in Germany. If the foreign activity of a domestic entity is carried out (solely) by interposition of a German PE – i.e. without establishing a foreign PE – then there are no trade-tax implications (e.g. profit gained from direct shipping of goods to a foreign country). If, on the other hand, the domestic entity carries out its foreign activities via a foreign PE (e.g. a factory abroad), then the income derived abroad must be exempted from paying German trade tax.

Example 8

A German corporation runs one production plant in Germany and one in France. The production plants constitute PEs. The profit attributable to the German PE is subject to (German) trade tax. The profit attributable to the French PE is not subject to (German) trade tax.

The existence (or nonexistence) of a DTT is of no relevance; the exemption of the PE's profits from trade tax is based on the German Trade Tax Act.

b) Domestic Business with Stake in Foreign Partnership

A German business (e.g. partnership or corporation) may participate in a foreign partnership as a partner. The profit or loss of the foreign partnership increases or reduces the taxable income of the domestic business.

Example 9

A German corporation holds an interest in a partnership with its registered seat in a non-DTT country. The partnership derives a profit that increases *(pro rata)* the taxable income of the German corporation.

If this were the end result, then the income of the foreign partnership would be taken into account when assessing the relevant trade tax despite the fact that the partnership, as an independent taxable entity for trade-tax purposes, does not maintain a PE in Germany. For this reason, the Trade Tax Act provides for an 'adjustment' of the taxable income of the German partner. The loss incurred by the foreign partnership must be added back to the profit of the domestic business (Sec. 8 no. 8 of the Trade Tax Act), i.e. it does not affect the amount of the trading income of the domestic business. Any profit gained from an interest in the foreign partnership must be reduced accordingly (Sec. 9 no. 2 of the Trade

Tax Act). Whether there is a DTT in place is irrelevant. In Example 9, the taxable income of the German corporation must be reduced by the amount of the partnership's profit.

The application of the add-back and reduction provisions can cause difficulty for structuring and taxation practice if, from a German perspective, the foreign entity is not to be classified as a partnership. Moreover, a trade-tax issue may arise if, from a German perspective, a partner's earnings from a foreign partnership are not to be classified as a profit share (but rather e.g. as interest).

c) Domestic Business with Stake in Foreign Corporation

A domestic business may participate in a foreign corporation as a shareholder. Distributions of profits by the foreign corporation increase the taxable income of the domestic business.

Example 10

A German corporation has held, for three years, a 20% share in a corporation with its registered seat and place of management in Brazil. The Brazilian corporation runs a car factory. The Brazilian corporation pays a dividend in 2013. The dividend increases the taxable income of the German corporation.

The profit of the business must be reduced by dividends received from foreign corporations if the (direct and/or indirect) stake in the corporation has been at least 15% (without interruption) since the start of the trade-tax assessment period and the corporation exclusively or almost exclusively earns 'active income' within the meaning of the Foreign Tax Act (Sec. 9 no. 7 sentence 1 of the Trade Tax Act). The trade-tax assessment period is the calendar year. Since the German corporation in Example 10 holds a 20% stake in the Brazilian corporation, the holding already existed on 1 Jan. 2013 and the Brazilian corporation has active operations, the taxable income of the German business must be reduced by an amount equivalent to the dividend.

The reduction provision applies to a stake in a foreign corporation even if the foreign corporation – while it not deriving 'active income' within the meaning of the Foreign Tax Act – derives income as a national or functional holding company *(Landesholding/Funktionsholding)* (Sec. 9 no. 7 sentence 1 of the Trade Tax Act). A national holding company is a subsidiary that is maintained by profits from active sub-subsidiaries which have their registered seats and place of management in the same country in which the national holding company has its seat/management (Sec. 9 no. 7 sentence 1 no. 1 of the Trade Tax Act; e.g. where a US national holding company holds stakes in active US sub-subsidiaries). The national holding company must hold a stake of at least 25% in the active sub-subsidiaries, and the holding must have been in existence without interruption for at least 12 months prior to the balance-sheet date relevant for profit determination.

A functional holding company is an active subsidiary that is maintained from profits of active sub-subsidiaries, and with regard to which there is an economic connection between the activity of the subsidiary and the activities of the sub-subsidiaries (Sec. 9 no. 7 sentence 1 no. 2 of the Trade Tax Act; e.g. where a US functional holding company with production plant holds a stake in an active distribution entity with its registered seat and place of management in Japan).

If the corporation is an entity within the meaning of the Parent-Subsidiary Directive, a stake of 10% is sufficient.

In addition, a *(pro-rata)* deduction under Sec. 9 no. 7 of the Trade Tax Act may be available in a scenario involving a dividend from a foreign sub-subsidiary passing through the foreign subsidiary to the business (Sec. 9 no. 7 sentences 4 *et seqq.* of the Trade Tax Act). In such a scenario, a minimum stake of 15% in the sub-subsidiary via the subsidiary is required (e.g. where a business holds a 100% stake in a subsidiary, and the subsidiary in turn holds a 15% stake in the sub-subsidiary). Another requirement is that the sub-subsidiary, in the fiscal year for which it made the distribution (to the subsidiary of the business) (almost) exclusively derives 'active income' within the meaning of the Foreign Tax Act or derived income from stakes within the meaning of Sec. 9 no. 7 sentence 1 no. 1 of the Trade Tax Act.

d) Application of a Double Taxation Treaty

The taxation of the foreign income derived by a business may be excluded under a DTT. As a general rule, the topic of trade tax falls within the scope of application of the DTTs entered into by Germany. This applies irrespective of whether the other country levies trade tax (or a comparable tax). DTTs do not contain any special rule of distribution or any special method article regarding trade tax. If foreign income is exempt from tax in Germany under a treaty, then it is also exempt from trade tax.

Exemption of Income Derived by a Foreign Permanent Establishment

Under the German DTTs, income attributable to a foreign PE may only be taxed by the state in which the PE is located (cf. Art. 7 of the OECD Model Convention – hereinafter 'MC'). This also applies to trade tax. The existence of a PE must be assessed according to treaty-law standards (cf. Art. 5 of the OECD MC). For this reason, a PE may exist for treaty purposes even if there is no PE under national law (Sec. 12 of the General Tax Code). In this case, the profit of the PE is not to be included in the trade-tax base; the imposition of trade tax is excluded. Correspondingly, a loss incurred by the PE is not taken into account for German trade-tax purposes either (the exception being a final PE loss).

Exemption of Significant-Holding Dividends (Schachteldividenden)

The distribution of profit by a foreign corporation to a German shareholder (e.g. parent or controlling *GmbH*) may be exempt from German taxation under the applicable DTT if certain requirements are met (cf. e.g. Art. 20(2) sentence 3 of the German-Luxembourg DTT). This requires a specific minimum stake; in addition, the shareholder of the foreign corporation must be a corporation (*'Schachtelbeteiligung'*, essentially denoting a 'significant holding'). If the DTT requirements regarding a 'significant holding' are met, the exemption of the significant-holding dividends also extends to trade tax. In this scenario, there is no need to satisfy the requirements of trade-tax deduction provisions.

It must be noted in this context that the minimum shareholding under a DTT (e.g. 25%) is reduced to 15% under Sec. 9 no. 8 of the Trade Tax Act. This rule ensures that DTT-based relief for significant-holding dividends, also known as the participation exemption *(Schachtelprivileg)*, also extends to trade tax – regardless of the minimum stake (e.g. at least 25%) required under the treaty. Since the participation exemption can normally only apply in favor of a shareholder with the legal form of a corporation, it will practically only be possible for a corporation (which is subject to trade tax) to use this provision. A reduction by the amount equivalent to the profit distributed by the subsidiary under sec. 9 no. 8 of the Trade Tax Act requires – regardless of the pertinent DTT provision – a stake in the amount of at least 15% (only); a lower minimum stake, if any, under a DTT takes precedence.

No Crediting of Foreign Tax Against Trade Tax

If the foreign state, as the source state, also has a (nonexclusive) right to tax (foreign-source) income, then the German DTTs usually provide for credit of the foreign tax against the German income tax or corporate income tax (e.g. taxation of free-float dividends, interest and royalty income). Foreign tax cannot be credited against German trade tax owing to the lack of legal bases in terms of DTTs or trade-tax law. Unless trade-tax provisions for the (unilateral) avoidance of taxation are applicable, the income derived in the source state is, in this case, subject to trade tax in Germany.

e) Taking Account of a Final Loss of a Foreign Permanent Establishment

A foreign PE has a final loss if, for factual reasons, the loss can no longer be used (e.g. discontinuance of the foreign PE, conversion of the foreign PE into a foreign corporation).

Example 11

A German corporation maintains a PE in France. In 2009 and 2010, the corporation suffers losses that are attributable to the PE. For this reason, the German corporation closes down its PE in 2010. The accrued 'final' loss of the PE is EUR 10m.

The German Federal Tax Court is of the opinion that it is possible to use, for trade-tax purposes, the final loss of a foreign PE.[2] The court held that, regardless of where the loss was caused territorially, it must be permitted once for deduction like a domestic loss, and that there was a need to avoid a loss disappearing

---

2 Federal Tax Court of 9 June 2010 – I R 107/09, BFH/NV 2010, p. 1744.

into a 'fiscal no-man's land'. It is necessary to consider this case law when preparing tax-related defence advice.

In our estimation, with reference to the territorial principle of trade tax, the German legislature will (by passing a law) 'counter' the use, for trade-tax purposes, of final losses of a foreign PE. When structuring cross-border situations, the risk of this change to trade-tax law must be considered.

f) Implications from Application of the Foreign Tax Act

When determining the trading profit of the domestic (i.e. German) business, the Foreign Tax Act must be observed. If a structure raises Foreign-Tax-Act issues, then this may also extend to the imposition of trade tax:

- An (off-balance-sheet) increase in income under Sec. 1 of the Foreign Tax Act affects, via Sec. 7 of the Trade Tax Act, the trading profit. As a result, any transfer-pricing adjustment made, for example, will affect the trading profit of the domestic business.

- If the property of the German business includes a (direct or indirect) stake in a foreign corporation that is subject to low taxation – and provided the statutory requirements are met – the German CFC (controlled-foreign-corporation) rules or 'add-back taxation' (*Hinzurechnungsbesteuerung*, Secs. 7 to 14 of the Foreign Tax Act) may become applicable. Via Sec. 7 of the Trade Tax Act, the add-back amount (Sec. 10 of the Foreign Tax Act) has a direct impact on the trading profit. The consequence of this is that the add-back amount – despite excessive taxation consequences in some cases – is generally subject to trade tax. A reduction under Sec. 9 no. 3 of the Trade Tax Act occurs only if there is a PE within the meaning of Sec. 12 of the Trade Tax Act in the foreign country. If the foreign corporation is neither covered by the Parent-Subsidiary Directive nor has 'active income' within the meaning of Sec. 8(1) nos. 1–6 of the Foreign Tax Act, then a reduction of the trading profit under Sec. 9 no. 7 of the Trade Tax Act is excluded as well. Since the add-back amount cannot be regarded as falling under the heading 'profits from shares in a foreign corporation', which under a DTT are tax-free, no reduction of the trading profit based on Sec. 9 no. 8 of the Trade Tax Act may be applied.[3]

- Under Sec. 12 of the Foreign Tax Act, the shareholder/partner may apply for credit of the tax attributable to the add-back amount; in this case, the tax deduction under Sec. 10(1) of the Foreign Tax Act is suspended with the effect of increasing the add-back amount. Via Sec. 7 of the Trade Tax Act, the increase in the add-back amount has a direct impact on the trading profit.

V. Summary

Trade tax as a (purely) domestic German tax has the potential to significantly impact on the trade-tax burden in certain cross-border scenarios. For this rea-

---

3 Tax Court of Düsseldorf of 28 Nov. 2013 – 16 K 2513/12 G; EFG 2014, p. 304.

son, trade-tax aspects must always be considered as well when fashioning inbound or outbound structures. Appropriate structuring can minimize trade-tax liability (or avoid it altogether). Points worth considering when devising a structure having regard to trade tax include – (i) avoidance (or specific structuring) of a German PE (e.g. by way of directly acquiring real estate rather than establishing a PE), (ii) taking advantage of reductions available under trade tax (e.g. establishment of a national or functional holding company, avoidance of profit distribution following the acquisition of a 'significant holding' in the course of the fiscal year) or (iii) the establishment of a tax group for the purpose of setting off (domestic) profits and losses within the group.

Dr. Arne von Freeden LL.M.

Lawyer, Certified Tax Lawyer, Tax Advisor

Areas of Specialization

- Business taxation
- Mergers & acquisitions and corporate reorganizations
- International tax law
- Tax litigation and procedural law

Telephone (ext.) +49 228/95 94-266 /-383
Email: arne.von-freeden@fgs.de

The Cornerstones and Quirks of Real Estate Transfer Tax

by Oliver Hötzel

Contents

I. Overview
II. Structure of Real Estate Transfer Tax
  1. Scope of Application
  2. Taxable Events
    a) Basic Event and Additional Events
    b) Share Transfer and Share Aggregation
    c) Changes of Partner
  3. Tax Exemptions
  4. Tax Assessment Basis
  5. Tax Rate
  6. Taxpayer
  7. Accounting Treatment of Real Estate Transfer Tax
  8. Notification Duties
  9. Reversal of Sale
III. Real Estate Transfer Tax in Selected Business Transactions
  1. Purchase of Shares in Corporations
  2. Change of Partner
  3. Purchase and Subsequent Merger of a Target
IV. Conclusion

I. Overview

German real estate transfer tax (*Grunderwerbsteuer*) is placing an ever greater burden on all kinds of businesses. The main reason is that this tax is imposed not just on the direct purchase and sale of commercial properties (office buildings, production sites etc.), but also, under certain conditions, on the purchase and sale of shareholdings or interests and on business restructurings.

Moreover, real estate transfer tax rates, which in the past were 2% for all of Germany, have since been raised to between 3.5% and 6.5% depending on the federal state, and therefore now average roughly 5%. The hike in tax rates was also accompanied by a significant increase in, and complication of, the events that trigger the tax (i.e. taxable events), particularly in the case of a change in or of business ownership.

The fundamental cornerstones of the German Real Estate Transfer Tax Act (*Grunderwerbsteuergesetz*) are described below. Thereafter, the special features of real estate transfer tax will be elucidated for some typical business transactions.

II. Structure of Real Estate Transfer Tax

1. Scope of Application

Real estate transfer tax applies to real estate situated in Germany and to *grundstücksgleiche Rechte*, which are effectively rights equivalent to real estate. The

German Civil Code (*Bürgerliches Gesetzbuch*) defines what falls within its scope of application. This also includes hereditary leasehold rights (*Erbbaurechte*) and buildings held on third party real estate.

It is important to distinguish the real estate itself from certain appurtenances which do not come within the scope of the Real Estate Transfer Tax Act. Appurtenances include 'fixtures and other nontaxable equipment' (*Betriebsvorrichtungen*). In practice, it is often difficult to make a distinction between the real estate on the one hand and fixtures and other nontaxable equipment on the other. However, it is worth addressing this issue because doing so may well lower any given assessment basis for real estate transfer tax.

Likewise, mineral exploitation rights (e.g. gravel extraction and other mining rights) must be deducted from the assessment of the real estate value.

2. Taxable Events

a) Basic Event and Additional Events

The basic event triggering taxation is the transfer of real property from one owner to another. It is important to remember that, in Germany, real estate is transferred in a two-step process. First, a real estate purchase contract is concluded in the presence of, and formally recorded by, a civil law notary (the *Verpflichtungsgeschäft*, which is a legally consequential act that creates an obligation). Then, as a second step, the ownership of the real estate in question is formally conveyed through an 'agreed title conveyance' (*Auflassung*) and an entry in the land register (the *Erfüllungsgeschäft*, which is a legally consequential act that discharges the obligation). The event triggering real estate transfer tax is the conclusion of a real estate purchase contract, and not the actual transfer of title when the land register entry is made.

In addition to this basic event, there are various other additional events which do not result in a formal legal transfer of ownership, but nevertheless lead to an economically comparable outcome. The reason for such additional events for triggering taxation is that real estate transfer tax law is very strictly construed. The 'substance over form' principle, which exists for tax accounting purposes and for other taxes such as corporate income tax and trade tax, does not apply. Hence, there is also no such thing as 'beneficial ownership'. This distinction becomes very obvious, e.g. in leases, which frequently attribute real estate to the lessee for accounting purposes, even though there has been no transfer for real estate transfer tax purposes.

The same principle applies to German trust relationships (*Treuhandverhältnisse*). If ownership of real estate passes to a trustee, then such transaction will trigger real estate transfer tax, even where the trustor is a beneficiary and remains solely entitled to the corpus and the income generated by the real estate. In the tax accounts, the real estate will instead be attributed to the trustor.

Due to this strictly formal approach to real estate transfer tax law, the legislature was compelled to incorporate into the law certain additional events triggering real estate transfer tax in specific scenarios. This is to cover cases which do not involve a transfer of legal title in real estate, but in actual fact lead to a similar outcome.

In practice, good examples of such a situation are when rights under a purchase agreement have been assigned and a right to use and enjoy real estate has been acquired.

One particularly important aspect for businesses is that the mere transfer of shares in an entity owning real estate could trigger real estate transfer tax under certain conditions. The prerequisites for corporations (including the *GmbH* and *AG*) differ from those for partnerships (including the *KG*, *GmbH & Co. KG*, *GbR*, and *OHG*).

b) Share Transfer and Share Aggregation

There is one rule that applies equally to both corporations and partnerships alike, namely that real estate transfer tax will be triggered if at least 95% of the ownership interests or shareholdings are transferred to a single purchaser ('share transfer') or if a single person by way of acquisition accumulates at least 95% of the ownership interests or shares in the business ('share aggregation'). If e.g. one person already holds 90% of the shares and acquires a total of 5% from another shareholder, then by virtue of purchasing that percentage, real estate transfer tax will be triggered on the business's entire real estate holdings.

In this regard, it is necessary to consider various implications that arise because the 95% interest does not need to be held by simply one person. Instead, the shares of various related entities will be aggregated in the following situations:

a) All shares of corporations which hold at least a 95% stake in one another will be aggregated.

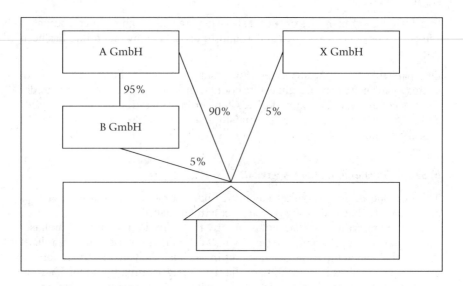

Under this structure, the shares of A GmbH are aggregated because it has a direct 90% holding and a 5% indirect holding in the entity owning real estate.

b) All shares in corporations which constitute a tax group for real estate transfer tax purposes (*grunderwerbsteuerliche Organschaft*) will be aggregated. A tax group for real estate transfer tax purposes will be deemed to exist if one corporation is financially, economically and organizationally integrated into another entity. Financial integration can exist when the owner holds more than 50%. Organizational integration can exist when at least some of the board members of both entities are identical so that the parent is able to assert its will over the subsidiary *via* the board members. Economic integration has to be construed broadly and will be presumed to exist if e.g. the parent is a holding company and the subsidiary is an operating company. This is very dangerous in practice because often one is completely unaware that the various entities constitute a tax group. This is the case particularly when the organizationally integrated entities are resident outside Germany, where there is no real awareness of issues related to German real estate transfer tax.

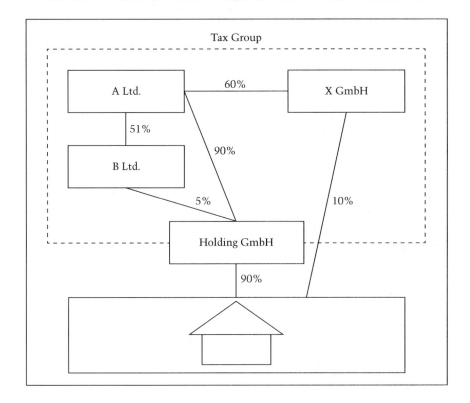

In the above example, share aggregation within the tax group exists because the group holds a 95% share in Holding GmbH so that the shares which Holding GmbH has in the entity owning real estate may be attributed to the tax group.

c) In 2013, legislation was tightened and now requires all shares in an entity holding real estate which are held by various interrelated companies to be added together on a *pro rata* basis. No minimum threshold exists for such aggregation, but rather each equity holding is included *pro rata* at each level. This new legislative provision is intended to prevent the creation of 'RETT blocker structures,' which had been previously deployed (see part III. 1. below).

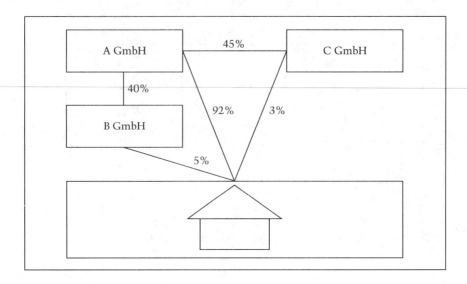

There is an aggregation of shares in the above case because A GmbH would be attributed a 95.35% holding in the entity owning real estate (92% + (40% x 5%) + (45% x 3%) = 95.35).

c) Changes of Partner

There is another taxable event that comes into play exclusively for partnerships. If at least 95% of the partners in a partnership which holds real estate should change within a period of five years, then the partnership must pay real estate transfer tax on its real estate holdings. Unlike share aggregation, where there has been an acquisition or aggregation of a 95% interest by one single person, a change of partner can also involve numerous partners. However, the prerequisite is that partner ownership interests be transferred to new partners. Shifts in the percentages held by existing partners will not trigger the tax.

Under certain conditions, an indirect change of partners can also trigger the tax. This always entails the risk in international structures that a change of partner at any given tier (frequently also outside Germany) can trigger German real estate transfer tax, even if the foreign partners are completely unaware of this possibility.

3. Tax Exemptions

For many of the events that would trigger real estate transfer tax, there is a tax exemption which prevents an actual tax obligation from arising. These tax exemptions are very different in nature and relate, for example, to:

- transfers made between relatives or spouses;
- events which are subject to gift or inheritance tax;

- *pro rata* tax exemptions if real estate is transferred from partners to the partnership or *vice versa*; or
- intragroup restructuring measures subject to very restrictive conditions.

In business practice, the two last exemptions are of major interest. If a partner sells real estate to a partnership in which he has an ownership interest, or if he contributes such an asset to the partnership, then that event will be exempted to the extent of that partner's *pro rata* interest in the partnership. Thus, if the transferor is the only partner (owner), then the transfer will be completely exempt. The same rule applies where the partnership sells the real estate to its partners.

It should be remembered, however, that the percentage of ownership interests in the partnership may not change for a period of five years following such a transfer. If such change does occur, then the tax exemption will be revoked retroactively.

A similar exemption also applies to real estate transfers between two partnerships which are owned by at least some of the same partners. This exemption is granted insofar as the partners in question hold the same percentage of ownership interests in both partnerships. The percentage of ownership interests must be maintained for a period of five years in that case as well. Another requirement is that the same percentage of ownership interests has existed for at least five years prior to the real estate transfer.

The exemption for intragroup real estate transfers, which was introduced in 2010, is intended to ease internal restructurings. Requirements for this exemption are so strict and so complex, however, that the provision has only limited application. Nevertheless, certain events which would have triggered real estate transfer tax in the past are now frequently tax-exempt in practice.

This provision is applicable if

- real estate is acquired by way of a corporate transaction, in particular through reorganization, merger, division, capital contribution etc.; and
- the transfer is made within a group which consists of a controlling entity and at least one controlled entity; and
- the controlling entity has held a minimum of 95% in the controlled entity for more than five years; and
- the 95% ownership interest is held for at least five years.

4. Tax Assessment Basis

The Real Estate Transfer Tax Act has various bases for assessment, the application of which depends on the relevant facts.

If real estate is sold, the purchase price is used as an assessment basis. If the purchase price also includes fixtures and other nontaxable equipment etc., then such items must be deducted from the purchase price.

In any case, the principle that the actually agreed purchase price serves as the basis of assessment will govern even if that price (e.g. on intragroup sales) were deliberately set too low. In other words, if a real estate owner sells its real estate to a related party for 10% of the market value, then this purchase price will still be used to compute the real estate transfer tax arising. This can obviously be used for structuring purposes. What is not acceptable, however, is merely a symbolic purchase price, such as EUR 1. It is not entirely clear where that line should be drawn.

A separate assessment basis applies to corporate transactions such as reorganizations or capital contributions, and to share aggregations and a change of partners. In those cases, the value of real estate is generally calculated using the income approach, which is based on the future earnings value of the real estate and on that of the building as calculated according to customary local rents. In either case, the gross value of the real estate is applied; debts or liabilities may not be deducted from that amount.

If, however, any undeveloped land is acquired, for which property development obligation was agreed, then the value of the development will also be factored into the assessment basis for real estate transfer tax.

5. Tax Rate

The tax rate is determined separately by the individual German federal states. In 2014, the following tax rates applied:

Federal State	Tax Rate
Baden-Württemberg	5.0%
Bavaria	3.5%
Berlin	6.0%
Brandenburg	5.0%
Bremen	5.0%
Hamburg	4.5%
Hesse	6.0%
Mecklenburg-Pomerania	5.0%
Lower Saxony	5.0%
North Rhine Westphalia	5.0%
Rhineland-Palatinate	5.0%
Saarland	6.5%
Saxony	3.5%
Saxony-Anhalt	5.0%

Federal State	Tax Rate
Schleswig-Holstein	6.5%
Thuringia	5.0%

6. Taxpayer

In general, real estate transfer tax is owed by both the seller and the purchaser. Nevertheless, the parties usually agree by contract that the purchaser will pay the real estate transfer tax.

If shares are aggregated, the taxpayer will be the purchaser(s) in whose hands the aggregation occurs.

One special feature applies to a change of partner. In that case, the partnership itself is the taxpayer. Where partnership interests are purchased, this fact must be taken into account because the purchaser will automatically acquire any real estate transfer tax due as a liability of the partnership. This also applies to earlier changes of partner which were previously unnoticed. Therefore, tax clauses in purchase agreements on partnership interests must address and regulate the issue of real estate transfer tax.

7. Accounting Treatment of Real Estate Transfer Tax

An important element determining the economic effect of real estate transfer tax is whether it should be accounted for as an additional cost of acquisition or can be immediately deducted as an operating expense. In this regard, a distinction should be made between various sets of circumstances:

When real estate is purchased, real estate transfer tax constitutes an incidental cost of acquiring the real estate. Real estate transfer tax must therefore be recognized and can be used to reduce income tax or corporate income tax only in the form of future depreciation (to the extent attributable to buildings) or by creating a higher book value for a subsequent sale.

The accounting is handled differently for the transfer or aggregation of shares. Recently, the Federal Tax Court (*Bundesfinanzhof*) held, contrary to the position taken by the tax authorities, that real estate transfer tax should not be considered an incidental cost of acquiring shares or the real estate held by the business.[1] It is therefore immediately tax deductible as an operating expense.

The accounting treatment of the purchase of partnerships is still uncertain. The tax authorities maintain the view that real estate transfer tax levied on any real estate held by a partnership must be recognized. The reasoning behind this view is that German income tax law presupposes that, in cases involving the purchase of partnership interests, the purchaser is acquiring the individual business assets of the partnership (partnership pass-through transparency). On

---

1 Federal Tax Court, 20.4.2011 – IR 2/10, Federal Tax Gazette II, 2011, p. 761.

the other hand, the better view should probably be that even where partnership interests are sold, it should be possible to immediately deduct real estate transfer tax as a business expense. This issue will remain unresolved, however, until the Federal Tax Court has rendered a final decision.

8. Notification Duties

In order to ensure that real estate transfer tax can also be levied in full, parties to a transaction face extensive reporting duties.

Since a normal real estate purchase contract must be formally recorded by a German notary, the notaries are under an obligation to file notification with the local tax office. In these cases, the parties typically do not need to do anything else.

On taxable events, for which a notary's recordation is not involved, and for share aggregations and changes of partner, the taxpayer is required to report the transaction in question to the tax authorities within two weeks. The same duty of notification also applies to transactions in which a waiting period related to a tax exemption is breached. If the notification is not filed in a timely manner, then such failure could constitute tax evasion. Based on recent developments, it appears that the tax authorities are highly sensitive in this area. Since indirect changes in shareholding or interests can also trigger tax or lead to a breach of a waiting period, taxpayers are sometimes unaware of such taxable events. In this case, they might fail to discharge their notification duties, thus being exposed to significant risk.

9. Reversal of Sale

If the original sale of real estate or sale of ownership interests in a business is reversed, then real estate transfer tax will also not be levied. The following cases should be distinguished:

Where only a contract was concluded and the title to the property has not yet passed, real estate transfer tax will not be levied if the reversal is either based on an agreement and takes place within two years after the tax arose or because certain contractual obligations have not been performed (no time limit).

If title already passed, then real estate transfer tax will not be charged, either, for the original transfer or for the reverse transfer, provided that either the reverse transfer occurred within two years or the original acquisition contract was null and void or the re-acquisition was made because certain contractual obligations were not performed (no time limit).

For all transactions requiring notification (such as share aggregation and a change of partner), the provisions governing the reversal of a sale will apply only if the notification was duly and timely made. This entails a significant inherent risk. If, for example, all ownership interests in a partnership are acquired and such acquisition transaction is reversed within two years, then real estate transfer tax will be assessed twice in the event that the original acquisition had not been timely notified.

III. Real Estate Transfer Tax in Selected Business Transactions

1. Purchase of Shares in Corporations

In an acquisition of all the shares in a corporation, real estate transfer tax is an important issue. Since the tax rates can be up to 6.5% of the value of the real estate concerned, this tax can lead to a very significant additional charge. This is particularly the case, of course, in the purchase of entities whose assets consist almost entirely of German real estate. Here a transaction will usually not be concluded if real estate transfer tax is unavoidable.

Until early 2013, transactional parties used 'RETT Blocker structures' in which typically Purchaser GmbH would buy 94.9% of the shares in a corporation. The remaining 5.1% of the shares would be purchased by a partnership in which a third party would hold a 0% interest and Purchaser GmbH would hold a 100% interest. As the interposed partnership effectively blocked the aggregation of shares for the purposes of real estate transfer tax, Purchaser GmbH held a 100% beneficial interest in the target without triggering real estate transfer tax.

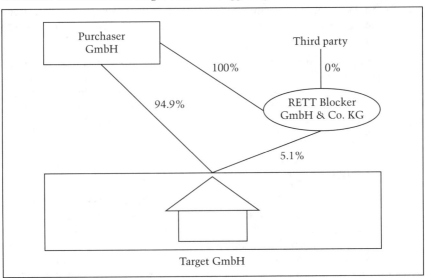

In mid-2013, a legislative change was enacted according to which all direct or indirect holdings are now factored into the computation (see above under part II.2.b)cc)). Under this new law, the previously described structure no longer blocks real estate transfer tax.

Against this background, the structuring options that can be implemented are now rather limited. In essence, the following approaches could be considered:

- 94.9% of an entity holding real estate is purchased by the primary purchaser. The remaining 5.1% of the shares in the target are acquired by a 'friendly' third party. The parties should make sure that relations between the main purchaser and the third party are not close enough for their respective shares to be aggregated for the purposes of real estate transfer tax.
- 5.1% of the shares are retained by the original seller. This person receives a guaranteed dividend in an amount that gives it an incentive to remain an owner. The purchaser enters into a control agreement with the target, which allows it to unconditionally assert its control over the target even against the will of the 5.1% shareholder. By virtue of a purchase option, the purchaser is assured that it or a third party designated by it can acquire the 5.1% holding at a later time and at a set price.
- Since only a change in ownership is relevant, real estate transfer tax can be avoided by entering into certain types of loan agreement. Instead of acquiring a shareholding in the target, the 'purchaser' grants a profit-sharing loan to the target or invests therein as a silent partner. The terms attached to the loan or to the silent partnership ensure that the purchaser receives or bears all the target's profits or losses and the full amount of any increase or decrease in the value of the its business, respectively. Such a granting of a loan or participation as a silent partner is usually combined with an acquisition of less than 95% of the shares in the target. In this way, the purchaser can effectively be in the same position it would have been in if it had acquired 100% of the shares.

It is important to remember that in all structuring measures, a number of details must be observed and parties should always check whether the structure could be necessarily deemed as abusive. Since frequently no clear answer can be found in these cases, parties should consider obtaining a binding advance ruling. The more aggressive the structure is, the less likely it is that the requested advance ruling will in fact be issued.

2. Change of Partner

When interests in partnerships are purchased, two different taxable events can arise. On the one hand, the previously described principles regarding share transfer to a single purchaser or share aggregation in the hands of a single purchaser will apply without limitation to the purchase of a partnership interest. On the other hand, a transaction could be subject to real estate transfer tax if 95% of the partners (directly or indirectly) change within five years. This latter triggering event takes precedence over and supersedes the aggregation of shares/share transfer.

If a partnership is acquired in its entirety, then there will be a complete change of partners, and real estate transfer tax will be triggered.

Unlike the case of share aggregation or share transfer, the tactic of having a 'friendly' third party purchase the remaining 5.1% of the ownership interests at the same time that 94.9% of the ownership interests are acquired will not be helpful here, inasmuch as the taxable event will also be triggered once a transfer is made to various purchasers.

As an avoidance strategy, however, the idea of having the previous partners/sellers hold back 5.1% of the ownership interest should once again be considered. After five years, the purchaser could purchase the remaining 5.1% of the ownership interests because only changes of partner that occur during a five-year period are aggregated. However, in that case, the aggregation of shares would also trigger a taxable event, which means that the strategy is initially subject to real estate transfer tax. Nevertheless, in that case, a tax exemption of 94.9% would apply because the previous partners had held this amount for more than five years. Thus, only a total of 5.1% of the ownership interests would be subject to real estate transfer tax.

If one wishes to avoid this 5.1% real estate transfer tax as well, then one could have the remaining 5.1% purchased by a friendly third party after the expiry of five years. This approach would avoid not only an immediate change of partner but also the aggregation of shares. In order to obtain some certainty that the remaining 5.1% of the ownership interest would in fact be acquired, the purchaser may wish to be granted an option that would give it the right after five years to designate a third party who could purchase the shares at a price previously defined. A unilateral option in this context should be not be harmful. If the parties agree to a combined call and put option, then such arrangement would pose a significant risk that the 5.1% purchase will be deemed to have already occurred.

In any case, even where partnership interests are purchased, it is possible to avoid real estate transfer tax by relying on other, previously described instruments such as a profit-sharing loan or a silent partnership.

3. Purchase and Subsequent Merger of a Target

It is often the case that the purchaser seeks to merge the purchased target into an acquisition vehicle or another group company. Such an approach can be feasible either from a tax perspective (in order to improve the deductibility of interest payments) or for purely corporate policy reasons.

In general, purchasing all of a target's shares will trigger real estate transfer tax liability as described above. This subsequent merger constitutes an additional event triggering real estate transfer tax because the real estate is transferred directly from the target to the acquiring entity. If the target is merged into the purchaser, then two events triggering real estate transfer tax will have occurred. Since both transactions involve the same real estate, however, the first real estate transfer tax will be credited against the second real estate transfer tax. In other words, real estate transfer tax is levied only once.

If, on the other hand, the target is merged into a subsidiary of the purchaser, then real estate transfer tax has to be paid twice. In order to avoid this double taxation, the target can sell the real estate to the purchaser's subsidiary prior to the share purchase. This arrangement would then trigger real estate transfer tax only once. If the shares are then sold and the merger takes place, then no additional real estate transfer tax would be owed because the target no longer holds any real estate. It is important in this regard that the chronological link between the contracts and the actual transfers are managed in such a manner that the desired result does in fact occur. In any case, corporate income tax effects have to be taken into account.

IV. Conclusion

Since tax rates are constantly on the increase, real estate transfer tax creates a significant burden for businesses. This is particularly true when businesses are sold or restructured, given that real estate transfer tax is tied to the gross value of the relevant real estate (i.e. liabilities may not be deducted).

In international business structures, past experience has shown that undesired and unknown events frequently arise which trigger real estate transfer tax. This risk is particularly high because board members living and working outside Germany might be unaware that ownership changes or restructurings can have significant real estate transfer tax consequences in Germany.

Even though the potential structuring strategies for avoiding real estate transfer tax on acquisitions have been limited by legislative changes recently, there are still various measures in practice which can avoid or at least reduce real estate transfer tax.

The Real Estate Transfer Tax Act does provide for one tax exemption for certain types of intragroup restructuring. Nevertheless, given the complexity of the provisions and due to the strict requirements for qualifying for such an exemption, not all restructuring measures can be implemented without triggering real estate transfer tax liability.

Due to these many uncertainties, parties are frequently advised to take certain precautionary measures such as securing a binding advance ruling from the local tax office responsible.

Dr. Oliver Hötzel

Public Auditor, Tax Advisor

Areas of Specialization

- Mergers & acquisitions and corporate reorganizations
- Structuring of real-estate investments
- Taxation of corporate groups
- Tax accounting

Telephone (ext.) +49 228/95 94-637

Email: oliver.hoetzel@fgs.de

6. Tax Procedure

Tax Disputes and Litigation in Germany

by Michael Hendricks

Contents

I. Introduction and Overview
II. Subject Matter of a Legal Dispute
III. Tax Disputes Following a Tax Audit
IV. Administrative Appeal Procedure Before the Tax Authorities
V. Court Proceedings in the Lower Tax Courts
   1. Normal course of litigation
   2. Termination of court proceedings without issuance of a judgment
VI. Appellate Proceedings Before the Federal Tax Court
VII. Non-Admission Complaint Before the Federal Tax Court
VIII. Constitutional Complaint to the Federal Constitutional Court
IX. Role of the European Court of Justice
X. Temporary Legal Protection
XI. Legal Protection Against International Double Taxation

I. Introduction and Overview

In Germany, there is a well-established culture of tax disputes. Where a taxpayer considers the tax imposed by the authority to be incorrect in law, he has the constitutional right to seek a court review of the decision taken by the relevant public authority (Art. 19(4) German Constitution – *Grundgesetz*). Taxpayers do quite frequently make use of this option. As a rule, tax disputes are handled in a constructive way by all private parties and tax authorities involved. This is also true of tax officials when their administrative actions are subjected to scrutiny; in general they do not take it personally if a tax claim they have issued is reviewed by a court. Only in a very small minority of cases does the dispute between the taxpayer and the authority escalate into an emotional conflict.

A taxpayer's initial response to a potentially incorrect tax assessment notice does not necessarily end in court proceedings. Where the taxpayer considers the tax assessment notice to be unlawful, he must initially object to the tax authority that issued the notice. This extrajudicial remedy is referred as an 'administrative appeal' (*Einspruch*). These administrative proceedings, which must be conducted prior to initiating litigation in court, are intended to reduce the workload of the courts. A further purpose of such administrative appeal is to enable the authorities to review their own tax assessment notice (self-regulation by the tax administration).

The right to file an administrative appeal against a tax assessment notice or another act of the tax authorities is widely used by taxpayers. According to statistics from the German Federal Finance Ministry, the number of administrative appeals filed in recent years (2009 to 2013) has ranged from 3.6 million to 5.24 million per year. Such administrative appeal filings are very frequently successful, meaning that court proceedings can be avoided. In more than two-thirds of all cases, the administrative appeal results in the challenged measure (e.g. the tax assessment notice) being modified as requested by the taxpayer. On average, such appeal proceedings take between three and twelve months.

Where the administrative appeal is not successful, the tax authorities are required to issue a formal notice of denial ('administrative appeal decision' – *Einspruchsentscheidung*). The taxpayer may then submit this administrative appeal decision to a tax court for a review of its lawfulness. Independent of and unrelated to the tax authorities, the tax courts rule on the soundness of decisions taken by the tax authorities. There are 18 such lower tax courts in Germany in total. The most recent statistics available (2009 to 2012) show that 41,000 new claims were brought on average before the German tax courts per year. The average length of proceedings ranges between 10 and 25 months (depending on the tax court) although the length of the proceedings will depend to a very large degree on the complexity of the dispute and the workload of the panel dealing with the matter. In addition, the duration of the proceedings will depend upon whether there are questions of fact to be determined. Experience has shown that where fact-finding proves difficult, proceedings will tend to be lengthy.

As a rule, the tax courts render their decisions by issuing a judgment. The court's judgment affirms, sets aside or modifies the tax authority's administrative appeal decision. Due to the intensive workload associated with rendering a judgment, judges will avoid doing so if a different solution is more feasible. Where the court has read into the case and considers the outcome to be clear, it advises the parties of its preliminary opinion. In many cases, the tax authorities are encouraged to modify the challenged state measure (e.g. the tax assessment notice) in favor of the taxpayer in order to avoid a judgment going against the authority. It can also be the case that the court advises the taxpayer to withdraw his claim. Approximately two-thirds of all cases are concluded in this way, without any judgment being issued. In a maximum of roughly 20 % of cases in which a judgment is issued does the tax court rule in favor of the taxpayer, either in whole or in part. The fact that taxpayers lose their cases more frequently than they win them is likely related to the fact that taxpayers do not have to be represented by counsel before the lower tax courts. Many taxpayers will litigate without engaging an experienced lawyer or tax advisor to represent them.

An unsuccessful party that does not accept the judgment may appeal to the German Federal Tax Court in Munich. In principle, this option applies only if the lower tax court has allowed an appeal to the Federal Tax Court. Appellate proceedings before the Federal Tax Court take roughly 20 months on average. The ratio of successful appeals by taxpayers is over 40 %.

Court fees are charged for proceedings before both types of court. The amount of those fees will depend on the amount in dispute. In the lower tax court, the costs on an amount in dispute of EUR 500,000, for example, will run to EUR 14,144, whereas appellate proceedings before the Federal Tax Court will trigger court costs of EUR 17,680. However, these court costs will be borne by the taxpayer only if he fails to prevail in the proceedings. Where he wins the case, the taxpayer is not charged any court costs. No administrative charges have to be paid for administrative appeal proceedings before the tax authorities, irrespective of their outcome.

As a general principle, the taxpayer must always bear the cost of any advisors he engages (lawyer or tax advisor). However, if the taxpayer prevails in litigation or appellate proceedings, the tax authority is required to reimburse the taxpayer for the fees he has paid to such advisors (the amount of which is regulated by law).

II. Subject Matter of a Legal Dispute

As a rule, the dispute between the taxpayer and the tax authority will be about the lawfulness of a tax assessment notice. In certain scenarios, however, the issuance of a tax assessment notice is preceded by preliminary decisions that are binding with respect to the subsequent tax assessment notice (Sec. 182 of the German General Tax Code – *Abgabenordnung*). In that case, the preliminary decision will then be the subject matter of the court litigation. Thus, pursuant to legal doctrine in Germany, partnerships themselves are not subject to income tax or corporation tax, but rather such tax is payable only by the private individuals or corporate entities holding a stake in the partnership (transparency principle). The profit attributed to the partners is determined by the tax authority with jurisdiction over the partnership and assessed by a special administrative act ('assessment ruling' – *Feststellungsbescheid*) which, in turn, is binding for purposes of the partners' personal tax assessment notices.[1] If one of the partners regards the assessment ruling as contrary to law, then in such case he cannot challenge his personal tax assessment notice, but rather is required to take action against the partnership assessment ruling. The requirement is that the taxpayer must always challenge the assessment ruling in which the error 'is rooted'. Preliminary assessment rulings of this kind exist in a number of different scenarios. This holds true, in particular, with respect to international tax cases (e.g. in cases involving CFC rules on 'addback taxation' – *Hinzuberechnungsbesteuerung*). With respect of local taxes (e.g. trade tax), there are similar preliminary assessment rulings (e.g. 'basic nonpersonal tax assessment notice' – *Steuermessbescheid*). If these assessment rulings are contrary to law, the taxpayer is required to object to them generally within a period of one month: On no account should he wait for issuance of the tax assessment notice that is based on such preliminary decisions.

---

1 cf. e.g. *Piltz*, StBp. 1989, pp. 193 *et seqq.*

Criminal sanctions are not imposed within tax dispute proceedings. If the tax authorities are of the view that a taxpayer has committed a tax offense, then criminal proceedings will be initiated against the taxpayer. Where the suspicion against the taxpayer is confirmed, criminal sanctions may be imposed on the taxpayer. However, these cases are not handled by the tax authorities alone, but rather the Public Prosecutor's Office takes the lead in proceedings. Any criminal sanctions will not be imposed by a tax court, but by the general criminal courts.

III. Tax Disputes Following a Tax Audit

As a rule, the German tax authorities will accept information provided for by the taxpayer in his tax return. Ordinarily, a tax dispute arises in the course of a tax audit. The tax authorities are entitled to implement findings they have made in a tax audit by amending previous assessment notices (tax assessment notices or preliminary tax assessment rulings). If the findings made during a tax audit result in an increased level of tax, then the authorities may thus modify previous assessment notices to the detriment of the taxpayer. Before the assessment notices are modified, the auditor initially prepares a report of his findings at the end of the audit ('audit report'). However, that audit report cannot be appealed. The taxpayer may submit only the assessment notices modified as a consequence of the audit report (tax assessment notices/preliminary tax assessment rulings) for judicial review.

As a rule, the question of whether a tax audit of a taxpayer is carried out will depend on the size of the business entity and its turnover/profit. In the case of large enterprises and corporate groups, every tax year is audited. In the case of very small enterprises and taxpayers with low levels of income, an audit is performed by way of exception rather than as the rule. Particular or unusual events may result in an audit even in cases of low turnover or profit (e.g. in the case of discrepancies in the taxpayer's tax return or where there are reorganization measures).

IV. Administrative Appeal Procedure Before the Tax Authorities

If the legal propriety of a tax assessment notice or similar measures has to be judicially reviewed, then an administrative appeal procedure (*Einspruchsverfahren*) must first be carried out before the tax authority (Sec. 44(1) of the German Tax Court Code – *Finanzgerichtsordnung*). The purpose of these procedures is to reduce the workload of the courts and to ensure self-regulation by the tax authorities. The appeal must be filed with the authority that issued the tax assessment notice within one month of service of the notice. The appeal must specify the points being appealed. However, submission of grounds of appeal (supportive appellate brief) is not required within that one-month period; these grounds may be submitted subsequently. It is also possible to file an appeal initially as a precaution (e.g. because it is not clear by the end of the one-month period whether the assessment notice is lawful). As no charges are levied on appeal proceedings before a tax authority, in practice taxpayers very frequently avail themselves of this option. In certain cases, no appeal proceedings before the tax authority are possible. In those cases, the taxpayer must waive any appeal proceedings before the authority and directly file an appeal in court against the assessment notice. In practice, this tends to be the exception.[2]

An appeal against an assessment notice (or similar measures) must be filed with the tax authority that issued the notice/ruling. At the tax authority, the initial decision on the appeal is made by the tax official who was responsible for the assessment notice. Where he does not see a good justification for the appeal, he forwards the case to another office within the tax authority, which deals exclusively with such appeals ('Legal Remedies Office' – *Rechtsbehelfsstelle*). This ensures that the final decision is not made by the official who was responsible for the assessment notice being challenged.

V. Court Proceedings in the Lower Tax Courts

Where the initial appeal procedure within the tax authority meets with no success, the tax authority rejects the appeal by an administrative appeal decision (see section I. above). The taxpayer now has the option of having that administrative appeal decision reviewed by a court. In general, jurisdiction in tax matters is vested in the lower tax courts. In rare cases, the appeal must be brought before the general administrative courts.[3]

1. Normal course of litigation

As a rule, a taxpayer must file his claim with the competent tax court within one month of notification of the administrative appeal decision. The question of which of the 18 tax courts has jurisdiction then arises. This will depend on what tax authority has issued the administrative appeal decision. The claim must specify what decision is being challenged. In addition, the statement of claim must indicate what the taxpayer considers the legal breach to be (Sec. 65 of the Tax Court Code). It is not necessary to submit the grounds of claim within the one-month period. Upon receipt of the claim, the panel dealing with the matter will set a deadline for submitting the grounds of the claim. As a rule, grounds for the statement of claim must be filed within four to six weeks from the date of filing the claim. In complex cases, the deadline for submitting grounds of the claim may be extended upon request. After the grounds of the claim have been submitted, the tax authority is given the opportunity to make written submissions in reply. The taxpayer is then permitted to comment on the submissions by the tax authority. As a rule, the parties' written arguments will be completed roughly six months following the submission of the grounds of the claim.

---

2 In some federal states (*Länder*), there is no possibility of pursuing legal remedies before the tax authorities when challenging trade tax assessment notices.
3 Thus, trade tax assessment notices must be challenged in the administrative courts rather than in the tax courts.

The further course of the proceeding will depend to a very large degree on what questions are at issue in the dispute. Where the dispute primarily centers on questions of fact, the court will take evidence. The court takes evidence primarily by hearing witnesses and reviewing documents. In certain individual cases, the court will engage experts. The taking of evidence takes place in the course of a court hearing. As a rule, the litigation will be concluded more quickly where the parties' dispute is exclusively on questions of law. After conducting the hearing, the tax court decides by means of a court judgment whether the taxpayer's claim is admissible and well-founded.

The tax courts sit in 'panels' to rule on claims. A panel consists of three professional judges and two lay judges (meaning a total of five judges). Experience has shown that the lay judges have only little influence on the decision. Although they do have fully-fledged voting rights in the case, their vote will usually follow that of the professional judges. Within the group of the three professional judges, the chief judge has particular influence. As presiding judge, he is responsible for the organization of the panel's work. The chief judge ordinarily puts his particular 'stamp' on the decision-making practices of his panel. Where the legal dispute is particularly simple both in terms of the facts and in terms of the legal issues to be determined, the legal case may be transferred to a judge sitting as a sole judge (Sec. 6 of the German Tax Court Code). Only a professional judge may sit as a sole judge. The transfer of a case to a sole judge is intended to accelerate litigation. As previously noted, the average duration of court proceedings is roughly 24 months.

2. Termination of court proceedings without issuance of a judgment

As drafting a judgment entails considerable time and expense and a judgment does not necessarily create legal peace between the parties, judges frequently seek to terminate the proceedings without a judgment. Where the panel considers the case to be clear, the parties are frequently given an indication of the direction in which the court is leaning. If the judges deem the claim to be well-founded, then the authority is advised to modify the challenged state action (e.g. the tax assessment notice) in favor of the taxpayer, in order to avoid a judgment against the tax authority. Where the situation is reversed, the court will advise the taxpayer to withdraw his claim to avoid dismissal of the claim. Roughly two-thirds of all proceedings are terminated in this way, without any judgment being issued.

When a tax dispute is pending, the German tax administration is not allowed to accept a compromise on questions of law. It is inferred from the constitutional principle of the rule of law that, in respect of questions of law, the tax authorities are strictly bound by the law. For this reason, cases cannot be resolved by amicable settlement where the dispute is over a question of law. Nevertheless, where the dispute is not one of law, but rather involves a question of fact (i.e. the question of what facts transpired), the tax authority is permitted to reach an amicable settlement with the taxpayer to agree what facts should be taken as the basis for taxation in the specific case. Nevertheless, the competent officials will only ever consent to a resolution of this kind if they are able to establish in a sufficiently clear manner that the compromise is exclusively on questions of fact rather than questions of law. In practice, this is possible very often. As a rule, such a settlement is already concluded at the time of a tax audit. However, this tool is also frequently used in the course of litigation in the tax courts.

VI. Appellate Proceedings Before the Federal Tax Court

If the lower tax court issues a judgment that the unsuccessful party considers to be unlawful, then that party may appeal to the Federal Tax Court. In principle, however, this option only ever applies where the lower tax court has allowed an appeal to the Federal Tax Court as a part of its ruling on the claim (Sec. 115(1) of the German Tax Court Code).

Where the appeal has been allowed, the unsuccessful party may request a review of the judgment by the Federal Tax Court. However, the sole point of challenge before the Federal Tax Court is that the lower tax court incorrectly adjudicated questions of law. The challenge must be directed against a breach of German federal law. As a matter of principle, in such appellate proceedings, the taxpayer cannot argue that the lower tax court's decision was based on incorrect findings of fact. If the unsuccessful party considers the findings of fact of the lower tax court to be incorrect, then that party may seek to have the judgment set aside only if he demonstrates to the Federal Tax Court that the judgment in question arose through a breach of procedural rules ('challenge of procedural error' – *Verfahrensfehler*). Where the Federal Tax Court accepts that such procedural error was made, the legal dispute is ordinarily remanded to the lower tax court (Sec. 126(3) no. 2 of the German Tax Court Code). In these cases, the proceedings of first instance must then be relitigated.

The deadline for filing an appeal in the Federal Tax Court ends one month from the date of service of the judgment of the lower tax court. The appeal to the Federal Tax Court must, in principle, be followed by grounds of appeal filed two months from the date the lower tax court's judgment was served (Sec. 120 of the German Tax Court Code). The average duration of Federal Tax Court appellate proceedings is currently approximately 20 months. The Federal Tax Court likewise has panels consisting of five judges. However, at the Federal Tax Court, the panels are made up exclusively of professional judges. Just as in the lower tax courts, the decision-making practices of a panel will be particularly influenced by the chief judge of that panel.

VII. Non-Admission Complaint Before the Federal Tax Court

If the litigation ends by judgment issued and if the lower tax court has not admitted the appeal to the Federal Tax Court, the unsuccessful party may file a non-admission complaint – a complaint against denial of leave to appeal (*Nichtzulassungsbeschwerde*) – with the Federal Tax Court (Sec. 116 of the Tax Court Code). A complaint of this kind will succeed if the unsuccessful party is able to demonstrate that the lower tax court should actually have admitted the appeal to the Federal Tax Court. That party must demonstrate that a question of law which was of crucial relevance to the ruling of the lower tax court has hitherto not been addressed by the Federal Tax Court ('question of fundamental significance' – *grundsätzliche Bedeutung*) or that the lower tax court has departed from a Federal Tax Court decision (*Divergenz*). A complaint will also be successful if the taxpayer demonstrates to the Federal Tax Court that the judgment came about by a breach of procedural rules ('challenge of procedural error' – *Verfahrensfehler*). The deadline for filing a complaint ends one month from the date the lower tax court judgment is served (Sec. 116(2) of the German Tax Court Code). As a basic principle, grounds for the complaint must be submitted two months from the date of service of the lower tax court's judgment (Sec. 116(3) of the Tax Court Code). On average, the Federal Tax Court will rule in the case within six months' time from the date the complaint was filed.

VIII. Constitutional Complaint to the Federal Constitutional Court

Where the taxpayer has no success with the remedies he pursues, then after exhausting all the levels of appeal he may seek redress before the German Federal Constitutional Court in Karlsruhe by way of constitutional complaint (Sec. 90 of the Federal Constitutional Court Act – *Bundesverfassungsgerichtsgesetz*). An appeal of this kind will make sense only if the taxpayer is able to demonstrate that there has been a breach of constitutional law (i.e. a breach of the Constitution). The appeal must be filed and grounds for the appeal submitted within one month of notice of the final court decision. Constitutional complaints against decisions of lower tax courts or of the Federal Tax Court have occasionally been successful in the past. Thus, the Federal Constitutional Court has, for example, ruled that certain cases involving a tightening of statutory rules have produced an impermissible retroactive effect, or that the courts have infringed a party's right to a fair hearing.[4] The duration of a constitutional complaint procedure will depend very much on the situation of the individual case. Whereas a ruling on some constitutional complaints is issued within only a few months, constitutional complaints with a particularly broad scope will often remain pending for several years.

IX. Role of the European Court of Justice

The task of the European Court of Justice is to ensure uniform application of European Union law in all of the member states. However, a taxpayer does not have the option of seeking redress himself in the European Court of Justice. This is a major distinction relative to the Federal Constitutional Court, to which a taxpayer may directly address a constitutional complaint after having exhausted all levels of appeal.

---

4 cf. e.g. Federal Constitutional Court of 7 July 2010 – 2 BvR 748/05, 2 BvR 753/05, 2 BvR 1738/05, BVerfGE, pp.127 and 61.

In practice, the European Court of Justice rules in tax matters primarily in connection with two types of cases. In order to counter the risk of divergent application and interpretation of European Union law by the national courts, the European Court of Justice rules by a 'preliminary ruling' on the interpretation of EU law (Art. 267 of the Treaty on the Functioning of the European Union). The proceedings are commenced when a national court submits a corresponding 'reference' to the European Court of Justice. References from the realm of tax law ordinarily pertain to the interpretation of EU Directives (in particular, questions in respect of the VAT Directive[5]). Frequently, the national court will also raise the question of whether a particular national legal provision is compatible with the fundamental freedoms under the Treaty on the Functioning of the European Union. As a basic principle, the lower tax courts have discretion whether to make a reference to the European Court of Justice for a preliminary ruling. Where a question is material to the litigation, they are permitted to make a reference (Art. 267(2) of the Treaty on the Functioning of the European Union), but are not obliged to do so. By contrast, the Federal Tax Court – as the national court of last instance – does have a duty to refer questions of interpretation that are material to the outcome of a judgment to the European Court of Justice for a ruling (Art. 267(3) of the Treaty on the Functioning of the European Union).[6]

In 'infringement procedures', the European Court of Justice will issue a ruling where the European Commission is of the view that a member state has breached an obligation under the treaties and thus seeks redress in the European Court of Justice (Art. 258 of the Treaty on the Functioning of the European Union). As a rule, infringement procedures are initiated because a member state has breached EU law or failed to implement an EU Directive or has done so incorrectly. In tax matters, infringement procedures of this kind are not at all rare.[7]

X. Temporary Legal Protection

The proceedings described above are intended to bring about a final resolution of the matters in dispute. One question that should be distinguished from such matters is whether the taxpayer is required to initially pay the amount of tax being demanded by the tax authority. Even where an appeal has been filed against a tax assessment notice, the amount demanded in the tax assessment notice will, as a general principle, still be due. This holds true even if the tax

---

5 cf. e.g. Federal Tax Court of 22 July 2010 – V R 19/09, Federal Tax Gazette Part II, 2010, p. 1090.
6 In 2013, the Federal Tax Court submitted a total of eight cases to the European Court of Justice in preliminary ruling proceedings.
7 The Commission did, for example, initiate infringement procedures against Germany because Germany initially failed to implement the requirements under the EC Mutual Assistance Directive (Council Directive 77/799/EEA of 19 Dec. 1977), although the deadline for implementation had passed, cf. Hendricks, *Internationale Informationshilfe im Steuerverfahren*, Cologne, 2004, pp. 74-75.

assessment notice (in the form of the tax authority's administrative appeal decision) is the subject-matter of a claim before the lower tax courts.

In order to prevent the tax from falling due, the taxpayer must submit an application for a 'suspension of enforcement' parallel to his appeal or his statement of claim. The application should be directed to the authority that issued the assessment notice. The authority is required to grant the application if, upon an initial review, serious doubts as to the lawfulness of the challenged assessment notice exist (in other words, where it is not certain that the tax assessment notice is lawful). If the payment represented a particular hardship for the taxpayer, then the taxpayer may likewise be granted a suspension of enforcement (Sec. 361 of the General Tax Code).

Where the tax authority refuses to grant a suspension of enforcement, the taxpayer may challenge that decision and have it reviewed by the lower tax court with jurisdiction over him (Sec. 69 of the Tax Court Code). The lower tax court then also examines the question of whether, following an initial review, there are any serious doubts as to the lawfulness of the challenged assessment notice or whether a suspension is justified by any particular hardship. This decision of the lower tax court may be reviewed by the Federal Tax Court if the lower tax court allows an appeal against its decision to the Federal Tax Court.

Decisions on applications for a suspension of enforcement are rendered with particular speed. The tax authorities ordinarily rule on an application of this kind within a few business days. Where the decision is reviewed by the lower tax court, its decision is ordinarily issued within three to six months from the time the case is filed with the court.

XI. Legal Protection Against International Double Taxation

If, in cases that have an international factual basis, a double taxation situation arises, then the taxpayer may attempt to defend himself against double taxation by using the tools described (in particular, administrative appeal procedures and litigation). Where it cannot be absolutely ascertained which of the states involved is incorrectly applying the relevant double taxation treaty, domestic litigation may remain unsuccessful (because each of the national courts will deem the respective tax assessment notice to be lawful). In such cases, the taxpayer should submit (where applicable, in parallel with domestic legal remedies) an application for mutual agreement procedures or – where possible – for bilateral state arbitration.

All of the double taxation treaties entered into by Germany provide (at the very least) that mutual agreement procedures should be carried out. Under most of the treaties, the taxpayer must apply for a mutual agreement procedure no later than three years from the date the double taxation arose (under a few treaties, the deadline is two or four years). In response to the application by the taxpayer, the competent authorities of the states in question will endeavor to eliminate the double taxation by mutual agreement. In Germany, this application is, as a rule, filed with the Federal Central Tax Office in Bonn. Taxpayers do not have any entitlement to elimination of double taxation under a mutual agreement procedure. However, in a majority of the cases involving Germany, a mutual agreement is reached by which the double taxation is either eliminated or at least attenuated.

The risk of failing to avoid double taxation can be minimized if the taxpayer is able to apply for an initiation of a bilateral state arbitration procedure under the applicable legal provisions. Where arbitration of this kind is contemplated, a decision on the conflict of taxation is rendered in the form of an arbitral award by an independent arbitrator. That award is binding on both states. This procedure ensures that double taxation is eliminated in all cases. To date, there are still only very few German double tax treaties that provide for an arbitration procedure. However, in respect of allocation of income as between related parties and allocation of income as between headquarters and permanent establishments, the EC Arbitration Convention stipulates that the taxpayer has a right to apply for compulsory arbitration if a mutual agreement procedure has not succeeded in eliminating the double taxation. In its scope of application, the EC Arbitration Convention represents a major legal basis for combating double taxation in respect of facts and circumstances of an intra-European nature. In practice, the Convention has proven itself of long-term value, at least from the perspective of Germany.

Prof. Dr. Michael Hendricks

Lawyer, Tax Advisor, Diplom-Finanzwirt

Areas of Specialization
- Tax litigation and procedural law
- European and international tax law
- Business taxation
- Taxation of reorganizations

Telephone (ext.) +49 228/95 94-335
Email: michael.hendricks@fgs.de

Tax Audits in Germany

by Stefan Schloßmacher / Joachim Schmitt

Contents

I. Introduction
II. Tax Audit of Business Enterprises
III. Discretionary Selection
IV. Audit Order
V. Audit Procedure in Practice

VI. Obligation to Cooperate
VII. Access to Digital Data
VIII. Final Meeting
IX. Remedy
X. Joint Audit

I. Introduction

Against the background of the OECD's Base Erosion and Profit Shifting (BEPS) initiative, tax authorities worldwide have been sharpening the tools at their disposal for combatting abuse. One of their main instruments for doing so takes the form of the tax audit, which is becoming ever stricter. The stance adopted by the German tax authorities in such audits certainly follows the international pattern, and multinational enterprises (MNEs) are increasingly having to seek professional advice in this connection.

In Germany, the tax audit in the form of a field audit is a special administrative procedure. In accordance with their legal mandate (Sec. 85 of the General Tax Code – *Abgabenordnung*), the German tax authorities have to assess and collect taxes uniformly according to the relevant tax laws. The legality and uniformity of taxation form the core elements of the tax authorities' constitutional mandate to levy taxes under the rule of law. As an executive power, the tax authorities are not only entitled, but also obligated according to the constitution, to assess and collect the taxes owed by law. In this context, tax audits play a special role. According to the Federal Tax Court, they serve the goal of ensuring tax equity through the uniform enforcement of tax laws.[1]

As a general rule, the German tax authorities have to establish the facts in an *ex officio* capacity (Sec. 88(1) of the General Tax Code). A system of official assessment is in force, as opposed to self-assessment in e.g. the United Kingdom, Ireland, Canada, Italy, or the US. The tax authorities in Germany bear the final responsibility for ascertaining the facts and determining the nature and scope of this procedure, and are not bound by the assertions made and evidence submitted by taxpayers. While the tax authorities are required to determine the facts, the taxpayer's obligation is to cooperate. The taxpayer is legally obligated to help clarify the matter and to disclose all facts known to it (Sec. 90 of the

---

1 Federal Tax Court of 2 Oct. 1991 – X R 89/89, Federal Tax Gazette Part II, 1992, p. 220.

General Tax Code) that are relevant for taxation. For instance, the laws assign extensive duties to the taxpayer, including bookkeeping, record-keeping, and cooperation as well as duties to provide information and documentation. The local tax office's duty to ascertain the facts is reduced to the extent that these duties are breached by the taxpayer. These mutual duties are defined according to the opportunities of influencing the presentation and determination of the facts. The taxpayer has more responsibility for clarifying facts and circumstances – and the local tax office has less – the more that facts and evidence are related to the sphere of information and activity controlled by the taxpayer.[2] Under these principles, the taypayer's obligation to cooperate is greater for facts with a foreign link.

In practice, the tax authorities are not always able to meet the strict requirements of clarifying the facts. These authorities cannot obtain absolute certainty regarding every tax-relevant fact due to enforcement weaknesses necessarily resulting from mass administration; instead, they have to define areas on which to focus. Regular tax audits are one of the most important instruments for clarifying facts, in addition to the investigation of tax offenses, fiscal control in customs and excise tax matters, special audits, investigation of individuals, or the selective clarification of facts. To clarifyof the relevant facts, tax auditors examine all tax relationships for one or more periods and one or more types of taxes (such as personal income tax, corporate income tax, trade tax, and value added tax). Tax audits differ from the investigations of individuals or of tax offenses through their broad scope. Their purpose is the comprehensive clarification of all tax-related facts and tax bases, and they are not limited to selective verification such as follow-up reviews or on-site assessment.

II. Tax Audit of Business Enterprises

Individual taxpayers and business entities – regardless of their legal form – can be subject to a tax audit. Sec. 193 of the General Tax Code permits the tax authorities to audit taxpayers who maintain a commercial operation or farm and forestry undertaking or provide independent services, regardless of whether the taxpayer resides in Germany or abroad or has been established under German or foreign laws. For instance, a British private limited company with a permanent establishment in Germany can be subject to a tax audit. Audit procedures beyond Germany's borders are not permitted in principle, unless they are permitted by the responsible foreign authorities.[3] Tax auditors do not have the necessary powers of intervention and sovereignty to determine facts related to foreign jurisdictions. A forward-looking amendment of these rules is only possible in connection with joint audits, i.e. collaborative tax audits on the part of German tax authorities and foreign tax authorities.

---

2 Federal Tax Court of 9 July 1986 – I B 36/86, Federal Tax Gazette Part II, 1987, p. 487.
3 Federal Tax Court of 19 Dec. 1996 – V R 130/92, Federal Tax Gazette Part II, 1998, p. 279.

In practice, tax audits focus on business enterprises and entrepreneurs. They do not depend on preconditions or triggering events, but rather the law presumes under Sec. 193(1) of the General Tax Code that the relationships relevant for taxation necessitate a review on the part of tax authorities. The necessity of an audit is deemed irrefutable under the law, whereas tax audits of other taxpayers are only permitted if the relationships relevant for taxation require clarification and an office audit is inexpedient based on the nature and scope of the facts to be audited, or a taxpayer does not comply with his obligation to cooperate.

The administration is hardly capable of auditing every business enterprise completely and consistently each year, so that a selection must be made, for which the tax authorities have formulated several 'size' categories according to the Tax Audit Regulations.[4] Business enterprises are divided into the categories of large, medium, small and micro, depending on sales revenues or taxable profits. For instance, commercial businesses with sales as low as EUR 7,300,000.00 are deemed to be large. The frequency of audits is considerably lower for smaller enterprises. The rate differs from state to state, reflecting Germany's federal structure. According to a statistical survey, the audit frequency in Germany amounted to 4-5 years for large enterprises, 14.45 years for medium-sized enterprises, and 28.69 years for small enterprises.[5]

As a rule, an audit period begins where the preceding audit period ended for corporate groups and large enterprises. Entities that belong to a corporate group are audited in conjunction with the group under uniform direction, with uniform audit criteria being applied. This is also the case for German member entities of a foreign corporate group.

III. Discretionary Selection

According to Sec. 193 of the General Tax Code, a tax audit is conducted at the discretion of the tax authorities. No special justification is necessary to audit commercial operations. The tax authorities also determine the timing and scope of the audit. They alone decide which types of taxes and which facts will be examined[6]; they can also decide whether to have the matter investigated as a potential tax offense. They are also allowed to select at random the taxpayer to be audited. The tax court can only examine whether the bounds of discretion have been exceeded or whether discretion was used in a way inappropriate to the purpose of the authorization. For example, the principle of equal treatment constitutes one limitation to their discretion, so that taxpayers may not be selected or the frequency of audits determined for improper reasons. Due to the

---

[4] General Administrative Rules of 15 March 2000, Federal Tax Gazette Part I, 2000, p. 368, and of 20 July 2011, Federal Tax Gazette Part I, 2011, p. 710.
[5] See Federal Ministry of Finance, Results of Tax Audits 2010, Table 3; Federal Ministry of Finance, Monthly Report 9/2011, pp. 60 et seqq.
[6] Federal Tax Court of 10 April 1990 – VIII R 415/83, Federal Tax Gazette Part II, 1990, p. 721; Federal Tax Court of 9 Nov. 1994 – XI R 16/94, official collection of unpublished Federal Tax Court decisions 1995, p. 578.

scope of the tax authorities' discretionary powers, the taxpayer is also not entitled to demand that a tax audit be conducted.[7]

IV. Audit Order

The tax authorities responsible for the tax audit issue an audit order before the tax audit begins that imposes a duty on the taxpayer to tolerate the tax audit. It specifies the scope of the audit and the taxpayer whose tax relationships have to be audited and designates the type of taxes to be audited, the audit period, and legal bases for the tax audit. An audit order is required for every type of tax and each audit period. It is customary to summarize several audit orders in writing. If any of this information is missing, the audit order is invalid; as a result, for example, the tax authorities cannot block the voluntary disclosure of tax evasion according to Sec. 371(2) no. 1a of the General Tax Code under which provision a taxpayer may avoid incurring penalties. As a rule, the taxpayer is notified of the expected start date and of the location of the field audit in the audit order. The audit order takes effect upon notification, notice being given a reasonable amount of time – as a rule, four to six weeks – prior to the beginning or extension of the audit. The official representatives of legal entitieshave to be notified of audit orders. It is also possible to notify an authorized tax advisor.

The audit order maybe appealed. It can be challenged if, for instance, it was issued by unauthorized authorities, the audit is to be based on periods when the statute of limitations has expired, or a justified request for postponement was rejected.

V. Audit Procedure in Practice

Tax auditors must identify themselves immediately after arriving for the audit according to Sec. 198 of the General Tax Code and record the date and time of starting the audit because the start of the audit blocks the expiration of the assessment deadline and ends the possibility of avoiding a penalty through voluntary disclosure of tax evasion (Sec. 371(2) no. 1c of the General Tax Code). A room or workstation suitable for conducting the tax audit and the necessary resources have to be provided to the auditor free of charge (Sec. 200(2) sentence 2 of the General Tax Code). The tax audit takes place during regular business and working hours (Sec. 200(3) sentence 1 of the General Tax Code). The auditors are entitled to enter and inspect business premises, whereby the owner or his agents has to be consulted. In contrast, tax auditors may not enter private dwellings.

Accordingto their legal mandate, the tax authorities are obligated to carry out the audit not only to the taxpayer's disadvantage, but its benefit as well (Sec. 199(1) of the General Tax Code). In practice, this aspect is often neglected and the auditor strives to achieve an increase in taxable income. Precisely because of the international exchange of information and future joint tax audits

---

7 Federal Tax Court of 8 Nov. 1984 – IV R 33/82, Federal Tax Gazette Part II, 1985, p. 352.

involving tax authorities from various EU countries, emphasis once again has to be placed on this mandatesince joint audits can be entirely expedient and justified for the taxpayer if, for example, classification conflicts or conflicting evaluations can be avoided – in the taxpayer's favor as well. In this way, double or multiple taxation could be avoided in advance, as well as protracted mutual agreement procedures that in practice do not provide legal protection, as desired.

Based on practical experience, audit areas in international tax law and involving cross-border facts include, among other things, financing structures (hybrid instruments), profit shifting and business restructurings, transfer pricing, loss carryforwards, cross-border reorganizations, constructive dividends and constructive capital contributions, double-dip arrangements, cost allocation agreements, split benefit agreements, license agreements, withholding taxes, and private equity structures.

The tax auditors are obligated to clarify all the relevant facts. However, it is permissible to focus on the essential aspects of the audit and limit its duration to the necessary minimum. Depending on the significance, audit area, and requirements, various audit and estimation methods are applied (statement of monetary transactions, statement of increase in net worth, chi-squared test, time-series comparison, external comparative analysis, calculation of historical cost, summary of personal spending). Should a tax offense or breach of administrative rules be suspected during the audit, the responsible local tax office for criminal tax matters and tax investigation has to be informed immediately. If the suspicion is directed towards the taxpayer, clarification of the facts may only be continued after the taxpayer has been notified that criminal proceedings have been instituted. In addition, the taxpayer has to be instructed that it may no longer be compelled to cooperate in the tax assessment proceedings in accordance with its right against self-incrimination.

It is advisable to prepare tax audits with the advisor in important cases. Such preparation makes internal control of the audit areas possible and also serves the purpose of carrying out the audit without major delays. A review of contractual relationships can be important as well as the selection of witnesses. The legal arguments must also be prepared for the discussion of legally critical issues with the tax auditors.

VI. Obligation to Cooperate

Taxpayers must cooperate in establishing the facts. The taxpayer designated in the audit order or its representative is primarily obligated to cooperate. In addition to principals, other witnesses such as the responsible bookkeeper, the head of the tax department, and the chief accountant maybe also be asked to provide information. If these witnesses are not sufficiently cooperative and do not provide information or the information is insufficient to clarify the facts or does not promise success, the tax auditor can also seek information from other employees of the taxpayer not named in the audit order. In this case, the taxpayer has the right to be present during the questioning.

The tax auditor may demand information useful for determining the tax base. As a rule, information is requested in writing in difficult cases. The written request for information must specifically explain the issue at hand, so that the significance of the information for the tax opinion is clear to the addressee. Insofar, the request for information must be sufficiently specific. Books, records, and business correpsondence and other documents have be presented for inspection and review according to Sec. 200(1) sentence 2 of the General Tax Code. All documents required for the tax bases must be presented, not only the documents that must be retained, but also all documents voluntarily prepared and retained for internal information.[8]

The tax auditor may not personally search for the documents at the business premises or obtain them by otherwise acting on their own authority, but instead can only request that the documents be presented. If the electronic bookkeeping has been outsourced to a foreign country, the electronic ledgers and other electronic records must be transmitted back to Germany upon request and presented to the tax auditors. Under certain circumstances,any breach of the duty to cooperatecan result in a fine of up to EUR 250,000.00 for the delay (Sec. 146(2b) of the General Tax Code). The violation of record-keeping or retention duties, in principle, entitles the local tax office to estimate the taxable income and the tax bases according to Sec. 162 of the General Tax Code.[9] Failure to cooperate can lead to the assumption in some cases that the taxable income generated in Germany and determined on the basis of these the records is higher than the income declared. If no records at all or only unusable records are presented, the tax authorities have to impose considerable fines according to Sec. 162(4) of the General Tax Code.

VII. Access to Digital Data

Tax auditors have the right to access databases and stored data if they are relevant for tax purposes. In addition to their right to print out the data, they can personally inspect the stored data and examine the system. In this context, the tax authorities' generally accepted principles of computerized accounting systems (*Grundsätze ordnungsmäßiger datengestützter Buchführungssysteme*) have to be followed.[10] They obligate the taxpayer to set up an internal control system, to maintain data security, and to document and internally audit the implemented systems' processes. Furthermore, the principles of data access and the verifiability of digital documents (*Grundsätze der Verwaltung zum Datenzugriff und zur Prüfbarkeit digitaler Unterlagen*)[11] specify the retention of accounting records, ledgers and invoices as well as their use in software systems for all digital data. If the tax audit requires access to data that is stored by

---

8 Federal Tax Court of 17 Oct. 2001 – I R 103/00, official collection of unpublished Federal Tax Court decisions, 2002, p. 134.
9 Federal Tax Court of 26 Feb. 2004 – XI R 25/02, Federal Tax Gazette Part II, 2004, p. 599.
10 Federal Ministry of Finance of 7 Nov. 1995, Federal Tax Gazette Part I, 1995, p. 738.
11 Federal Ministry of Finance of 16 July 2001, Federal Tax Gazette Part I, 2001, p. 415.

a taxpayer, the tax auditor can choose between the following three types of data access:

- direct read access,
- indirect access *via* summaries, and
- provision of data media in various formats.

Various formats are permitted for the provision of data media. Tax auditors do not have the right to install their own software on the taxpayer's system. The Federal Finance Ministry has meanwhile also made a recommendation for an appropriate description standard. The data can then be imported by the tax auditor into auditing software.

Furthermore, tax auditors can request that the data be mechanically evaluated according to their specifications and that the documents and records be presented to them on machine-readable data media. In this case, the taxpayer bears the cost of data analysis (Sec. 147(6) of the General Tax Code). In addition to direct access, the auditor can request technical assistance from the taxpayer, meaning that the data must be processed according to the auditor's instructions.

There is an extended obligation to cooperate with respect to facts with a foreign link. This extended obligation to cooperate relates not only to the clarification of facts according to Sec. 90(2) of the General Tax Code, but instead also to the verification of the business purpose of expenses claimed.[12] To this extent, the taxpayer's obligation to cooperate is an obligation to provide evidence. Business enterprises operating internationally with foreign parent companies and subsidiaries are also obligated to provide records regarding the nature and content of their business relationships. These special record-keeping duties serve in particular the audit of the appropriateness of international transfer prices. The Regulation on Transfer Pricing Documentation (*Gewinnabgrenzungsaufzeichnungsverordnung*) of 13 Nov. 2003[13] includes special rules governing the documentation duties that, among other things, specify which facts can be attributed to the taxpayer in connection with its activitiess with related parties (for example, subsidiaries or parent as defined under Sec. 1(2) of the Foreign Tax Act (*Außensteuergesetz*)) and whether and to what extent the taxpayer based these business relations on terms and conditions that demonstrate that it complied with the arm's length principle.

---

12 Federal Tax Court of 25 Nov. 1986 – VIII R 189/85, official collection of unpublished Federal Tax Court decisions, 1987, p. 486.
13 Federal Law Gazette Part I, 2003, p. 2296, last amended by Article 9 of the law on 14 Aug. 2007, Federal Law Gazette Part I, 2007, p. 1912, taking account of the Act Implementing the Mutual Assistance Directive (*Amtshilferichtlinie-Umsetzungsgesetz*) of 26 June 2013, Federal Law Gazette Part I, 2013, p. 1809.

VIII. Final Meeting

During the audit, in particular of large corporate groups, work and interim meetings are held. This enables both the tax authorities and the employees of the tax department to present their respective views for evaluating the tax-related facts. According to Sec. 201 of the General Tax Code, the result of the audit has to be presented after the audit is completed during a legally prescribed final meeting if the findings result in a change in the tax bases. The final meeting is held to discuss, in particular, disputed facts, and the legal analysis of the audit findings as well as their impact on the taxpayer's taxes. The final meeting ensures due process and is extremely important in practice. If everyone is well prepared, the taxpayer's perspective can often be successfully conveyed to the auditors in this meeting, resulting solutions to tax issues. Therefore, the final meeting can play a major role in achieving satisfaction. Careful preparation is crucial for the successful completion of the tax audit. The taxpayer has to develop a line of counterargument to the tax auditor's determination of the facts and legal remarks.

In addition, a written audit report on the conclusions of the tax audit is prepared a description of the tax-relevant audit findings from an actual and legal perspective as well as the adjustment to the tax bases. This report is also required by law (Sec. 202 of the General Tax Code). The purpose of the audit report is to document the administrative decisions and to enable the taxpayer to comprehend the findings of the tax audit. Upon request, the tax authorities have to send the audit report to the taxpayer prior to its evaluation, giving it a reasonable period of time to comment.

IX. Remedy

As a rule, the conclusions of a tax audit cannot be appealed. An appeal can be filed only if administrative acts (*Verwaltungsakte*) are issued or, for instance, tax assessment notices are issued based on the tax audit, because, as a rule, the tax auditor's audit procedures are of a factual nature and do not justify administrative acts.

X. Joint Audits

In addition to the simultaneous tax audits already established, which are coordinated tax audits for the purpose of exchanging information subsequently, the national tax authorities involved are, in future, likely to increase their international cooperation in the form of joint tax audits. Above and beyond a simple right to be present, the tax auditors receive active audit and intervention rights in the respective foreign state in coordination with the foreign auditors. In turn, the tax auditors of foreign administrations receive access rights in Germany. Pilot projects that have so far been initiated include joint tax audits with the Netherlands and Italy (region of Venetia). The experience has been rather sobering. Specifically, there are considerable difficulties, such as language issues, differing audit methods, varying responsibilities, numerous open legal issues (rules on statutes of limitations and enforceability) or questions of due process.

The goal of joint tax audits is to establish a uniform definition of facts. The jointly-determined facts should then facilitate the avoidance of double taxation and classification conflicts. Audit areas of a joint audit include, for example: complex business restructuring processes, split benefit agreements (including royalty payments), cost allocation agreements, hybrid financial instruments, back-to-back loans, structured transactions, double-dip leases, service agreements and cost sharing agreements, private equity funds, and dealings with source issues.

An important question that has not yet been sufficiently clarified is the issue of the legal basis for joint audits. In this context, the existing legal bases for a 'simple' exchange of information (for instance, Art. 26 OECD MC; Mutual Assistance Directive – Council Directive 2011/16/EU) have to be differentiated from the legal bases that also permit further rights of intervention on the part of the foreign auditor.

The Council Directive on Administrative Cooperation of 26 June 2013[14] provides in Sec. 10 for the right of officials of other member states to be present in offices of the German tax authorities for the 'purpose of exchanging information' with another member state. According to requirements established by the tax authorities, officials of other member states may also be present for official investigations that are conducted on sovereign German territory. These rules focus on the exchange of information; as a result, the tax auditor is not granted any further rights. In addition, it is unclear how existing instruments of due process will provide the taxpayer with effective legal protection. Countries may be obligated to hold information confidential and in particular to mutually protect business and professional secrets (Art. 16(1) and Art. 17(4) of Council Directive 2011/16/EU of 15 Feb. 2011). But so far only a few cases are known in which this protection could be effectively implemented. The Tax Court of Cologne rejected the provision of information to foreign tax authorities in connection with temporary legal protection. It deemed the nondisclosure requirements of the foreign authorities for the prevention of irreparable damage to be insufficient.[15] If the audit rights of foreign tax auditors are extended, this legal protection will have to be developed significantly.

---

14 Federal Law Gazette Part I, 2013, p. 1809.
15 Tax Court of Cologne of 20 Aug. 2008 – 2 V 1948/08, German Tax Law Review, 2009, p. 238.

Prof. Dr. Joachim Schmitt

Lawyer, Certified Tax Lawyer, Public Auditor, Diplom-Kaufmann

Areas of Specialization

- Reorganization law and the taxation of reorganizations
- Taxation of corporate groups
- Taxation of partnerships
- Tax accounting
- Corporate law

Telephone (ext.) +49 228/95 94-335
Email: joachim.schmitt@fgs.de

Dr. Stefan Schloßmacher

Lawyer, Tax Advisor

Areas of Specialization

- Taxation of corporate groups
- International tax law
- Corporate law
- Insurance

Telephone (ext.) +49 228/95 94-324
Email: stefan.schlossmacher@fgs.de

Ruling Practice in Germany – Achieving Legal Certainty on Taxation

by Martin Cordes

Contents

I. Introduction
II. Advance Ruling Under Sec. 89 of the General Tax Code
  1. General
  2. Formal Requirements
  3. Reasons for Exclusion
  4. Applicant
  5. Binding Effect
  6. Competence
  7. Obligation to Pay Fees
III. Binding Commitment Following a Tax Audit Under Secs. 204 *et seqq.* of the General Tax Code
IV. Wage-Tax Ruling Under Sec. 42e of the Income Tax Act
V. Advance Pricing Agreement on Transfer-Pricing Inquiries
VI. Conclusion

I. Introduction

The German taxation procedure is designed as an assessment procedure. As a rule, the tax authorities decide on the specific taxation fact pattern only in retrospect, i.e. when assessing the tax payable *(Steuerveranlagung)*. For income tax and VAT, the principle of taxing a specific period applies. This means that a binding decision is given only for the current assessment period. The decision on a similar fact pattern in the subsequent period may be different.

For various reasons, however, it can be of crucial importance for enterprises to achieve clarity regarding the tax consequences before deciding whether to make a disposition. Tax scenarios nowadays are complex and of individual nature . Therefore, questions on the tax consequences of planned scenarios normally cannot be answered on the basis of existing statutes, including administrative instructions and case law without residual uncertainties as to interpretation. The situation is compounded by the sometimes imprecise wording of statutes and administrative instructions as well as by frequent amendments to statutes. Case law is published only several years later. Consequently, there is a need for tax-law instruments that enable enterprises to achieve the necessary certainty in tax planning nonetheless. In this regard, German tax law principally provides four mechanisms which will be explained in more detail below:

- Advance ruling *(verbindliche Auskunft,* Sec. 89 of the German General Tax Code – *Abgabenordnung)*
- Binding commitment following a tax audit (Secs. 204 *et seqq.* of the General Tax Code)

- Wage-tax ruling (*Lohnsteueranrufungsauskunft*) (Sec. 42e of the German Income Tax Act – *Einkommensteuergesetz*)
- Advance Pricing Agreement (APA) on transfer-pricing inquiries (Sec. 178a of the General Tax Code)

A 'mutual agreement as to the facts' *(tatsächliche Verständigung)* must be distinguished from the aforementioned options of clarifying the tax treatment before the scenario is realized. A mutual agreement as to the facts involves a binding agreement between the tax authorities and the taxpayer on fact patterns from the past which can no longer be clarified without unreasonable effort on the part of the taxpayer and/or the tax authorities. Naturally, this is only possible for fact patterns that have already been realized.

II. Advance Ruling Under Sec. 89 of the General Tax Code

1. General

The 'advance ruling' under Sec. 89 of the General Tax Code corresponds to what is frequently understood by the term 'ruling'. Expressed in simple terms, an advance ruling is the prior clarification with the tax authorities of the tax consequences of a planned scenario or a planned transaction. The advance ruling was formerly based on the principles of 'good faith' *('Treu und Glauben')*. Since 2006, Sec. 89 of the General Tax Code has contained statutory rules on the advance ruling. These statutory rules are supplemented by the Tax Information Regulation *(Steuer-Auskunftsverordnung)*, a regulation equivalent to a statute in terms of legal significance, as well as by the provisions contained in the General Tax Code Application Decree *(Anwendungserlass zur Abgabenordnung)*, an administrative instruction.

The advance ruling is issued following an application submitted to the tax authorities by the taxpayer or the taxpayer's authorized representative. The application must outline both the present fact pattern and the planned scenario as well as the legal opinion held by the taxpayer for which confirmation is being sought. The tax authorities must decide on this application. The decision on whether or not an advance ruling is granted with the desired content has a formal and a substantive element. The first question is whether the formal requirements for the granting of an advance ruling as outlined below have been met. If so, the second stage is about whether the tax authorities follow the taxpayer's opinion on the tax consequences presented in the application. The substantive assessment is based on the individual tax statutes (e.g. the Income Tax Act, the German Corporate Income Tax Act (*Körperschaftsteuergesetz*) and the German VAT Act (*Umsatzsteuergesetz*)).

2. Formal Requirements

The following formal requirements must be observed:

- The scenario must not yet have been realized (General Tax Code Application Decree, entry on Sec. 89 of the General Tax Code, marginal no. 3.4.2).

  This means that the planned scenario may not be implemented until after the advance ruling has been granted. Taking initial civil-law preparatory steps is not harmful in this context. The crucial legal act that gives rise to the tax consequences forming the subject matter of the inquiry, however, must not yet have become valid in any event. The reasoning given by the legislature and the German tax authorities is: If implementation has already validly taken place, the decision in course of the normal tax-assessment process can be awaited as the disposition has already been made. If, in practice, the parties involved wish to establish a legally binding relationship with each other, one possibility would be to conclude the relevant contract (e.g. a contribution agreement) subject to the condition precedent of a positive advance ruling being granted.

- There must be a special tax-related interest on the part of the applicant (Sec. 1(1) no. 3 of the Tax Information Ordinance).

  In most cases, this special tax-related interest can be justified as follows: Without the advance ruling, the planned scenario (e.g. reorganization) cannot be realized. This is because the tax risks associated with the implementation of the planned measures and/or the amount of the additional tax burden in the event of the tax authorities coming to a different opinion would be too high without the advance ruling.

- No alternative scenarios; no general questions of law (General Tax Code Application Decree, entry on Sec. 89 of the General Tax Code, marginal no. 3.5.1, sentence 3).

  The application for the advance ruling must ask specific questions of law that refer to the scenario concerned (for example: "Can O-GmbH merge with its parent company, P-GmbH *Gesellschaft mit beschränkter Haftung* – privately held corporation), without triggering taxes on income?"; "Can the real estate owned by X-KG (*Kommanditgesellschaft* – limited partnership) be transferred to Y-KG without triggering real estate transfer tax (RETT)?"). By contrast, no advance ruling can be given on general questions regarding the taxation of a specific fact pattern (for example: "What are the tax implications of a merger of O-GmbH into P-GmbH?") or abstract questions of law without reference to a specific situation (for example: "Can a subsidiary GmbH be merged into its parent GmbH without triggering tax?").

The application for the advance ruling must include the following details (Sec. 1(1) of the Tax Information Regulation):

1. exact details of the applicant (name; for natural persons, place of residence or habitual abode; for corporations, the seat or place of management; tax number, if any),

2. a comprehensive and conclusive presentation of the scenario not yet realized at the time the application is submitted to the tax authorities,
3. the description of the special tax-related interest of the applicant,
4. a detailed description of the legal problem with a detailed explanation of the taxpayer's own legal opinion,
5. the asking of specific questions of law,
6. a declaration that no application for an advance ruling on the scenario to be assessed has been submitted to any other tax authorities mentioned in Sec. 89(2) sentences 2 and 3 of the General Tax Code (tax offices or Federal Central Tax Office), and
7. an affirmation that all information required for the assessment and for the granting of the ruling has been supplied and that this information is true and correct.

3. Reasons for Exclusion

The tax authorities have defined certain cases for which, despite the formal requirements having been met, no advance ruling is to be granted.

Mentioned first in this context are requests for information predominantly aimed at gaining a tax advantage (e.g. examination of tax shelters, establishment of the limits to the acts of a diligent business manager; cf. General Tax Code Application Decree, entry on Sec. 89 of the General Tax Code, marginal no. 3.5.4, sentence 1). The tax authorities do not provide any more detailed distinctions or explanations, so that there is no guarantee of consistency of treatment between the various tax offices with local competence. Consequently, there may be differences between individual tax offices whether or not as a harmful attempt to gain a tax advantage is given.

The administrative instruction also provides that the tax office may (but need not) refuse to grant an advance ruling if a statutory provision, a judgment by the highest court or an administrative instruction concerning the underlying question of law is to be expected in the foreseeable future (General Tax Code Application Decree, entry on Sec. 89 of the General Tax Code, para. 3.5.4, sentence 2).

4. Applicant

The application must specify who the applicant is. The legal person(s) on whose tax assessment the advanced ruling is applied is/are to be named as applicant(s). This is important because the applicants are the addressees of the advance ruling granted, and the advance ruling has the desired protective effect only *vis-à-vis* addressees. Therefore, it is necessary to ensure that the right applicants are named.

Peculiarities are given for example regarding partnerships or contribution cases. A partnership is not subject to income tax or corporate income tax. The income generated in the partnership is taxed on the level of the partners. However, the income is determined on the level of the partnership. A 'determination notice' (*Feststellungsbescheid*), a declaratory decision determining the income and other certain bases of taxation is issued to the partnership. The procedure is important, as the 'determination of bases of taxation' is binding at the level of the partnership. It can be contested only by the partnership's legal representatives lodging an administrative appeal. By contrast, it is not possible to challenge the amount of the partnership income with an appeal against the assessment of corporate income tax or income tax for the partner. Consequently, in cases involving partnerships, the partnership must always be named as applicant in order to achieve the desired binding effect of the advance ruling.

In contribution cases falling under Sec. 20 and Sec. 24 of the German reorganization tax act (*Umwandlungsteuergesetz*) the decision whether or not tax neutrality is possible is subject to the taxation procedure of the corporation or partnership, which receives the contributed assets and not - what of course would be more logical - subject to the taxation procedure of the person who contributes the assets. Consequently, in contribution cases the corporation or partnership, which receives the contributed assets, has to be named as applicant.

5. Binding Effect

The central element of the advance ruling is its binding effect. This achieves the intended protective effect. 'Binding effect' means that the tax authorities must, once the taxpayer has realized the planned scenario, adhere to the legal opinion as confirmed in the advance ruling. In particular, the tax authorities are not permitted to take a different position, possibly less favorable to the taxpayer, during the later assessment procedure. The taxpayer can enforce the binding effect in court if need be.

The prerequisite for the binding effect is that the scenario is realized exactly as described in the application for the ruling. Therefore, it can only be recommended that the scenario described in the application for the ruling is followed precisely during later implementation. Even slight deviations from the scenario described in the application may serve as a basis for the tax authorities to call the binding effect into question. As a result, it is also of crucial importance to outline in the application both the present fact pattern and the planned scenario fully and as precisely as possible. In the context of restructuring scenarios and similar, it may also be useful enclosing the draft contractual documentation, for example.

6. Competence

As a rule, the authority competent to grant the advance ruling is the tax office that is competent locally for the applicant in the event of the scenario in question being realized (Sec. 89(2) sentence 2 of the General Tax Code). That tax office is then bound, with respect to the later realization of the scenario, by the advance ruling granted (see above). In the event of restructuring scenarios especially, particularities may apply in connection with determining the competent tax authority. If the advance ruling is granted by a tax office that is not competent, there is a risk that the advance ruling will have no binding effect.

Owing to the structure of the German tax authorities, several tax offices may be competent for the advance ruling on a planned scenario. This may be the case particularly if the scenario has ramifications for multiple types of tax (e.g. corporate income tax and RETT). In a case that different local tax offices are competent because different types of taxes are relevant, either (a) the application for the advance ruling must be submitted to each of the two tax offices, together with the question of law for which that tax office is responsible (e.g. to the tax office of city A for corporate income tax, and to the tax office of city B for RETT), or (b) an application is made for the tax offices to reach an agreement *inter se*, regarding competence, according to which one of the tax offices involved may grant a ruling with binding effect also on the other tax office (cf. Sec. 27 of the General Tax Code).

In some cases, no competent tax authority can be determined. This is primarily the case in the context of planned investments, when the place of investment has not yet been decided. In that case, under Sec. 89(2) sentence 3 of the General Tax Code, the Federal Central Tax Office is competent for processing the application for a ruling and for granting the advance ruling instead of any local tax office. A ruling granted by the Federal Central Tax Office binds the tax office that later carries out the taxation of the scenario once it has been realized.

7. Obligation to Pay Fees

An application for the granting of an advance ruling is subject to a fee pursuant to Sec. 89(3) sentence 1 of the General Tax Code. More specifically, the fee payable is always determined on the basis of the value of the subject matter underlying the ruling (value-based fee). The subject-matter value is determined by the tax implications for the taxpayer making the application (General Tax Code Application Decree, entry on Sec. 89 of the General Tax Code, marginal no. 4.2.2, sentence 1). To this end, in a first step the tax burden that would arise if the tax authorities were to follow the legal opinion of the taxpayer is calculated (possibly EUR 0 if the taxpayer assumes that no tax will be triggered). Subsequently the tax burden in the event that tax authorities take a different legal position has to be determined. The difference arising therefrom represents the subject-matter value. The taxpayer is responsible for calculating this value himself and for presenting it in the application. A fee table (Sec. 34(2) of the German Court Costs Act *(Gerichtskostengesetz)*, which determines the fee based on the subject-matter value, is subsequently applied to that value. When the subject-matter value is used, the minimum fee is EUR 196. The fee may increase to a maximum of EUR 109,736 (where the subject-matter value exceeds EUR 30 million). The amount of the fee is independent of the complexity of the question of law. For this reason, the maximum fee may be charged even for simple questions of law where the subject-matter value exceeds the pertinent thresholds. The Federal Tax Court expressly confirmed this position taken by the tax authorities.[1]

If the subject-matter value can be neither determined nor estimated, the fee must be charged as a time-based fee instead. In these cases, the fee is based on the actual time spent by the tax authorities on granting the advance ruling. For each half-hour of processing time or part thereof, a fee of EUR 50 is charged. In practice, a time-based fee is charged only in rare exceptional cases and is very difficult to assert *vis-à-vis* the tax authorities. Normally the value-based fee, which is usually higher, will be used.

The fee set is payable within one month of issue of the fee notice. The fee may also be set before the advance ruling is granted. It is also possible to make the granting of the advance ruling conditional upon prior payment by the taxpayer. The fee is set in a notice against which the taxpayer can file an administrative appeal. In the opinion of the tax authorities, the fee for advance rulings regarding taxes on income is not tax-deductible. However, this point is controversial; accordingly, the further legal developments should be monitored.

It should be noted that the tax authorities may treat an application for an advance ruling as several separate applications. This is particularly the case in the context of restructurings that take place in several stages. In these cases, the procedure for setting fees has not been finally determined. There is a general risk of multiple fees being assessed. This means that, in cases of high subject-matter values, the maximum value may be applied several times and the amount of EUR 109,736 may not be the absolute ceiling, but may be exceeded by multiple fees being assessed.

III. Binding Commitment Following a Tax Audit Under Secs. 204 et seqq. of the General Tax Code

Scenarios already realized are usually subjected retrospectively to a legal examination as part of a tax audit. Tax audits usually concern the evaluation of fact patterns with reference to the past. Upon application by the taxpayer, the tax authorities can grant a binding commitment for the future following a tax audit (cf. Sec. 204 of the General Tax Code). This is particularly useful for the tax treatment of permanent situations which have already been examined and for which the tax treatment agreed is recorded permanently for the future. This avoids the disadvantages of taxation of specific periods described at the beginning. The application for a binding commitment should be made before the end of the final audit conference (cf. General Tax Code Application Regulation, entry on Sec. 204 of the General Tax Code, marginal no. 3, sentence 3). Regarding legal form, it must be noted that the advance commitment must be signed by an official competent for the tax assessment. A commitment given only by an official responsible for the tax audit without the involvement of the official responsible for the tax assessment is invalid.

---

1 *Inter alia* Federal Tax Court of 30 March 2011 – I R 61/10, Federal Tax Gazette Part II, 2011, p. 536.

The commitment binds the tax authorities in relation to a future assessment of the scenario (cf. Sec. 206 of the General Tax Code). The taxpayer gains legal certainty and need not fear any future changes in the tax treatment of the permanent fact pattern.

The binding commitment ceases to have effect if there is any change in the tax statutes relevant for the substantive assessment of the fact pattern or scenario (cf. Sec. 207(1) of the General Tax Code). This is understandable because changed tax statutes make a new assessment necessary, and the former legal position cannot be adopted. The tax authorities are generally entitled to revoke the effect of the binding commitment for the future (cf. Sec. 207(2) of the General Tax Code). It has not been finally clarified how and from what time any revocation of the binding commitment takes effect if the taxpayer has made long-term dispositions on the basis of the binding commitment. In this case, an examination is advisable.

Unlike for an advance ruling, no fees are charged for a binding commitment. In principle, there are no overlaps between an advance ruling and a binding commitment because the binding commitment is normally given for the assessment of permanent fact patterns already ongoing. An advance ruling may not normally be granted in such a scenario because the situation has already been realized and no new decision on a disposition is being made. The situation is different if a current permanent situation is to be modified. In this case, an advance ruling can be obtained. By contrast, no binding commitment is possible because the modification has not been the subject matter of a tax audit.

IV. Wage-Tax Ruling Under Sec. 42e of the Income Tax Act

For the taxation of wages, a special procedure – the 'wage-tax deduction procedure' *(Lohnsteuerabzugsverfahren)* – is applied in Germany. Under that procedure, the employer is under a duty to withhold the wage tax due on the wages and to pay the same over to the tax office. The employer is liable for the employee's wage tax if the amount withheld and paid over by the employer is too low.

Both employer and employee may apply for a wage-tax ruling under Sec. 42e of the Income Tax Act with the tax office competent for wage tax and inquire whether a fact pattern is being treated correctly for wage-tax purposes. The legislator provides this opportunity in order to exclude liability risks on the part of the employer in the wage-tax deduction procedure. The legal right to such a wage-tax ruling refers solely to specific business matters associated with the deduction and payment of wage tax. By way of example, these include questions on whether specific elements of remuneration constitute wages, or on the employee status of certain persons.

Sec. 42e of the Income Tax Act affords the parties involved a legal right to a clear and binding ruling. There are two major differences compared to the advance ruling under Sec. 89 of the General Tax Code, over which the wage-tax ruling takes precedence as *lex specialis*. First, a wage-tax ruling on the wage-tax deduction procedure must be granted free of charge, whereas an advance ruling under Sec. 89(3) et seqq. of the General Tax Code always triggers a fee. Second, a wage-tax ruling can also refer to fact patterns that have already been realized, whereas it is an explicit requirement of the advance ruling under Sec. 89(2) sentence 1 of the General Tax Code that the scenario has not yet been realized.

The wage-tax ruling is binding on the tax office irrespective of which of the parties involved made the inquiry. If, for wage-tax purposes, the employer later treats the fact pattern in accordance with the wage-tax ruling obtained, then liability is excluded even if the ruling granted turns out to be incorrect. However, it is binding only within the context of the wage-tax deduction procedure. In the context of the employee's tax assessment, there is no such binding effect on the employee's tax office from the wage-tax ruling. In addition, there is no such binding effect if the employer or the employee does not act in accordance with the ruling. If the scenario as presented in the inquiry differs in essential respects from the fact pattern as it has actually been realized, there is no binding effect either.

Given the existing legal right to be granted a wage-tax ruling, this can be enforced in court in case of doubt. In this case, the tax court must subject the wage-tax ruling to a comprehensive examination in terms of content. Consequently, effective legal protection is guaranteed by way of a timely clarification of wage-tax inquiries.

V. Advance Pricing Agreement on Transfer-Pricing Inquiries

The determination of transfer prices is of great importance for international business dealings between affiliated entities. The arm's-length principle applies in this respect. In this context, there may frequently be a dispute with the competent tax authorities regarding for example the applicable transfer-pricing method to be applied to the specific fact pattern or other issues determining the arm's-length price. In the event that a country involved unilaterally undertakes corrective measures, there are considerable risks of double taxation if no corresponding corrective measure is taken in the other country. In many cases there would be a theoretical right to claim for a correction in the other country by means of mutual agreement or arbitration proceedings. However, in practice, this balancing correction works only in relation to very few countries and even then requires a great deal of time and expense.

In order to avoid such a risk of double taxation, an Advance Pricing Agreement (APA) can be applied for.[2]

If a taxpayer submits a written APA application to the Federal Central Tax Office, he must outline therein all documents and calculations used for the application of the transfer-pricing method sought. This transfer-pricing method may refer only to certain transactions or types of transactions with a different coun-

---

2 See the letter issued by the German Federal Finance Ministry on 5 Oct. 2006, Federal Tax Gazette Part I, 2006, p. 594.

try within a specific period. Afterwards follows an advance mutual agreement procedure between the tax authorities of the countries involved. In contrast to the advance ruling under Sec. 89 of the General Tax Code, the legal basis for this procedure is the double taxation treaty (DTT) entered into between the countries (cf. Art. 25 of the OECD MC).

On the basis of the advance mutual agreement procedure, the tax office then gives a binding advance commitment *vis-à-vis* the taxpayer as to which transfer-pricing method is to be applied to the scenario outlined. However, the binding effect on the tax authorities regarding the binding advance commitment only arises provided that the scenario underlying the APA application is in fact realized. The period for which the advance commitment is to have binding effect must be stated in the application. It shall normally be between three and five years.

Under Sec. 178a of the General Tax Code, a fee is payable for the APA application. The fee is generally EUR 20,000 (EUR 10,000 in smaller cases). In contrast to the fee for an advance ruling under Sec. 89 of the General Tax Code, the fee for an advance commitment does not depend proportionally on the subject-matter value. The fee of EUR 20,000 is also considerably lower than the maximum fee for an application for an advance ruling.

VI. Conclusion

It is frequently of crucial importance for enterprises to have legal certainty about the tax consequences of planned decisions. First, in some cases (especially those involving reorganizations), any uncertainties as to the tax treatment are unacceptable because, in the absence of tax neutrality, the tax burden would represent a serious financial risk to the enterprise. Second, a careful financial planning requires – even in the case of less important matters – legal certainty on taxation in order to avoid, as far as possible, subsequent tax payments and possibly interest on these subsequent payments, for example in the context of tax audits. German tax law provides various instruments to achieve legal certainty.

The most important instrument is the advance ruling under Sec. 89 of the General Tax Code. An advance ruling serves to clarify, with binding effect, the tax consequences of a planned scenario with the tax authorities before the scenario is realized. This requires that the planned scenario, including a detailed description of the applicant's own legal point of view, be presented in an application for an advance ruling and that confirmation by the tax authorities of the legal opinion presented therein be requested. If the tax authorities consent to the application and the scenario is subsequently realized as presented in the application, then the tax authorities are bound by the legal opinion contained in their ruling. Points to note in this context include the competence of the tax authorities and the obligation to pay a fee. These points should be clarified before submitting the application.

Other instruments intended to create legal certainty are the binding commitment following a tax audit (Secs. 204 *et seqq.* of the General Tax Code), the wage-tax ruling (Sec. 42e of the Income Tax Act) and the APA for transfer-pricing inquiries. Each of these mechanisms refers exclusively to certain special areas and, in these special areas, takes precedence over an advance ruling under Sec. 89 of the General Tax Code.

By way of conclusion, German tax law provides adequate instruments for enterprises to achieve legal certainty on the taxation before a disposition is taken.

Dr. Martin Cordes

Tax Advisor, Diplom-Finanzwirt, Diplom-Kaufmann
Areas of Specialization
- Business taxation (esp. tax planning)
- Corporate reorganizations
- International tax law
- International transfer pricing/transfer pricing documentation
- Tax audits
- Tax litigation

Telephone (ext.) +49 228/95 94-218
Email: martin.cordes@fgs.de

II. Private Clients and Succession Planning

Unlimited and Limited Inheritance Tax Liability of Individuals and Business Entities

by Frank Hannes

Contents

I. Overview
 1. Who Is Affected?
 2. What Is Taxed?
 3. How Are Taxes Imposed?
 4. Structuring Strategies for Avoiding or Reducing Tax Liability
II. Unlimited Inheritance and Gift Tax Liability
 1. Tax Residents
 2. Domicile
 3. Ordinary Abode
 4. Extended Unlimited Inheritance and Gift Tax Liability
 5. Foreign Civil Service
 6. Executive Management and Registered Office of Corporate Entities, Associations of Persons and Estates
 7. Effective Date
III. Limited Inheritance and Gift Tax Liability
 1. Domestic Assets
 2. Special Features Regarding the Limited Inheritance and Gift Tax Liability
 3. Option to Assume Unlimited Tax Liability
IV. Extended Limited Inheritance Tax Liability

I. Overview

1. Who Is Affected?

German inheritance tax liability can affect any person, regardless of citizenship, who has his or her domicile or usual abode in Germany and therefore qualifies as a tax resident (*Inländer*). A person can also become subject to tax liability in Germany simply by having inherited property or received a gift from a tax resident or by having given a gift to a tax resident, even without having his or her domicile or usual abode in Germany.

German citizens will also be deemed tax residents if they are no longer domiciled in Germany, but have not yet continuously resided for more than five years in a foreign country. Irrespective of the five-year period, tax-resident status also applies to German citizens who are in a civil service relationship with a German governmental entity and who receive as consideration for that work a wage or salary from German public funds, and to any of their relatives who belong to their household and have German citizenship, unless the foreign country in which they live does not tax more than the assets located there. Not only natural persons, but also corporate entities, associations of persons and estates can qualify as tax residents if their executive management or registered office is located in Germany. Any person who inherits property or receives a gift from a tax resident, or donates a gift to a tax resident, must also comply with special tax obligations. These range from reporting the transfer to the competent tax office and filing a tax return to paying inheritance and gift taxes.

Even if the testator, donor, heir or donee does not qualify as a tax resident, a succession of property (*Vermögensanfall*) in Germany could still trigger inheritance and gift tax liability. This is particularly the case when the estate or gifts are domestic assets located in Germany. The foregoing applies to certain asset types that are itemized under the statutory provisions, to the extent that they are situated in Germany or can be attributed to a German permanent establishment.

2. What Is Taxed?

If the inheritance or gift tax liability in Germany is based on the testator or donor's tax resident status, the inheritance and gift tax liability under the law will be unlimited. The entire succession of property would be subject to German taxation, irrespective of where the property making up the testator's estate or the donor's gifts are located in the world.

If the tax liability is instead based solely on the classification of the estate or gift property as domestic assets, tax liability is limited in Germany. In that case, Germany will tax only the succession of property related to the domestic assets in question.

3. How Are Taxes Imposed?

The concepts of inheritance tax and gift tax are handled synonymously under the German Inheritance Tax Act (*Erbschaftsteuergesetz*). Accordingly, with respect to the type of taxation, no distinction is made between gifts made *inter vivos* or gifts made by last will or testament. The amount of inheritance and gift tax is determined primarily by three factors: the value of the taxable gift (transfer), its reduction through personal and property tax allowances, and the progressive tax rate.

The fair market value serves as the basis of valuation. It is calculated by determining the price which would have been obtained in a sale in the ordinary course of business based on the condition and qualities of the property transferred by will or by gift. For certain types of assets – agricultural and forest assets, landholdings and business assets – the German Valuation Act (*Bewertungsgesetz*) provides for special rules on calculating the fair market value.

In addition to the personal tax allowances – spouse: EUR 500,000; children: EUR 400,000; grandchildren: EUR 200,000, and so on – the law recognizes special tax exemptions, for example for business property, residential real estate, self-used family homes (homesteads) and artistic and cultural property. As a rule, the property-related tax exemptions apply to foreign assets, but only if they are situated in the EU or EEA.

The taxes are computed on the basis of a progressive tax rate that is split into three tax categories tied to familial relation with (or kinship to) the testator or donor.

Value of taxable gifts (Sec. 10) up to and including EUR ...	Percentage rate in the tax categories		
	I	II	III
75,000	7	15	30
300,000	11	20	30
600,000	15	25	30
6,000,000	19	30	30
13,000,000	23	35	50
26,000,000	27	40	50
more than 26,000,000	30	43	50

Spouses and children are grouped in tax category I. Siblings, nieces and nephews belong to tax category II.

4. Structuring Strategies for Avoiding or Reducing Tax Liability

Structuring strategies for tax optimization can focus on avoiding the creation of tax liability exposure in Germany. The main steps here are for the testator/donor and the transferee to leave Germany – German citizens must also either surrender their German citizenship or satisfy a five-year waiting period – and for the assets to be regrouped in a way that they are not part of the domestic assets. If only limited tax liability exists from the outset, the focus will be on regrouping the domestic assets into other assets. If a tax liability in Germany is unavoidable, the structuring strategy will aim to reduce the taxable transfer, to better exploit any tax allowances and tax exemptions, and to lower the tax rate mostly through the timing and personal apportionment of the gifts.

II. Unlimited Inheritance and Gift Tax Liability

1. Tax Residents

Unlimited tax liability for the entire succession of property (global assets) will apply if either the testator or donor or the heir or donee is, or is deemed to be, a tax resident. If, however, only the transferee qualifies as a tax resident, the taxation based on the unlimited tax liability will naturally be limited only to his gift.

A person's citizenship is immaterial to whether he or she can be qualified as a tax resident. As with foreign citizens, German citizens will be considered tax residents if they have their domicile or ordinary abode in Germany.

2. Domicile

The requirements prescribed by the Act for achieving domicile status are not very high. A person will have a domicile any place where he possesses a residential dwelling under circumstances that create the impression that he maintains and uses that dwelling. There is no requirement that the primary domicile be located in Germany. Even if the use of the residential dwelling is limited to just a few weeks a year and the taxpayer otherwise resides primarily outside Germany, he will still be seen as having a domicile in Germany. A well-known case on this matter is the 'hunting lodge' case, in which the taxpayer established unlimited tax liability in Germany because he routinely used his semi-detached house several weeks during the year to go hunting, yet otherwise did not reside in Germany. In the case of a married couple, unlimited tax liability will be assumed for both spouses if one of them has a domicile in Germany. Even a taxpayer's childhood bedroom in his or her parents' house may create domicile status, specifically if the taxpayer can use the room at any time, has a key to the house, and stores clothing and other items in that room to use during visits to Germany. For such usage Germany does not recognize any minimum stay duration corresponding to the 183-day rule found in double taxation treaties. In any case, whether the taxpayer wishes to remain in Germany for a longer period of time is immaterial. Even foreign students or employees who live in Germany for a few years and thereafter return to their homeland will normally establish a domicile during that period of time and thereby become subject to unlimited tax liability.

The low requirements for qualifying as a domicile in Germany mean that many people may be deemed to have multiple domiciles in various countries – a situation that not infrequently leads to double or multiple taxation exposure. Germany deals with this problem in two ways: bilaterally through double taxation treaties (which, however, are not all that common in the field of inheritance tax), and unilaterally by giving taxpayers credits for tax owed outside Germany.

3. Ordinary Abode

In practice, a person's qualification as a tax resident based on his ordinary abode in Germany is less common because that feature becomes relevant only if the person does not already have a fixed domicile in Germany. A person will have his ordinary abode in the place where he spends his time under circumstances that create the impression that he stays in that location or area more than just temporarily. This will always be presumed if the stay lasts for more than six months, unless the stay was solely for purposes of visiting, rest and recovery, managed treatment or similar private purposes and did not continue for more than one year.

4. Extended Unlimited Inheritance and Gift Tax Liability

For foreign citizens, the unlimited inheritance and gift tax liability will end once their German domicile is surrendered or their ordinary abode is changed. German citizens, on the other hand, remain subject to unlimited tax liability for five years after they have surrendered their domicile and changed their ordinary abode in Germany. This 'extended unlimited tax liability' (*erweiterte unbeschränkte Steuerpflicht*) also affects persons with dual citizenship of Germany and another country. German citizens whose unlimited tax liability is based solely on their ordinary abode in Germany are not affected. For a person's own life planning, it is worth mentioning that taking up short-term domicile in Germany will again reinitiate the five-year waiting period.

5. Foreign Civil Service

The unlimited inheritance tax liability established through a civil service relationship with a German government entity likewise affects only German citizens. It is triggered only if the German civil servant working abroad is not already taxed in the foreign country like a taxpayer subject to unlimited tax liability. The same applies to any persons who are related to the foreign civil servant.

6. Executive Management and Registered Office of Corporate Entities, Associations of Persons and Estates

Corporate entities, associations of persons and estates are deemed tax residents if their executive management or registered office is situated in Germany. A requirement in that case, however, is that such organization actually be subject to inheritance tax liability, in other words, as a transferor or transferee within the meaning of the Inheritance Tax Act. This is not the case for partnerships, which are treated as transparent (pass-through) entities under the Inheritance Tax Act, meaning that the relevant criterion is not the registered office and executive management of the partnership but rather the tax-resident status of each partner. In contrast, since corporations are non-transparent for inheritance tax purposes, the location of their executive management and registered office will determine their exposure to unlimited tax liability (as is the case for foundations or trusts). The executive management will always take place wherever the focal point of the senior business management is situated, where the key decisions regarding the day-to-day business operations are made. The registered office is more formal and is determined by the relevant laws, partnership agreement, articles of association, foundation charter or similar documents. In practice, the potentially more contentious issue involves the location of executive management. If they wish to avoid German tax liability, foreign family foundations and trusts should be particularly careful to ensure that the governing bodies are located for the most part only outside Germany and that they make their key decisions on day-to-day business operations outside Germany.

7. Effective Date

Since the classification as a tax resident can be influenced by the surrender of domicile or change in the usual abode, by the expiration or termination of the civil service relationship, or by a change in the registered office or relocation of executive management, the question arises as to what the applicable date is for determining a person's status as tax resident. If, in the case of a transfer by last will and testament, the testator is a tax resident, the date of his death will be dispositive. If, on the other hand, the testator was not a tax resident and thus the tax-resident status of the transferee becomes relevant, the effective date can be structured for planning purposes. In that case, the date on which the tax liability arose will be the dispositive date for purposes of examining the tax-resident status. Where the transfer is conditional or limited in time, the tax liability will not arise until the condition has been met or the time period has expired. By structuring the transfers by will accordingly, the timing of the transfer or the date of the tax event can be deferred to a later date and the transferee can be given an opportunity to surrender a tax-resident status that may have been acquired up to that point. Nevertheless, action must be taken to ensure that the transferee 'parks' any estate assets with a non-resident for an interim period. For the ultimate transferee, however, the time in which the assets are parked with an intermediate transferee is not entirely free of risk. Reasonable structuring opportunities will also arise for transferees on *inter vivos* transfers, which can be more easily scheduled. For purposes of defining the tax-resident status of both the donor and the donee, the dispositive issue is the time and date on which the gift transfer is completed.

III. Limited Inheritance and Gift Tax Liability

Even if none of the parties participating in the asset transfer are tax residents, a transfer by will or *inter vivos* gift can still become subject to tax liability in Germany. Whenever domestic assets are donated or devised, Germany imposes an inheritance or gift tax.

1. Domestic Assets

Only the types of assets that are expressly defined as domestic assets in a statutory list are deemed domestic assets subject to limited tax liability. Domestic assets in this case do not refer to all assets situated domestically (i.e. in Germany). There is a whole series of assets which are situated in Germany but do not qualify as domestic assets; examples include German accounts and moveable personal property located in Germany such as household goods or works of art. Even the great majority of in-kind claims that are directed at acquiring domestic assets are not classified as domestic assets. On the other hand, domestic assets are not confined to assets situated domestically. More specifically, the domestic business assets included among the domestic assets do not in fact need to be situated in Germany. Instead, all assets that serve to promote the trade operated in Germany will be deemed domestic business assets if a permanent establishment is maintained in Germany or a permanent representative has been appointed there. Domestic business assets therefore also include all assets that serve a domestic permanent establishment, regardless of whether they are located in or outside Germany.

According to the list set forth in Sec. 121 of the Valuation Act, the following items of property constitute domestic assets:

1. Domestic agricultural and forestry assets;
2. Domestic real estate assets;
3. Domestic business assets. These include the assets that serve to promote a trade operated in Germany, provided that a permanent establishment is maintained in Germany or a permanent representative has been appointed there;
4. Shares of a corporation, if the company has its registered office or executive management in Germany and the shareholders, either by themselves or with persons considered closely related within the meaning of Sec. 1(2) of the Foreign Tax Act (as amended from time to time), directly or indirectly hold a minimum of one-tenth of the company's registered share capital;
5. Inventions, utility models and topographies recorded in a domestic book or register and which do not fall under item 3;
6. Assets that do not fall under items 1, 2 and 5 and that are furnished to a domestic trade operation, including by way of lease;
7. Mortgages, abstract land charges (*Grundschulden*), annuity charges (*Rentenschulden*) and other claims or rights, if they are directly or indirectly secured by domestic landholdings, by domestic rights that are analogous to real property (*grundstücksgleiche Rechte*) or by ships recorded in a domestic ship registry. Exempted are bonds and receivables securitized through an issued bond (*Teilschuldverschreibung*);
8. Receivables from an investment holding as a silent partner in a commercial trade and from a profit-participating loan, if the debtor/obligor has a domicile or usual abode, registered office or executive management in Germany;
9. Rights of use to the assets set forth in items 1–8.

2. Special Features Regarding the Limited Inheritance and Gift Tax Liability

A number of special rules are associated with the limited tax imposition on domestic assets and can prove to be quite detrimental to the taxpayer with limited tax liability. For example, commensurate with the limited tax exposure, such taxpayer also has only one limited debt deduction. Only those debts and charges which are economically connected to the domestic assets will be deductible. Accordingly, income tax liabilities of a testator are deductible only to the extent that they have an economic connection to the domestic assets. Even the personal allowance is significantly lower. Whereas for unlimited tax liability, everyone enjoys a EUR 20,000 allowance and close relatives have an allowance ranging from EUR 100,000 up to EUR 500,000, the Act provides taxpayers with limited tax liability with only a single standard allowance of EUR 2,000. Moreover, any taxpayers who are subject in Germany to limited tax liability do not have the right to receive a credit for any foreign inheritance or gift taxes.

3. Option to Assume Unlimited Tax Liability

The European Court of Justice has held that the detriment incurred by taxpayers with limited tax liability, particularly as it relates to the personal allowances, violates European law.[1] The German legislators reacted not by providing equal status to taxpayers with limited and unlimited tax liability, but by opting to provide taxpayers with limited tax liability with the opportunity to acquire unlimited tax liability status. Since 1 January 2012, a taxpayer with limited tax liability status can petition to be taxed like a taxpayer who has unlimited tax liability status. This option exists irrespective of how high the share of domestic assets is relative to the total succession of property and also irrespective of the citizenship of the taxpayer with limited tax liability status. Only the transferee holds this option, however – not the transferor, even though the latter is liable for the tax as a joint and several obligor. This applies even if he has contractually assumed the taxes. Another requirement is that either the transferee, as the petitioner, or the testator or donor, must have his domicile in a Member State of the EU or the EEA.

If the option is exercised, the transfer (gift) as a whole is subject to unlimited tax liability. Thus, not only are the domestic assets subject to German taxation, but also all other transferred assets, regardless of where they are situated in the world. The unlimited tax liability extends not only to the specific succession of property, which seems to have triggered the option, but also to all transfers which the transferee received from the same person during the previous 10 years and which he will thereafter receive. On the other hand, the taxpayer who is now subject to unlimited tax liability will also be granted the personal allowances available to a taxpayer with unlimited tax liability, with such allowances depending on the familial relation and ranging between EUR 20,000 and EUR 500,000. All debt which he assumed will also reduce the value of the transferred property or gifts he receives. In the end, he may, as a taxpayer with unlimited tax liability, credit against his German taxes the inheritance or gift taxes he had to pay outside Germany, provided such payments involved asset items that are not part of the domestic assets. Nevertheless, the option will have likely been considered in light of the extension of property to encompass the global assets and the chronological extension to encompass transfers made within a period of 20 years.

---

1 EuGH v. 22.4.2010 – C-510/08 – Mattner, DStR 2010, 861.

IV. Extended Limited Inheritance Tax Liability

The scope of the domestic assets taxable in Germany is extended even more under certain conditions, to include all income-generating elements of the transferred property (where income tax liability is unlimited) that would not qualify as foreign source income within the meaning of Sec. 34c(1) of the Income Tax Act. The extended domestic assets also include specifically:

- Claims for the return of principal from debtors located in Germany;
- Cash deposits and cash credit balances held at financial institutions in Germany;
- Stocks and shares in a corporation at whatever percentage of ownership;
- Investment funds and open-ended real estate funds, plus business credits with cooperatives in Germany;
- Claims for annuities and other recurring payments held against debtors in Germany as well as usufruct rights and rights of use to assets located in Germany;
- Insurance claims against insurance companies in Germany.

Such extended limited inheritance tax liability does not arise, however, unless the testator or donor has satisfied certain conditions. The personal situation of the transferee is irrelevant. The extended limited inheritance tax liability arises if:

- The testator or donor, as a German citizen, was subject to unlimited tax liability for a total of at least five years during the 10 years immediately before his emigration from Germany;
- He has established a domicile in another foreign territory in which his income is subject to lower taxes;
- He has a significant direct or indirect economic interest in Germany;
- Sec. 2(1) of the German Foreign Tax Act (*Außensteuergesetz*) is inapplicable, but not because of a double taxation treaty;
- The inheritance tax liability attributable to the transferred property has not achieved at least 30% in the foreign country and the person is at the same time subject to limited inheritance tax liability.

Pursuant to an order issued by the German tax administration, taxpayers who are subject to extended limited tax liability can opt to assume unlimited inheritance tax liability under the conditions described above.

Prof. Dr. Frank Hannes

Lawyer, Certified Tax Lawyer, Tax Advisor

Areas of Specialization

- National and international estate planning and succession planning
- Tax and corporate-law advice for family-owned businesses
- The law of foundations and the structuring of private wealth
- Tax litigation, civil litigation and executorship
- Partnership law, esp. from a tax perspective
- Legal aspects of business valuation

Telephone (ext.) +49 89/80 00 16-21

Email: frank.hannes@fgs.de

Foundation and Trust in Succession Planning

by Bernd Noll

Contents

I. Introduction
II. The Taxation of Foundations in Germany
  1. Types and Advantages of Foundations
  2. Civil-Law Principles
  3. Tax Treatment of a Foundation from a German Perspective
    a) Establishing the Foundation
    b) Current Taxation
    c) Dissolution of the Foundation
III. The Taxation of Trusts in Germany
  1. Trusts and German Private International Law
  2. Tax Treatment of the Trust in Germany
    a) Inheritance and Gift Tax
    b) Taxes on Income
    c) Establishment of a Foreign EU/EEA (Interim) Foundation
IV. Summary

I. Introduction

In today's age of open borders, international mobility is continually on the increase. This has implications for many areas, not least succession planning. One of the consequences of cross-border mobility can be that families, notably parents and their descendants, live in different countries. One day, this inevitably leads to the question of how to organize succession. In this regard, it needs to be borne in mind in particular that different countries also have different legal systems. Therefore, prior to succession planning, the position as regards the law of succession, corporate law and tax law in the countries involved must be clarified.

Specific questions can arise if, in the context of succession planning, the establishment of a foundation *(Stiftung)* or of a trust is intended. From the perspective of a property owner resident in Germany and holding property in Germany, a trust – unlike a foundation – can be ruled out from a civil-law perspective (and, more precisely, from the perspective of the German law of rights *in rem (Sachenrecht)* – hereinafter 'German property law', as trusts do not exist in the German legal system. Such trust is therefore also excluded as heir in the case of succession under German law. This is why, from a German perspective, one encounters those cases mainly where persons resident abroad have established a trust and subsequently move to Germany, or where the beneficiaries of such trust are resident in Germany.

This article provides insights into international succession planning using foundations and trusts, e.g. if descendants resident in Germany are subject to tax in Germany or if the estate includes German property. The following sets out the treatment of foundations and trusts in Germany. In the specific context, opportunities for optimization will be discussed in more detail.

II. The Taxation of Foundations in Germany

In Germany, there is no statutory definition of the term 'foundation'. It is general consensus that a foundation with legal capacity established under private law is a pool of assets *(Vermögensmasse)* established by the act of will of the founder and dedicated for a specific purpose which, by way of state recognition, has obtained legal independence as a legal entity for (in principle) an indefinite period.

1. Types and Advantages of Foundations

It is possible in Germany to establish foundations in different legal forms and for any lawful purpose. Among foundations established under private law, a distinction is made in particular between (i) private foundations and/or those for private benefit and (ii) public (usually charitable) foundations.

Charitable foundations are aimed exclusively at benefiting the public in material, spiritual and moral terms, whereby the property is permanently out of reach of the founder and his heirs in a legally certain manner. Other than for altruistic motives, charitable foundations play a role in the context of succession planning only if there are no descendants as heirs or if the property is not meant to pass to these descendants. Much more common in the context of succession planning are private foundations in the form of what is known as family foundations, which are established for the benefit of one family or certain families. Here, the motivation mainly lies in the long-term safeguarding of substantial assets and in providing for the family financially.

The advantages of succession planning via foundations are manifold. With a foundation, there are no (hereditable) shares, which is why in the future the property is preserved as a unit, and a fragmentation in subsequent generations is avoided. Given that, as a rule, foundations are established for an indefinite period, a 'perpetual' continued existence of the undertaking is guaranteed. As there are no shares in a foundation, both the heirs and their creditors are denied immediate access to the foundation property. In this sense, the foundation also serves the purpose of asset protection because claims under the law of succession – in the form of claims to compulsory shares, or claims under the matrimonial property regime in the case of a divorce – are excluded.

2. Civil-Law Principles

Establishing a German foundation first requires an act of formation *(Stiftungsgeschäft)*. A foundation can be established either by an act of formation *inter vivos* or by an act of formation *mortis causa*. A further prerequisite is the recognition of the foundation by the competent foundation authority. Finally, the act of formation of the foundation needs to actually be realized by transferring the property dedicated to the foundation (the foundation's *Grundstockvermögen* or 'basic property') to the foundation.

The establishing of a foreign foundation is governed by the law on foundations of the country in which the foundation is to be based.

3. Tax Treatment of a Foundation from a German Perspective

The advantages and objectives mentioned under item 1 can be accomplished both via a German and via a foreign foundation. However, substantial differences arise in this respect from a tax perspective. First, it has to be considered that following the decision of the Federal Tax Court of 28 June 2007[1], in Germany, a foundation is recognized for tax purposes only if it is able 'freely in fact and in law' to dispose of the foundation property given to it ('opaque foundation'). If, however, the right to decide on investment and use of the foundation property is reserved for the founder alone, and if he is also entitled, by issuing instructions to that effect, to bring about the partial or full retransfer of the foundation property at any time, then he has controlling powers over the foundation and its property that are so comprehensive that the foundation property continues to be attributed to the founder ('transparent foundation'). In structuring the transfer agreement and the foundation's constitution, the above is to be taken into account.

The establishing of a transparent foundation does not lead to any tax consequences. The foundation property and the earnings resulting from such property are to be taxed at the level of the founder himself. Upon the death of the founder, the foundation property becomes part of his estate and, 'bypassing the transparent foundation', passes to the founder's successor under the law of succession. In the case of an opaque foundation, different tax consequences arise in the various phases of the 'lifecycle' of the foundation; these are set out below.

a) Establishing the Foundation

aa) Taxes on Income

The initial transfer of property into the foundation *(Erstausstattung)* does not trigger any liability to pay taxes on income, neither with respect to German nor to foreign foundations, as this event falls within the private-property sphere *(Vermögenssphäre)*. Likewise, the founder is not liable to pay taxes on income, because he gives away the foundation property without consideration and thereby does not conduct a disposal transaction. Any hidden reserves contained in the foundation property are thus not realized by the above action. According to Sec. 6(3) of the German Income Tax Act *(Einkommensteuergesetz)*, this also applies to a German business and to shares of the contributing party in a commercial partnership. The transfer of property to a foreign foundation may ex-

---

[1] Federal Tax Court of 28 June 2007 – II R 21/05, Federal Tax Gazette Part II 2007, p. 669.

ceptionally have consequences for taxes on income if the foundation property constitutes 'significant shares' (amounting to at least 1%) in a corporation. In this case, pursuant to Sec. 6 of the German Foreign Tax Act *(Außensteuergesetz)*, the hidden reserves contained in the shares are subject to tax on income under German exit taxation *(Entstrickung)*. It is unclear, however, whether upon a transfer to an EU/EEA foundation this 'exit tax' *(Wegzugsteuer)* is deferred – in principle 'perpetually' – pursuant to Sec. 6(5) sentence 3 no. 1 of the Foreign Tax Act.

bb) Inheritance and Gift Tax

The establishing of a German foundation is subject to inheritance tax or gift tax, either as an act of formation *mortis causa* (Secs. 2(1) no. 1(d), 3(2) no. 1 sentence 1 of the German Inheritance and Gift Tax Act [*Erbschaft- und Schenkungsteuergesetz*]) or as an act of formation *inter vivos* (Sec. 7(1) no. 8 sentence 1 of the Inheritance and Gift Tax Act). The inheritance or gift tax is calculated according to the fair market value of the foundation property given away. The tax bracket and tax allowances depend on the family relationship between the founder and the most remote beneficiary named in the foundation's constitution. The tax rate for descendants in tax bracket I is between 7% and 30%, depending on the property value; for third parties, in tax bracket III, it is 30% or 50%. Transfers of property to pre-existing foundations ('contributions to foundations') always fall within tax bracket III, thus resulting in a tax rate of 30% for acquisitions of up to EUR 6 million and, above that, in a tax rate of 50%.

If, on the other hand, a foreign foundation is established, inheritance or gift tax arises only (a) if the founder is resident in Germany for tax purposes *(Steuerinländer)* within the meaning of Sec. 2(1) no. 1 of the Inheritance and Gift Tax Act or (b) if the foundation property constitutes 'domestic property' *(Inlandsvermögen)* within the meaning of Sec. 121 of the German Valuation Act *(Bewertungsgesetz)*. Resident taxpayers are considered to include – in addition to natural persons who have a place of residence or their habitual abode in Germany – German nationals without residence or habitual abode in Germany if they have not permanently resided abroad for more than five years. In the case of a departure to the USA, that time limit is even longer, namely ten years. Domestic property within the above sense includes domestic real estate, domestic business assets or shares in corporations with seat or management in Germany.

If business assets are transferred to foundations, then the inheritance tax privileges under Secs. 13a and 13b of the Inheritance and Gift Tax Act apply in relation to both German and foreign foundations. This results in a tax exemption of 85% and, under certain conditions, as much as 100%. Property so privileged includes shares in corporations and co-entrepreneurial interests in partnerships, provided such corporations and partnerships have their seat or management in the European Union or in a contracting state of the European Economic Area (EEA) Agreement.

b) Current Taxation

As regards current taxation, a distinction is made hereinafter between taxation at foundation level (aa) and taxation at the level of the beneficiaries (bb). Subsequently, examples demonstrate how differences in taxation can be used in the current taxation of foundations and natural persons.

aa) Foundation Level

(1) Taxes on Income

A foundation with management or seat in Germany is subject to unlimited corporate income tax liability. The corporate income tax rate in Germany is 15% and is calculated in relation to income. Profit distributions by German and foreign corporations are 95% tax-free if the ownership interest amounts to at least 10% (Sec. 8b(1), (4), (5) of the German Corporate Income Tax Act (*Körperschaftsteuergesetz*). In addition to corporate income tax, a solidarity surcharge of 5.5% of the corporate income tax to be assessed is charged, so that the total corporate income tax charge amounts to 15.83%. To the extent that the foundation operates a German trade or business *(Gewerbebetrieb)* or commercial business *(wirtschaftlicher Geschäftsbetrieb)*, it is subject to trade tax *(Gewerbesteuer)*. The trade tax charge is approximately 14%–15%, so the total charge of tax on income of a German foundation amounts to a maximum of approximately 30%.

However, in a scenario where neither the management nor the seat of the foundation are in Germany, the foundation is subject to German corporate income tax if it generates 'domestic income' within the meaning of Sec. 49 of the Income Tax Act. This includes, for instance, (i) income from a trade or business for which a German permanent establishment (PE) is being maintained, (ii) certain income from German sources of capital, and (iii) income from the renting-out of German real estate. To the extent that the income is not generated by a German PE, the definitive corporate income tax charge remains 15%.

(2) Inheritance and Gift Tax

In addition, every 30 years, a German foundation is subject to 'substitute inheritance tax' *(Erbersatzsteuer)* under Sec. 1(1) no. 4 of the Inheritance and Gift Tax Act. Pursuant to Sec. 15(2) sentence 3 of the Inheritance and Gift Tax Act, this involves simulating – every 30 years – a case of succession along with a transfer of property to two descendants, which results in the whole of the foundation property being subjected to inheritance tax. The subject-matter tax exemptions, such as for business assets pursuant to Secs. 13a and 13b of the Inheritance and Gift Tax Act, are applicable not only upon establishing the foundation but also in relation to substitute inheritance tax.

By contrast, foreign foundations are not subject to substitute inheritance tax. Taxation in this case is limited to inheritance and gift tax upon the initial transfer of property.

bb) Level of the Beneficiaries

(1) Taxes on Income

Contributions *(Zuwendungen)* made by a German foundation are subject to income tax on the level of the beneficiaries as income from capital investments within the meaning of Sec. 20(1) no. 9 sentence 1 of the Income Tax Act. This tax liability is discharged through retention of withholding tax on capital investments *(Kapitalertragsteuer)* of 25% (known as 'final withholding tax'). It is possible for the German tax burden to be reduced if the beneficiary is nonresident for tax purposes and a double-taxation agreement is applicable.

If contributions are made by a foreign foundation, then the beneficiaries who are subject to unlimited income tax liability are subject to German income tax pursuant to Sec. 20(1) no. 9 of the Income Tax Act and thus subject to the same tax burden as a domestic foundation.

What also needs to be considered in the case of foreign foundations is the German controlled-foreign-company rules or 'add-back taxation' *(Zurechnungsbesteuerung)* pursuant to Sec. 15 of the Foreign Tax Act. Under that provision, income derived by foreign family foundations is directly attributed to (a) the founder or (b) to the beneficiaries or persons entitled on dissolution *(Anfallsberechtigte)* (hereinafter the 'Persons Entitled on Dissolution'), respectively – provided these are subject to unlimited income tax liability – if the foundation has its seat or management outside the European Union or a contracting state of the EEA Agreement. If, however, contributions are made by the foundation at a later date, then these are not subject to income tax once more. If the foundation has its place of management or seat within the EU/EEA area, then no add-back taxation is applicable pursuant to Sec. 15(6) of the Foreign Tax Act if (i) there is an agreement with Germany regarding administrative assistance and (ii) the foundation property is out of reach, 'in law and in fact', for the persons entitled to income *(Bezugsberechtigte)* (hereinafter the 'Persons Entitled to Income') and the Persons Entitled on Dissolution (cf. the comments regarding the 'opaque foundation' under item 3).

From the perspective of taxes on income, the 'interposition' of a domestic or foreign foundation is advantageous especially with regard to generating German-source income, e.g. in respect of income from the renting-out of real estate located in Germany.

Whereas natural persons are subject to income tax at a rate of 42% or 45% (plus solidarity surcharge), the foundation is subject to corporate income tax at a rate of 15% (plus solidarity surcharge). If contributions are made to the beneficiaries, then they are subject to final withholding tax of 25% plus solidarity surcharge. In such a scenario, the overall tax burden amounts to approx. 38%; this results in a tax benefit of up to 9% compared to generating the income directly.

(2) Inheritance and Gift Tax

It has so far been the unanimous view that benefits in line with the foundation's constitution granted by a German or by a foreign foundation are not subject to gift tax, because such benefits are based on a legal obligation established in the foundation's constitution. In individual cases, however, the German tax authorities have now also subjected, to gift tax, benefits in line with the foundation's constitution granted by foreign foundations with the result that, together with the income tax burden mentioned above, a double taxation burden may arise.

However, according to the intent of the legislature, the provision occasionally quoted in this regard, namely Sec. 7(1) no. 9 sentence 2 of the Inheritance and Gift Tax Act – pursuant to which the acquisition by a 'person entitled in the interim' *(Zwischenberechtigter)* of a pool of assets governed by foreign laws is subject to inheritance tax –, was meant to be applicable in relation to trusts. In a recent decision in the context of preliminary legal proceedings, the German Federal Tax Court therefore expressed serious doubts about whether the term 'pool of assets governed by foreign law' also covers a foundation governed by foreign law. The Federal Tax Court is expected to decide in the same way in the main proceedings.[2] In addition to these considerations under EU law, there are also (German) constitutional concerns against this double taxation with income tax and inheritance/gift tax that should be put forward in appeal proceedings. At present, in a similar case, there is a complaint of unconstitutionality pending with the Federal Constitutional Court.[3]

c) Dissolution of the Foundation

aa) Inheritance and Gift Tax

Upon dissolution of a foundation, the foundation property is distributed to certain persons already specified in the foundation's constitution (the 'Person Entitled on Dissolution'). If the foundation involved in the dissolution is a German one, then this event is in principle subject to gift tax under Sec. 7(1) no. 9 sentence 1 of the Inheritance and Gift Tax Act. It is the property accrued to the individual Persons Entitled on Dissolution that is subject to tax. The applicable tax bracket is determined by the family relationship of the respective Person Entitled on Dissolution *vis-à-vis* the founder (Sec. 15(2) sentence 2 of the Inheritance and Gift Tax Act). According to the prevailing opinion, if the founder himself is entitled on dissolution, then the reacquisition of the property by the founder falls within tax bracket III, resulting in a tax rate of between 30% and 50%. Any substitute inheritance tax incurred may be credited to a limited extent in the case of a timely dissolution.

If a foreign foundation is dissolved, then this is subject to German gift tax only to the extent that one or more of the Persons Entitled on Dissolution are resi-

---

[2] Federal Tax Court of 21 July 2014, ref. no. II B 40/14, BFH/NV 2014, p. 1014.
[3] Federal Constitutional Court of 7 Sept. 2010 – 1 BvR 1432/10, proceedings pending.

dent in Germany for tax purposes or if the foundation property constitutes domestic property. Again, subject-matter tax exemptions, such as for business assets, apply in this case.

bb) Taxes on Income

In addition, in the opinion of the tax authorities[4], the retained earnings are subject to income tax on the level of the Persons Entitled on Dissolution (final withholding tax: 25%). In this respect, once more, a double tax charge rises, namely income and gift taxes. In this case, too, the initiation of appeal proceedings should be considered against such double taxation.

III. The Taxation of Trusts in Germany

The legal institution of the trust originates in the Anglo-American legal sphere but has since also been integrated into other countries' legislations, such as that of Liechtenstein. A trust may be thought of as a legal relationship in which the settlor of a trust transfers ownership of assets to another person, the trustee, with the proviso that the trustee shall hold these assets for the benefit of a third party (beneficiary).

1. Trusts and German Private International Law

The rules on recognition and conflict of laws laid down in the Hague Convention on the Law Applicable to Trusts and on their Recognition are not applicable, because the Federal Republic of Germany has not ratified the convention. In view of the absence of a corresponding legal institution in Germany, the classification of a trust under German private international law is more complicated and also not uncontroversial.

The establishment of a trust is composed of (i) the declaration of trust, a unilateral legal act in which the settlor determines the person of the trustee and the extent of his obligations, as well as the beneficiary or beneficiaries, and (ii) the transfer of the assets to the trustee. The establishment of a trust is therefore a mixed legal institution. In classifying the trust, one also has to distinguish between a trust established during the settlor's lifetime (*inter vivos* trust) and a trust established *mortis causa* (testamentary trust). The *inter vivos* trust is largely classified under the law of obligations by way of analogous application of Arts. 3 *et seq.* of the Rome I Regulation. According to those provisions, the trust is governed by the law chosen by the settlor and, in the absence of such choice of law, the trust is governed by the law of the country with which the legal transaction is most closely connected. The testamentary trust, on the other hand, is classified under the law of succession. To the extent that German law of succession is applicable to the settlor pursuant to Art. 25 of the

---

4 German Federal Finance Ministry of 27 June 2006, ref. no. IV B 7-S 2252-4/06, Federal Tax Gazette Part I 2006, p. 417.

Introductory Act to the German Civil Code (*Einführungsgesetz zum Bürgerlichen Gesetzbuch*), it is not possible to choose the testamentary trust as a legal institution, as no such institution exists under the German law of succession, which is conclusive in this regard. However, to the extent that the disposition is formally valid in Germany under the Hague Convention on the Conflicts of Laws Relating to the Form of Testamentary Dispositions, the administration of property upon death as intended by the testator needs to be reinterpreted as a recognized legal institution with an equivalent function, such as executorship, provisional succession *(Vorerbschaft)* and subsequent succession *(Nacherbschaft)*, dependent foundation *mortis causa (unselbständige Stiftung von Todes wegen)*, or legacy of usufruct *(Nießbrauchvermächtnis)*.[5]

However, from the perspective of German property law, the establishment of the trust must be assessed separately. The effectiveness of the transfer of assets to the trustee is governed by the legal system applicable to the property right in question. Accordingly, for property located in Germany, German property law is applicable. The trust is characterized by a dualism of ownership: between (i) the trustee as the legal owner of the trust property and (ii) the beneficiary as the equitable owner who holds rights akin to ownership rights. This division of rights *in rem* is alien to German property law and therefore prohibited on the basis of the *numerus clausus* of German rights *in rem*. It is therefore impossible for the transfer of the property (which in terms of property law is governed by German law) to the trustee to represent – in line with the intended concept of the trust – special property of the trustee that is separate from his other property. In legal-structuring practice, such nonrecognition, in terms of German property law, of the trust as a legal entity can be taken into consideration by interposing a foreign entity capable of being a trust. Thus, for instance, the interests in a German partnership could be transferred to a US corporation whose company shares are then capable of being effectively transferred to a trust.

2. Tax Treatment of the Trust in Germany

a) Inheritance and Gift Tax

For the purposes of inheritance tax, in Germany trusts been treated as equivalent to foundations since 1999. Accordingly, both the establishment and the dissolution of the trust lead to the consequences under inheritance and gift tax set out above with regard to the foundation. As a general rule, in relation to a contribution the recipient is the tax debtor. For the scenario of the trust establishment, Sec. 20(1) sentence 2 of the Inheritance and Gift Tax Act stipulates that the trust and/or the trustee is/are the tax debtor(s) or, in the case of an establishment of a trust *inter vivos*, also the settlor in a subsidiary manner. In contrast to the ordinary distributions of a foundation's earnings (i.e. those covered by the foundation's constitution) regarding which it is the general view

---

5 Cf. Federal Tax Court of 8 June 1988, ref. no. II R 243/82, Federal Tax Gazette Part II 1988, 808; Higher Regional Court of Bavaria of 18 March 2003, ref. no. 1Z BR 71/02, Periodical for the law on succession and property succession, ZEV 2003, p. 503 (508); Higher Regional Court of Berlin of 3 April 2012, ref. no. 1 W 557/11, ZEV 2012, p. 593.

that they are free from inheritance tax, distributions by the trust during its administration are, in principle, subject to inheritance tax as acquisitions by interim beneficiaries within the meaning of Sec. 7(1) no. 9 sentence 2 of the Inheritance and Gift Tax Act. The simultaneous burdening with income tax of this acquisition as benefits by a foreign pool of assets pursuant to Sec. 20(1) no. 9 sentence 2 of the Income Tax Act leads to double taxation, which can only be taken into consideration within the narrow limits of Sec. 35b of the Income Tax Act by way of relief regarding income tax within the subsequent four assessment periods. Against this background, the taxation of the earnings distributed from the trust in line with the trust's constitution in the context of the Inheritance and Gift Tax Act is to be criticized as being contrary to the system. This could be countered in the context of interpreting the term 'person entitled in the interim' – this term being dogmatically unconvincing anyway – so as to say that distributions to the trust's beneficiaries in line with the trust's constitution are precisely not intended to be subject to the Inheritance and Gift Tax Act regime. What also appears defensible is a grammatical interpretation of the interim entitlement *(Zwischenberechtigung)* neither as an entitlement at the outset *(Anfangsberechtigung)* nor an entitlement at the end *(Endberechtigung)*, so that distributions in the context of trust administration at least to the trust founder himself and to the (final) Person Entitled on Dissolution would not be subject to tax pursuant to Sec. 7(1) no. 9 sentence 2 of the Inheritance and Gift Tax Act.

Under an *a fortiori* argument, the case law of the Federal Tax Court concerning the tax transparency of foreign family foundations is to be applied to the 'formation of, or transfer into, pools of assets'. A necessary prerequisite for the trust establishment being subject to tax is, therefore, the free power of disposition on the part of the pool of assets and/or its institutions *(Organe)*. With reference to the Federal Tax Court judgment dated 28 June 2007[6], the free power of disposition cannot be excluded solely on the grounds that the transfer of property to the trust is subject to the reservation of the right of revocation ('revocable trust').

In a judgment dated 15 July 2010[7], the Tax Court of Baden-Württemberg held – with reference to the case law of the Federal Tax Court in the case of a grantor's trust – that the property was not attributable to the trust and that therefore there was no tax liability. The Tax Court of Baden-Württemberg held that a trust in which the trust settlor is *'the sole beneficiary [...] and in which the trust administrators are under an obligation – no later than at the age of 30 or 37 years, respectively, and at the time of the dissolution of the trust which then takes place – to refund the entire trust property, and moreover in which the trust property becomes part of the estate in the event of the (earlier) death of the trust settlor'*, served only the trust settlor's own interests. The court went on to say that the segregation of assets *(Vermögensbindung)* within the

---

6 Federal Tax Court, 28 June 2007, ref. no. II R 21/05, Federal Tax Gazette Part II 2007, p.669.
7 Tax Court of Baden-Württemberg of 15 July 2010, ref. no. 7 K 38/07, EFG 2011, p. 164.

meaning of Sec. 7(1) no. 8 sentence 2 of the Inheritance and Gift Tax Act had, by contrast, to be for a purpose usually benefitting third parties.

b) Taxes on Income

Unless the trust is the economic owner within the meaning of Sec. 39 of the German Tax Code *(Abgabenordnung)* of the trust property, the trust is subject to limited corporate income tax liability, as a foreign pool of assets without legal capacity pursuant to Sec. 2 no. 1 of the Corporate Income Tax Act, with its source income within the meaning of Sec. 49 of the Income Tax Act. If the economic ownership of the trust is negated, then the property is to be attributed for tax purposes to the settlor, so that the income is to be taken into account on the level of the settlor in the context of income tax.

Pursuant to Sec. 15(4) of the Foreign Tax Act, the add-back taxation is applicable to the 'family trust' *mutatis mutandis*. The property and the income of a trust with management and seat abroad is attributed (pursuant to Sec. 15(1) of the Foreign Tax Act) to the settlor and, in a subsidiary manner, to the Persons Entitled to Income and/or Persons Entitled on Dissolution if these are subject to unlimited income tax liability in Germany. It would seem fair to say that the question of when an entitlement to income or entitlement on dissolution is present should depend on the same criteria as in the case of a family foundation. In particular in the context of a discretionary trust (i.e. when there are several beneficiaries in accordance with the trust's constitution, but the 'whether' and 'how' of the distributions is at the discretion of the trustee), it will be problematic at what point the beneficiaries obtain a legal status sufficiently secure as to lead to them having to be regarded as Persons Entitled to Income. At any rate, the Federal Tax Court has treated as a Person Entitled to Income within the meaning of Sec. 15(1) of the Foreign Tax Act the only beneficiary of a discretionary trust who actually receives distributions.[8]

The exemption, provided for in Sec. 15(6) of the Foreign Tax Act, from attribution (to the founder or to the Persons Entitled to Income/Persons Entitled on Dissolution) applies to EU/EEA trusts in the same way as to family foundations.

c) Establishment of a Foreign EU/EEA (Interim) Foundation

In order to avoid the aforementioned disadvantages of add-back taxation (Sec. 15(4) of the Foreign Tax Act) and of an 'interim-beneficiary taxation' *(Zwischenberechtigungsbesteuerung)* (gift tax, Sec. 7(1) no. 9 sentence 2 of the Inheritance and Gift Tax Act), it may be advisable to transfer the beneficiary status *vis-à-vis* the trust to a foreign EU/EEA foundation.

The transfer of the beneficiary status has two advantages compared to the previous legal situation:

---

[8] Federal Tax Court of 2 Feb. 1994, ref. no. I R 66/92, Federal Tax Gazette Part II 1994, p. 727.

aa) Elimination of an Add-back Taxation Under Sec. 15 of the Foreign Tax Act

If the foreign EU/EEA foundation is a foundation within the meaning of Sec. 15(6) of the Foreign Tax Act (in this respect cf. item II. 3.b)bb)(1)), then the property and income of the trust are no longer attributed, because the foreign EU/EEA foundation, as a person who is not subject to tax (in Germany), is a Person Entitled to Income. An attribution would therefore come into consideration in relation neither to the original beneficiary nor to the foreign EU/EEA foundation.

bb) Elimination of the Taxation of Distributions Under Sec. 7(1) No. 9 Sentence 2 of the Inheritance and Gift Tax Act

In addition, a taxation of distributions by the trust pursuant to Sec. 7(1) no. 9 sentence 2 of the Inheritance and Gift Tax Act is also excluded. Admittedly, the original beneficiary himself would still be subject to unlimited gift tax liability. However, it would not be he who receives the distributions but the foreign EU/EEA foundation, which in this respect exudes a kind of 'shielding effect'. Yet, at the level of the foundation, the distributions would not be subject to German gift tax because the foundation is not personally subject to tax.

IV. Summary

Cross-border succession planning requires precise planning, taking into account in particular the characteristics of civil law and tax law of all countries involved. Comprehensive preparation is crucial in this regard, which is why the most exacting demands should be placed on the legal advisor.

In the context of international succession planning, another option that presents itself is the establishment of a foundation. The advantages of such structuring include, for instance, a cohesion of the estate that in principle is 'perpetual', the prevention of the family property falling into the hands of third parties, and asset protection. In addition, the establishment of a foundation also enables the use of tax advantages resulting from the different systems of taxation applicable to foundations and natural persons. This article therefore offers a brief insight not only into the current position regarding taxation of foundations and trusts in Germany, but also into options of tax optimization via foundations and trusts. The advantages of such structures have only been outlined briefly and have not been covered exhaustively.

Dr. Bernd Noll

Lawyer, Certified Tax Lawyer

Areas of Specialization

- National and international succession and wealth planning
- Tax and corporate-law advice for family-owned businesses
- (Family) foundations
- Tax structuring of expatriation and immigration for individuals
- Taxation of partnerships

Telephone (ext.) +49 228/95 94-218

Email: bernd.noll@fgs.de

Inheritance and Gift Tax Planning Strategies for Individuals Subject to Nonresident Taxation (Foreigners)

by Christian von Oertzen

Contents

I. Introduction
II. Bases of Nonresident Inheritance and Gift Tax Liability
III. Requirements of Nonresident Inheritance and Gift Tax Liability
IV. Inheritance and Gift Tax Planning Strategies
  1. 'Children Buyout'
  2. Changing the Type of Property
  3. Heir/Legatee Strategy
4. Holding Company Strategy (Using Directive 2 Section 3 of the German Inheritance Tax Directives)
5. Debt Deduction Strategy
6. Escape into Resident German Inheritance and Gift Tax Liability
7. Graduated Transfer of Shares in Corporations
8. Assumption of German Gift Tax
V. Conclusion

I. Introduction

This article sets out various tested and recognized estate and gift tax planning options related to German nonresident inheritance or gift taxation, i.e. in the event of a tax liability for persons who have no residence or habitual abode in Germany and are not German nationals, but who own German assets.

II. Bases of Nonresident Inheritance and Gift Tax Liability

Tax planning for the above-mentioned group of persons begins at the basis of inheritance and gift tax. Characteristics of nonresident inheritance tax liability are:

- limited tax take in relation to the 'domestic assets' within the meaning of Sec. 121 of the German Valuation Act (*Bewertungsgesetz*);
- limited deduction of debts; liabilities of the estate are deductible only to the extent that debts have an economic connection with the taxable assets. The creation of the debt must be based directly on circumstances relating to the encumbered taxable asset;

- a limited tax-free amount of EUR 2,000 (Sec. 16(2) of the German Inheritance and Gift Tax Act – *Erbschaftsteuer- und Schenkungsteuergesetz*), which is against EU laws[1];
- no crediting of foreign inheritance and gift taxes against the German tax.

The objectives of inheritance and gift tax planning in the event of nonresident tax liability are to:

- avoid gratuitous transfers;
- avoid the existence of taxable domestic assets;
- ensure full deductibility of the debts if there are liabilities;
- structure the domestic assets in other respects such that the taxable amount is reduced (the usual options in relation to tax structures in the case of resident inheritance tax liability will apply here, for example, the 'escape into tax-privileged business assets').

Sometimes, inheritance and gift tax planning will also mean deliberate inclusion in resident taxation in Germany. This may be done by taking up residence in Germany or by way of an application under certain conditions (Sec. 2(3) of the Inheritance and Gift Tax Act).

Examples of all the above structuring objectives are set out in section IV. below. Some of these structuring options are also applicable in the case of an extended nonresident inheritance tax liability (Secs. 2 and 4 of the German Foreign Tax Act (*Außensteuergesetz*).

III. Requirements of Nonresident Inheritance and Gift Tax Liability

One of the special features of German inheritance tax is the legal technique which links personal unlimited (resident) tax liability either to the domestic residence or habitual abode of the testator/donor or the heir/donee (Sec. 2(1) no. 1a of the Inheritance and Gift Tax Act). At the same time, there is a 'retrograde' resident tax liability for German nationals in the first five years after their relocation to another country linked both to the testator/donor and the heir/donee (known as the 'gift and inheritance tax shadow', Sec. 2(1) no. 1b of the Inheritance and Gift Tax Act), as well as a subsequent extended nonresident taxation for the sixth to tenth year after the relocation to a low tax jurisdiction within the meaning of the German CFC legislation in relation to a German testator/donor (Secs. 2 and 4 of the Foreign Tax Act). Only once these hurdles have been overcome will nonresident tax liability apply, including the limited tax take in relation to the domestic assets within the meaning of Sec. 121 of the German Valuation Act (Sec. 2(1) no. 3 of the Inheritance and Gift Tax Act).

---

1 Recently the European Court of Justice decided that the German provisions concerning the German tax-free amount of EUR 2,000 is against EU laws also in relation to third countries. It has to be assumed that the German legislator will soon change the law and will allow recipients from third countries in the meaning of the EU treaties the same option right as mentioned in Sec 2(3) of the Inheritance and Gift Tax Act for EU nationals (on the downside effect of the option right see IV. 6.).

IV. Inheritance and Gift Tax Planning Strategies

1. 'Children Buyout'

That structure is based on the consideration that the Inheritance and Gift Tax Act covers only transfers which are fully or partly gratuitous, but not transactions against payment. If 'domestic assets' within the meaning of Sec. 121 of the Valuation Act exist in addition to nontaxable foreign assets such as foreign securities or capital assets, the nontaxable (foreign) assets should be given to the children as a gift tax-free transfer, and that money should be used to purchase the taxable domestic assets ('escape into valuable consideration').

Example

A father, F, and his son, S, have lived in Monaco for more than ten years. F still owns real property in Germany with a value for tax purposes of EUR 2.5 million (taxable private assets). The fair market value is EUR 2.8 million. He also owns foreign capital assets with a value of EUR 5 million.

a) Alternative 1

F gives to S the real property as a gift.

Legal consequence:

S is subject to nonresident taxation (Sec. 2(1) no. 3 of the Inheritance and Gift Tax Act, in conjunction with Sec. 121(2) no. 2 of the Valuation Act).

Taxable amount:	EUR 2,500,000
less personal tax-free amount (Sec. 16(2) of the Inheritance and Gift Tax Act):	EUR 2,000[2]
Taxable amount:	EUR 2,498,000
Tax rate of 19%	
Tax:	EUR 474,620

In terms of income tax, S continues the depreciation made by F, i.e., he rolls over the previous values (Sec. 11d(1) of the German Regulations of the Implementation of Income Tax Laws (*Einkommensteuer-Durchführungsverordnung*).

b) Alternative 2

F gives to S financial assets with a value of EUR 2.8 million without any conditions.

S purchases the real property from his father at the fair market value.

Legal consequence:

The monetary gift does not relate to domestic assets within the meaning of Sec. 121 of the Valuation Act. No tax liability in Germany accrues.

---

2 See footnote 1.

S purchases the real estate at the fair market value. Therefore, no taxable event within the meaning of Sec. 7(1) of the Inheritance and Gift Tax Act occurs, and no gift tax accrues in Germany. If F owned the real estate for longer than 10 years, the sale is not subject to capital gains tax.

S has incurred acquisition costs in the amount of EUR 2.8 million. From these high acquisition costs, S makes a depreciation within the scope of nonresident income tax liability and thereby reduces his taxable rental income within the scope of Sec. 49(1) no. 6 of the German Income Tax Act (*Einkommensteuergesetz*).

2. Changing the Type of Property

Sec. 121 of the Valuation Act lists the assets which constitute taxable domestic assets. With a timely restructuring to assets which do not constitute domestic assets within the meaning of Sec. 121 of the Valuation Act, nonresident taxation can be avoided in full.

Example

Facts and circumstances as above.

During his lifetime, F contributes his domestic real property to an operating foreign corporation that also manages other assets and whose management deals with the investment and management of property. F then gives to S his shares in the foreign corporation as a gift.

Legal consequence:

No domestic inheritance tax liability because no domestic assets within the meaning of Sec. 121 of the Valuation Act are transferred.

Sec. 42 of the German General Tax Code (*Abgabenordnung*) (abuse of legal structuring options) cannot be considered, as the foreign corporation is not a base company and non-tax-related reasons exist for the contribution of the domestic real property to the foreign corporation.

The foreign corporation is subject to nonresident corporate tax on the rental income within the meaning of Sec. 49(1) no. 2f) of the Income Tax Act, in conjunction with Sec. 2(1) of the German Corporate Income Tax Act (*Körperschaftsteuergesetz*). The subsequent sale of the real property is subject to corporate income tax within the meaning of Sec. 2(1) of the Corporate Income Tax Act, in conjunction with Sec. 49(1) no. 2f) of the Income Tax Act.

The consequences of the contribution to the foreign corporation in terms of income tax must be considered.

3. Heir/Legatee Strategy

German inheritance tax law distinguishes between a direct accrual of the domestic assets to the heir/donee and a claim to a benefit in kind directed at the procurement of domestic assets. In the prevailing view held in case law and legal literature, as well as by the tax authorities, a legacy directed to a taxable domestic asset is not subject to nonresident taxation. In addition, the legacy burden is deductible at the level of the heir, provided that the legacy relates to domestic assets. The economic connection required under Sec. 10(6) sentence 2 of the Inheritance and Gift Tax Act exists. This suggests a structure such that the ultimate acquirer of the domestic assets becomes a legatee, and the person to whom other assets are to be transferred becomes an heir.

Example

a) Alternative 1

The father (a nonresident taxpayer) appoints his two sons (also nonresident taxpayers) as heirs in equal shares. According to the testator's instructions for the apportionment of the estate, Son 1 is to receive the German real property with a value for tax purposes of EUR 3 million, while Son 2 is to receive the Monaco real property and the other EUR 3 million in the estate (capital assets).

Legal consequence:

In the event of succession, Son 1 and Son 2 are subject to nonresident tax liability in relation to their domestic real property, as any instructions for the apportionment of the estate are irrelevant in terms of inheritance tax.

Taxable acquisition for each son:	EUR 1,500,000
less personal tax-free amount (Sec. 16(2) of the Inheritance and Gift Tax Act):	EUR 2,000[3]
Amount per son subject to inheritance tax:	EUR 1,498,000
Tax rate of 19%	
Tax:	EUR 284,620
Total tax burden:	EUR 569,240

b) Alternative 2

By a testamentary disposition, the father appoints Son 2 as his sole heir. Son 1 receives the German real property by way of a legacy.

Legal consequence:

Although Son 2 is subject to nonresident inheritance tax liability in Germany, the taxable acquisition amounts to EUR 0, as the legacy burden may be deducted in full from the domestic acquisition (Sec. 10(6) of the Inheritance

---

3 See footnote 1.

and Gift Tax Act). The liability does not constitute a general liability of the estate within the meaning of Directive 2.2 section 7 of the German Inheritance Tax Directives. The legacy is inseparable from the German real property. The heir must surrender the German real property for the fact alone that he inherits it.

Son 1 is not subject to nonresident inheritance tax liability in Germany, as no domestic assets accrue to him in the event of succession but, rather, only a claim to a benefit in kind which is directed at domestic assets. That claim does not, however, constitute domestic assets within the meaning of Sec. 121 of the Valuation Act.

Tax savings: EUR 569,240

4. Holding Company Strategy (Using Directive 2 Section 3 of the German Inheritance Tax Directives)

One of the most problematic provisions of Sec. 121 of the Valuation Act is no. 4, pursuant to which taxable domestic assets already exist if the heir/donor, alone or together with persons closely related to him within the meaning of Sec. 1(2) of the Foreign Tax Act, holds a direct or indirect interest of at least one-tenth of the share capital of a domestic corporation. The wording might give the impression that an indirect interest is sufficient to create taxable domestic assets for inheritance tax purposes.

Example

The testator, T, has pooled his interests in a holding company (top holding), which is an operating enterprise. Through an intermediary holding company (Euroholding), he owns a 15% interest in Germany. T now transfers his shares in the top holding company to his son.

Legal consequence:

According to the wording of Sec. 121 no. 4 of the Valuation Act, inheritance tax will accrue in Germany because the participation threshold is exceeded.

In Directive 2 section 3 of the Inheritance Tax Directives, the tax authorities made it clear that a merely indirect participation is not sufficient to create domestic assets subject to nonresident inheritance tax liability, if the interposed corporation is neither a fiduciary relationship for the German shares nor a base company.

This clarification results in the following holding strategy:

Example

The testator, T, wishes to acquire a share of 15% in a domestic corporation and considers transferring it after several years to his son, who is not subject to resident or extended nonresident taxation in Germany, by way of anticipated succession.

a) Alternative 1

T acquires a direct share and gives it to his son as a gift.

Legal consequence:

Nonresident inheritance tax liability in Germany, with the basis of assessment being the fair market value of the shares, as determined in accordance with Sec. 11(2) of the Valuation Act.

b) Alternative 2

The testator, T, acquires a share in the limited liability company through an interposed holding company and transfers the shares in that holding company.

Legal consequence:

If the company is an operating foreign corporation, and if there are economic or other substantial reasons to interpose the company, or if the company carries on business operations of its own, nonresident inheritance tax liability in Germany will not apply.

The transfer of the shares in the top holding company, which facilitates access to the 15% share in the limited liability company in Germany, may be conducted without incurring any inheritance or gift tax.

5. Debt Deduction Strategy

As the claim to taxation in Germany is limited, the option to deduct liabilities from the tax payable will also be limited (Sec. 10(6) sentence 2 of the Inheritance and Gift Tax Act). Liabilities may be deducted only if they have an economic connection with the taxable domestic assets. Such connection will exist only if the creation of the debt is directly caused by events which relate to the encumbered asset. The limited option to deduct liabilities from the tax payable should be noted in relation to tax planning.

Example

The testator, T, acquires an interest of 15% in a domestic limited liability company. Given his other asset structures, he is able to pay the full purchase price on his own. That interest is to be transferred to his son. The value for tax purposes of the interest is EUR 150,000. T has no other descendants or relatives.

a) Alternative 1

The testator, T, dies.

Legal consequence:

The son is subject to nonresident domestic inheritance tax, with the basis of assessment being the value determined in accordance with Sec. 11(2) of the Valuation Act in the amount of EUR 150,000.

This results in the following inheritance tax:

Value of the interest in the limited liability company for tax purposes:	EUR	150,000
less personal tax-free amount (Sec. 16(2) of the Inheritance and Gift Tax Act):	EUR	2,000[4]
Total:	EUR	148,000
Tax rate of 11%		
Tax:	EUR	16,280

b) Alternative 2

The testator dies, but had debt-financed the acquisition of the interest. At the time of his death, the amount payable under the loan in connection with the acquisition of the interest in the limited liability company is EUR 100,000.

Taxable acquisition:	EUR	150,000
less liabilities (Sec. 10(6) sentence 2 of the Inheritance and Gift Tax Act):	EUR	100,000
Taxable amount:	EUR	50,000
less personal tax-free amount (Sec. 16(2) of the Inheritance and Gift Tax Act):	EUR	2,000[5]
Taxable amount:	EUR	48,000
Tax rate of 7%		
Tax:	EUR	3,360
Tax savings:	EUR	12,920

6. Escape into Resident German Inheritance and Gift Tax Liability

Should only a gift *inter vivos*, or the appointment as an heir, come into question for a person, and if the value of the gifts does not exceed the tax-free amounts of resident tax liability, one should consider establishing a domestic residence of the acquirer in order to deliberately assume resident German inheritance tax liability and to make use of the resultant advantages. Resident inheritance tax liability of the testator should not be created, as this would result in resident tax liability in relation to his entire worldwide assets. If resident inheritance tax liability is created for the beneficiary only, it will apply only to his worldwide acquisitions.

Alternatively, an application under Sec. 2(3) is possible in order to be treated as an unlimited tax-liable recipient. In this provision the donee can opt to be

---

4 See footnote 1.
5 See footnote 1.

treated as a resident taxpayer if the testator or donor or the donee has a residence in a member state of the European Union or the EEA (Sec. 2(3) of the Inheritance and Gift Tax Act). The downside of this option right is that any further transfer to the recipient from the same donor or testator within ten years before the gift opted and after the gift opted to be treated as resident is treated as taxable in Germany. In practical terms this means that in a 20-year period any donation or transfer from the same donor to that recipient is taxable in Germany.

Example:

The father, F, a nonresident taxpayer, wishes to give to his son, S, as a gift his domestic interest (15%) in a limited liability company. The holding solution is out of the question. The value for tax purposes of the interest is EUR 450,000.

a) Alternative 1

F gives to S his interest as a gift without any further planning.

Legal consequence:

Taxable acquisition:	EUR	450,000
less personal tax-free amount (Sec. 16(2) of the Inheritance and Gift Tax Act):	EUR	2,000[6]
Taxable amount:	EUR	448,000
Tax rate of 15%		
Tax:	EUR	67,200

b) Alternative 2

F gives his interest to S as a gift after S has established a secondary residence in Germany or makes an application under Sec. 2(3) of the Inheritance and Gift Tax Act.

Legal consequence:

Taxable amount:	EUR	450,000
less personal tax-free amount (Sec. 16(1) no. 2 of the Inheritance and Gift Tax Act):	EUR	400,000
Taxable amount:	EUR	50,000
Tax rate of 7%		
Tax:	EUR	3,500
Tax savings:	EUR	63,700

---

6 See footnote 1.

7. Graduated Transfer of Shares in Corporations

Capital shares in corporations with a domestic seat or place of management will be subject to nonresident taxation only if the donor, or testator, holds at least one-tenth of the share capital. Special circumstances arise if the shareholder with other shareholders entered into voting agreements or other agreements between the shareholders to organize their ownership. Only if that threshold is exceeded will transfers of any such domestic assets be taxable in Germany in accordance with Sec. 2(1) sentence 1 no. 3 of the Inheritance and Gift Tax Act, in conjunction with Sec. 121 no. 4 of the Valuation Act. If neither the donor not the donee are subject to resident inheritance and gift tax liability in Germany, the objective should be to effect transfers of shares in corporations in which the donor holds an interest of less than one-tenth. In calculating the donor's capital shareholding, the ten-year time limit pursuant to Sec. 2(1) sentence 2 no. 3 in conjunction with Sec. 14 of the Inheritance and Gift Tax Act must be observed. For determining the acquisition of a domestic capital interest within the meaning of Sec. 121 no. 4 of the Valuation Act, any previous acquisitions from the capital interest will be added to the current percentage of the interest held, if any such acquisitions occurred no longer than ten years ago.

Example

Both A and B are nonresident taxpayers, while C is a resident taxpayer. The father, A, plans to give his two sons, B and C, his shares in the domestic limited liability company by way of a gift. The father holds a 15% stake in the corporation and has not yet transferred any portions of his interest in the limited liability company. No prior gifts have been made. The value of the share for tax purposes is EUR 1,000,000. It is planned that B and C each acquire an interest of 7.5% of the company's share capital.

a) Alternative 1

Simultaneous donation in Year 1:

Taxes of C:

Value for tax purposes:	EUR	500,000
less personal tax-free amount (Sec. 16(1) of the Inheritance and Gift Tax Act):	EUR	400,000
Taxable amount:	EUR	100,000
Tax rate of 11%		
Tax:	EUR	11,000

Taxes of B:

Value for tax purposes of domestic assets, owing to the donor's share in the transfer of 15%:	EUR	500,000
less personal tax-free amount (Sec. 16(2) of the Inheritance and Gift Tax Act):	EUR	2,000[7]

---

7 See footnote 1.

Taxable amount:	EUR	498,000
Tax rate of 15%		
Tax:	EUR	74,700
Total tax:	EUR	85,700

b) Alternative 2

Donation to C in Year 1, and to B in Year 11:

Taxes of C as above:	EUR	11,000
Taxes of B, as the donor held less than 10% of the share capital at the time of the donation and acquisitions in the last ten years will not be added:	EUR	0
Tax savings in Germany as compared to Alternative 1:	EUR	74,700

8. Assumption of German Gift Tax

If domestic assets within the meaning of Sec. 121 of the Valuation Act are given as a gift by a donor to a donee both subject only to nonresident taxation, an assumption of the gift tax by the donor will not increase the tax burden in Germany.

Example

Taxpayer A, who is subject to nonresident taxation, gives to his son, who is subject to nonresident taxation, real property located in Germany as a gift and assumes German gift tax.

Basically, Sec. 10(2) of the Inheritance and Gift Tax Act provides that the gift tax assumed by the donor qualifies as an additional gift and is subject to German gift tax. The provisions of Sec. 10(2) of the Inheritance and Gift Tax Act do not, however, apply to gifts as between parties subject to nonresident taxation. The tax debt assumed by the donor is a pecuniary claim not included in the list in Sec. 121 of the Valuation Act. Therefore, the tax debt to be assumed does not constitute domestic assets, so that no additional gift tax accrues in Germany on the amount of the gift tax assumed. From the perspective of German tax advice, it is recommended that the donor assume the gift tax, as this will not trigger any additional domestic gift tax at the level of nonresident taxpayers.

V. Conclusion

Several stable and safe estate and gift tax planning strategies are available for foreigners. This chapter describes a number of them.

Dr. Christian von Oertzen

Lawyer, Certified Tax Lawyer, TEP

Areas of Specialization

- National and international estate planning and succession planning
- Tax and corporate-law advice for family-owned businesses
- Structuring of private wealth
- Expatriation and immigration planning
- Law of foundations, associations and not-for-profit organizations
- Executorships and probate matters

Telephone +49 69/717 03-0

Email: christian.von-oertzen@fgs.de

Immigration and Emigration of Individuals

by Johannes Baßler

Contents

I. Introduction
II. Basics
III. Pitfalls
  1. Inadvertent Unlimited Tax Liability
  2. Attribution of Deemed Foreign Income
    a) Attribution of Foreign Income to Shareholders (CFC Legislation)
    b) Attribution of Foreign Income to Beneficiaries of Foundations and Trusts
  3. Exit Taxation
IV. Closing Remarks

I. Introduction

A number of periods in German history have been marked by substantial migration into and out of the country. After the Thirty Years' War, many regions were ravaged by plagues and looting troops and their rulers struggled to repopulate their fiefdoms by attracting immigrants from abroad. During the 19th century, approximately four million Germans sought a brighter future in the United States while many Polish-speaking people migrated to the Ruhr district to work in the expanding coal and steel industry. Economic turmoil after World War I sparked emigration, especially to South America, and the years following 1933 saw a wave of people fleeing abroad from Nazi terror. Starting with the economic boom in the 1950s, Germany gradually developed into a country of immigration. Today, people from other European countries and beyond are attracted by its prosperity and Germany welcomes them – sometimes more cordially, sometimes less – in order to mitigate the social and economic repercussions triggered by a shrinking domestic population.

The mobility of individuals has always been a policy issue, and from time to time it has even been a **tax policy issue**. The predominant patriotic thinking during World War I denounced emigration as tax desertion since the emigrants' German tax liability was substantially restricted or even ended when they left the country. That is why the 'Law against tax evasion' (*Gesetz gegen die Steuerflucht*) was introduced in 1918 subjecting German nationals even without domestic residence or habitual abode to unlimited tax liability. The law expired in 1925, but when the German government sharply raised tax rates in 1931 during the Great Depression, it also introduced the 'Reich flight tax' (*Reichsfluchtsteuer*) as part of its capital control measures. This wealth tax was levied from individuals emigrating from Germany on the totality of their property at a rate of 25%. Originally enacted as a sunset law to expire at the end of 1932, it was extended and modified several times and eventually became a cynical instrument in the hands of the Nazi government to despoil Jewish people fleeing from its terror. But German income tax legislation did not only impede emigration. For most of the 20th century, it also aimed to attract people from abroad by offering them lump-sum taxation (at a usual discount of 50%) for a period of ten years after immigration. Although the provision aimed to encourage the re-immigration of German nationals, it was never formally limited to this group of people and was open to any immigrant.

Today, tax law is less of an instrument of German migration policy. The way modern tax law deals with immigration and emigration is determined by the principle task of taxation: yielding revenue for the state. Making sure that everyone contributes his fair share to the public financing requirements has become the main objective of German tax policy with the notion of a fair share being open to continual debate. Indeed, the provision of lump-sum taxation of immigrants was abolished in 1988 since it contravened the principle of equal taxation. On the emigration side, an exit tax was introduced in 1973 (the notorious Reich flight tax was abolished in 1953) and substantially modified in 2006, triggering income tax on undisclosed capital gains that will no longer be subject to German taxation.

II. Basics

Like almost all modern tax regimes, German direct taxation distinguishes between two types of taxpayers. Individuals who have a personal allegiance to the Federal Republic of Germany are subject to **unlimited tax liability** and taxed on their worldwide income and property[1]. All others are taxed only on their German source income and their property located in Germany[2] (**limited tax liability**). The personal allegiance of the taxpayer is defined by whether either his residence or his habitual abode is located in Germany (Sec. 1(1) sentence 1 of the German Income Tax Act – *Einkommensteuergesetz*, Sec. 2(1) no. 1 sentence 2(a) of the German Inheritance and Gift Tax Act – *Erbschaft- und Schenkungsteuergesetz*). Immigration and emigration of individuals from a tax law perspective therefore refer to acquiring or losing a personal allegiance to Germany: An immigrant becomes subject to unlimited tax liability ('tax resident') by taking up residence or establishing his habitual abode there, whereas the emigrant shakes off these ties. Both events have immediate effect, i.e. the immigrant becomes tax-resident (and subject to unlimited tax liability) from the moment he takes up German residence or establishes a habitual abode. The same principle applies to emigrants.

An individual's personal allegiance to Germany resulting from his **nationality** is not relevant for tax law purposes. There are three exceptions to this:

---

[1] Germany currently does not levy a wealth tax but a person's assets are relevant for inheritance and gift tax purposes.
[2] For a more detailed discussion on what is domestic property cf Hannes, p. 348 et seq. above.

- For inheritance and gift tax purposes, German nationals are tax residents for a period of five years after having abandoned their German residence or habitual abode (Sec. 2(1) no. 1(b) of the Inheritance and Gift Tax Act, referred to as 'extended unlimited tax liability'[3]). For German nationals emigrating to the US this period is prolonged to ten years.
- German nationals emigrating to a tax haven after having been subjected to unlimited tax liability for five years out of the last ten are subjected to an extended form of limited income and inheritance and gift tax liability (referred to as 'extended limited tax liability') for ten years if they continue to have substantial economic interests in Germany (Sec. 2(4) of the German Foreign Tax Act – *Außensteuergesetz*).
- Nationality may play a (subordinate) role when it comes to determining the taxpayer's residence pursuant to a double taxation treaty (Art. 4 para. 2 (d) of the OECDMC).

Residence is a very broad concept under German tax law. It requires the taxpayer to maintain a dwelling under circumstances from which it may be inferred that he will maintain and use such dwelling (Sec. 8 of the German General Tax Code – *Abgabenordnung*). There is basically no minimum standard for the dwelling to qualify as a residence. Even modest accommodation qualifies as long as it is, by its nature, designed to enable human habitation (Circular on the Application of the General Tax Code, Sec. 8, no. 3). Access to a bathroom is required although it may be shared with others; a cooking facility is not required.[4] A minimum of furniture is required; a completely unfurnished flat is not deemed to be a residence.

The taxpayer maintains the dwelling if he can use it at his discretion. This requires a sort of authority over the dwelling. This is usually based on a legal position such as property or a lease contract but an implied authority is sufficient. For example, each spouse is deemed to maintain the dwelling where the couple usually stays even if only one of them is the proprietor or the lessee. A hotel room can qualify as a residence, but under usual circumstances the use is assumed to be temporary, not permanent. There is an important exception to this if the room is let for more than six months or for an indefinite period of time. The repeated use of one and the same room for a more limited period of time does not establish residence. But if the hotelier, to please his guest, stops letting this room to others in order to have it permanently available for him, the room might constitute a residence for this guest, especially if he leaves personal belongings in it during his absence. Unlike many other tax laws, German tax law does not require a minimum length of physical presence during the tax year. An instructive case was a taxpayer whose employer sent him for four years to Saudi Arabia. The employee was accompanied by his wife. During that period, the couple used their German dwelling only for three to eight weeks a year and were still held to be resident in Germany since the apartment

---

3 cf. Hannes, p. 347 above.
4 Federal Tax Court of 10 April 2013 – I R 50/12, BFH/NV 2013, p. 1909.

was equipped, furnished and ready for them to use at any time during the year.[5] This mere availability indicated the employee's intention to keep and to use the apartment, which is sufficient for the purposes of residence. No actual use is required. In contrast, maintaining a suitable dwelling for a temporary purpose (six months at maximum) does not constitute a residence.

A person's **habitual abode** is defined as where he is present under circumstances indicating that his stay at that place or in that area is not merely temporary (Sec. 9 sentence 1 of the General Tax Code). A continuous stay in Germany of not less than six months' duration invariably and from the beginning of that stay constitutes a habitual abode there (Sec. 9 sentence 2 of the General Tax Code). The person's sojourn in Germany does not have to end in the same calendar year in which it starts. Stays undertaken for visiting, recuperation, curative or similar private purposes and not lasting more than 12 months are excepted (Sec. 9 sentence 3 of the General Tax Code). Brief interruptions such as vacations, business trips, and journeys abroad for medical treatment or recreation are not deemed to disrupt a continuous sojourn. Those transitional interruptions, especially if they occur regularly and inherently connected, have to be distinguished from situations in which the personal circumstances indicate a temporary nature of the individual's presence in Germany.[6] To do this, all aspects of the individual's personal situation, his social and economic ties and interests in the broadest sense have to be taken into account.

Cross-border commuters who travel to their place of work or business in Germany from a neighboring country each day do not have their habitual abode in Germany. In contrast, an individual has established his habitual abode in Germany if he spends the working days of the week in Germany and returns home only on the weekends. This was clearly illustrated in the case of a TV presenter who lived with her family in Switzerland. In order to produce her TV show, she flew to Germany on Mondays and returned to Switzerland on Thursday evenings or Friday mornings from mid-January to the end of June and from mid-August to mid-December for three consecutive years with two one-week breaks at the beginning of April and at the beginning of October. The court held that her stays in Switzerland on weekends and during the various breaks during the year were of a mere temporary nature and the person was therefore held to have her habitual abode in Germany.[7] For highly mobile individuals, the analysis of their situation includes not only the tax year in question but also the preceding (and, if applicable, subsequent) periods. A preceding tax year with an easily identifiable habitual abode could serve as a starting point: Since any individual has only one habitual abode at a given time, changes in his personal situation must be analyzed to determine whether they carry sufficient weight for a shift in the habitual abode (Circular on the Application of the General Tax Code, Sec. 9, nos. 3, 4).

---

5 Federal Tax Court of 19 March 1997 – I R 69/96, Federal Tax Gazette part II, 1997, p. 447.
6 Federal Tax Court of 30 Aug. 1989 – I R 215/85, Federal Tax Gazette part II, 1989, p. 956.
7 Federal Tax Court of 22 June 2011 – I R 26/10, BFH/NV 2011, p. 2001.

III. Pitfalls

Individuals may inadvertently become tax residents in Germany because of the broad scope of the concepts of residence and habitual abode. In fact, they may 'immigrate' to Germany without being aware of it (cf. section 1 below). This could trigger a sharp rise in the tax burden and could even lead to criminal prosecution for tax evasion. But even people who intentionally immigrate to Germany may be confronted with peculiar and complicated rules on the attribution of deemed foreign income (cf. section 2 below). Finally, taxpayers emigrating from Germany should be aware of the exit tax (cf. section 3 below).

1. Inadvertent Unlimited Tax Liability

A classic example of individuals becoming inadvertently subjected to German unlimited tax liability is owners of summer cottages. Early precedents do not regard these houses as suitable dwellings due to their remote location and their standard of construction and equipment.[8] As these properties become more and more comfortably equipped, they become similar to normal housing. That they may still appear as mere 'barns' compared to the taxpayers' properties abroad is irrelevant. Irrespective of the cottage's construction and equipment standard, it is widely held as not constituting a residence when used sporadically and for holiday purposes only. However, case law is somewhat ambiguous in this respect. An early judgment of the Federal Tax Court[9] held that staying for five to six weeks for recreation purposes does not constitute a residence. In a similar setting, however, a person was deemed to be resident because she stayed in Germany twice a year for four to six weeks during the deer hunting season.[10] Some judgments link their interpretation to the duration of the stay (no residence if the stay does not exceed three weeks a year); others explicitly do not.

Another source of dispute is the required implied authority over the dwelling. Sleeping on a friend's sofa indefinitely does not grant authority over his dwelling. The other side of the coin is marked by the case of a celebrated tennis professional who also became well-known in tax law circles more than a decade ago. Criminal proceedings were lodged against him because he had his (principle) residence abroad (in a tax haven) but possessed the key to the granny-flat in his sister's house in Germany. Although there was no formal lease arrangement between brother and sister, the possession of the key gave him implied authority over the flat pursuant to the meaning of residence. Therefore, he was held to be also resident in Germany and convicted for tax evasion. Although possession of the key constitutes strong evidence that the taxpayer in fact maintains the dwelling, it is not an irrefutable assumption. The decisive element is the opportunity to use the dwelling at one's personal convenience. This may not be true despite possession of the key. Frequently, children keep

---

8 Federal Tax Court of 24 April 1964 – VI 236/62 U, Federal Tax Gazette part III, 1964, p. 462.
9 Federal Tax Court of 6 March 1968 – I 38/65, Federal Tax Gazette part II, 1968, p. 439.
10 Federal Tax Court of 23 Nov. 1988 – II R 139/87, Federal Tax Gazette part II, 1989, p. 182.

keys to the dwellings of their parents even after having settled down and established their own households. Nevertheless, they are not resident at their parents' home because the authority over the dwelling is exclusively vested with their parents. This may also apply to separate premises at the parents' home exclusively dedicated to the children's use such as a granny-flat or guest house. As long as the children are expected to inform their parents in advance each time they plan to use the premises, the parents could deny the use and so authority over the premises is still with the parents. Otherwise, i.e. if the children use the premises at their own discretion, the dwelling is (also) maintained by them.

The importance of the person's discretion to use a dwelling was well illustrated by a series of cases recently brought before and decided by the Federal Tax Court.[11] An airline required its flight attendants and pilots to maintain overnight accommodation within a certain perimeter of their assignment airport. Those of the employees living outside the perimeter, and specifically those living abroad, formed groups of roughly four to ten people and each group rented an apartment within the perimeter. The apartments were spartanly equipped and used only occasionally by the lessees. Nevertheless, the German tax administration considered each apartment as a residence for each lessee of the group and consequently all lessees as being resident in Germany. It disregarded the fact that not all of the lessees could use the apartment at the same time. Some of the apartments were simply too small. In other cases in which the apartment was theoretically large enough to accommodate all lessees at the same time, the lease agreement limited the number of persons permitted to use the apartment concurrently and there were organizational arrangements in place (such as the number of keys available) to make sure that the lessees complied with the agreement. Therefore, an individual member of the group could not use the apartment at his personal discretion. For this reason the court held that none of the group members maintains the apartment.

It should become clear that the legal concepts of residence and habitual abode offer substantial leeway for the tax authorities to allege a person's tax residence in Germany. Individuals with relevant connections to Germany should have their situation reviewed regularly.

2. Attribution of Deemed Foreign Income

People not familiar with tax law are often surprised to learn that someone can be taxed on earnings that he or she never actually pocketed. Rules on controlled foreign companies (CFCs) are a classic example of this and Germany features among those jurisdictions which have put in place a rather complex set of rules in this respect (cf. section a) below). Furthermore, German tax law

---

11 Federal Tax Court of 10 April 2013 – I R 50/12, BFH/NV 2013, p. 1909; 13 Nov. 2013 – I R 38/13, not published.

provides for rules with a similar objective which does not apply to foreign corporations but to beneficiaries of foreign foundations and trust structures (cf. section b) below).

a) Attribution of Foreign Income to Shareholders (CFC Legislation)[12]

Pursuant to German CFC rules, passive income of a foreign corporation which is taxed abroad at a rate of less than 25% is attributed to its domestic shareholder, be it a corporation or an individual, subject to specific shareholding requirements (Sec. 7 *et seq.* of the Foreign Tax Act).[13] Therefore, an immigrant with a relevant shareholding could easily fail to recognize that the part of the foreign corporation's profit equal to his stake quota is to be added to his taxable revenue. Passive income pursuant to the act means profits other than those derived from an active business (Sec. 8(1) of the Foreign Tax Act). The act lists what is deemed an active business: agriculture, manufacture of goods, energy production, and exploration of natural resources. Other business activities, such as banking operations, trade and commerce, provision of services, and leasing of property, requires the connected business organization and/or the added value to be effectively located abroad in order to be deemed as an active business[14]. In fact, not every tax-resident shareholder of a low-taxed foreign corporation is affected by the German CFC rules.

Certain shareholding requirements have to be met but their scope is particularly broad. A CFC under German law does not have to be controlled by a single domestic shareholder or by a group of affiliated shareholders. It is sufficient that the majority of shares or voting rights are held by shareholders who are either German tax residents or subject to German extended limited tax liability (Sec. 7(2) of the Foreign Tax Act, for extended limited tax liability cf. section II above). No link, affiliation or alignment of any kind between these shareholders is required; they may well be unrelated parties and are still taxed on that part of the corporation's passive income which is equivalent to their respective stake quota in the corporation. That is why individuals who immigrate with a shareholding in a foreign corporation may face taxation on deemed income they would never have imagined. Even worse, immigration may possibly spark an additional tax burden for those other shareholders who had already been German residents but did not control the majority of shares in the corporation. The CFC rules also apply to listed companies. Only foreign investment funds (UCITS or AIF pursuant to Sec. 1(1b) of the German Investment Tax Act [*Investmentsteuergesetz*]) are exempted.

---

12 For more detailed discussion of Controlled Foreign Company Legislation cf Schönfeld, p. 41 et seg. above.
13 There is an important exception to this rule for corporations having their registered office or principle place of management in an EU or EEA member state where they exercise a real economic activity.
14 The complexity of the rules to distinguish active income from passive income is notorious and cannot be described in detail in this context.

Shareholders of a low-taxed foreign corporation can even be taxed more aggressively on the corporation's profit if it is deemed as financial **investment income** (*Einkünfte mit Kapitalanlagecharakter*, Sec. 7(6a) of the Foreign Tax Act) which is a subset of the corporation's passive income. If the corporation's investment proceeds account for at least 10% of its gross proceeds, its financial investment income is attributed to any shareholder holding at least 1% of its share capital or voting rights (Sec. 7(6) sentences 1, 2 of the Foreign Tax Act). Furthermore, the minimum shareholding requirement ceases to apply and the corporation's financial investment income is attributed to every tax-resident shareholder independent of the extent of his shareholding if all (or nearly all) of the corporation's gross proceeds account for investment proceeds provided, however, that the corporation's shares are not quoted on a stock exchange. Again, the corporation's financial investment income can be attributed only to the extent of the shareholder's stake quota. Nevertheless, immigrating to Germany with a shareholding in a low-taxed foreign corporation could be accompanied by unwelcomed tax effects.

The law provides an **EU/EEA privilege** as an important exception to the CFC rules outlined above: No deemed income arises if the corporation's registered office or its principle place of management is located in an EU/EEA member state where it pursues an actual business activity (Sec. 8(2) of the Foreign Tax Act). The law additionally requires information relevant for taxation to be mutually exchanged between Germany and this other country. Due to the Council Directive 2011/16/EU on the administrative cooperation in the field of taxation[15], information exchange clauses in double taxation treaties (Norway and Iceland), and a tax information exchange agreement with Liechtenstein, this prerequisite is currently met in relation to all EU/EEA member states.

The EU/EEA privilege is of practical significance since a number of EU/EEA countries, including Denmark, the Republic of Ireland and the United Kingdom, levy corporation tax at a lower rate than 25%. Due to a reduced corporation tax rate of 20% for the first tax bracket, the effective corporation tax rate in the Netherlands is also below this threshold. A source of disputes in practice is the level of activity necessary to meet the requirement of an actual business activity. The EU/EEA privilege as a whole, as well as the activity requirement, was inspired by the judgment of the European Court of Justice in the *Cadbury Schweppes* case.[16] In this decision, the court distinguished between 'the actual pursuit of an economic activity' (*loc. cit.* no. 54) on the one hand and 'wholly artificial arrangements which do not reflect reality' (*loc. cit.* no. 55) on the other. From this it could be derived that the required level of activity of the foreign corporation is low and that this legal element should only exclude 'artificial arrangements' from benefiting from the privilege. The German administration,

---

15 OJ 2011, L64 p. 1.
16 European Court of Justice of 12 Sept. 1996, C-196/04, ECR 2006, I-7995.

however, requires more substance in the activity, especially that the corporation has its own personnel which is sufficiently skilled to pursue the corporation's activity autonomously and self-dependently.[17]

b) Attribution of Foreign Income to Beneficiaries of Foundations and Trusts

Surprising tax effects may also arise for immigrants who are beneficiaries of a foundation whose registered office and principle place of management is located abroad and whose majoritarian beneficiaries are the founder, his/her relatives and their descendants ('foreign family foundation', Sec. 15(2) of the Foreign Tax Act). The income and property of this kind of foundation are attributed to its founder, if he or she is a tax resident in Germany, or at a proportionate share to its tax-resident beneficiaries (Sec. 15(1) of the Foreign Tax Act); the same rule applies *mutatis mutandis* to settlors and beneficiaries of a foreign trust (Sec. 15(1) sentence 4 of the Foreign Tax Act).[18] It is important to note that contrary to CFC legislation, the rule applies irrespectively of the foundation's tax burden in its country of domicile. Its application is not limited to foreign family foundations or trusts domiciled in tax havens.

The rule was enacted to hamper the transfer of assets to offshore structures that were implemented by resident taxpayers to reduce their German income tax and wealth tax liability. Unfortunately, it overshoots the mark considerably since it does not require the founder/settlor to have ever been tax-resident in Germany. It thereby also hits beneficiaries immigrating to Germany, even if neither the founder/settlor nor his property ever had ties to Germany. This is obviously an unjust taxation.

There are more defects of the law to deplore. The *pro rata* attribution of income presupposes a sort of participation of the beneficiary in the entity which in fact does not exist. Usually, there is no such thing as a share of the beneficiary in the entity. That is why *pro rata* attribution of income and capital is usually interpreted as a repartition of profit and assets per capita. This is justified if the beneficiaries enjoy equal treatment. Frequently enough, however, the deed of foundation or trust grants the management discretionary authority to decide how much and to whom (within the family) funds are to be distributed. An attribution of income per capita obviously leads to unjust taxation. This is all the more evident if the deed of foundation or trust temporarily bars a group of beneficiaries from any entitlement to distributions, e.g. before having reached a certain age or during the lifetime of their parents. Attribution of income to such beneficiaries is hardly justified. The situation becomes vague if family members under a certain age are denied any distributions of funds unless in the case of hardship and distress. There is no well-established rule that the attribution of income to a person having not reached the necessary age actually de-

---

17 Federal Finance Ministry, Circular of 8 Jan. 2007, Federal Tax Gazette part I, 2007, p. 99.
18 The attribution of property is currently of no relevance, however, since Germany does not levy a wealth tax at present and the attribution does not apply for inheritance and gift tax purposes (Sec. 15(1) sentence 2 of the Foreign Tax Act).

pends on whether he is in a situation of distress. Therefore, such a person should brace himself for having the foundation's income attributed to him by the tax administration.

Similar to the CFC rules, the provision on the attribution of profits to beneficiaries provides for a **privilege** for foundations or trusts having their registered office or their principle place of management in an **EU/EEA member state**. No deemed income arises if this country provides information relevant for the taxation of the beneficiary (see above) and if he does not have any legally or factually based authority to have the assets of the foundation or trust at his disposal (Sec. 16(6) of the Foreign Tax Act). This criterion targets the large number of foundations in Liechtenstein which were originally established in the 20th century to fraud on German income tax. An important feature of these structures was a contract between the founder and the Liechtenstein-based members of the management body by which the former was entitled to instruct the latter on how to execute their function, especially on the distribution of funds. The founder thereby had access to the foundation's assets and could control them as if they were never transferred to the foundation and still belonged to him. Pursuant to general principles of German tax law, such sham entities are simply disregarded and their funds are directly attributed to the founder. But the legislators wanted to make sure that even if these general principles do not apply, foundations that are 'remotely controlled' by their founders do not benefit from the EU/EEA privilege. This may lead to the assumption that immigrants who are merely beneficiaries of EU/EEA foundations or trusts could easily benefit from the privilege. This is not true, however, if the beneficiary is entitled to have the foundation or trust dissolved and its funds distributed to him. The authorities question whether the beneficiary is really not entitled to factually control the foundation's funds if its dissolution is subject to his absolute discretion.

The essence of these rules on the attribution of income of foreign entities (corporations and family foundations or trusts) to the resident taxpayer is that immigration of individuals concerned requires tax planning in advance. There are measures available to mitigate the impact of these attribution rules, such as interposing a foundation which benefits from the EU/EEA privilege. Off-the-shelf structures rarely fit, however, so individual planning is usually required.

3. Exit Taxation

For the majority of emigrants, emigration does not trigger an extra tax burden. It does so, however, for individuals who have been subject to German unlimited tax liability for at least 10 years and who own a shareholding in a corporation of at least 1% of the corporation's share capital. It is of no importance whether the shareholding is in a domestic or a foreign corporation.

If such a taxpayer ceases to be tax-resident in Germany, income tax will be levied on the capital gain on the shares as if the shareholding had been sold at fair market value at the time of emigration ('exit tax', Sec. 6(1) of the Foreign Tax Act, Sec. 17(1) of the Income Tax Act). The same is true if the taxpayer, instead of giving up his tax residence in Germany, merely shifts his center of vital interest (pursuant to the clause in the double taxation treaty between Germany and the other state being modeled on Art. 4 para. 2 (a) of the OECD-MC) to another country provided this move deprives Germany of taxing capital gains on the shares in the future pursuant to the applicable double taxation treaty (Sec. 6(1) sentence 2 no. 2 of the Foreign Tax Act). There are other situations in which exit tax is levied. Since they are related more to the emigration of the shares than of the person (e.g. transfer of shares as a gift to a non resident person), they are beyond the scope of this article.

Exit taxation is usually justified by being the last resort of the tax jurisdiction to tax the capital gains that have accrued under its sovereignty. If the escape of capital gains from the territorial scope of a tax jurisdiction is imminent, that jurisdiction is entitled to levy the tax on those gains without them being recognized. The German exit tax, however, does not depend on whether emigration of the taxpayer actually deprives Germany of taxing the capital gains in the future. If shares in foreign corporations are at stake, Germany will of course forfeit any chance of eventually taxing the capital gains after the taxpayer has moved abroad: Neither is he still subject to unlimited tax liability, nor are the capital gains subject to limited tax liability except if the taxpayer has claimed the business reorganization privilege in the past. The setting is different if the emigrant has a shareholding in a domestic corporation. The gain on such a shareholding, if recognized, will be German source income, and the emigrant, wherever he is resident at that time of recognition, will be subject to German limited tax liability unless a double taxation treaty bars Germany from taxing the gain (cf. Art. 13 para. 5 of the OECDMC). Therefore, emigration of the taxpayer does not generally deprive Germany from taxing gains on shares should they later be recognized. Still, exit tax is triggered by any emigration of the taxpayer.

The double taxation treaty between Germany and the emigrant's new country of residence does not hamper the levying of exit tax according to the tax administration.[19] The moment triggering exit tax is deemed to precede the time of becoming tax resident in the other country (and thereby being protected by the clause of the double taxation treaty modeled on Art. 13 para. 5 of the OECDMC) for a logical second. There is support for this view from the case law of the Federal Tax Court[20], but it is strongly criticized in academic writing. The Federal Finance Ministry tries to avoid the problem by including an exit tax clause in new conventions. This clause, which is part of the German basis of negotiations, expressly stipulates that the clause akin to Art. 13 para. 5 of the OECDMC does not hamper the contracting state in treating a person who has become a resident of the other contracting state after having been resident in the contracting state for five years as if the person had sold his shareholding when changing residence. Indeed, the clause has a second objective. It seeks to prohibit double taxation on the capital gains which have been subject to exit

---

19 Circular on the Application of the Foreign Tax Act, Federal Tax Gazette 2004 part. Special Edition No. 1/2004, p.3, no. 6.1.5.1.
20 Federal Tax Court of 17 Dec. 1997 – I B 108/97, Federal Tax Gazette Part II, 1998, p. 558.

tax. This could easily occur if the tax law of the emigrant's new country of residence calculates the capital gains on the shares on the basis of their historical acquisition costs without taking the exit tax into consideration. Upon recognition, capital gains would then be taxed by this state although they have already been subject to exit taxation upon emigration in the other state. Therefore, the treaty clause requires the emigrant's new country of residence to calculate a gain recognized subsequent to the change of residence on the basis of the value of the shares which was subject to exit tax.

Germany levies an exit tax irrespective of why the taxpayer gives up his residence or habitual abode in Germany. This could mean a particular hardship for taxpayers who leave Germany only temporarily. If the taxpayer can establish his intention to return and actually returns with the shares within five years, no exit tax becomes due; any tax paid is then reimbursed (Sec. 6(3) sentence 1 of the Foreign Tax Act). The administration may extend this period for another five years if the taxpayer shows credibly that his absence is based on professional grounds and he continuously intends to return (Sec. 6(3) sentence 2 of the Foreign Tax Act).

Exit tax is also levied if the taxpayer leaves Germany for another EU country. If he is an EU national and subject to income tax in the EU country which is comparable to German income tax, the exit tax is not immediately due for payment but deferred indefinitely without interest and without any collateral (Sec. 6(5) sentences 1, 2 of the Foreign Tax Act). The taxpayer (or his heir) is required to annually file a declaration with the fiscal administration stating his current address and that he is still in the possession of the shares. This **EU privilege** was effectively imposed by the jurisprudence of the European Court of Justice, especially in the Hughes de Lasteyrie du Saillant case.[21] Deferred payments become due if the shareholder is no longer subject to an income tax in another EU member state or if the shares are transferred to a person who does not meet this requirement. Of course, the exit tax becomes due for payment if the corporation is dissolved or if the shareholder simply sells the shares (Sec. 6(5) sentence 4 of the Foreign Tax Act). There is an exception for business reorganizations such as share-for-share exchanges or mergers; in both cases, the deferral can be upheld subject to certain requirements. An important aspect of the EU privilege is that the exit tax claim is waived if the person becomes a tax resident again in Germany (Sec. 6(3) sentence 4 no. 1 of the Foreign Tax Act). More important, it is sufficient that the shares return, i.e. Germany may again tax a gain on the sale of the shares.

IV. Closing Remarks

It has already been mentioned that tax law has not been an instrument of German migration policy for quite some time. This is consolatory since the rules currently in place effectively deter immigration as well as emigration at least of wealthier people, which would seem strange as an objective of migration policy.

---

21 European Court of Justice – C-9/02, ECR 2004, I-2409.

From a strictly revenue-yielding point of view, the rules in place merit a nuanced judgment. Whereas the exit tax as a matter of principle can be justified as an instrument of *ultima ratio* (capital gains subject to the German tax jurisdiction are taxed prior to the end of the German tax liability), the rules on the attribution of profit and assets of foreign corporations, foundations and trusts seem to frequently lead to unfair taxation of immigrants. These rules aim at hampering structures designed to shelter revenue from German taxation by stockpiling it in foreign entities. The rules are justifiable if the shelter appears to be artificially created, even if designed as a shelter against taxes levied by another state, especially the taxpayer's former country of residence. Frequently enough however, the foreign structure was put in place in good faith and prior to any factual link to the German tax jurisdiction. The indistinctive application of the attribution rules in those settings clearly overshoots the mark.

Dr. Johannes Baßler

Lawyer, Tax Advisor

Areas of Specialization

- Tax and corporate-law advice for family-owned businesses
- Expatriation of individuals and business entities
- National and international succession planning
- Taxation of capital investments

Telephone (ext.) +49 228/95 94-218

Email: johannes.bassler@fgs.de

Using German Tax Incentives for Nonprofit Organizations Across National Borders

by Stephan Schauhoff

Contents

I. Introduction
II. German Tax Law
　1. Tax Advantages for Nonprofit Organizations in Germany
　2. Tax Advantages in Germany for Foreign Nonprofit Entities
III. Investments in Germany
IV. Cooperation with Nonprofit Entities Resident in Germany
V. Organized Events in Germany
VI. Collecting Donations for a Foreign Nonprofit Entity
VII. Gifting German Assets
VIII. Summary

I. Introduction

For charitable (nonprofit) entities which are resident outside Germany the question comes up every now and again whether and to what extent such organizations can utilize the German advantages afforded to nonprofit entities. Sometimes a foreign charitable entity will invest in German real estate or make capital investments in Germany and receive dividends from a stock corporation resident in Germany or subscribe bonds issued by German debtors. Some charitable organizations resident outside Germany also want to collect donations in Germany and, to that end, need an opportunity to pass on their charitable tax deductions to their benefactors. Finally, there are a number of charitable foundations resident in Germany or other larger organizations which cooperate with 'friendly' foreign nonprofit organizations but which are required to observe the restrictions imposed by German charity law with respect to such cooperative arrangements. Then there are those other foreign charitable entities which would like to organize or initiate fundraising events or solicit sponsorship payments and which often ask whether and to what extent such activities could expose their organization to tax liability in Germany. Moreover, there are certain foreign nonprofit organizations, such as well-known universities, which expect to receive in Germany large gifts or bequests from persons who are resident in Germany and affiliated with them, and which ask about the extent to which the relevant transfer could be carried out without triggering inheritance or estate tax. The following chapter will address and answer all of these issues.

II. German Tax Law

1. Tax Advantages for Nonprofit Organizations in Germany

German tax laws offer comprehensive tax advantages for nonprofit organizations that are resident in Germany. The organization must be an entity, even though for tax purposes it does not matter whether the entity is a corporation, foundation or association. The key tax advantages are:

- If donations are made to a nonprofit entity resident in Germany, then the donor may for tax purposes deduct the donation and thereby lower his taxable income in Germany. Experience has shown that the potential amount of deductible donations is considerably higher in Germany than in numerous foreign jurisdictions. For example, in any given year, a taxpayer may claim tax relief on up to 20% of his income donated to a nonprofit organization. Moreover, German law allows spouses to gift up to EUR 2 million in capital to charitable foundations over a period of ten years and to have these amounts treated as tax-deductible donations.

- All passive income generated from assets owned by a nonprofit entity, whether in the form of rent from real estate or interest or dividends, remains generally exempt from income tax. Withholding tax is typically not retained from payments that are made to nonprofit entities if those nonprofit entities receive the dividends. At the very least, the nonprofit entities will generally receive a withholding tax refund if such tax is in fact withheld from any dividend.

- However, income from asset management is not the only income that is tax-exempt. Even commercial activities which a nonprofit entity undertakes may generate tax-exempt income if the commercial activity directly serves the charitable purpose and such activity either falls under a special exemption for 'charitable purposes businesses' (*Zweckbetriebsbefreiung*) within the meaning of Secs. 66 *et seqq.* of the German Tax Code (*Abgabenordnung*) or does not create any harmful competition for commercial undertakings.

- Donations made nonprofit entities are not subject to inheritance and gift tax. Nonprofit entities are granted favorable VAT treatment on certain activities, and they are not usually required to pay any real estate tax on any real estate which is used or managed by it for charitable purposes.

These extensive tax advantages primarily apply only to entities which are themselves resident in Germany. On the other hand, however, the price for such tax advantages is a set of extensive restrictions that are imposed on nonprofit entities:

- The bylaws of the nonprofit entity must contain very specific provisions which are prescribed by German law.
- Management must pursue charitable purposes only and may not, in addition to an entity's charitable purpose, focus on any other purposes such as managing a corporate group or acquiring a certain asset. The management of the assets or management of a corporate group must always be an incidental

purpose and must serve simply as a means of procuring proceeds in order to be able to pursue the entity's own charitable purposes.

- Every nonprofit entity must act altruistically. It may not predominantly further the economic interests of its owners, members or founders, and must instead act solely in the interests of the common good.
- The actual management in practice must demonstrate that the entity's intent is to create a benefit in the interests of the common good. Mere assistance – such as managing assets or services for other nonprofit organizations – without promoting its charitable purpose, is allowed if the entity gains financially from the profits of the services it provides.
- Remunerating the managing directors or other governing bodies of nonprofit entities is readily permissible, but will be subject to a 'reasonableness test'. The remuneration must be in line with the scope of the job and with the standard remuneration for similar management board or supervisory board work.
- Extensive verification is required under German law to determine whether a nonprofit entity has redistributed – in a timely manner – the income which it receives in furtherance of its charitable purpose. No later than two years after the income is received must the entity redistribute it for the charitable purposes. Despite this principle, there are numerous opportunities for retaining some of the incoming income, either temporarily or permanently. For example, one-third of the net income from asset management may be routinely retained in order to preserve the real value of the assets. The reasoning behind this is that the assets can lose their value through inflation, which is typically offset by setting aside one-third of the income.

We are familiar with the laws and regulations on nonprofit organizations in a number of different jurisdictions, including Europe and the United States. When comparing these various laws and regulations, German law, on the one hand, offers considerable tax advantages yet, on the other hand, also prescribes very detailed rules for maintaining charitable status. It is therefore not easy for foreign entities to satisfy the many tax requirements for charitable status in Germany.

2. Tax Advantages in Germany for Foreign Nonprofit Entities

In general, the tax advantages described above can be claimed only by nonprofit entities that are resident in Germany, as expressly stipulated in Sec. 5(2) no. 2 of the German Corporate Income Tax Act (*Körperschaftsteuergesetz*). According to the case law handed down by the European Court of Justice and as similarly regulated under Sec. 5(2) no. 2 of the Corporate Income Tax Act, the only exception here is for tax-exempt entities that are resident in another member state of the European Union.[1] Under this case law, any entities which are resident outside Germany and enjoy tax benefits in their jurisdiction, are

---

1 European Court of Justice of 14 Sept. 2006 – C-386/04 – Centro di Musicoligia Walter Stauffer, ECR 2006, p. I-8203.

not automatically entitled to receive in Germany the tax advantages for nonprofit organizations recognized in their own countries. Instead, each Member State of the European Union is given the flexibility to structure its own national charity laws. There is no supranational European directive or regulation governing this area. There are also no provisions in any European treaties concluded to date which indicate that the member states are seeking to harmonize their respective charity laws. Thus, an entity resident outside Germany must generally prove that, on the basis of its own bylaws and its own management practices, it satisfies the requirements of Secs. 51 *et seqq.* of the General Tax Code applicable to charitable entities resident in Germany. European law does not demand that entities which are exempted under the laws of other member states but which do not satisfy the requirements of Secs. 51 *et seqq.* of the General Tax Code be afforded tax-exempt status. The foreign tax entity must cooperate extensively when the German tax authorities examine whether its bylaws and actual management practices are in accordance with tax-privileged purposes as defined by German law (Sec. 90(2) of the General Tax Code). If it fails to discharge this duty of cooperation, then tax exemption status will be lost. In addition, a review of the bylaws and management practices of the foreign entity could be carried out by way of formal administrative assistance. In any case, an opinion from the foreign country that the entity is recognized as charitable in that country will in no way satisfy this requirement. Instead, the German tax authorities require detailed proof. In our experience, we have frequently seen problems as to the recognition of the foreign charitable entity in Germany. Specifically:

- The bylaws of the foreign entity must contain the fundamental principles that are required under German charitable law. One of these principles specifically also involves the obligation to permanently leave any assets which are tied to the common good in that location in order to cover the scenario in which the entity voluntarily dissolves or ends its charitable work. To address this situation, the bylaws must provide that in such a situation, the assets would be transferred to another nonprofit entity or to a public-law entity in order for them to be used for charitable purposes.

- The entity must pursue charitable purposes within the meaning of German law. Section 52 of the General Tax Code contains extensive provisions as to which purposes are considered charitable. In our experience, these requirements are, to a large extent, comparable with those established in many other European countries. Frequently, German regulations even go beyond the requirements laid down in foreign jurisdictions, which means that there are seldom problems.

- The annual financial statements of the foreign nonprofit entity must show that all funds were used exclusively for charitable purposes. These accounts should also satisfy the requirement for showing that the funds were redistributed in a timely manner. A disproportionately high retention of profits could jeopardize the foreign entity's status.

- Finally, Sec. 51(2) of the General Tax Code provides that if the purposes leading to tax-exemption are realized outside Germany, as is typically the case for foreign nonprofit entities, such activity should contribute to the reputation of the Federal Republic of Germany abroad. The provision has in many cases been considered a breach of European law because it can be assumed from the very outset that entities which are resident in Germany contribute to the reputation of the Federal Republic of Germany. Foreign entities can establish connecting factors to Germany, e.g. by realizing some of these purposes in Germany as well or – to the extent they operate only outside Germany – by supporting individuals living in Germany in accordance with the German charity laws and by otherwise establishing a connection to Germany. In practice, the German tax authorities frequently do not enforce this unfortunate statutory language against foreign entities, which means that there remains some legal risk here.

If a foreign organization resident in Europe is able to satisfy all of these criteria for charitable status, then the rental or investment income which it generates in Germany will be likewise tax-exempt, the organization does not owe real property tax, and it will enjoy the ability to pass through the deductible donations to its benefactors. The above-mentioned high obstacles presented by the German charity law do, however, also prevent entities resident in other member states of the EU from having the regular opportunity to claim the above-mentioned tax benefits. Thus, the following discussion will address the main activities conducted by foreign nonprofit entities in Germany and provides an opinion on how such entities can effectively use the tax advantages afforded by charitable status.

III. Investments in Germany

Investments in assets located in Germany are frequently attractive even for foreign nonprofit entities. However, an investment in assets by a foreign nonprofit entity will routinely result in limited tax liability in Germany. Income generated from leasing real estate or from the sale thereof will usually be taxable in Germany, although the use of business entities and their sale will generally allow for the same structuring potential for real estate investments as exists for foreign persons operating a business for profit. As explained, a tax benefit could be available for nonprofit entities from other member states of the European Union. Yet even here, the tax advantage is often lost inasmuch as the bylaws or the management practice of the European nonprofit entity does not accord with German charity rules and regulations. In any case, this issue must be carefully examined prior to any investments and, if necessary, coordinated with the competent German tax authorities in order to avoid any unwelcome surprise.

Thus, one solution which is often recommended is to make the investments not through the foreign nonprofit entity itself, but instead through a German corporation – a nonprofit *GmbH* – which can be interposed. The corporate purpose set forth in the bylaws of a German nonprofit *GmbH* can stipulate that the corporation seeks to promote the charitable purposes of the shareholders residing outside Germany by using its income in accordance with Sec. 58 no. 1

of the General Tax Code. In that case, the foreign nonprofit parent must simply be sure to in fact use the funds which are allocated to its German nonprofit subsidiary in accordance with the requirements of German charity law. In our experience, it is much easier to present such evidence than it is for a foreign entity to gain charitable status in Germany. This structuring tactic is also available to nonprofit entities from countries outside the European Union. German law allows a nonprofit corporation to transfer all the funds which it generates through its investments in assets to an entity located outside Germany, provided that this entity uses the funds in accordance with German concepts of charity to pursue a similar purpose and provided that this occurs in a timely manner and that very clear contractual provisions ensure that the funds are used outside Germany in conformity with the German charity laws. Then it is not necessary to prove that the foreign entity itself conforms to the German charity law.

IV. Cooperation with Nonprofit Entities Resident in Germany

There are numerous German foundations and associations that run projects outside Germany. Many larger developmental aid organizations are headquartered in Germany. These organizations must constantly prove to the German tax authorities that when donations are made to other nonprofit entities which are located outside Germany and with which those organizations are involved in joint projects, these foreign entities must comply with German charity law. In this respect, German law draws a distinction as to whether the foreign organization operates on the basis of a service contract and therefore as a subcontractor of the German charitable organization, or whether a grant has been made to the cooperation partner. In the latter case, an entity's charitable status will be safeguarded only if there are assurances made in a contract that the use of the allocated funds will be in accordance with German charity law, if the contract memorializes the relevant requirements, and if the German organization has documentation which makes it possible to see that the funds were in fact used in accordance with its charitable purpose under the German law. Foreign charitable entities should show understanding if German donors wish to execute contractual agreements before committing any funds.

V. Organized Events in Germany

If a foreign nonprofit entity organizes a conference in Germany – e.g. a training conference or an academic symposium – then the admission fees or sponsoring contributions collected will routinely be tax-exempt only for the nonprofit entities that are resident in Germany. Only entities from other member states of the European Union may enjoy the same tax advantages if the above-mentioned conditions are met. Even for these organizations, the obstacles are often high, which means that the structuring recommendations routinely apply: Forming a nonprofit corporate subsidiary, ideally in the form of a German *GmbH*, in Germany in order to run the conference and, if applicable, transferring any net income to the foreign parent organization after the conference has ended. By drafting the bylaws appropriately, the tax advantage in Germany can be achieved much more easily in terms of administration.

VI. Collecting Donations for a Foreign Nonprofit Entity

Although it is considerably behind the United States, Germany is one of the largest markets in the world for soliciting donations. On a *per capita* basis, it is one of the largest market for donations in the world. We are aware of a number of foreign organizations which had hoped to collect donations on the German market. Although the European Court of Justice decided in the matter of *Persche*[2] that organizations resident in other member states of the European Union can pass on a charitable deduction in Germany, such an opportunity exists only if the foreign organizations comply with all key aspects of the German law. It is also completely impractical from the German legal perspective for a donor's local tax office to be responsible for reviewing whether the foreign organization meets German legal requirements. If the organization, for example, has identified several hundred donors, then many hundred tax offices could have the responsibility for deciding the legal issue and do so very differently. Thus, it is usually recommended that the foreign organization establish a nonprofit association or nonprofit *GmbH* in Germany which would collect the donations and then forward them to their foreign parents in accordance with Sec. 58(1) of the General Tax Code. This alone is the only possible structure in practice which can successfully ensure that tax advantages will be available for donations in Germany.

VII. Gifting German Assets

Persons residing in Germany sometimes seek to donate some of their property to a charitable organization resident outside Germany or to designate such an organization as an heir or legatee. In general, such benefits are subject to German inheritance and gift tax. However, Germany has in a number of cases entered into reciprocity agreements with other countries, according to which Germany will exempt such gifts or bequests from inheritance or gift tax, provided that the foreign country in turn does not tax gifts or bequests made to nonprofit entities which are resident in Germany. Such reciprocity provisions are included in a number of double taxation treaties, such as the ones with the United States or France. Notwithstanding the above, Sec. 13(1) no. 17 of the German Inheritance Tax Act (*Erbschaftsteuergesetz*) states that even if the foreign organization itself should not completely meet the requirements of the German nonprofit laws, a bequest in Germany will be exempted from inheritance tax, provided that the use of the donated or bequeathed amount is designated for charitable purposes within the meaning of the German charity law (e.g. by imposing restrictions in the donation agreement or in the last will and testament). Thus, the transfer of any property should be carefully structured in order to achieve the corresponding inheritance or gift tax exemption.

---

2 European Court of Justice of 27 Jan. 2009 – C-318/07 – Persche, ECR 2009, p. I-359.

VIII. Summary

The German charity law offers extensive tax advantages which even foreign organizations can utilize in any given case. It is normally recommended that the foreign organization itself not attempt to obtain the tax advantage without interposing its own nonprofit subsidiary in Germany. The law itself – except for inheritance or gift tax – states that this structure is available only for organizations from other member states of the European Union. Yet even these organizations must overcome high statutory and regulatory hurdles in Germany because the organization must meet almost all of the detailed requirements under German charity law, which often cannot be done and even then, not to the satisfaction of the German tax authorities. Thus, in all of these cases, we recommend forming a nonprofit *GmbH* in Germany as a structuring alternative in order to be able to utilize the German donor market for foreign charitable organizations or be able to invest in assets in Germany, whether in real estate or capital assets, as a foreign nonprofit organization. Even if greater harmonization of European charity law is a desirable objective, it is not one which is expected to be achieved in the near future.

Dr. Stephan Schauhoff

Lawyer, Certified Tax Lawyer

Areas of Specialization

- Legal and tax advice to not-for-profit organizations such as foundations and associations
- Tax issues concerning public institutions
- Taxation of sports organizations, sportsmen and sponsors
- Legal and tax advice for family-owned businesses
- Legal and tax advice on private wealth
- Tax litigation

Telephone (ext.) +49 228/95 94-238

Email: stephan.schauhoff@fgs.de

Taxation of Sportsmen and Artists

by Carsten Schlotter

Contents

I. Introduction
II. Problem Areas and Issues of Tax Collection and Legal Remedies
III. Typical Cases Leading to Limited Tax Liability
    a) Artists and Sportsmen Subject to Limited Tax Liability
    b) Structures for Circumventing Taxation Through the Interposition of Nonresident Entities

I. Introduction

Nonresident taxpayers frequently perceive the taxation of artists and sportsmen in Germany to be a difficult and complex subject. This is certainly not just because the enforcement of (limited) tax liability is taken very seriously in Germany. This complexity is primarily due to the fact that the income derived from artists' and sportsmen's activities may be classified in different ways. In addition, the various taxation procedures applicable raise a large number of issues for the taxpayer. The discussion below will present typical legal issues related to limited tax liability facing nonresident artists and sportsmen in conjunction with the taxation of their activities in Germany.

II. Problem Areas and Issues of Tax Collection and Legal Remedies

The legislature has not provided a single answer to the question of collecting tax owed by artists and sportsmen. Nonresident artists and sportsmen liable to German tax law are often surprised that German tax law distinguishes between different levels of procedural law at which the questions raised have to be answered. If income is subject to limited tax liability, the first question that arises is whether the nonresident taxpayer himself must assess his earnings for tax in Germany or whether the payer retains the tax due by retaining withholding tax. Only a few categories of income being subject to limited tax liability are subject to German withholding taxation. If, for tax purposes, a compensation package can be categorized as various types of income, individual portions of income may be subject to withholding tax, while the taxpayer himself must assess other portions of his income in Germany.[1] Naturally, complex classification issues arise when distinguishing different types of income.

Another problem stems from the fact that the German system of withholding tax is also heterogeneous: The law makes a distinction between withholding

---

1 Federal Tax Court of 7 Sep. 2011 – I B 157/10, Federal Tax Gazette Part II, 2012, pp. 590 et seq.

tax according to Sec. 50a of the German Income Tax Act (*Einkommensteuergesetz*) and withholding tax under wage taxation. Since Jan. 1, 1996, the particular type of income has been decisive in determining whether withholding tax should be retained by the payer according to Sec. 50a(4) of the Income Tax Act or withheld by the domestic employer pursuant to Sec. 38 of the Income Tax Act. Sec. 50a(1) no. 1 of the Income Tax Act establishes the principle that wage taxation takes precedence over withholding tax under Sec. 50a(4) of the Income Tax Act in the case of income from employment, insofar as this income is subject to German wage taxation according to Sec. 38(1) sentence 1 no. 1 of the Income Tax Act. This is always the case if there is a **domestic** employer. However, in the case of income from providing independent services or carrying on a trade or business, and when there is no obligation to collect wage tax on income from employment, i.e. when income from employment is received from a **foreign** employer, which does not fall within the scope of Sec. 38(1) of the Income Tax Act, withholding tax according to Sec. 50a of the Income Tax Act is applicable. German tax law therefore does not limit the requirement to withhold tax to domestic payers.[2] The payer has until the 10th day of the month following the end of the calendar quarter in which the tax-triggering event occurred to file a self-assessment and to remit the withheld amount to the relevant tax office (Sec. 73e of the German Income Tax Implementation Regulation – *Einkommensteuer-Durchführungsverordnung*). Both systems are secured by the liability of the withholding agent.

Unlike the deduction of wage tax, Sec. 50a of the Income Tax Act essentially requires the relevant tax to be withheld pursuant to Sec. 50d(1) sentence 1 of the Income Tax Act regardless of any treaty law. This distinction is by no means purely academic in nature. It becomes relevant, for example, in the issue of taking double taxation agreements into account during the tax withholding phase. If a payer is required to withhold tax according to Sec. 50a of the Income Tax Act, he is only permitted not to do so or to apply a lower tax rate if the payee is able to provide a 'certificate of exemption from withholding tax' (hereinafter 'certificate of exemption') according to Sec. 50d(2) of the Income Tax Act prior to the tax being withheld (cf. Sec. 50d(2) sentences 5 and 8 of the Income Tax Act). The payee must formally request this certificate of exemption from the Federal Central Tax Office in Bonn in a separate administrative procedure **prior to** the tax actually being withheld. What is distinctive about this procedure is that the Federal Central Tax Office authority focuses on tax treaty law.[3] In the taxation of artists and sportsmen, an application for a certificate of exemption can only be considered when income cannot be categorized as income being subject to Art. 17 of the OECD MC. Unlike the case in many legal systems, the payer may therefore not autonomously take exemptions into consideration under tax treaty law. If a recipient fails to apply for an exemption, a refund procedure will have to be performed. The situation is different for wage

---

[2] Federal Tax Court of 22 Aug. 2007 – I R 45/02, Federal Tax Gazette Part II, 2008, pp. 190 et seq.
[3] Federal Tax Court of 19 Nov. 2003 – I R 22/02, Federal Tax Gazette Part II, 2004, pp. 560 et seq.

taxation because, in that instance, the employer required to collect the wage tax may take into consideration issues of tax treaty law when withholding wage tax without any previous exemption procedure. If an employer wishes to ensure tax exemption for wage tax purposes under tax treaty law, the employer's local tax office and not the Federal Central Tax Office is responsible for this.

The full amount of income is generally subject to withhold tax according to Sec. 50a of the Income Tax Act. Travel costs of the payee that are reimbursed or assumed by the payer (withholding agent) are not considered to be income insofar as this amount does not exceed the actual costs incurred for travel and accommodation plus the standard allowance for meals according to Sec. 4(5) sentence 1 no. 5 of the Income Tax Act. If the payee is an EU or EEA national who is domiciled or has a usual abode within the territory of any of these states, or is a corporation, association of individuals or legal estate that is an entity established under the law of a member state of the EU or of the EEA, having its registered office and place of effective management within the territory of any of these states, the payer may deduct from his income the business expenses or income-related expenses (Sec. 50a(3) sentences 1 and 3 of the Income Tax Act) that have a close business connection therewith under the circumstances laid down in Sec. 50a(1) nos. 1 and 2 of the Income Tax Act. For this close connection, a causal link is not sufficient (e.g. in the case of overhead expenses). It is irrelevant, however, whether the expenses were incurred domestically or abroad. The payee must provide the payer with proof of the business or income-related expenses in a format that is verifiable for the relevant tax office (for instance, by providing copies of invoices). Documentation and record-keeping obligations also exist for the payer. In non-EU/EEA cases, business or income-related expenses may not be deducted.

Withholding tax according to Sec. 50a of the Income Tax Act is essentially considered to be definitive (Sec. 50(2) of the Income Tax Act). A tax assessment would only come into play in narrowly defined legally permissible exceptions. If gross income is taxed, the tax rate is 15% of the income. In the case of net taxation, the tax rate is 30% of the remaining income after deducting business or income-related expenses if the payee is a natural person or partnership. If a corporation, association of individuals or legal estate is acting as payee, the tax rate is 15% of the remaining income after deducting business or income-related expenses. An additional solidarity surcharge in the amount of 5.5% must be levied on the tax.

In chains of payment, tax must, in principle, be deducted at each level of that chain (e.g. a foreign concert agency passes payments on to foreign artists that it has engaged). Since nonresident payers are also required to withhold tax, he has to withhold tax at the second level when paying artists or sportsmen. Payments that are passed on can regularly be deducted as business or income-related expenses under the provisions stipulated in Sec. 50a(3) of the Income Tax Act. By way of exception, Sec. 50a(4) of the Income Tax Act permits the second-tier payer not to withhold tax if the gross amount of the remuneration he has received has already been taxed, but not, for example, if the first-tier payee has claimed business or income-related expenses.

Appellate procedures are complex as well. The significance of the withholding-tax system for the payer, who is required to withhold the tax on the one hand, and the payee on the other frequently raises questions as to which of the parties involved is entitled to file a claim or appeal.[4] Problems arise in particular when there are uncertainties as to whether income is subject to limited tax liability or exemptions apply under tax treaty law. Since the party required to withhold tax is, under case law, also permitted to do so, if there are uncertainties as to limited tax liability, the nonresident payee must clarify the issue in a special procedure.[5] The payee may apply for a notice of exemption if he is not entitled to file a self-assessment. If he is entitled to file a self-assessment, that procedure has to be used. In contrast, if the payer appeals against the withholding, a full review of this will include the answer to the question whether the payee is subject to limited tax liability.[6] If exemptions under tax treaty law are in dispute, particular procedural steps have to be followed. It is therefore procedural issues that make the taxation of nonresident artists and sportsmen particularly complex. This is often a reason why nonresident taxpayers attempt to negotiate net payments with domestic payers. In that regard, however, it should be noted that even in the case of an agreement for net remuneration, the nonresident payee continues to be the actual taxpayer within the meaning of the law. Well advised domestic payers therefore seek assurances from the nonresident payee in contractual agreements of cooperation in the taxation process, request that they be granted powers of attorney, and ask for assignment of refund claims (in order to apply under tax treaty law for refunds from the Federal Central Tax Office). It is also useful to explicitly agree on any obligations to co-operate in appellate procedures. The lack of explicit agreements often leads to complex matters of dispute as to the scope of the obligation to cooperate.

III. Typical Cases Leading to Limited Tax Liability

a) Artists and Sportsmen Subject to Limited Tax Liability

Focusing first on the artists and sportsmen themselves, it should be noted that their income regularly consists of two elements: First, artists or sportsmen receive payments based on appearances; second, artists and sportsmen frequently receive income for an advertising activity as well. Various types of income are already affected as a result of these basic activities of nonresident artists and sportsmen under German tax law.

---

4 Federal Tax Court of 13 Aug. 1997 – I B 30/97, Federal Tax Gazette Part II, 1997, pp. 700 et seq.; Federal Tax Court of 7 Nov. 2007 – I R 19/04, BFH/NV 2008, pp. 442 et seq.
5 Federal Tax Court of 7 Nov. 2007 – I R 19/04, BFH/NV 2008, pp. 442 et seq.
6 Federal Tax Court of 28 Jan. 2005 – I R 73/02, Federal Tax Gazette Part II, 2005, pp. 550 et seq.

aa) Payments for Appearances

Payments for appearances received by artists or sportsmen may be classified as income from employment, providing independent services and carrying on a trade or business. Sportsmen less frequently receive income for providing independent services, and this is more often a consideration for artistic activity when artists render an intrinsically artistic performance with the required level of originality (Sec. 49(1) no. 3 in conjunction with Sec. 18 of the Income Tax Act). That income for providing independent services is subject to German taxation if the activity is or was carried out or utilized domestically, or if a permanent establishment is maintained in Germany for the activity. In addition, an artist may receive income from employment within the meaning of Sec. 49(1) no. 4 of the Income Tax Act in conjunction with Sec. 19 of the Income Tax Act if the artist is engaged in dependent employment. Sportsmen receive income from employment if they are engaged in a team (e.g. soccer, handball or basketball). Income from employment has the requisite link to Germany if the activity is or was carried out or utilized domestically (e.g. income of soccer players playing in Germany). The income of boxers, golfers or tennis players is not categorized as income from employment. This income is treated as originating from a trade or business activity and is subject to German limited tax liability (Sec. 49(1) no. 2(d) of the Income Tax Act) if the activity is carried out in Germany.

In Germany, performance-related income earned by artists and sportsmen is subject to withholding tax according to Sec. 50a(1) no. 1 of the Income Tax Act. The payer, who must withhold the tax on behalf of the payee, who is subject to limited tax liability (taxpayer), is thereby the withholding agent. As already stated, the system of withholding tax on performance-related income is not at all homogenous, so that it must be determined whether wage taxation or withholding tax according to Sec. 50a of the Income Tax Act is applicable. The Federal Republic of Germany is entitled to tax performance-related income from domestic appearances if the relevant double taxation treaty contains a provision comparable to Art. 17 of the OECD MC.

bb) Advertising Income Received by Artists and Sportsmen

Significant problems arise when attempting to distinguish between the types of income when it comes to the tax treatment of advertising fees received by non-resident artists or sportsmen. It should be noted that advertising services are provided in different ways. In terms of the income classification, it is essential to distinguish between active, appearance-based advertising (e.g. advertising on a jersey or supplier contracts) and income from the passive licensing of personality rights for advertising purposes.[7]

---

[7] Federal Tax Court of 19 Dec. 2007 – I R 19/06, Federal Tax Gazette Part II, 2010, pp. 399 et seq.; Federal Tax Court of 7 Sep. 2011 – I B 157/10, Federal Tax Gazette Part II, 2012, pp. 590 et seq.

Income from active advertising services, which is directly (i.e. in terms of time or place) associated with a sporting or artistic performance (e.g. advertising on a sports jersey), has to be categorized as income from employment if the artist or sportsman is required to perform the promotional activity as part of his employment contract.[8] If the advertising is not included in the employer's marketing strategy (e.g. in the case of personal supplier contracts of a player), the income is treated as trade or business income (e.g. advertising contracts between a team player and a third party).[9] What is also considered to be trade or business income is appearance-based advertising income earned by sportsmen whose sporting activity is deemed to be of a trade or business nature (e.g. tennis players). Advertising income of this nature that has a close link to the sporting or artistic performance in Germany in terms of time or place is subject to limited tax liability in Germany due to this close connection with the performance according to Sec. 49(1) no. 2(d) of the Income Tax Act. For advertising income associated with a sporting or artistic performance, the withholding taxation rules for the appearance itself are applicable (see above).[10]

If active promotional appearances do not directly relate to the performance, this does not alter the classification as trade or business income, since there is an activity that markets the sportsmen's personality. However, the income is only subject to limited tax liability if a domestic permanent establishment exists. The fact that the popularity was only achieved by means of performances is not sufficient reason in this case to assume that a performance was utilized, or to establish a causal connection within the meaning of Sec. 49(1) no. 2(d) of the Income Tax Act.

Income that is received for the passive utilization of personality rights must be treated separately. This income falls under Sec. 49(1) no. 2f of the Income Tax Act. There is already a domestic connection when these rights are utilized by a contractual partner at a domestic permanent establishment. Tax on income from the licensing of personality rights has to be withheld according to Sec. 50a(1) no.(3) of the Income Tax Act. If the contracting parties have combined a number of advertising services within the context of one single advertising contract (e.g. participation in promotional events, licensing of personality rights, etc.), the services must be regarded as separate for taxation purposes, and compensation packages has to be **subdivided** (if necessary, by means of an estimate).[11] It is advisable to take this into consideration when drafting the contact.

---

8 Federal Tax Court of 22 Feb. 2012 – X R 14/10, Federal Tax Gazette Part II, 2012, pp. 511 et seq.
9 Federal Tax Court of 22 Feb. 2012 – X R 14/10, Federal Tax Gazette Part II, 2012, pp. 511 et seq.; Federal Tax Court of 7 Sep. 2011 – I B 157/10, Federal Tax Gazette Part II, 2012, pp. 590 et seq.
10 Federal Tax Court of 19 Dec. 2007 – I R 19/06, Federal Tax Gazette Part II, 2010, pp. 399 et seq.
11 Federal Tax Court of 7 Sep. 2011 – I B 157/10, Federal Tax Gazette Part II, 2012, pp. 590 et seq.

The need to distinguish forms of income also continues in cases that fall under a double taxation treaty, since the different portions of income must be classified within the context of Arts. 17, 12 and 7 of the OECD MC.

cc) Special Considerations for Artists Who Create Works of Art

A distinction has to be drawn between payments effected to artists for public appearances and payments to 'artists who create works of art' (e.g. painters, sculptors, composers and writers), who do not make public appearances. This income is taxable in Germany as income from providing independent services if this work is performed or utilized in Germany, or if it is attributable to a domestic permanent establishment (Sec. 49(1) no. 3 of the Income Tax Act).

Since 2009, only performance-related income received by artists has been subject to withholding tax (Sec. 50a(1) no. 1 of the Income Tax Act), while the income received by artists who create works of art is no longer subject to withholding taxation. Rather, nonresident taxpayers must themselves assess the tax on this income earned in Germany. However, it should be noted that artists who create works of art frequently also receive income from the licensing of rights. In this regard, withholding tax according to Sec. 50a(1) no. 3 of the Income Tax Act still applies. Since 2009, the distinction between a payment for the activity itself and for the licensing of rights has therefore been of considerable importance. Compensation packages should be subdivided according to business criteria by making estimates if necessary if the portion allotted to the transfer of rights is not entirely insignificant. When drafting contracts with artists who create works of art, the different activities should therefore be strictly separated and the payments should be clearly differentiated.

dd) Income from a Trade or Business for the Utilization of an Artistic or Sporting Activity

In Germany, limited tax liability does not only apply to income from an artistic or sporting performance itself, but also to trade or business income from the **utilization** of the performance. There is a special need to distinguish such income from performance income when ancillary copyright protections are created in conjunction with the performance. In this context, it should also be noted that, according to German law, a distinction must be made between the licensing of rights and the final sale of rights since the tax is only withheld on income from the licensing of rights according to Sec. 50a(1) no. 3 of the Income Tax Act. A sale of rights is also assumed when the right is *de facto* used up (e.g. advertising in sports fields).[12]

> **Example:** A nonresident singer gives a concert in Germany and allows a domestic company to sell the live recording on sound storage media. The payment received by the singer for the utilization of his ancillary copy-

---

12 Federal Tax Court of 16 May 2001 – I R 64/99, Federal Tax Gazette Part II, 2003, pp. 641 et seq.

rights falls under Sec. 49(1) no. 3 of the Income Tax Act and is, in essence, subject to tax withheld according to Sec. 50a(1) no. 3 of the Income Tax Act. In a case that falls under a double taxation treaty, however, Art 12. of the OECD MC applies.

Singers or producers making nonpublic studio recordings in Germany may be liable to tax according to Sec. 49(1) no. 2(f) of the Income Tax Act. If nonresident entertainers make appearances, the tax authorities assume in the case of recordings that the fee for the entertainment activity is paid for the entertainment itself and cannot partly be allocated to the transfer of ancillary copyrights for later broadcasts.

In many cases, 'third parties' (persons other than the artist or sportsman) earn income from the utilization artistic or sporting activities. It is of paramount importance to clarify whether the activities of the third party have to be classified as income from utilization of an artistic or sporting activity or whether the activity of the third party is seen from the perspective of German tax law as an artistic of sporting activity **itself**. A third party other than the artist or sportsman may receive performance income under German tax law as well (e.g. income received by a foreign corporation that enters a race car and driver as a motorsports team in an international racing series; the same applies for a cycling team).[13] Utilization means any financial exploitation of the value of the performance, with the performance being utilized by the artist or sportsman, by the organizer, or by a third party.[14] Limited tax liability according to Sec. 49(1) no. 2d) of the Income Tax Act regularly applies to trade or business income, which also explicitly includes income accrued by third parties. Utilization income is for example received by agencies that act as intermediaries by engaging sportsmen or artists, or nonresident sporting event organizers who market a performance in Germany. Utilization may also occur through the granting or licensing rights by sports organizers. Rights management entities in the chain of utilization who deal in image rights for performances in Germany may also receive utilization income. According to Sec. 49(1) no. 2(d) of the Income Tax Act, the domestic utilization of a foreign performance is also subject to limited tax liability. In this context, still many detailed issues are contentious.

The licensing of television rights, in particular, raises a number of complex questions as to both the classification of income within the criteria for limited tax liability, and the scope of withholding taxation according to Sec. 50a of the Income Tax Act. What is decisive, among other things, is whether copyright-protected image signals are licensed or not.

> **Example:** A domestic broadcast company acquires a copyright-protected image signal for a foreign event from a foreign broadcast company. The foreign broadcast station receives income subject to limited tax liability

---

13 Federal Tax Court of 6 June 2012 – I R 3/11, Federal Tax Gazette Part II, 2013, pp. 430 et seq.
14 Federal Tax Court of 4 March 2009 – I R 6/07, Federal Tax Gazette Part II, 2009, pp. 625 et seq.

according to Sec. 49(1) no. 2(d) of the Income Tax Act. Since this is a copyright-protected image signal, the withholding of tax according to Sec. 50a(1) no. 3 of the Income Tax Act (licensing of rights) applies. If this were not a copyright-protected image signal, the foreign broadcast station would have to file a self-assessment in Germany because Sec. 50a(1) no. 2 of the Income Tax Act does not provide a withholding taxation for the taxation of the utilization of foreign performances in Germany. Under tax treaty law, a distinction must be made between Art. 17, Art. 12 and Art. 7 of the OECD MC.

Even if German limited tax liability applies broadly to utilization income under national law, where a double taxation treaty exists, the income categories that Germany has a right to tax are considerably narrower. According to the case law of the Federal Tax Court, Art. 17(2) of the OECD MC is only suited to a limited degree to making utilization income subject to German taxation.[15] Thus in the view of the Federal Tax Court, the income of a nonresident sporting-event organizer does not fall within the scope of tax treaty law according to Art 17(1) of the OECD MC.[16] The organizer provides organizationally independent services, which would be classified under a different business category than that applying to sportsmen. Since the actual structure of Art. 17(2) of the OECD MC only extends the group of persons liable to tax, but not the categories of taxable income according to Art. 17(1) of the OECD MC, the income of organizers likewise does not come under the scope of Art. 17(2) of the OECD MC.[17]

Independent services that are indirectly connected with a performance do not fall under 'utilization' (e.g. ancillary technical services). However, in some cases, they may lead to income for 'related services' within the meaning of Sec. 49(1) no. 2(d) of the Income Tax Act and are therefore subject to German limited tax liability. For that the primary service and the related service must be rendered by the same provider. Regardless of this, the tax authorities only recognize contract splitting within narrow limits.

ee) Loan and Transfer Fees

Since 2010, Sec. 49(1) no. 2(g) of the Income Tax Act has contained a special provision for the taxation of loan and transfer fees, which targets the income of foreign clubs (especially soccer clubs) that is generated by the (temporary) renunciation of a legal position under employment and association law in relation to a sportsman (e.g. soccer player). According to case law, this income was previously not subject to German limited tax liability (either from the perspec-

---

15 Federal Tax Court of 4 March 2009 – I R 6/07, Federal Tax Gazette Part II, 2009, pp. 625 et seq.
16 Federal Tax Court of 4 March 2009 – I R 6/07, Federal Tax Gazette Part II, 2009, pp. 625 et seq.; Federal Tax Court of 13 June 2012 – I R 41/11, Federal Tax Gazette Part II, 2012, pp. 880 et seq.
17 Federal Tax Court of 4 March 2009 – I R 6/07, Federal Tax Gazette Part II, 2009, pp. 625 et seq.

tive of Sec. 49(1) no. 2(d) of the Income Tax Act, or Sec. 49(1) no. 2(f) of the Income Tax Act). It has not been conclusively clarified whether the payments received by nonresident players' agents are included in limited tax liability according to Sec. 49(1) no. 2(g) of the Income Tax Act. As a rule, however, Germany should not have the right to tax payments according to Sec. 49(1) no. 2(g) of the Income Tax Act in cases that fall under a double taxation treaty. Art. 17 of the OECD MC does not provide a basis for Germany's right to tax, nor should the requirements laid down in Art. 12 of the OECD MC be met. Art. 7 of the OECD MC would therefore apply. Nonresident clubs do not usually have a permanent establishment in Germany. According to Sec. 50a(1) no. 3 of the Income Tax Act, only payments for the loan of a player are subject to withholding tax. Tax on payments for a permanent transfer is not subject to withholding taxation; there is an obligation to file a tax assessment. Insofar as a payment is subject to withholding tax, it should be noted that an application for a certificate of exemption must be filed with the Federal Central Tax Office in a timely manner (cf. the explanation on p. 406).

b) Structures for Circumventing Taxation Through the Interposition of Nonresident Entities

The taxation of nonresident artists and sportsmen, which is already complicated, is exacerbated in practice by the fact that foreign entities that handle artists and sportsmen can act as intermediaries, creating a means by which income of a natural person may be shifted to the income sphere of an entity. The aim in this scheme is, among other things, to allocate the income to a foreign permanent establishment. Such arrangements exist not only for performance income, but also for royalties (e.g. when personality rights are used).

The interposition of those entities as a means of structuring such arrangements counteracts German law in many respects. Under Sec. 49(1) no. 2(d) of the Income Tax Act limited tax liability is extended to third persons other than the artist or sportsman since it is irrelevant who receives the income. This notwithstanding, German tax law already asks in advance whether the interposed entity is the one to which the income should be attributed. These structures have to be measured against the rules of abuse of legal structuring. According to the case law of the Federal Tax Court, Sec. 42 of the German Tax Code *(Abgabenordung)* is also applicable, on its own merits, to interposed entities that handle artists/sportsmen, even if only nonresident taxpayers hold stakes in these entities. In particular, if a pure letterbox company is involved, the interposition of a corporation is not recognized.[18]

If the interposed entity is recognized as an independent taxable entity under German tax law, a further point has to be considered. German tax law draws a strict distinction between income received by the interposed entity for the performance in Germany, and the income received by an artist or sportsman from

---

18 In the case of artists or sportsmen that are domiciled in Germany, provisions for the taxation of German controlled foreign corporations (CFC) must also be observed.

the interposed entity in connection with an appearance in Germany. If an artist or sportsman subject to limited tax liability receives income from a taxpayer which itself has received income subject to limited taxation of the particular activity, the requirements for limited tax liability must be examined at both levels. Both levels must therefore be considered separately, and in essence are subject to German limited tax liability. In that regard, however, the provision laid down in Sec. 50a(4) of the Income Tax Act, which has already been described, must be observed.

Dr. Carsten Schlotter

Lawyer, Tax Advisor

Areas of Specialization

- Corporate reorganizations
- Tax accounting
- International tax law
- Constitutional aspects of tax law
- Tax litigation
- Taxation of artists and sportsmen, advertising and sponsoring of sport, and advice for sports organizers

Telephone (ext.) +49 228/95 94-238

Email: carsten.schlotter@fgs.de

III. Corporate, M&A and Labor/Employment Law

Legal Forms in German Corporate Law

by Christoph Schulte

Contents

I. Introduction
II. Partnerships
  1. *Gesellschaft bürgerlichen Rechts (GbR)*
    a) Formation
    b) Governance, Structure and Financials
    c) Transfer of Interests
  2. *Offene Handelsgesellschaft (OHG)*
  3. Kommanditgesellschaft (KG)
    a) Usual Structure
    b) ... & Co. KG Structure
  4. *Partnerschaftsgesellschaft (PartG/PartG mbB)*
III. Corporations and Limited-Liability Entities
  1. *Gesellschaft mit beschränkter Haftung (GmbH)*
    a) Formation
    b) Governance, Structure and Financials
    c) Transfer of Shares
  2. *Aktiengesellschaft (AG)*
    a) Formation
    b) Governance, Structure and Financials
    c) Transfer of Shares
  3. *Kommanditgesellschaft auf Aktien (KGaA)*
    a) Usual Structure
    b) ... & Co. KGaA Structure
  4. Societas Europaea (SE)
IV. Codetermination *(Mitbestimmung)*
V. Group Structures
VI. Insolvency

I. Introduction

German corporate law, in principle, provides for two basic types of legal form: corporate entities and partnerships. In general, the shareholders of corporations and other limited-liability entities must contribute a prescribed minimum legal capital to their company, and they are not liable for its debt. In a partnership, the general partners, as a minimal requirement, are personally liable for the partnership's liabilities, but they are not subject to legal capital requirements. Partnerships must consist of at least two partners, while most limited-liability entities could also be established by a single shareholder. In practice, however, it is often the other way round: The law governing most limited-liability entities is geared toward a rather high number of shareholders who are not necessarily familiar with one other; and most types of partnership are aimed at a rather low and constant number of partners whose relationships with one other are based on trust. Consequently, partnerships tend to enjoy broader freedoms as to the regulation and administration of their entity's internal and external affairs compared to limited-liability regimes, which usually include mandatory provisions on creditor and minority shareholder protection.

Finally, both corporations and partnerships can assume rights and incur obligations on their own behalf, but only corporations are regarded as separate legal persons.

The most important and common types of partnership are the *GbR* (*Gesellschaft bürgerlichen Rechts* – civil law association), the *KG* (*Kommanditgesellschaft* – limited partnership), and the *OHG* (*Offene Handelsgesellschaft* – general partnership). Most limited-liability entities under German law are incorporated as a *GmbH* (*Gesellschaft mit beschränkter Haftung* – privately held corporation), *AG* (*Aktiengesellschaft* – stock corporation), *SE* (*Societas Europaea* – European company) or *KGaA* (*Kommanditgesellschaft auf Aktien* – partnership limited by shares). A number of other legal forms such as the European Economic Interest Group and the *e.G.* (*eingetragene Genossenschaft* – registered cooperative society) are only relevant for limited specific purposes; they will not be covered in detail in this chapter.

II. Partnerships

1. *Gesellschaft bürgerlichen Rechts (GbR)*

a) Formation

The *GbR* is the most simple and traditional way to establish a partnership under German law. It is governed by Secs. 705 *et seqq.* of the German Civil Code (*Bürgerliches Gesetzbuch*) and comes into existence whenever two or more individuals join in the pursuit of a common goal on the basis of a binding contract. The partners do not necessarily have to be aware of the legal significance of their cooperation since the required contract can be concluded verbally or based on a tacit understanding. However, for practical reasons, most *GbR* agreements are (and should be) concluded in writing and specify the *GbR*'s name, purpose, partners, the allocation of profits and losses among the partners, management powers, accounting standards, distribution policies, and the procedure for dissolving the *GbR*. The *GbR* is not registered in a public commercial register, and the partnership agreement is not available to the public.

b) Governance, Structure and Financials

As a general rule, the affairs of a *GbR* are managed jointly by all partners. Also, all partners jointly represent the partnership *vis-à-vis* third parties, and partnership resolutions require the consent of each partner. Individual partnership agreements do allow the establishment of majority-based resolutions, and management and representation duties can be concentrated on one or several partners. The partners may not, however, delegate the *GbR*'s management to outside managers who are not members of the partnership.

In practical terms, the *GbR*'s liabilities are the private liabilities of its partners. If the partnership's own funds and resources turn out to be insufficient to serve the partnership's obligations *vis-à-vis* its creditors, the latter are free to hold each partner fully liable. Due to this unlimited personal liability, the partners are completely free to choose the type and size of their contributions to the partnership's resources without being restricted by minimum legal capital requirements. Furthermore, a *GbR* is not legally required to prepare or publish regular annual accounts.

In practice, this legal form is often used to carry out small-scale, low-risk operations with limited resources and where there is no need to protect the business owners from personal liability (e.g. the administration of real estate property). It is also popular among smaller and medium-sized professional partnerships between attorneys, patent attorneys, tax advisors, medical practitioners, architects and other noncommercial professionals.

c) Transfer of Interests

The existence and identity of a *GbR* is strongly linked to the identity of its partners. Therefore, if the partnership agreement does not stipulate otherwise, the partnership will be dissolved as soon as one partner leaves the partnership (including the death of a partner). As a general rule, a partner's interest in the partnership can be transferred to a third party only with the approval of all the remaining partners.

2. *Offene Handelsgesellschaft (OHG)*

The *OHG* is basically a *GbR* with a commercial purpose of greater magnitude; it is regulated primarily in Secs. 105 *et seqq.* of the German Commercial Code (*Handelsgesetzbuch*). Whenever a *GbR* carries out a structured, long-term commercial venture, it will automatically be transformed into an *OHG*.

Like in a *GbR*, the partners are jointly and severally liable for the *OHG*'s debt and also do not have to contribute a certain minimum amount of capital. The *OHG* is managed and represented jointly by all its partners, with the option of appointing one or several partners as the sole managers and/or representatives of the entity, and likewise does not grant partners the option of appointing outside managers. As a general rule, partnership resolutions require approval by all partners; majority requirements can be stipulated in the individual partnership agreement. All partners are subject to a statutory noncompete obligation.

Unlike the *GbR*, however, the *OHG*'s existence is not tied to the identity and continuing membership of each partner. Partners can leave the *OHG* and, under certain circumstances, can also be forced to leave without affecting its existence.

An *OHG* and its basic legal data (e.g. name, registered seat, partners, and partners' authority to represent the partnership) must be registered with the local commercial register. Apart from this registration, however, there are no formal requirements for the establishment and administration of an *OHG* that would be comparable to the situation of a limited-liability entity. As with the *GbR*, most partnership agreements and resolutions will be in writing for practical reasons.Because of the partners' unlimited personal liability, this kind of partnership is very rare nowadays.

3. Kommanditgesellschaft (KG)

a) Usual Structure

A *KG*'s usual structure – set out in Secs. 161 *et seqq.* of the Commercial Code – resembles most features of an *OHG* but distinguishes between general partners (*Komplementäre*) and limited partners (*Kommanditisten*). While the general partners find themselves in the same position as the partners of an *OHG* or a *GbR*, *inter alia* in terms of personal liability, management authority and authority to represent the partnership *vis-à-vis* third parties, the limited partners are excluded from managing the *KG* and from acting as its representatives. Instead, they merely contribute a contractually fixed and published amount of capital to the *KG*'s funds, which limits their personal liability. As soon and as long as a limited partner contributes the registered amount, he cannot be held liable for the obligations of the *KG*.

b) ... & Co. KG Structure

The general partner in a *KG* can also be a limited-liability entity, typically a *GmbH*. Private individuals will then be involved only as shareholders and managers (*Geschäftsführer*) of the *GmbH* and as limited partners of the *KG*. The group's business is carried out solely at the level of the *KG*, while the main purpose of the *GmbH* is to act as the *KG*'s general partner and to assume unlimited liability accordingly. It is also at the level of the *GmbH* where the relevant decision-making takes place: The *GmbH* managers will perform the *GmbH*'s duties as the general partner of the *KG* and will also be responsible for acting as the *KG*'s manager and legal representative. If no private individual as a general partner is liable for the *KG*'s debt, the name of a *KG* must end with *GmbH & Co. KG* in order to highlight the fact that only a *GmbH* and no private individuals can be held liable for the KG's debt.

In practice, this legal form is particularly popular among family-owned enterprises due to its partnership-like flexibility, the corporation-like limitations on personal liability, and the lack of legal capital requirements that would otherwise limit distributions of profits and assets to partners and shareholders.

4. Partnerschaftsgesellschaft (PartG/PartG mbB)

A special legal form exists exclusively for attorneys, patent attorneys, tax advisors, medical practitioners, architects and other noncommercial professionals, which is known as a *Partnerschaftsgesellschaft* (*PartG*) or *Partnerschaftsgesellschaft mit beschränkter Berufshaftung* (*PartG mbB*). This form is defined by the German Act on Professional Partnerships (*Partnerschaftsgesellschaftsgesetz*), and it replaces the *GbR* for the groups listed above. The unique feature of both options is the limitation of the partners' personal liability. In the *PartG*, professional liability is limited to the partnership's own funds and to the funds of the partner(s) responsible for the critical engagement; in the *PartG mbB*, the partners' professional liability is completely replaced by an extended professional liability insurance policy. For liability claims which extend beyond professional matters (e.g. rent arrears), however, all partners are jointly and severally liable for the *PartG*'s or *PartG mbB*'s debt.

III. Corporations and Limited-Liability Entities

1. *Gesellschaft mit beschränkter Haftung (GmbH)*

a) Formation

The *GmbH* – a German privately held corporation regulated in the *GmbH* Act (*GmbH-Gesetz*) – is by far the most popular and common legal form for incorporating businesses under German law. In order to initially set up a *GmbH*, one or more prospective shareholders must draft and notarize the *GmbH*'s bylaws, nominate at least one manager, contribute the necessary legal capital (at least EUR 25,000) to the corporation, and register it with the local commercial register. Once the *GmbH* is registered in the commercial register, the shareholders are in general no longer liable for its debts. To enjoy limitation of liability for their obligations, new corporations must wait until registration in the commercial register is complete before beginning their business activities. Alternatively, in 'shelf' company formation (*Vorratsgründung*), a service provider acts as the initial shareholder of a multitude of inactive but registered *GmbH*s and then sells them to the founding shareholders. The latter then merely customize the *GmbH*'s bylaws to their particular needs.

The *GmbH*'s shares may be held by an unlimited number of shareholders (or just one), who are personally identified and whose names are published in the *GmbH*'s shareholders' list.

b) Governance, Structure and Financials

Most *GmbH*s are governed by a one-tier structure with at least one manager (see above), who may (but does not have to) be a shareholder. Optionally, a *GmbH* may opt for a two-tier structure with a supervisory board (*Aufsichtsrat*) similar to that of an *AG* or, as a less formal alternative, an advisory board (*Beirat*). A supervisory board is mandatory only for *GmbH*s that are subject to co-determination since the employees' representatives will typically have to be members of the corporation's supervisory body (see below).

The shareholders are empowered not only to make fundamental decisions (e.g. mergers with other entities, amendments to the *GmbH*'s bylaws, removal or appointment of the manager); they are also free to issue detailed and binding directives to the managers on almost any subject as they see fit.

Due to the (usually) low number of shareholders and members of management, many aspects of a *GmbH*'s legal structure can be tailored to the corporation's individual needs. For example, in a family-owned business, the bylaws could provide for family-specific share transfer restrictions, multiple voting rights for particular family members, voting restrictions for outside shareholders, issue-specific majority requirements, mandatory sell-out rights or the equal representation of each family branch in the management and/or supervision of the entity. On the other hand, a *GmbH* with just one shareholder can be administered by this shareholder alone (who can elect himself as the sole managing director) with the opportunity to release himself from the restrictions against self-dealing (Sec. 181 of the Civil Code); however, every transaction between him and the corporation must be documented in writing.

A *GmbH*'s business purpose may be purely commercial, but also nonprofit organizations, attorneys and tax advisors can opt for the *GmbH* form to pursue their activities. Generally speaking, the *GmbH* can be tailored to a broad variety of business environments and is particularly suitable for small and medium-sized enterprises with a low and constant number of shareholders. Also, many subsidiaries and joint ventures of larger companies are incorporated as *GmbH*s.

The *GmbH* must maintain legal capital of at least EUR 25,000. However, instead of establishing a EUR 25,000 *GmbH*, start-up businesses in particular and other small and very small enterprises with limited financial resources have the option of incorporating as an *Unternehmergesellschaft (haftungsbeschränkt)* (entrepreneurial company (limited liability)). The latter shares most of the characteristics and legal foundations of the *GmbH* but allows for legal capital of as low as EUR 1.

As a rule, the shareholders are not liable for the corporation's debts. This advantage is not applicable (i) if the corporation is not registered in the commercial register or (ii) the registered capital is (partially) paid back to the shareholders (capital maintenance) or (iii) the registered capital is not (entirely) paid in.

c) Transfer of Shares

The process of transferring a *GmbH*'s share carries significantly more formal requirements than the transfer of an *AG* share. Most importantly, a share can be transferred only on the basis of a notarized written contract. Additional transfer requirements (e.g. a vote of approval of the shareholders' meeting) can be set out in the *GmbH*'s bylaws. The new shareholder must be registered in a shareholders' list. Otherwise he is not entitled to exercise shareholder's rights.

2. *Aktiengesellschaft (AG)*

a) Formation

An *AG* is a German stock corporation. Its legal foundation is primarily the Stock Corporation Act (*Aktiengesetz*). As with the formation of a *GmbH*, the founding shareholders of an *AG* must draft and notarize the bylaws, nominate management and supervisory board members, deposit the necessary legal capital, and register the corporation with the commercial register. It is also possible to form a shelf company.

In practice, many *AG*s come into existence not in the course of an ordinary formation but by way of reorganization; i.e. they are initially established in another legal form (such as a *GmbH*) and subsequently reorganized into an *AG* along with the growth of the corporation's business or shareholder basis or in order to prepare for an initial public offering.

b) Governance, Structure and Financials

An *AG* is managed by a two-tier structure with a management board (*Vorstand*) and a supervisory board. The shareholders' meeting (*Hauptversammlung*) elects only the members of the supervisory board (at least three members depending on the registered capital), while management board members are selected and monitored only by the supervisory board. For both the management and the supervisory board members, the term is limited to five years.

Generally, the role of *AG* shareholders and the *AG* shareholders' meeting is very limited. They elect supervisory board members, and a number of fundamental and strategic decisions are subject to their approval (e.g. mergers with other entities and amendments to the *AG*'s bylaws). At the same time, shareholders are strictly cut off from the company's day-to-day management and most other management decisions. In particular, they are not authorized to issue binding directives to board members on their own initiative.

As a consequence, the management board runs the *AG*'s business almost completely independently of the potentially interfering decisions and opinions of shareholders – and also of the supervisory board members. Only with respect to specific and important management decisions set out in the bylaws or in the board's internal rules of procedure (e.g. capital investments exceeding a certain euro amount or long-term contracts exceeding a certain number of years) does the management board require a vote of approval by the supervisory board.

Due to the large number of shareholders (in most cases), the need to protect minority shareholders and the allocation of decision-making authority among three organs, the legal administration of an *AG* entails more standardized and inflexible requirements than that of a *GmbH*. Many aspects of the *AG*'s legal structure are predetermined by statutory law and can be adapted to individual circumstances only insofar as this is explicitly permitted. For example, the supervisory board must consist of at least three members, a higher number of board seats must be a multiple of three, the management board members must be different from the supervisory board members, the shareholders will often have to be invited publicly to the *AG*'s annual meeting, and the minutes of the shareholders' meeting must generally be recorded by a German notary. Furthermore, if the corporation's stock is traded on a regulated market, the *AG* will have to comply with the requirements of the relevant capital-market laws and regulations, which could, for example, include the publication of quarterly reports, *ad-hoc* announcements and the stricter regulation of takeover transactions.

An *AG*'s legal capital must consist of at least EUR 50,000 and be divided into either par-value shares (*Nennbetragsaktien*) or shares without a par value (*Stückaktien*). If these shares are registered shares (*Namensaktien*), each shareholder will be listed in the *AG*'s nonpublic shareholders' list. Otherwise, i.e. if the *AG* has issued bearer shares (*Inhaberaktien*), the *AG* has no means of directly and individually identifying its shareholders.

c) Transfer of Shares

AG shareholders can transfer their shares quickly and, by and large, without the need to observe too many legal technicalities. If share certificates have not been issued, a shareholder can transfer a bearer share by assigning it without a notarial deed. The same applies when a registered share is transferred; however, the new shareholder's name will then additionally have to be included in the *AG*'s shareholders' list (which is not publicly accessible) and appear on the share certificate itself.

Publicly traded *AG*s will regularly have their shares deposited with a clearing institution and linked to the relevant electronic trading platform. Because of this enhanced transferability, the *AG* is by far the most common legal form for publicly traded companies in Germany. Currently, 23 of 30 DAX companies and 40 of 50 MDAX companies are structured as an *AG*.

3. *Kommanditgesellschaft auf Aktien (KGaA)*

a) Usual Structure

The *KGaA*'s regular structure is that of a hybrid corporate entity with elements of a partnership: Similar to a limited partnership, the *KGaA*'s equity shareholder basis is split into general partners and limited-liability shareholders (*Kommanditaktionäre*). The former are in charge of managing the *KGaA*, acting as representatives of the entity, and they are jointly and severally liable for its debts. In general, the rules for a *KG* are applicable. On the other hand, the rules for *AG*s are largely applicable for the limited-liability shareholders.

Like the *AG*, the *KGaA* is a separate legal person with two-tier corporate governance and legal capital of at least EUR 50,000. Its limited-liability shares are transferable as quickly and easily as shares of an *AG*, and, importantly, they can be traded on equity capital markets. The limited-liability shareholders' meeting votes on certain fundamental issues and elects the supervisory board members. The supervisory board itself, however, is not entitled to replace the general partners with managers of its own choice. This is a substantial difference to an *AG*.

The *KGaA* is typically chosen by business owners who seek to extend their equity capital basis without jeopardizing their control position such as large-scale family-owned businesses. Currently, one DAX entity and a number of private banks are structured as a *KGaA*.

b) ... & Co. KGaA Structure

Similar to a *... & Co. KG*, the general partner of a *KGaA* can also be a corporation such as a *GmbH* or an *AG*, or a partnership such as a *GmbH & Co. KG*. Private individuals will then be involved only as shareholders and managers of this limited-liability entity and as limited-liability shareholders of the *KGaA*. In instances, for example, in which an *AG* acts as the sole general partner of a *KGaA*, the *AG* management board is equally responsible for managing the affairs of the *AG* and – through the *AG*'s position of general partner – also the affairs of the *KGaA*. In order to clarify that no private individual is liable for the *KGaA*'s debt, the name of the entity must end in *AG & Co. KGaA*.

This legal form is particularly useful for enterprises that seek to combine the benefits of a regular *KGaA* structure (strong control position of a single shareholder and full access to equity capital markets) with an *AG*-like exclusion of personal liability. For example, six of the current 18 *Bundesliga* football teams are structured as a *GmbH & Co. KGaA*, and the DAX contains two *AG & Co. KGaA*s and one *SE & Co. KGaA*.

4. Societas Europaea (SE)

A German *SE*'s characteristics and legal foundations are very similar to those of an *AG*. In particular, the rules applying to capital maintenance, share transferability, the shareholders' meeting and publication requirements are derived from the Stock Corporation Act and, therefore, are almost identical. Only a limited number of rules are directly based on European law and thus distinguish the *SE* from its *AG* counterpart:

Firstly, an *SE* can choose between a traditional two-tier structure, similar to that of an *AG*, and a one-tier structure with one single administrative organ, similar to that of a US corporation. The *SE*, therefore, is the only German legal form that can combine a one-tier board structure with full access to equity capital markets.

Secondly, codetermination (or non-codetermination) in most *SE*s is not based on statutory law but on an agreement between management and employee representatives (see below).

And finally, an *SE* can transfer its registered seat from one EC Member State to another without having to be dissolved, in order to take on a new legal form or to merge with a foreign entity.

The number of German stock corporations being established as *SEs* is still low when compared to the *AG* but has been growing since 2006, when the first DAX corporation – Allianz *AG* – was reorganized into an *SE*. Currently, three of 30 DAX corporations and seven of 50 MDAX corporations are *SEs*.

IV. Codetermination *(Mitbestimmung)*

Depending on its legal form and on the number of employees it has, a German partnership or limited-liability entity may be governed not only by shareholders, partners and managers but also by employee representatives.

Usually, an *AG*, *KGaA*, *GmbH* or *e.G.* is subject to codetermination if the number of its regular employees rises above 500; one-third of the supervisory board members are then elected by the entities' employees. In entities with more than 2,000 regular employees (including the employees of any subsidiaries), the share of supervisory-board seats allotted to employee representatives rises to one-half. Such codetermined boards, however, will always be chaired by a shareholder representative who can exercise a casting vote to resolve any deadlock. Therefore, even with a maximum of codetermination, employee representatives will not play a decisive role within the board as long as the shareholder representatives exercise their votes uniformly.

Partnerships, on the other hand, are mostly free of any type of codetermination, irrespective of the size of their workforce. However, if an *AG*, *KGaA*, *GmbH* or *e.G.* acts as the sole general partner of a *KG* (...*&* Co. *KG* structure; see above) and is dominated by this *KG*'s limited partners, the *KG*'s employees will be considered employees of the *AG*, *KGaA*, *GmbH* or *e.G.* for the purpose of codetermination law. If this causes the 2,000-employee threshold to be exceeded, the *KG*'s employees are entitled to elect representatives to the general partner's supervisory board.

In most *SEs*, codetermination rules (or non-codetermination) are not derived from statutory law or otherwise dependent on the number of employees, but are based on an agreement between management and employee representatives. This agreement is concluded in the course of the *SE*'s initial establishment and, generally, must not fall below the level of codetermination which exists in the entities setting up the *SE*. For example, an *AG* with a supervisory board consisting of 50% employee representatives cannot be reorganized into an *SE* with a 25% codetermined board. Apart from this aspect, however, the individual codetermination regime can be adapted to the particular needs of the respective *SE* (e.g. with regard to the overall board size, election mechanisms and information rights), and the number of employee representatives does not necessarily increase with the overall number of employees. Particularly due to the latter aspect, the *SE* has become a popular tool for medium-sized entities to freeze a *status quo* of limited or nonexisting codetermination.

V. Group Structures

Entities with one or more subsidiaries have the option of establishing a more permanent group structure by entering into an affiliation agreement. Several types of such agreement are possible under German stock corporation law; the most prominent ones are the control agreement (*Beherrschungsvertrag*) and the profit and loss transfer agreement (*Gewinnabführungsvertrag*).

A control agreement entitles the controlling entity to issue direct and binding directives to the controlled entity's management. It is typically concluded between a subsidiary *AG* and its parent in order to strictly align the *AG*'s management with the strategy and decision-making at the top of the group. Otherwise, even in a wholly-owned subsidiary *AG*, the *AG* management board's decision-making would (at least in theory) remain independent of the shareholders and supervisory board members, and focus solely on the entity's own benefit. Under a control agreement, the controlled entity's management must even carry out directives that are directly detrimental to the controlled company – for example, to sell off a profitable business unit in order to support another group member. On the other hand, the controlling entity must compensate the controlled subsidiary for any annual loss suffered in the course of the contractual relationship.

Under a profit and loss transfer agreement, the controlled entity must transfer its entire annual profit to its parent, and the parent – like under a control agreement – is responsible for annual losses at the level of the subsidiary. From a practical perspective, the two companies are merged together, and they are also regarded as a single entity under corporate tax law if the agreement is entered into for a term of at least five consecutive years. Corporate groups tied together by profit and loss transfer agreements will thus, for corporate-tax purposes, be able to automatically offset profits earned by one group member against losses suffered by another group member.

A control agreement and a profit and loss transfer agreement can also be combined; both types of agreement must be registered with the subsidiary's commercial register.

VI. Insolvency

Formal insolvency proceedings can be opened for any of the above-mentioned entities. The application can be filed by either a creditor or by the insolvent business entity itself. The purpose of insolvency proceedings is to determine whether the entity can survive and to make sure that all creditors will be treated equally.

Under certain circumstances, the legal representatives of an affected entity may even be under a legal obligation to file an application for insolvency without undue delay. Namely, management board members of limited-liability entities – in particular, *AG*s, *GmbH*s, *SE*s and *KGaA*s – must file for insolvency as soon as their entity is overindebted (*überschuldet*) or unable to service its debt (*zahlungsunfähig*). The same applies to ... *& Co. KG* and ... *& Co. KGaA* entities in which the general partner position is assumed by a limited-liability entity (see above). Generally speaking, the obligation to file for insolvency and to constantly monitor the relevant financial criteria is regarded as one of the most important legal duties of management board members under German business law. Board members who are derelict in these obligations may incur personal liability and even criminal prosecution.

Once the responsible court has opened an insolvency proceeding, it will usually appoint an insolvency administrator, who takes control of the entity. The procedure's basic purpose is still very often limited to securing the entity's assets, liquidating them for the benefit of the creditors, and, in the end, terminating the entity's legal existence.

Dr. Christoph Schulte

Lawyer, Tax Advisor

Areas of Specialization

- Corporate law
- Mergers & acquisitions and corporate reorganizations
- Takeover law
- Capital markets law
- Business taxation

Telephone +49 69/717 03-0

Email: christoph.schulte@fgs.de

Private M&A in Germany

by Jens Eggenberger

Contents

I. Basics
  1. Some Basic Facts about the German M&A Market
  2. Major Players in the German M&A Market
     a) Buyers/Sellers
     b) Other Players
  3. Types of Transaction
     a) Asset vs. Share Deal
     b) Different Phases/Steps of a Transaction
     c) Structuring Options for an Asset/Share Deal
II. Pitfalls
  1. Potential Pitfalls in Asset Deals
     a) Notarization Requirements
     b) Section 613a of the German Civil Code (*Bürgerliches Gesetzbuch*) ('TUPE')
     c) Authorizations Required for the Business
     d) Environmental Liability
     e) Consent of Third Parties Required
  2. Potential Pitfalls in Share Deals
     a) Transfer Restrictions
     b) Notarization Requirements
     c) Change-of-Control Clauses
     d) (Hidden) Liabilities
     e) Pre-emption Rights
III. Schemes
  1. Information
  2. Purchase Price Adjustments
  3. Representations and Warranties
     a) Title
     b) Financial Situation
     c) Authorizations
     d) Human Resources
  4. Calculation of Damages
  5. Hold-Harmless Provisions/Indemnifications
  6. Covenants
  7. Distressed M&A
     a) M&A Transactions Prior to the Institution of Insolvency Proceedings
     b) M&A Transactions After the Institution of Insolvency Proceedings

I. Basics

1. Some Basic Facts about the German M&A Market

German M&A activities started to rise significantly at the turn of the millennium, when certain gains resulting from the sale of specific shareholdings started to receive very favorable tax treatment. The German legislature intended, *inter alia*, to provide an incentive to dissolve the numerous crossholdings between financial institutions such as banks and insurance companies as well as large corporations in Germany (*Deutschland AG*). In particular, financial institutions often made use of this opportunity.

A major downturn in M&A activities occurred in 2009, resulting from the financial/debt crisis starting in 2008. In 2013, the total deal volume with German targets was the highest since 2008. While naturally several – somewhat differing – statistics exist, the total volume with German targets rose to over

USD 100 billion. However, the number of deals continued to decline compared to 2011 and 2012: Of these, roughly 20 deals were valued at over USD 1 billion and accounted for approximately 70-75% of the total 2013 volume. Roughly 55% of the volume can be attributed to non-German buyers.

Currently, most experts in the M&A industry generally expect German M&A activities to either continue to grow in the coming years or – at least – to remain stable. However, a growing number of entrepreneurs seem to be hesitant to sell their businesses due to a lack of lucrative investment options for the funds received from such sales. These individuals generally expect that interest in the Eurozone will probably remain low for the coming years, and prices for real estate have already soared in the last few years.

2. Major Players in the German M&A Market

a) Buyers/Sellers

In Germany a large number of – even very large – businesses are still family owned (the German *Mittelstand*). These family-owned entities include small and medium-sized enterprises (SMEs) that are known in all European countries, but also very powerful market-leaders. For several years now, German family-owned businesses have been active in M&A deals in Germany. While these families are usually reluctant to sell their businesses (which have, in many cases, been in the family for decades or even generations), they often have to be sold if managerial or supervisory activities cannot be assumed by the next generation due to the lack of a qualified successor within the family. At the same time, family members (often through a professionally managed family office) have become more active in investing the funds received from these sales, *inter alia* in German businesses.

b) Other Players

By now, M&A deals in Germany generally follow international, i.e. US/UK, standards. Buyers and sellers are typically represented by lawyers. Legal, financial and economic due diligence examinations are generally performed by buyers and their advisors. In transactions exceeding a value of EUR 50-100 million, the parties usually hire investment banks and/or other corporate finance advisors or other M&A consultants.

3. Types of Transaction

Some of the various structuring options for a deal are highlighted below. While the structure that is chosen for a specific deal should of course respect the business rationale behind the envisaged deal, the tax implications of these options for all parties involved will need to be assessed in detail in order to make the deal – overall – as tax-efficient as possible. For this, it is indispensable that M&A lawyers and tax advisors work together seamlessly.

a) Asset vs. Share Deal

In most cases, M&A transactions are structured either as an asset deal or as a share deal directly between buyer and seller (sometimes a combination is used; e.g. if German assets and certain foreign subsidiaries are sold). While share deals are clearly more common in Germany, asset deals are often preferred by the buyer for tax reasons or in the case of distressed businesses (although such deals are somewhat more complicated).

aa) Asset Deal

Under an asset deal structure, the shares in the target remain with the seller as the buyer is only acquiring the target company's assets. Asset deals generally require extensive documentation as every single asset to be transferred *in rem* to the buyer needs to be stated expressly in the deal documentation. This is especially tedious if only a part of the business is sold; if certain assets are forgotten, this might create both economic problems for the buyer and tax issues for the seller. Depending on the assets involved, the notarial recording of the sale and transfer agreement might additionally be required (in particular, if real estate is concerned).

The buyer of assets generally does not assume any of the seller's liabilities (certain exceptions apply, *inter alia* regarding specific tax liabilities and employment contracts). Special attention is required if the assets of an entity in financial distress are bought as creditors of that entity might later try to challenge the effectiveness of the transfer (*Anfechtung*).

bb) Share Deal

Even though buyers often prefer asset deals for tax reasons, sellers regularly wish to sell their shareholdings. As the entity itself is bought in a share deal, the buyer will assume all risks and liabilities inherent to the entity. Therefore, a proper due diligence of the target should precede any share deal.

b) Different Phases/Steps of a Transaction

Roughly speaking, a transaction can be divided into aa) the preparatory phase, bb) the due diligence phase, cc) the contract negotiation phase, dd) signing, ee) preclosing phase and ff) closing.

aa) Preparatory Phase

In the preparatory phase, the seller considers the advantages and disadvantages of a disposal of the business, often by examining the commercial and tax implications of the envisaged sale. If a decision to sell has been made, a restructuring of the seller's group might additionally be necessary (or might at least seem useful) to render the sale possible at all or in order to facilitate the deal. Sometimes retention letters are exchanged with key staff members to prevent them from terminating their employment during this crucial period.

Following the decision to sell, potential buyers will be contacted. Usually the seller will not act alone; often an investment bank or a corporate finance advisor will contact potential buyers on behalf of the seller, who remains anonymous at this stage. The advisor will provide a short summary of the entity and the business ('teaser') containing only very limited data about the target. If the potential buyer shows an interest in acquiring the entity, that buyer will be asked to agree to a confidentiality agreement. After this has been signed, the buyer will be provided with an information memorandum containing more detailed data about the target.

(i) Letter of Intent (LoI)

In particular if only one potential buyer seems to be seriously interested in the target, the parties often conclude a nonbinding letter of intent (LoI). In such LoI, the parties express their general willingness to conclude the transaction and agree on very basic terms such as the general transaction structure, the purchase price (or at least a price range), and the general scope of representations and warranties given by the seller. The LoI constitutes an agreement on a strictly nonbinding basis; therefore the LoI needs to be drafted very carefully in order to ensure this nonbinding character under German law. Generally, an LoI is prepared and negotiated with the assistance of M&A lawyers.

(ii) Confidentiality Requirements

A lack of confidentiality might affect M&A transactions at a very early stage. Confidentiality agreements (CAs/NDAs) are intended to, *inter alia*, prevent the risk that confidential information on the target (or the fact itself that the target is being sold) is leaked to third parties or might be used improperly by the potential buyer after the negotiations have ended without a deal having been struck.

The purpose of confidentiality agreements is to provide the seller with a claim against the buyer if the buyer or its advisors fail to comply with the confidentiality agreement. It may, however, turn out to be very difficult for the seller to bring a claim against the buyer. According to principles of German law, the seller has to provide facts proving that the breach of confidentiality (directly) resulted in damage suffered by the target and/or the seller. Traditionally, contractual penalties were agreed in case the confidentiality undertakings were breached in order to avoid having to provide this proof. Under current market conditions, however, it has become increasingly difficult for the seller to insist on a contractual penalty clause, which is often rejected by potential buyers.

Another problem might arise if the potential buyer uses the information gained in the M&A process to induce key staff members to terminate their employment with the seller. Usually nonsolicitation clauses are included in confidentiality agreements: According to these clauses, the buyer undertakes to abstain from luring key staff members away from the seller. However, this offers only limited protection to the seller as such clauses do not constitute a general prohibition on employing the seller's former staff members. These clauses would usually also be invalid as a matter of mandatory German law. If an employee decides by himself to terminate his employment relationship with the seller and to agree on a new employment with the buyer, the nonsolicitation clause will usually not protect the seller.

bb) Due Diligence Phase

If the seller decides to pursue the transaction with a specific interested party or a number of interested parties, these potential buyers will be granted access to the data room. Most data rooms in German transactions are nowadays organized as electronic data rooms. Often the data room will initially contain only very limited information on the entity; further documents permitting an in-depth insight into the entity will usually be provided only at a later stage and access to this data is then often restricted (e.g. only a limited number of persons, 'view-only', 'red' data room etc.).

The level of due diligence and the intended work product need to be defined in advance; buyers nowadays often prefer a mere high-level/ 'red' flag report limited to material issues to a fully-fledged due diligence report summarizing any and all documents contained in the data room. Therefore, it is indispensable that M&A lawyers with outstanding expertise are retained. Based on their legal and business knowledge, they are able to identify – as regards the specific transaction – potentially high-risk areas as well as those which normally do not carry any risks.

cc) SPA Negotiations

Generally, SPA negotiations start while the due diligence is still ongoing. The seller will try to obtain coverage for any (potential) risks identified in the due diligence by requesting representations and warranties and/or indemnifications by the seller in this regard. SPA negotiations are generally led by lawyers (both in-house lawyers and outside counsel).

dd) Signing

The agreement between the parties becomes binding at signing. If real estate or shares in a privately held German corporation (*Gesellschaft mit beschränkter Haftung, GmbH*) are sold, a notarial recording of the deed before a German notary is required to ensure that it is effective. Failure to comply with notarial recording requirements will render the agreement null and void.

ee) Preclosing Phase

During the preclosing phase the parties prepare the *in rem* transfer of the shares or assets sold. Often clearance by merger control authorities as well as internal approvals need to be obtained; sometimes some structuring needs to be done prior to closing.

ff) Closing

At closing, the payments due at that point in time are effected and the *in rem* transfer of the shares or assets sold takes place as soon as the payments have been confirmed. Some of the managers usually step down from their positions, and new managers are appointed by the buyer. More closing actions might be necessary depending on the specific arrangements made.

c) Structuring Options for an Asset/Share Deal

Although roughly 80% of all deals are asset or share deals, there are also a few structuring options which might be preferable in some situations. Some examples are described below:

The shareholders of the target can resolve to effect a **capital increase against cash** and to grant the subscription rights for such capital increase solely to the acquirer (absent such resolution, the shareholders are generally entitled under German law to the subscriptions rights *pro rata* to their shareholdings). In the case of an acquisition by way of a capital increase, the acquirer will generally face the same issues as in a share deal. Representations and warranties should, however, be granted by the original shareholders: First, representations and warranties granted by the corporation will economically also be borne by the acquirer, in particular if the original shareholders have left. Second, payments by the corporation to the acquirer if the representations and warranties are breached might constitute a violation of German corporate law. It is also the original shareholders that need to accept post-transactional noncompete clauses (if required and to the extent permitted under relevant competition laws).

Instead of a capital increase against cash, a **capital increase in kind** can be effected. For example, if two businesses are combined, the assets of one of the businesses can be transferred to the acquirer as a contribution in kind (and the transferor will receive the relevant shares) (**asset-for-share exchange**). In this scenario, representations and warranties need to be given in both directions. In a **debt-equity swap**, a receivable against the target is contributed into the corporation against the issuance of new shares.

An acquisition can also be structured by way of a merger or spin-off according to the provisions of the German Reorganization Act (*Umwandlungsgesetz*).

II. Pitfalls

Even though M&A procedures in Germany follow international standards, some particularities caused by German law need to be respected. This section will highlight the most common pitfalls under asset and share deal structures. Schemes that might be used in order to prevent these pitfalls will be presented in Section III.

1. Potential Pitfalls in Asset Deals

a) Notarization Requirements

For asset deals, a notarial recording is required if real estate is to be sold and transferred. The notarization requirement might extend to the entire commercial understanding of the parties (i.e. also side agreements etc.) if the sale of the real estate is – according to the understanding of the parties – dependent on the sale of the remaining assets. Failure to comply with this requirement might render the whole agreement ineffective.

b) Section 613a of the German Civil Code (*Bürgerliches Gesetzbuch*) ('TUPE')

Under an asset deal structure, the buyer will usually not assume any agreements concluded by the seller unless the seller, the buyer and the third party agree that the buyer will become a party to the respective agreement instead of the seller. An important exception to this rule exists in terms of employer-employee relationships. According to Sec. 613a of the German Civil Code, the acquirer of a business or of a part of a business will automatically become the employer of the employees working in the acquired business (similar to 'TUPE' in the UK).

c) Authorizations Required for the Business

Asset deals might become somewhat risky if the target requires public-law permits for running its business. These authorizations might have been awarded to the seller in person (potentially a long time ago) and will therefore remain with the seller even if the assets of the entity are sold. Generally, these public-law permits cannot be transferred by an agreement between the seller and the buyer. The buyer might therefore need to apply for new authorizations which might be difficult to obtain – in particular if the applicable regulations have changed since the initial permits were granted.

d) Environmental Liability

Under German law, the owner of real estate might be held liable for environmental clean-up measures if the real estate turns out to be polluted – this principle generally also applies even if it is evident that the pollution had been caused by the property's former owner or a tenant.

e) Consent of Third Parties Required

Usually, in an asset deal contracts as well as liabilities pertaining to the business are also transferred to the acquirer (sometimes contracts even need to be split up). In order to be legally valid, these transfers will generally require the consent of the relevant contracting party and creditor, respectively. If this consent cannot be obtained, the parties can sometimes use remedial measures in order to reach the business goal that is envisaged – such as trust arrangements, profit-sharing schemes etc. These can, however, only be the last resort: In any case, the parties have to use their best efforts to obtain such consent.

2. Potential Pitfalls in Share Deals

a) Transfer Restrictions

When a share deals occurs, share transfer restrictions might have to be taken into account. In partnerships (including limited partnerships) statutory transfer restrictions apply, unless the partnership agreement provides that a transfer of interests in the partnership does not require the consent of all partners.

In privately held corporations, the share transfer is generally not restricted unless the bylaws provide for transfer restrictions. Nevertheless, such transfer restrictions based on the bylaws are very common in privately held corporations. Transfer restrictions will, however, not apply to listed corporations. The above-mentioned transfer restrictions effectively ban an *in rem* transfer of the shares as long as the required consent has not been granted. A transfer without the required consent will consequently be ineffective.

b) Notarization Requirements

Notarization is required for share deals involving shares in a privately held German corporation. It is important to be aware that the notarization requirement regarding any part of the transaction will normally render a notarial recording of the full commercial understanding necessary (including all appendices and/or side agreements etc.). Failure to comply with this notarization requirement might render the whole agreement ineffective.

c) Change-of-Control Clauses

The target might be bound by agreements containing a change-of-control provision. This provision entitles the contracting party to terminate the agreement if the counterparty's owner changes.

d) (Hidden) Liabilities

Naturally, the target remains liable for all of its liabilities in a share deal. The acquirer of an entity will therefore normally insist on performing a due diligence in order to identify the specific amount and the nature of the target's liabilities. Furthermore, the seller will claim representations regarding the correctness of the target company's balance sheet/liabilities etc.

e) Pre-emption Rights

Under German law, shares may be pledged or pre-emption rights may apply. This might enable third persons to acquire the shares sold. The buyer will usually demand representations from the seller that the shares sold have not been pledged and that no pre-emption rights apply to the sold shares.

III. Schemes

The schemes that are usually used to minimize the risks resulting from the above-mentioned pitfalls follow US/UK standards. These standards need, however, to be slightly modified in order to comply with German law requirements.

1. Information

The buyer can minimize risks inherent to the acquisition if it manages to gain a good understanding of the company's legal and financial situation. Usually the buyer will conduct a due diligence examination in order to obtain a deeper insight into the entity. Sometimes, however, opportunities to conduct a due diligence examination are rather limited for confidentiality reasons, especially if the seller insists on confidentiality *vis-à-vis* the management. In such a case the buyer will seek protection by demanding extensive representations and warranties from the seller.

2. Purchase Price Adjustments

Seller and buyer will usually at first disagree on the purchase price. Moreover, the target's value might change between the date of the valuation and the closing date. Purchase price adjustment clauses are therefore commonly used to deal with the different valuations made by the seller and the buyer, and to reflect any changes in the target's value between signing and closing. To prevent a dispute on the purchase price adjustment, the SPA usually provides for a binding decision by an auditor appointed by a third party acting as arbitrator.

Recently, buyers and sellers have often agreed on a 'locked-box' concept in order to facilitate transactions. A locked-box clause will set a fixed purchase price based on a valuation reflecting the target's value at a certain date; interest for the period from the valuation date until the closing date will usually be added to compensate sellers for the time value of money. The SPA provides that no 'leakage' (e.g. distribution) towards the seller is permitted after this date. To avoid disputes, the parties will need to set detailed rules in the SPA stating what kind of payments (if any) will be permitted under the locked-box concept.

3. Representations and Warranties

German statutory law is often considered to be inadequate when measured against the reality of the international M&A business. It is therefore common standard to waive the application of the legal regime provided by German statutory law and to agree on a contractual regime of (i) representations and (ii) the calculation of damages. The most common representations are presented below.

a) Title

As a rule, the seller will always agree to make representations as to its title in the shares sold. These representations will, *inter alia*, state that the shares sold have been validly issued in compliance with applicable law and that the seller holds full and unrestricted legal and beneficial title to the shares. This representation normally extends to the legal and beneficial title to stakes in subsidiaries held by the target. The seller will also need to accept representations that the shares are neither pledged nor otherwise encumbered with any third-party rights and that the shares are not subject to any pre-emption rights, trust arrangements, silent partnerships, subparticipations or similar arrangements.

b) Financial Situation

Sellers will generally be more reluctant to agree to make representations as to the company's financial situation. Nevertheless, sellers usually accept at least some representations in this regard.

c) Authorizations

Depending on the nature of the business, a representation stating that all required authorizations have been granted might be very important. This representation can be extended by stating that seller is not aware of any circumstances that would enable the public authorities to withdraw any of the required authorizations.

d) Human Resources

The buyer will regularly ask for some representations on HR issues. These representations are often limited to a statement on the number of staff employed and/or a statement on the number of staff members entitled to a salary exceeding a certain amount. As a rule, the seller further accepts a representation stating whether any employment- or labor-related lawsuits have been filed recently. In particular, due diligence and representations on HR issues need to respect data protection and privacy laws.

4. Calculation of Damages

The SPA (or APA) regularly entitles the buyer to damages if the representations are incorrect. Usually only claims exceeding a certain amount will be taken into consideration according to the SPA/APA (*de minimis*); damages can only be claimed if the total of all claims exceeds a certain amount ('threshold'). The seller's liability for most representations and warranties (other than title) is normally capped at an amount equal to 10-30% of the transaction value.

5. Hold-Harmless Provisions/Indemnifications

Hold-harmless provisions entitle the buyer and/or the target to be held harmless from the seller if certain risks materialize. Hold-harmless clauses are generally favorable if a specific risk has been identified, and they are therefore usually used to protect the buyer if a third party makes a claim against the buyer and/or the target (e.g. the environmental authorities issue an order to decontaminate real estate held by the target; the tax authorities charge taxes for a period prior to the economic effective date, or a third party sues the company for known infringement of IP rights having occurred in the past). Contrary to what is usual for representations, the buyer's knowledge of a specific risk does not preclude him from claiming indemnification. The above-mentioned limitations (*de minimis*, 'threshold' and 'cap') do not generally apply to these hold-harmless provisions.

6. Covenants

Usually some time passes between signing and closing. During this period, merger clearance and/or other authorizations, if required, need to be obtained. This period might entail risks for the buyer as the seller might conduct the business in an unusual (potentially improper) way. Usually covenants are used to force the seller to continue to operate the target's business in the way it was run prior to signing ('going concern'). Covenants, however, need to be modified according to antitrust law requirements. Under German merger control principles, it is unlawful for the buyer to gain control over the target until merger clearance has been granted. Covenants restricting the seller might be considered as a way to gain control over the target. Therefore covenants should basically be limited to ensure that the business is run in accordance with past practice.

7. Distressed M&A

Sometimes entities suffering financial difficulties are attractive targets for competitors. This, however, entails some particularities that need to be observed. To evaluate the potential acquisition structures, an important distinction needs to be made between M&A transactions agreed on prior to and M&A

transactions agreed on <u>after</u> the institution of insolvency proceedings of the target. Asset deals will generally be favored by buyers in distressed situations as the risk of buying a legal entity suffering financial difficulties is often considered to be too high.

a) M&A Transactions Prior to the Institution of Insolvency Proceedings

Under German law, the acquisition of assets owned by an entity suffering financial difficulties is generally permitted. The sale might, however, under certain circumstances be challenged by creditors of the seller under German law. Briefly, this may be the case if the assets have been sold at a price below their fair value. It is therefore of great importance to be able to prove that the assets have been sold by the distressed company at their fair market value.

After insolvency proceedings have been opened, the court-appointed administrator might challenge the effectiveness of the sale. If the sale has not been concluded at the time the administrator is appointed, the administrator has the right to choose whether he wishes to close or to withdraw from the transaction. If the sale had already been closed, the administrator may nevertheless challenge the effectiveness of the deal, in particular if the assets have been sold at a price below their fair market value.

In SPA negotiations, the buyer will need to consider that any representations and indemnifications given by the seller might turn out to be useless in practice if insolvency proceedings are later instituted against the seller.

b) M&A Transactions After the Institution of Insolvency Proceedings

After insolvency proceedings have been instituted against the target and an administrator has been appointed by the insolvency court, the legal capacity to sell the company's assets has shifted from the target to the administrator by operation of law. The administrator will usually consider whether the entity's business can be sold as a whole or whether the assets can only be sold separately. To enable the administrator to sell the entity's business as a whole, several forms of relief are applicable as this is the route preferred by the German legislature. It is worth mentioning that the administrator can easily terminate employment agreements in order to restructure the business. Labor courts accept that the administrator bases his decision to terminate employment agreements on the overall strategy/goal of restructuring the target's business. On the other hand, it is important to note that insolvency administrators are usually very reluctant to grant any representations in SPAs.

Dr. Jens Eggenberger LL.M.

Lawyer, Attorney-at-Law

Areas of Specialization

- National and international M&A transactions
- National and international joint ventures
- Private equity and venture capital
- Management participation
- Corporate reorganizations

Telephone (ext.) +49 228/95 94-637

Email: jens.eggenberger@fgs.de

M&A Involving Listed Corporations

by Stephan Göckeler

Contents

I. Basics
1. General Background
2. Notification Requirements as to Shareholdings
3. *Ad-hoc* Disclosure
4. Takeover Legislation
5. Life as a Listed Company
6. Squeeze-out, Delisting and Downgrading and Other Corporate Actions

II. Pitfalls and Schemes
1. Listed Corporation as Target
2. Listed Corporation as Seller
3. Listed Corporation as Buyer

I. Basics

1. General Background

M&A transactions involving German listed corporations require special attention. Specific legal rules apply to these corporations. The most important ones will be addressed in more detail below. It also has to be kept in mind that, apart from the major corporates listed in the DAX or MDAX, the German *Mittelstand* owns substantial parts of Germany's listed corporations. Many of these businesses are still majority owned or at least substantially influenced by one or a few families. As a result, besides the legal particularities of listed corporations, specific factual circumstances have to be taken into account, such as restricted tradability due to the limited traded volume of shares in quite a number of German listed corporations.

Neither German nor EU law provides for a general definition of the term 'listed corporation' and the consequences attached thereto. Therefore, whenever rules are relevant, it has to be determined whether and to what kind of 'listed corporations' they apply. As an example, the German Securities Trade Act (*Wertpapierhandelsgesetz*) applies in most of its relevant parts only to those corporations having securities admitted for trading in an 'organized market'. In Germany, this is the regulated market (*regulierter Markt*) which is publicly organized and supervised, but not other stock exchange segments such as the 'free market' (*Freiverkehr*), which are privately organized. However, e.g. the insider rules in Secs. 12 *et seq.* of the Securities Trade Act also apply to corporations whose shares are traded in the free market. Thus, the first principal mistake to avoid is to ignore these precise definitions and the scope of application resulting therefrom.

443

Nevertheless, as a general rule of thumb, the relevant borderline between listed and nonlisted corporations has to be determined on the basis of (i) the securities (in particular shares and bonds) which have been issued and (ii) the market to which such securities are admitted or in which they are traded or tradable. As was described for the Securities Trade Act, the distinction often is whether the securities are traded in the regulated market or in any other nonregulated, privately organized market.

The following overview of M&A involving listed corporations focuses on the base case being those corporations which have issued shares that have been admitted to the German regulated market, but also addresses other scenarios in a general way. It should be noted, however, that whenever an M&A transaction involves corporations that have issued securities of whatever kind which are not privately held by a known and limited number of persons, it has to be checked whether special rules apply.

2. Notification Requirements as to Shareholdings

In order to establish transparency as to the relevant shareholder structure of a listed corporation, Sec. 21(1) of the Securities Trade Act provides that any person reaching, crossing or falling short of 3%, 5%, 10%, 15%, 20%, 25%, 30%, 50% or 75% of the voting rights in a listed corporation (regulated market) has to notify this fact to the corporation and the German Federal Financial Services Supervisory Agency (*Bundesanstalt für Finanzidienstleistungsaufsicht*). The same applies to financial or other instruments according to Secs. 25 and 25a of the Securities Trade Act. These provisions have been introduced to prevent a secret or hidden creeping up to the level of control, which has been experienced in a number of prominent cases, such as *Schaeffler/Continental* and *Porsche/VW*.

In addition to Secs. 21, 25 and 25a of the Securities Trade Act, Sec. 22 of the Securities Trade Act provides for a number of cases in which the rights of a person are attributed to another person, such as the rights of a subsidiary to its parent, the rights of a trustee to the beneficiary, or even under certain circumstances the rights of a shareholder to its proxy. Another scenario in which (voting) rights are attributed is the case of 'acting in concert' (Sec. 22(2) of the Securities Trade Act), in which all rights of all persons acting in concert are attributed to each of such persons, resulting in a multiple number of persons being required to notify their own rights and all attributed rights pursuant to Secs. 21, 25 and 25a of the Securities Trade Act.

Any notification received by a listed corporation pursuant to Secs. 21, 25 and 25a of the Securities Trade Act has to be published by the corporation and will be available to the public.

The major legal consequence in the case of noncompliance with the notification requirements described above consists of a loss of rights, such as voting rights or, unless in the case of unintentional acting, dividend rights (Sec. 28 of the Securities Trade Act) which may extend to a period of six months after the rectification of noncompliance.

3. *Ad-hoc* Disclosure

The '*ad-hoc* disclosure' obligation is part of the specific insider rules provided for in Secs. 12 *et seq.* of the Securities Trade Act. Under Sec. 15(1) of the Securities Trade Act, a listed corporation (regulated market) has to immediately disclose any insider information that directly relates to that corporation. This disclosure obligation already applies from the date of the corporation's application for listing. In the context of a contemplated M&A transaction, this disclosure obligation in particular raises the question of whether and when the listed corporation has to publicly disclose the fact of the contemplated transaction.

The corporation, however, has the right to exempt itself from the disclosure if (i) such nondisclosure is necessary to protect its legitimate interests, (ii) no misleading of the public has to be feared and (iii) it can ensure confidentiality (Sec. 15(3) of the Securities Trade Act). In most cases, corporations rely on this self-exemption in order not to be required to disclose the envisaged transaction at an early stage in which the consummation of the transaction is not definite and could be jeopardized by disclosure.

4. Takeover Legislation

Since 2002, German law has provided in the form of the German Securities Acquisition and Takeover Act (*Wertpapiererwerbs- und Übernahmegesetz*) for certain rules dealing with public offers to acquire shares in listed corporations (organized markets). The main provisions focus on public offers, both voluntary and mandatory, and in particular on takeover offers aiming to obtain control, defense measures by the target, the exclusion of minority shareholders after a takeover (squeeze-out) and a selling option for the minority shareholders after a take-over (sell-out).

Mandatory public offers are such offers that a person has to extend to all shareholders of a listed corporation. Such obligation arises pursuant to Sec. 35 of the Securities Acquisition and Takeover Act if a person directly or indirectly obtains control over a listed corporation. Control means the holding of at least 30% of the voting rights in the relevant corporation, Sec. 29(2) of the Securities Acquisition and Takeover Act. If a person obtains such control, the obligation to make the mandatory takeover offer exists by operation of law. In calculating whether the 30% threshold is reached, voting rights held by certain other persons are attributed to a person in certain scenarios under Sec. 30 of the Securities Acquisition and Takeover Act, similar to the attribution of shareholdings according to Sec. 22 of the Securities Trade Act (see 2. above).

All other offers, i.e. such offers that are not made under an obligation pursuant to Sec. 35 of the Securities Acquisition and Takeover Act, are voluntary offers and are based on a decision of the offeror to make such public offer. In the case of voluntary offers that are directed at the acquisition of control (i.e. at least 30% of the voting rights as just described), the special rules for takeover offers pursuant to Secs. 31 *et seq.* of the Securities Acquisition and Takeover Act apply.

The most important rules applicable for mandatory and voluntary takeover offers provide for (i) a certain minimum level of consideration to be offered (weighted three-month average stock price or highest share price paid by the offeror within six months prior to the offer), (ii) the inadmissibility of partial offers, (iii) guidelines for defense measures of the targeted listed corporation, (iv) the squeeze-out option and (v) the sell-out right of the minority shareholders.

In case of noncompliance with the obligation to extend a mandatory public takeover offer, Sec. 59 of the Securities Acquisition and Takeover Act (similar to Sec. 28 of the Securities Trade Act in the case of noncompliance with notification requirements, cf. 2. above) provides for loss of shareholder rights, such as voting rights and dividend rights. In a recent court decision, it was held by the German Federal Court of Justice (*Bundesgerichtshof*), however, that noncompliance with the takeover rules does not entitle the other shareholders to request a takeover offer.

5. Life as a Listed Company

As is true for most other jurisdictions, listed corporations in Germany are subject to increased disclosure and information requirements, besides the notification and disclosure rules set out above. These increased requirements relate e.g. to a different and more detailed type of reporting as part of the annual financial statements, the need to prepare consolidated accounts under International Financial Reporting Standards (IFRS) and quarterly reports. A special feature exists in the form of the 'enforcement proceeding', which allows the German Financial Reporting Enforcement Panel (*Deutsche Prüfstelle für Rechnungswesen*) to review the published accounts, to disclose incorrect accounts and, together with the Federal Financial Services Supervisory Agency, to enforce their adjustment.

Surprising and challenging to foreign investors may be the role of the general shareholders' meeting (*Hauptversammlung*) as part of a listed German corporation. Especially in the last decades, there has been a special development in this respect. To better understand the German specifics, it has to be noted that under the German Stock Corporation Act (*Aktiengesetz*) and other relevant laws (such as the German Reorganization Act (*Umwandlungsgesetz*) the shareholders' meeting has a (limited) number of functions, the most important being (i) dividend resolutions, (ii) discharge (*Entlastung*) of management and supervisory board, (iii) election of members of the supervisory board, (iv) election of an auditor, (v) capital increases, capital decreases and other changes to the corporation's statutes (*Satzungsänderungen*), and (vi) other major corporate actions such as a merger (*Verschmelzung*) or change of legal form (*Formwechsel*). The crucial point, however, is that, as a general rule, almost any shareholder who objects to a resolution has the right to file a shareholder suit and thereby to challenge a resolution adopted by the shareholders' meeting. Such shareholder suit might lead to deadlock or at least a deferral of the consummation of the resolution, especially if registration in the commercial register (*Handelsregister*) is needed for the effectiveness of the measure resolved. As a result, listed German corporations have, in the past, experienced an increased tendency to bring such shareholder suits including a substantial number which could be regarded as abusive. However, German legislature and court practice have set effective standards to counterbalance these suits and to protect the corporations' flexibility and room to maneuver. Nevertheless, the specific German shareholders' landscape has to be taken into account.

6. Squeeze-out, Delisting and Downgrading and Other Corporate Actions

As just described, if a buyer does not acquire 100% in the listed target, which is, as a matter of fact, almost impossible, he faces a scenario as a majority or minority shareholder with a number of known and unknown co-shareholders. In such a situation, the investor may be able to make use of certain special features offered by German law to improve its situation. The most important ones are:

Squeeze-out: If a shareholder holds 95% or more of the target's registered capital (*Grundkapital*), such shareholder may resolve the squeeze-out of the other (minority) shareholders against payment of appropriate compensation in cash. As a result, such shareholder increases his 95%+ shareholding to a 100% shareholding without any minority shareholders remaining in the corporation. The major steps of such squeeze-out are (i) decision of 95%+ shareholder and notification of target *AG*, (ii) evaluation of the target and calculation of a cash compensation offer by the shareholder, (iii) examination of the offered compensation by an independent, court-appointed auditor, (iv) report by the offering shareholder to the other shareholders backed by a bank guarantee, (v) resolution by the general shareholders' meeting, and (vi) registration of the resolution in the target's commercial register. Upon such registration, the minority shareholders cease to be shareholders and are entitled to receive the offered cash compensation. Shareholders could try to defer or block the registration by filing a shareholder's suit. However, in recent years the number of such suits has significantly declined, especially in the case of squeeze-out proceedings. Rather, the shareholders generally file an application for a special court procedure, which does not defer or block the registration and thereby the effectiveness of the squeeze-out, but which is focused on the court review of the appropriateness of the offered compensation, also called 'judicial valuation proceedings' (*Spruchverfahren*). Therefore, the shareholder implementing a squeeze-out procedure has to take into consideration that he might be forced by a court decision to pay a higher price for the minority shares than initially offered. In case of a successful takeover offer (cf. 4 above), Secs. 39 a *et seq.* of the Securities Acquisition and Takeover Act provide for a special squeeze-out procedure and, *inter alia*, a presumption of the appropriateness of the offered consideration if the offeror has acquired at least 90% of the shares in the corporation on the basis of the takeover offer and the offered price.

Delisting and Downgrading: For more than a decade, it has been heavily disputed whether the delisting or downgrading of a listed corporation requires, in addition to stock exchange requirements, a resolution by the general shareholders' meeting and also an offer by the major shareholder or by the corporation (if legally permissible) to acquire the shares of the shareholders that would like to sell their shares in the case of delisting and downgrading. Whereas the Federal Court of Justice held in 2002 that such resolution and offer was required, it changed its opinion in 2013 after a decision rendered by the Federal Constitutional Court (*Bundesverfassungsgericht*). As a result, no such resolution or offer is required, and it is within the management board's discretion (in general subject to the supervisory board's approval) to decide and pursue a delisting or downgrading. However, the relevant stock exchanges may have certain delisting requirements providing protection of minority shareholders.

Other Corporate Actions: Other possible corporate actions are the execution of a profit and loss transfer agreement (*Gewinnabführungsvertrag*) or a control agreement (*Beherrschungsvertrag*) or a formal integration of the target *AG* into the buyer (*Eingliederung*). In practice, the most relevant corporate action is the execution of a profit and loss transfer agreement. The effect is that the aggregate profits of the target in a fiscal year will be attributed and paid to the majority shareholder. Furthermore, the profit and loss transfer agreement can be used to establish group taxation for German tax purposes, cf. e.g. Secs. 17 *et seq.* of the German Corporate Income Tax Act (*Körperschaftsteuergesetz*). As compensation, the minority shareholders receive the right to a guaranteed dividend (*Garantiedividende*) or to sell their shares for an appropriate price. In addition, the majority shareholder has to compensate the corporation for any losses. Comparable to the squeeze-out procedure, the process to implement a profit and loss transfer agreement consists of a number of steps, the major ones being: (i) evaluation of the target and calculation of compensation and a guaranteed dividend offered by the shareholder, (ii) examination of the offered compensation and dividend by an independent, court-appointed auditor, (iii) report by the corporation to the shareholders, (iv) resolution by the general shareholders' meeting, and (v) registration of the resolution in the target's commercial register. Again, the minority shareholders can challenge the validity of the general shareholders' meeting by filing a shareholder suit or initiate a court review of the amount of the guaranteed dividend and the offered sale price (cf. *Spruchverfahren* under I.6 above).

II. Pitfalls and Schemes

Most of the potential pitfalls and possible prevention schemes depend on whether the listed corporation is involved in the contemplated transaction as target, seller or buyer.

1. Listed Corporation as Target

As set out above (cf. I.2.), one of the major legal consequences in the case of noncompliance with the notification requirements pursuant to Secs. 21, 25 and 25a of the Securities Trade Act is a loss of voting rights (Sec. 28 of the Securities Trade Act). Whereas in the past it was possible to rectify such noncompliance with immediate effect, e.g. by filing the notification in the course of a general shareholders' meeting, Sec. 28 sentence 3 of the Securities Trade Act now provides for the loss of voting rights in the case of intentional or even grossly negligent noncompliance for a period of six months after correct notification.

Therefore, when planning the acquisition of a listed corporation, it has to be carefully evaluated and observed whether and at what point in time notification requirements arise to avoid the loss of voting rights. Especially the extended period of six months after the correct notification in case of noncompliance may prevent the new shareholder from implementing corporate actions.

Also, the potential ad-hoc disclosure obligation of the target AG pursuant to see. 15 59 the Securities Trade Act. (cf. I.3. above) and a possible self-exemption need to be considered, also from a timing, structuring and procedural aspect.

Another pitfall to be avoided is incorrect or incomplete notification, e.g. in case of an acquirer with a number of direct and indirect shareholders or if several persons team up or otherwise jointly act to acquire a German listed corporation (acting in concert). There are court cases in which the notifications made by the relevant shareholders were successfully challenged, resulting in important resolutions of the general shareholders' meeting, e.g. with respect to corporate actions, being avoided.

If an investor intends to acquire 30% or more of the voting rights in a German listed corporation (regulated market only), it has to consider German takeover legislation (cf. I.4 above). In such a scenario, the investor faces the question whether to acquire the available stake, e.g. from the major shareholder and thereby to cross the 30% threshold, resulting in the obligation to extend a mandatory public takeover offer or whether to make a voluntary takeover offer. Often, the path of a voluntary offer is chosen because it gives the investor broader flexibility as to the terms and conditions of the offer.

Further, any shareholder in a German listed corporation needs to implement a compliance system able to detect any relevant subsequent changes in the shareholder structure which need to be notified and to make the necessary notification in order to avoid a loss of rights. It has been observed that in quite a number of cases undetected relevant transfers have been carried out including changes due to legal succession, e.g. to heirs in the case of a shareholder's death, all resulting in notification requirements pursuant to Secs. 21, 25 and 25a of the Securities Trade Act or in the acquisition of control and the obligation to extend a mandatory public takeover offer under Secs. 29 *et seq.* of the Securities Acquisition and Takeover Act. In this context, it should be noted that Secs. 36 and 37 of the Securities Acquisition and Takeover Act provide certain rules for special situations, such as inheritance or group restructuring cases, in which the Federal Financial Services Supervisory Authority can be asked not to consider the shareholding or to grant an exemption from the need to file a takeover offer. It is important to consider these options before the situation arises as application under Sec. 36 of the Securities Acquisition and Takeover Act can only be filed after the takeover, whereas application pursuant to Sec. 37 of the Securities Acquisition and Takeover Act can already be filed prior to a takeover.

In a takeover situation, two additional common pitfalls need to be avoided. Under the Securities Acquisition and Takeover Act, the price to be offered to all shareholders must be at least equal to the highest price paid by the offeror within six months prior to the takeover offer. In addition, if the buyer pays a higher price within one year after the takeover offer, all shareholders are entitled to such higher price. As a consequence, it is not possible to pay a premium to the selling majority shareholder; also earn-out or other variable purchase price mechanisms are rather difficult (although not impossible). In addition, the buyer needs to be careful not to pay a higher price for shares within one year after the takeover in order to avoid being obligated to pay such higher price to all other shareholders.

Further, as a result of the notification requirements and the need to comply with takeover legislation (even if it can be avoided by means of an application as just described), the investor should consider the appropriate structure from the beginning rather than being forced to change the structure subsequent to an acquisition (e.g. in order to establish a German holding corporation for group taxation purposes) and the risk of inadvertently not complying with notification requirements and takeover legislation, resulting in loss of rights and other sanctions.

Once an investor has acquired a (substantial) stake in a German *AG*, it has to be careful not to unintentionally become liable for certain losses or disadvantages such *AG* incurs. Under Sec. 311 of the German Stock Corporation Act (*Aktiengesetz*), a controlling shareholder (in general more than 50%), in the absence of a formal control agreement, may not exercise its influence to cause the *AG* to engage in a disadvantageous transaction or to otherwise incur disadvantages. Otherwise, the controlling shareholder has to compensate the *AG* (Secs. 311 and 317 of the Stock Corporation Act). In any case, the *AG* has to prepare a report on any transactions with the controlling shareholder which will be reviewed by the supervisory board and the auditor, but which will not be published (Secs. 312 *et seq.* of the Stock Corporation Act).

2. Listed Corporation as Seller

If the listed corporation acts as the seller in a transaction, the two major issues to be considered are (i) whether shareholder approval is required and (ii) to ensure compliance with insider rules, in particular the *ad-hoc* disclosure obligation.

Pursuant to Sec. 179a of the Stock Corporation Act, shareholder approval is required if an *AG* sells its entire assets. It is the general understanding that also cases in which substantially all of the *AG*'s assets are sold are subject to Sec. 179a of the Stock Corporation Act. In addition, the Federal Court of Justice and other courts have developed an opinion according to which even other disposals may require shareholders' approval (what is termed *Holzmüller-* or *Gelatine-Rechtsprechung*). These limitations need to be observed, especially because noncompliance may result in an invalid sale and purchase agreement even if the buyer acts in good faith. Thus, it is of importance not only for the selling listed corporation but also for the potential buyer in order to secure the validity of the sale agreement and its consummation. Therefore, a detailed analysis needs to be made in the preparatory phase, ideally in cooperation with the selling listed corporation. If the result of such analysis is that shareholders' approval is required, the parties need to include the shareholders' meeting and the publicity and disclosure of the contemplated transaction connected therewith into their step plan and timetable. It should also be noted that the approval requirement is not just a formality, but also results in the need for a reasonably detailed description of the transaction including the major content of the agreement and, at least in most cases, the valuation and the determination of the purchase price. Again, the resolution of the general shareholders' meeting can be challenged by any shareholder by means of a shareholder suit.

As to *ad-hoc* disclosure, the most prominent question is the timing of the disclosure and whether and under which circumstances the listed corporation is entitled to exempt itself from the disclosure requirement under Sec. 15(3) of the Securities Trade Act in order to allow confidential treatment of the proposed transaction until the agreement is signed. As the *ad-hoc* disclosure rule aims at early disclosure, it has to be evaluated at every stage of the transaction whether disclosure is required and whether self-exemption may be available.

3. Listed Corporation as Buyer

In the first place, if a listed corporation is involved in a transaction as the (potential) buyer, it has to comply with insider rules, especially the *ad-hoc* disclosure obligation.

Also, the need for a shareholders' resolution approving the acquisition has to be checked. However, as a general rule, any acquisition which is both in line with the corporation's statutory purpose (*Unternehmensgegenstand*) and on an appropriate scale falls within the discretion of the management board (usually subject to the supervisory board's approval), and does not require a general shareholders' meeting and its consent. Nevertheless, the parties need to be aware hereof, and there may be situations which require the shareholders' consent. Also, if the target does not fit into the statutory purpose of the company, it is the prevailing opinion that the management may not consummate the transaction before the company's statutes have been properly changed (including registration in the commercial register) as a first step. Such change, again, requires a shareholders' meeting and an approving resolution with the risk of a shareholder suit besides the fact that it takes some time and requires disclosure of the transaction.

Dr. Stephan Göckeler

Lawyer, Attorney-at-Law

Areas of Specialization

- Corporate law
- Mergers & acquisitions and corporate reorganizations
- Privatizations
- IPOs and capital markets law
- Corporate financing and private equity

Telephone (ext.) +49 228/95 94-637

Email: stephan.goeckeler@fgs.de

Cross-Border Reorganizations

by Philipp Rulf

Contents

I. Introduction
II. Basics
  1. Historical Development and the Legal Sources of the Reorganization Law Governing Cross-Border Reorganizations
  2. Forms of Cross-Border Reorganizations
     a) Cross-Border Mergers
     b) Cross-Border Changes of Legal Form
     c) Cross-Border Divisions
III. Pitfalls
  1. Legal Uncertainties
     a) Implementation of the Merger Directive
     b) Merger of Partnerships
     c) Procedures and the Application of Law in the Context of Cross-Border Divisions and Changes of Legal Form
  2. Participation, in an SE Merger, of a Legal Entity not Mentioned in Art. 2(1) of the SE Regulation
  3. Employee Participation
  4. Planning and Coordination
IV. Schemes
  1. Procedures for Cross-Border Mergers Under Secs. 122a et seqq. of the Reorganization Act
     a) Merger Capability of the Participating Legal Entities
     b) Draft Terms of Merger
     c) Initiation of the Procedure for Employee Participation
     d) Merger Report and Examination
     e) Merger Resolution
     f) Furnishing of Security in the Event of Outbound Mergers
     g) Registration Proceedings
  2. Procedure for Cross-Border Mergers Under Art. 2(1) of the SE Regulation
     a) Merger Capability of the Participating Legal Entities
     b) Other Requirements for a Merger
     c) Employee Participation
     d) Registration Proceedings
  3. Other Situations

I. Introduction

The significance of cross-border reorganizations has grown constantly over the last few years. In times of increasing Europeanization, the practical need to no longer restrict processes of reorganization to a national arena has meanwhile largely been catered for by corresponding legislation at national (German) and European level. Nevertheless, legal advisors are still faced with many challenges when it comes to the planning and implementation of cross-border reorganizations. Some of these challenges are of a legal nature; others are purely factual. Legal problems already arise from the fact that the existing national and European rules do not cover the whole area of reorganization law; rather, there are some quite significant gaps that give rise to legal uncertainties. Challenges of a factual nature lie particularly in the planning and coordination of the (possibly multilingual) process of reorganization. The principles underlying cross-border reorganizations are outlined below in order to show the challenges and problems in advising clients in practice and to make proposals for the structuring of processes of reorganization to address the difficulties described. The analysis focuses on cross-border mergers, probably the most important scenario in practice.

II. Basics

1. Historical Development and the Legal Sources of the Reorganization Law Governing Cross-Border Reorganizations

German reorganization law recognizes four types of reorganization: merger *(Verschmelzung)*, division *(Spaltung)*, transfer of assets *(Vermögensübertragung;* omitted from the following analysis) and change of legal form *(Formwechsel)*. These have been governed by the German Reorganization Act *(Umwandlungsgesetz)* since 1 Jan. 1995 and were originally available only to domestic entities. It was not until the second Act to Amend the Reorganization Act of 2007 that the legislature inserted into the Reorganization Act, by means of Secs. 122a *et seqq.* of the Reorganization Act, provisions for cross-border mergers involving foreign (EU or EEA) corporations. In so doing, the German legislature transposed the Directive on Cross-Border Mergers of Limited Liability Companies[1] ('Merger Directive', Directive 2005/56/EC).

The European Union took its first steps towards enabling cross-border reorganizations with the Merger Directive of 1978 (78/855/EEC – newly consolidated as Directive 2011/35/EU[2]) and the Division Directive[3] of 1982 (82/891/EEC). These two directives achieved some degree of harmonization of the national legal systems governing reorganization. In 2001, the EU created the possibility of cross-border mergers to form a *Societas Europaea* (SE) by means of EC Regulation No. 2157/2001 on the Statute for a European Company ('SE Regulation')[4]. This represents the first case of cross-border reorganization expressly provided for in law. Art. 2(1) of the SE Regulation allows stock corporations, which were founded under the law of a Member State and have their registered office as well as their head office within the EU, to merge into an SE if at least two of them are governed by the law of different Member States. Later, with the Merger Directive, the European Union also satisfied the need of small and medium-size enterprises to be able to merge across borders without the efforts involved in forming an SE.

---

1 OJ L 310 p. 1, corrected in OJ L 28 p. 40, most recently amended by Art. 2 of the Amending Directive 2012/17/EU of 13 June 2012, OJ L 156 p. 1.
2 OJ L 110 p. 1, most recently amended by Directive 2013/24/EU of 13 May 2013, OJ L 158 p. 365.
3 OJ L 378 p. 47, most recently amended by Art. 3 of the Amending Directive 2009/109/EC of 16 Sept. 2013, OJ L 259 p. 14.
4 OJ L 294 p. 1, most recently amended by Art. 1 para. 1(c) of the Council Regulation (EU) No 517/2013 of 13 May 2013, OJ L 158 p. 1.

By means of two judgments (*SEVIC* [5] and *VALE*[6]) from 2005 and 2012, respectively, the European Court of Justice held that the possibility of cross-border reorganizations was already guaranteed by the principle of freedom of establishment. The Court went on to say that, moreover, the principle of equivalence required that cross-border scenarios within the EU should not be regulated less favorably than national scenarios.

2. Forms of Cross-Border Reorganizations

a) Cross-Border Mergers

Cross-border mergers may occur in various permutations. Thus a German corporation can merge with foreign corporations by absorption or by forming a new entity. What is more, foreign corporations can merge into a German corporation ('NewCo cases'). The merger may be an inbound merger *(Hereinverschmelzung)* (absorption or new formation in Germany) or an outbound merger *(Hinausverschmelzung)* (absorption or new formation in an EU/EEA country outside Germany). As a rule, Secs. 122a *et seqq.* of the Reorganization Act apply to all of these cases. A merger resulting in an SE under Art. 2(1) of the SE Regulation represents a special case. In this regard, the provisions of the SE Regulation apply. In terms of systematics, with Sec. 122a(2) of the Reorganization Act the legislature has established a connection to the provisions of domestic (German) law of mergers. Accordingly, unless otherwise stipulated in Secs. 122a *et seqq.* of the Reorganization Act, the pertinent provisions of the first and second parts of the Reorganization Act applicable to corporations apply to the participation of corporations in cross-border merger processes. Sec. 122a(2) of the Reorganization Act makes it clear that the provisions of that Act apply only to entities participating in the merger which are governed by German law. According to the case law of the European Court of Justice, the bylaws are decisive in that respect. Consequently, a cross-border merger can even consist of two entities which have their place of management in Germany, but were founded in different Member States. Accordingly, with respect to the participating foreign entity, the relevant foreign law applies.

b) Cross-Border Changes of Legal Form

Cross-border changes of legal form can be 'outbound' or 'inbound'. An outbound change of legal form involves a change from a German legal form to that of another Member State; the inbound change of legal form is a change of legal form from that of another Member State to a German legal form. In contrast to a cross-border merger within the EU, there is no uniform EU legislation on cross-border changes of legal form, and German reorganization law also makes provision only for the participation of national legal entities. For this reason, it is necessary to refer to the principles developed by the European Court of Justice in its *VALE* decision.

---

5 European Court of Justice of 13 Dec. 2005 – C-411/03, ECR 2006, p. I-81.
6 European Court of Justice of 12 July 2012 – C-378/03, ECR 2012, p. I-621.

Art. 2(4) of the SE Regulation does provide a special rule governing a change of legal form ('transformation') from a national stock corporation into an SE. However, this form of reorganization does not allow the crossing of borders. This is because, under Art. 37(3) of the SE Regulation, the registered office must remain in the country in which the stock corporation to be converted has its registered office, and its registered office may not be relocated on occasion of the change of legal form. However, Art. 8 of the SE Regulation allows the transformed SE the possibility of relocating its registered office while preserving its identity ('without creating a new legal person').

c) Cross-Border Divisions

Regarding cross-border divisions there are no legal provisions at EU or federal (German) level either. In particular, Sec. 125 of the Reorganization Act indeed contains no reference to Secs. 122a *et seqq.* of the Reorganization Act. For this reason, it is necessary to refer to the case law of the European Court of Justice according to which cross-border divisions also fall within the scope of application of the principle of freedom of establishment and, therefore, should be possible.

III. Pitfalls

1. Legal Uncertainties

a) Implementation of the Merger Directive

Despite the harmonization efforts of the EU as evidenced by the Merger Directive, the ways in which the directive has been implemented into national law may, in some cases, vary considerably. This is because the Merger Directive grants national legislators considerable leeway in some respects. In addition, solutions to legal problems under the relevant opinion prevailing nationally may also differ from each other.

b) Merger of Partnerships

The legislature has incorporated rules for the merger of corporations in Secs. 122a *et seqq.* of the Reorganization Act.

On the other hand, pursuant to Sec. 122b of the German Reorganization Act and Art. 2(1) of the EU Merger Directive, partnerships are not covered by the scope of application of the Merger Directive and of Secs. 122a *et seqq.* of the German Reorganization Act – at least when it comes to Germany.

Even if it seems fair to say that the *SEVIC* decision by the European Court of Justice should be interpreted such that these entities are also, in principle, capable of being merged, there is in fact considerable legal uncertainty about this.

c) Procedures and the Application of Law in the Context of Cross-Border Divisions and Changes of Legal Form

Even if – as already outlined above – it should be clear on the basis of the case law of the European Court of Justice that cross-border divisions and changes of legal form are admissible in principle, there is considerable legal uncertainty in practice owing to the gap in terms of legal rules. For this reason, prior consultation with the commercial registers involved is strongly advised.

2. Participation, in an SE Merger, of a Legal Entity not Mentioned in Art. 2(1) of the SE Regulation

Scenarios may arise where the objective is to merge into an SE legal entities that are not capable of being merged within the meaning of Art. 2(1) of the SE Regulation. Examples include scenarios in which a transferring legal entity is to be a stock corporation originating in a third country, or in which an entity is to be merged that is not a stock corporation. Special structuring is required in such cases.

3. Employee Participation

An important aspect in the context of cross-border reorganizations is the participation of employees. For cross-border mergers, the German Act Governing the Codetermination of Employees in Cross-Border Mergers ('Employee Codetermination Act') *(Gesetz über die Mitbestimmung der Arbeitnehmer bei grenzüberschreitenden Verschmelzungen)* provides for a special procedure for codetermination on the part of the employees of the legal entities participating in the merger. Besides, the directive amending the SE Regulation and the relevant national implementing statutes (in Germany: Act on SE Participation [*SE-Beteiligungsgesetz*]) contain rules with regard to the involvement of employees. The purpose of these provisions is to maintain the highest level of codetermination existing in the participating entities. The idea is that the cross-border merger should not be effected at the expense of the employees. For this reason, the Employee Codetermination Act and the Act on SE Participation provide for a negotiating procedure between corporate management and employee representatives. Pursuant to Sec. 5 of the Employee Codetermination Act, this is necessary for cross-border mergers under Secs. 122a *et seqq.* of the Reorganization Act especially if, in the six months preceding publication of the draft terms of merger, (i) at least one of the participating entities employed more than 500 employees on average and (ii) a system of codetermination exists within the entity.

There are no provisions for other forms of reorganization.

4. Planning and Coordination

Providing advice and support for cross-border reorganization processes requires careful planning and coordination. The parties involved include not only the legal entities involved but also the relevant registering authorities, employee representatives, and creditors. For mergers especially, the time limits prescribed by statute for employment-law, corporate-law and possibly tax-law purposes must be coordinated in order to ensure that the merger process proceeds as promptly and smoothly as possible.

IV. Schemes

1. Procedures for Cross-Border Mergers Under Secs. 122a *et seqq.* of the Reorganization Act

The actual merger process is preceded by a planning phase in which the time frame for the merger is to be defined. A period of at least six months should normally be allowed. This period of time flows from the individual employment-law and corporate-law time limits and from preparation and buffer periods which should be factored in. Another important point in the course of planning is determining the relevant balance-sheet dates. In this respect, it is necessary in particular to comply with the time limit specified in Sec. 17(2) sentence 4 of the Reorganization Act, under which a closing balance sheet, which must not be older than eight months, has to be submitted to the commercial register together with the application to register an outbound merger (cf. Sec. 122k of the Reorganization Act). For this reason, it makes sense to use the most recent annual financial statement. If, on the other hand, the transferring entity is governed by foreign law, then there is a need to clarify, as early as at the planning stage, for how long the relevant annual financial statements may be used under foreign law. In many cases, they must not be older than six months.

It is also necessary to clarify at the planning stage what foreign legal systems must be considered in the merger process and how these are organized with regard to the implementation of the Merger Directive.

The merger process can be divided into three stages. First, the participating legal entities must meet the requirements for the cross-border merger (in particular by preparing the draft terms of merger and passing the merger resolution (see *a)* to *f)*). Second, an initial examination is made by the relevant registry as to whether the transferring legal entities have met the requirements for the merger. Finally, the registration court competent for the acquiring legal entity and/or the legal entity to be newly formed examines whether the relevant legal entity has met, for its part, all the requirements for an effective merger (see *g) Registration Proceedings*).

a) Merger Capability of the Participating Legal Entities

The structuring of cross-border mergers must begin as early as with regard to the legal form of the participating legal entities. Since German reorganization law makes no provision for cross-border mergers for partnerships and, accordingly, there is no legal certainty in this respect, it makes sense for the participating partnerships to change their legal form into corporations or to undertake a cross-border accrual *(Anwachsung)*. In the event of a cross-border accrual, the partnership must admit a foreign legal entity as partner. After the other partners have withdrawn, the assets of the partnership pass to the foreign legal entity by universal succession pursuant to Sec. 738(1) of the German Civil Code *(Bürgerliches Gesetzbuch)* (if appropriate, in conjunction with Secs. 105(2) and 161(2) of the German Commercial Code [*Handelsgesetzbuch*]).

b) Draft Terms of Merger

Under Sec. 122c of the Reorganization Act, the representative bodies of the entities to be merged must draw up draft terms of merger. In the context of cross-border mergers, these draft terms take the place of the merger agreement. They must also be available in German translation and be submitted, no later than one month prior to the general meeting in which the merger is to be resolved, to the competent registry (in Germany: the commercial register) for publication. Even if in this context it normally suffices to submit a draft, it needs to be noted that the draft submitted must not differ from the version to be subsequently authenticated by a notary in accordance with Sec. 122c(4) of the Reorganization Act. In some cases, twofold authentication will be required if the relevant foreign law provides for a corresponding formality. Even if the foreign provision involves lesser requirements in terms of formalities than German law, it is advisable, in case of doubt, to undertake the authentication in accordance with the requirements of all jurisdictions involved rather than to trust that an authentication by a German notary as a 'more powerful form' will be recognized by a foreign registering authority.

The requirements, in terms of contents, regarding the draft terms of merger are laid down in Sec. 122c(2) of the Reorganization Act. Some additional details are required compared to national mergers. These concern (i) the articles of association of the acquiring and/or the newly-formed entity, (ii) details on the valuation of the assets and liabilities that are being transferred as well as on the closing date of the balance sheets, and (iii) in the case of outbound mergers, the offer of a cash compensation to the shareholders.

c) Initiation of the Procedure for Employee Participation

Pursuant to Sec. 6(2) sentence 3 of the Employee Codetermination Act, employees must receive information about the planned merger without the need for a request and without delay after disclosure of the draft terms of merger. Disclosure of the draft terms of merger is effected by their notification in accordance with Sec. 122d of the Reorganization Act. Simultaneously with the employee representatives being informed, they must also be asked to form a special negotiating body (Sec. 6(1) sentence 1 of the Employee Codetermination Act). The negotiating body must be formed within ten weeks (Sec. 13(1) sentence 1 of the Employee Codetermination Act). The purpose of that body is to enter into negotiations with corporate management on the future structuring of employee codetermination. In the event that the negotiations fail, the Employee Codetermination Act provides for fallback rules; these also become applicable if they are accepted by corporate management from the outset, in which case the need for negotiations is dispensed with. This enables the merger process to be expedited significantly.

Although there is some discussion as to whether information could be given and/or employee representatives could be asked to form a committee even before notification of the draft terms of merger, this is not advisable in practice. First of all, such a course of action would not be covered by the wording of the statute. Second, there is a risk of sensitive information about the merger process becoming known to the public prior to notification of the merger.

The procedure for employee participation must be completed before an application for registration of the merger is made by the acquiring corporation (cf. Sec. 122l(1) sentence 2 of the Reorganization Act).

d) Merger Report and Examination

The duty of explanation within the framework of the merger report for cross-border scenarios under Sec. 122e of the Reorganization Act goes beyond the duty of explanation for national mergers. In the context of a cross-border merger, the effects of the merger not only on the shareholders but also on creditors and employees must be explained in the merger report. The report must be made accessible, no later than one month before the general meeting of the shareholders, to (i) the works council, if any, and otherwise to the employees as well as (ii) to the shareholders. In view of this obligation to notify the employees, shareholders may not dispense with the merger report. Even where corporations have no employees, the possibility of waiver – as partially recommended by way of teleological reduction of Sec. 122e sentence 3 of the Reorganization Act – should not be used. By contrast, an examination of the merger under Sec. 122f of the Reorganization Act may always be dispensed with. Both the merger report and the merger examination may be undertaken jointly for the legal entities involved.

e) Merger Resolution

Under Sec. 122g(1) of the Reorganization Act, shareholders may make their consent conditional on their express confirmation of the structure of codetermination of the employees of the acquiring or newly-formed entity. In addition, it needs to be noted that, in the event that all shares of a transferring entity are held by the acquiring entity, no resolution of merger by the transferring entity is necessary. The resolution must be authenticated by a notary.

f) Furnishing of Security in the Event of Outbound Mergers

If a German entity is merged into an entity in another country, security must be furnished to the creditors of the German entity to the extent that they are not entitled to demand satisfaction (Sec. 122j of the Reorganization Act). However, creditors have the right to be furnished security only if (i) the receivable to be secured arose before or up to 15 days after publication of the draft terms of merger or their preliminary version, and (ii) the creditors have registered the amount and description of their claim in writing within two months of notification of the draft terms of merger and have provided *prima facie* evidence that the merger endangers the satisfaction of their claims.

In addition, all members of the representative body of the German entity involved must give an assurance *vis-à-vis* the registry pursuant to Sec. 122k(1) sentence 3 of the Reorganization Act that adequate security has been furnished to all creditors entitled to security.

g) Registration Proceedings

Under the concept of Arts. 10 and 11 of the Merger Directive, the registration proceedings consist of two stages, resulting in dual scrutiny of the legitimacy of the merger process – once in the country of the outbound merger and once in the country of the inbound merger. For the outbound merger, the entities entitled to represent the transferring legal entity must register the merger with the responsible authorities of the Member States in which they are located. If, from a German perspective, it is an outbound merger, then the German commercial register is competent for the registration. The registration court checks whether the requirements for the merger have been met and then grants an advance certificate; in Germany, this is known as a 'merger certificate' (*Verschmelzungsbescheinigung*) (Sec. 122k(2) sentence 1 of the Reorganization Act). Even if the fiction in Sec. 122k(2) sentence 2 of the Reorganization Act provides that the notice of the entry of the merger in the commercial register can serve as a merger certificate, it is advisable in practice, when dealing with reorganizations, to demand a separate merger certificate. Otherwise there is a risk of the registering authority in the target country not recognizing the notice of merger as an advance certificate.

The merger must then be registered with the competent authority of the Member State in which the acquiring or the newly formed entity has its registered office. In that context, presentation of the advance certificates is required. The subsequent examination extends to (i) the formal examination of the advance certificates, (ii) satisfaction of the merger requirements and (iii) examination of whether the procedure for employee participation has been properly implemented. In Germany, an inbound merger by acquisition must be registered by the representative bodies of the acquiring entity; an inbound merger by way of formation of a new entity, by the representative bodies of the transferring entities (Sec. 122l(1) of the Reorganization Act). The German registration court examines the requirements pertaining to the German entity and subsequently enters the merger in the commercial register with constitutive effect. In other Member States, the merger is completed by the granting of a final merger certificate.

2. Procedure for Cross-Border Mergers Under Art. 2(1) of the SE Regulation

In the course of their planning, the parties involved must agree, *inter alia*, where the SE is to have its registered office. In the context of a merger by absorption, the registered office of the SE may differ from that of the acquiring entity. Accordingly, a German *AG* can merge with a stock corporation from Liechtenstein into an SE with its registered office in Germany. This corresponds to standard registration practice.

a) Merger Capability of the Participating Legal Entities

Art. 2(1) of the SE Regulation provides for the possibility of stock corporations, which have been formed under the law of a Member State and which have their registered office or place of management within the EU, to form an SE by means of a merger, provided that at least two of them are governed by the law of different Member States. For stock corporations from third countries, it may be possible to first effect a change of legal form into the territory of the EU/EEA and, thereafter, to merge to form an SE; in the context of entities that are not *AGs*, it is advisable – provided this is possible – to first change their legal form into a stock corporation.

b) Other Requirements for a Merger

The other requirements for a merger are similar to those of Secs. 122a *et seqq.* of the Reorganization Act and are also inspired, via Art. 18 of the SE Regulation, by the rules governing national mergers in particular.

Under Art. 20(1) of the SE Regulation, it is necessary to prepare **draft terms of merger** that are to include the statutes of the SE. If a German entity is to participate, then the draft terms must be submitted for publication to the commercial register in German (Sec. 5 of the SE Implementation Act *[SE-Ausführungsgesetz]*) in conjunction with Sec. 61 of the Reorganization Act). They also require authentication by a notary (Art. 18 of the SE Regulation in conjunction with Sec. 6 of the Reorganization Act). In addition, for cases where the future SE is to have its registered office abroad, Sec. 7 of the SE Implementation Act provides for objecting shareholders to be offered cash compensation for their shares.

In relation to German entities, the duty to prepare a **merger report** arises from Art. 18 of the SE Regulation in conjunction with Sec. 8 of the Reorganization Act. As a result, the possibility of waiver under Sec. 8 of the Reorganization Act is available. A **merger examination** must in turn take place in accordance with Art. 18 of the SE Regulation in conjunction with Secs. 9–12 of the Reorganization Act. Alternatively, pursuant to Art. 22 of the SE Regulation, a uniform merger examination may be undertaken for all participating legal entities. The consenting resolutions of the general meetings of the merging (German) *AGs*, required by Art. 23(1) of the SE Regulation, also require authentication by a notary pursuant to Art. 18 of the SE Regulation in conjunction with Sec. 13 of the Reorganization Act. With regard to the **furnishing of security** for an outbound merger, the above statements on mergers under Secs. 122a *et seqq.* of the Reorganization Act apply accordingly. For the SE merger, this flows from Secs. 8 and 13 of the SE Implementation Act.

c) Employee Participation

The aim of the SE Codetermination Act is to safeguard the acquired rights of employees to participation in corporate decisions (Sec. 1(1) sentence 2 of the SE Codetermination Act). The underlying principles of the employee participation procedure are similar to the corresponding rules of the Employee Codetermination Act. In this case, too, employees must receive information on the planned merger without delay after disclosure of the draft terms of merger (Sec. 4(2) sentence 3 of the SE Codetermination Act). In that context, a special negotiating body undertakes negotiations with corporate management on behalf of the employees. Pursuant to Sec. 20 of the SE Codetermination Act, the period available for the negotiations is generally six months; this period may be extended to one year if necessary. In the event that the negotiations fail, the SE Codetermination Act provides for fallback rules by way of Secs. 22 *et seqq.* of the SE Codetermination Act.

d) Registration Proceedings

Similarly to the case for cross-border mergers under Secs. 122a *et seqq.* of the Reorganization Act, Arts. 25 and 26 of the SE Regulation provide for a two-stage scrutiny of the legitimacy of the merger. During the first stage, it is examined whether the merger requirements are satisfied in relation to the transferring entities. For this reason, the registration for a German transferring *AG* must be accompanied by the same enclosures as are necessary in the context of domestic mergers (cf. Secs. 16(2) and 17 as well as Secs. 66 *et seqq.* of the Reorganization Act). In the event of an outbound merger, an additional declaration is required that security has been furnished to the creditors (Sec. 8 sentence 2 of the SE Implementation Act). If these requirements are satisfied, a certificate of legitimacy is granted.

That certificate must be submitted together with the draft terms of merger and the consenting resolution to the responsible authority in the EU Member State in which the SE is to have its registered office. That authority then examines in accordance with Art. 26(3) and (4) of the SE Regulation whether (i) the entities participating in the merger have consented to draft terms of merger with the same wording, (ii) an agreement for the participation of employees has been entered into, (iii) the formation of the SE complies with the statutory requirements of the state of establishment in accordance with Art. 15, and (iv) the requirements of Art. 2(1) of the SE Regulation have been met. The merger and the formation of the SE take effect upon registration (Art. 27(1) of the SE Regulation).

3. Other Situations

It would seem fair to say that, based on the case law of the European Court of Justice, cross-border changes of legal form and divisions are likely to be admissible. Nonetheless, the legal position is in no way certain. There are no rules with binding effect which could be relied on in the reorganization process. Even if the case law of the European Court of Justice would seem to indicate that in such cases the respective national rules of reorganization of the Member States affected apply, these are not tailored to cross-border situations. In particular the lack of consideration of the necessary employee participation and of other noncodified individual interests might result in the reorganization process being invalid or in a refusal by the responsible registries to effect registration. Added to this is the fact that the case law of the European Court of Justice, unlike German reorganization law, is open to reorganizations of all kinds. In the *VALE* case, the 'change of legal form' took place by an Italian entity with limited liability into its Hungarian equivalent – inconceivable from the perspective of German reorganization law. Accordingly, no change of legal form *stricto sensu* took place.

Therefore, in practice, consultation with the competent registries is of particular importance. In the course of such consultation, it is often possible to push through reorganizations for which there is no certain legal basis. Should no such consultation be possible or should it fail to lead to the desired result, then recourse should be sought via the legally certain merger alternatives described above.

Dr. Philipp Rulf

Lawyer

Areas of Specialization

- Corporate law
- Corporate reorganizations and changes of legal form
- Advice for family-owned businesses and their shareholders
- Commercial law

Telephone (ext.) +49 228/95 94-637

Email: philipp.rulf@fgs.de

Corporate Reorganizations in Germany

by Michael Erkens

Contents

I. Introduction
II. Basics
 1. Developments in Reorganization Law
 2. Types of Reorganizations
    a) Merger
    b) Division
    c) Change of Legal Form
 3. Basic Requirements for Each Form of Reorganization
 4. Shareholder Protection
 5. Creditor Protection
 6. Employee Protection
III. Pitfalls
 1. Judicial Valuation Proceedings (*Spruchverfahren*)
 2. Legal Actions Challenging the Validity of Reorganization Resolutions
 3. Apportionment of Assets in a Division
 4. Waiver of a Grant of Shares and Non Proportional Divisions
IV. Schemes
 1. Approach for Mergers
    a) Merger Agreement
    b) Merger Report and Merger Audit
    c) Merger Resolution
    d) Registration Procedure
 2. Approach for Divisions
    a) Division Agreement and Division Plan
    b) Division Report and Audit
    c) Division Resolution
    d) Registration Procedure
 3. Approach for the Change of Legal Form
    a) Reorganization Resolution
    b) Reorganization Report and Audit
    c) Compliance with the Corporate Formation Laws
    d) Registration Procedure

I. Introduction

In Germany, four different types of business restructuring governed by the German Reorganization Act of 28 Oct. 1994 (*Umwandlungsgesetz*) come under the single umbrella term of 'reorganization'. There are various reasons for such reorganizations, which could range from operational grounds to a change of public image or employee codetermination. Reorganizations are often tax-driven. Today's German reorganization laws are influenced not insignificantly by European rules and standards. In practice, standards have become established that permit the experienced advisor to structure reorganizations with legal certainty and at a reasonable cost, and to regularly do so in close coordination with the commercial registers and the German tax authorities.

II. Basics

1. Developments in Reorganization Law

The German law on reorganization recognizes four types of reorganization: merger, division (*Spaltung*), transfer of assets and the change of legal form. These reorganizations have been governed by the Reorganization Act since that legislation entered into force on 1 Jan. 1995. Prior to that time, the rules on merger and change of legal form were contained in a patchwork of different laws. Practitioners were only in part able to compensate for the lack of rules governing the division of business entities. Demergers were complicated and expensive. The Reorganization Act created for the first time a uniform set of rules that covered all the legal measures of reorganization and restructuring. These special rules offer a relatively simple and cost-effective procedure for the various types of reorganization, and at the same time avoid both the cumbersome processes associated with a reorganization carried out under civil and corporate law, and the unreasonable legal consequences resulting therefrom. The Reorganization Act has been amended several times since it became law.

2. Types of Reorganizations

The Reorganization Act distinguishes four types of reorganizations: merger, division, transfer of assets and change of legal form. The transfer of assets does not have any practical relevance.

a) Merger

Pursuant to Sec. 2 of the Reorganization Act, business entities may be merged, on being dissolved without going into liquidation, by granting shares to the shareholders of the transferring entities. The merger may be carried out by way of absorption (*Verschmelzung durch Aufnahme*) by transferring all of the assets (as a whole) of one or more entities to another existing one or by transferring the assets of two or more entities to a newly formed one.

A defining structural principle of the merger is that the assets are transferred by way of **universal succession** (*Gesamtrechtsnachfolge*). This feature demonstrates the key advantage of a merger consummated under the Reorganization Act as compared to an asset transfer by way of contribution in kind. The asset transfer is effected by registration of the merger in the commercial register at the registered seat of the acquiring entity (Sec. 20(1) no. 1 of the Reorganization Act). The significance of universal succession is that all assets and liabilities of the transferring entities are transferred by law. When the merger is registered, the transferring entities are dissolved. Their shareholders automatically become shareholders of the acquiring entity. Third-party rights to the shares of the transferring entities continue to exist but then apply to the shares of the acquiring entity.

b) Division

The concept of division under the Reorganization Act encompasses three different restructuring measures of demerger: split-up (*Aufspaltung*), spin-off (*Abspaltung*) and hive-down (*Ausgliederung*).

The feature common to divisions is that in each case, only parts of business entities are transferred, resulting in the partitioning of the assets of the transferring entities. As with mergers, the transfer of assets is conducted by means of (partial) **universal succession** and does not require the consent of third parties, i.e. persons other than the shareholders of the entities involved. The transfer of assets is made by registration of the division in the commercial register at the registered seat of the transferring entity (Sec. 131(1) no. 1 of the Reorganization Act). Under universal succession, a portion of the assets is transferred including the liabilities of the transferring entity related or allocated to those assets. As with mergers, the acquiring entities can be ones that already exist or ones that are newly formed as a result of the division. A combination of different types of division is also permissible (Sec. 123(4) of the Reorganization Act).

In the case of the **split-up**, a transferring entity splits up and transfers **all of its assets** into at least two other entities. Thus, the split-up is the opposite of a merger. When the split-up is registered, the relevant parts of the assets are transferred to the acquiring entities by way of universal succession. The transferring entity is dissolved without going into liquidation (Sec. 131(1) no. 2 of the Reorganization Act). The shareholders of the transferring entity automatically become shareholders of the acquiring entities in accordance with the apportionment stipulated in the split-up agreement (Sec. 131(1) no. 3 of the Reorganization Act). In the absence of the statutory provisions in the Reorganization Act, a split-up would entail considerable expense.

A division of greater practical relevance than the split-up is the **spin-off**. In a spin-off, the transferring entity simply spins off one or more parts of its assets into one or more acquiring entities. Once the spin-off is registered, the relevant assets are transferred to one or more acquiring entities by way of universal succession. Like the split-up, the shareholders of the transferring entity automatically become shareholders of the acquiring entities based on the apportionment prescribed in the spin-off agreement. Unlike the split-up, the transferring entity continues to exist after the spin-off is registered. The spin-off normally results in the creation of a sister company or the relevant assets are spun off to an entity that already exists.

Another type of division of great practical importance is the **hive-down**. As with the spin-off, the transferring entity in a hive-down transfers only one or more parts of its assets and remains in existence even after the hive-down is entered in the commercial register. Unlike the split-up and spin-off, however, the shareholders of the transferring entity in a hive-down do not receive any direct (*pro rata*) compensation for transferring the transferring entity's assets. The shareholder of the acquiring entity is instead the transferring entity itself.

This transaction results in the creation of a new subsidiary or in a hive-down to an existing subsidiary. The hive-down allows the parties to avoid the more costly method of singular succession (*Einzelrechtsübertragung*) by way of contribution in kind.

c) Change of Legal Form

The provisions on changing a business entity's legal form under Sec. 190 of the Reorganization Act permit it to adopt a different legal form or structure at a relatively low cost. The defining feature for the change of legal form is the legal **identity and continuity** of the restructuring entity. Its assets are not transferred; instead, merely its legal form (i.e. its legal structure or shell) is modified. While the legal entity enjoys continuity, the laws previously governing the restructuring entity change. When the new legal form is registered, the stakes held by the owners of the restructuring entity are governed by the provisions that apply to the new legal form or structure. Third-party rights to the shares in the transferring entities continue to exist but then apply to the shares in the legally reformed entity (Sec. 202(1) no. 2 of the Reorganization Act). Whether the members of the supervisory board retain their positions on the board depends on whether the supervisory board for the legally reformed entity has been constituted in the same manner (Sec. 203 of the Reorganization Act). The principals' terms of office, on the other hand, end when the change of legal form is registered.

3. Basic Requirements for Each Form of Reorganization

As corporate structural measures, a merger, division, and change of legal form are transactions that are prepared by the representative bodies of the entities involved. These enter into a **reorganization agreement** on the merger and division, the content of which is subject to certain minimum requirements provided by law (Secs. 5 and 126 of the Reorganization Act). In the case of a division by forming a new entity, a division plan is prepared instead of the division agreement.

The merger agreement and the division agreement/division plan require **shareholder approval** from the entities involved in order to become binding and enforceable (Secs. 13(1) and 125 sentence 1 of the Reorganization Act). Shareholder approval is also required for a change of legal form. Unlike for mergers and divisions, details of the change of legal form are stipulated in the reorganization resolution adopted by the shareholders' meeting (Sec. 194(1) of the Reorganization Act).

In each case, the reorganization will not enter into legal force until it has been **registered with the commercial register**.

4. Shareholder Protection

Each type of reorganization can harm the interests of the shareholders of the entities involved. In the event of a merger, split-up and spin-off, the shareholders of the transferring entity become shareholders of another entity once the reorganization is formally registered. In the case of a merger, the percentage of the stakes held by the shareholders decreases, and there is a risk of dilution. The shareholders of an entity which is involved in a merger, split- up or spin-off can also be disadvantaged if the exchange ratio for the shares is deemed inappropriate (*unangemessen*). In the case of a hive-down, the relevant assets are shifted to a subsidiary. This reduces the influence of the parent's shareholders on the assets transferred. Depending on the relevant legal form selected, a change of legal form can also reduce the shareholders' rights and their opportunities to exert influence.

In order to protect shareholders, the Reorganization Act provides for comprehensive **reporting and disclosure** duties for all reorganization measures. The scope and content of reorganization reports is generally prescribed by law (Secs. 8, 127 and 192 of the Reorganization Act). As to what details should be reported, each case is different and will require an exact review by legal counsel. The report should enable the shareholders to understand both the legal and economic aspects of the reorganization. The reports may be jointly prepared by the entities involved. A report is not required if all the shareholders of the entities involved waive the preparation of the report or all the shares of the transferring entity are held by the acquiring entity.

The Reorganization Act provides for an additional protective tool; namely, **the audit of the reorganization agreement or reorganization plan** by an independent expert (Secs. 9 and 125 sentence 1 of the Reorganization Act). The auditor will be appointed by the court upon application and must issue a written report about his audit. The subject matter of the audit is the reorganization agreement. The centerpiece of the audit must be the share exchange ratio and the amount of any potential cash settlement offer. Audit and audit report are not required under the same conditions as for the reorganization report.

The interests of the shareholders should also be protected through the **qualified voting majorities** that are prescribed under the Reorganization Act. If the reorganization harms the rights of certain shareholder groups or shareholders with special rights, then the approval of these groups or shareholders is also required. Each shareholder has the right within a one-month period to file a legal action in court challenging an alleged violation of the reorganization resolution. The legal action will lead to a **'suspension of registration'** (*Eintragungssperre*) (for more on this issue, see below under II.2).

Finally, the shareholders' pecuniary interests (*Vermögensinteressen*) are protected inasmuch as the shareholders may under certain circumstances demand either the right to withdraw from the transferring entity in return for **cash compensation** (Secs. 29 and 207 of the Reorganization Act) or – despite any share transfer restrictions in place - the sale of their shares (Secs. 33 and 201 of the Reorganization Act). The shareholders of the transferring entity are also entitled to an additional **cash payment** (premium), if the share exchange ratio is too low (Sec. 15 of the Reorganization Act).

5. Creditor Protection

The creditors of the entities involved can also be harmed by the reorganization being unable to influence or prevent the reorganization. When the merger has been completed, the creditors obtain a new debtor. In the case of a division, the assets of the transferring entity can diminish. Accordingly, in the case of a merger or a division where a new company is formed or in the case of a change of legal form, it is obligatory to comply with the formation rules of the new entity or of the new legal form. Otherwise, the creditors of the entities involved may demand security, provided that they make their claim in writing within six months (Secs. 22 and 204 of the Reorganization Act). In the case of divisions, the acquiring entities will also become jointly liable for any existing debt (Sec. 133 of the Reorganization Act). Holders of special rights are protected separately.

6. Employee Protection

Finally, the reorganization can have an effect on the employees of the entities involved. Although the reorganization is not subject to the consent of the employees, the reorganization agreement (or the reorganization resolution for a change of legal form) must describe the consequences that the reorganization will have for employees and their representatives and the measures taken in that regard (Secs. 5(1) no. 9, 126(1) no. 11 and 194(1) no. 7 of the Reorganization Act). The reorganization agreement or the draft reorganization agreement (the draft reorganization resolution for a change of legal form) must be submitted to the works councils concerned at least one month prior to the shareholders' meeting which is expected to resolve on the approval (Secs. 5(3), 126(3) and 194(2) of the Reorganization Act). The works councils may waive the one-month notice period.

III. Pitfalls

Where reorganization measures are taken, advisors have to keep a number of different aspects in mind, some of which are described as follows:

1. Judicial Valuation Proceedings (*Spruchverfahren*)

If, in connection with a merger or division, the transferring entity has a large group of shareholders or is even publicly listed, then determining the share exchange ratio becomes particularly important. Although the shareholders of the transferring entity cannot base a legal action challenging the validity of the reorganization resolution on the fact that the exchange ratio was set too low and thereby prevent the commercial register registration that validates the merger, such shareholders may, under Sec. 15(1) of the Reorganization Act, demand compensation from the acquiring entity in the form of an additional cash payment if indeed the exchange ratio is deemed to have been set too low. The appropriate additional payment is determined by a court upon application made. 'Judicial valuation proceedings' will also need to be conducted if the shareholders of the transferring entity are offered a cash payment that they believe to be too low. It is not uncommon for judicial valuation proceedings to last for several years. In judicial valuation proceedings, expensive expert opinions as to the appropriateness of the exchange ratio or of the cash payment are often prepared. Recent experience has shown that courts do not hesitate to award substantial additional payments or cash settlements. Such court decisions can render a previously viable merger completely unprofitable.

The shareholders of an acquiring entity, on other hand, can assert claims based on a possibly incorrect exchange ratio only by filing a legal action challenging the validity of the reorganization resolution (for more on this issue, see immediately below). This fact should be taken into consideration in the individual case when selecting the transaction structure.

2. Legal Actions Challenging the Validity of Reorganization Resolutions

As a main component of minority shareholder protection, the shareholders of an entity involved in a reorganization have the right to demand a judicial review of the validity of the resolution on the merger. If a lawsuit is filed within one month after the resolution is adopted, then the reorganization cannot be entered in the commercial register (Sec. 16(2) sentence 2 of the Reorganization Act). This is called a 'suspension of registration'. Even the most careful preparation cannot always prevent this fate. The economic consequences of such suspension can be very serious. If legal action is in fact taken, necessary steps need to be taken.

3. Apportionment of Assets in a Division

Whereas all the assets (as a whole) of the transferring entities are transferred to the acquiring entity in mergers, in divisions only those assets are transferred by way of 'partitioned universal succession' (*partielle Gesamtrechtsnachfolge*), which are assigned to the acquiring entity in the division agreement. In principle, the assets and liabilities may be freely apportioned to the entity involved (Sec. 126(1) no. 9 of the Reorganization Act). This flexibility is limited, however, with respect to employment relationships. In any case, the greatest degree of care should be exercised when defining the assets to be transferred. If the structure is set up properly, then the disclosure of hidden reserves can be avoided and the book values shown in the tax accounting may be retained.

4. Waiver of a Grant of Shares and Non Proportional Divisions

In practice, divisions are frequently used for intragroup restructurings and for organizing business successions. In these cases, there is often a need to regulate the equity interest held in the acquiring entity differently from that held in the transferring entity, or a need to waive the grant of shares entirely. In that case, the legal structuring options and their limitations have to be observed precisely.

IV. Schemes

1. Approach for Mergers

In the planning of a merger, it is essential to establish a timeframe. This timeframe will be based on the deadlines required under labor and corporate law, and on any preparatory and buffer time that has to be included. Given the numerous simplifications and streamlined processes, intragroup mergers are less costly; in contrast, mergers of publicly-listed corporations or entities with a large staff require greater planning.

In scheduling the steps of the merger, defining the relevant balance sheet dates is important as the documents to be filed when the merger is entered in the commercial register include a closing balance sheet from the transferring entities which must not be older than eight months. In this respect, the parties can usually rely on the annual financial statements for the most recently completed fiscal year. In other cases, an interim balance sheet will need to be prepared.

To the extent allowed by law, initial efforts should be made to coordinate with the controlling shareholders prior to the actual merger process. In many cases, it is advisable also involve the employee representatives in a timely manner. Publicly-listed corporations must pay attention to complying with capital-market rules.

a) Merger Agreement

The representative bodies of the entities that are seeking to merge will enter into a merger agreement. The merger agreement is the outcome of the negotiations conducted between the entities involved (to the extent they are not affiliated with one another in a corporate group) and forms the legal basis of the merger. The merger agreement must be formally notarized by a German notary (Sec. 6 of the Reorganization Act). The substantive requirements in the merger agreement are prescribed in Sec. 5(1) of the Reorganization Act. The core elements are the agreement to transfer the assets by way of universal succession and the establishment of the exchange ratio for the shares. In order to calculate the exchange ratio and, if necessary, the amount of the additional cash payment, a comparative analysis of the entities involved is required. In practice, this crucial task is performed by an auditor. The valuation report that he issues will be critically reviewed by the merger auditor and, in some cases, as part of judicial valuation proceeding. Thus, the valuation report is of considerable importance for the prospects of success in any such proceeding. Information about the exchange ratio is not necessary in the case of an intragroup upstream merger (Sec. 5(2) of the Reorganization Act). The merger agreement or a draft merger agreement must be submitted to the responsible works councils.

b) Merger Report and Merger Audit

In the merger report, the representative bodies of the entities involved must explain the legal and economic aspects of the merger and the merger agreement in detail, the main focus being on the share exchange ratio. The merger report has to be audited by an independent expert. In certain situations, the report and the audit are not necessary.

c) Merger Resolution

The shareholders' meetings of the entities involved must be convened in order to formally and finally approve the merger. The merger has to be approved by a qualified majority vote. The resolution needs to be notarized. In the event of an upstream merger within a stock corporation group and a holding of at least 90%, the consent of the shareholders' meeting of the acquiring stock corporation is not necessary. In that case, the minority shareholders of the transferring (stock) corporation may also be excluded (squeezed-out). This new process is a simpler method than the squeeze-out procedure available under the German Stock Corporation Act (*Aktiengesetz*) and the German Securities Acquisition and Takeover Act (*Wertpapiererwerbs- und Übernahmegesetz*), which require a holding of at least 95% in each case. The only exception to the requirement for a merger resolution from the transferring entity is if all of the shares of such are consolidated in the hands of the acquiring stock corporation.

d) Registration Procedure

For a merger to become valid, it must be entered in the commercial registers of all entities involved. The registration in the commercial register of the acquiring entity is constitutive. In the past, shareholders have occasionally sought to hinder or delay the registration of a merger by filing lawsuits challenging the merger. The legislature's 2009 enactment of the 'approval procedure' (*Freigabeverfahren*) was designed to counteract such activities. Under Sec. 16(3) of the Reorganization Act, any such legal action can be defeated by way of court order, if (i) the legal action is inadmissible or evidently unfounded, or (ii) none of the plaintiffs can prove a minimum shareholding of (nominal) EUR 1,000, or (iii) the interests of the entities involved in the merger and their shareholders in quickly consummating the merger outweigh the interests of the litigating shareholders in postponing the action and there is no significant breach of law.

2. Approach for Divisions

As is the case with mergers, divisions also require advance planning. Such planning is comparable to the planning phase for mergers in terms of scheduling and content. This can be attributed not least to the comprehensive references in the Reorganization Act to the laws and regulations governing mergers.

a) Division Agreement and Division Plan

The basis for a division by way of absorption (*Spaltung zur Aufnahme*) is the division agreement. In a division by way of formation of a new entity (*Spaltung zur Neugründung*), a unilateral division plan will be used instead of a division agreement. Both, agreement and plan must be notarized. The content will be to the greatest extent consistent with the content of the merger agreement. In addition, information on the identification and assignment of the asset and liability items to be transferred to the acquiring entity (Sec. 126(9) of the Reorganization Act) is most important. The parties are generally free to assign the assets and liabilities as they wish. For each asset and each liability item, a rule must be established that indicates which item is to be assigned to which entity. Universal succession, which is triggered by the division, allows transferring liabilities and contracts without the consent of the creditors. Nevertheless, the entities must at least be 'definable', identification made via asset schedules and balance sheets being sufficient. It is also possible to determine the assets by listing only those that are not to be transferred (*Negativabgrenzung*). In addition, clauses specifying the economic consequences of an unintended but incorrect assignment are recommended. Special transfer requirements must be observed. This primarily applies to real estate and rights equivalent to real estate. In practice, the identification of the assets to be transferred is generally the most important and time-consuming aspect of divisions, both for the entities involved and for their advisors. This is because if the assets are assigned in such a way that a business or business unit passes to the acquiring entity, then it will have the option of retaining the book values in the commercial and tax balance sheet. To that end, a 'binding ruling' should be requested from the tax authorities.

In the case of a split-up and spin-off, the shares of the entities involved must also be apportioned among the shareholders of the transferring entity (Sec. 126(1) no. 10 of the Reorganization Act). As a rule, the shares of the acquiring entity will be assigned to the shareholders of the transferring entity in proportion to the latter's holdings in the transferring entity. Yet, a *division that does not preserve the ownership percentages* is also permissible (Sec. 28 of the Reorganization Act). The permissibility of such a division is the basis for most experts to assume that a split-up or spin-off in exchange for no shares ('zero division' – *Spaltung zu Null*) is also permissible. This provides significant options for restructuring groups and business successions. It will specifically apply if a waiver of the share grant is prohibited, namely in the case of partnerships. This will therefore also allow a *GmbH & Co. KG* to be divided without granting shares to the *GmbH* as general partner.

b) Division Report and Audit

As with a merger, in the case a division, the representative bodies of the entities involved will generally prepare a written report and have it audited by an independent expert (Sec. 125 sentence 1 of the Reorganization Act). No audit is undertaken for a hive-down (Sec. 125 sentence 2 of the Reorganization Act).

c) Division Resolution

With regard to the resolution on the division to be adopted by the shareholders of the entities involved, there are no special qualities that are different from those of the resolution on mergers. For a split-up or spin-off which does not preserve the ownership percentages, Section 128 of the Reorganization Act requires, however, the approval of all shareholders of the transferring entity.

d) Registration Procedure

The division will not become valid and effective until it is entered in the commercial register of the transferring entity (Sec. 130(1) of the Reorganization Act). The transferring entity is dissolved only in the case of a split-up. When the split-up and spin-off are registered, the shareholders of the transferring entity become the shareholders of the acquiring entity. In the case of a hive-down, the transferring entity receives the shares of the acquiring entity.

3. Approach for the Change of Legal Form

The change of legal form is probably the simplest reorganization measure to implement. The setting of the cash compensation and compliance with the corporate formation laws applicable to the targeted legal structure are of particular importance.

a) Reorganization Resolution

The details on a change of legal form (legal structure) are prescribed not in an agreement or a plan (the case for a change of legal form from a stock corporation into an SE (*Societas Europaea* or European company) under the European Company Regulation), but in the reorganization resolution itself (Sec. 194(1) of the Reorganization Act). The draft of such resolution must be submitted in advance and in a timely manner to the responsible works councils (Sec. 194(3) of the Reorganization Act). The share capital under the previous legal form must be adjusted, if necessary, to comply with the requirements applicable to the new legal form. Since the change of legal form will modify the shareholders' participation and voting rights, the shareholders have to be given an offer to withdraw from the entity in return for a cash compensation, unless the resolution must be unanimously adopted (Secs. 194(1) no. 6 and 207 of the Reorganization Act). The judicial valuation proceeding is also admissible to challenge a shareholding ratio and cash compensation that are considered to have been set too low (Secs. 196 and 212 of the Reorganization Act). Unless the principle of officer/director continuity applies (*Grundsatz der Ämterkontinuität*), the new administrative bodies have to be appointed in the reorganization resolution.

b) Reorganization Report and Audit

The reorganization report must describe, in particular, the reasons for the change of legal form and explain the legal and economic aspects of the shareholders' future stakes in the new legal structure (Sec. 192(1) of the Reorganization Act). The law requires the reorganization report to be audited only with respect to the appropriateness of the cash compensation offered (Secs. 208 and 30(2) of the Reorganization Act).

c) Compliance with the Corporate Formation Laws

As with mergers and divisions in which new entities are created as part of the transaction, the corporate formation rules for the new legal structure must be observed when there is a change of legal form (Sec. 197 of the Reorganization Act). This is mainly intended to prevent the breach of capital subscription and contribution rules. In the event that a partnership is converted into a corporation, the nominal amount of the share capital may not exceed the assets of the restructuring enterprise after deducting the liabilities (Sec. 220(1) of the Reorganization Act).

d) Registration Procedure

When the new legal structure is entered in the commercial register, the change of legal form will enter into effect (Sec. 202(1) no. 1 of the Reorganization Act).

Dr. Michael Erkens

Lawyer, Tax Advisor

Areas of Specialization

- Corporate law
- Corporate reorganizations
- Mergers & acquisitions and joint ventures
- Corporate governance and compliance
- Corporate litigation and arbitration
- Business taxation

Telephone (ext.) +49 228/9594-208

Email: michael.erkens@fgs.de

Legal Aspects of Investments in German Real Estate

by Michael R. Wiesbrock

Contents

I. Land Register Inspection
1. Object of Purchase / Legal Ownership Situation / Hereditary Building Rights
   a) Basic Background
   b) Pitfalls
   c) Solution
2. Entries in Section II of the Land Register
   a) Easements
   b) Priority Notations
   c) Preemptive Right to Purchase and the Repurchase Right
3. *In Rem* Security Interests Entered in Section III

II. Lease Situations
1. Written Form Requirement
   a) Basic Background
   b) Pitfalls
   c) Solution
2. Incidental Costs
   a) Basic Background
   b) Pitfalls
   c) Solution
3. Repairs and Maintenance / Cosmetic Repairs
   a) Basic Background
   b) Pitfalls
   c) Solution
4. Exclusivity (No Compete) Covenant
   a) Basic Background
   b) Pitfalls
   c) Solution
5. Rent Security
   a) Basic Background/Pitfalls
   b) Solution
6. Maintenance and Service Contracts

I. Land Register Inspection

1. Object of Purchase / Legal Ownership Situation / Hereditary Building Rights

a) Basic Background

Any real-estate due-diligence review will initially involve a detailed examination of the subject matter underlying the transaction and the legal ownership status of the real estate by checking up-to-date excerpts from the land register. This is the most important source of information for assessing the legal status of any real estate.

b) Pitfalls

In practice, the seller of real estate is often not even entered in the land register and is therefore not the lawful owner. Often the reason for this omission can be traced back to intra-group transfers of real estate to a subsidiary of the selling group, according to which the conveyance of title was not recorded in the land register or traced back to corporate transactions (e.g. name changes, mergers, spinoffs, etc.) in which a correction in the land register was simply overlooked. In these situations, the seller is not in a legal position to convey title in the real estate to the purchaser. Indeed, the land register enjoys the presumption of public good faith and is deemed to be true and correct in favor of that person who is entered therein as the legal owner (Sec. 892 of the German Civil Code – *Bürgerliches Gesetzbuch*).

c) Solution

Since it is not unusual for years to sometimes pass before any changes are made in land registers, business frequently works with land register extracts that are relatively outdated. From the buyer's perspective, this can often have fatal consequences for transactions during a due-diligence review. The demand for, and inspection of, up-to-date land register extracts is therefore an essential component of any due-diligence examination and brings to light the above-mentioned risks. The circumstances surrounding the seller may have to be updated prior to the real estate purchase (e.g. by making the requisite changes). In certain cases, such an update may prove to be difficult in practice if certain (legal) entities involved refuse to cooperate or no longer exist.

2. Entries in Section II of the Land Register

The following encumbrances in section II of the land register are relevant and should be mentioned:

a) Easements

aa) Basic Background

Easements can afford third parties the right to use and enjoy certain aspects of real estate, e.g. when a land owner is obligated to accept certain transit rights or the laying of pipes, when it must desist from developing its real estate in a certain manner or must waive certain rights as protection against emissions (easement or limited personal easement). Contrary to the rights mentioned above, the *Nießbrauch* (analogous to a usufruct) instead generally grants a comprehensive right to use the real estate The *Nießbrauch* can be distinguished from an easement or from a limited personal easement mostly because of its comprehensive character. It may be concluded from the above discussion that easements could have a significant effect on the usability and hence the value of the real estate.

bb) Pitfalls

The restrictions on ownership resulting from easements harbor a major – and in practice frequently underestimated – potential risk from the buyer's perspective. Thus, for example, the completion of a construction project planned on a piece of land could fail simply because an easement conflicts with the construction method planned by the purchaser. There is no immediate solution to these kinds of serious obstacles in connection with a real estate transaction, which could result from an easement. Indeed, unlike the *in rem* security interests (*Grundpfandrechte*) recorded in section III of the land register, the restrictions listed in section II of the land register cannot be simply discharged by paying a certain amount of money. In order to release an easement from a piece of land, the person entitled to the easement must issue a statement of relinquishment and record a deletion notation in the land register. Accordingly, the contracting parties cannot effect a deletion notation by themselves.

cc) Solution

Every real estate transaction requires an extensive analysis of the easements contained in section II of the land register. It should be remembered here that the entire range of encumbrances and restrictions frequently cannot be derived from the land register alone, but must instead be inferred using the underlying instruments that actually created the encumbrances. Thus, the file containing the key documentation related to the property (including documents relating to the encumbrances) must be obtained and then carefully examined to determine which individual duties will be assumed by the purchaser of the real estate. For easements which represent an obstacle for completing a construction project planned on the land efforts should be made, if possible, to conclude a rescission agreement with the beneficiary. After a reasonable due diligence has been conducted, it may prove to be necessary to condition a real estate acquisition on the deletion of those encumbrances that threaten to derail the transaction.

b) Priority Notations

aa) Basic Background

A priority notation an *in rem* security device which is recorded in the land register and serves to secure a claim to demand the transfer of *in rem* rights, specifically the claim to acquire title. If section II of the land register contains an outside, higher-ranking priority notation of conveyance, then any title conveyance to someone other than the person listed as the beneficiary under that priority notation will be invalid.

bb) Pitfalls

From the purchaser's perspective, a higher-ranking priority notation represents a significant risk to the real estate transaction.

cc) Solution

If a higher-ranking priority notation is entered in the land register, then it should be examined carefully whether the acquisition process is to be stopped or if it is carried on then the purchase agreement must ensure that the higher-ranking priority notation is deleted before the title conveyance is executed. Ideally, it should be agreed that payment of the purchase price is conditioned on the deletion of the priority notation.

c) Preemptive Right to Purchase and the Repurchase Right

aa) Basic Background

A preemptive purchase right gives the person to whom it is granted (grantee) the authority to purchase the encumbered real estate if the owner of the real estate seeks to sell it to a third party. The preemptive purchase situation arises when a purchase contract related to the encumbered real estate is concluded with a third person. When the preemptive purchase right is triggered, the grantee will have the opportunity to exercise its preemptive right by giving unilateral notice. If it exercises this preemptive purchase right, then a new, independent purchase contract will be formed between itself and the person obligated under the preemptive purchase right (= owner of the real estate). The *in rem* preemptive purchase right will have the same effect *vis-à-vis* third parties as a priority notation; i.e. any disposal of the real estate will be invalid to the extent it could thwart the preemptive purchase right. Thus, the purchaser can be compelled to surrender the real estate in the event that the preemptive purchase right is exercised.

In addition to the legally consequential preemptive purchase right described above, there are also statutory preemptive purchase rights, which are regulated under German federal laws and under the laws of the individual German states. These laws relate primarily to statutes on environmental protection and landmark preservation.

A repurchase right is understood to mean an agreement, under which the real estate seller – by unilateral notice – can require the purchaser to convey the object of purchase back to the seller in exchange for the payment of the repurchase price.

bb) Pitfalls

The existence of a preemptive purchase right or a repurchase right can represent an 'unpleasant surprise' for the potential buyer of real estate. The buyer may have already expended enormous sums during the course of the purchase contract negotiations – e.g. for technical due diligence – and will have to bear those costs if the preemptive purchase right or repurchase right is exercised, unless a differently worded agreement is reached in advance of the discussions.

cc) Solution

The issue of which contractual and/or statutory preemptive purchase rights or repurchase rights exist should be reviewed as early as possible during the due-diligence process. In the event that such rights do exist, the question of whether they will in fact be exercised should be investigated.

With respect to statutory preemptive purchase rights, the competent government authorities should be contacted as early as possible. Binding waivers (no-action notices) are not, however, normally issued prior to the conclusion of the contract, which means that the real estate purchase contract needs to be made subject to a corresponding condition/reservation.

With respect to any contractually stipulated preemptive purchase rights and repurchase rights, the agreements that form the basis for the recordation in the land register should be inspected and analyzed. It is precisely the repurchase rights that are frequently impacted, when the real estate had been sold by a municipality or public agency in the past with the anticipated expectation of resale to a business owner; e.g. in the expectation that a certain number of jobs will be created in the business which is to be operated on the real estate. The investigation into the agreement forming the basis of the respective preemptive purchase right or repurchase right could reveal that the agreed reasons for a preemptive purchase or repurchase situation do not (any longer) exist. Should it emerge, however, that the requirements for a repurchase scenario do exist, then this could represent a deal breaker if perhaps the agreed repurchase price is set at a particularly low level.

If a problematic preemptive purchase right or repurchase right is encountered when dealing with the target property, then one could consider as a precautionary matter whether or not to reach a contractual arrangement with the seller, according to which the seller would bear the transaction costs in the event that the preemptive purchase or repurchase right is exercised.

3. *In Rem* Security Interests Entered in Section III

The *in rem* security interests recorded in section III of the land register tend to play a somewhat minor role in the due-diligence process. The reason is that such encumbrances generally are not assumed by the buyer and are therefore deleted during settlement of the contract. It should be remembered, however, that *in rem* security interests must be valued so that they can be deleted on payment of the purchase price. By conditioning the payment of the purchase price on the submission of the deletion notation documentation to the civil-law notary, the purchase agreement itself should ensure that the *in rem* security interests will be deleted.

II. Lease Situations

1. Written Form Requirement

a) Basic Background

In many cases, the value of a property primarily depends on the amount of rent collected. The key factor in determining the amount of the (anticipated future) rental income is the residual term of the existing leases as of the date the property is purchased. If a fixed term is agreed, then in principle there will be no right to terminate the lease earlier than the agreed expiration date. The result would be different if the written form requirement, as prescribed by law for long-term leases (Secs. 550, 578 and 126 of the Civil Code), is not observed. Sec. 550 of the Civil Code requires that a lease be memorialized in writing if its term is more than one year. If the lease is not in writing, then it will be deemed to have been concluded for an indefinite period of time. In that case, the lease agreement may be terminated at any time within the notice period prescribed by law, irrespective of the agreed fixed term. The statutory notice period for commercial leases is based on Sec. 580a(2) of the Civil Code. Under that provision, the notice of termination must be made no later than the third business day of a calendar quarter in order to take effect as of the end of the next calendar quarter.

The essence of the statutory written form requirement will be met if all of the parties' agreements are memorialized in writing. Written form, within the meaning of this requirement, is required not only for the original agreements made by the parties in connection with forming the lease, but also for any subsequent (material) amendments that arise during the course of the lease relationship (tenancy). A formal instrument or deed is deemed to meet the writing requirement only if it has been signed by both parties with their original signature (telefax or correspondence by letters will therefore not suffice). According to the most recent case law, an amendment instrument does not need to be physically affixed to the original instrument to create a single, integrated instrument. What is required, however, is that all material agreements are linked together through adequately definitive cross-references.[1]

b) Pitfalls

From the buyer's perspective, a notice of termination, which is issued by an 'anchor tenant' of a real estate property (mainly 'shopping centers') and is based on a failure to satisfy the writing requirement in a lease, constitutes the 'maximum credible accident (MCA)'. This is because not only does the loss of an anchor tenant have an adverse effect on the attractiveness and hence value of the real estate, but fewer visitors will adversely impact the revenues of the other tenants. Possible consequences could involve other customers enforcing rent abatements, asserting compensatory damage claims and issuing adjoining notices of termination. The failure to satisfy a writing requirement could also result in the landlord being unable to enforce rent increases in accordance with the agreed indexation provisions. These are just some of the reasons why from the landlord's perspective, the greatest degree of care needs to be exercised when complying with the writing requirement.

---

1 Federal Court of Justice of 9 April 2008 — XII ZR 89/06.

c) Solution

In light of the discussion above, it is very important to review lease agreements to assess whether the written form requirement has been satisfied. Given the fact that there has since been an almost incalculable number of decisions from the highest courts on the requirements for complying with the statutory writing requirements, the only persons who now truly understand the written form requirements are experts in lease law. If a lease review should reveal that the statutory writing requirements have been breached, then it will be important – where possible – to cure this breach by amending the lease. If no amendment can be made, then the buyer may use the writing requirement breaches to its advantage during negotiations in order to extract purchase price concessions.

2. Incidental Costs

a) Basic Background

Incidental costs have an enormous economic significance during the postacquisition management of commercial real estate. Only the phrase 'operating costs' is defined by statute (Sec. 1 of the Operating Costs Regulation – *Betriebskostenverordnung*). Where leasing commercial property is involved, however, the principle of party autonomy prevails with respect to the apportionment of incidental costs. The parties can therefore also agree to the payment of incidental costs other than the operating costs as defined in Sec. 1 of the Operating Costs Regulation. Accordingly, commercial landlords seek to pass on the incidental costs to tenants as much as possible.

b) Pitfalls

According to the case law handed down by the German Federal Court of Justice, in order to allocate or pass on incidental costs, there must generally be an express, substantively precise contractual agreement.[2] It should also be remembered that in practice more than 90% of the commercial leases are form contracts, and therefore contain standard terms and conditions. These types of agreement are subject to a strict reasonableness analysis under Sec. 307 of the Civil Code. The case law here has, on numerous occasions, held that incidental cost provisions set forth in form contracts are unenforceable due to a breach of Sec. 307 of the Civil Code.[3] If the applicable provisions are held to be unenforceable, then the incidental costs stipulated therein cannot be validly allocated and must be borne by the landlord (= purchaser).

---

[2] Federal Court of Justice of 6 April 2005 — XII ZR 158/01.
[3] See e.g. Federal Court of Justice of 3 Aug. 2011 — XII ZR 205/09, concerning the allocation of the 'center management costs' related to a shopping center.

c) Solution

During the due-diligence process, the enforceability of the incidental costs provisions contained in lease agreements should be reviewed using that careful standard terms and conditions (STC) reasonableness analysis. The review may reveal that individual cost items are unenforceable when analyzed under the current case law and can therefore be successfully challenged by tenants. If the landlord and tenant cannot reach agreement on the allocation of operating costs, then the buyer can use such unenforceable incidental cost allocation to its advantage during purchase price negations. Given the considerable economic importance of this issue, the matter should be queried and investigated during due diligence, including the extent to which tenants can challenge past incidental cost allocations. Such an enquiry can frequently reveal to the buyer the degree of trouble that could be entailed in acquiring the real estate.

3. Repairs and Maintenance / Cosmetic Repairs

a) Basic Background

A particularly important issue for investors when purchasing commercial real estate involves repairs, maintenance and cosmetic repairs. The allocation of costs between owner/landlord and tenants is of considerable economic importance for the postacquisition management of the property. Under German law and in the absence of any other contractual arrangement, the landlord must maintain the leased property during the entire lease term and must carry out cosmetic repairs (Sec. 535(1) sentence 2 of the Civil Code). As a rule, however, commercial lease contracts delegate the obligation to repair, maintain and cosmetically fix the property to the tenant.

b) Pitfalls

The above discussion on the allocation of incidental costs also applies to the shifting of the duty to repair, maintain and cosmetically fix the property. These provisions are often ruled unenforceable under the strict reasonableness analysis applicable to STCs pursuant to Sec. 307 of the Civil Code. Under the case law of the Federal Court of Justice, shifting the costs for repairs and maintenance of areas commonly used by other tenants (common areas) is unenforceable, if it is done without any quantitative limitation.[4] The unenforceability of such cost shifting clauses – which means that the statutory provision applies and the landlord will bear the obligation of repairing and maintaining – is particularly unfortunate because the shifting of the costs is routinely factored into the rent calculation.

---

4 Federal Court of Justice of 6 April 2005 — XII ZR 158/01.

c) Solution

The rules on cost allocation as set forth in the lease must undergo a careful STC reasonableness analysis during the course of the due diligence. If the unenforceable provisions cannot be cured by making the appropriate amendments to the lease agreements, then they may be used to reduce the purchase price during negotiations.

4. Exclusivity (No Compete) Covenant

a) Basic Background

During the due-diligence process and particularly in the case of shopping center purchases, the property buyer must be aware of the issues surrounding 'exclusivity (no compete) covenants', which give tenants the right to preclude other tenants who compete with them in business from leasing space on the property. This concept conceals one distinct risk: Under the generally prevailing view, the landlord of commercial property must refrain from itself competing against the tenant and from leasing space in its building or its immediate proximity to competitors, even without an express agreement in the lease.

b) Pitfalls

In the opinion of the Federal Court of Justice, a breach of the exclusivity covenant constitutes a qualitative defect in the leased property and thereby gives rise to the tenant's applicable statutory rights concerning defects. Accordingly, where the exclusivity covenant is breached, the tenant may reduce the rent, enforce compensatory damages or even terminate the lease without notice (extraordinary termination). Above all, the tenant will have a right, however, to demand that the landlord remove the competitor and thereby rescind the lease agreement with that competitor. Typically, such an arrangement will be possible only by paying a suitable settlement to the competitor, which could greatly impact the landlord – particularly if the residual term of the lease extends over numerous years.

c) Solution

During due diligence, the existing competitor situation should be specifically investigated, particularly in the case of shopping centers. Accordingly, the relevant leases should be reviewed to determine whether they contain contractual exclusivity (no compete) covenants. By making the appropriate amendments, legal disputes with potential competitors can be avoided.

5. Rent Security

a) Basic Background/Pitfalls

When a commercial property is purchased, another important issue involves the security that is agreed to in the leases and must be provided by the tenants. The reason here is the following: Pursuant to Sec. 566 of the Civil Code, the purchaser of commercial real estate will assume the rights and duties under any leases on that real estate. Consequently, after the expiration or termination of a lease, the buyer will face the obligation to repay the rent security, which may have been provided under that in the form of a cash security deposit. The buyer will owe this repayment duty to the tenant even if the cash security deposit was not transferred to it by the previous owner (former landlord). From the buyer's perspective, such a scenario could prove to be very unfortunate, particularly if the previous owner is now insolvent and the security deposit can no longer be segregated from that previous owner's other assets (because the assets have become part of the insolvency estate). In that situation, the purchaser's recourse against the previous owner is practically useless; the only claim it would have against the previous owner is an insolvency claim. The Federal Court of Justice rendered a decision addressing a similar case in 2012.[5]

b) Solution

From the buyer's perspective, there is a considerable incentive to review any agreed rent security clauses in the lease agreements and to ensure the preservation of such security by including an appropriate provision in the purchase agreement.

6. Maintenance and Service Contracts

The provision under Sec. 566 of the Civil Code as explained above – according to which existing lease agreements pass to the real estate purchaser by operation of the law – do not apply to maintenance and other service contracts with respect to real estate, where such contracts existed between the previous owner and third parties. If such contracts are to be assigned, then this must be expressly stipulated in the purchase contract. Occasionally, the seller will demand that the purchaser assume such contracts. Thus, the purchaser should review such contracts early enough during due diligence to develop an opinion about whether or not it wishes to assume the contracts.

---

[5] Federal Court of Justice of 7 March 2012 — XII ZR 13/10.

Dr. Michael R. Wiesbrock

Lawyer, Diplom-Kaufmann

Areas of Specialization

- Real-estate transactions and REITs
- Real-estate law and financing
- Mergers & acquisitions, venture capital and private equity
- Corporate law and general business law
- Capital markets law

Telephone +49 69/717 03-0

Email: michael.wiesbrock@fgs.de

Delisting as a Component of Taking Private Transactions

by Dieter Leuering

Contents

I. Taking Private Transactions
II. Delisting
III. Requirements for Regular Delisting
 1. The Previous View Held by the Federal Court of Justice: Macrotron
 2. An About-Turn by the Federal Court of Justice: Frosta
IV. Effects on Taking Private Transactions
 1. Effects on Regular Delisting and Downgrading
 2. Effects on Cold Delisting

I. Taking Private Transactions

In recent years we have seen an increasing number of transactions, in Germany and elsewhere, in which undervalued companies in neglected stock exchange segments are bought out by investment and private equity firms. The investor aims to buy the company at a low price, increase its value by means of strategic measures, and then resell it. Generally, the companies are held by the new owners for around three to five years. It is also conceivable that the company would later be taken public again under its new structure should it become of interest to institutional investors once more. This type of transaction is not limited to any particular industries. The decisive factor here is rather the price-earnings ratio: If it is under 10, the entity may be a promising target.

The acceptance of such transactions is related, among other things, to the generally discernible opening of companies toward investors. Private equity firms were once decried as „Heuschrecken" (locusts), but the criticism leveled against them is slowly dissipating. In the past new equity capital was generally raised by means of an IPO; today a private equity firm can achieve the same goal. Such firms are generally not merely invested in the equity, but together with the other owners seek to sustainably increase the target company's value. Taking in such capital can therefore further professionalize the management of the company.

A key component of these transactions is delisting, i.e. the complete disappearance of the company from the stock exchange list. In semantic juxtaposition to the term 'going public', these transactions are thus also described as 'taking private'. In the literature, the terms delisting, withdrawal from the stock exchange, going or taking private, or P2P (public to private), are sometimes used synonymously. In some cases they are differentiated, but authors vary in their usage; as yet no uniform terminology has emerged.

II. Delisting

Delisting can be brought about using various methods. One is for the purchaser to intervene in the structure of the company such that the tradable shares cease to exist by operation of law. Transactions under this heading are referred to as 'cold' delisting. The following instruments are recognized by German law:

- Transferring dissolution, i.e. the sale of all individual assets of the listed company to an unlisted purchasing company, which is typically controlled by the majority shareholder, by way of an asset deal and the subsequent dissolution and winding-up of the publicly listed stock corporation;
- Changing the corporate form of the target company; a merger (going private merger) or a change of corporate form are possible with this method;
- Organizational incorporation (*Eingliederung*), provided the purchaser consolidates at least 95% of the shares of the target company under a single owner; this has the effect of excluding the outside shareholders from the integrated company;
- Squeezing out the minority shareholders, i.e. transferring the remaining shares in the target company to the purchaser in return for a reasonable cash settlement, provided the purchaser holds at least 95% of the shares of the target company (in certain situations 90% will suffice).

The legal requirements and consequences of these methods cannot be examined in detail here, so an example must suffice. If, for instance, the purchaser acquired 95 % of the shares of the target company by way of a public takeover offer, then it may also collect the remaining shares of the target company by way of a squeeze-out against the will of the outside (minority) shareholders. In this case, the management of the stock exchange will revoke the admission of the shares because "proper trading on the stock exchange is no longer guaranteed for the long term" (Sec. 39(1) of the German Stock Exchange Act – *Börsengesetz*).

This cold delisting stands in contrast to regular delisting. According to Sec. 39(2) of the Stock Exchange Act, the management of the stock exchange may revoke the admission to the regulated market at the request of the issuer. The revocation of the admission has the opposite effect of admission. It ends the public-law usage relationship established by the admission between the stock exchange and the issuer to use the stock exchange facilities for trading the admitted securities in the relevant market segment. This termination, like the admission, is an administrative act. The background for this delisting may be a taking private transaction; however, it may also be the wish of management to escape the strict regulations of the capital market (particularly the obligations subsequent to admission).

Although regular delisting restores a public company to a private one, it changes nothing about the shareholders, and the company is not subsequently held by a closed group. Nonetheless, it is worth taking a further look at regular delisting.

III. Requirements for Regular Delisting

The legal basis for regular delisting is found in Sec. 39(2) of the Stock Exchange Act and the application of the relevant stock exchange rules; there is no specific legal basis in company law. In the Macrotron decision of 2002, the Federal Court of Justice laid out specific requirements for when a delisting is carried out at the request of the issuer, but it has recently abandoned this case law.

1. The Previous View Held by the Federal Court of Justice: Macrotron

In its Macrotron decision of 25 Nov. 2002 on the requirements for a complete withdrawal from the stock exchange[1], the Federal Court of Justice assumed that the revocation of the admission to trade shares on the regulated market at the request of the issuer (regular delisting) required *firstly* the approval by resolution of the shareholders' meeting of the affected company and *secondly* a mandatory offer by the company or the majority shareholder to purchase the shares of the minority shareholders. The reasoning behind this was that the Federal Court of Justice deemed that the adverse effect on the ability to sell the shares associated with the revocation adversely affected the constitutionally protected share ownership.

This view of the matter was surprising since the Federal Constitutional Court had decided on 5 Feb. 2002 that the exchange value of property rights in and of itself does *not* fall within the scope of protection of the freedom of ownership, which is why reductions in the exchange or market value of an item of property brought about by an official action do not generally affect the constitutionally protected rights of property. "This also applies in principle to the market value of securities".[2]

It was therefore not completely surprising that the Federal Constitutional Court stated on 11 July 2012, in a constitutional complaint directed *inter alia* against the Macrotron decision, that the revocation of the admission of securities to trading on the regulated market at the request of the issuer *does not* violate the guarantee of the right of property in the German Federal Constitution (*Grundgesetz*), i.e. Art. 14(1) of the Federal Constitution.[3] The scope of protection of the guarantee of the right of property merely includes the legal ability to sell the shares (i.e. the legal power to sell at any time on a market), whereas a mere increase in the actual ability to sell as a mere value factor of the share ownership is not protected. Thus, the admission for trading on the regulated market at most affects the opportunities for sale of a shareholder. However, as

---

1 Federal Court of Justice/ Civil Matters (*Bundesgerichtshof/ Zivilsachen*) 25.11.2002 – II ZR 133/01, 153, 47 = New Journal of Company Law (*Neue Zeitschrift für Gesellschaftsrecht*) 2003, p. 280.
2 Federal Constitutional Court 5.2.2002 – 2 BvR 305/93, reported in the legal periodical *Neue Juristische Wochenschrift* (NJW) 2002, p. 3009.
3 Federal Constitutional Court 11.7.2010 – 1 BvR 3142/07, 1569/08, Decisions (*Bundesverfassungsgericht- Entscheidungen*) 132, 99 = reported in NJW 2012, p. 3081.

a matter of principle, the functioning of a market is not protected by the constitutional right of property.

The court further stated that the principles set out by the Federal Court of Justice in the Macrotron decision for cases of delisting were permissible from a constitutional perspective, but not required.

2. An About-Turn by the Federal Court of Justice: Frosta

The Federal Court of Justice recently had to put its case law on regular delisting to the test. The underlying facts of the case were as follows: The management board of the publicly listed stock corporation submitted, with the consent of the supervisory board, an application for revocation of the admission to the stock exchange (Sec. 39(2) of the Stock Exchange Act) in connection with switching from the regulated market of the Berlin stock exchange to the Entry Standard of the Open Market of the Frankfurt stock exchange. Unlike a complete delisting, this merely meant changing over to a less regulated stock market segment (known as downgrading or downlisting). In the process, no settlement payment offer was submitted to the shareholders, nor was any approval obtained from the shareholders' meeting. Two shareholders subsequently instituted special award proceedings in order to have a reasonable cash settlement payment assessed for the shares held by them. The shareholders were unsuccessful with their demands both at the first instance and on appeal.

Even though the decision was based merely on a case of downgrading, and not on a complete withdrawal from the stock exchange, the Federal Court of Justice abandoned the principles it had developed in the Macrotron ruling.[4] Even with respect to cases of a complete withdrawal from the stock exchange, the Federal Court of Justice has now decided that it is not necessary to make any offer for a cash settlement payment to the shareholders of a publicly listed stock corporation for the purchase of their shares during a withdrawal from the stock exchange. The Federal Court of Justice also decided that no prior approval by resolution of the general shareholders' meeting is required for such a withdrawal. The Federal Court of Justice has thereby moved away from the principles for regular delisting it put forth in the Macrotron ruling.

The Federal Court of Justice shares the opinion of the prior instances, that no special valuation proceedings to determine a cash settlement payment need to be conducted, because the shareholders have no claim to a cash settlement payment in the case of a revocation of the admission of the shares to trading on the regulated market at the instigation of the company. The revocation of the admission to trading on the regulated market under Sec. 39(2) of the Stock Exchange Act at the request of the company does not lead to any adverse effect on the share ownership. The basis of the case law of the Federal Court of Justice[5] has been removed by the decision of the Federal Constitutional Court, accord-

---

4 Federal Court of Justice 8.10.2013 – II ZB 26/12, reported in NJW 2014, p. 146.
5 Federal Court of Justice/ Civil Matters 153, 47 25.11.2002 – II ZR 133/01 = reported in NZG 2003, p. 280 – Macrotron.

ing to which the revocation of the admission to trading on the regulated market of the stock exchange does not affect the constitutional right of property of the shareholders.[6]

According to this, the revocation of the admission to trading on the stock exchange does not deprive the shareholder of any legal positions which are allocated to the shareholder for his/her/its private benefit; the revocation has no adverse effect on the substance of the share ownership in terms of membership law or property law. Only the legal ability to sell falls under the protection of Art. 14(1) of the Federal Constitution. The actual ability to sell represents simply an earning or trading opportunity.

Furthermore – contrary to what is sometimes put forth in the literature – there is no subsequent requirement, either based on a *mutatis mutandis* application of Sec. 207 of the German Reorganization Act (*Umwandlungsgesetz*) or under Sec. 243(2) sentence 2 of the German Stock Corporation Act (*Aktiengesetz*), to submit a mandatory offer. Also, Sec. 29(1) sentence 1 of the Reorganization Act should not be applied *mutatis mutandis* to the withdrawal from the stock exchange. No general principle can be inferred from the norm that a switch from the regulated market leads to a cash settlement payment in every case. Opposing the recognition of such a general principle is that no cash settlement payment is intended for every case of cold delisting in which measures could indirectly lead to the termination of the admission, such as integration into a nonlisted publicly held corporation.

In addition, no other obligation to make an offer for a cash settlement payment exists based on any overall analogy to statutory provisions of other structural measures under company law (Secs. 305, 320b, 327b of the Stock Corporation Act, Secs. 29, 207 of the Reorganization Act). Since withdrawal from the stock exchange is not specified among the cases in which an approval by resolution of the shareholders' meeting is required pursuant to Sec. 119(1) of the Stock Corporation Act, there is also no obligation under the Stock Corporation Act to procure a resolution of the shareholders' meeting.

IV. Effects on Taking Private Transactions

If one considers the effects of the Federal Court of Justice's about-turn regarding the practice of delisting, a distinction must be made between the effects on regular delisting and downgrading on the one hand, and the effects on cold delisting on the other.

1. Effects on Regular Delisting and Downgrading

The effects on regular delisting and downgrading are obvious: The decision of the Federal Court of Justice makes it distinctly easier for companies to insti-

---

[6] Federal Constitutional Court Decision 132, p. 99 11.7.2012 – 1 BvR 3142/07, 1569/08 = reported in NJW 2012, p. 3081.

tute a regular delisting in the future, since neither a settlement payment offer nor approval by resolution of the shareholders' meeting is required. The decision also brings more legal certainty for cases of downgrading. Although the higher regional courts (*Oberlandesgerichte*) previously supported the position that a settlement payment is not necessary in this case there has been no case law from the highest courts on this issue to date.[7]

For listed publicly held corporations, the reversal of case law by the Federal Court of Justice specifically means that, in future, listed publicly held corporations or majority shareholders will not be confronted by the costs associated with a cash settlement payment offer in the context of delisting or mere downgrading. This applies to the cash settlement in and of itself, but also, to an extent, to the immense costs resulting from a special valuation proceeding to examine the reasonableness of the cash settlement payment. Another area of activity for litigious shareholders may therefore lose its appeal.

With respect to the costs associated with a withdrawal from the stock exchange, the requirement to prepare and conduct an extraordinary shareholders' meeting, which – depending on the size of the corporation – can involve considerable resources, also no longer applies. The risk that the resolution of the shareholders' meeting will be contested and the associated costs thereof to the company also no longer apply.

2. Effects on Cold Delisting

Of greater interest are the indirect effects on cold delisting, which open new structuring possibilities: For many structural measures, the law provides for the awarding of a reasonable cash settlement payment. Pursuant to the DAT/Altana case law of the Federal Court of Justice[8], the amount of the cash settlement depends on the stock exchange price of the relevant share. Outside shareholders are generally to be compensated during structural measures in consideration of the market value of the shares. However, if the company value per share calculated on the basis of the income value method per share is higher than the stock exchange value, then this must be paid.

> For example: If one investor holds more than 95% of the shares of a publicly listed stock corporation, he may transfer the shares of the other shareholders to himself in return for a reasonable cash settlement payment (squeeze-out, Secs. 327a *et seqq.* of the Stock Corporation Act). If the company is listed, the average weighted stock exchange price of the shares during the three-month period prior to the announcement of the measure represents the lower limit of the settlement payment. This is awkward if the cash settlement payment calculated based on the stock exchange price is

---

7 Higher Regional Court of Munich 21.5.2008 – 31 Wx 62/07, New Journal of Company Law 2008, p. 755 and Superior Court of Justice (*Kammergericht*) 30.4.2009 – 2 W 119/08, New Journal of Company Law 2009, p. 752.
8 Federal Court of Justice/ Civil Matters 12.3.2001 – II ZB 15/00, 147, 108 = reported in NJW 2001, p. 2080.

significantly higher than the company value calculated on the basis of income value. The same applies if a listed publicly held corporation is merged into an unlisted publicly held corporation; according to Sec. 29(1) of the Reorganization Act, a cash settlement payment offer must be made to the opposing shareholders.

After a delisting – in the absence of a stock exchange price – only the (in this case lower) future earnings value can be used as a basis.

Dr. Dieter Leuering

Lawyer, Certified Commercial and Corporate Lawyer, Certified Tax Lawyer
Areas of Specialization
- Corporate law
- Capital markets law
- Mergers & Acquisitions
- Corporate reorganizations
- Corporate litigation and arbitration

Telephone (ext.) +49 228/95 94-199
Email: dieter.leuering@fgs.de

German Corporate Governance Code

by Jens Eric Gotthardt

Contents

I. Introduction
  1. Corporate Governance
  2. Background to the Code
II. Objective
III. Legal Nature and Range of Application
  1. Legal Nature
  2. Range of Application
IV. Structure
  1. Prevailing Law
  2. Recommendations
  3. Suggestions
V. Contents
  1. Two-Tier Management System
  2. Essential Details of the Code
    a) Shareholders and General Meeting
    b) Cooperation Between Executive Board and Supervisory Board
    c) Executive Board
    d) Supervisory Board
    e) Transparency
    f) Accounting and Auditing
VI. Development
VII. Summary

I. Introduction

1. Corporate Governance

There is no direct German translation for the expression 'corporate governance', nor is there a uniform national or international definition of this term. In Germany, 'corporate governance' is generally understood to mean corporate management and supervision.

The Code itself explains in its preamble: *"The German Corporate Governance Code sets out essential statutory requirements for the management and supervision of German listed corporations (corporate management) and includes internationally- and nationally-recognized standards of good and responsible corporate management."*

The Organization for Economic Cooperation and Development (OECD) defines 'corporate governance' as follows: *"Corporate governance is the system by which business corporations are directed and controlled. The corporate governance structure specifies the distribution of rights and responsibilities among different participants in the corporation, such as the board, managers, shareholders and other stakeholders, and spells out the rules and procedures for making decisions on corporate affairs. By doing this, it also provides the structure through which the corporation's objectives are set and the means of attaining those objectives and monitoring performance."*

Responsible corporate management and supervision is therefore at the heart of all attempts at definition.

2. Background to the Code

Principles of corporate governance, i.e. principles for responsible corporate management and supervision, are – in Germany as in other countries – traditionally found in legal norms. By contrast, in countries with an Anglo-Saxon legal tradition, law-making in this area tends to be relatively restrained. In these countries, the business community itself has developed codes of best practice, to which corporations voluntarily submit in order to create the necessary transparency for the capital markets.

In Germany, the idea of drafting its own code in this area first arose after the string of national and international collapses of listed corporations that occurred in the 1990s. It became evident in connection with these collapses that the possibility of separation of ownership and corporate management in corporations carried considerable risks for the entities concerned. The interests of the owners on the one hand and of management on the other are frequently at odds with each other. As a rule, the owners are interested in a continuous and sustainable positive development of the corporation. Management, by contrast, is often focused on short-term results and high profits. As a result of the absence of their ownership and the responsibility for the ultimate fate of the corporation that comes with ownership, management is prepared to take higher risks for the sake of maximizing profits and, ultimately, maximizing salaries. The interests of the owners may therefore, as a result of the decoupling of business decisions and business responsibility, be pushed into the background.

In order to avoid the aforementioned conflict of interest, and following the Anglo-Saxon example of self-regulation, in May 2000, the government Corporate Governance Commission was established as the first such commission in Germany. This commission was tasked with investigating the possibility of introducing a regulatory framework for combining the principles of good corporate management and supervision. By way of conclusion to its activities, the Commission presented the suggestion that a 'code of best practice' be drafted. Subsequently, in September 2001, the German Federal Ministry of Justice set up a new government commission on corporate governance chaired by Gerhard Cromme. This commission was composed of high-ranking representatives from trade and industry as well as academia. It was given the task of drafting a German Corporate Governance Code ('GCGC') on the basis of the prevailing law. On 26 Feb. 2002, the Commission completed the GCGC. Its initial version was published in the electronic Federal Gazette on 20 Aug. 2002.

II. Objective

The introduction of the GCGC is meant to provide a unified regulatory framework. The presentation of the prevailing German law contained in this set of rules is intended to make German listed corporations and their corporate governance more transparent to investors. This is aimed in particular at promoting investors' trust in German listed corporation as well as in the German capital market more generally. The Code is intended to convey the principles of good corporate governance as required from a German perspective. Finally, the Code is meant to encourage corporations to adopt value-oriented behavior, i.e. behavior that abides by the law and is also morally unobjectionable.

The Code explains in its preamble: *"The objective of the Code is to make the German corporate-governance system transparent and comprehensible. It seeks to promote trust on the part of international and national investors, clients, employees and the public in the management and supervision of German listed corporations."* Finally, the Code is intended to inform national as well as international investors about German corporate governance principles and to provide listed stock corporations *(Aktiengesellschaften* or *AGs)*, for purposes of their self-regulation, with recommendations for recognized corporate-governance standards.

III. Legal Nature and Range of Application

1. Legal Nature

The GCGC has acquired a prominent position in the field of corporate-governance regulation. The percentage of corporations who comply with the recommendations of the Code has risen steadily since its introduction, although the recommendations of the Code are not in themselves binding. Compliance with the recommendations of the Code is voluntary.

The Code itself does not have the status of law. While it was drafted by a government commission which edits it annually, there is (i) no statutory regulation governing how this commission is constituted and (ii) no statutory procedure regarding decision-making within the commission. Consequently, the government commission does not possess any democratic legitimation and is not empowered to issue binding regulations.

Similarly, the Code does not constitute customary law; if this were the case, this would make it a binding regulation similar to a law. In fact, from among customary laws, only commercial custom might be applicable in this regard. Commercial customs are the customs and uses of merchants which supplement the will of those merchants even if they might not be aware of them. The GCGC, however, did not come about through customs between merchants; instead, it was developed by specifically-commissioned professionals.

According to prevailing opinion, the Code represents nothing more than behavioral recommendations. It is designed to act as a self-regulatory instrument for the German business community. It does contain descriptive presentations of prevailing law, which of itself, by definition, implies obligation. However, the Code merely summarizes these in an understandable way. From this, however, a binding nature of the Code cannot be inferred. The only part of the Code that constitutes exclusively original content is the recommendations and suggestions within the Code, and these precisely do not lay claim to being binding.

Corporations may refrain, in principle, from following the recommendations and suggestions of the Code without having to fear legal repercussions. This classification as a 'behavioral recommendation' is aimed at avoiding an over-regulation of the German capital market. Nonetheless, the Code is intended to serve as a guideline for the business community regarding good corporate governance.

The Code received a particular boost through the Transparency and Disclosure Act *(Transparenz- und Publizitätsgesetz)* adopted in July 2002, through which the ***Entsprechenserklärung*** (**'Declaration of Conformity'**) was inserted into the German Stock Corporation Act *(Aktiengesetz)* (Sec. 161 of the Stock Corporation Act): *"The executive board and supervisory board of any corporation listed on the stock exchange shall declare once every year that the recommendations of the 'Government Commission German Corporate Governance Code' published by the Federal Ministry of Justice in the official section of the Federal Gazette have been and continue to be complied with, or else, which of the recommendations have not been or are not being applied and why so."* Issuing the Declaration of Conformity is not at the corporation's discretion but is mandatory. While the Code itself does not become binding through the issuing of the Declaration, the mandatory issuing of a Declaration at least introduces a statutory requirement for the executive board and the supervisory board to examine the Code.

The failure to issue a Declaration of Conformity represents a breach of duty under the Stock Corporation Act. Such a breach can in principle lead to the liability of directors and officers *(Organhaftung)*. However, in order for such executive liability to be triggered, concrete evidence of damage and causation are required, so that ultimately there is scant risk of liability. Infringements of the Declaration of Conformity have recently become particularly relevant in German case law in the context of appeals against discharge decisions under the Stock Corporation Act. The Federal Court of Justice explains in this respect that an inaccurate Declaration of Conformity creates a legal offense for which *"every member of the bodies that are required to make the Declaration is liable, to the extent that the members of the bodies in question knew or ought to have known of the initial or subsequent inaccurateness of the Declaration and despite this did not procure its correction."*

2. Range of Application

The German Corporate Governance Code is directly aimed at all listed corporations as well as corporations with 'access to the capital market' within the meaning of the Stock Corporation Act. Pursuant to the Stock Corporation Act, listed corporations are those *"whose shares are admitted to a market regulated and supervised by officially-recognized bodies, operated regularly and accessible to the public either directly or indirectly"*. Corporations with access to the capital market within the meaning of the Stock Corporation Act are *"[corporations] that [have] issued, for trading on an organized market (within the meaning of Sec. 2(5) of the German Securities Trade Act – Wertpapierhandelsgesetz), exclusively securities other than shares, and whose issued shares are traded, at their own behest, on a multilateral trading system within the meaning of Sec. 2(3) sentence 1 no. 8 of the German Securities Trade Act".*

In addition to the above, the GCGC also has a 'ripple effect' on other corporations. For example, in the Code itself, all capital-market oriented corporations are encouraged to comply with the GCGC.

Furthermore, there is now a plethora of separate Corporate Governance Codes for particular types of entity, for example for family businesses ('Corporate Governance Code for Family Businesses') and public companies ('Corporate Governance Code for Public-Sector Companies'). The constant development of new codes demonstrates that the system of self-regulation is met with steadily increasing acceptance in Germany.

IV. Structure

1. Prevailing Law

First and foremost, the GCGC is about setting out those corporate-governance principles that have been enacted in Germany. It does so by summarizing, in clear and understandable language, the prevailing legal rules. It does not lay any claims to completeness in this regard, but rather serves to provide an overview of the principles of corporate governance that prevail in Germany.

2. Recommendations

Second, the Code contains recommendations. As already explained above, the recommendations of the Code do not constitute binding regulations. However, in accordance with Sec. 161 of the Stock Corporation Act, a declaration as to compliance or noncompliance with them must be made, and any noncompliance must be explained further. This principle is generally referred to as the **'comply or explain' principle**. This principle thus gives rise to a **duty to provide a statement** as to whether or not the recommendations of the Code are being complied with, and in the event that they are not, a **duty to provide pertinent reasons**. The executive board and the supervisory board are obliged, through the binding requirement to submit a Declaration of Conformity, to examine the contents of the Code. In so doing, they must decide whether compliance with the Code is advisable for them in a given instance or whether particularities of their corporation or of the market make deviations from the recommendations of the Code necessary or expedient.

3. Suggestions

Third, the Code contains suggestions. These are intended to influence the corporation's future development but are not yet consolidated to a degree that they contain management or supervisory principles. However, suggestions may certainly be promoted to recommendations at a later stage by the government commission.

V. Contents

The Code is divided into six parts that address the topics **'Shareholders and the General Meeting'**, **'Cooperation Between Executive Board and Supervisory Board'**, **'Executive Board'**, **'Supervisory Board'**, **'Transparency'** and **'Accounting and Auditing'**. As already mentioned above, the focus across all of these topics is to set out prevailing law.

1. Two-Tier Management System

In order to be able to illustrate the topics of the Code in greater detail, the **two-tier management system** that is legally prescribed in Germany needs to be explained. 'Two-tier management system' means that corporate management and corporate supervision are carried out by two separate bodies. These two bodies are the executive board and the supervisory board. The executive board manages the business of the corporation and reports to the supervisory board. The supervisory board, in turn, supervises the executive board and supports the executive board in an advisory capacity. Unlike the case in countries with an Anglo-Saxon legal tradition, the two-tier management system is used in Germany. In countries with an Anglo-Saxon legal tradition, a single-tier system of corporate management and supervision is applied. In such a system, the management function is not separated from the supervisory function; instead, both roles are carried out by the same single body. Both systems have advantages and disadvantages. Advantages of the single-tier system include in particular the swifter flow of information and the resulting ability to reach decisions more quickly. Quicker decision-making enables a more flexible adaptation to changing circumstances. By contrast, the two-tier management system that is predominant in Germany enables management to be supervised more independently. Furthermore, dividing the management and supervision functions between two separate bodies leads to a clearer separation of powers, which in turn promotes greater transparency.

The following diagram shows the essential tasks and functions of the corporation bodies in the two-tier management system:

German Corporate Governance Code

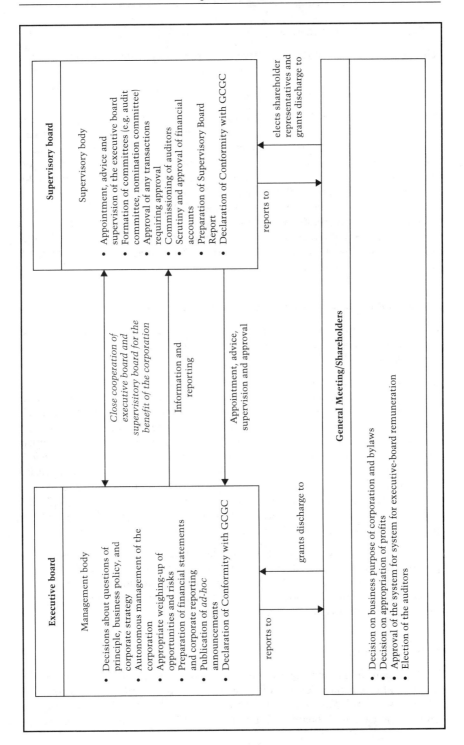

2. Essential Details of the Code

The essential details of the Code are briefly presented and summarized below:

a) Shareholders and General Meeting

With respect to the shareholders, the GCGC provides a brief description of the rights to which the shareholders are typically entitled under German stock-corporation law. In that context, the focus is on the description of the exercise of shareholders' membership rights at and in connection with the general meeting. In this regard, the Code contains the recommendation that, for shareholders, the personal exercise of their rights and their voting by proxy should be made as easy as possible, e.g. by appointing a representative for the exercise of shareholders' voting rights, who is bound by the shareholder's instructions, and who can also be contacted during the general meeting. The Code further recommends that shareholders be enabled to follow general meetings using modern communication channels (e.g. the Internet).

b) Cooperation Between Executive Board and Supervisory Board

Close collaboration for the benefit of the corporation runs through the GCGC as the central idea behind the cooperation between the executive board and the supervisory board.

The key point in the cooperation between the executive board and the supervisory board is the provision of sufficient information, since this is essential for the supervisory board to be able to properly carry out its supervisory and advisory functions. This requires regular and prompt provision of information by the executive board. The executive board must, in particular, inform the supervisory board about *"relevant issues of strategy, planning, business development, risk position, risk management and compliance"*. The executive board has a duty to provide information; the supervisory board has a duty to request it. The means that the executive board must, at its own initiative, supply the supervisory board with information, while the supervisory board must, in turn, make active efforts to obtain information from the executive board.

In addition to the recommendations of the GCGC that mirror the statutory provisions with respect to the cooperation of the executive board and the supervisory board, items 3.7 and 3.8 contain recommendations for the conduct of the executive board and the supervisory board in the event of a takeover offer and for the details of D&O insurance.

c) Executive Board

In the recommendations of the GCGC relating to the executive board, the main emphasis is on recommendations on executive-board remuneration. The Code sets out the following criteria that ought to be considered when determining the executive-board remuneration in order to ensure that such remuneration is reasonable: *"the tasks of the individual member of the executive board; his or her personal performance; the economic situation, performance and future prospects for the corporation as well as the appropriateness of the remuneration, taking into account corporations of comparable size in similar industries and the remuneration structure in place in other areas of the corporation".*

The Code recommends that that the remuneration structure be geared towards a sustainable development of the corporation. To this end, the Code goes on to recommend that the variable remuneration elements, in particular, be based upon a multi-year assessment basis. In addition, any calculation should take into account positive as well as negative developments.

The Code also recommends creating a transparent remuneration structure by disclosing the executives' remuneration (including their names). This is meant in particular to make possible a clear division into fixed and variable remuneration and, with respect to variable remuneration, the monitoring of compliance with remuneration requirements.

d) Supervisory Board

The emphasis of the GCGC recommendations with respect to the supervisory board is on recommendations regarding the supervisory board's composition.

In the context of its composition, the supervisory board is recommended to pay attention to diversity, in particular, striving to include an appropriate number of women.

Depending on the specific circumstances of the corporation and the number of board members available, the Code further recommends the supervisory board set up professionally-qualified committees. The formation of committees facilitates dealing with various topics in a more effective and professionally more qualified manner.

In addition to professional qualifications, any composition of the supervisory board should take diversity into account. Furthermore, corporations are advised to avoid conflicts of interest by appointing a number of independent supervisory board members. Supervisory board members are considered independent if they do not have a personal or other relationship with the corporation or with persons associated with the corporation. In particular, it is recommended that the supervisory board include no more than two former members of the executive board, and the Code additionally recommends that members of the executive board not become members of the supervisory board any earlier than two years after the end of their term as executive board members, unless they are elected as a result of a nomination by shareholders holding more than 25% of the voting rights in the corporation.

e) Transparency

The recommended way to achieve transparency is the forwarding of information to shareholders. Information provided to shareholders must include not only information that is subject to mandatory domestic publication but also information published abroad as a result of capital-market regulations existing in such foreign countries.

f) Accounting and Auditing

Shareholders and third parties are informed, in particular, through the consolidated group statements and the consolidated group report. Relevant international accounting principles must be taken into account in the preparation of reports. The executive board prepares the consolidated group accounts, which are examined and audited by the supervisory board and the external auditor, respectively.

The supervisory board issues the audit assignment to the external auditor and enters into a fee agreement with him. The Code recommends that the external auditor and the supervisory board agree that, during the course of his activity, the external auditor bears an obligation to provide information and to report to the supervisory board. In particular, the auditor is advised to inform the supervisory board if, in his audit, he comes to the conclusion that there are inaccuracies in the Declaration of Conformity made by the executive board and by the supervisory board.

VI. Development

The German Corporate Governance Code is revised on an ongoing basis by the Government Commission on Corporate Governance. The commission is what is known as a 'standing commission'. It currently has 14 members. The composition of the commission has changed several times. Most recently, Manfred Gentz took over as chair on 30 Sept. 2013.

The Code is revised and adapted roughly on an annual basis. Up to now, the only years in which the Code has not been revised were 2004 and 2011. In the context of these revisions, the Code is continuously adapted to new statutory developments. In addition, amendments are made with the objective of focusing on particular issues by emphasizing specific legal principles. For example, in the context of such adaptations, the individualized disclosure of executive-board-member remuneration was introduced, together with the recommendation to aspire to having women appropriately represented in the composition of the executive board. In the most recent amendment, recommendations for streamlining the Code and making it more readable were incorporated.

VII. Summary

The Code provides a good body of rules for responsible corporate management and supervision. It has become a standard for the DAX 30, the 30 largest German corporations listed on the Frankfurt Stock Exchange. However, smaller German corporations also follow the recommendations of the Code in large numbers.

The widespread acceptance of the Code demonstrates that, as a result of compliance with the Code, trust in German listed corporations and with it trust in the German capital market is growing. In particular, in this context, one of the decisive factors in raising capital is to achieve transparency.

Dr. Jens Eric Gotthardt

Lawyer, Tax Advisor

Areas of Specialization

- Mergers & acquisitions and corporate reorganizations
- Private equity and venture capital
- Corporate law
- Value-added tax law

Telephone (ext.) +49 228/95 94-324

Email: jens-eric.gotthardt@fgs.de

Recent Developments in Corporate and Financial Restructuring

by Stefan Simon

Contents

I. The New German 'Rescue Culture'
  1. Overview: Revision of Insolvency Law and the Debenture Act
  2. The Revision of German Insolvency Law Promotes In-Court Corporate Restructurings
     a) Introduction of New 'Insolvency Corporate Governance' Comparable to the US Debtor in Possession
     b) Automatic Stay Protection of a Debtor by New 'Umbrella Proceedings'

  c) The Insolvency Scheme as the Centerpiece of Corporate Restructuring
  3. Bonds and Debentures
  4. The Current Draft of Insolvency Proceedings for Corporate Groups

II. New Opportunities and Pitfalls for In-Court Restructurings

I. The New German 'Rescue Culture'

1. Overview: Revision of Insolvency Law and the Debenture Act

In the past, the German corporate restructuring culture mainly focused on out-of-court restructurings. Out-of-court restructurings were quick, quiet, and effective. However, as the corporate finance culture grew more diverse – in the past, German businesses were mainly financed by local banks – the need for effective in-court restructurings became apparent. Unlike the case in other jurisdictions such as the United States or France, corporate restructuring by formal bankruptcy court proceedings was very rare.

Although the 1999 German Insolvency Code provided for several restructuring tools, e.g. an insolvency scheme (*Insolvenzplan*) and self-administration, in practice insolvency administrators were forced to liquidate the corporation and to generate the going concern value of the entity by way of an asset deal. As a result, the management of the corporation often did not file for insolvency proceedings at an early stage in order to restructure the business entity because the outcome of insolvency proceedings was to a large extent unpredictable, and the shareholders had to face the possibility of losing their investment completely.

A further weak spot of German insolvency legislation was that an insolvency plan/rescue plan could not interfere with the rights of a bankrupt corporation's shareholders. Once the European Insolvency Regulation came into force in 2002, several traditional German corporations, e.g. the automotive supplier Schefenacker, moved its center of main interest to the UK shortly before filing for insolvency in order to come under the jurisdiction of what was presumed to be the much more flexible English Insolvency Act and its corporate rescue culture. Having gained the impression of this new form of 'forum shopping' and due to the financial crisis, the German legislature revised several statutes in order to promote the in-court restructuring of corporations under German law. In 2009 the new German Debenture Act (*Schuldverschreibungsgesetz*) first came into force, which is a tool for 'tailor-made' bond restructurings. In 2012 the new German Act for the Further Facilitation of the Restructuring of Companies (*Gesetz zur weiteren Erleichterung der Sanierung der Unternehmen* – hereinafter 'Restructuring Facilitation Act') entered into force. Both laws have passed the practical test very successfully and have changed German restructuring culture. Serious weaknesses of German insolvency law have been eliminated and significant advantages of the new Restructuring Facilitation Act have been introduced including compensation for lost wages due to insolvency (*Insolvenzausfallgeld*). This means that the wages of the employees of a corporation in insolvency proceedings are paid by the employment authority and the corporation may protect its liquidity. For these reasons, it is safe to say that a modern and competitive corporate and financial restructuring law now exists in Germany. The last step of these legislative actions will be the introduction of a new law on the restructuring of corporate groups, which is now before the German parliament.

2. The Revision of German Insolvency Law Promotes In-Court Corporate Restructurings

German insolvency law was last reformed on 1 March 2012 with the Restructuring Facilitation Act. Now the Insolvency Code (*Insolvenzordnung*) provides for an abundance of possibilities as to in-court corporate restructurings as follows:

a) Introduction of New 'Insolvency Corporate Governance' Comparable to the US Debtor in Possession

This change of governance has led to the promotion of self-administration proceedings comparable to 'debtor in possession' according to Chapter 11 of the US Bankruptcy Code. The debtor now is able to remain fully in control of the proceedings. He will only be assisted by the 'examiner' (*Sachwalter*), who is entrusted with monitoring the ongoing insolvency proceedings and the way the management is handling it. The managers who were in office during the opening proceedings will remain in their position. Usually they will be – or have already been – supported by a Chief Restructuring Officer (CRO) who is knowledgeable of restructuring processes. In some cases creditors will even call for a full replacement of the former management board in favor of a new CRO. It is common practice before filing for insolvency in self-administration for a reputable insolvency law expert to join the management. In this way, the debtor is able to fully flesh out the court restructuring beginning with the application for insolvency up to the draft of the insolvency scheme, which means that the business continues to function outside insolvency proceedings. The creditors do gain a substantial influence via their creditors' committee, which has to intervene in certain transactions. Even during the opening proceedings, liquidity can be vastly improved by the option of financing the wages of the employees via 'insolvency payment prefinancing' (*Insolvenzgeldvorfinanzierung*). The insolvency payment is granted by the Federal Employment Agency and will only have to be repaid to the extent of the 'insolvency quota' (*Insolvenzquote*) – this means that the funding is almost gifted to the business entity. This is a restructuring tool which is unique worldwide; labor-intensive businesses gain an advantage under insolvency law in comparison to other European jurisdictions by being located in Germany.

When the new law came into force, it was not clear whether the new law allowed debtor-in-possession financing ('DIP financing'), which is very common in US in court restructurings. DIP financing is a special form of financing provided to entities in insolvency proceedings. Usually, this debt is considered senior to all other debt or equity issued by a corporation. When the new law came into force, there was legal uncertainty as to whether the debtor in possession may create such a senior-ranking claim (*Masseverbindlichkeit*) in the crucial period after filing for insolvency, mainly three months ('opening proceedings' – *Eröffnungsverfahren*). Most of the German insolvency courts accepted the option of DIP financing, but most of them require specific advance authorization on their part to create specific senior-ranking claims during the opening proceedings. As there is still no uniform case law (the Federal Court of Justice has yet to decide) and the restructuring of an entity is reliant on this financing in the opening procedures, one should always check in advance how the prospective court handles these kinds of questions. This allows the debtor to use the full array of options open to the responsible court, even if this means moving the corporation's registered seat prior to the application if necessary to a court more sympathetic toward the concept of debtor in possession and restructurings.

b) Automatic Stay Protection of a Debtor by New 'Umbrella Proceedings'

A new type of 'umbrella proceedings' (*Schutzschirmverfahren*) has been introduced which is similar to the automatic stay associated with proceedings in accordance with Chapter 11 of the US Bankruptcy Code. If the debtor has filed for insolvency according to the rules of debtor in possession, he may also apply for 'umbrella proceedings'. The 'umbrella' grants a period of up to three months to work out an insolvency scheme. Furthermore, unlike conventional self-administration, the debtor has the exclusive right to propose the examiner who is appointed by the court and has to supervise the debtor during insolvency proceedings. During this time the insolvency court must, upon request, order the suspension of – or provisional restriction on – enforcement measures against the debtor unless real estate is involved.

In order to be granted these umbrella proceedings, the debtor must not be 'illiquid' but only 'overindebted' or under threat of becoming illiquid. It will also have to present a certificate issued by a specially qualified person stating that the restructuring does not manifestly lack the prospect of success. If the court accepts these prerequisites, it will grant the umbrella proceedings.

The umbrella proceedings are advantageous compared to the 'regular' self-administration proceedings as the court – if it has received an application from the debtor – will have to grant the status of senior-ranking claims to financing established by the debtor and has no discretion. For the regular debtor in possession, it is still not finally decided by the courts whether the debtor may apply at all to have these senior-ranking claims established.

c) The Insolvency Scheme as the Centerpiece of Corporate Restructuring

The centerpiece of corporate in-court restructurings in Germany is the insolvency scheme. The new German restructuring law now provides for a package of improved measures: In particular, corporate-law-related structural measures can be part of an insolvency scheme and can thus be used against shareholders which block the restructuring. The following measures can be taken:

- Implementation of a capital increase and/or a capital reduction. The capital increase can be a part of the insolvency scheme and can – after adoption by the creditors' meeting – be implemented without a shareholders' resolution according to corporate law. This can be an effective tool for a distressed-company investor to acquire the corporation.

- Transfer of shares in the restructured corporation. Transfers of shares – e.g. to an investor – may be incorporated into the insolvency scheme and may be executed even against the will of the shareholders if the necessary majorities amongst the creditors are met. Thus the disruptive potential of shareholders whose shares have lost their value can be neutralized.

- Reorganization measures, especially the spin-off (*Ausgliederung*) of valuable parts of a business by an insolvency scheme. Often certain parts of an entity are still of great value while other parts are creating a loss and have thus led to insolvency. By way of the spin-off, it is possible to transfer these profitable parts to a new entity, thus separating them from the less profitable parts and making them easily transferable. In doing so, the less profitable parts of the business can be disposed of, while the entity can continue doing business with only the profitable parts. Once all debtors have been repaid according to the provisions of the insolvency scheme, the business is released from the insolvency proceedings.

- Change of legal form. This is the change of a *GmbH*, a German privately held corporation, into an *AG*, a German stock corporation, to prepare for an initial public offering (IPO). However, the recent Suhrkamp case, which was widely discussed in the German public, has initiated a legal discussion in regard to the boundaries and the risk of misuse of this new measure.

- It is now also possible to incorporate a debt-to-equity swap in an insolvency scheme. This was, for example, conducted in the insolvency scheme of IVG Immobilien AG and Pfleiderer AG. The debt does not have to be swapped at its nominal value; instead, an – at times substantial – deduction has to be made in line with the business entity's ability repay its debt. Thus even large-scale debt may not lead to the whole corporation being swapped to the benefit of the debtors. Pfleiderer (a wood-processing corporation) was one of the first entities to enter insolvency under the new Restructuring Facilitation Act. With a debt of about EUR 1 billion its insolvency scheme planned for a capital reduction to zero (effectively removing all its previous shareholders) combined with a capital increase by capital contribution in kind made by an investor who had previously bought more than half of the debt below its nominal value. This shows the option for investors to gain access to a corporation via insolvency proceedings which would otherwise not have been possible.

IVG had planned a very large commercial building at Frankfurt Airport and, as a result of it selling and letting much more slowly than anticipated, bankruptcy ensued. The umbrella proceedings were used to establish an insolvency scheme fit to rid the corporation of all its debt: Holders of a EUR 400 million bond and creditors of a syndicated loan of EUR 1.3 billion were to swap these debts in an insolvency scheme and thus take over the corporation as a whole, 80% going to the lenders and 20% to the bondholders.

These debt-to-equity swaps are usually commenced by first transferring the debt into a trust SPV, which in turn contributes this debt in kind under the capital increase. Once the debt-to-equity swap has been fully executed, part of the newly created shares will be sold by the trust SPV on the capital market. The former creditors may then choose to receive either shares in the debtor or part of the proceeds from the sale of the shares.

It has to be noted, though, that many restructuring cases still take place outside these formal proceedings. For example, the restructuring of SolarWorld AG, the world's leading solar-panel producer, which consisted of a complex debt-to-equity swap and thus a waiver of considerable financial amounts by both stockholders and bondholders took place outside formal insolvency proceedings. The advantages and disadvantages of both in-court restructuring as well as out-of-court restructuring have to be weighed up for each individual case. In the case of SolarWorld, there was a homogenous creditor structure, which makes it possible to gain the consent of all the creditors, which is a prerequisite for an out-of-court restructuring. According to German law, an out-of-court restructuring scheme (*außergerichtlicher Sanierungsvergleich*) needs the consent of all creditors to become effective against this creditor, whereas an in-court restructuring scheme is binding and effective against all creditors of a debtor once it is adopted by the majorities in the creditors' meeting. Therefore, unlike in out-of-court restructurings, a waiver or deferral of a claim made by creditors may become effective, although the specific creditor has voted against the in-court restructuring scheme.

3. Bonds and Debentures

Besides the overall insolvency of a corporation, German law also allows for a restructuring of bonds (*Anleihen*) and debentures (*Schuldverschreibungen*). On

5 Aug. 2009, a new Debenture Act entered into force. Whereas previously a bond once issued could effectively not be changed at all, sometimes meaning the bondholders lost everything because the issuer went bankrupt, this new law allows the majority of bondholders to decide in favor of any necessary restructuring of a bond. Thus the bondholders may vote, for example, to swap their old bonds for new bonds of lesser nominal value. The majority of bondholders may also vote for a swap of their old bonds for new stocks (debt-to-equity swap).

This was how SolarWorld AG was restructured. SolarWorld AG had suffered under a crushing debt of more than EUR 1 billion in bonds and certain loans. As the corporation was threatened with 'overindebtedness', shareholders, bondholders and lenders agreed upon a capital reduction by about 1:145 followed by a substantial capital increase through contribution in kind of the debt of bondholders and lenders. The bondholders of the two issued bonds agreed on this in two consecutive bondholder meetings.

If a corporation which issued a bond faces financial distress, any required restructuring will usually need to include the bondholders and stockholders. The German Debenture Act provides that the creditors can adopt resolutions to amend the terms of the bond in a bondholders' meeting. Unless the terms of the bond require larger majorities, any material amendment (such as a change of maturity, reduction of interest claims, debt-equity swaps and subordination of claims) to the terms of the bond requires a supermajority of at least 75%, minor amendments require a majority of only 50%. As it is possible for a common representative to be named in the bondholders' meeting, further negotiations between the bondholders, the debtor and other creditors are greatly facilitated: The common representative actually represents all bondholders, even those who did not vote for him at the bondholders' meeting.

It is not uncommon for individual bondholders to be dissatisfied with the results of such bondholders' meetings and may thus file a suit, which may block the restructuring of the bond. Because of this, the Debenture Act provides for release proceedings (*Freigabeverfahren*) to obtain a judgment that the bondholders' actions do not prevent the effectiveness of the amendments to the terms of the bond.

This provides the legal framework for the tailor-made restructuring of bonds governed by German law and allows that the bondholders amend the terms of the bond by majority vote.

4. The Current Draft of Insolvency Proceedings for Corporate Groups

In the future, Germany and the European Union are determined to continue advancing insolvency law. The next step currently in the making is a law on the insolvency of corporate groups. Unlike US legal tradition, no insolvency law in Germany or any other EU member state addresses the insolvency of corporate groups. This makes an in-court restructuring of a corporate group consisting of several legal entities quite complicated because the lack of a specific insolvency law on corporate groups means that each entity has its own responsible court and has to file for insolvency separately. If the different responsible insolvency courts do not coordinate their decisions, the group as an economic entity may break apart, especially if the courts appoint different insolvency administrators. A group-based restructuring in this case is very difficult.

Until now it has been common practice to allow corporate groups to enter into insolvency proceedings governed by one insolvency administrator. Yet this common practice has lacked sufficient legal certainty and is not granted if different insolvency courts are responsible.

The respective draft legislation brought before the German parliament on 30 Jan. 2014 now aims to establish a common venue for all members of a corporate group. It is also planned to establish a common insolvency administrator or insolvency examiner for all members of the group. Also, the corporations, administrators and courts are now explicitly obliged to cooperate and coordinate with one another to find group-wide restructuring solutions. Furthermore, a court may order special coordination proceedings (*Koordinationsverfahren*). The respective draft legislation focuses on the concept of the coordinated joint administration of the group proceedings. There are no plans, however, to introduce a model of substantive consolidation by merging different estates of the legal entities into one 'group insolvency estate', which occurs in some jurisdictions such as the US.

At the same time there are plans to introduce similar legislation at the European level. The European Insolvency Regulation, which came into force in 2002 after decades of negotiations between the EU member states, is about to be amended and will also contain a stance in regard to the insolvency of corporate groups which is very similar to the planned German model. It will also change the European Insolvency Regulation to be more focused on restructuring rather than liquidation.

II. New Opportunities and Pitfalls for In-Court Restructurings

A major concern with the in-court restructuring of a business is the danger of sliding into 'uncontrolled' insolvency proceedings. This may result in the directors and officers entirely losing their administrative powers if the insolvency court does not order the self-administration proceedings as described under 2.a), but instead appoints an insolvency administrator who is in the 'driver seat' and will decide autonomously on the 'road map' of insolvency proceedings. This momentum brought by the insolvency administrator may well result in the entity being liquidated rather than restructured.

In order to avoid this, it is advisable to look for restructuring options and requirements already at an early stage. It is decisive to prepare both the application for insolvency as well as the application for self-administration in the best possible way. Essential creditors should be integrated as soon as possible and be recruited as members of the creditors' committee. If the creditors' committee unilaterally approves self-administration and the person to become the insolvency examiner, the court is obliged to follow this decision.

Generally, the parties involved need to weigh up the advantages and disadvantages of an in-court restructuring as opposed to an out-of-court restructuring. Each way does have its merits depending on the situation:

In-Court Restructuring:

- Possible prefinancing of insolvency payments for employees means easy liquidity for three months.
- Super senior DIP financing
- Clarity for investors who buy a business after insolvency or through an insolvency scheme
- Clear array of possible instruments with court-sanctioned functions
- Support by court-appointed professionals (examiner)
- Measures binding on all creditors

Out-of-Court Restructuring:

- Even higher flexibility
- No publicity, saving 'indirect insolvency costs'
- Lower costs as court and examiner do not have to be paid
- No further administrative efforts and interference such as possible obstructions through examiner, creditors' committee and court

Before entering into insolvency proceedings, a master plan should be developed which details the desired outcome as well as the way envisaged to lead there. Thus it is necessary to actively include the creditors in thought processes as they will decide the fate of a corporation if it does enter into insolvency proceedings. If the way of insolvency proceedings is chosen, it is of great importance to name a possible candidate for the examiner and to name candidates for the creditors' committee. This grants the debtor substantial influence over the course of the proceedings as many very important decisions will have to be approved by the creditors' committee.

Insolvency may even provide for a way to solve certain problems imposed by corporate law which could not easily be solved outside of insolvency proceedings. If a business is already struggling financially, it should also see the opportunities presented through this. Many options such as squeeze-out of a troublesome shareholder may be achieved through insolvency. If the business is still outside a material insolvency with its duty to apply for insolvency, one can well prepare for orderly insolvency proceedings in the form of debtor in possession. As long as illiquidity threatens, it is possible to enter these proceedings of one's own accord. If a business plans these proceedings in detail beforehand, the actual proceedings can be fully used to its advantage and may be kept as short as possible.

Prof. Dr. Stefan Simon

Lawyer, Tax Advisor

Areas of Specialization
- Corporate governance
- Corporate reorganizations
- Capital markets law
- Mergers & acquisitions

Telephone (ext.) +49 228/95 94-187
Email: stefan.simon@fgs.de

Corporate Litigation in Germany

by Lambertus Fuhrmann

Contents

I. Introduction
 1. Subject of This Article
 2. Overview of the German Court System
 3. Overview of Types of Proceedings
  a) Contentious Civil Proceedings
  b) Noncontentious Proceedings
 4. Some Special Features of German Civil Proceedings
II. Corporate Litigation in German Stock Corporations
 1. Overview
 2. Actions for Annulment
  a) Subject of Action
  b) Requirements
  c) Legal Effect
  d) 'Predatory Litigants'
 3. Release Proceedings
  a) Subject of Proceedings
  b) Requirements
  c) Legal Effect
 4. Judicial Valuation Proceedings
  a) Subject of Proceedings
  b) Procedural Principles
  c) The Problem: The Costs and the Interest
 5. Special Audit Proceedings Under Stock Corporation Law
  a) Subject of Proceedings
  b) Requirements
  c) Legal Effect
 6. Actions for Disclosure
 7. Other Proceedings
  a) Overriding the Shareholders' Meeting
  b) Liability of Board Members
  c) Actions of Board Members Against Their Unlawful Dismissal
III. Corporate Litigation in Privately Held Corporations
 1. Overview
 2. Actions for Annulment
 3. Release Proceedings
 4. Judicial Valuation Proceedings
 5. Special Audits and Right of Supervision
 6. Other Proceedings
  a) Liability of Managers and Their Unlawful Dismissal, Action Against
  b) Actions for Annulment
IV. Corporate Litigation in Partnerships
 1. Overview
 2. Actions for Annulment Relating to Flaws Resolutions
 3. Dismissal and Exclusion
 4. Partners' Contributions
 5. Actions for Disclosure

I. Introduction

1. Subject of This Article

This article deals with contentious corporate proceedings before German civil courts with a focus on legal disputes in German listed stock corporations (*Aktiengesellschaften*). Since other legal forms in Germany, namely privately held corporations (*Gesellschaften mit beschränkter Haftung*) and limited partnerships (*Kommanditgesellschaften*), also play a role in international business, legal disputes in or in connection with these legal forms are also addressed. Special focus is placed on actions relating to flawed resolutions (hereinafter 'actions for annulment' – *Anfechtungsklagen*), judicial valuation proceedings (*Spruchverfahren*), proposals for special audits, actions for disclosure and compensation proceedings. Administrative proceedings initiated by authorities, criminal proceedings, proceedings before administrative courts and proceedings before arbitration courts are not addressed.

2. Overview of the German Court System

Corporate legal disputes of all kinds are brought before ordinary courts of law (in contrast to special courts such as labor, tax, social-security and administrative courts).

The responsible regional court (*Landgericht*) having local jurisdiction is the first instance for all pecuniary disputes (having a value in dispute of more than EUR 5,000 – proceedings having a lower value in dispute are not addressed here), such as actions for annulment, actions relating to the amount of settlement payments (hereinafter 'judicial valuation proceedings') and the like. As a general rule, the regional court in the jurisdiction of which the corporation has its registered seat is the responsible court. In most cases, however, the individual German states have concentrated the jurisdiction of actions for annulment and judicial valuation proceedings at particular regional courts in order to ensure a higher level of professional competence.

Appeals against the decisions of the regional court have to be lodged with the higher regional court (*Oberlandesgericht*). This is also a trier of fact, i.e. the first-instance decision is fully reviewed. This comprises both the establishment and evaluation of facts and the application of law. Appeals against the higher regional courts' decisions on appeals have to be lodged with the Federal Court of Justice (*Bundesgerichtshof*), but only if the higher regional court has expressly allowed the appeal or if the Federal Court of Justice accepts a lawsuit for decision following a successful appeal against denial of leave to appeal (cf. Sec. 543(1) of the German Code of Civil Procedure – *Zivilprozessordnung*).

3. Overview of Types of Proceedings

Corporate litigation makes a distinction between two main types of proceedings, referred to as 'contentious' civil proceedings and 'noncontentious' proceedings. Noncontentious proceedings are usually those proceedings where the court, similarly to an authority, takes action on application made and investigates the facts of the case *ex officio* (Sec. 26 of the Act on Court Procedure on Family Matters and Noncontentious Matters – *FamFG*).

a) Contentious Civil Proceedings

Contentious civil proceedings are governed by the German Code of Civil Procedure. The most important procedural principles are referred to as 'principle of party presentation' (*Beibringungsgrundsatz*) and 'principle of party control' (*Dispositionsmaxime*). Principle of party presentation means that the parties must bring the matter in dispute themselves. The judge does not become involved in the investigations and does not conduct investigations on his own initiative. Principle of party control means that the parties retain control of the matter in dispute at any time, e.g. withdraw actions, effect arrangements or waive legal remedies. Actions for annulment are contentious civil proceedings. However, the German Stock Corporation Act (*Aktiengesetz*) contains substantial deviations from the principles set out in the Code of Civil Procedure, which are applicable to stock corporations, European companies and partly also to German privately held corporations.

b) Noncontentious Proceedings

Noncontentious proceedings are mainly governed by the Act on Court Procedure on Family Matters and Noncontentious Matters. However, judicial valuation proceedings as the most important corporate proceedings within this field fall within the scope of a special law referred to as the German 'Act on Judicial Valuation Proceedings' (*Spruchgesetz*). These proceedings deal with the determination of an appropriate (*angemessen*) cash settlement for external shareholders following reorganization measures. Unlike the case in contentious civil proceedings, what is referred to as the 'modified principle of party presentation' applies to noncontentious proceedings, namely in the underlying settlement proceedings of the Act on Judicial Valuation Proceedings. Although the party doubting the appropriateness of the settlement amount must outline the basis of his doubts, the requirements for a logical presentation are not nearly as high as in contentious civil proceedings. The amount of settlement is then determined by the court by way of official investigation (Sec. 26 of the Act on Court Procedure on Family Matters and Noncontentious Matters).

4. Some Special Features of German Civil Proceedings

a) Within the scope of contentious jurisdiction, German courts have a statutory requirement of representation by legal counsel: Each party must be represented by a lawyer admitted by the trial court. In noncontentious proceedings, this does not apply in the first instance before the regional court, where no legal representation is required.

b) The court language is German. Some German states are currently attempting to establish special divisions where proceedings can also be held in English. However, corporate legal disputes are not expected to be brought before these divisions, since most shareholders who file an action speak German as a first language. Referring them to a foreign language would therefore not be appropriate.

c) The quality of the individual courts and/or trial courts is very different. Firstly, the organization of courts is incumbent upon the German states, which is why the personnel and material resources of courts, the professional requirements for judges and the practical application of procedural provisions vary in the individual German states. At least, the legal fragmentation in actions for annulment has been reduced considerably through consolidation to a small number of regional courts. The same applies to judicial valuation proceedings. In addition, it should be noted that many state courts are overburdened with the complex accounting-, tax- and valuation-related aspects that often play a major role in corporate litigation.

d) The length of the proceedings at the individual courts also varies greatly. Civil proceedings in Germany are certainly delayed by obsolete delivery regulations (always via the court by post). Considerations about introducing an obligatory electronic court post office box for all lawyers and courts are still in their infancy. In addition, the courts are fairly generous with requests for extension of deadlines by individual parties. In nearly every civil procedure, there is a party stating at least once that it is not able to meet a deadline set by the court 'due to overburdening of the lawyer in charge'. Against this background, even if a contentious procedure goes well, a period of one to two years is to be expected in the first instance. In unfavorable cases, periods of up to five years are possible. The appeal procedure before the regional court and the Federal Court of Justice then takes at least an additional one to two years. This means that if a matter in dispute reaches the Federal Court of Justice, the proceeding may take five to six years as a best-case scenario, which is definitely too long.

An exception to this practice is what is termed 'release proceedings' (*Freigabeverfahren* – described below in greater detail). Since this is a summary procedure with only one instance, namely the higher regional court, usually only a period of between three and nine months is to be expected.

e) In contentious civil proceedings, the legal charges for potential experts and the lawyer's fees incurred by the parties are apportioned according to the proportion of won or lost proceedings (Secs. 91 and 92 of the Code of Civil Procedure).

This is different in judicial valuation proceedings: In the first instance, the costs of legal defense and of the expert appointed by the court have to be paid for by the corporation in nearly all cases. In turn, the shareholders who file the action usually bear their lawyers' fees themselves (Sec. 15(2) of the Act on Judicial Valuation Proceedings).

f) Civil proceedings are usually public. Every procedure (except for some release and summary proceedings) is preceded by hearings. Since nearly all corporate litigation proceedings are conducted in writing, hearings usually involve little debate and are dominated by the judge. Many courts attempt to propose an arrangement, including a statement of their own legal opinion. Apart from that, the procedure is predominantly based on the written presentation of facts. 'Stirring summations' are rather rare and usually have limited effect.

II. Corporate Litigation in German Stock Corporations

1. Overview

The stock corporation is the legal form in which a foreign investor most frequently comes into contact with German procedural law in the field of corporate litigation, for example in connection with a corporate takeover and subsequent reorganization. In these cases 'predatory shareholders' often raise actions for annulment of a shareholders' resolution aimed at the corporate reorganization.

The procedure of actions for annulment is usually the same: At the beginning, there is a shareholders' resolution, for example on a merger or share transfer. One or more shareholders file an action for annulment of this resolution. This action entails what is referred to as 'suspension of registration', i.e. as long as the action is pending, the measure may not be entered in the commercial register and therefore does not become legally effective, either. The defendant corporation then resorts to legal defense by filing a petition for release. If the release is allowed, the action for annulment is usually concluded either by a decision in favor of the defendant corporation or by way of settlement. This is because the party applying for annulment of the resolution does not necessarily speculate on winning the proceeding but often only on exerting pressure on the corporation with the suspension of registration.

2. Actions for Annulment

a) Subject of Action

The subject of an action for annulment is a shareholders' resolution. Other resolutions, such as those passed by the management board or the supervisory board, may not be contested. Actions for annulment are governed by Secs. 243 *et seqq.* of the Stock Corporation Act; the Code of Civil Procedure is also applicable. These lawsuits are aimed at the annulment of the contested shareholders' resolution.

b) Requirements

In addition to the general procedural requirements set out in the Code of Civil Procedure, an action for annulment of a shareholders' resolution can only be filed by a person who:

- was already a shareholder of the corporation when the shareholders' meeting was convened and the resolution was passed;
- raised an objection against the shareholders' resolution at the shareholders' meeting, and this objection was recorded in the minutes signed by a German notary;

- submitted all means of defense including offering of evidence within a period of one month of the resolution being passed; and
- gives notice of a breach of law or the statutes by the shareholders' resolution in a qualified manner.

An action against – alleged – inappropriate settlement amounts is usually excluded. Such objections have to be raised as part of a judicial valuation proceeding (Sec. 1 of the Act on Judicial Valuation Proceedings).

c) Legal Effect

The decision whether or not to annul a resolution has what is termed an *inter omnes* effect, i.e. it is not only binding on the parties in dispute but also in relation to third parties (Sec. 248(1) sentence 1 of the Stock Corporation Act). This decision takes effect *eo ipso*; it requires no enforcement or other implementation. This means that a decision in favor of the plaintiff bringing the action automatically entails the annulment of the shareholders' resolution. The annulment takes effect *ex tunc*. The procedure is only different with those resolutions which have been entered in the commercial register. If the court has granted a release, a measure has therefore been entered in the commercial register, and the resolution is then declared null and void, but the entry is nevertheless maintained.

d) 'Predatory Litigants'

Until a few years ago, the suspension of registration in Germany was being systematically abused by an entire group of 'predatory litigants' aiming to hinder large-scale restructuring measures and thereby gain special advantages – secretly, of course. During the suspension of registration, shareholders' resolutions could not be implemented, which was used by the litigants as a – concealed – lever to effect favorable arrangements for fellow shareholders under the cloak of 'Robin Hood' and then once again gain special advantages in the form of secret payments. This 'business model' has by now been largely eliminated by legislators by limiting the corporation's release options to one instance at higher regional courts (Sec. 246a of the Stock Corporation Act). As a result, competent and prompt processing of such petitions is ensured. Furthermore, the judicial valuation practice at many higher regional courts is currently clearly *pro societate*. In addition, such an action can be regarded as an abuse of law in individual cases.[1]

3. Release Proceedings

a) Subject of Proceedings

Release proceedings (*Freigabeverfahren*) as the response of the defendant stock corporation to contested capital-increase or capital-reduction resolutions, inte-

---

1 Frankfurt/Main Higher Regional Court of 13 Jan. 2009 – 5 U 183/07, NJW-Spezial, 2009, p. 112.

gration resolutions and squeeze-out resolutions are governed by the Stock Corporation Act. These proceedings in response to contested merger, spin-off and reorganization resolutions fall within the scope of the German Reorganization Act (*Umwandlungsgesetz*).

b) Requirements

The requirement for the court to grant a release decision is that the action for annulment of a restructuring resolution is inadmissible or manifestly unfounded or that the defendant corporation has an overriding interest in implementing the relevant measure. Furthermore, the petition has to be allowed if the party filing the action fails to prove that his shareholding amounts to a *pro rata* amount of at least EUR 1,000 (Sec. 246a(2) of the Stock Corporation Act).

c) Legal Effect

A positive release decision means that the registration procedure 'pending' due to an action for annulment can be continued and the contested resolution can be entered in the commercial register. The principal action for annulment remains pending and – theoretically – the responsible court could still declare the contested resolution null and void; however, since the responsible regional court would then have to act against 'its' higher regional court, this is only to be expected in exceptional cases. Moreover, a declaration of nullity at a later point would not entail the annulment of the contested, albeit implemented, resolution.

4. Judicial Valuation Proceedings

a) Subject of Proceedings

Judicial valuation proceedings are governed by the Act on Judicial Valuation Proceedings. The provisions of the Act on Court Procedure on Family Matters and Noncontentious Matters (Sec. 17(1) of the Act on Judicial Valuation Proceedings) are also applicable. These proceedings are aimed at the determination of an appropriate cash settlement or additional cash payment following restructuring resolutions, such as transfer of shares against payment of cash settlement, merger, spin-off, reorganization or approval of a control and profit and loss transfer agreement.

b) Procedural Principles

The petition must be filed with the responsible regional court within three months after registration and announcement of the relevant restructuring measure (e.g. a merger) by publication (Sec. 4(1) of the Act on Judicial Valuation Proceedings).

Petitions are always filed by shareholders or former shareholders. The principle of official investigation applies, i.e. the court determines the appropriate cash settlement amount *ex officio*. Since judges do not possess the required valuation competence, they usually commission external experts. The most recent list price of the shares (where stock exchange trade still took place) marks the lower value limit. The expert's opinion is aimed at determining whether the share has a 'higher value'.

c) The Problem: The Costs and the Interest

Any shareholder affected by one of the above-mentioned restructuring measures may institute judicial valuation proceedings largely without risking high costs, which is why this is done in Germany on a regular basis. Judicial valuation proceedings often involve fairly high costs for the corporation and usually take a long time. There are now even special funds specializing in the acquisition of shares from corporations where structural measures are about to be taken or have been implemented with the sole aim being to effect an increase in the cash settlement by way of a judicial valuation proceeding. Courts often decide in favor of the minority shareholders who file the petition, i.e. the procedure fairly often entails an increase in the settlement amount. The increase frequently amounts to 20% or more of the settlement amount originally offered by the corporation or the principal shareholder.

5. Special Audit Proceedings Under Stock Corporation Law

a) Subject of Proceedings

The shareholders' meeting of a stock corporation can resolve by a simple majority of votes that a special audit be conducted. The subject of this audit is business transactions that may date back up to ten years in listed corporations (Sec. 142(2) of the Stock Corporation Act).

b) Requirements

If the shareholders' meeting rejects a particular proposal, minority shareholders whose nominal capital shares amount to at least 1% or EUR 100,000 are entitled to demand such a special audit if facts exist which give them reason to suspect that dishonest conduct or a gross breach of law or the statutes has occurred. The minority shareholders can also be involved in the selection of the special auditor to be appointed by a court (Sec. 142(2) and (4) of the Stock Corporation Act).

c) Legal Effect

If the court allows the petition, the court-appointed auditor must be commissioned and paid for by the corporation. He has to be granted access to the corporation and provided with all necessary documents (Sec. 145 of the Stock Corporation Act).

6. Actions for Disclosure

Irrespective of the amount of his share capital and the date of acquisition, every shareholder has the right to receive information from the corporation. This right can be asserted in different ways:

- The option of direct assertion of rights is set out in Sec. 131 of the Stock Corporation Act. According to this, the corporation is obliged, at the shareholders' meeting, to provide information, upon request, about affairs relating to the corporation or affiliated corporations to every shareholder, provided that this is required for the proper assessment of the relevant item on the agenda.
- Since this right is used frequently, the management establishes a back office during the general meeting in order to be able to answer the expected raft of questions efficiently, correctly and within a reasonable period of time.
- Questions from shareholders must be answered truthfully and completely. A particular approach of giving short and concise answers in a comprehensible manner and in accordance with the facts has become established.
- Denial of information is only admissible if objective reasons exist, e.g. if the corporation incurs a considerable disadvantage due to questions not relating to the agenda or the corporation's affairs. If the corporation fails to answer admissible questions, the shareholder is entitled to file an action for disclosure pursuant to Sec. 132 of the Stock Corporation Act. However, this regulation is of limited practical relevance.
- Questions that are unjustly not answered or answered incorrectly result indirectly in the respective shareholders' resolution becoming contestable. In some respects, case law is very strict about this.[2] In fact, with their lists of questions and the accidental failure to answer individual questions, predatory litigants make entire restructuring resolutions contestable. For this reason, great importance is attached to a prompt, comprehensive and correct response to such questions at German shareholders' meetings.

7. Other Proceedings

a) Overriding the Shareholders' Meeting

German stock corporation law distinguishes between two types of responsibilities of the shareholders' meeting, namely those written in the law (cf. Sec. 119 of the Stock Corporation Act) and the unwritten responsibilities established by

---

[2] cf. Federal Court of Justice of 18 Oct. 2004 – II ZR 250/02, NJW, 2005, p. 828; Federal Court of Justice of 16 Feb. 2009 – II ZR 185/07, NJW, 2009, p. 2207.

case law.[3] Written responsibilities of the shareholders' meeting include the approval of the accounts (in certain cases), the appointment of board members, capital measures, but also the approval of certain agreements, e.g. control and profit and loss transfer agreements, merger and spin-off agreements or similar reorganization agreements. The shareholders' meeting is protected by law from being overridden in terms of these written responsibilities. The measure in question does not legally exist without its approval. Conflicts are excluded. This is different with the unwritten responsibilities of the shareholders' meeting. Such responsibilities are assumed in particular if the management board of a stock corporation wants to dispose of assets that account for at least 70-80% of the overall assets.[4] If it fails to obtain this approval, the measure is effective in any case where the contracting party was not aware of the fact that the power of representation was abused.

b) Liability of Board Members

According to Sec. 93 as well as Secs. 116 and 93 of the Stock Corporation Act, members of the corporation's management and supervisory boards are personally liable if they fail to exercise the due diligence of a prudent and conscientious manager in the execution of their duties. Claims for compensation brought by the corporation against board members or former board members are asserted by the supervisory board, which is generally obliged to do so according to case law.[5]

If the supervisory board fails to comply with this duty, the shareholders' meeting may resolve by a simple majority of votes, according to Sec. 147(1) sentence 1 of the Stock Corporation Act, that claims for compensation be asserted against the management board and/or the supervisory board.

c) Actions of Board Members Against Their Unlawful Dismissal

Board members of stock corporations are not employees. If a service agreement is terminated without notice by the stock corporation and the board members want to defend themselves against it or bring an action for the continued payment of their remuneration, this is done by way of a common action for performance before an ordinary court of law.

---

3 cf. Federal Court of Justice of 25 Feb. 1982 – II ZR 174/80, NJW, 1982, p. 1703 (*Holzmüller*); Federal Court of Justice of 26 April 2004 – II ZR 155/02, NJW-RR, 2004, p. 1619 (*Gelatine I*).
4 Federal Court of Justice of 26 April 2004 – II ZR 155/02, NJW-RR, 2004, p. 1619 (*Gelatine II*); Cologne Higher Regional Court of 15 Jan. 2009 – 18 U 205/07, BeckRS, 2009, 04001.
5 Federal Court of Justice of 21 April 1997 – II ZR 175/95, NJW, 1997, 1926 (*ARAG vs. Garmenbeck*).

III. Corporate Litigation in Privately Held Corporations

1. Overview

As a rule, the privately held corporation is the legal form which is selected by a strategic foreign investor in order to take on a joint commercial activity in Germany together with one or more other persons (joint venture). The constitution of a privately held corporation is not nearly as complex as that of a stock corporation. In particular, apart from the rare case of codetermination, privately held corporations do not have any supervisory board and the principles of self-managed action (freedom from instructions) as well as strict earmarking of assets are not applicable to this legal form. Foreign investors can also become involved in shareholders' disputes in privately held corporations, for example, if there is a conflict of interests with the joint-venture partner, possible co-investors or the local management.

2. Actions for Annulment

Actions for annulment in privately held corporations are not laid down in the law. A number of provisions set out in Secs. 243 *et seqq.* of the Stock Corporation Act are applied by analogy, but not in all respects. In particular, the *GmbH* Act, the law on privately held corporations, stipulates no definite prior holding period and no definite minimum quorum for the action for annulment to be admissible. The objection to the resolution need not be first recorded in the minutes, either. It is questionable whether the one-month period under corporate law is applied in the event of annulment. Such a one-month period can be stipulated in the statutes (although only as a minimum period). In the absence of any relevant regulations in the statutes, the legal situation is uncertain. Quite a few courts apply the one-month period by analogy; others say that the action has to be filed within a reasonable period. What this means in the individual case is unclear.

The practical relevance of actions for annulment is great. They protect minority shareholders. In particular, minority shareholders can also file an action for annulment after filing a reasonable proposal (e.g. proposal for removal of a negligent manager – *Geschäftsführer*) and the majority shareholder (employing the respective manager) blocks this resolution contrary to the principle of good faith. The minority shareholders can contest the negative resolution, in addition to filing what is termed an 'action for declaratory relief', which states that the opposite (in the above example, the removal of the manager) has taken place.

3. Release Proceedings

Release proceedings in privately held corporations only take place within the meaning of the Reorganization Act since the *GmbH* Act does not cover capital measures (increases/reductions). In practice, release proceedings play hardly any role, as squeeze-out or integration under corporate law does not exist in the *GmbH* Act.

4. Judicial Valuation Proceedings

Judicial valuation proceedings also only apply to measures within the meaning of the Reorganization Act. However, this rarely occurs in practice. In most cases, reorganization resolutions are most likely doomed to failure due to the majority situation (75%) if no agreement is reached on the valuation. If, in exceptional cases, a judicial valuation proceeding is instituted, the same procedural principles apply as to stock corporations.

5. Special Audits and Right of Supervision

The legal instrument of special audit proposed by a minority shareholder is not known in the *GmbH* Act. Unless stipulated otherwise in the statutes, a special audit can therefore only be conducted by majority resolution. For this reason, it is advisable to lay down protective rights for minority shareholders (e.g. right to information, right to access books and accounts or similar rights) in a joint-venture agreement.

According to Sec. 51a of the *GmbH* Act, the management (*Geschäftsführung*) has to inform every shareholder about the corporation's affairs. Unlike the case in stock corporations, this right can also be exercised outside formal shareholders' meetings, and the shareholders themselves have the right to inspect the books and accounts of the corporation. The statutes may not stipulate deviating regulations to the detriment of the shareholders (Sec. 51a(3) of the *GmbH* Act). If the management fails to comply with such a request, the respective shareholder is entitled to file an action for disclosure (Sec. 51b of the *GmbH* Act).

6. Other Proceedings

a) Liability of Managers and Their Unlawful Dismissal, Action Against

In the event that the privately held corporation brings actions against its managers or vice versa, the corporation is legally represented by the shareholders' meeting. If the privately held corporation intends to assert claims for compensation against managers or former managers, a shareholders' resolution is required. This can be passed by a simple majority of votes, unless the statutes prescribe a greater majority. In exceptional cases, a resolution rejecting the assertion of claims for compensation may be contrary to the principle of good faith. This can be assumed in cases where the majority shareholder attempts to obstruct legitimate claims of the privately held corporation together with a general manager. In this case, the minority shareholders are entitled to contest the resolution.

b) Actions for Annulment

The explanations relating to stock corporations apply by analogy.

IV. Corporate Litigation in Partnerships

1. Overview

Partnerships, in particular silent partnerships, *KGs* (limited partnerships) and *OHGs* (general partnerships) are rather uncommon as vehicles of foreign investors. However, many closed-end real estate, patent, ship, aircraft and other special funds are held in the legal form of a *GmbH & Co. KG* (limited partnership with a privately held corporation as the general partner). These structures, also referred to as 'public partnerships', are subject to a special litigation regime generally established by case law.

2. Actions for Annulment Relating to Flaws Resolutions

Secs. 243 *et seqq.* of the of the Stock Corporation Act do not apply, not even by analogy. Although the partners can stipulate their analogous application in the partnership agreement, the initiators of partnerships with 'sophisticated' constitutions, namely investment entities, are most likely to have no interest in the clear regulation of this matter. They often prefer to keep the legal situation unclear in order to make lawsuits as difficult as possible.

In partnerships with a personalized structure, actions for annulment within the meaning of corporate law do not exist under case law. In fact, partners who do not agree to a resolution have to file an action for declaratory relief against all fellow partners to annul the resolution. Case law has come to recognize that this is hardly feasible in public partnerships. In this case, it is sufficient to file an action against the management of the privately held corporation acting as the general partner.[6] The further formal requirements and the deadline for filing an action are unclear; however, the one-month period under corporate law is most likely not to apply, even by analogy. In fact, a partner who waits several months before filing an action may forfeit his rights.

3. Dismissal and Exclusion

Apart from what is referred to as 'public partnership', German legislators assume that partnerships are very close professional associations of few persons, which are essentially based on mutual trust. Against this background, the main issues in partnerships are actions for dismissal and exclusion rather than actions relating to flawed resolutions.

As a general rule, interests in partnerships are not freely transferable. Legislators take the view that the transfer of e.g. a limited partner's interest consti-

---

[6] Federal Court of Justice of 7 June 1999 – II ZR 278/98, NJW, 1999, p. 3113.

tutes a change in the entity that is subject to the approval of all partners (Sec. 116(2) of the German Commercial Code – *Handelsgesetzbuch*). Numerous partnership agreements depart from this regulation, prescribing simple or qualified majority voting or even declaring that no approval at all is required for the transfer of interests to fellow partners or family members.

The principle that a partner cannot permanently be a 'prisoner of his partnership' applies in any case. The limit of admissible restrictions on dismissal cannot be defined in general and abstract terms. In the individual case, agreements are ineffective where the notice period is so long that the consequences cannot be estimated at the time of concluding the agreement.[7] The limit of what is tolerable is reached if notice periods exceed 10-15 years. In individual cases, however, even periods of 12[8] or 17[9] years were not contested.

If the partnership agreement prescribes a stringent restriction of transferability and also does not mention dismissal, case law assumes that the option of terminating membership in the entity exists by virtue of law.

This right of termination may also not be excluded in fact by granting an inappropriate settlement to the terminating party. The limit of what is tolerable is reached if the market value and the settlement amount are entirely out of proportion. Case law does not prescribe any specific proportion[10], whereas legal scholars agree on approximate values amounting to 50% of the real value. The market value is determined according to the same principles as the settlement value in stock corporations. Where the partnership agreement was too strict from the very beginning, it is deemed to be null and void by case law, with the consequence being that the terminating partner can claim the full market value in settlement.[11] Where the clause originally led to tolerable results but has become 'intolerable' in the course of the further economic development of the partnership, case law adjusts the settlement amount only to the lowest tolerable value.[12]

4. Partners' Contributions

A common issue in partnerships is the contributions owed by the individual partners, be it in the form of payments, noncash contributions or the performance of work. According to German corporate law, partnerships are not legal entities. Because of the legal construction of a community of joint owners, legislators, judges and legal theorists have difficulties establishing a generally

---

7 Cf. Federal Court of Justice of 18 Sep. 2006 – II ZR 137/04, NJW, 2007, p. 295.
8 Cf. Federal Court of Justice of 21 March 2005 – II ZR 310/03, NJW, 2005, p. 1784.
9 Cf. Munich Higher Regional Court of 13 Jan. 2011 – 23 U 3628/10, BeckRS, 2011, 01289.
10 Cf. Federal Court of Justice of 20 Sep. 1993 – II ZR 104/52, NJW, 1993, p. 3193.
11 Cf. Federal Court of Justice of 16 Dec. 1991 – II ZR 58/91, NJW, 1992, p. 892.
12 Cf. Federal Court of Justice of 13 June 1994 – II ZR 38/93, NJW, 1994, p. 2536.

applicable and comprehensible definition of legal capacity for partnerships. However, it is certain that the partnership as such can bring an action and can be sued in a legal dispute concerning the payment of contributions. Fellow partners need not be involved in the legal dispute.

5. Actions for Disclosure

The rights to information in general partnerships are governed by Sec. 118 of the Commercial Code. Limited partners' rights to information in limited partnerships are laid down in Sec. 164 of the Commercial Code. This section is not mandatory, i.e. a partnership agreement can largely restrict the limited partners' rights to information. Failure to provide information that is admissible under the law or the partnership agreement entitles the partners concerned to assert their rights by filing an action.

Dr. Lambertus Fuhrmann

Lawyer, Tax Advisor

Areas of Specialization

- Annual general meetings
- Corporate law
- Corporate litigation and general litigation
- Mergers, demergers, reorganizations and squeeze-outs

Telephone (ext.) +49 228/95 94-237

Email: lambertus.fuhrmann@fgs.de

Forms of Distribution Under German Commercial Law

by Jan Christian Giedinghagen

Contents

I. Introduction
II. Basics
  1. Commercial Agent
    a) Essential Features
    b) Distinction from Other Forms of Distribution
  2. Commercial Broker
    a) Essential Features
    b) Distinction from Other Forms of Distribution
  3. Commission Agent
    a) Essential Features
    b) Distinction from Other Forms of Distribution
  4. Authorized Dealer
    a) Essential Features
    b) Distinction from Other Forms of Distribution
  5. Franchisee
    a) Essential Features
    b) Distinction from Other Forms of Distribution
III. Pitfalls
  1. Distinction from Employees
  2. General Terms and Conditions
  3. Restrictions on Competition
  4. Claim for Compensation upon Termination
  5. International Context
IV. Schemes

I. Introduction

Like distribution law in other countries, German distribution law recognizes various forms of selling goods by way of an intermediary. Types of distribution intermediary frequently encountered in practice are the commercial agent *(Handelsvertreter)*, the (commercial) broker *([Handels-]Makler)*, the commission agent *(Kommissionär)*, the authorized dealer *(Vertragshändler)* and the franchisee *(Franchisenehmer)*. What all of these types of distribution intermediaries (under commercial law) have in common is that, as sales vehicles, they are aimed at facilitating customer acquisition and thus the sale of goods or services of an entrepreneur. Customer acquisition is thus characterized by the engagement of an independently active sales intermediary who is remunerated directly or indirectly by the entrepreneur for his – usually causal – assistance in customer acquisition. In this context, depending on the type of contract and its structure, the sales intermediaries are frequently integrated into the entrepreneur's sales organization.

Depending on the legal classification and choice of legal form of the sales intermediary, the challenge is to bear in mind a wide variety of legal aspects in the planning and structuring of the contractual relationship with the entrepreneur. This frequently involves, besides the rules of commercial and civil law, taking into consideration the requirements of employment law, corporate law, antitrust and competition law, license and trademark law and tax law as well as, in an international context, the rules of private international law.

In addition, in some cases there are also aspects relevant to valuation, in particular the question whether or in what amount the entrepreneur is obliged, upon termination of the contractual relationship, to pay compensation to the sales intermediary for the provision of the customer base or, as the case may be, at what value a successor or the entrepreneur can take over the business of the sales intermediary. The value can also play an important role in the context of divorce proceedings or succession planning.

Various possible structures exist depending both on the type of transactions to be brokered and on the underlying legal relationship. Frequently, the nature of the transactions to be brokered depends, in turn, on the product to be distributed.

II. Basics

1. Commercial Agent

a) Essential Features

The law pertaining to commercial agents is set out in Secs. 84–92c of the German Commercial Code *(Handelsgesetzbuch)*. The provisions[1], in existence in part since the entry into force of the German Commercial Code in 1900 and fundamentally revised in 1953, were later also an important basis for the harmonization of the European minimum requirements laid down in the EU Commercial Agents Directive, although the provisions go further than the regulatory content of that Directive.[2]

Pursuant to Sec. 84(1) sentence 1 of the Commercial Code, a commercial agent in the legal sense is an independent person carrying on a trade or business *(selbständiger Gewerbetreibender)* who is permanently engaged to transact business as an intermediary of another entrepreneur or to enter into such transactions in the name of such entrepreneur.

Independent commercial agents need to be distinguished in particular from employees. What both have in common is the emphasis placed on the principle that the services must be provided in person. With respect to independence, the decisive distinguishing criterion is that the commercial agent is essentially free to organize his activity and working time on his own.

Permanent engagement as a prerequisite for the position of a commercial agent relates to the obligation to enter into or procure an undetermined number of transactions for the entrepreneur. There is thus a contract for the performance of continuing obligations *(Dauerschuldverhältnis*, hereinafter 'continuing obli-

---

1 Law amending the Commercial Code of 6 Aug. 1953, Federal Law Gazette, Part I 1953, p. 771.
2 Council Directive 86/653/EEC, OJ 1986 L 382/17.

gation') between the commercial agent and the entrepreneur.[3] A contract relating to the procurement of specific individual transactions is therefore not a commercial-agency agreement.

The commercial agent acts in the name and for account of the entrepreneur. Consequently, the commercial agent does not himself become a contracting party of the customer. Rather, the commercial agent attempts to find purchasers for the products or services of the entrepreneur and procure or directly bring about contracts relating to these. In contrast to the EU Commercial Agents Directive, which is applicable in the EU and the European Economic Area (EEA), the German law on commercial agents is not limited to procurement with respect to trade in goods, but also extends to the procurement of services.[4]

The commercial agent is thus not exposed to entrepreneurial risks such as the sales risk. In this connection, he will at most need to accept losses to his commission owing to the absence of corresponding sales. The commercial agent is thus not an independent trader but an independent assistant to the entrepreneur.

Furthermore, there are two types of commercial agent, namely procurement representatives and contracting representatives. Procurement representatives make possible, prepare or bring about the closing of transactions by the entrepreneur. In this context, by carrying out his activities, the commercial agent must at least have partly induced the conclusion of the contract.[5] In this respect, the idea underlying the statutory provisions is for the commercial agent to be under a duty to try to use his influence on the customer in order to bring about that customer's readiness to conclude a contract with the entrepreneur for the first time, or to reinforce such readiness. Normally, the mere assumption of continuous customer support for existing customer relationships is not sufficient in this regard.[6] Subsequently, the actual conclusion of the contract is brought about by the entrepreneur himself.

By contrast, in the context of concluding contracts, the contracting representative is himself directly involved, as a proxy, in making the declarations which lead to the contract being entered into. This requires a separate authorization by the entrepreneur, which is often already provided in the commercial-agency contract by agreeing a corresponding power of attorney to conclude contracts.

In consideration for his procurement or contracting activity, the commercial agent receives a commission in accordance with Sec. 87 of the Commercial Code. It can be structured in a variety of ways. By way of deviation from the statutory default case of performance-related commission, an additional activity-based commission is sometimes agreed in recognition of further activities taken on by the commercial agent for the entrepreneur beyond pure procure-

---

3 German Federal Court of Justice 19.5.1982 – I ZR 68/80, NJW 1983, p. 42.
4 On the limitations of the EU Commercial Agents Directive cf. Art. 1(2) of Council Directive 86/653/EEC, OJ 1986 L 382/17.
5 German Federal Court of Justice 5.4.2006 – VIII ZR 384/04, NJW-RR 2006, p. 976.
6 German Federal Court of Justice 19.5.1982 – I ZR 68/80, NJW 1983, p. 42.

ment or contracting activities (e.g. storage of goods). The concrete structural details of the commission can prove to be of particular significance for the later calculation of commercial-agent compensation (which is discussed below).

As a general rule, upon termination of the commercial-agency relationship, the commercial agent also has a claim to commercial-agent compensation pursuant to Sec. 89b of the Commercial Code. More specifically, the nature of this claim is that of compensation for the customer base that has been provided to, and further used by, the entrepreneur. The background is that, owing to his activity in the name of and for the account of the entrepreneur, the commercial agent is not able to build his own customer base. Pursuant to Sec. 89b(2) of the Commercial Code, the maximum amount of this protective claim for the benefit of the commercial agent is an amount equivalent to the annual commission, calculated on the basis of the average for the last five years of his activity; if the contractual relationship lasted less than five years, then the average of such shorter period is applied. In this context, the applicability and calculation of this compensation claim are in part highly contested and constitute one of the most common points of discussion and conflict upon termination of a commercial-agency relationship.

b) Distinction from Other Forms of Distribution

Since there is a continuing obligation between the commercial agent and the entrepreneur, the commercial agent is far more closely connected to the entrepreneur than is the case with, for example, a broker – entrusted with an individual assignment – or with a commission agent.

Due to his pure procurement activity for the entrepreneur, the commercial agent receives remuneration only in the form of commission from the entrepreneur. In contrast to this, the authorized dealer and the franchisee receive their remuneration directly from the end customer.

2. Commercial Broker

a) Essential Features

The law relating to commercial brokers is set out in Secs. 93–104 of the Commercial Code.

The commercial-broker contract represents a special form of broker agreement under Secs. 652 *et seqq.* of the German Civil Code *(Bürgerliches Gesetzbuch)*. In contrast to the 'civil broker' *(Zivilmakler)* under Sec. 652 of the Civil Code, the commercial broker under Sec. 93 of the Commercial Code acts commercially and only procures contracts relating to *Gegenstände des Handelsverkehrs* ('objects forming the subject of trading transactions', hereinafter 'commercial objects'). Commercial objects are assets which represent a commercial value and which are characterized by the fact that they can easily be traded (e.g. goods, securities, and insurance). They do not include, for example, the procurement of land, loans or marriages.

Accordingly, owing to the products that he procures, the commercial broker is a special type of civil broker, and the rules relating to commercial brokers are special rules which, by adding a commercial-law perspective, supplement the general brokerage law as set out in Secs. 652 *et seqq.* of the Civil Code.

Pursuant to Sec. 93(1) of the Commercial Code, the commercial broker assumes the procurement of contracts regarding the acquisition or sale of commercial objects for other people without being permanently entrusted to do so by them on the basis of a contractual relationship. However, the broker is under no obligation to become active.

As a rule, the right to commission on the part of a commercial broker arises only once (i) the commercial broker has become active and (ii) as a result of the activity of the broker, a contract has been concluded between the principal and the customer. Accordingly, the commercial broker must likewise at least have partly induced the conclusion of the contract. It is worth noting in this respect that the principal nonetheless retains his full freedom to contract. Consequently, he can decide on the 'if' and 'how' of the entering into the transaction at his own discretion.

To the extent that the parties to the procured contract have not agreed otherwise on the brokerage fee, Sec. 99 of the Commercial Code stipulates that each of the parties has to bear half of the fee.

b) Distinction from Other Forms of Distribution

In contrast to commercial agents, authorized dealers and franchisees, the commercial broker is not permanently entrusted with business procurement. What distinguishes him from a commission agent is that he procures contracts at his own discretion and enters into the transaction himself in exceptional cases only. The commission agent, on the other hand, acts in his own name.

The classic broker agreement should further be distinguished from sole agency, under which the principal undertakes not to involve any other brokers. In this type of arrangement, the broker is obliged to actively engage in procurement, but at the same time reduces his risk of receiving no commission despite having engaged in brokerage activities.

3. Commission Agent

a) Essential Features

The law governing commission business is set out in the Commercial Code in Secs. 383–406. Under Sec. 383(1) of the Commercial Code, the commission agent undertakes, on a commercial basis, to purchase (purchasing commission) or sell (sales commission) goods or securities for the account of another (the principal) in his own name.

The contract entered into between the commission agent and the principal is referred to as the commission contract. The contract between the commission agent and the third party is referred to as the execution transaction. Here, the commission agent acts in his own name, since it is exclusively he – rather than the principal – who will acquire rights and obligations under the execution transaction.

Under Sec. 384(1) half-sentence 1 of the Commercial Code, the commission agent is obliged to carry out the business with the care of a prudent businessman. This implies in particular the duty of finding a third party who is interested in the products of the entrepreneur, i.e. the principal. In carrying out the business, the commission agent must act in the interests of the principal, cf. Sec. 384(1) half-sentence 2 alternative 1 of the Commercial Code. The conclusion generally drawn from this is that the commission agent must agree contractual provisions which are as favorable as possible for the principal.

Pursuant to Sec. 384(1) half-sentence 2 alternative 2 of the Commercial Code, in the execution of the business, the commission agent must comply with the instructions of the principal. This right to issue instructions is interpreted as very extensive. The commission agent may usually not disregard such instructions. In the event that the commission agent does not comply with the instructions of the principal, he is obliged (pursuant to Sec. 385(1) half-sentence 1 of the Commercial Code) to pay damages to the principal. Pursuant to Sec. 385(1) half-sentence 2 of the Commercial Code, the principal also needs not treat as legally binding on him any transaction that has been entered into against his instructions.

If the transaction has been executed, then the commission agent may demand his commission pursuant to Sec. 396(1) sentence 2 of the Commercial Code. In this context, the basis for his claim is the commission contract.

b) Distinction from Other Forms of Distribution

The commission agent acts only on the basis of individual assignments. It is this aspect in particular which distinguishes the commission agent from the commercial agent, who is appointed by the entrepreneur on a lasting basis. In the absence of such a cooperation established on a permanent basis, the possibility of classification as an employee is also excluded since an employment relationship presupposes working together on a permanent basis.

Furthermore, it is in his own name that the commission agent enters into a contract with the customer. This, in turn, distinguishes him from the commercial broker in particular. However, in contrast to the authorized dealer and the franchisee, the commission agent is not integrated into the organization of the entrepreneur. Authorized dealers, franchisees and commission agents enter into their transactions in their own name, but authorized dealers and franchisees also do so for their own account.

4. Authorized Dealer

a) Essential Features

The form of distribution of the authorized dealer is not regulated by statute in Germany.

An authorized dealer is a merchant *(Kaufmann)* whose enterprise is integrated into the sales organization of another entrepreneur in such a way that the authorized dealer undertakes on a permanent basis, through a contract with the entrepreneur, in his own name and for his own account, i.e. through his own business *(Eigengeschäft)*, to distribute the goods in a particular contractual territory for the entrepreneur and to promote their sale in accordance with the guidelines of the entrepreneur.

Owing to the lack of statutory rules with respect to this form of distribution, there are various scenarios with respect to the integration of the authorized dealer into the sales organization of the entrepreneur. However, in general, the form of distribution of the authorized dealer allows the entrepreneur to minimize the risks associated with having his own distribution system by involving several authorized dealers, who are in turn entrusted with the sales of the products to the end customers. It is precisely this direct client relationship of the authorized dealers, who are in immediate contact with the client, which cannot be ensured in such intensity in the context of a business entity of a certain size.

Generally speaking, with regard to the classification of the authorized dealer as an employee or as self-employed (i.e. independent), the comments regarding the commercial agent apply. However, the activity aimed at generating proceeds through resale usually leads to the position as an independent dealer.

In this form of distribution, there is a performance relationship between the entrepreneur and the authorized dealer as well as subsequently, in the context of a resale, between the authorized dealer and his customer (consumer or additional dealer). The authorized dealer receives his remuneration directly from the customer rather than from the entrepreneur.

Depending on the degree of his integration into the sales organization of the entrepreneur, under certain circumstances the authorized dealer may also have a claim to compensation upon termination of the contractual relationship, analogous to that set out in Sec. 89b of the Commercial Code. According to consistent case law of the German Federal Court of Justice, the provision of Sec. 89b of the Commercial Code which is tailored to the situation of the commercial agent has to be applied *mutatis mutandis* to the authorized dealer if (i) the authorized dealer were integrated into the sales organization of the manufacturer or the supplier in such a way that, in economic terms and to a significant extent, the tasks he had to fulfill were comparable to those of a commercial agent, and (ii) the authorized dealer, on the other hand, is under an obligation to transfer his customer base to the manufacturer or supplier (entrepreneur) so that, upon termination of the contract, they can take advantage of the customer base immediately and readily.[7]

b) Distinction from Other Forms of Distribution

An authorized dealer distributes goods in his own name and for his own account, i.e. he purchases goods in order to resell these independently and at his own risk. The basis for this is a relationship established on a permanent basis and with commitment to another enterprise. This distinguishes the authorized dealer in particular from the commercial agent, the commercial broker, and the commission agent.

5. Franchisee

a) Essential Features

The franchisor makes available to the franchisee the use of a business strategy in exchange for consideration. Owing to this integration into the distribution system of the entrepreneur, the franchise system is generally characterized by an extremely strong vertical integration. From the perspective of the customers, the enterprise and the franchisees thus appear as a single entity. Within this franchise system, however, franchisees resemble authorized dealers in several respects. For instance, franchisees also act for their own account and in their own name and enter into direct contractual relationships with end customers.

As is the case with authorized dealers, the law governing franchisees has not been made the subject of separate statutory codification in Germany.

As a result, in practice there are different kinds of franchising, owing not least to the fact that this type of distribution system is used for the distribution of goods and services alike. For the same reason, the legal classification of the franchise contract is not without difficulty. Since a franchise contract is usually composed of different types of contract, it can be described as a 'mixed contract'.

The fact that the details of this contractual relationship hinge on the individual case makes it impossible to enumerate the mutual rights and obligations of the contracting parties in an exhaustive way. What can be said in general, however, is that that this system is meant to facilitate, (a) for the franchisor, the sale of his goods, and (b) for the franchisee, success in terms of sales on the basis of his integration into a – possibly already well-established – business strategy. Depending on whether the relationship is fashioned as a partner franchising or subordinate franchising, there is an intense obligation on both parties, in this context in particular, to promote each other's interests.

---

7 German Federal Court of Justice 13.1.2010 – VIII ZR 25/08, IHR 2010, p. 265.

Another aspect of fundamental importance is the franchisor's obligation to transfer the know-how underlying his business strategy to the franchisee. Similarly, agreement must be reached with respect to the use of rights which are directly connected to the business strategy and its marketing (e.g. trademarks, logos, copyrights and possibly patent rights). Depending on the type of franchising, the challenge is to ensure protection for the franchisor by way of contractual provisions aimed at safeguarding locations *(Standortsicherung)*.

The contentious issue of whether – and if so, under what conditions – the franchisee has a right to compensation upon termination of the franchise relationship (analogous to the claim set out in Sec. 89b(1) of the Commercial Code) has not yet been conclusively clarified.

b) Distinction from Other Forms of Distribution

To the extent that the relationship between the franchisee and the franchisor is a continuing obligation, the role of the franchisee can be distinguished from that of the broker and the commission agent.

The franchisee acts in his own name and trades for his own account, which sets him apart from the commercial agent, who trades in the name of and for the account of another.

In contrast to the authorized dealer, the franchisee is yet more closely integrated into the business strategy of the entrepreneur. While the form of distribution of the authorized dealer focuses on the distribution of goods *per se*, franchising is additionally characterized by the franchisee's intensive integration into the organization and marketing strategy of the franchisor. Unlike the franchisee, the authorized dealer does not necessarily receive continuous support from the entrepreneur; at the same time, the authorized dealer is not necessarily bound by the entrepreneur's instructions to the same degree as the franchisee.

III. Pitfalls

In the context of contract drafting, a multitude of legal issues need to be borne in mind, depending on the respective form of distribution.

1. Distinction from Employees

Significant issues include the adequate distinction of the independent sales intermediary from the employee. This distinction is particularly important for sales intermediaries who are integrated into the sales organization of the entrepreneur. If they have to be classified not as independent professionals but as employees, then they fall within the statutory social security regime. Disregarding the resulting obligations may even trigger criminal-law consequences.

2. General Terms and Conditions

The law regarding general terms and conditions *(Allgemeine Geschäftsbedingungen)* is a common reason for the ineffectiveness of contractual provisions in distribution contracts. General terms and conditions are contractual provisions which have been pre-formulated for an indeterminate number of different contracts, and which the applying party (the entrepreneur) requires the other party to agree to in the context of conclusion of the contract in question. Owing to the fact that these provisions are prescribed by the entrepreneur unilaterally – i.e. without individual negotiation between the parties – and as such become the basis of the contract, German civil law has set out certain control rules in Secs. 305 to 310 of the Civil Code, which set limits on the use of general terms and conditions. A breach of these rules normally results in the application of those very statutory rules that the entrepreneur was seeking to avoid.

3. Restrictions on Competition

Entrepreneurs who do business in Germany also need to heed the rules of European and German antitrust law. Of fundamental significance in this respect are (i) the prohibition on agreements with a restrictive effect on competition under Art. 101 of the Treaty on the Functioning of the European Union and Sec. 1 of the German Antitrust Act *(Gesetz gegen Wettbewerbsbeschränkungen)* and (ii) the prohibition on abusive practices under Art. 102 of the Treaty on the Functioning of the European Union and Secs. 19 *et seqq.* of the German Antitrust Act. In this context, the thresholds for the applicability of the European rules are often quickly exceeded. A breach of the antitrust-law rules can lead to (partial) invalidity of the contract and to claims for damages as well as to the imposition of fines by the responsible antitrust authorities.

4. Claim for Compensation upon Termination

In all (commercial-law) forms of distribution which are characterized by the integration of the sales intermediary into the sales organization of the entrepreneur, the additional question arises as to whether, upon termination of the contractual relationship, the distribution partner – just like the commercial agent – has, in principle, a claim for compensation with respect to a customer base that he has built up (or helped to build), with such claim being based on an analogous application of Sec. 89b of the Commercial Code.

As explained above, provided certain preconditions are met, the application of this rule also to the authorized dealer and, only recently, even the trademark licensee has been upheld by the case law of the highest courts.[8] Whether and to what extent it might even be applicable to a franchisee has as yet not been

---

[8] For the application of Sec. 89b of the Commercial Code in the context of the trademark licensee cf. German Federal Court of Justice 29.4.2010 – I ZR 3/09, GRUR 2010, p. 1107, NJW 2010, p. 2354.

conclusively clarified. The unexpected assertion of such a claim by the sales intermediary at the end of the contract can come as an unwelcome surprise for the entrepreneur.

5. International Context

In the context of distribution contracts with cross-border elements, one question that always arises is which country's law and jurisdiction are applicable. In order to avoid later uncertainties, contractual agreements are therefore reached on the choice of law and the choice of jurisdiction, which are intended to govern both the applicability of substantive law and the later, possible competence of a particular court and the associated procedural law. However, if they lead to a breach of legal provisions that are mandatory in the area in which the sales intermediary is active, then they may be ineffective.

IV. Schemes

Any implementation of a distribution system – regardless of its size and of which sector it relates to – requires early planning by the parties who will be involved. Along with civil- and commercial-law considerations, a host of issues from other areas of law often make it absolutely essential to obtain prior advice that is legally sound and comprehensive. The target should be a choice of structure that realizes the desired sales system in a cost-efficient and legally secure manner.

For the issue of the distinction between an independently active sales intermediary and an employee, for instance, what is decisive is, on the one hand, the taking into consideration of the legal structure of the distribution relationship as a whole, and, on the other hand, its later actual execution. If any doubts remain, it might be advisable – in order to achieve a binding clarification of the social-security status of the sales intermediary in Germany – to initiate a 'status-determination procedure' *(Statusfeststellungsverfahren)* with the competent authority, the Federation of German Pension-Insurance Institutions *(Deutsche Rentenversicherung Bund)*.

However, caution should be exercised in connection with other protective norms as well. The title of the contract as such is not decisive for the legal classification of the contractual relationship. Far more significant is the question on what distribution level the respective sales intermediary is active, and what rights and obligations he has. The exact legal classification often gains practical relevance only once a conflict arises thereon. At that point in time, however, it is no longer possible to influence things by way of structuring. It is therefore important to take care – in good time, i.e. in the run-up to commercial activities – to choose the right form of distribution and to regulate, as unambiguously and comprehensively as possible, the objective pursued as well as the resulting rights and obligations of the parties, bearing in mind all protective provisions prescribed by statute.

The need for an early examination and possible taking of measures becomes particularly obvious in connection with compliance with antitrust-law requirements regarding vertical restrictions on competition such as contractually agreed pricing specifications, territorial protection provisions or (post-contractual) restraints on competition. For the assessment of whether a distribution contract is subject to antitrust-law rules, it is of significance whether one is dealing with a contract with (a) a 'genuine commercial agent' *(echter Handelsvertreter)* under Sec. 84 of the Commercial Code or (b) a 'ungenuine commercial agent' *(unechter Handelsvertreter)*, e.g. in the form of an authorized dealer or a franchisee. While the contract involving a genuine commercial agent is excluded from antitrust-law restrictions in principle, such restrictions do apply – subject to the European block-exemption regulations – to a contract with an authorized dealer or a franchisee. In the opinion of the EU Commission, the decisive criterion for the distinction between genuine and ungenuine commercial agents is whether the sales intermediary bears a business and cost risk of his own.[9]

In order to avoid breaches of mandatory law on general terms and conditions, the entrepreneur should neither prepare his own general terms and conditions nor adopt those of a third party without legal review. If, as is often the case, the individual negotiation of terms and conditions between the parties is out of the question, then here, too, essentially the only course of action is to ensure the timely review and drafting of possible general terms and conditions by a legal expert prior to entering into the contract.

Depending on the form of distribution, careful prior contractual drafting – where necessary taking into account elements relevant for valuation purposes – can serve to avoid, or at least mitigate in economic terms, a possible claim for compensation as set out in Sec. 89b of the Commercial Code on the part of the contractual partner.

In international contexts, a hasty, unverified choice of law or agreement on jurisdiction in the distribution contract is not advisable. If one wishes to avoid nasty surprises later on, then it is important, before entering into the contract, to include in the legal review not only the governing law of the contract but also the mandatory law that applies to the proposed area of activity of the sales intermediary. By way of example – as mentioned above – the compensation claim by a commercial agent who, under a commercial-agent contract governed by German law, is active in Germany or in the EU/EEA area is governed by the provisions of Sec. 89b of the Commercial Code, in accordance with Arts. 17 and 18 of the EU Commercial Agents Directive. With respect to those rules, it is impermissible to agree any deviations to the detriment of the commercial agent prior to the termination of the contract. According to case law, this applies even where the commercial agent is active in Germany (or another EU/EEA Member State) – despite the fact that the entrepreneur has his seat outside of the EU/EEA area – and the parties have contractually agreed on the

---

9 Cf. EU Commission Communication, Guidelines on Vertical Restraints, OJ 2010 C 130/01.

law of the state of the entrepreneur as their governing law, and that law precisely does not provide for any compensation for commercial agents.[10] Pursuant to Sec. 92c(1) of the Commercial Code, a sole exception applies if, despite the applicability of German law, the commercial agent is active exclusively outside the EU/EEA area. In this case, a contractual deviation is permitted in principle, even if it is to the detriment of the commercial agent. The preparation and drafting of a cross-border contract ought to be carried out by at least two legal advisors, and more specifically by one from the home state of the entrepreneur and one from the relevant foreign jurisdiction.

---

10 Cf. European Court of Justice 9.11.2000 – Rs C-381/98, EuZW 2001, p. 50, and German Federal Court of Justice 5.9.2012 – VII ZR 25/12, IHR 2013, p. 35.

Dr. Jan C. Giedinghagen LL.M.

Lawyer

Areas of Specialization

- Law of partnerships and corporations
- Corporate law and corporate governance
- Mergers & acquisitions and corporate reorganizations
- Capital markets law
- Commercial law

Telephone (ext.) +49 228/95 94-383

Email: jan.giedinghagen@fgs.de

Matrix Structures as a Means of Steering Groups Under Corporate Law and Labor-and-Employment Law

by Tobias Nießen

Contents

I. Introduction
II. Corporate-Law Implications of Cross-Company Matrix Structures
  1. Classification of the Underlying Legal Relationship
  2. Corporate-Law Limitations of Matrix Structures
    a) German AG (*Aktiengesellschaft* or *Stock Corporation*) in a Contract-Based Group
    b) German *AG* in a *De-Facto* Group
    c) Group Companies in the Legal Form of a German *GmbH*
III. Labor-and-Employment-Law Implications of Matrix Structures

1. Employment-Law Aspects
2. Labor-Law Aspects
  a) Participation Rights of the Works Council / Economic Committee
  b) Effects on the Existing Structures in Terms of Organizational Units (*Betriebe*)
  c) The Employees' Affiliation with an Organizational Unit (*Betriebszugehörigkeit*)
3. Protection of Employee Data
IV. Conclusion

I. Introduction

In a group, the legal structures are often not congruent with the economic structures. First, the fact that groups are developed successively and holdings/activities are acquired step by step or built from scratch means that groups are not usually developed in a homogeneous legal manner. Second, based on tax, social, corporate-policy or legal considerations, these groups are often not structured in what would constitute, viewed in isolation, optimal operating structures. In the modern economic world, economic dealings within complex organizations are therefore often not primarily defined by the legal form or legal structure of the group but by market function and market process.

In group practice, the question therefore frequently arises how to optimize the existing structures both from an economic and from a legal perspective. In this connection, what is also often of interest are organizational forms which are incongruent with the legal form, i.e. those which allow group-wide decision-making powers to be pooled in one organizational unit within the group. In this respect, it is often necessary to implement function-oriented steering structures which go beyond the boundaries of corporate law; this is especially the case with groups involving an international presence and structure.

In legal terms, such group-wide 'steering' (*Steuerung*) can be implemented in different ways. In the context of indirect steering models, steering is carried out via the management board of the respective corporation which, in turn, issues instructions to the respective specific employees affected in its corporation. In the context of direct steering models, by contrast, the respective employees affected are managed and instructed directly by the 'steering' entity, i.e. without involving the management board of the 'steered' entity as an intermediary. Matrix structures are increasingly used for this purpose. In the context of matrix structures, the respective steering unit and/or its employees are authorized, as a rule, either (a) to exercise the right, based on corporate law, to issue instructions (whether this arises from a control agreement or from the position of shareholder in a German *GmbH – Gesellschaft mit beschränkter Haftung* or privately held corporation), together with an authorization of the 'steered' employees to receive, and follow, these instructions or (b) to exercise, on behalf of the contractual employer, the right conveyed under the employment contract to issue (subject-specific) instructions.

However, when using matrix structures, there are corporate-law and labor-and-employment-law limitations, in particular, which must be observed under German law – quite apart from further-reaching questions e.g. of a tax-law nature.

II. Corporate-Law Implications of Cross-Company Matrix Structures

1. Classification of the Underlying Legal Relationship

As regards the implementation of matrix structures, it is necessary to differentiate between (i) the act of granting power of attorney and (ii) the legal relationship which forms the basis of such granting of power of attorney. Irrespective of the mode of implementation, the granting of power of attorney as such always constitutes an authorization within the meaning of Sec. 164 of the German Civil Code *(Bürgerliches Gesetzbuch)*. If the exercised right to issue instructions stems from an existing control agreement or – in the case of a German *GmbH* – from the position of (majority) shareholder, then the control agreement or the exercising of the shareholder rights constitutes the underlying legal relationship. As regards the granting of authorization to exercise the right conveyed under the employment contract to issue (subject-specific) instructions, one needs to differentiate as follows: If the activity of the authorized company solely amounts to exercising the right to issue instructions as conveyed under the employment contract, then, as a rule, this constitutes a pure management agreement *(Geschäftsbesorgungsvertrag)* or – where no fee is payable – a mandate *(Auftrag)*. By contrast, if the instructions are not restricted to sporadic directions but rather – owing to quality and quantity of the instructions – the operations of the business or business segment are effectively run by the authorized party, then this may qualify as an *echter (Teil-)Betriebsführungsvertrag* ('genuine agreement on management of a business/business segment'). This is an agreement by way of which a third party undertakes to manage the business of the owner entity in the name and in the interest of that entity. If the rights granted to the authorized party are so far-reaching that it is entitled to exercise significant final decision-making competences, and if the supervisory and influencing rights as well as the competences of the entity granting the power of attorney are curtailed for the most part with respect to the 'steered' area, then this effectively constitutes a (partial) control agreement which is only effective if it complies with the provisions of Secs. 293 *et seqq.* of the German Stock Corporation Act *(Aktiengesetz)*.

2. Corporate-Law Limitations of Matrix Structures

Irrespective of the specific structure chosen, in the context of implementing matrix structures, legal limitations pertaining to groups need to be observed. These differ depending on the type of corporation and type of group involved.

a) German AG (*Aktiengesellschaft or Stock Corporation*) in a Contract-Based Group

If the steered corporation has the legal form of a German *AG* and is affiliated with the steering entity on the basis of a control agreement, then the executive board has a duty under Secs. 308 and 310 of the Stock Corporation Act to examine whether the instructions issued by the controlling corporation are lawful. In the context of a control agreement, comprehensive power of attorney granted by the dependent corporation to the controlling entity – which enables the controlling entity to act directly for the dependent corporation without explicit instruction to the executive board – is regarded as impermissible if, as a result of this, the supervisory function of the executive board of the dependent corporation, which exists as a general rule and which according to the prevailing view may not be delegated, would be undermined. According to that prevailing view, delegation and implementation of an instruction are regarded as permissible only if care is taken to ensure that the executive board is informed about such instruction early enough so as to enable the executive board to prevent implementation of this instruction where the legal requirements are not met. The supervisory duty on the part of the executive board of the dependent corporation is sometimes thought to imply that, even in cases where there is a combination of a control agreement and additional 'steering agreements' – such as an agreement on management of a business – it is necessary to ensure that the executive board of the dependent corporation be in a position to supervise all direct instructions issued to employees. However, according to the opposing view, the delegation to lower-tier corporate levels of the executive board's supervisory and examination duties is possible, with the consequence that not every single instruction would need to be examined by the executive board itself.

If one regards the delegation, to lower-tier levels, of the right to examine the individual instructions as possible in principle, then there are still rights and duties which even under the right to issue instructions, arising from the control agreement, must be carried out by the management board of the dependent corporation itself and may not be delegated; the management board therefore needs the information necessary to exercise these rights and to meet these duties. This concerns, in the first place, the tasks mandatorily assigned to the management board by statute, e.g. ensuring that the required accounting is undertaken (Sec. 91(1) of the Stock Corporation Act), securing the continued existence of the corporation (Sec. 91(2) of the Stock Corporation Act), filing an application for insolvency (Sec. 15a of the German Insolvency Code – *Insolvenzordnung*), or preparing the financial statements and management report and submitting these to the supervisory board (Sec. 170 of the Stock Corporation Act). Creating matrix structures must not lead to the management board no longer having access to the information necessary to meet the duties assigned to it by statute, especially since this management board is not exculpated if it is unable to meet its duties for this reason. In this respect, it is therefore necessary to ensure through corresponding reporting duties *vis-à-vis* the management board of the dependent corporation itself – and, if so, in parallel to the matrix structures geared towards the controlling entity – that the management board possesses the necessary information in good time.

Furthermore, the general duties of care which apply when delegating tasks to lower-tier corporate levels need be observed in any event. In this respect it is necessary that, in each instance, the delegate, on the basis of its abilities, be carefully (i) selected (diligence in selecting), (ii) briefed (diligence in briefing) and (iii) monitored (diligence in monitoring). Accordingly, specific requirements arise in this regard not only on the second level of monitoring the functionality and effectiveness of the required reporting system but already with regard to structuring the reporting duties and processes themselves. Proper selection and monitoring in particular make it necessary, as early as at the stage of implementing matrix structures, to precisely define and allocate responsibilities among the employees, taking into account their qualifications, and to take organizational precautions to prevent breaches of duty from the outset.

In the context of the monitoring duty, on the second level, the management board is responsible – also once the reporting system has been implemented – for ensuring a reasonable degree of supervision. In general, the monitoring duty requires (i) constant supervision independent of actual deficiencies arising – e.g. by way of regular reporting duties – as well as (ii) supervision which prevents irregularities even without constant direct supervision, e.g. by way of unannounced spot checks. Where there are reasons for suspicion, these must not only be investigated; rather, inspections must be carried out in addition in order for possible structural causes to be ascertained and responded to. Again, this responsibility continues to lie with the management board of the dependent corporation despite delegation.

In practice, guidelines on future reporting lines are therefore regularly implemented in the context of introducing matrix structures in order to ensure that the statutory duties still incumbent on the management board are met. Furthermore, adjustments to the compliance system of the steered corporation also usually become necessary in order to reflect the modified structures and reporting lines here, too. Moreover, the members of the management board are often indemnified against liability. In this respect it should be noted, however, that the limitation of liability in favor of the management board is not always possible, e.g. in view of mandatory duties under public law or in the case of breaches of the capital-protection rules. In such cases, only indemnification in terms of the internal relationship *vis-à-vis* the employing entity and the other group companies is conceivable.

b) German *AG* in a *De-Facto* Group

If the instructed German *AG* is part of a *de-facto* group, then steering 'by way of corporate law' through (a) a right to issue instructions which arises from a control agreement, or (b) the shareholder meeting, as in the case of a German *GmbH*, is not possible; instead, steering can take place by way of authorizing the exercise of the right, conveyed under the employment contract, to issue (subject-specific) instructions. The starting point for determining the scope and limits of such matrix structures is Sec. 76(1) of the Stock Corporation Act, pursuant to which the executive board is obliged to manage the corporation on its own responsibility. It is in line with the predominant view that the executive board must personally carry out its management duty under Sec. 76(1) of the Stock Corporation Act and may only delegate – or have carried out by third parties – those activities which are considered part of general management *(Geschäftsführung)* within the meaning of Sec. 77 of the Stock Corporation Act but not simultaneously part of the directional management *(Leitung)* within the meaning of Sec. 76(1) of the Stock Corporation Act. The management board at the level of the instructed corporation therefore continues to be obliged to observe the directional management duties *(Leitungsverantwortung)* incumbent on it. In addition, while direct instructions from third parties to employees of the corporation are not excluded, the executive board of the instructed corporation does have examination and supervisory duties – similar to the case of a contract-based group.

Restrictions with respect to *de-facto* groups also arise under Secs. 311 and 312 of the Stock Corporation Act. Section 311 of the Stock Corporation Act stipulates that a controlling entity may not use its influence over the *AG* to cause the dependent *AG* (i) to carry out a legal transaction prejudicial to it, or (ii) to take, or omit to take, measures in a way detrimental to the *AG*, unless the disadvantages are compensated for. Accordingly, the executive board of the dependent corporation has an additional organizational duty in that it must (i) ensure that it become aware of any influencing within the meaning of Sec. 311 of the Stock Corporation Act and (ii) check whether any such influencing is of a detrimental nature and, if so, whether any disadvantages are being compensated for in such cases. Furthermore, the executive board of the dependent corporation must ensure that all occurrences required to be included in the 'dependent-corporation report' (cf. Sec. 312 of the Stock Corporation Act) are in fact documented.

c) Group Companies in the Legal Form of a German *GmbH*

Sec. 43(1) of the *GmbH* Act *(Gesetz betreffend die Gesellschaften mit beschränkter Haftung)* obliges the management *(Geschäftsführung)* of German *GmbHs* to exercise, in comporate matters, the care of a prudent businessman. Under Sec. 37(1) of the *GmbH* Act, the management have a duty *vis-à-vis* their corporation to comply with such limitations of their authority of representation as may be stipulated by the bylaws or the resolutions of the corporation. Thus, in the case of a *GmbH* – unlike in that of an *AG* – there is the possibility of issuing instructions by way of shareholder resolutions. Ultimately, however, direct instructions issued by the shareholder meeting to the employees of the corporation are in general not readily permissible even in the case of a *GmbH*; instead, it is necessary in such scenarios, too, to grant authorization to exercise the right conveyed under the employment contract to issue instructions. Even within the right to issue instructions laid down in Sec. 37 of the *GmbH* Act, certain rights and duties of the management are statutorily assigned to them personally and may not be delegated to lower-tier corporate levels. Therefore, in this context as well, the management board must be provided with the information necessary to discharge these minimum duties. Furthermore, the management are always responsible for general compliance and thus for ensuring that the corporation acts in a lawful manner. For this purpose, the management of a *GmbH* have an irrevocable right to be informed and involved so that they can discharge these duties. In particular, the management must create an appropriate organizational structure geared towards them, which ensures that duties are properly discharged and enables them to monitor these requirements in an effective manner. If a dependent *GmbH* is affiliated by way of a control agreement, then the above-mentioned comments on the *AG* in a contract-based group apply accordingly.

III. Labor-and-Employment-Law Implications of Matrix Structures

In the context of introducing matrix structures, the structure of the specific model in the individual case is of significant importance from a labor-and-employment-law perspective. Different labor-and-employment-law consequences can arise depending on how the right to issue instructions is fashioned as well as in light of the related integration, if any, of the instructed employees into the organizational structures of the instructing party.

1. Employment-Law Aspects

Pursuant to the case law of the German Federal Labor Court, there is the possibility of transferring to an external third party the right to issue (subject-specific) instructions, without the consent of the employee being required. Unless otherwise agreed under a collective agreement or in the individual employment contract, the employer may transfer the right to give subject-specific instructions to another person – including to a third party outside the business – who can then exercise this right, as the superior, *vis-à-vis* his subordinate employees. However, with respect to the right to issue disciplinary instructions, this only applies to a limited extent. For instance, it is generally accepted that the employer may authorize a third party to give notice of dismissal, whereas the right of termination as such mandatorily remains with the contractual employer.

Transferring the right to issue (subject-specific) instructions is not usually barred by Sec. 613 sentence 2 of the German Civil Code either. Under Sec. 613 sentence 2 of the Civil Code, in the case of doubt the employer's claim to the employee's services is nontransferable. Where the functional steering is not restricted to transferring the right to issue instructions but the work provided is, at least in part, for someone other than the contractual employer, consent is required by Sec. 613 sentence 2 of the Civil Code. What is decisive in this respect is whether (a) the third party from outside the entity assumes the steering in practical terms as an 'employee of the respective company', e.g. because he has special knowhow and the employee continues to work exclusively for his contractual employer, or whether (b) the third party from outside the business assumes the steering e.g. in order to pursue cross-company (group) purposes. The latter case does not merely involve a 'replacement of superior'; rather, the employees affected by the steering provide their work services (in part) also for the benefit of third parties, something that is only possible with the consent of the employee concerned. However, such consent may be given by way of anticipated or implied consent. The former is the case, for example, where, in scenarios where the management function is exercised by a group company, an express 'matrix clause' or reservation of group-wide secondment or relocation has been agreed in the employment contract. Such implied consent is present e.g. where the employee concerned enters into an agreement on objectives, which is based on the new matrix structure.

Furthermore, in the context of implementing matrix structures, it must be ensured that this does not constitute temporary hiring-out of employees *(Arbeitnehmerüberlassung)* requiring consent. Pursuant to Sec. 1(1) sentence 1 of the German Temporary Employment Act *(Arbeitnehmerüberlassungsgesetz)*, employers desiring to temporarily hire out, as lenders and in the context of their economic activity, employees to third parties for work require a permit. A hiring-out occurs when, based on an agreement which is at least implied, the (contractual) employer provides employees employed by it to a third party, who then deploys them in accordance with its own needs and objectives in its business to advance its business purposes. The employees must then carry out their work in accordance with the instructions of the borrower and be integrated into the business operation of the borrower, and from then on, the lender must, with the employees he has temporarily hired out, exclusively pursue business purposes other than his own. In order to avoid a hiring-out, care should be taken that the instructed employees are not integrated into the business of the instructing party and that the contractual employer continues to pursue its own business purposes.

2. Labor-Law Aspects

a) Participation Rights of the Works Council / Economic Committee

aa) Involvement of the Economic Committee

Pursuant to Sec. 106 of the German Works Constitution Act *(Betriebsverfassungsgesetz)*, the employer must inform the economic committee about the business entity's economic affairs in a timely and comprehensive manner, submitting the necessary documents, and must discuss these with the committee. 'Economic matters' do not only include changing the business organization or the business purpose but also other occurrences and projects which could significantly affect the interests of the employees of the entity. Depending on the nature and scope of the functional steering, this will normally constitute an economic matter, particularly where ultimately a relevant number of employees (in qualitative and quantitative terms) are to be steered.

bb) Duty to Draw Up a Reconciliation-of-Interests and Social Plan

Sections 111 and 112 of the Works Constitution Act stipulate that the employer must inform the works council in a timely and comprehensive manner about proposed operational changes which could lead to significant disadvantages for the workforce (or considerable parts thereof), and must discuss the planned operational changes with the works council. Moreover, the employer has a duty to attempt a reconciliation of interests with the works council regarding the operational changes as well as to agree a social plan if the legal requirements are met.

When implementing a matrix structure, one needs to consider whether this constitutes a fundamental alteration to the business organization within the meaning of Sec. 111 sentence 3 no. 4 of the Works Constitution Act both with respect to the business of the instructing party and to that of the employees receiving the instructions. What is decisive in this respect is whether the creation of the matrix structures significantly affects the structure of the business or the organization of the management structure in the individual case. Where, for example, the existing (departmental) structures are completely transformed into a business-unit structure, this will probably be regarded as a fundamental alteration to the business organization. The same is also likely to apply if existing hierarchy levels are removed in favor of the matrix structure.

cc) Consent Requirement for Individual Personnel Measures

Further involvement of the works council is necessary in view of Sec. 99 of the Works Constitution Act if implementing the matrix structure means, for the instructed employee, relocation within his contractual employer's business or being recruited into the business of the instructing party.

What may, in particular, constitute relocation is a scenario involving changes to the responsibilities, the actual activities carried out or the work organization within which the activities must be carried out. Removing or extending personnel responsibility can also lead to a change of activity which, as relocation, requires the involvement of the works council.

Recruitment by the instructing party takes place – irrespective of whether an employment contract has been signed – when the employee is integrated into the instructing party's business in order to realize the purpose of the business by carrying out, together with the employees employed there, instruction-based activity. Depending on the design of the matrix structure, this can be assumed where, in the case of cross-company steering, the employee serves the business purpose of the instructing party, and that party is entitled to determine especially the time and place of the activity.

b) Effects on the Existing Structures in Terms of Organizational Units (*Betriebe*)

Introducing a matrix structure does not normally affect the structure of existing organizational units *(Betriebe)* within the meaning of the German Works Constitution Act. More specifically, even in the case of comprehensive steering by a foreign entity, in general the German Works Constitution Act still applies to the German permanent establishment since, according to case law, for a business unit within the meaning of Sec. 4(1) sentence 1 of the Works Constitution Act, the required minimum degree of organization already exists if instruction rights of the employer are exercised within the organizational unit at all.

Depending on the intensity of the cooperation between the contractual employer and the instructing party, there may, however, be a risk of a 'joint organizational unit' *(Gemeinschaftsbetrieb)* within the meaning of Sec. 1(1) sentence 2 of the Works Constitution Act arising between the two parties. This would have substantial consequences in particular for terminations on operational grounds because, in the compulsory process of selection on social grounds, all employees belonging to a joint organizational unit would have to be taken into account. However, in addition to pursuing a uniform work purpose, one of the prerequisites for a joint organizational unit is the existence of a uniform management structure, especially with respect to staff and social matters. Therefore, a joint organizational unit does not usually exist if, in the framework of the matrix structure, solely the right to issue subject-specific instructions is delegated, while the contractual employer retains the main disciplinary powers.

The divergence between operational structure and management competences does, however, raise the issue of group-wide harmonization of the works-council structures.

An adjustment of the works-council structures as provided for by statute is possible, for instance, where the group's organization is product- or project-related (Sec. 3(1) no. 2 of the Works Constitution Act). A deviating works-council structure can also be agreed if, given the group's organization, this is more conducive to an effective and expedient representation of the employees' interests. In this respect, the Federal Labor Court requires that the deviating agreement be better suited in this respect than the structure prescribed by statute. Whether this is the case materially depends on the circumstances of the individual case.

c) The Employees' Affiliation with an Organizational Unit (*Betriebszugehörigkeit*)

The organizational unit (within the meaning of the German Works Constitution Act) with which an employee is affiliated needs to be determined both (i) with respect to the employee's right to vote in works-council elections (Secs. 7 and 8 of the Works Constitution Act) as well as (ii) (partially based thereon) with respect to the other thresholds of works-constitution law, e.g. with regard to determining the relevant size of the works council (Sec. 9 of the Works Constitution Act). In this respect, it is also possible that an employee is affiliated with two different organizational units.

Owing to his contractual connection, an employee usually remains affiliated with the organizational unit of his contractual employer even after the matrix structure has been introduced, provided he continues to be integrated into that employer's structure in terms of organizational units. However, depending on the degree to which the employee is integrated into the organization unit of the instructing party, the question arises whether the employee is not also affiliated with the instructing party's organizational unit. This results not least from the fact that the Federal Labor Court, in its more recent case law on the hiring-out of employees, has deviated from its previously-held view under which an employee's affiliation with a particular organizational unit always required an employment contract binding that employee to the owner of the organizational unit.

3. Protection of Employee Data

Particularly with respect to the central collection and administration of employee data within the group which often accompanies the implementation of matrix structures, the question arises how the necessary data transfer between the individual group companies can be placed on a legal basis. Since there is no statutory provision for an intragroup exemption, the group-wide collection, processing and use of personal data is only permissible under Sec. 4(1) of the German Federal Data Protection Act *(Bundesdatenschutzgesetz)* if permitted by statute or by any other legal provision, or if the person concerned has consented. The latter is hardly practicable owing to the strict consent requirements laid down in Sec. 4a(1) of the Federal Data Protection Act and the fact that consent is freely revocable at any time. Section 32(1) sentence 1 of the Federal Data Protection Act, which permits data processing for employment-related purposes, is unlikely to be of any assistance in most cases, unless the employment contract includes a specific reference to the group, e.g. by including a clause providing for group-wide secondment and relocation. The same applies to the permission laid down in Sec. 28 of the Federal Data Protection Act. Finally, group-wide processing of employee data in matrix cases is also unlikely to constitute mere 'processing by an agent' within the meaning of Sec. 11 of the Federal Data Protection Act because the transmission of data is specifically intended to enable the recipient of the data to autonomously exercise his HR competence, and in this respect the authorizing entity no longer has the full control over the data. On the basis of prevailing opinion, the most legally secure basis for a group-wide exchange of data is therefore the entering into a corresponding works agreement as 'another legal provision' within the meaning of section 4(1) of the Federal Data Protection Act.

IV. Conclusion

Introducing (group-wide) cross-company steering models by granting authorization to other group companies to exercise the (functional) instruction right is possible, in principle, both from a corporate-law and from a labor-and-employment-law perspective. These therefore constitute an alternative to restructuring measures carried out under corporate law.

However, when establishing a matrix structure, it must be borne in mind that the executive board or the management of the authorizing corporation has examination and supervisory duties. The related risks of care and liability should definitely be counteracted by way of suitable measures such as, in particular, creating clear and binding reporting channels and a suitable compliance system as well as indemnification against liability, as appropriate. From an employment-law perspective, the consent of the employee affected by the matrix structure may be necessary, depending on each single case. Furthermore, what needs to be clarified in each instance is the extent to which the implementation of matrix structures leads to employee-representation bodies having rights of involvement. Finally, in light of the data-protection-law aspects which are regularly associated with group-matrix structures, it is advisable to conclude a corresponding group works agreement.

Dr. Tobias Nießen

Lawyer

Areas of Specialization

- Corporate law
- Labor and employment law
- Corporate reorganizations

Telephone (ext.) +49 228/95 94-198

Email: tobias.niessen@fgs.de

Corporate Codetermination and Its Avoidance

by Michael Winter

Contents

I. Corporate Codetermination
1. Codetermination on the basis of parity pursuant to the Codetermination Act of 1976
   a) Companies covered
   b) Codetermination at the ultimate parent company
   c) Formation of a supervisory board subject to parity-based codetermination
   d) Responsibilities of supervisory boards subject to parity-based codetermination
2. One-third codetermination pursuant to the One-Third Participation Act
   a) Companies covered
   b) Codetermination in the company heading the group
   c) Formation of a supervisory board subject to one-third codetermination
   d) Responsibilities of supervisory boards subject to one-third codetermination

II. Strategies to Avoid Codetermination
1. Using partnerships, particularly the *GmbH & Co. KG*
   a) 'Reallocating' the general partner *GmbH*
   b) *Stiftung & Co. KG*
   c) *SE & Co. KG*
   d) Foreign corporation & Co. *KG*
2. Distributing the employees to multiple group companies
3. Using foreign legal forms
4. Using SE structures
5. Freezing codetermination through a cross-border merger
6. Reducing codetermination using a *KGaA*

I. Corporate Codetermination

German law allows for participation and codetermination by employees at both the operational and the corporate level. Operational codetermination is exercised primarily through works councils (*Betriebsräte*), which are entitled to codetermination rights pursuant to the Works Constitution Act (*Betriebsverfassungsgesetz*) in social, personnel and financial matters. Corporate codetermination refers to the involvement of the employees in corporate decisions and is secured through employee representation on a supervisory board.

Not every company is obligated to set up a supervisory board and appoint employee representatives to it; only certain medium-sized and large companies that meet the relevant requirements specified in the codetermination laws. These codetermination laws are (i) the Codetermination Act (*Mitbestimmungsgesetz*) of 1976, (ii) the One-Third Participation Act (*Drittelbeteiligungsgesetz*) of 2004, (iii) the Codetermination Act for the Coal, Iron and Steel Industry (*Montan-Mitbestimmungsgesetz*) of 1951, (iv) the Supplementary Codetermination Act (*Montan-Mitbestimmungsergänzungsgesetz*) of 1956, (v) the SE Employee Participation Act (*SE-Beteiligungsgesetz*) of 2004, (vi) the SCE Participation Act (*Beteiligungsgesetz für Europäische Genossenschaften*) of 2006 and (vii) the Act on Employee Codetermination in Cross-Border Mergers (*Gesetz über die Mitbestimmung der Arbeitnehmer bei einer grenzüberschreitenden Verschmelzung*) of 2006. The Codetermination Act of 1976 (see section 1 below) and the One-Third Participation Act (see section 2) have a considerable practical impact; around 650 companies are subject to the first and around 1,500 are subject to the second. The other laws affect relatively few companies that are engaged in mining or iron and steel manufacturing, have the legal form of European Company or (almost nonexistent) a European Cooperative Society, or that emerged from a cross-border merger (see II.4 below with respect to the SE Participation Act and II.5 below regarding the Act on Employee Codetermination in Cross-Border Mergers).

1. Codetermination on the basis of parity pursuant to the Codetermination Act of 1976

a) Companies covered

According to the Codetermination Act of 1976, a supervisory board must be set up, and half its members must be employees ('parity'), if the company

- has the legal form of a German publicly held corporation [*Aktiengesellschaft*] (AG), a partnership limited by shares [*Kommanditgesellschaft auf Aktien*] (KGaA), a limited liability company [*Gesellschaft mit beschränkter Haftung*] (GmbH) or cooperative [*Genossenschaft*] and
- normally employs more than 2,000 employees in Germany.[1]

Together, the requirements considerably narrow the group of companies potentially subject to codetermination. Thus, the listing in the Codetermination Act of 1976 of legal forms subject to codetermination is conclusive. Partnerships (*Personengesellschaften*) are not listed and are therefore not subject to codetermination. The same applies to foreign legal forms. Furthermore, the Codetermination Act of 1976 is limited to Germany: Employees who are employed on a permanent basis abroad (whether in a permanent establishment or a foreign subsidiary) are not included and do not count in the calculation of the number of employees. Also excluded from codetermination are companies that directly or predominantly serve political, religious, educational, charitable, scientific or artistic purposes (*Tendenzunternehmen*, e.g. magazine and book publishers) and religious groups.

The reason that **partnerships** are not subject to codetermination is that the partners are assigned the position of management by operation of law and are subject to personal liability regardless of negligence or fault. A limited partnership [*Kommanditgesellschaft*] (KG) in which solely natural persons take the position of general partner (*Komplementär*) thus remains free from the codetermination requirements. At companies with the legal form of a *Kapitalge-*

---

[1] Sec. 1(1) of the Codetermination Act of 1976.

sellschaft & Co. KG, the organizational and liability structure is more like that of a corporation (*Kapitalgesellschaft*), for which the Codetermination Act of 1976 includes a special attribution rule[2]: The employees of the KG are deemed the employees of the general partner, provided

- the general partner is a German AG, KGaA, GmbH or cooperative,
- the majority of the limited partners (based on shares or votes) also possess the majority of the shares or votes in the general partner and
- the general partner does not have any business of its own which normally has more than 500 employees.

This attribution rule does not in any way extend the scope of the Codetermination Act of 1976 to limited partnerships (KGs); rather, the employees of the KG are attributed to the general partner corporation (*Komplementär-Kapitalgesellschaft*) thus facilitating codetermination for the general partner. This attribution requires firstly that the general partner is a German corporation subject to codetermination, and secondly that there is sufficient corporate unity between the corporation and the KG. The latter is expressed in the requirements of identical majority shareholders (*Mehrheitsidentität*) and that the general partner has no large business of its own.

> **Example:** A foreign investor acquires the majority interest in a German KG and in the associated general partner GmbH (*Komplementär-GmbH*). The GmbH itself has no employees, but the KG has 2,500 employees in Germany.
>
> The general partner GmbH is subject to codetermination because its 2,500 employees are attributed to the KG. Consequently, a supervisory board subject to parity-based codetermination, i.e. having six shareholder representatives and six employee representatives, must be set up for the GmbH. To secure the influence of this supervisory board on the KG in addition, the GmbH may not be contractually excluded from the management of the KG.

b) Codetermination at the ultimate parent company

Codetermination should occur when important corporate decisions are made, thus (also), in groups, in the German company heading the group. This should apply even if the company heading the group is restricted, for example, to management and cross-sectional tasks and therefore itself has significantly fewer than 2,000 employees in Germany. According to the Codetermination Act of 1976[3], all employees in a subordinate group company are deemed employees of the company heading the group, provided this has the legal form of a German corporation. Consequently, a codetermined supervisory board may need to be set up in the German company heading the group, in which all German group employees are actively and passively eligible to vote.

---

2 Sec. 4(1) of the Codetermination Act of 1976.
3 Sec. 5(1) of the Codetermination Act of 1976.

Even if the company heading the group has its registered office abroad and thus is not subject to the German codetermination requirements, this alone does not yet prevent codetermination from being set up in a German intermediate holding company. This is conceivable if, firstly, the foreign company heading the group has granted a certain amount of independent leeway to the German intermediate holding company so that the intermediate holding company can exercise uniform management over subordinated group companies (the legal concept of a 'group within a group'). Secondly, even if the foreign company heading the group makes all important decisions itself and 'bypasses' the intermediate holding company, a supervisory board subject to parity-based codetermination may alternatively have to be set up in any case.[4] Attempts to avoid codetermination in the intermediate holding company, for example by entering into cross-border domination agreements directly between the foreign company heading the group and the German second-tier subsidiaries, have not proven effective in the past.

> **Example:** A foreign investor has an interest in a German GmbH & Co. KG with 1,800 employees and in a German GmbH with another 400 employees via an intermediate holding company with no employees, having the legal form of a German GmbH. A supervisory board subject to parity-based codetermination may need to be set up in this intermediate holding company because the intermediate holding company, to the extent that it has independent leeway in decision-making, could be viewed as the company heading a '(small German) group within a (larger international) group'. Alternatively, codetermination may have to be set up in it in any case because this is not possible with respect to the foreign company heading the group.

If the company heading the group has the legal form of a *Kapitalgesellschaft & Co. KG*, the employees of the general partner corporation may also be attributed to it, with the result that a codetermined supervisory board may have to be set up at the general partner corporation.

c) Formation of a supervisory board subject to parity-based codetermination

At companies subject to codetermination, a supervisory board must be formed, unless – as is the case for AGs, KGaAs and cooperatives – one is required already pursuant to the requirements of the specific legal form. This particularly concerns the German GmbH. The supervisory board is composed of six shareholder representatives and six employee representatives if the group has up to 10,000 employees in Germany, eight shareholder representatives and eight employee representatives if the number is up to 20,000, and ten shareholder representatives and ten employee representatives if it is more than 20,000.[5] The employee representatives must also include two or three external representatives from trade unions represented in the company.[6] The shareholder repre-

---

4 Sec. 5(3) of the Codetermination Act of 1976.
5 Sec. 7(1) of the Codetermination Act of 1976.
6 Sec. 7(2) of the Codetermination Act of 1976.

sentatives are elected by the shareholders' meeting or general meeting, or they are appointed by the shareholders entitled to so do as per the articles and memorandum of association. In contrast, the employee representatives are elected directly by the employees or by their elected delegates. The voting procedure is detailed in voting regulations.

d) Responsibilities of supervisory boards subject to parity-based codetermination

The Stock Corporation Act and the Codetermination Act of 1976 assign certain responsibilities to the supervisory board that may not be curtailed by the articles and memorandum of association. Deviations are specifically with respect to the constitution of a GmbH subject to codetermination, which does not have a mandatory supervisory board in its non-codetermined form:

- In the GmbH that is subject to codetermination, the supervisory board is **responsible for personnel decisions** regarding management.[7] This includes the right to appoint and dismiss members of management along with ancillary responsibility for concluding, amending and canceling the employment contracts of managing directors. The management must consist of at least two members, since a labor director must be appointed as a member of management having equal rights in every sense.[8] The minimum responsibility of the labor director is in the area of personnel and social matters of the employees of the company.

- An additional central task of the supervisory board is to **supervise the management**. The Codetermination Act of 1976[9] provides the supervisory board with certain tools for this, specifically (i) the right of inspection and examination, (ii) the right to call and attend a shareholders' meeting, (iii) the right and the obligation to approve a catalog of measures requiring consent and (iv) other rights to information. However, in the case of a GmbH, the supervision authority of the supervisory board is secondary to the responsibility of the shareholders' meeting for the control and supervision of the management, because the reservation of consent of the supervisory board may be overridden by the shareholders: If the supervisory board withholds its consent to a management measure, this can be replaced by the consent of the shareholders' meeting. Conflicts of authority between the shareholders' meeting and a mandatory supervisory board tend to be rare because the majority shareholder can regularly appoint the shareholder representatives and, in cases of conflict, the deciding vote falls to the **chair of the supervisory board** – who counts as one of the shareholder representatives.[10] The right of the shareholders to issue instructions to the managing directors, which is characteristic of the structure of the GmbH, also remains in GmbHs which are subject to codetermination.

---

7 Sec. 31 of the Codetermination Act of 1976.
8 Sec. 33 of the Codetermination Act of 1976.
9 Sec. 25 of the Codetermination Act of 1976.
10 Secs. 29(2), 27(2) of the Codetermination Act of 1976.

2. One-third codetermination pursuant to the One-Third Participation Act

a) Companies covered

According to the One-Third Participation Act a supervisory board is required to be formed in a company and one-third of it filled with employee representatives ('tripartite') if the company

- has the legal form of a German AG, KGaA, GmbH, cooperative or mutual insurance company and
- normally employs more than 500 employees in Germany.[11]

A codetermination right may further exist regarding AGs registered prior to 10 August 1994, provided they are not family-owned. Companies that directly or predominantly serve political, religious, educational, charitable, scientific or artistic purposes, and religious groups, are exempt from one-third codetermination.

Partnerships are not subject to one-third codetermination. The One-Third Participation Act, unlike the Codetermination Act of 1976, contains no attribution rules according to which the employees of a KG could possibly be attributed to the general partner corporation.

> **Example:** A GmbH & Co. KG with identical shareholders has no employees in the GmbH but 600 employees in the KG. The GmbH & Co. KG remains entirely free from codetermination requirements. If the KG were changed into the form of a GmbH, e.g. for tax reasons or because a foreign investor was more familiar with this legal form, the new GmbH would be subject to one-third codetermination.

b) Codetermination in the company heading the group

In groups, the employees of other companies in the group are not attributed to the controlling company for the purposes of determining whether the threshold of 500 employees has been exceeded, unless a corporate domination agreement exists with these group companies or (now rarely the case) they have been integrated into the controlling company under stock corporation law.[12] Thus, unlike under the Codetermination Act of 1976, the mere existence of a *de facto* group is insufficient for attribution. Rather, attribution may occur only within a group affiliated by contract (*Vertragskonzern*) or an integrated corporate group (*Eingliederungskonzern*).

> **Example:** A GmbH & Co. KG has 200 employees. A subsidiary GmbH, which is connected via a domination and profit and loss transfer agreement, has an additional 400 employees. It is being considered whether to change the form of the KG to a GmbH.

---

11 Sec. 1(1) of the One-Third Participation Act.
12 Sec. 2(2) of the One-Third Participation Act.

The GmbH resulting from the change of form would (unlike the previous KG) be subject to one-third codetermination, since the employees of the subsidiary company would be attributed to it and the threshold of 500 employees would be exceeded. This attribution can be avoided by terminating the domination agreement (alone); an isolated profit and loss transfer agreement does not lead to the attribution of group employees.

c) Formation of a supervisory board subject to one-third codetermination

A supervisory board is required to be formed in companies subject to codetermination. One-third of the supervisory board must be made up of employee representatives. If the supervisory board has only three or six members, the employee representatives must be employees of the company; in larger supervisory boards, trade union representatives may also be appointed. The employee representatives are always elected through direct vote, not through delegates.

d) Responsibilities of supervisory boards subject to one-third codetermination

The provisions of the Stock Corporation Act on the internal order, adoption of resolutions and responsibilities of the supervisory board are applicable with respect to AGs and KGaAs subject to one-third codetermination. In GmbHs subject to one-third codetermination, the supervisory board – unlike under the Codetermination Act of 1976 – has no personnel responsibilities. The One-Third Participation Act does not refer to the corresponding provisions of the Stock Corporation Act, with the result that the shareholders' meeting of the GmbH remains responsible for the appointment and dismissal of the managing directors. The supervisory board is thus merely a body charged with controlling and advising the managing directors *alongside* the shareholders. In this function, the supervisory board specifically has rights to information, inspection and examination and the option to call and attend shareholder meetings.

II. Strategies to Avoid Codetermination

The parity-based codetermination requirements in particular are frequently found by foreign investors, but also German owners of family companies, to be too broad. Points of criticism include the sheer size of the supervisory board with 12 to 20 members (which makes confidential consultations difficult), the presence of external trade union representatives and – untypically for GmbHs – the supervisory board's personnel responsibilities with respect to the management.

Strategies to avoid parity-based or one-third codetermination include:

- using partnerships, particularly the GmbH & Co. KG (see section 1 below);
- distributing the employees among multiple group companies (see section 2);
- using foreign legal forms (see section 3);

- using an SE (see section 4);
- freezing codetermination by way of a cross-border merger (see section 5);
- reducing the scope of codetermination through a KGaA (see section 6).

1. Using partnerships, particularly the *GmbH & Co. KG*

The GmbH & Co. KG is a KG in which a GmbH (or alternatively an AG) assumes the position of general partner. As a partnership, it is innately well-suited for avoiding the codetermination aimed at corporations. However, this applies without restriction only in the area of one-third codetermination. As soon as the applicable threshold for parity-based codetermination of 2,000 German group employees is exceeded, a supervisory board subject to codetermination on the basis of parity may need to be set up for the general partner GmbH, insofar as the employees of the KG and subordinate group companies are attributable to it (see I.1.a. above). This can, however, also be avoided by (i) changing from the GmbH & Co. KG to a KG in which only natural persons take the position of the personally liable shareholder, (ii) 'reallocating' the general partner GmbH or (iii) substituting the general partner GmbH with a foundation (*Stiftung*), SE or foreign legal form which is not subject to the Codetermination Act of 1976.

a) 'Reallocating' the general partner *GmbH*

Employees of a KG (and its subsidiaries) shall be attributed to the general partner only if both companies form a 'corporate unit' and coordinated decision-making occurs. For this, the majority of the limited partners must generally also possess the majority of the shares or votes in the general partner (identical majority). Furthermore, it should suffice if, instead of having an identical majority shareholding, the coordinated decision-making in the KG and general partner is legally secured through, for example, a trust agreement or a voting agreement. If the general partner is 'reallocated' in this way, so that not all the limited partners have an identical shareholding, but, for instance, the shares are held by a minority limited partner, there will be no identical majority. However, a certain risk remains that in such situations, an (unwritten) trust agreement will be assumed to exist between the minority limited partner and the other limited partners and the general partner GmbH could, as a result, be deemed subject to codetermination.[13]

b) *Stiftung & Co. KG*

In a *Stiftung & Co. KG*, a foundation with legal capacity assumes the position of general partner. As such, the foundation has no shareholders and is merely

---

13 See Higher Regional Court (*Oberlandesgericht*) of Celle, 30 Aug. 1979 – 9 Wx 8/78, Higher Regional Court for Civil Matters Decisions (*Oberlandesgericht Zivilsachen-Entscheidungen*) 1980, p.136.

geared towards the mission of the foundation. Permissible missions for a family-oriented general partner foundation include keeping the company a family company and securing reasonable provisions for the founder and his family. Nowadays, the legal form combination of a foundation and a KG is predominantly viewed as permissible. Since foundations, like KGs, are not among the legal forms subject to codetermination pursuant to the Codetermination Act of 1976 or the One-Third Participation Act, a Stiftung & Co. KG remains entirely free from the codetermination requirements.

c) SE & Co. *KG*

The European Company (*Societas Europaea*, SE) is not among the legal forms subject to codetermination pursuant to the Codetermination Act of 1976 or the One-Third Participation Act. Corporate codetermination is separate for an SE having its registered office in Germany and is conclusively governed by the provisions of the SE Participation Act, which implements the SE Directive.[14] The directly applicable SE Regulation views the SE as a legal form for large companies acting internationally, and therefore assumes that the future SE will have employees from the outset. It makes the formation of the SE generally dependent on negotiating with the employee representatives in advance regarding codetermination in the future SE (participation process) and also regularly on the conclusion of an agreement regarding the participation of the employees in the SE (participation agreement). Today it is recognized that a lack of employees is not an obstacle to the formation of an SE and thus an SE with no employees can also be formed.[15] A participation procedure must be conducted when an SE without employees is later 'activated' by starting to conduct business and by achieving a sufficient number of employees to conduct the participation procedure.[16] It has not yet been conclusively clarified whether this also applies if the SE itself remains without employees on a permanent basis, but is the general partner of a KG with employees. Some legal scholars have expressed the opinion, with good reasons, that an employee-free, codetermination-free SE remains free from the codetermination requirements if it becomes the general partner of a KG with more than 2,000 employees.

d) Foreign corporation & Co. *KG*

Since the codetermination law on which codetermination is based pertains solely and conclusively to German company (corporation) forms, foreign company forms are not subject to German corporate codetermination. According to the widespread prevailing opinion, this applies even if the *de facto* place of

---

14 Directive 2001/86/EC of 8 Oct. 2001, Official Journal of the European Communities No. L 294 p. 22; see Sec. 47(1) No. 1 of the SE Participation Act.
15 Higher Regional Court of Düsseldorf of 30 March 2009 – I-3 Wx 248/08, German Notary Journal (*Deutsche Notar-Zeitschrift*) 2009, p. 699.
16 Sec. 18(3) of the SE Participation Act by analogy.

management is Germany. Thus, a foreign corporation that takes the place of a German general partner GmbH is not subject to the codetermination requirements under German law.

Example: With respect to a Liechtenstein GmbH or AG, the highest courts have confirmed that it must be recognized as a foreign company, regardless of whether its place of management is Germany[17]. The same applies to companies from other EU/EEA states, notably Dutch B.V.s or British Ltd.s, which may also be the general partner of a German KG. A Liechtenstein GmbH has the advantage that its external appearance changes as little as possible; the Liechtenstein GmbH also has the legal form designation 'GmbH.' The German KG may continue to operate as 'GmbH & Co. KG.'

2. Distributing the employees to multiple group companies

German corporations should, in all events, avoid having one corporation employ more than 500 employees in Germany, thereby growing into the area of one-third codetermination. As long as fewer than 2,000 employees are employed in Germany in the group overall, codetermination can be avoided by suitably distributing the employees to several group companies (and by refraining from concluding any domination agreements between these group companies).

3. Using foreign legal forms

For the reasons specified in 1.d) above, foreign legal forms may also be used to avoid codetermination. Thus, foreign companies that wish to operate in Germany may refrain from establishing a German legal entity and may operate in Germany through a dependent branch. However, companies formed pursuant to the laws of another EU/EEA country must be recognized as a foreign legal form even if they operate predominantly or even exclusively in Germany. This is because the cross-border mobility of national company forms in the EU/EEA area is protected by the freedom of establishment. The European primary law guarantees this not only for natural persons, but also for companies formed pursuant to the legal provisions of an EU/EEA country and that have their place of incorporation or management in the EU/EEA area.[18] Consequently, the corporate structure of the foreign legal form will continue to be determined pursuant to foreign law. This corporate structure also includes corporate codetermination. A company from the EU/EEA area operating in Germany will thus be subject to corporate codetermination only if the national laws governing the company provide for this.

---

17 Federal Court of Justice (*Bundesgerichtshof*) of 19 Sept. 2005 – II ZR 372/03, Federal Court of Justice, Civil Matters (*Bundesgerichtshof/Zivilsachen*) vol. 164, p. 148.
18 Art. 49, 54 of the Treaty on the European Union.

4. Using SE structures

The European Company (SE) can be used to 'freeze' an existing level of codetermination – whether it is one-third codetermination or even freedom from codetermination. This is because the SE Directive and the SE Participation Act (see 1.c) above) aim to secure the rights acquired by the employee to participate in company decisions in the SE also. According to the 'before and after principle', the participation rights of the employees existing in the original company should, in principle, also exist in the SE. The configuration of the employee participation in the SE is negotiated between company management and the employees. These negotiations occur against the backdrop of statutory reference provisions which would take effect if the negotiations fail. These provide for an SE works council by operation of law, and for codetermination by operation of law, but only where the original company was subject to codetermination.[19] If codetermination by operation of law applies, then the prior highest level of codetermination will be maintained. Thus, if a German company with codetermination on the basis of parity is involved in the formation of an SE, codetermination on the basis of parity is provided also for the SE. In contrast, if the original companies are not subject to codetermination or are subject merely to one-third codetermination, this lower level of codetermination will be maintained, even if the SE later exceeds the thresholds of 500 or 2,000 employees in Germany.

> **Example:** Large companies use the SE in many cases to reduce the size of the supervisory board while maintaining the previously existing codetermination on the basis of parity. This is because the size requirements in the Codetermination Act of 1976 (see I.1.c) above) do not apply to SEs. Allianz SE and BASF SE used the SE formation to reduce their supervisory boards from 20 members to 12 members in each case.

5. Freezing codetermination through a cross-border merger

Whereas the timely formation of an SE can also permanently secure freedom from codetermination, an existing tripartite codetermination can be frozen only by way of a cross-border merger. Cross-border mergers of German corporations with other EU/EEA corporations can be carried out in Germany in a legally secure manner on the basis of the EU Merger Directive and the provisions of the Reorganization of Companies Act enacted to implement the EU Merger Directive[20]. The result of a cross-border merger is not a supranational legal form, but a company governed by national law. Under codetermination law, the country of establishment principle generally applies here. The company

---

19 Secs. 22 *et seqq.*, 34 *et seqq.* of the SE Participation Act.
20 Directive 2005/56/EC of 26 Oct. 2005, Official Journal of the European Communities L 310, p. 1; Secs. 122a *et seqq.* of the Reorganization of Companies Act.

resulting from the cross-border merger will thus be subject to the employee codetermination regulations, if any, which apply in the Member State in which this company has its registered office.[21]

Example: If a British Ltd. with no employees is merged into a German GmbH with 400 employees, who are to be kept, the German GmbH will continue to be subject to German codetermination law. If it later has more than 500 employees, it will become subject to one-third codetermination.

However, the country of establishment principle will be superimposed by a complex negotiation procedure assumed by the SE if a codetermined company is already involved in the merger.[22] If the negotiations fail, then, like in the case of the SE, a statutory reference provision will apply, which in most cases uses not the country of establishment principle, but the highest codetermination level of the companies involved ('before and after principle'). As a result, the cross-border merger is therefore solely suitable for freezing an existing one-third codetermination or – as in the case of the SE – for reducing the size of the supervisory board compared to the requirements of the Codetermination Act of 1976 in cases where codetermination on the basis of parity previously existed.

6. Reducing codetermination using a *KGaA*

The partnership limited by shares (KGaA) is a legal entity in which – like in a KG – at least one shareholder has unlimited liability towards the creditors of the company and – as in the case of an AG – the other shareholders are invested in the registered share capital, which is divided into shares, without being subject to personal liability. The KGaA is a legal form in between a KG and an AG; it is eligible for listing on the stock exchange and has a certain importance primarily for family-controlled companies and, for instance, soccer clubs seeking access to the capital market. The general partner position in the KGaA may also be assumed by a corporation.[23] As German corporations, KGaAs are subject to codetermination under the One-Third Participation Act and the Codetermination Act of 1976. However, codetermination in KGaAs is materially reduced, so the form of a *Kapitalgesellschaft & Co. KGaA* can certainly be an alternative to GmbHs and AGs fully subject to the codetermination requirements, as well as to codetermination-free foreign companies or companies with the legal form of *Foreign Corporation & Co. KGaA*. This is because the general partner corporation itself remains free of codetermination; the codetermination takes place instead in the supervisory board of the KGaA, and this has only limited rights.

---

21 Sec. 4 of the Act on the Codetermination of Employees in Cross-Border Mergers.
22 Sec. 5 of the Act on the Codetermination of Employees in Cross-Border Mergers.
23 Federal Court of Justice (*Bundesgerichtshof*) of 24 Feb. 1997 – II ZB 11/96, Federal Court of Justice, Civil Matters (*Bundesgerichtshof/Zivilsachen*) p. 134, p. 392.

Thus, unlike AGs, the supervisory board of a KGaA has no personnel authority with respect to the management (of the general partner); it may not issue reservations of consent and has no authority with respect to approving financial statements and internal rules of procedure. Finally, no labor director needs to be appointed for a KGaA. The form of a KGaA therefore clears away several points of criticism against codetermination from the perspective of foreign investors and family-controlled companies.

Dr. Michael Winter

Lawyer, Tax Advisor

Areas of Specialization
- Corporate law
- Advice for family-owned businesses
- Mergers & acquisitions and corporate reorganizations
- Cross-border mergers/SEs
- Codetermination law

Telephone (ext.) +49 228/95 94-199

Email: michael.winter@fgs.de

IV. Tax Crime

Voluntary Disclosure of Tax Evasion Under German Law

by Jörg Schauf

Contents

I. Introduction
II. The Person Filing the Disclosure
III. Addressee, Form and Content of the Voluntary Disclosure
   1. Form and Content of the Amended Tax Returns
   2. Addressee of the Voluntary Disclosure
IV. Validity Requirements
   1. Requirement of Completeness
      a) Completeness from a Chronological Perspective
      b) Completeness from a Substantive Perspective
      c) Insignificance of Minor Discrepancies
      d) Correction of Incorrect Preliminary Value-Added Tax Returns
   2. Subsequent Payment of Evaded Taxes
   3. No Grounds to Block Exemption from Punishment
      a) Infection Effect
      b) Notification of an Audit Order
      c) Notification of the Initiation of Criminal Proceedings
      d) Appearance of an Auditor
      e) Detection of an Offense
      f) Evasion Amount over EUR 50,000
V. Outlook

I. Introduction

Any person who has committed intentional tax evasion (Sec. 370 of the German General Tax Code – *Abgabenordnung*) will be exempted from punishment if he files a voluntary disclosure (*Selbstanzeige*) in accordance with Sec. 371 of the General Tax Code. In legal terms, this voluntary disclosure constitutes personal (i.e. limited to the specific person filing the voluntary disclosure) grounds for exemption from punishment (*persönlicher Strafaufhebungsgrund*). The criminal liability previously incurred is cleared with retroactive effect.

The legislative purpose and justification for voluntary disclosure is primarily to allow the tax authorities to tap into previously unknown sources of tax revenue. In addition, the tax evader is offered an incentive to return to tax compliance. In practice, voluntary disclosure is very important, not only in cases of concealed income from investments made by individuals, but in particular also in business entities that are required to declare extensive and legally complex facts and circumstances. Voluntary disclosure offers the officers of such entities the chance to be exempted from punishment by correcting the incorrect information and paying the back taxes.

In recent years, the requirements for the validity of voluntary disclosures – especially for business entities – have been tightened considerably, primarily through the more restrictive case law of the First Criminal Division of the Federal Court of Justice, which has had jurisdiction over appeals on questions of law in tax offense cases since 2008[1] and the German Act for Combatting Unreported Income (*Schwarzgeldbekämpfungsgesetz*) dated 28 April 2011, through which the wording of Sec. 371 of the General Tax Code was largely reformulated. Fueled by the German government's purchases of CDs containing bank data on German clients of foreign banks (a practice begun in 2010) and by the revelation of some voluntary disclosures made by well-known tax evaders, a political debate has been brewing for years about the controversial institution of voluntary disclosure. Opponents of voluntary disclosure steadfastly demand that it be abolished entirely. Complete abolition is unlikely to occur for the time being. Nevertheless, there are currently attempts underway to further tighten the requirements for the valid voluntary disclosure of tax evasion.

As in the past, it remains possible to be completely exempted from punishment for tax evasion by filing a voluntary disclosure, a peculiarity of German criminal law. Very few other countries in the world have comparable legislation or regulations.

II. The Person Filing the Disclosure

In principle, voluntary disclosure may be filed by any party to the crime, regardless of whether the person is a sole perpetrator or co-perpetrator, or an indirect perpetrator or participant (abettors, aiders, Secs. 2 and 27 of the German Criminal Code – *Strafgesetzbuch*). Since voluntary disclosure constitutes personal grounds for exemption from punishment, the statutory requirements must be personally fulfilled by the relevant party to the crime. There is no obligation, however, for the voluntary disclosure to be filed in person. It is merely necessary that it is based upon the intent of the party to the crime and was initiated by that person. The amended tax return may also be filed by a third party provided such third party was validly commissioned and authorized in advance. According to prevailing opinion – in any case where the commissioning party (principal) itself has not obtained any direct tax benefit or where the reduced taxes are later paid – it is not necessary for the commissioned party (agent) to outwardly indicate that it is filing the return on behalf of another (i.e. undisclosed agency).

With respect to legal entities, it will generally suffice for the voluntary disclosure to be filed by an agent or by a representative who is granted authority by law or under the bylaws. With respect to corporations, it will therefore suffice for the voluntary disclosure to be made by the responsible governing bodies (managers (*Geschäftsführer*) or management board). Such voluntary disclosure is also effective for the other governing bodies and employees, even if they are not expressly named in the restatement of income. Nonetheless, all parties

---

[1] Particularly Federal Court of Justice of 20 May 2010, 1 StR 577/09.

who were involved in the preparation and delivery of the tax return should file a 'notification of joinder' (*Anschlusserklärung*). Under this notification, they declare that they are aware of the voluntary disclosure for the corporation and that the disclosure should apply to them as well.

III. Addressee, Form and Content of the Voluntary Disclosure

1. Form and Content of the Amended Tax Returns

Sec. 371(1) of the General Tax Code requires that incorrect information be corrected, incomplete information be completed, or omitted information be provided. The voluntary disclosure must enable the tax administration to properly assess the tax without having to conduct any major investigations of its own. It is therefore mandatory that every voluntary disclosure contains corrected data.

In contrast, it is not necessary for the voluntary disclosure of tax evasion to be described as such. A voluntary disclosure may even be contained in a tax return filing. Voluntary disclosures filed by business entities often pertain to not one, but rather several types of tax (frequently, in addition to corporate income tax, also trade tax and value-added tax). Thus, it is not necessary for a voluntary disclosure to specify the type of tax to which it refers in order for it to be valid. Case law recognizes that a voluntary disclosure may, without any special indication, relate to various types of tax, i.e. all those which may be involved and for which sufficient details are provided. Accordingly, for a voluntary disclosure to be valid, it will suffice if the tax-relevant information, including the corrected figures (e.g. on revenue), is described precisely enough for the tax authorities to correctly assess the applicable taxes.

If the figures to be corrected cannot be produced in a timely manner due to the complexity of the situation, then as a first step, estimated figures may be communicated to the local tax office. Nevertheless, these should leave a sufficient margin for error so as not to jeopardize the validity of the voluntary disclosure. After evaluation of the relevant documents and accounting, the exact figures are then reported as a second step. This procedure is recommended if there is reason to believe that the detection of an offense is directly imminent. After an offense has been uncovered, a voluntary disclosure can no longer exempt the disclosing party from punishment (see D. III. 5 below for further details).

2. Addressee of the Voluntary Disclosure

The correct office to which a voluntary disclosure should be directed (the addressee) is every tax authority (Sec. 6(1) of the General Tax Code). Contrary to earlier opinion, this office does not have to be the locally responsible tax authority with jurisdiction over the subject-matter. Due the obligation to forward the matter to the responsible tax office in the given case (Sec. 111 of the General Tax Code), the taxpayer can assume, by virtue of reporting the tax evasion to one tax office, that the source of tax revenue has been disclosed 'to the tax authorities as a whole'. For cases in which the subsequently reported circumstances result in tax adjustments both at the level of the business entity and the partner/shareholder, this means that the complete disclosure of the circumstances only to the local tax office responsible for the entity's place of business will also constitute a valid voluntary disclosure of tax evasion for the necessary adjustments at the partner/shareholder level. Nonetheless, it is recommended in practice, as a precautionary measure, to inform all relevant tax authorities of the need for an adjustment when several tax authorities have jurisdiction (e.g. by forwarding a copy of the letter which was sent to the local tax office responsible for the place of business to the local tax office responsible for the partner's/shareholder's place of residence).

IV. Validity Requirements

When filing a voluntary disclosure, certain statutory requirements must be observed. Otherwise, the voluntary disclosure will not exempt the disclosing party from punishment. As already mentioned in the introduction, the legislative and regulatory environment has been tightened substantially in this respect recently.

1. Requirement of Completeness

A key aspect of the amendment to Sec. 371 of the General Tax Code pursuant to the Act on Combatting Unreported Income of 28 April 2011 was the statutory abolition of 'partial voluntary disclosure of tax evasion' (*Teilselbstanzeige*). The legislature thereby followed the decision rendered by the Federal Court of Justice on 20 May 2010[2], which had held that partial voluntary disclosure of tax evasion was no longer valid even under the old legislation. A valid voluntary disclosure now requires the taxpayer to fully correct all tax offenses which have not been time-barred. Consequently, what is required is a full confession specific to the type(s) of taxes involved. According to the amended version of Sec. 371(1) of the General Tax Code, voluntary disclosure thus refers to a 'system of adjustments' (*Berichtigungsverbund*) which can consist of several substantive offenses.

a) Completeness from a Chronological Perspective

From a chronological perspective, the voluntary disclosure must include all tax offenses which have not yet been time-barred. This limitation period for criminal prosecution must be distinguished from the tax assessment limitation period (Sec. 169 of the General Tax Code), which is irrelevant for determining completeness within the meaning of Sec. 371(1) of the General Tax Code. The limitation period for prosecuting simple tax evasion is five years (Sec. 78(3) no. 4 of the Criminal Code in conjunction with Sec. 369(2) of the General Tax Code). In particularly serious cases of tax evasion, the limitation period is extended to ten years (Sec. 376(1) of the General Tax Code). Particularly serious

---

2 Federal Court of Justice of 20 May 2010 – 1 StR 577/09.

tax evasion includes large-scale tax understatement (Sec. 370(3) sentence 2 no. 1 of the General Tax Code). According to the case law of the Federal Court of Justice, large-scale tax evasion regularly exists where the amount evaded is at least EUR 50,000 if the offender received unjustified payments from the tax authorities (e.g. input VAT refunds). If the offender conceals tax-relevant facts from the tax administration, then large-scale tax evasion is assumed from EUR 100,000. In larger entities, those thresholds are quickly exceeded, which generally results in the ten-year limitation period.

b) Completeness from a Substantive Perspective

From a substantive perspective, the completeness requirement refers to the type of tax reported in the given case. The separate 'types of taxes' (*Steuerarten*) within the meaning of Sec. 371(1) of the General Tax Code are, at any rate, personal income tax, corporate income tax, trade tax, value-added tax, etc. In this respect, a valid voluntary disclosure requires that all intentional inaccuracies be corrected during the period of possible criminal prosecution. In contrast, other thoughtless or even negligent inaccuracies do not have to be disclosed for a valid voluntary disclosure under Sec. 371 of the General Tax Code.

According to prevailing opinion, the wording of Sec. 371 of the General Tax Code should be limited so that the completeness requirement covers only the types of taxes owed by one and the same taxpayer. If a manager or member of the management board files a voluntary disclosure due to incorrect wage tax reports (*Lohnsteueranmeldungen*) in a corporation, then it is valid without him having to simultaneously correct intentional inaccuracies in his own personal income tax return during the relevant adjustment period. Wage tax is a special form of personal income tax collection. The taxpayer is not, however, the corporation or its governing bodies, but rather the employee (Sec. 38(2) sentence 1 of the German Income Tax Act (*Einkommensteuergesetz*)).

For personal income tax purposes, partnerships under German law are pass-through or transparent organizations, i.e. income is earned solely by the partners of the partnership; they are the taxpayers. Nonetheless, the income is determined firstly at the level of the partnership in a 'uniform and separate determination of tax bases' (*Gewinnfeststellungsbescheid* – Sec. 180(1) of the General Tax Code), which forms the basis for the assessment of personal income tax at the partner level. Until now, it is still an open question whether the adjustment of the determination of tax bases must be disclosed simultaneously with all other errors in the partners' personal income tax returns. If other inaccuracies in the partners' income tax returns also had to be adjusted when correcting the determination of tax bases, then a voluntary disclosure in the business area of partnerships would be virtually excluded. If all bases of taxation for all partners had to be included, then it would be very difficult to satisfy the completeness requirement – particularly in larger partnerships. In order to maintain the possibility of a voluntary disclosure among partnerships as well, the determination of tax bases for the purposes of Sec. 371 of the General Tax Code must be recognized as a separate 'type of tax'.

c) Insignificance of Minor Discrepancies

A voluntary disclosure is valid only if the evaded taxes are reported in the correct amount. If a voluntary disclosure is filed initially on the basis of an estimate, then a margin of error should always be added (upward deviations are harmless). According to the new legislation, minor discrepancies below the correct number will generally also not render the entire voluntary disclosure invalid. According to the case law of the Federal Court of Justice, however, a discrepancy having an effect of more than 5% of the understated amount within the meaning of Sec. 370(4) of the General Tax Code is not minor. Nevertheless, in the view of the Federal Court of Justice, a discrepancy which is below this threshold may also be considered significant based on an overall evaluation of the circumstances at the time of filing the voluntary disclosure, and is usually the case when discrepancies were deliberate.

So far, it is unclear whether the insignificance of a discrepancy has to be investigated in isolation based on the respective offense (i.e. for example, evasion or personal income tax 03) or in reference to the 'system of adjustments' (e.g. evasion of personal income taxes 01 to 05). In our opinion, it depends on an overall perspective. This has the advantage that after filing a voluntary disclosure, individual offenses can be 'offset' if the restatement of income turns out to be too low for individual years.

d) Correction of Incorrect Preliminary Value-Added Tax Returns

The completeness requirement is problematic for business entities when correcting intentionally incorrect or preliminary VAT returns filed late. If a preliminary VAT return is intentionally not filed in a timely manner, then such omission technically constitutes the complete evasion of VAT. Yet the late filing of a preliminary VAT return is considered a voluntary disclosure resulting in exemption from punishment. As a result, any preliminary return that is filed late must be complete and correct because otherwise it constitutes an invalid partial voluntary disclosure of tax evasion.

Additional difficulties arise for larger entities because, due to the large amount of VAT-relevant information, preliminary VAT returns frequently have to be adjusted several times. Since the responsible parties are at least aware when the first preliminary return is filed that it is incorrect and must be corrected, and yet approve of that situation, these parties are committing conditionally intentional tax evasion by filing a false preliminary return. A consistent application of the amended legislation should result in entities being denied the opportunity in future to correct their preliminary returns several times. Based on the complexity of preliminary VAT returns of large entities, this is neither proper nor practical and cannot have been the intention of the legislature. In our opinion, this drawback must be countered by a restrictive interpretation of this wording of the legislation.

2. Subsequent Payment of Evaded Taxes

Where taxes have already been understated or tax advantages have already been derived, an offender will be exempted from punishment only insofar as he pays the taxes which were evaded to his benefit within the reasonable period of time allowed to him for that purpose (Sec. 371(3) of the General Tax Code). As long as the taxes are not subsequently paid, he merely has a conditional right to be exempted from punishment. The person to whose benefit the taxes are evaded is the taxpayer himself. What applies in relation to taxes evaded for the benefit of corporations is uncertain. According to the – questionable – opinion held by the Federal Court of Justice, the manager of a *GmbH* (German privately held corporation) evades the corporate income tax of the *GmbH* to his own benefit because he can be held liable for this tax (Secs. 69 and 71 of the General Tax Code).

3. No Grounds to Block Exemption from Punishment

The validity of the voluntary disclosure also requires that no reasons exist to block exemption from punishment pursuant to Sec. 371(2) of the General Tax Code.

a) Infection Effect

As already suggested, the amended wording of Sec. 371(2) of the General Tax Code has considerably broadened the scope of the blocking effect. If the requirements for blocking exemption from punishment pursuant to Sec. 371(2) nos. 1 or 2 of the General Tax Code have been satisfied for only one of the offenses covered by the voluntary disclosure, then all tax offenses which have not been time-barred will be blocked for the relevant type of tax (known as the 'infection effect').

This broadening of the blocking effect becomes particularly apparent in terms of the blocking reason based on the notification of a tax audit order (under 2.). This notification of a special VAT audit for (only) two preliminary tax return periods will preclude a valid voluntary disclosure of VAT evasion even if intentionally incorrect statements were also made during the preliminary return periods to be audited. It is generally no longer possible to correct tax offenses which occurred outside the audit period. Instead, a voluntary disclosure pertaining only to those offenses not covered by the tax audit order would be incomplete, and thus constitute an invalid, partial voluntary disclosure of tax evasion. For entities which are subject to a follow-up tax audit, this has the result of effectively eliminating the prospect of filing a valid voluntary disclosure. A voluntary disclosure can of course be validly filed even after notification of the tax audit order if all offenses to be corrected occurred outside the audit period.

b) Notification of an Audit Order

The blocking effect takes effect as soon as the audit order has been notified (Sec. 371(2) no. 1(a) of the General Tax Code). A correction of intentional tax offenses is accordingly no longer possible following notification of the tax audit order. Nevertheless, the verbal notification of the audit, which is customary in practice, as well as the scheduling agreement, which is made in advance, will not, however, trigger the blocking effect because Sec. 196 of the General Tax Code prescribes notification in writing. In contrast, it has been unclear so far whether an implied notification (Sec. 122(2) no. 1 of the General Tax Code) will apply also in penal proceedings for tax offenses. The result would be that if a tax audit order, which is frequently sent by regular mail, is received prior to the expiration of the three-day fictitious period, then a voluntary disclosure would still be possible. This approach is, however, contrary to the intent of the legislature, which specifically wanted to prevent the correction of intentional tax offenses upon learning of an imminent tax audit. Thus, regardless of the form in which notification is served (formal delivery), for the purposes of Sec. 371(2) no. 1(a) of the General Tax Code, the actual receipt of the audit order should be applicable. Nevertheless, the onus for providing proof of service lies with the investigative authorities.

The substantive scope of the blocking effect is formally determined in accordance with the content of the tax audit order. Thus, the tax audit order causes a blocking effect only with respect to the types of taxes to which it refers. If, for example, a tax audit order is issued for the corporate income tax, trade tax and VAT owed by a *GmbH*, then the voluntary disclosure of understated personal income tax will remain possible for the shareholders. Due to the infection effect, however, the substantive scope of the blocking effect can exceed the tax assessment periods covered by tax audit order (see above).

Another issue is the question of whether, in the case of partnerships, a tax audit order which refers to the separate and uniform determination of the tax bases also has a blocking effect with respect to the personal income tax owed by the partners. According to an older decision of the Federal Court of Justice dating from 1988[3], such effect will not arise. On the other hand, it is questionable whether the Federal Court of Justice would make the same decision today. As the courts' interpretation of law on voluntary disclosure has become stricter, there is a chance that the Federal Court of Justice could now assume a blocking effect for the partners by virtue of factual connection.

Finally, the blocking effect requires a valid tax audit order. A void tax audit order has no legal effect from the outset. In contrast, the legality of the tax audit order is irrelevant, i.e. even an illegal tax audit order can trigger the blocking effect. The situation is different, in our opinion, if an illegal (but not void) tax audit order is challenged and is subsequently revoked by the tax authorities or the tax court, and a voluntary disclosure has been submitted in the interim. Systematically, the decision in an administrative or judicial appeal to revoke an

---

[3] Federal Court of Justice of 15. Jan. 1988 – 3 StR 465/87.

audit order is retroactive to the date of issuance. Accordingly, a successful challenge of the tax audit order would exclude the blocking effect.

With respect to the blocking reason of an ongoing tax audit, prevailing opinion is overwhelmingly that once the tax audit is concluded, a voluntary disclosure can be revived. Generally, a tax audit can be deemed concluded when the audit report is delivered (see Sec. 202(1) of the General Tax Code).

c) Notification of the Initiation of Criminal Proceedings

Voluntary disclosure is also blocked if the offender or his representative is notified of the initiation of criminal proceedings or proceedings for the imposition of administrative fines related to a tax offense (Sec. 371(2) no. 2(b) of the General Tax Code). Thus, the **initiation** of criminal proceedings by itself will not suffice. The notification must be valid, which first of all requires that it be directed to a specific person. Only that person will be barred from making a voluntary disclosure. Furthermore, the notification must be sufficiently precise. In any case, it must include the types of tax and the tax assessment period.

The scope of this blocking reason is as follows: A voluntary disclosure is valid based on the completeness requirement only if it covers all tax offenses (which have not yet been time-barred) of a specific type of tax. If criminal proceedings were initiated due to (only) one of the offenses specified in a voluntary disclosure, then the whole disclosure will be invalid. This represents a tightening of the legal framework compared to the legal situation prior to the 2011 Act on Combatting Unreported Income when, under the previous law, a voluntary disclosure was blocked only for the assessment periods covered in the criminal proceedings.

d) Appearance of an Auditor

Voluntary disclosure is excluded also if a tax official has already appeared to conduct a tax audit or investigate a tax crime or a tax offense (Sec. 371(2) no. 1(c) of the General Tax Code). A tax official has appeared for a tax audit or investigation if he arrives at the place at which the audit is to be performed (known as the 'doormat theory'). The enactment of the blocking reason based on the notification of a tax audit order (Sec. 371(2) no. 1(a) of the General Tax Code) has rendered significantly less important (in practice) the blocking reason based on the appearance of an auditor.

e) Detection of an Offense

Another blocking reason exists if one of the tax offenses were already fully or partially detected at the time of the correction, supplementation or subsequent furnishing of particulars and the offender were aware of this fact or should have expected this fact on duly considering the facts of the case (Sec. 371(2) no. 2 of the General Tax Code). The offense is detected if the objective facts establishing the elements of tax evasion and the facts from which intentional behavior can be concluded are known. For these purposes, it is sufficient if a conviction is likely based on the preliminary conclusion that an offense has been committed. Detection of the offense must be assumed at the latest when the information about a prospectively unknown source of income has been compared with the tax returns of the taxpayer, and the comparison showed that some sources of tax revenue were not specified or not fully specified. Nevertheless, under certain circumstances, detection of the offense can be assumed even before the information has been compared with the tax returns, particularly if, in criminological experience, the type of tax source detected is a significant indicator of the incompleteness of the particulars furnished in the tax return.

The offense does not have to be detected by the tax office. Public prosecution departments, the police or judges may also detect offenses. In this respect, it must be taken into account, however, that these persons generally have no knowledge of the contents of the tax files, so the outcome of the case cannot be evaluated until the case has been passed to the responsible tax office. Only where there is special evidence indicating undeclared income in connection with the source of tax revenue can detection of the offense be deemed already made at the time when the police, public prosecution department or judge learns thereof.

It will suffice if the authorities know about the tax evasion itself; the specific amount of the evaded tax is irrelevant. Detection of the offense also does not require knowledge of the offender's name. It will suffice if the offender can be identified based on the known facts of the case.

Upon detection of the offense, voluntary disclosure is excluded only if the offender knew of the offense or should have expected the offense upon duly considering the facts of the case. The courts tend to quickly assume that a suspect 'should have expected' detection of the offense. Nonetheless, it always depends on all the circumstances of the individual case and the individual judgment of the offender. Thus, in our opinion, in the case involving the press report about the tax authorities' purchase of a CD containing 1,000 files of 100,000 German bank clients and details about the banks at which the taxpayer has an offshore account (regardless of the question of detection), the taxpayer upon due consideration of the facts cannot be expected to conclude that his tax evasion has been detected.

f) Evasion Amount over EUR 50,000

Criminal prosecution will proceed if the understated tax or the unjustified tax advantage obtained for the individual himself or for another exceeds EUR 50,000 per offense (Sec. 371(2) no. 3 of the General Tax Code). Nevertheless, the offender will be exempted from punishment if he pays not only the tax evaded to his benefit, but an additional amount to the treasury (Sec. 398a of the General Tax Code) coming to 5% of the evaded tax. Thus, in these cases, the validity of the voluntary disclosure of tax evasion depends on the payment of the 5% surcharge. However, in this respect, the infection effect described above is not activated. The tax authorities have to consider any excess of the threshold amount separately for each offense. If the surcharge is not paid in a timely manner, then the voluntary disclosure will remain valid for offenses under the EUR 50,000 threshold.

Frequently, several persons are involved in evading the taxes owed by an entity. A strict interpretation of the statute's wording would mean that if there are several offenders, each offender would be subject to the obligation to pay the 5% surcharge. In this manner, significant amounts would frequently accrue in the case of entities. To make matters worse, the wording of Sec. 398a no. 2 of the General Tax Code does not limit the surcharge to the tax advantage directly gained by the offenders as a result of the offense. The legislature obviously did not consider this aspect. The constitutionality of the 5% surcharge can therefore be questioned. This could be countered, on the one hand, by limiting the obligation to pay the surcharge to offenders who were acting in their own self-interest and, on the other hand, by structuring the obligation to pay the surcharge as a joint and several debt (*Gesamtschuld*) when offenders act jointly. In our opinion, any payment made by one offender should also inure to the benefit of the others.

V. Outlook

We can expect to see a further tightening of the law on the voluntary disclosure of tax evasion. On 9 May 2014, the finance ministers of the federal states agreed on the basic points for tightening the rules on voluntary disclosure. On 24 September 2014 the Government has released their proposal for an Act amending the relevant provisions in the General Tax Code. These rules specifically include the following: The penalty surcharge (Sec. 398a of the General Tax Code) is to be increased significantly. In the future, if the amount evaded is higher than EUR 25,000 or in cases of particular serious tax evasion only offenders who pay a penalty surcharge of 10% will be exempted from punishment. If the amount evaded exceeds EUR 100,000, the surcharge will be 15%; it will be 20% if the amount exceeds EUR 1,000,000. In addition, the immediate payment of evasion interest of 6% p.a. will be an additional requirement for the valid voluntary disclosure. Furthermore, the voluntary disclosure will only be regarded as valid if the evaded taxes for the last ten years are corrected, regardless of whether the limitation period for criminal prosecution has ended yet. The effect of this will be an equivalent extension of the 'system of adjustments'. The amendments to the provisions on voluntary disclosure (Sec. 371 of the General Tax Code) will contain clarification for self-assessed taxes (in particular, VAT): A corrected or late (preliminary) tax return will be considered a – valid – partial voluntary disclosure. It is intended that the above-mentioned amendments will come into force on 1 Jan. 2015. Entities, above all, can expect to see an additional tightening of the rules on voluntary disclosure as a result of the planned reforms.

Dr. Jörg Schauf

Lawyer, Certified Tax Lawyer

Areas of Specialization

- Tax investigation and tax crime defense
- White-collar crime defense
- Voluntary disclosure of tax evasion
- Search and seizure
- Preventive advice in connection with audits
- Compliance & risk management

Telephone (ext.) +49 228/95 94-672
Email: joerg.schauf@fgs.de

Changed Criminal Tax Law Framework

by Karsten Randt

Contents

I. Introduction
II. Legal Development
III. The Statutory Preconditions for Tax Evasion
   1. Tax Reduction and Unjustified Tax Advantage Including Nonrecognition of Fiscal Benefits (*Kompensationsverbot*)
   2. Acts Through Which Tax Evasion is Committed Including Duty to Disclose Differing Legal Position
   3. Violation of Tax Notification Obligations Including the Correction Obligation Pursuant to Sec. 153 of the General Tax Code
   4. Subjective Component of Tax Evasion: Intent
   5. Legal Consequences of Especially Serious Tax Evasion in Particular (Sec. 370(3) of the General Tax Code)
IV. Conclusion

I. Introduction

Governments and the public have a significant interest in receiving taxes in full and on time. Without that tax revenue, the federal, state, and municipal governments would not be able to fulfill sufficiently the public duties incumbent upon them.[1] Since comprehensive fiscal controls are hardly possible at a time when the assessment of taxes is a mass business, taxpayers are regularly tempted to not fulfill their fiscal duties.

Even though the resulting tax losses on an individual level are only marginal compared to Germany's overall tax revenue, the violation of these duties by numerous taxpayers adds up to annual tax losses in the billions from an economic perspective. In 2012 alone, an additional EUR 3.1 billion in (real) taxes was assessed as the result of tax investigation audits.[2] Since that result applies only to a very limited number of taxpayers and only to the cases discovered, the actual amount of taxes lost can hardly be estimated. According to a study conducted in 2012, the tax lost by Germany due to evasion is estimated at 1.1% of gross national product from 1999 to 2010, i.e. approximately USD 27.5 billion for 2010.[3]

As a consequence, both counter-steering measures on the part of the legislature and a change in investigation practice have become apparent over the last few years. This has entailed more severe punishment in the form of imprisonment

---

[1] FGJ/*Joecks*, Steuerstrafrecht, 7th edition, introduction, marginal no. 9.
[2] Federal Finance Ministry monthly report of 21 Oct. 2013.
[3] *Buehn/Schneider*, Size and Development of Tax Evasion in 38 OECD countries, available on the website of the Johannes Kepler University at <http://www.econ.jku.at/members/Schneider/files/publications/2012/TaxEvasion_buehn.pdf>.

without suspension and a crackdown on conduct potentially coming under the scope of criminal law. The rule of thumb is that imprisonment without suspension can always be expected where tax evasion exceeds EUR 1 million.

Within this changed framework, the greatest difficulty now in practice is how to act with the right degree of moderation. Not every tax return that is partially incorrect or incomplete was filed with intent. Specifically in complex corporate structures, it is naturally impossible to avoid clerical errors due to the mass of data. In international cases and an even more difficult legal starting position, organizational interlinking and coordination also play an essential role in the fulfillment of fiscal obligations.

Errors that occurred in this context were rarely investigated under criminal law in the past. Today, however, the exception has become the rule.

Even though no traditional corporate criminal law has (yet) been introduced in Germany, there are ways under the law of administrative offenses also to sanction organizational misconduct by imposing fines or disallowing corresponding economic benefits. These provisions have emerged from the shadows and are taken into account alongside the authorities' evaluation of the facts of any given case.

Accordingly, the risk of prosecution under criminal tax law and/or the law of administrative offenses already arises in corporate tax law whenever tax returns require correction. This may prove to be the case if objections are discovered during tax audits (which regularly occurs) if corrected returns are filed by a business entity because certain errors were noted by the entity itself, but also when the legal classification of the facts is not clear. This clearly means that the question of criminal liability may in the end depend on whether the relevant intentional conduct is assumed. Unlike in the case of ordinary criminal law, forensic evidence is not available. Accordingly, it has to be established whether it can be derived from the circumstances surrounding the taxpayer's conduct connected with the tax return whether he merely made a clerical error, did this in a grossly negligent manner, or was knowingly aiming at tax evasion, or whether he considered such tax evasion to be possible and accepted it. These circumstances also make tax crime defense more difficult and should, in order to specifically avoid these dangerous waters, make businesses strive to achieve continuous improvements in their organizational structure so as to rule out or reduce potential errors.

II. Legal Development

The tendency of some taxpayers not to fulfill their fiscal obligations has a long tradition. It goes hand in hand with the question of fiscal justice, and the tension between just and excessive taxation. The enforcement of the respective tax claims is not only subject to 'simplified' provisions of administrative law, but also protected by provisions of criminal law.

Criminal customs law, for example, which was governed uniformly by Art. 3 of the Treaty between the North-German Federation, Bavaria, Württemberg,

Baden, and Hesse 1867, contained the crime of *Defraudation* (Sec. 135 of the Union Customs Act), which dealt with the evasion of import duties.[4] During the following decades, including after 1871/72, however, the development of criminal tax law and administrative law was characterized by state-specific rules, which contained tax laws against intentional or knowing tax evasion.[5] Only the German Code of Criminal Procedure (*Strafprozessordnung*) of 1 Feb. 1877, which became effective on 1 Oct. 1877, reflected renewed efforts to codify criminal tax law uniformly by introducing the part on 'proceedings in the case of violations of provisions on the collection of public dues and levies' (Secs. 459 to 469 of the Code of Criminal Procedure).[6] Substantive criminal tax law was reformed in the third part of the *Reich* Tax Code (*Reichsabgabenordnung*) of 13 Dec. 1919 in Secs. 355 to 384 of the *Reich* Tax Code 1919. Even though Sec. 359 of the *Reich* Tax Code 1919 determined the characteristics of tax evasion and insofar introduced a general provision on intentional tax reduction,[7] the provision continued to refer 'to the individual laws' in terms of the main sanctions, whereby the opportunity was missed to fully abandon legislation by individual states. After several further legal reforms, which dealt in particular with the threat of punishment and made the state-specific rules obsolete, the statutory preconditions for tax evasion were not reformed until the German General Tax Code (*Abgabenordnung*) of 1977 entered into force in (essentially) today's version (Sec. 370 of the General Tax Code).[8] After its most recent adjustment by Art. 12 of the German Implementation Act on the Tax Recovery Directive (*Beitreibungsrichtlinie-Umsetzungsgesetz*[9]), Sec. 370 of the General Tax Code now states:

Sec. 370 Tax Evasion

(1) A penalty of up to five years' imprisonment or a monetary fine shall be imposed on whoever

1. *provides the revenue authorities or other authorities with incorrect or incomplete information concerning matters that are relevant for taxation,*

2. *fails to inform the revenue authorities of facts that are relevant for taxation when obliged to do so, or*

3. *fails to use revenue stamps or revenue stamping machines when obliged to do so*

   and as a result reduces taxes or derives unwarranted tax advantages for himself or for another person.

(2) The attempt is punishable.

---

4 Federal Law Gazette, 1867, p. 81, Reichstagsprotokolle 1867, annex no. 5.
5 cf. in this regard comprehensively FGJ/*Joecks*, introduction marginal nos. 31-35.
6 *Reich* Law Gazette, 1877, p. 253.
7 *Reich* Law Gazette, 1919, p. 1993.
8 Federal Law Gazette Part I, 1976, p. 613.
9 Federal Law Gazette Part I, 2011, p. 2592.

(3) In particularly severe cases, a penalty of between six months and ten years' imprisonment shall be imposed. A case shall generally be deemed to be particularly severe where the perpetrator

1. deliberately reduces taxes on a large scale or derives unwarranted tax advantages,

[...]

(4) Taxes shall be deemed to have been understated in particular where they are not assessed at all, in full or in time; [...] The preconditions of sentences 1 and 2 shall also be fulfilled where the tax to which the act relates could have been reduced for other reasons or the tax advantage could have been claimed for other reasons.

[...]

III. The Statutory Preconditions for Tax Evasion

The wording of the statutory preconditions for tax evasion already hints at several aspects of criminal law. Sec. 370(1) of the General Tax Code, for example, is structured as a blanket provision according to prevailing opinion.[10] This means that even though the provision contains a threat of punishment, (most of) the statutory preconditions for the punishable conduct in question are described in the provisions of the individual tax laws and the General Tax Code.[11] This necessary link to the tax provisions has raised several questions from the perspective of criminal law, e.g. on the application of the determinateness principle set out in Art. 103(2) of the German Constitution (*Grundgesetz*) in light of the specification for fulfilling the statutory preconditions through Federal Tax Court case law or on the question of the application of the milder law within the meaning of Sec. 2(3) of the German Criminal Code (*Strafgesetzbuch*) in the case of tax reforms.[12] Furthermore, questions arise as to the criminal law implications of the continued application of a tax provision that was found to be unconstitutional[13] and the authorities' ability to prosecute if the interpretation of a relevant tax law question has changed after tax evasion was committed.[14]

These numerous discourses, some of them involving legal theory, in light of particular aspects of criminal law are of rather a general nature and are only marginally relevant in practice, if at all. Practical problems arise, however, from the outcome of the offense in the form of the tax reduction and unwar-

---

10 Federal Constitutional Court of 16 June 2011 – 2 BvR 542/09, wistra 2011, p. 458; Federal Court of Justice of 28 Jan. 1987 – 3 StR 373/86, wistra 1987, p. 139; Klein/ Jäger, Abgabenordnung, Sec. 370 marginal no. 5 with further references.
11 SSW/*Satzger*, Sec. 1 marginal no. 53.
12 *Rolletschke*, DStZ 2000, p. 211.
13 Federal Court of Justice of 7 Nov. 2001 – 5 StR 395/01, wistra 2002, p. 64; Klein/Jäger, Sec. 370 marginal no. 6.
14 Federal Court of Justice of 9 Dec. 1966 – 4 StR 119/66, NJW 1967, p. 116; Federal Court of Justice of 17 July 1986 – 4 StR 543/85, NJW 1986, p. 2650; OLG Köln of 4 Dec. 1992 – 2 Ws 236/92, wistra 1994, p. 272.

ranted tax advantage that are specified in Sec. 370(4) of the General Tax Code and the punishable actions described in Sec. 370(1) nos. 1 to 3 thereof.

1. Tax Reduction and Unjustified Tax Advantage Including Nonrecognition of Fiscal Benefits (*Kompensationsverbot*)

Section 370(1) of the General Tax Code presupposes a tax reduction or unjustified tax advantage. In particular, taxes are reduced pursuant to Sec. 370(4) sentence 1 of the General Tax Code if they are not assessed at all, in their full amount, or in time. However, taxes do not include incidental tax payments within the meaning of Sec. 3(3) of the General Tax Code such as interest (Secs. 233 *et seq.* of the General Tax Code), default or late payment surcharges (Secs. 152 and 240 of the General Tax Code).

From the perspective of value-added tax (VAT) law, it must be noted that the tax owed for VAT stated without justification pursuant to Sec. 14c(2) of the German VAT Act (formerly Sec. 14(3) of the VAT Act 1999) qualifies as tax for the purposes of Sec. 370(1) and (4) sentence 1, 1st half-sentence of the General Tax Code since it is treated as tax under procedural law and must be declared in an advance VAT return (Sec. 16(2) sentence 4, and Sec. 18(4b) of the VAT Act). If the tax owed on this basis is not remitted, tax evasion may therefore arise.

In criminal tax proceedings, it is generally not possible to argue as a defense that, based on the application of the tax provisions as interpreted by the tax administration, no tax reduction has occurred or no unjustified tax advantage has been obtained because reasons for a reduction subsequently became relevant for tax purposes. These reasons must be disregarded, as laid down in Sec. 370(4) sentence 3 of the General Tax Code. This provision was introduced by a previous legislature against the background that the criminal court should not carry out a comprehensive new fiscal evaluation.[15] According to established case law, an exemption applies only in those cases where true statements also lead directly to tax advantages with a direct and close economic link to false statements.[16] Case law was developed extensively for individual cases. The nonrecognition of expenses covers e.g. accruals for claims for damages or previously unclaimed input VAT deductions[17], but not profits carried forward (Sec. 10d(2) of the German Income Tax Act – *Einkommensteuergesetz*)[18] or operating expenses[19] with a close economic link to the reduction.

---

15 Federal Court of Justice of 3 June 1954 – 3 StR 302/53; MüKo-StGB/*Schmitz/Wulf*, Sec. 370 marginal no. 144.
16 Federal Court of Justice of 5 Feb. 2004 – 5 StR 420/03, wistra 2004, 147; Federal Court of Justice of 26 June 1984 – 5 StR 322/84, wistra 1984, p. 183, each with further references.
17 Federal Court of Justice of 24 Oct. 1990 – 3 StR 16/90, wistra 1991, p. 107; OLG Düsseldorf of 24 Nov. 1987 – 2 Ss 203/87 – 93/87 III, wistra 1988, p. 118.
18 Now Federal Court of Justice of 2 Nov. 2010 – 1 StR 544/09, NStZ 2011, p. 294; Tax Court Nds. V. 11 June 2012 – 11 K 257/10, PStR 2010, p. 210.
19 Federal Court of Justice of 20 July 1988 – 3 StR 583/87, wistra 1988, 356; Federal Court of Justice of 31 Jan. 1978 – 5 StR 458/77, GA 1978, p. 307.

2. Acts Through Which Tax Evasion is Committed Including Duty to Disclose Differing Legal Position

According to Sec. 370(1) nos. 1 and 2 of the General Tax Code, criminal sanctions apply to whoever provides the tax authorities or (other authorities) with incorrect or incomplete information as to facts that are relevant for taxation or fails to inform the tax authorities of facts that are relevant for taxation when obliged to do so. The 'facts that are relevant for taxation' as well as the (fiscal) duties constitute the connecting factors that trigger the application of these tax law provisions. Furthermore, whoever fails to use revenue stamps or revenue stamping machines when obliged to do so, is also punished (Sec. 370(1) no. 3 of the General Tax Code).

When filing tax returns in the officially provided form (Sec. 150(1) of the General Tax Code), from which tax-relevant facts can be derived, the taxpayer regularly faces the problem that evaluations of tax law and the establishment of the facts are so interdependent that the taxpayer's legal evaluation determines the scope and content of the facts communicated.[20] The tax-relevant facts that are last communicated are therefore usually the result of a comprehensive evaluation of tax law (or should be at least).

Until the end of the 1990s, this problem did not arise in criminal tax law from a practical perspective. On the contrary, fiscally disputed issues were not addressed so that the interpretation of the relevant tax provisions could be discussed during a tax audit – if these evaluations became apparent to the auditor – and, if necessary, adjustments could be made.

In a decision rendered by the German Federal Court of Justice on 10 Nov. 1999[21], the court addressed the problem of having to disclose legal views within the meaning of Sec. 90(1) sentence 2 of the General Tax Code in connection with filing returns and found that the taxpayer was allowed to hold 'openly or covertly an incorrect legal view to his own benefit'. The tax-relevant facts on which the legal view is based, however, have to be stated correctly and completely in order to enable the tax office to assess the tax correctly if the taxpayer takes a differing legal view. The result of this decision was that the disclosure obligation was based on the tax authorities' doctrine of the 'typified recipient's horizon'. According to this, the taxpayer has to state information in a way that the tax authorities receiving such may typically understand his tax return.[22] If the interpretation or subsumption by the taxpayer deviates from case law, the guidance of the tax authorities or regular administrative practice, and if this deviation is not evident for the public official processing the tax return, it has to be disclosed.[23]

---

20 *Rolletschke*, Steuerstrafrecht, 4th edition, marginal no. 21.
21 Federal Court of Justice of 10 Nov. 1999 – 5 StR 221/99, NStZ 2000, p. 203.
22 Tipke/Lang/*Seer*, Sec. 23 marginal no. 24; differing opinion FGJ/*Joecks*, Sec. 370 marginal no. 128.
23 Federal Court of Justice of 23 Feb. 2000 – 5 StR 570/99, NStZ 2000, p. 320.

In practice, the tax structure of a business deviating from the view held by the tax authorities contains the risk, at least since the decisions taken at the turn of the last century, that such a structure is considered to be in violation of Sec. 90(1) sentence 2 of the General Tax Code and – if the further preconditions set out in Sec. 370(1) of the General Tax Code are fulfilled – that it will be classified as tax evasion by the decision-maker in the business entity. When tax returns are prepared, the principle of the fiscal freedom to structure (in some cases probably even creativity in structuring) has to yield to the principle of precaution considering criminal law.

3. Violation of Tax Notification Obligations Including the Correction Obligation Pursuant to Sec. 153 of the General Tax Code

Section 370(1) no. 2 of the General Tax Code, which stipulates that failure to notify the tax authorities of the facts that are relevant for taxation is conduct which fulfills the statutory preconditions for tax evasion, covers in particular the violation of tax notification obligations, to the extent that these are related to fiscally relevant facts.

Tax notification obligations can be found in numerous individual tax laws. From a business perspective, these obligations include e.g. the obligation to file tax returns (Sec. 149 of the General Tax Code in conjunction with the individual tax laws), the obligation to file corporate income tax returns (Sec. 31(1) sentence 1 of the German Corporate Income Tax Act – *Körperschaftsteuergesetz* – in conjunction with Sec. 25 of the German Income Tax Act) and trade tax returns (Sec. 14a of the German Trade Tax Act – *Gewerbesteuergesetz*), or the obligation to file wage tax returns (Sec. 41a of the Income Tax Act). The obligation to cooperate during a tax audit (Sec. 200 of the General Tax Code) and the VAT-related obligations to file advance returns and annual tax returns (Sec. 18 of the German VAT Act – *Umsatzsteuergesetz*) are also among the original fiscal obligations incumbent upon business entities.

In practice, the correction obligation pursuant to Sec. 153 of the General Tax Code in particular is gaining importance from a criminal tax law perspective. According to this provision, the taxpayer or person acting for the former (Secs. 34 and 35 of the General Tax Code) is required to correct previously filed returns if it is recognized after filing, but prior to the expiration of the assessment deadline (*Festsetzungsfrist*), that the returns were incomplete or incorrect and that this could or did lead to a reduction of taxes. It must also be observed here from a corporate law perspective that the correction obligation pursuant to Sec. 153 of the General Tax Code not only applies to the taxpayer or persons acting for the former, but that the obligation is also incumbent upon the universal successor. If it should be discovered, e.g. during a corporate reorganization (Sec. 2 of the German Reorganization Act – *Umwandlungsgesetz*), that the legal predecessor has filed incorrect or incomplete tax returns, the universal successor is required to make the correction.

The problem regularly arises for the obligated party that a correction also leads to the uncovering of tax evasion (or tax reduction within the meaning of Sec. 378 or the General Tax Code) aimed at a previous incomplete return at the same time, so that the correction may insofar give rise to self-disclosure.

The criminal tax law risk in connection with the correction obligation pursuant to Sec. 153 of the General Tax Code only played a minor role prior to the decision rendered by the Federal Court of Justice on 20 May 2010[24] and the reform of self-disclosure of unreported or understated income pursuant to Sec. 371(1) of the General Tax Code through Art. 2 of the German Act to Combat Tax Evasion and Money Laundering (*Schwarzgeldbekämpfungsgesetz*) of 28 April 2011.[25] This was because the correction regularly contained effective partial self-disclosure through which exemption from punishment could be obtained. However, the situation has now changed significantly through the comprehensive self-disclosure that is now required. The basic problem of self-disclosure or any question as to the duty to incriminate oneself thus arises again, at least for cases of tax evasion.

Another practical problem in connection with the correction obligation pursuant to Sec. 153 of the General Tax Code arises when determining the point in time at which self-disclosure or correction is still permitted. A tax reduction must be reported without undue delay (within the meaning of Sec. 121(1) of the German Civil Code – *Bürgerliches Gesetzbuch*) after the incorrectness or incompleteness has been discovered subsequently (Sec. 153(1) sentence 1 of the General Tax Code), so that a decision to file a report or correction should not be protracted for too long to avoid exposure to the risk of tax evasion. At the same time, however, a comprehensive self-incriminating report must be coordinated. A business entity and its decision-makers are thus under pressure in two ways.

From an entrepreneurial perspective, violation of the correction obligation pursuant to Sec. 153 of the General Tax Code also entails the risk that has emerged increasingly over the last few years: The tax evasion that is attributed to the decision-makers may directly or indirectly lead to a company-related fine (Sec. 30 of the German Administrative Offenses Act – *Ordnungswidrigkeitsgesetz*) via the allegation of violating supervision obligations (Sec. 130 of the Administrative Offenses Act), which may amount to up to EUR 10 million since 30 June 2013[26] if the related offense were committed intentionally. The current cases from the financial and banking industry show that the investigating authorities hardly have any reservations anymore about prosecuting and imposing very large fines.[27]

---

24 Federal Court of Justice of 20 May 2010 – 1 StR 577/09, NJW 2010, p. 2146.
25 Federal Law Gazette Part I, 2011, p. 676.
26 Federal Law Gazette Part I, 2013, p. 1738.
27 cf. e.g. the high corporate monetary fine against the private bank Julius Bär, Credit Suisse, or UBS, all of which had to pay a high multi-million amount.

4. Subjective Component of Tax Evasion: Intent

Section 370(1) of the General Tax Code also requires intentional conduct. Even though this cannot be derived directly from the statutory preconditions for tax evasion, it corresponds to the principle of criminal law which determines in Sec. 15 of the Code of Criminal Procedure that only intentional conduct may be punished, unless the law explicitly stipulates that negligent conduct is also punishable. The principles of criminal law also apply to criminal tax law via the referring provision of Sec. 369(2) of the General Tax Code.

The general understanding of intent is the will to fulfill all the objective statutory preconditions.[28] Due to the particular features of the interaction between criminal tax law and tax law provisions, intent connected with tax evasion according to the 'tax claim theory' require that the offender know about the breach of the existing tax claim in terms of its merits and the amount, and want to reduce it in spite of this knowledge (contingent intent).[29] It is deemed sufficient here if the offender recognizes, based on a 'parallel layman's' evaluation of the situation, that the tax claim exists and that he breaches it in a harmful manner. Certain knowledge of the tax claim is not required.[30] Where members of the tax-advising profession and businesses with employees or decision-makers that are well-versed in tax matters are involved, it is often difficult from a practical perspective to deny contingent intent considering the low level of requirements.

5. Legal Consequences of Especially Serious Tax Evasion in Particular (Sec. 370(3) of the General Tax Code)

Tax evasion pursuant to Sec. 370(1) of the General Tax Code as a misdemeanor within the meaning of Sec. 12(2) of the Criminal Code may result in a prison sentence of up to five years or a monetary fine. In particularly serious cases of tax evasion, the prison sentence ranges from six months to ten years pursuant to Sec. 370(3) sentence 1 of the General Tax Code.

Commercial and organized tax evasion could incur imprisonment from one year to ten years under Sec. 370a of the General Tax Code until it was repealed on 21 Dec. 2007. This form of tax evasion therefore constituted a felony within the meaning of Sec. 12(1) of the Criminal Code, but it was deleted because of constitutional law concerns and included as no. 5 in Sec. 370(3) of the General Tax Code.

At the same time, the law dated 21 Dec. 2007 deleted the criterion of 'gross selfishness' also due to concerns as to the determinateness defined in Sec.

---

28 SS/*Sternberg-Lieben/Schuster*, Sec. 15 marginal no. 9 with further references.
29 Federal Court of Justice of 8 Sept. 2011 - 1 StR 38/11, wistra 2011, p. 465; Federal Court of Justice of 13 Nov. 1953 – 5 StR 342/53, NJW 1954, p. 241; Federal Court of Justice of 29 April 2008 – VIII R 28/07, wistra 2009, p. 76; FGJ/*Joecks*, Sec. 370 marginal no. 235.
30 Federal Court of Justice of 8 Sept. 2011 *loc.cit.*; Federal Court of Justice of 16 Dec. 2009 – 1 StR 391/09, HFR 2010, p. 866.

370(3) no. 1 of the General Tax Code so that serious tax evasion pursuant to no. 1 now regularly exists where the offender has reduced taxes or obtained unjustified tax advantages on a large scale.

Section 370(3) of the General Tax Code simply provides for the determination of criminal sanctions. The provision is structured using the rule-example technique, which means that Sec. 370(3) of the General Tax Code merely shifts the sentencing framework if a serious case of tax evasion has to be assumed. It can be derived from the examples in nos. 1 to 5 when this is the case. The determinateness principle is not violated if a court also assumes an unknown case of serious tax evasion outside the cases stipulated. The reason for this is that, as the determinateness principle set out in Art. 103(2) of the Constitution is expressed through the prohibition of analogies and retroactive effects, it only applies to the statutory preconditions, but not to the sentencing framework in connection with the legal consequence of imprisonment.[31]

The most important exemplary rule is Sec. 370(3) no. 1 of the General Tax Code, which has already been mentioned; it refers to large-scale tax reduction. Until the reform, the large scale was reached only in the case of a reduction in the seven-digit range (at the time still DM).[32] In addition, the requirement of gross selfishness existed and was fulfilled by the offender if his conduct was based on the pursuit of his own advantage in a particularly objectionable manner.[33] After the reform, it is now assumed against the decision of the Federal Court of Justice of 2 Dec. 2008 that in respect to the question of the large scale in Sec. 370(3) no. 1 of the General Tax Code, reference to the large scale within the meaning of Sec. 263(3) no. 2 of the Criminal Code has to be made and that it must therefore already be assumed when the evaded amount exceeds EUR 50,000.00.[34] This threshold value applies if the tax authorities have suffered a true financial loss, whether through refunds or credits or through offsets against other tax liabilities if the offender claims tax reductions without justification.[35] A threshold value of EUR 100,000.00 does apply to endangering tax revenues, however.[36]

Over the last few years, it can be noted that specifically sentencing has become harsher. Even though some proceedings are still discontinued subject to conditions pursuant to Sec. 153a of the Code of Criminal Procedure, the imposition of both prison sentences and monetary fines has increased nevertheless.[37] In

---

31 cf. *Eisele*, JA 2006, p. 309.
32 FGJ/*Joecks*, Sec. 370 marginal no. 270 with further references.
33 Prevailing opinion cf. *Fischer*, Sec. 264 marginal no. 46 with further references.
34 Federal Court of Justice of 2 Dec. 2008 – 1 StR 416/08, NJW 2009, p. 528.
35 Federal Court of Justice of 15 Dec. 2011 – 1 StR 579/11, wistra 2012, p. 191.
36 Federal Court of Justice of 12 July 2011 – 1 StR 81/11, wistra 2011, p. 396; Federal Court of Justice of 15 Dec. 2011 *loc.cit.*; the continued application of two threshold values after the Act to Combat Tax Evasion and Money Laundering became effective on 28 April 2011 is disputed in scholarly literature; no Federal Tax Court case law exists to date.
37 Federal Finance Ministry monthly report of 21 Oct. 2013.

addition, since the Federal Court of Justice decision of 7 Feb. 2012[38], the imposition of a monetary fine for evaded amounts in the six-digit range is deemed to be appropriate only if important mitigating reasons exist; if evaded amounts reach the million-euro range, a suspended prison sentence may be considered only if particularly important mitigating reasons exist.

From a practical perspective, the statutory limitation provisions must also be observed, especially in the case of particularly serious tax evasion. While 'ordinary' tax evasion defined in Sec. 370(1) of the General Tax Code regularly becomes statute-barred after five years (Sec. 78(3) no. 4 of the Criminal Code), the differing provision of Sec. 376 of the General Tax Code has applied to particularly serious tax evasion within the meaning of Sec. 370(3) of the General Tax Code since the Annual Tax Act 2009. As a consequence, criminal offenses that were not already statute-barred on 25 Dec. 2008 (when the revision came into effect), become statute-barred only after ten years. From a tax perspective, this does not have any effect on the limitation period for assessment due to the parallel between the statutory limitation for prosecution and assessment (Sec. 169(2) sentence 2 of the General Tax Code). Something else may apply only if a legal successor's own tax evasion creates a suspending effect via Sec. 171(7) of the General Tax Code.

IV. Conclusion

Over the last few years and decades, criminal tax law has become noticeably harsher both *de facto* and *de jure*, particularly in the context of tax evasion. Due to the continuously changing legal situation and the much stricter application of tax provisions, taking into account the harsher case law of criminal and tax courts, businesses are coming increasingly under pressure to work in a fiscally transparent manner in order to avoid, in particular, criminal tax law consequences. Furthermore, sanctioning business entities for the misconduct of their employees and decision-makers via Secs. 30 and 130 of the Administrative Offenses Act has increased significantly over the last few years, in particular, and will continue to do so. In order to avoid fiscal and criminal consequences, it will therefore be increasingly necessary to advise businesses to establish a comprehensive 'criminal compliance' system within the organization. A relaxation of the legal situation may hardly be expected considering the continuing efforts to reform measures to combat tax evasion.

---

38 Federal Court of Justice of 7 Feb. 2012 – 1 StR 525/11, NStZ 2012, p. 1458.

Dr. Karsten Randt

Lawyer, Certified Tax Lawyer, Certified Criminal Lawyer
Areas of Specialization
- Tax investigation and tax crime defense
- White-collar crime defense
- Voluntary disclosure of tax evasion
- Search and seizure
- Internal investigations in order to identify tax risks

Telephone (ext.) +49 228/95 94-671
Email: karsten.randt@fgs.de

V. Public Auditing, Accounting and Business Valuation

A Comparison of Valuation Principles in Germany and Internationally

by Torsten Kohl

Contents

I. Starting Point
II. Comparison of Selected Issues
 1. Standard of Value
 2. Valuation Methods
 3. Determining Future Cash Flows
 4. Capitalization Rate
 5. Interim Conclusion
III. Specific Characteristics
IV. Final Assessment

I. Starting Point

Business valuation is currently a widely discussed subject. The issues concerned are comparable in Germany and internationally. Although we find similarities in the structure of these issues, the defining elements vary between Germany and the international context.

In Germany, business valuation principles are largely dominated by the certified public auditors (*Wirtschaftsprüfer*) and are codified in Standard S 1, Principles for the Performance of Business Valuations (2008 version), issued by the Institute of Public Auditors in Germany (*Institut der Wirtschaftsprüfer*, abbreviated as IDW). This standard reflects both prevailing practice and prevailing opinion. Applying it therefore offers a relatively high level of assurance that the principles and recommendations it contains will be acknowledged and accepted for business, tax, and accounting valuations. The standard represents a binding basic framework for certified public auditors in Germany. The EB1 standard issued by the Austrian Chamber of Public Accountants (*Kammer der Wirtschaftstreuhänder*) and the standards issued by the American Institute of Certified Public Accountants have a similar status.[1]

In addition to these examples, other accounting and auditing organizations as well as various professional associations of valuers and appraisers or similar organizations act as standard-setters.[2] However, the authoritativeness of their standards differs in that there are both binding professional standards and mere

---

1 cf. *Hayn/Laas*, Grundlagen der Unternehmensbewertung, in: *Peemöller* (ed.), Praxishandbuch der Unternehmensbewertung, 4th ed. 2009, p. 133 and p. 147.
2 Examples include the American Society of Appraisers, the Canadian Institute of Chartered Business Valuators, the European Group of Valuers' Association, the Institute of Business Appraisers and the International Valuation Standards Council.

recommendations for their members. As well as these professional bodies, financial analyst associations such as the Society of Investment Professionals in Germany (*Deutsche Vereinigung für Finanzanalyse und Asset Management*) and the Chartered Financial Analyst Institute issue pronouncements. Unlike those mentioned above, these pronouncements do not have any binding effect.

In addition to these organizations and standard-setters, other rules relating to external financial reporting must be complied with that also require the business in question to be valued. A number of the International Financial Reporting Standards (IFRSs), for example, require measurement at fair value. Particularly relevant examples are IAS 36 and IFRS 13, the overarching standard governing measurement. Finally, the professional pronouncements and the standards for external financial reporting are rounded off by a range of interpretive guidance issued by a number of organizations. In Germany, for example, the Institute of Public Auditors issues 'Accounting Principles' (*Stellungnahmen zur Rechnungslegung*), which the members may ignore only if their non-application is justified. In the field of business valuations, this refers in particular to Accounting Principle No. 10 issued by the Auditing and Accounting Board (*Hauptfachausschuss*), which deals with certain valuation principles to be applied in German GAAP financial statements.

A common feature of these standards is that they address similar issues, in particular the definition of the relevant standard of value, the treatment of individual valuation methods, and details of how future cash flows and the capitalization rate are derived. Lower-level issues relating to the derivation of future cash flows include the treatment of management factors, synergy effects, and taxation at the level of the owners. When defining the capitalization rate, distinctions are made in particular in the way risk premiums are applied to reflect a lack of marketability or size.[3] The valuation of small and medium-sized enterprises (SMEs) is an area with its own specific issues; these are covered in Germany by a separate Practice Statement issued by the Institute of Public Auditors.[4]

In light of this diversity of domestic and international pronouncements, the question that arises frequently from an international perspective is whether there is such a thing as an authoritative approach to valuations in Germany. To enable an assessment of the subjects outlined above, the national rules governing these complex issues will be presented in the following and compared with the international standards and other pronouncements.

---

3 cf. Hayn/Laas, Grundlagen der Unternehmensbewertung, in: Peemöller (ed.), Praxishandbuch der Unternehmensbewertung, 4th ed. 2009, p. 145 *et seq.*
4 The Practice Statement addressing the valuation of small and medium-sized enterprises is 'Fragen und Antworten: Zur praktischen Anwendung der Grundsätze zur Durchführung von Unternehmensbewertungen nach IDW S 1 i.d.F. 2008'.

II. Comparison of Selected Issues

1. Standard of Value

A primary feature of the principles underlying the IDW S 1 standard is the distinction between the 'objectified' and the 'subjective' business value. The objectified business value represents an 'intersubjectively verifiable' value of future earnings from the perspective of an owner with standardized characteristics. It contrasts with the 'subjective value for decision-making purposes', which is based on individually tailored assumptions related to the specific engagement instead of the heavily standardized assumptions used for the objectified value. As a rule, the objectified business value is used when a valuer acts as a neutral expert. By contrast, if the valuer is acting as a consultant, he will determine a subjective value for decision-making purposes, or an arbitration value if he is acting as a mediator in arbitration proceedings.[5] The different functions that a valuer may have are an expression of what is referred to as 'functional business valuation'.[6]

Comparable products of this functional theory of business valuation can be found not only in Germany, but also in certain international standards in which different standards of value or functions are defined depending on the purpose of the valuation. For this reason, the insights and effects of the functional theory of business valuation are not limited to the national context. However, it must be acknowledged that there is no discussion of standards of value in most of the international valuation standards above and beyond the definition of fair value. Rather, international standards of value frequently tend to define rules for determining an objective market value that are as concrete as possible, in the form of a fair value, fair market value, or investment value.

The background to these different rules can be explained by the prominence of the IDW S 1 standard. As a general principle, this standard is designed to be applied to all business valuations performed by certified public auditors in Germany. By contrast, many international pronouncements relate to financial accounting scenarios in which the concrete standard of value is already defined in the underlying accounting standards.

To establish comparability between national and international pronouncements, it is therefore necessary to focus in specific instances on the specific function in which the valuer has acted in accordance with German standards.

2. Valuation Methods

In principle, IDW S 1 requires 'German income approach' methods (*kapitalwertorientierte Verfahren*) to be used for valuation. The dividend discount and discounted cash flow methods are mentioned as equivalent models.[7] They will have identical outcomes, provided the underlying assumptions are the same. A

---

5 cf. IDW S 1 (2008 version), para. 12.
6 cf. *Matschke/Brösel*, Unternehmensbewertung, 4th ed. 2013, p. 23.
7 cf. IDW S 1 (2008 version), para. 7.

characteristic feature of German income approach methods is that the value of the business is derived from forecasted future cash flows that are discounted using the capitalization rate. In addition, the determination of a liquidation value is mentioned for cases in which a business is being liquidated.[8] Other valuation principles such as the net asset method are therefore not relevant on their own.[9] These German income approach methods are supplemented by models that use multiples. Under IDW S 1, these can be used to assess the plausibility of the German income approach methods.[10] The same applies if quoted market prices are available. In such cases, and especially if valuations are required under stock corporation law, special rules must be observed under which the quoted market price must be used as the minimum value.[11]

This approach results in certain differences compared with the 'international' valuation methods, which often use a market approach in addition to the international income approach. Whereas the international income approach also discounts future earnings or cash flows, the market approach uses transaction prices or quoted market prices of similar businesses or other assets. In the international context, these approaches are considered to be equivalent to the German income approach.[12] Within the context of the IDW S 1 principles, on the other hand, they may be used only for assessing plausibility.[13]

The advantages often associated with such multiple-based methods are that they are simple to use and the methods themselves and their results can be communicated easily.[14] However, the quality of these methods depends heavily on the comparability and robustness of the selected peer-group businesses. As a rule, businesses are highly individual entities, and the business to be valued cannot normally be compared with its peers without any limitations. If it is possible to identify and isolate differences between the business to be valued and its peers in the course of a valuation, those differences will have to be adjusted by factoring in premiums or discounts if a multiple-based approach is used. However, this would eliminate the advantage of a simple valuation method.

In terms of how multiple-based methods are structured, most of the standards recommend earnings-based multiples, whereby a distinction is made between profit, EBIT, EBITDA, and cash flow multiples.[15]

---

8 cf. IDW S 1 (2008 version), para. 5.
9 cf. IDW S 1 (2008 version), para. 6.
10 cf. IDW S 1 (2008 version), para. 143.
11 cf. IDW S 1 (2008 version), para. 16.
12 Examples include the American Institute of Certified Public Accountants' Statement of Standards for Valuation Services No. 1 and the American Society of Appraisers' Business Valuation Standards, which regard these approaches as equivalent.
13 cf. IDW S 1 (2008 version), para. 143.
14 cf. *Ernst/Schneider/Thielen*, *Unternehmensbewertungen erstellen und verstehen*, 4th ed. 2010, p. 10 *et seq.*
15 Examples include SFAS No. 157 Fair Value Measurements issued by the Financial Accounting Standards Board and Practice Standard No. 110 issued by the Canadian Institute of Chartered Business Valuators.

If the income approach is used as a common basis for internationally customary valuations, a number of other subareas become apparent that are governed by different requirements. In the first instance, this relates to the definition and structure of future cash flows and the measurement of the capitalization rate.

3. Determining Future Cash Flows

Income approach methods and approaches based on the value of future earnings both revolve around the process of deriving future cash flows. For valuations in compliance with IDW S 1, this generally means using forecasts prepared by the business, the plausibility of which is assessed by the valuer. The period modeled in the forecasts is termed the 'detailed planning phase', during which the future cash flows of the business are projected on the basis of the business plan, taking into account the planned investments and distributions. IDW S 1 does not specify any particular timeframe for this detailed planning phase, although periods of between three and five years are mainly encountered in practice. As a rule, this detailed planning phase will be followed by a 'perpetuity', the amount of which is of considerable importance for the value determined for the business. To calculate it, the valuer must estimate the sustainable cash flows that can be generated by the business in a state of equilibrium.

This approach does not differ fundamentally from comparable international standards, which mainly also recommend using a two-phase model. The first phase uses the detailed planning period and the business's detailed plans, after which the sustainable cash flows are derived.[16] There are some differences in the recommendation on how to derive the sustainable cash flows. Certain standards also suggest using multiple-based methods to derive the residual value.

However, the specific assumptions used to derive the cash flows are more important. IDW S 1, for example, contains certain requirements on how to account for management factors as well as the current business strategy and business plans.[17] For example, if the valuer is calculating an objectified business value, only the cash flows that will result from continuing the business on the basis of the unchanged business strategy and the business's financial options may be used.[18] A key feature of these assumptions is that the present management will continue to be part of the business to be valued. Management formulates and implements the business strategy. The standardized approach for this objectified value therefore uses this current business strategy. Further-reaching subjective features or business-specific structuring options may be applied only when determining the subjective business value.[19]

---

16 Canadian Institute of Chartered Business Valuators Practice Standard No. 110, which requires the use of a detailed planning phase of — as a rule — three to five years, as well as of a discounted residual value, is one example of the international application of the two-phase model.
17 cf. IDW S 1 (2008 version), para. 38 *et seqq*.
18 cf. IDW S 1 (2008 version), para. 39.
19 cf. IDW S 1 (2008 version), para. 56.

The same applies to the definition of the existing or transferable earnings power. Objectified business valuations can be based only on the existing earnings power at the valuation date and the existing earnings drivers. Potential future measures that have not yet been initiated or other measures that are not documented in the business strategy may not be used when determining objectified business values.[20] The background to this requirement is the desire not to factor any business-specific ideas about future measures into standardized valuations. For this reason, IDW S 1 imposes stiff requirements regarding the implementation of future planned measures. One of them is that they must already have been initiated by the valuation date and that they must be documented in the business strategy.[21] Merely vague ideas do not qualify for inclusion in any objectified business value. One indication that the measures are sufficiently concrete is that they have been approved by the supervisory board and are reflected in the business plans that have also been approved by the supervisory board.

By applying these standardized requirements, IDW S 1 in some cases goes beyond what is required by comparable international standards, which contain little in the way of guidance and requirements about the extent to which management factors or future investments should be incorporated when deriving future cash flows.[22]

This is also the case with how synergy effects are addressed. Synergy effects are those effects that cannot be achieved by the business by itself, but only in combination with other businesses. In Germany, these issues are discussed in detail both in IDW S 1 and in court rulings. The rulings have been incorporated into the approach adopted in IDW S 1, which makes a distinction between 'real' and 'pseudo' synergy effects. 'Pseudo' synergy effects are effects that can also be achieved without the measures underlying the valuation or that can be achieved in the case of a large number of buyers or other businesses.[23] By contrast, 'real' synergy effects are those that can only be achieved in the case of a small number of specific businesses.[24] In the course of a subjective business valuation relating to a transaction, it is clear that the buyer will decide the maximum price that it is willing to pay by taking into account both 'real' and 'pseudo' synergy effects. For an objectified business valuation, however, the distinction between these two types of synergy effects is of particular importance. 'Pseudo' synergy effects must also be taken into account in objectified business valuations provided that the related measures have already been initiated or documented. One example of 'pseudo' synergy effects involves loss carry-forwards, whose value increases the faster they are used. One synergy effect may be that of increasing potential earnings, and thus the speed at which loss carry-forwards can be utilized. As a rule, this sort of scenario will apply to a large number of businesses. However, 'real' synergy effects that can only be achieved with a

---

20 cf. IDW S 1 (2008 version), para. 23 and para. 32.
21 ibid.
22 cf. *Berger/Knoll*, BewP 4/2009 p. 5 *et seq.*
23 cf. IDW S 1 (2008 version), para. 34.
24 cf. IDW S 1 (2008 version), para. 50 *et seq.*

single buyer may not be taken into account in the course of standardized business valuations pursuant to IDW S 1. This corresponds to current court rulings relating to company and civil law cases.

Another feature of the German standard is that it addresses potential tax effects at the level of the owners. In the course of objectified business valuations, the standardized approach is to apply the personal income tax position of the owners.[25] This is reflected both in the derivation of the cash flows in the numerator and in the derivation of the capitalization rate. The latter is an expression of 'tax equivalence', in which the numerator and the denominator must be determined using standardized methods. International standards do not distinguish in the same way between the personal taxes of the owners and the business taxes. In fact, some standards actually reject the notion that personal income taxes should be taken into account.

However, it should be noted that even IDW S 1 permits the explicit consideration of personal taxes in the case of certain situations in connection with valuation scenarios related to stock corporation law. This approach is termed 'direct standardization'.[26] IDW S 1 also permits 'indirect standardization', meaning that the effects of the personal income taxes of the owners are not explicitly factored into the calculation of the capitalization rate or the cash flows. Rather, it is assumed that the net cash flows from the business to be valued are subject to a level of personal taxation that is similar to that of the cash flows from an alternative investment. When deriving corresponding capital market data, such effects are therefore expected to be implicitly contained in the capital market data used for the valuation.[27] As a rule, this 'indirect standardization' approach corresponds to the approach adopted in the international standards.[28]

4. Capitalization Rate

Along with the cash flows, the capitalization rate (also referred to in IDW S 1 as the 'discount rate') is the second component used in business valuations. The concept of the capitalization rate is largely identical in the national and the international standards. The standards that address these issues regard the cost of capital as compensation for an alternative investment in equities. Equally, they uniformly define it as a combination of the components 'risk-free rate' and 'risk premium'. Some standards also offer a uniform definition of the growth discount. To determine the risk premium, most of the standards use the capital asset pricing model (CAPM), in which the market risk premium is derived from long-term returns obtainable on the capital markets.[29]

---

25 cf. IDW S 1 (2008 version), para. 28 and para. 43 *et seqq.*
26 cf. IDW S 1 (2008 version), para. 45.
27 cf. IDW S 1 (2008 version), para. 93.
28 cf. *Berger/Knoll*, BewP 4/2009 p. 9.
29 cf. *Berger/Knoll*, BewP 4/2009 p. 7.

IDW S 1 also requires the CAPM to be used, but there is a difference in its application: If the personal tax rates of the owners have to be considered as part of the 'indirect standardization' approach described above, the 'tax CAPM' must be used to ensure tax equivalence. The tax CAPM considers the effects of personal taxation when deriving the market risk premium.[30]

5. Interim Conclusion

We find many similarities and common features in the way that the standards in Germany and internationally approach the valuation of a business. One major difference, though, is that IDW S 1 emphasizes that the reason behind the valuation drives the way it is structured ('functional business valuation'). One consequence of this approach is the definition of an 'objectified business value' that valuers are supposed to draw on when they act as neutral experts. This objectified business value is based on a range of standardized assumptions, for example regarding the applicable business strategy, the need for specific details with respect to future investments, and the perspective of the owners.

In addition to these standardized assumptions, one difference in substance is the hierarchy of income approach methods and multiple-based methods. Whereas IDW S 1 uses only multiples to assess plausibility, these are often treated as equivalent to income approach methods in the international context.

III. Specific Characteristics

A number of specific characteristics become evident when special aspects in the form of minority discounts, control premiums, and marketability discounts are analyzed.

The concept of the 'control premium' or 'minority discount' addresses how the existing value of a business is attributed to the individual ownership interests. This reflects the opportunities for influencing a business that are governed by statutory requirements and that increase as certain ownership interest thresholds are exceeded.

When ownership interests are valued, the objectified business value is generally based on the extent to which individual ownership interests share in the cash flows. For this reason, the objectified value of an ownership interest corresponds to its proportionate interest in the value of the business. This principle applies irrespective of the size of the ownership interest[31] and therefore leaves no room for possible minority discounts or control premiums. Beyond this standardized approach, however, it may be appropriate to take into account the specific characteristics attributable to the ownership interest to reflect opportunities for owners to exercise influence or restrictions on their ability to do so.

---

30 cf. IDW S 1 (2008 version), para. 92.
31 cf. IDW S 1 (2008 version) para. 13.

As a rule, international standards contain similar provisions that recommend the application of such premiums or discounts.[32]

An analysis of marketability aspects produces a similar picture. This refers to potential discounts to reflect the relative absence of marketability. To take account of the fact that a business being valued is less marketable than a more liquid form of equity, international standards commonly expect appropriate risk premiums to be applied to the capitalization rate ('marketability risk premium' or 'marketability discount').[33]

By contrast, applying a general risk premium to the capitalization rate is not permitted in an objectified valuation.[34] The same applies to transaction costs triggered by a change in owners.[35]

Finally, international standards also frequently allow the option of applying a 'size risk premium' (or 'size discount').[36] This represents an increase in the risk premium to reflect the size of the business. IDW S 1 does not permit the application of such a risk premium in an objectified business valuation. Rather, it addresses the issue of the transferability of earnings power in the case of SMEs. If an SME has only a small number of earnings drivers that are consumed over time and are heavily dependent on its owner or owners, its earnings power is only partly transferable. For valuation purposes, therefore, the current earnings power may not be converted into a perpetuity without adjustment. It may even be appropriate to reduce such an earnings power to zero over a short period for valuation purposes. For this reason, both national and international standards address the specific characteristics of the size of a business, although there are differences in the way they do so. While the international standards generally apply risk premiums to the capitalization rate, IDW S 1 adjusts the cash flows.

IV. Final Assessment

Alongside many common features, a number of special characteristics have been identified and addressed. For simplification purposes, these can be grouped into two categories. On the one hand, there is a discussion as to whether certain matters should actually be taken into account. In this context, IDW S 1 specifies a range of standardized assumptions that are designed to achieve a high level of objectivity. However, such standardized assumptions apply predominantly to the

---

32 For example, these premiums and discounts are contained in the Uniform *Standards of Professional Appraisal Practice* standards issued by the Appraisal Foundation, the *National Association of Certified Valuators and Analysts' Professional Standards*, and the Internal Revenue Service's Business Valuation Guidelines.
33 cf. Hayn/Laas, *Grundlagen der Unternehmensbewertung*, in: Peemöller (ed.), *Praxishandbuch der Unternehmensbewertung*, 4th ed. 2009, p. 147.
34 cf. *Fragen und Antworten: Zur praktischen Anwendung der Grundsätze zur Durchführung von Unternehmensbewertungen nach IDW S 1 i.d.F. 2008*, para. 5.1.
35 cf. *Fragen und Antworten: Zur praktischen Anwendung der Grundsätze zur Durchführung von Unternehmensbewertungen nach IDW S 1 i.d.F. 2008*, para. 5.3.
36 cf. Hayn/Laas, *Grundlagen der Unternehmensbewertung*, in: Peemöller (ed.), *Praxishandbuch der Unternehmensbewertung*, 4th ed. 2009, p. 147.

concept of the objectified business value. An important factor in obtaining a meaningful comparison in individual cases is therefore an assessment of the reason for the valuation. Together with the standardized assumptions, the question arises as to how certain effects should be taken into account. In the case of some issues, there are common features between all standards in a number of areas (for example in how the specific features of SMEs should be reflected). By contrast, there are significant differences in the concrete approach adopted by different standards, which in turn underscores that a standalone comparison of individual components can lead to the wrong conclusions being drawn.

Dr. Torsten Kohl

Public Auditor, Tax Advisor

Areas of Specialization

- Business valuation
- Purchase price allocation and impairment tests according to International Accounting Standards
- Advice on M&A transactions
- Fairness opinions
- Expert opinions within arbitration proceedings

Telephone (ext.) +49 228/95 94-201

Email: torsten.kohl@fgs.de

Financial Statements: Disclosure Requirements and Ways of Avoiding Them

by Marc Schmidt

Contents

I. Introduction
II. Classification of Entities
   1. Microcorporations
   2. Small Corporations
   3. Medium-sized Corporations
   4. Large Corporations
III. Scope of Documents to be Published
   1. Large corporations
   2. Simplified preparation and publication rules for medium-sized corporations
   3. Simplified preparation and publication rules for small corporations
   4. Simplified preparation and publication rules for microcorporations
   5. Preparation and publication exemptions for companies that fall under the Disclosure Act
IV. Format and Content of Published Information
   1. Basic principles
   2. Exercising publication exemptions
V. Timing of publication
VI. Avoiding Publication Requirements through Inclusion in Consolidated Financial Statements
   1. Exemption from the requirement to prepare/publish consolidated financial statements
   2. Exemption for corporations from the requirement to publish single-entity financial statements in accordance with Sec. 264(3) of the Commercial Code
   3. Exemption for commercial partnerships from the requirement to publish single-entity financial statements in accordance with Sec. 264b of the Commercial Code
VII. Sanctions in the Event of Failure to Comply with the Publication Requirements

I. Introduction

In Germany, the requirement to disclose financial statements and the scope of documents that have to be published are driven largely by the legal form and size of the entity.

Under German commercial law, the following legal forms are generally required to publish or otherwise disclose their financial statements in the Federal Gazette (*Bundesanzeiger*):

- corporations (AG, GmbH, KGaA);
- commercial partnerships without a natural person as a general partner (e.g. GmbH & Co. KG, GmbH & Co. OHG with a corporation as a general partner);
- banks and financial services institutions;
- pension funds;
- insurers;

- registered cooperatives;
- branches of certain foreign corporations, e.g. UK/Irish limited companies (Sec. 325a of the Commercial Code (*Handelsgesetzbuch*)),
- all legal forms (e.g. sole traders or civil law partnerships) that are required by Sec. 1 of the Disclosure Act (*Publizitätsgesetz*) to publish their financial statements. These are companies whose total assets exceed EUR 65,000,000, whose sales exceed EUR 130,000,000, and that employ on average more than 5,000 employees at the balance sheet date and the two following balance sheet dates, whereby at least two of these three criteria must be satisfied.

The scope of the documents that have to be published depends on the size of the entity. For publication purposes, size is generally determined by sales, total assets, and the number of employees.

Especially small and medium-sized enterprises (SMEs) are often highly critical of the financial statement disclosure requirements. They expect that disclosure of their company's profitability in particular will adversely affect their customer and supplier relationships, so finding ways of avoiding the requirements to publish their single-entity financial statements is an important issue in Germany.

The following article starts by describing the scope of the publication requirements currently in force in Germany, as well as the sanctions that may be imposed in the event of noncompliance, before addressing the options available for avoiding publication of single-entity financial statements.

II. Classification of Entities

The scope of the documents that have to be published is linked to the size of the entities. The following subclassifications of the size criteria are relevant in this context for corporations and for commercial partnerships without a natural person as a general partner:

1. Microcorporations

Microcorporations are corporations whose total assets at the balance sheet date do not exceed EUR 350,000 or whose sales are not more than EUR 700,000, and that do not employ on average more than ten employees during the year. Microcorporations may not exceed two of the three criteria on two successive balance sheet dates.

2. Small Corporations

Small corporations are corporations whose total assets at the balance sheet date do not exceed EUR 4,840,000 or whose sales are not more than EUR 9,680,000, and that do not employ on average more than 50 employees during the year. Small corporations may not exceed two of the three criteria on two successive balance sheet dates.

3. Medium-sized Corporations

Medium-sized corporations are corporations whose total assets at the balance sheet date do not exceed EUR 19,250,000 or whose sales are not more than EUR 38,500,000, and that do not employ on average more than 250 employees during the year.

This means that corporations are classified as medium-sized corporations if they exceed at least two of the three criteria defined for small corporations, but do not exceed at least two of the three criteria applicable to medium-sized corporations.

4. Large Corporations

As a rule, large corporations are those that exceed at least two of the three criteria for medium-sized corporations. Additionally, the large corporation rules apply to the following entities regardless of their size:

- credit institutions;
- financial services institutions;
- pension funds;
- insurers;
- entities that make use of a regulated market within the meaning of Sec. 2(5) of the Securities Trading Act (*Wertpapierhandelsgesetz*) for their securities in issue within the meaning of Sec. 2(1) sentence 1 of the Securities Trading Act or that have applied for such securities to be admitted to trading on a regulated market.

III. Scope of Documents to be Published

1. Large corporations

Large corporations must publish the following documents in electronic form:

- the annual financial statements, comprising the balance sheet, income statement, and notes;
- plus, in the case of publicly traded corporations that are not required to prepare consolidated financial statements (Sec. 264(1) sentence 2 of the Commercial Code), a cash flow statement and a statement of changes in equity, as well as segment reporting (if prepared voluntarily);
- the management report;
- in the case of corporations and commercial partnerships without a natural person as a general partner whose financial statements are subject to an audit requirement, the auditor's report or nonaffirmative auditor's report;
- the report of the supervisory board (including for corporations that are required to have a supervisory board and for GmbHs with a voluntary supervi-

sory board, but not for commercial partnerships without a natural person as a general partner that have voluntarily established a supervisory board);
- the proposal on the appropriation of net profit and the resolution on its appropriation, stating the net income or net loss for the fiscal year, where that figure is not evident from the financial statements;
- for listed corporations, the declaration of conformity (Sec. 161 of the Stock Corporation Act (*Aktiengesetz*)) with the German Corporate Governance Code;
- any changes to the financial statements resulting from the resolution adopting the financial statements;
- any changes to the auditor's report or nonaffirmative auditor's report resulting from a supplementary audit;
- if the financial statements have already been adopted or – in the case of consolidated financial statements – approved, the date of adoption or approval.

If the balance sheet and income statement are published, the complete classification formats required by Sec. 266(2) and (3) of the Commercial Code (balance sheet) and Sec. 275(2) or (3) of the Commercial Code (income statement) must be applied.

Under Sec. 325(2a) of the Commercial Code, separate IFRS financial statements prepared in accordance with the international accounting standards designated in Sec. 315a of the Commercial Code may be published in place of the German GAAP annual financial statements.

The scope of the documents that are required to be published listed above also applies to the publication of the consolidated financial statements and the group management report, with the necessary modifications.

2. Simplified preparation and publication rules for medium-sized corporations

In principle, the scope of documents to be published described under 1) above also applies to medium-sized corporations/medium-sized commercial partnerships without a natural person as a general partner. As an exception to these requirements, Sec. 327 of the Commercial Code allows publication exemptions that are explained in the following:
- The balance sheet classification under Sec. 266(2) and (3) of the Commercial Code need only comply with the condensed format applicable to small corporations. This means that only those line items that are designated by letters and Roman numerals in the classification format set out in Sec. 266(2) and (3) of the Commercial Code need be reported. However, in those cases the following line items prescribed by Sec. 266(2) and (3) must additionally be presented **separately** in the balance sheet or the notes:

- **Assets**
  - A I 1 Internally generated industrial rights and similar rights and assets;
  - A I 2 Goodwill;
  - A II 1 Land, land rights, and buildings, including buildings on third-party land;
  - A II 2 Technical equipment and machinery;
  - A II 3 Other equipment, operating and office equipment;
  - A II 4 Prepayments and assets under construction;
  - A III 1 Shares in affiliated companies;
  - A III 2 Loans to affiliated companies;
  - A III 3 Other long-term equity investments;
  - A III 4 Loans to other long-term investees and investors;
  - B II 2 Receivables from affiliated companies;
  - B II 3 Receivables from other long-term investees and investors;
  - B III 1 Shares in affiliated companies.
- **Equity and liabilities**
  - C 1 Bonds,
  - of which convertible;
  - C 2 Liabilities to banks;
  - C 6 Liabilities to affiliated companies;
  - C 7 Liabilities to other long-term investees and investors.
- For the income statement classification, under Sec. 276 of the Commercial Code the line items prescribed by Sec. 275(2) nos. 1–5 or, if the cost of sales (function of expense) format is used, the line items prescribed by Sec. 275(3) nos. 1–3 and no. 6 of the Commercial Code may be combined into a single heading designated 'Gross profit/loss'.
- Disclosure of the following items may be omitted in the notes in the course of publication:
  - a breakdown by the individual liabilities headings of the total amount of liabilities with a remaining term of more than five years and of liabilities that are secured by liens or similar rights (Sec. 285 no. 2 of the Commercial Code);
  - the cost of materials and its breakdown, if the cost of sales (function of expense) format is used (Sec. 285 no. 8(a) of the Commercial Code);
  - an explanation of other provisions that are not presented separately in the balance sheet (Sec. 285 no. 12 of the Commercial Code).

3. Simplified preparation and publication rules for small corporations

Under Sec. 326(1) of the Commercial Code, small corporations are only required to file the following documents with the operator of the electronic Federal Gazette:

- the balance sheet;
- the notes, except for disclosures relating to the income statement.

The other documents described for large corporations under 1) above do not have to be published by small corporations/commercial partnerships without a natural person as a general partner.

In addition to the publication exemptions, small corporations/commercial partnerships without a natural person as a general partner can also elect to apply the following optional exemptions when preparing their financial statements:

- preparation of a condensed balance sheet (compared with balance sheet formats under Sec. 266(2) und (3) of the Commercial Code) that only includes those items designated by letters and Roman numerals (Sec. 266(1) sentence 3 of the Commercial Code);
- preparation of the balance sheet or the notes without a presentation of changes in the individual items of fixed assets (statement of changes in fixed assets) (Sec. 274a no. 1 of the Commercial Code);
- preparation of the notes, except for disclosures on receivables for which no legal claim has yet arisen (Sec. 274a no. 2 of the Commercial Code);
- preparation of the notes, except for disclosures on liabilities for which no legal claim has yet arisen (Sec. 274a no. 3 of the Commercial Code);
- preparation of the balance sheet or the notes without the separate presentation or alternative disclosure of prepaid expenses in accordance with Sec. 250(3) of the Commercial Code (Sec. 274a no. 4 of the Commercial Code);
- preparation of the notes, except for disclosures on deferred taxes (Sec. 274a no. 5 of the Commercial Code);
- preparation of the notes, except for disclosures on extraordinary income and extraordinary expense as well as income and expenses attributable to another fiscal year (Sec. 276 sentence 2 of the Commercial Code);
- preparation of the notes in accordance with Sec. 288(1) of the Commercial Code, except for the disclosures required under Sec. 284(2) no. 4, Sec. 285 nos. 2–8(a), no. 9(a) and (b), and nos. 12, 17, 19, 21, 22, and 29 of the Commercial Code.

4. Simplified preparation and publication rules for microcorporations

The rules for microcorporations were introduced by the Act Amending Accounting Law for Microcorporations (*Kleinstkapitalgesellschaften-Bilanzrechtsänderungsgesetz*), which came into force on 28 Dec. 2012. These rules are applicable to all financial statements with balance sheet dates after 30 Dec. 2012, so they apply for the first time to annual financial statements for the year ended 31 Dec. 2012.

In contrast to all other companies required to publish their financial statements, microcorporations/microcommercial partnerships without a natural person as a general partner do not have to file their financial statements with the operator of the electronic Federal Gazette. They can also satisfy the publication requirements by filing only their balance sheet in electronic form with the operator of the electronic Federal Gazette and issuing lodging instructions. The key advantage of this procedure is that the financial statements cannot simply be downloaded by anybody over the Internet, because they can only be accessed on application and by paying a fee. Note, though, that anybody can make such an application without the need to give any reasons. However, a condition for taking advantage of this option is that the legal representatives of the microcorporation/microcommercial partnership without a natural person as a general partner must notify the operator of the Federal Gazette that two of the three relevant size criteria set out in Sec. 267a of the Commercial Code are not exceeded.

As a general rule, the same rules apply to microcorporations as for small corporations unless stipulated otherwise by law. As a further exemption compared with small corporations, the balance sheet classification may be condensed as follows:

Assets	Equity and Liabilities
A. Fixed assets	A. Equity
B. Current assets	B. Provisions
C. Prepaid expenses	C. Liabilities
D. Excess of PA* over PEB** liability	D. Deferred income

* PA = plan assets
** PEB = postemployment benefit

Sec. 264(1) sentence 5 of the Commercial Code exempts microcorporations/microcommercial partnerships without a natural person as a general partner from the requirement to prepare notes if they disclose the contingent liabilities in accordance with Sec. 251 of the Commercial Code and the contingent liabilities assumed in favor of members of governing bodies as below-the-line items under the balance sheet. Stock corporations and partnerships limited by shares have to disclose additional information about treasury shares. If the exemption option for the notes is exercised, additional below-the-line disclosures may be required if special circumstances result in the financial statements not presenting a true and fair view of the net assets, financial position, and results of operations.

There is some dispute about whether these below-the-line items must be published in addition to the balance sheet. However, leading commentaries take the view that they do not have to be published.

The reduced disclosure requirements for microcorporations/microcommercial partnerships without a natural person as a general partner, coupled with the option to lodge the balance sheet in such a way that it cannot be accessed directly online, offer attractive options – especially for holding companies that prepare exempting consolidated financial statements in accordance with Sec. 264(3) of the Commercial Code – for avoiding the burdens imposed by the disclosure requirements.

5. Preparation and publication exemptions for companies that fall under the Disclosure Act

The primary scenario for application of the Disclosure Act relates to sole traders and partnerships with at least one natural person as a general partner, provided that they exceed the size criteria described in the Introduction. The following comments are therefore restricted to those companies.

The Disclosure Act is additionally applicable to:

- associations whose purpose is associated with a commercial business operation;
- foundations with legal capacity that operate a commercial business; and
- corporations/foundations/institutions under public law that are classified as merchants.

As a general principle, the scope of the documents required to be published is governed by the rules applying to large corporations (cf. III. no. 1), to the extent that the Disclosure Act requires those documents to be prepared.

Under Sec. 5 of the Disclosure Act, partnerships and sole traders do not have to prepare notes or a management report, so those documents also do not have to be published.

In addition, Sec. 9(2) of the Disclosure Act sets out additional publication exemptions for partnerships and sole traders, under which they are not required to publish an income statement or the resolution on the appropriation of net profit if the following information is disclosed:

- sales within the meaning of Sec. 277(1) of the Commercial Code;
- income from equity investments (in a single amount);
- the number of employees;
- wages, salaries, social security, and post-employment benefit costs;
- disclosures on measurement and depreciation and amortization policies, including material changes in those policies.

Under Sec. 13(3) sentence 2 of the Disclosure Act, this also applies to the consolidated income statement of partnerships, with the necessary modifications.

However, one consequence of publishing the condensed income statement in the consolidated financial statements is that those consolidated financial statements can only be classified as exempting subgroup consolidated financial statements of a subsidiary under Sec. 291 of the Commercial Code if that subsidiary could also exercise the exemption for its consolidated financial statements.

Sec. 9(3) of the Disclosure Act additionally allows partnerships to combine the following equity accounts into a single 'Equity' heading:

- capital shares of the partners;
- reserves (capital and revenue reserves);
- retained profits or accumulated losses brought forward;
- profit or loss (net of the share of past losses of partners not covered by capital contributions).

Furthermore, consolidated financial statements that comply with the Disclosure Act can be prepared without a cash flow statement and a statement of changes in equity, so these documents also do not have to be published.

Not publishing the income statement and combining the reported equity into a single heading avoids the need to disclose the net income or loss for the year. The same principle applies to consolidated financial statements under the Disclosure Act, with the result that this piece of legislation offers attractive options for avoiding the disclosure requirements. In practice, this means that many commercial partnerships with a legal person as a general partner also admit a natural person as a general partner so that they can take advantage of the more favorable options available under the Disclosure Act. Because the thresholds for applying the Disclosure Act are relatively high (total assets > EUR 65,000,000, sales > EUR 130,000,000, and an average of more than 5,000 employees), the assets and liabilities of individual companies are often transferred in practice to several brother/sister partnerships using tax-neutral transactions so that each of them comes in below the Disclosure Act thresholds. The end effect is that it is possible to avoid having to apply the disclosure requirements in their entirety.

IV. Format and Content of Published Information

1. Basic principles

As a general rule, both the format and the content of the financial statements as prepared by the entity must be used for publication purposes. The principles of completeness and accuracy apply in this respect.

The principle of completeness means that the financial statements and management report as prepared by the entity cannot be condensed in any way. For example, the narrative text in the notes and the management report must be reproduced word for word, and the classification formats in the balance sheet and income statement must also be included in full in the published documents.

The principle of accuracy refers to the way the financial statements are reproduced. Apart from preparation and publication exemptions that may be exercised for publication purposes, the financial statements must be reproduced exactly as they were prepared or have already been adopted. Any errors in the version as prepared must be included in the version that is published.

As a general principle, the documents to be published must be filed in German. Exceptions apply only to branches of corporations/commercial partnerships without a natural person as a general partner that are domiciled outside Germany (Sec. 325a(1) sentence 3 of the Commercial Code).

2. Exercising publication exemptions

In derogation of the principles of completeness and accuracy, preparation exemptions (Secs. 264(1) sentence 4 *et seq.*, 266(1) sentence 3 *et seq.*, 274a, 275(5), or 276, 286(4), and 288 of the Commercial Code) or departures from the account format under Sec. 328(4) of the Commercial Code can be applied for publication purposes only, within the framework of the publication exemptions under Secs. 326 and 327 of the Commercial Code. As a result, the publication exemptions described in detail for the individual size criteria can be modified solely for the purposes of publication, irrespective of the financial statements as prepared.

If publication exemptions are exercised, it should be remembered that the auditor's report, as issued by the auditor, refers to the financial statements as prepared by the entity. Consequently, if the auditor's report referring to the financial statements as prepared by the entity is published together with financial statements for which publication exemptions under Secs. 326 and 327 of the Commercial Code have been exercised, the entity publishing this financial information must indicate that the auditor's report refers to the complete set of financial statements.

V. Timing of publication

As a rule, Sec. 325(1) of the Commercial Code requires the entity's legal representatives to publish the annual financial statements and the management report without delay following their submission to the shareholders. At the latest, they must be published within the first twelve months of the fiscal year following the balance sheet date. In the case of entities that make use of a regulated market within the meaning of Sec. 2(5) of the Securities Trading Act or that have applied for their securities to be admitted to trading on a regulated market, this period is reduced to four months.

VI. Avoiding Publication Requirements through Inclusion in Consolidated Financial Statements

If certain conditions are met, publication of the single-entity or consolidated financial statements can be avoided by applying the provisions of Secs. 264(3), 264b, 291, and 292 of the Commercial Code. The following graphic summarizes the exemption options that are generally available to companies:

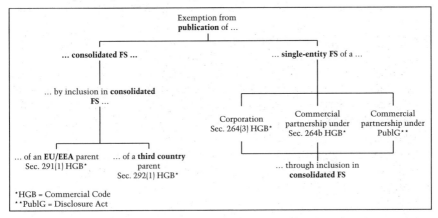

1. Exemption from the requirement to prepare/publish consolidated financial statements

As a general principle, consolidated financial statements are also subject to a publication requirement. The requirement to prepare and publish subgroup consolidated financial statements can be avoided by including them in the ultimate parent's consolidated financial statements:

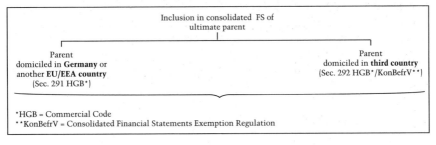

The requirements for exemption are that the consolidated financial statements/group management report of the ultimate parent

- comply with, or at a minimum are equivalent to, the requirements of the 7th EC Directive;
- are audited;

625

- are published in German, in Germany; and
- that the notes to the financial statements of the entity to be exempted include disclosures in accordance with Sec. 291(2) no. 3 of the Commercial Code.

This allows both the preparation and the publication of subgroup consolidated financial statements to be avoided in Germany if the entity is included in the consolidated financial statements of an ultimate parent, and those consolidated financial statements are published in German, in Germany.

This exemption option does not apply if securities issued by the entity to be exempted have been admitted to trading on a regulated market in the EU or if the shareholders of the parent to be exempted request preparation and publication of the consolidated financial statements. In the case of a GmbH, at least 20% of the voting rights are required for such a request, and at least 10% in the case of an AG or KGaA.

2. Exemption for corporations from the requirement to publish single-entity financial statements in accordance with Sec. 264(3) of the Commercial Code

If the single-entity financial statements of a corporation are included in a parent company's consolidated financial statements, publication of those single-entity financial statements can be avoided if the following conditions are met:

- all shareholders of the company to be exempted give their consent (each year);
- the parent has declared that it will absorb losses either directly or indirectly, whereby a voluntary standalone undertaking to absorb losses or equivalent liability undertaking is sufficient;

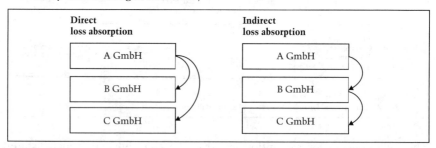

- the declaration of loss absorption (DLA) must relate to the year following the fiscal year for which financial statement exemptions will be exercised, and it must be effective up to the end of that following year;

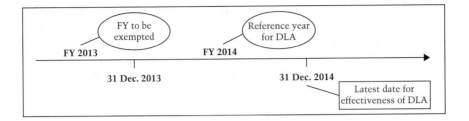

- the subsidiary is included in the consolidated financial statements of the parent (including consolidated financial statements prepared on a voluntary basis);
- the consolidated financial statements are audited;
- disclosure in the notes to the parent's consolidated financial statements of the subsidiary for which the exemption option is being exercised;
- publication:
  - of the consolidated financial statements;
  - of the declaration of loss absorption;
  - of the exemption in the Federal Gazette.

If the conditions set out above are satisfied, the entity is also exempted from the requirement to have the financial statements audited, to prepare a management report, to prepare notes, and to apply the specific recognition, classification, and presentation provisions for corporations under Secs. 264 *et seqq.* of the Commercial Code.

There is one significant limitation on the ability to exercise the exemption from the requirement to publish annual financial statements in the case of corporations that prepare consolidated financial statements as a parent company. Sec. 264(3) of the Commercial Code cannot be applied to these entities, with the result that their single-entity financial statements have to be published in accordance with Sec. 325 of the Commercial Code.

The Act Amending Accounting Law for Microcorporations extended the exemption options to cases where subsidiaries are included in the consolidated financial statements of a parent that is domiciled elsewhere in the EU/EEA. Formerly, the exemption option under Sec. 264(3) of the Commercial Code applied only to subsidiaries that were included in the consolidated financial statements of a German parent. Under the revised Sec. 264(3) of the Commercial Code, all that is now required is a declaration of loss absorption under the law of the EU/EEA parent's country of domicile. The non-German consolidated financial statements must be published in German, in Germany, with the operator of the electronic Federal Gazette. This revision applies for the first time to financial statements for fiscal years beginning after 31 Dec. 2012.

There was some dispute in the past about whether inclusion in the consolidated financial statements of a parent domiciled elsewhere in the EU/EEA was in fact sufficient grounds for avoiding publication.

In a judgment dated 6 Feb. 2014, the European Court of Justice (ECJ) ruled that the statutory provisions in force until the Commercial Code was reformed by the Act Amending Accounting Law for Microcorporations, and that governed publication of the financial statements of corporations that are members of groups, were not compliant with European law. As a result, exemption from the publication requirement can also be exercised for periods prior to 31 Dec. 2012 in cases where a subsidiary is included in the consolidated financial statements of a parent domiciled elsewhere in the EU/EEA.

3. Exemption for commercial partnerships from the requirement to publish single-entity financial statements in accordance with Sec. 264b of the Commercial Code

Commercial partnerships without a natural person as a general partner can also avoid publication through inclusion in consolidated financial statements if the following conditions are met:

- the parent is domiciled in the EU/EEA (including Germany);
- the commercial partnership is included in the audited EU/EEA consolidated financial statements of the parent;
- the consolidated financial statements are published in German in the electronic Federal Gazette;
- exercise of the exemption option under Sec. 264 b of the Commercial Code is disclosed in the notes to the parent's consolidated financial statements;
- the exemption is published in the electronic Federal Gazette.

In contrast to the rules applying to corporations, neither the consent of the partners nor a declaration of loss absorption is necessary to apply the exemption option. Moreover, in contrast to a comparable corporation, the partnership is also exempted from publishing its single-entity financial statements if it itself prepares the exempting consolidated financial statements as the parent.

VII. Sanctions in the Event of Failure to Comply with the Publication Requirements

The operator of the electronic Federal Gazette is responsible for reviewing whether entities required to publish their financial statements have filed the necessary documents within the required time limit and in full (Sec. 329 of the Commercial Code). This review is conducted on the basis of the data stored in the electronic companies register, with which all merchants are registered.

If the review establishes that an entity has not complied with its publication requirements within the required time limit, a notification is sent to the Federal Office of Justice (*Bundesamt für Justiz*), which is the central authority responsible for initiating administrative fine proceedings in accordance with Sec. 335 of the Commercial Code.

In the event of a such a notification being sent, the Federal Office of Justice is required to initiate administrative fine proceedings 'by virtue of its office'. In the course of these administrative fine proceedings, the entity is initially given a six-week period to publish the documents. If they are not published within this period, an administrative fine of at least EUR 2,500 is imposed. At the same time, the entity is given a further six weeks to publish the documents, with the threat of another administrative fine of up to a maximum of EUR 25,000 if it fails to do so. These proceedings end only once all of the documents have been published. The administrative fine proceedings are directed at the members of the body authorized to represent the entity.

The imposition of a fine can be appealed in the first instance by lodging an administrative appeal with the Federal Office of Justice, and in the next instance by instituting appellate proceedings with the Regional Court of Bonn. Since the reform of the administrative fine proceedings under commercial law, which applies for the first time to fiscal years ending on 31 Dec. 2012, the ruling by the Regional Court of Bonn can then be appealed to the Higher Regional Court of Cologne. However, this is only the case if the Regional Court of Bonn has allowed an appeal.

Because the administrative fine proceedings are instituted by the Federal Office of Justice 'by virtue of its office,' entities that do not file the necessary documents for publication, or do not file them within the required time limit, face seamless monitoring and prosecution. As a result of this approach, more than 90% of all entities required to publish their financial statements now do so within the required time limit. The ability to repeatedly impose administrative fines of up to EUR 25,000 means that, in the long term, entities cannot avoid the publication requirements.

Marc Schmidt

Public Auditor, Tax Advisor, Diplom-Kaufmann

Areas of Specialization

- Auditing
- Tax accounting
- Tax audits
- M&A transaction services

Telephone (ext.) +49 228/95 94-177

Email: marc.schmidt@fgs.de

Accounting for Advertising Spots

by Andreas Söffing

Contents

I. Preliminary Remarks
II. Fundamental Principles Governing the Application of the Classification Criteria
III. The Individual Classification Criteria
 1. Who Bears Responsibility for the Financial Risks?
 2. Constructive Influence on Production of the Film
 3. Exploitation Rights
IV. Summary and Concluding Remarks

I. Preliminary Remarks

The issue of how to account for film rights has been exercising the courts, tax authorities, specialist literature, and accounting practitioners for many years. The first question to be answered is whether film rights are tangible or intangible assets. Because films are normally stored on physical media (e.g. film reels or videotape), it is possible to argue that those physical media represent tangible assets. However, the party commissioning a film production is less interested in taking possession of the physical media than in obtaining the copyright in the film, so film rights are classified as intangible assets.[1] Specifically, the intangible asset relates to the right of the film producer under Sec. 94(1) of the German Copyright Act (*Urheberrechtsgesetz*) to reproduce and distribute the combined image and sound media on which the film has been recorded, to use them for public screenings or broadcasts, or to otherwise make them available to the public, and to prohibit the combined image and storage media from being distorted or abridged.

The question of whether this intangible asset must be shown in the commissioning party's tax accounts is governed by Sec. 5(2) of the German Income Tax Act (*Einkommensteuergesetz*), which states that only purchased intangible noncurrent assets must be shown. For the party commissioning a film production, the film rights are generally classified as noncurrent assets because they will not as a rule be resold, but are intended to be broadcast on multiple occasions and will thus serve business operations in the long term.[2] The question then arises whether the rights under Sec. 94 of the Copyright Act were purchased or internally generated. As Sec. 94 of the Copyright Act assigns the

---

[1] Federal Tax Court of 20 Sep. 1995 — X R 225/93, Federal Tax Gazette Part II, 1997, p. 320 [p. 321].
[2] Federal Tax Court of 20 Sep. 1995 — X R 225/93, Federal Tax Gazette Part II, 1997, p. 320 [p. 322].

rights of use and exploitation rights to the 'producer' of a film, court rulings and guidance from the tax authorities hold that a right is only internally generated if the reporting entity is required to be classified as a 'film producer' within the meaning of Sec. 94 of the Copyright Act.

> "The question of who a film producer is does not depend on whether they make a creative and artistic contribution to the production of the film, but rather whether they bear the business risk of producing the film (see Jan Bernd Nordemann, in: Fromm/Nordemann, Copyright Act, 10th ed., Sec. 94, marginal no. 12). The key factor is therefore the question of who has assumed financial responsibility and has undertaken the organizational measures needed to produce the film as the finished product of the efforts of all those who participated in its creation, and thus as a film suitable for exploitation (Federal Court of Justice GRUR 1993, 472 – Film Producers). What counts here is not advance production work on the film, but production of the first fixation of a film – in the case of commercial productions, this is the 'answer print'; whoever controls this from a content and organizational perspective, is financially responsible for it, and acquires or would subsequently have to acquire the intellectual property rights needed to produce the film and also, at least temporarily, the exploitation rights to the film, is the producer. An overall assessment must be made to arrive at a judgment, based on additional financial criteria (including cost overrun risk, acceptance risk, completion and exploitation risk), about which of the parties involved in a production embodies the primary focus of the business activity (Wandtke/Bullinger/Manegold, Copyright Act, Sec. 94, marginal no. 31)".[3]

The courts and the tax authorities have developed a wide variety of criteria in order to decide whether the commissioning party or the contractor is the producer in the case of commissioned productions. If the commissioning party is regarded as the producer, this scenario is referred to as a 'unreal' commissioned production because, although the commissioning party commissions a film producer to produce a film, the commissioning party ultimately takes the decisions needed to produce the film and, in the final analysis, bears financial responsibility and must therefore be regarded as the producer of the film.[4] In this case the film is an internally generated intangible asset that, under Sec. 5(2) of the Income Tax Act, may not be shown as an asset in the balance sheet. If the commissioning party is not ultimately responsible for the production, it is classified as a 'real' commissioned production for which the contractor is regarded as the producer of the film. As a result, the prohibition on showing the production as an asset under Sec. 5(2) of the Income Tax Act does not apply because the film is purchased by the commissioning party.

The classification criteria used to date have been developed by the courts and the tax authorities, especially in conjunction with scenarios where television

---

3 Higher Regional Court of Cologne of 10 Dec. 2012 — 6 U 92/10, GRUR-RR 2011, p. 161–162.
4 Federal Tax Court of 20 Sep. 1995 — X R 225/93, Federal Tax Gazette Part I, 1997, p. 320 [p. 321].

broadcasters or film funds are the commissioning party. The question therefore arises as to whether these criteria can be applied unchanged to the production of advertising spots, or whether they need to be modified in this case. Because the useful lives of advertising spots are normally considerably shorter, the accounting effects of this classification are likely to be less serious than in the case of television or film rights. Nevertheless, it is evident that this question is also increasingly being addressed by the tax authorities in the case of advertising spots.

II. Fundamental Principles Governing the Application of the Classification Criteria

The criteria for distinguishing between 'real' and 'unreal' commissioned productions developed by the courts and the tax authorities can be used to establish whether the commissioning party or the contractor ultimately takes the necessary decisions, and who bears responsibility for the financial risks. These criteria are an important indicator in this respect. However, the actual overall picture derived from the facts and circumstances is what is really decisive in distinguishing between 'real' and 'unreal' commissioned productions. For example, the commissioning party's right under the law of agency to issue instructions to the contractor is irrelevant if the commissioning party cannot constructively issue instructions to the contractor because the commissioning party's decisions are controlled by the service provider or this right is frustrated for other reasons, for instance because the commissioning party has insufficient knowledge of motion picture technology.[5] Conversely, however, an 'unreal' commissioned production will also have to be assumed if the actual facts and circumstances indicate that the commissioning party ultimately takes the necessary decisions and bears responsibility for the financial risks – even if some of the classification criteria that have been developed are not satisfied, or not to any significant extent.

The existing distinction between a 'real' and an 'unreal' commissioned production is driven largely by the classification of the circumstances under copyright or civil law, and especially by the question of who the producer of the film is within the meaning of Sec. 94 of the Copyright Act in the specific production scenario. This distinction can then be used to answer the question of whether the film or television right is an internally generated intangible asset that may not be shown as an asset, or a purchased intangible asset that has to be shown as an asset (see Sec. 5(2) of the Income Tax Act). Because Sec. 5(2) of the Income Tax Act is a financial accounting rule, the answer to the question of whether the right should be shown as an asset or not will have to pay greater attention to the principle of substance over form in addition to the situation under copyright and civil law (Sec. 39 of the German Tax Code – *Abgabenordnung*).

---

5 see German Federal Finance Ministry circular dated 23 Feb. 2001, Federal Tax Gazette Part I, 2001, 175 marginal no. 12b.

III. The Individual Classification Criteria

1. Who Bears Responsibility for the Financial Risks?

In accordance with court rulings and guidance from the tax authorities, the following indicators can be used to test whether financial responsibility rests with the commissioning party (which suggests an 'unreal' commissioned production) or with the contractor (suggesting a 'real' commissioned production):

- The contractor is required to prepare a full budget for its production costs that forms part of the contract and is approved by the commissioning party.[6] The financial responsibility necessary for classification as an 'unreal' commissioned production thus requires the commissioning party to have a high degree of transparency about the costs incurred by the contractor.
- The commissioning party is able to influence the cost estimates.[7] As well as transparency about costs, classification as an 'unreal' commissioned production thus also requires the commissioning party to have decision-making powers about the composition of the production costs.
- Agreement of a fixed fee plus reimbursement of expenses incurred by the contractor for the account of the commissioning party.[8] Another key factor is that the cost risk resulting from the film production is also borne ultimately by the commissioning party and not by the contractor.
- Insurance is taken out to cover the film production risk (in particular a completion guarantee and shortfall insurance for which the commissioning party is the policyholder).[9] We do not believe that it makes any difference whether the commissioning party is the policyholder or whether the commissioning party has required the contractor to take out this insurance under the production agreement.

The question of who bears responsibility for the financial risks of an advertising spot revolves around the risks and opportunities associated with the film production. The greater the responsibility shouldered by the commissioning party for the financial risks associated with the film production, the stronger the indications are that this is an 'unreal' commissioned production. Financial responsibility has to distinguish between the exploitation risk (and opportunities) on the one hand and the completion or acceptance risk (production risk) on the other.

In the case of an advertising spot, the financial exploitation risks and opportunities are likely to be attributed solely to the commissioning party. As a rule, the contractor does not participate in the financial success or failure of the ad-

---

[6] German Federal Finance Ministry circular dated 23 Feb. 2001, Federal Tax Gazette Part I, 2001, p. 175.
[7] German Federal Finance Ministry circular dated 23 Feb. 2001, Federal Tax Gazette Part I, 2001, p. 175 marginal no. 12b.
[8] German Federal Finance Ministry circular dated 23 Feb. 2001, Federal Tax Gazette Part I, 2001, p. 175 marginal no. 12c.
[9] German Federal Finance Ministry circular dated 23 Feb. 2001, Federal Tax Gazette Part I, 2001, p. 175 marginal no. 12d.

vertising spot. The issue of whether the advertising spot results in the desired revenue increases or positive effects on the image of the advertised product, brand, or business entity does not affect the contractor. Likewise, the commissioning party has to pay the production costs that are due to the contractor regardless of the financial success or failure of the advertising spot.

In the case of an advertising spot, the contractor's financial risk is thus limited at most to the completion or acceptance risk. This production risk is largely limited to the risk of miscalculating the budget. In terms of both amount and probability of occurrence, however, this is likely to be considerably lower than the commissioning party's 'market risk'. Moreover, many agreements stipulate price adjustments if the originally agreed performance elements are subsequently modified, so the financial risk associated with any subsequent adaptation or modification to the performance elements is also shifted from the contractor to the commissioning party.

Provided that the specific provisions of production agreements ensure that cost transparency, the composition of the costs, and the cost risk are largely the responsibility of the commissioning party rather than the contractor, then the commissioning party will usually be responsible for the financial risks. Not too much significance can be attached to the classification criterion "Insurance is taken out to cover the film production risk (in particular a completion guarantee and shortfall insurance) for which the commissioning party is the policyholder" in the case of advertising spots because these do not generate any income, and shortfall insurance is therefore not necessary in the first place.

2. Constructive Influence on Production of the Film

A production is classified as an 'unreal' commissioned production if the commissioning party has significant opportunities to influence production of the film, this influence has a direct impact on the fate of the film, and the opportunities to influence production of the film are not constructively ruled out.

"The fund decides on all significant measures relating to production of the film, in particular choosing the subject, the screenplay, and the cast, calculating the budget, the production schedule, and financing of the film. The actual facts and circumstances are decisive".[10] Other criteria cited are approving the agreements with the people involved in producing the film, enforcing changes in the way production of the film is organized, and approving the cast and crew. These opportunities to influence production of the film may not be constructively ruled out.[11]

These criteria were developed by the tax authorities and the courts in particular in the context of film and television funds as commissioning parties. Potential fund sponsors mentioned in the 'Media Decree' issued by the German Fed-

---

10 see German Federal Finance Ministry circular dated 23 Feb. 2001, Federal Tax Gazette Part I, 2001, p. 175, marginal no. 12b.
11 German Federal Finance Ministry circular dated 23 Feb. 2001, Federal Tax Gazette Part I, 2001, p. 175, marginal no. 10.

eral Ministry of Finance include distributors, investment advisors, and leasing companies. These are an entirely different type of commissioning party than would be encountered in the case of advertising spots. If commissioning parties like this are involved, the issue of the ability to influence the production of the film will doubtless have to be examined in greater detail, because the purpose of the venture is also to generate an investment product or raise capital for a film project. As a result, additional objectives are being pursued above and beyond the film in addition to influencing its content. The situation is different in the case of advertising spots where the commissioning party is a business entity that wishes to use the advertising spot to advertise a particular product, a brand, or the business entity itself. Production of this advertising spot has to be coordinated closely with the marketing strategy for the product or the business entity, which means that influence on the production of the advertising spot necessarily has to be very strong.

3. Exploitation Rights

A production is classified as an 'unreal' commissioned production if the agreements entered into by the commissioning party also ensure that all rights necessary for producing and exploiting the film are attributable to the fund; if rights are only established when the film is being produced, there must be a mechanism in place for ensuring that these rights are granted without restriction to the commissioning party.[12] In the case of an 'unreal' commissioned production, the commissioning party is the producer within the meaning of Sec. 94 of the Copyright Act. This means that the commissioning party has the exclusive right to reproduce and distribute the image media or combined image and sound media on which the film has been recorded, to use them for public screenings or broadcasts, or to otherwise make them available to the public.

Conversely, this means that a production is classified as a 'real' commissioned production if the original rights under copyright law to use the film to be produced are directly and inherently attributable to the contractor, with the result that the contractor holds the exploitation rights to the film, at least temporarily.[13] In the case of a 'real' commissioned production, the contractor is the producer within the meaning of Sec. 94 of the Copyright Act.

Therein lies the key difference between a television or cinema film on the one hand and an advertising spot on the other. An advertising spot is intended to present a particular product, brand, or business entity. The original rights to this product or brand are held by the commissioning party, and do not accrue initially to the contractor. This means that, as a rule, the contractor will never hold the unrestricted exploitation rights to the advertising spot. The contractor will therefore be unable to hold the exclusive right to reproduce and distribute the advertising spot or to otherwise make it available to the public. The ques-

---

12 German Federal Finance Ministry circular dated 23 Feb. 2001, Federal Tax Gazette Part I, 2001, p. 175, marginal no. 12a ('Media Decree').
13 See also Higher Regional Court of Cologne of 10 Dec. 2010 — 6 U 92/10, GRUR-RR 2011, p. 161.

tion therefore arises whether, in the case of advertising spots for which the brand rights are held by the commissioning party, the contractor can in fact ever be the producer of the film within the meaning of Sec. 94 of the Copyright Act, because the commissioning party has the right to object in relation to the use of its brand, including under Sec. 14 of the German Trademark Act (*Markengesetz*). If the reasons set out above mean that the contractor cannot be viewed as the producer of the film, the production of an advertising spot in the form described above can only ever be an 'unreal' commissioned production, and not a 'real' commissioned production.

Another question that arises from a financial accounting perspective is whether, in such cases, the contractor actually developed an asset that could be purchased by the commissioning party. Based on the rulings of the Federal Tax Court, the right of the producer of the film under Sec. 94 of the Copyright Act is an intangible asset under both financial accounting and tax law. If the contractor cannot be the producer of an advertising spot for the reasons set out above, then no rights of the producer of the film under Sec. 94 of the Copyright Act can be transferred. A consequence of this in turn would be that Sec. 5(2) of the Income Tax Act could not apply because there is no asset.

Finally, another classification criterion applied is the distinction in German law between a *Werkvertrag* (a contract for work and services to deliver a specific outcome) and a *Dienstvertrag* (a general contract to render services). One criterion supporting classification as a 'real' commissioned production is when the completed film must first be accepted by the commissioning party.[14] This civil law perspective can be countered by arguing that, in financial accounting law, the principle of substance over form predominates, and that acceptance of a completed advertising spot is also a common form of performance review under contracts classified as a *Dienstvertrag*. Use of the term 'acceptance' does not therefore automatically allow the conclusion to be drawn that the commissioned production can be defined as a contract classified as a *Werkvertrag*.

IV. Summary and Concluding Remarks

(1) The criteria developed by the courts and the tax authorities can also be used for advertising spots to distinguish between 'real' and 'unreal' commissioned productions. However, the differences between television and cinema films on the one hand and advertising spots on the other must be taken into account. A consequence of these differences is that, based on both the individual classification criteria and on the overall picture derived from the facts and circumstances, advertising spot productions are more likely to be 'unreal' than 'real' commissioned productions.

(2) Financial responsibility for the exploitation risks and opportunities associated with advertising spots is likely to be borne exclusively by the commissioning party. The issue of whether the advertising spot results in the de-

---

14 See Federal Tax Court of 20 Sep. 1995, Federal Tax Gazette Part II, 1997, p. 320.

sired revenue increases or positive effects on the image of the advertised product, brand, or business entity as a whole does not affect the contractor.

(3) In the case of advertising spots, the specific provisions of production agreements will normally ensure that cost transparency, the composition of the costs, and the cost risk are largely the responsibility of the commissioning party.

(4) Not too much significance can be attached to the classification criterion "Insurance is taken out to cover the film production risk (in particular a completion guarantee and shortfall insurance) for which the commissioning party is the policyholder" in the case of advertising spots because these do not generate any income directly, and shortfall insurance is therefore not necessary in the first place.

(5) The classification criteria developed by the courts and the tax authorities have been applied primarily to scenarios where film funds or television broadcasters are the commissioning party. Potential fund sponsors mentioned in the 'Media Decree' include distributors, investment advisors, and leasing companies. As a rule, advertising spots involve an entirely different type of commissioning party – a business entity that wishes to advertise its own product, brand, and business entity. As a rule, the commissioning parties of advertising spots do not have additional, in particular monetary, objectives in the same way as a film fund, for example. It must therefore be assumed that a party commissioning an advertising spot will have a much stronger influence on the design of the advertising spot, and thus on the film production, than a party commissioning a television or cinema film. This in turn corresponds to greater financial responsibility for the party commissioning an advertising spot (see no. 3 above).

(6) As a rule, the exploitation rights from production of an advertising spot will never be attributed without restriction to the contractor, because the original rights to the product or brand that is being advertised will be held by the commissioning party, not the contractor. In the case of advertising spots, it is therefore questionable whether the contractor can ever actually be the producer of the film within the meaning of Sec. 94 of the Copyright Act, and whether – from a financial accounting perspective – an identifiable asset can actually be transferred by the contractor to the commissioning party.

Prof. Dr. Andreas Söffing

Tax Advisor, Diplom-Kaufmann

Areas of Specialization

- Tax audits
- Tax litigation
- Structuring advice
- Corporate reorganizations and changes of legal form
- Mergers & acquisitions
- Business succession and wealth planning
- Exit taxation

Telephone +49 69/717 03-0

Email: andreas.soeffing@fgs.de

Tax Compliance – A Challenge for Tax Departments

by Jesco Idler

Contents

I. Introduction
II. Legal Requirements
  1. More Stringent Tax Requirements for Corporations
    a) More Stringent Cooperation and Documentation Duties
    b) Improved Access and Investigatory Potential
    c) Limitation of Fiscal Confidentiality
  2. Recent Corruption Scandals and Implications for Tax Law
    a) Occasion for Investigation: Allegations of Corruption
    b) Tax Considerations
    c) Inadequate Tax Compliance System
  3. Increasingly Stringent Requirements in Corporate Governance
    a) Legislative Reforms
    b) Recent Case Law
III. Structure of a Tax Compliance System
  1. Introduction of a Compliance Program
  2. Compliance Organization and Conduct Guidelines
  3. Communication
  4. Ongoing Control and Improvement
IV. Conclusions and Outlook

I. Introduction

The 1990s saw the beginning of a discussion on deficits in the organization of corporate governance and oversight in Germany. Since then, there have been many changes in legislation, to some extent driven by similar initiatives undertaken by legislatures in other countries.

However, despite more stringent compliance requirements, high-profile cases have come to light – especially recently – involving corruption and fraud in Germany (e.g. Siemens, Daimler, VW, MAN, Ferrostaal, and ThyssenKrupp). As these corruption proceedings go through the courts, the definitions as to the duties of corporate governing bodies and the consequences of their breach under criminal and civil law are gradually becoming more concrete.

Independently of this development, recent proceedings have made it clear that the detection of improper business practices can have significant fiscal – and therefore financial – ramifications. And not only that, more stringent requirements in terms of the taxpayer's documentation and disclosure duties in combination with the German tax authorities' broader access and investigatory powers mean that tax audits are increasingly likely to result in proceedings of the nature mentioned above. Not only has the probability of discovery of tax offenses risen steadily in recent years; curtailment of fiscal confidentiality means that the tax authorities are increasingly seizing upon nonfiscal offenses and reporting them to the criminal authorities for prosecution.

These developments are drawing attention to an aspect of the general discussion on compliance issues that has up to now been neglected in Germany, i.e. the importance of tax compliance systems. Although awareness that tax compliance plays an important role in the overall context of corporate compliance is growing, the necessary systematic approach is too often lacking: Efforts are directed solely at selected tax risks that corporations attempt to address through preventive measures. However, it takes a comprehensive tax compliance system to provide an appropriate response to regulatory requirements and overcome the strategic challenge involved in avoiding the risks of liability and criminal prosecution.

Given this situation, this chapter provides an overview of the tension between the requirements of tax law on the one hand and general legal requirements on the other. Proceeding from this basis, the second part outlines the elements that are fundamental to a tax compliance system.

As used below, compliance systems are understood to mean the entirety of all measures intended to ensure legal conduct on the part of members of corporate governing bodies, their close relatives and employees, i.e. compliance with legal requirements and prohibitions. These systems incorporate a corporation's mission-critical statutory provisions and monitor compliance with such provisions. To that effect, tax compliance systems involve compliance with requirements and prohibitions embodied in tax law, which represent a subset of all relevant legislation. The principles and measures adopted by a corporation in this context therefore serve – for present purposes – not only to identify, assess and manage tax exposure, but also to permit avoidance or recognize breaches of law in time.

II. Legal Requirements

1. More Stringent Tax Requirements for Corporations

a) More Stringent Cooperation and Documentation Duties

In Germany, cooperation and documentation duties have in recent years been steadily expanded, in particular as regards cross-border transactions. At the same time, sanctions for violations have become considerably stricter. That now gives the government a broad array of legal instruments that can be used for investigatory purposes.

For example, the documentation duties required of taxpayers that maintain business relationships with related parties within the meaning of Sec. 1(2) German Foreign Tax Act (*Außensteuergesetz*) became more stringent in 2003[1]. The intention of the provision contained in Sec. 90(3) of the German General Tax Code (*Abgabenordnung*), was to facilitate the examination of the allocation of income among affiliated undertakings in different countries by the tax administration. As a result, decisions involving the determination of transfer prices,

---

1 Tax Preference Reduction Act (*Steuervergünstigungsabbaugesetz*) of 16 May 2003, Federal Law Gazette Part I, 2003, p. 660 *et seqq*.

for example, must be documented (arm's length standard). The required records must be provided at the request of the tax authorities. Special provisions of law governing sanctions were introduced for the purposes of prosecuting violations of these documentation duties. In cases of failure to submit documentation or filing of unusable documentation, Sec. 162(3) of the General Tax Code requires the taxpayer to refute the tax administration's assumption of a reduction in income and reverses the burden of proof. Late filing is penalized under Sec. 164(4) of the General Tax Code by applying surcharges in excess of anything previously known under German tax law.

In 2009[2], extensive documentation and disclosure duties were also introduced for business relationships between nonrelated parties. Germany has since 2009 entered into treaties with numerous countries (including Gibraltar, Guernsey, the Isle of Man, several Caribbean countries, and Singapore) governing legal and administrative assistance as well as the exchange of information. The goal is to curtail the use of tax havens for evading taxation. It can be expected that the German tax authorities will in the future request information from foreign countries even more frequently than in the past.

Furthermore, business relationships between nonrelated parties have been subjected to significantly stricter scrutiny by the tax administration in recent years in terms of the taxpayer's disclosure and documentation duties. The provision contained in Sec. 90(2) of the General Tax Code applies to all cross-border transactions, including those with nonrelated parties. According to this provision, taxpayers are not only required to disclose relevant information, but must also provide proof. They must provide the supporting documents to the tax authorities as 'available proof' (*präsente Beweismittel*). Violation of this more stringent disclosure requirement results in a lowering of the standard of proof pursuant to Sec. 162(2) sentence 1 of the General Tax Code. Accordingly, the tax authority will regularly proceed from assumptions that exhibit a certain degree of probability to the detriment of the taxpayer. The administration's approach in practice to the application of this provision has recently been found to be significantly more restrictive than only a few years ago.

The provisions contained in Sec. 160 of the General Tax Code take on special importance in international contexts when related parties are not involved. According to Sec. 160(1) sentence 1 of the General Tax Code, deduction of operating expenses for tax purposes will regularly be disallowed when taxpayers fail to comply with the request of the tax authorities to disclose the identity of creditors or recipients. If the recipient of a payment cannot be identified, Sec. 160 of the General Tax Code imposes a kind of fiscal sanction by disallowing its recognition as an operating expense. This does, however, presuppose that the tax administration has first requested the information from the taxpayer. A typical scenario in this context would involve payments to 'letterbox companies', which usually have their registered offices in tax havens such that it is not possible to know who is the ultimate recipient behind the company. In

---

2 Anti-Tax-Evasion Act (*Steuerhinterziehungsbekämpfungsgesetz*) of 29 July 2009, Federal Law Gazette Part I, 2009, p. 2302 *et seqq.*

practice, the tax administration has also applied this provision significantly more stringently in recent years, in particular following the introduction of stricter conditions for the disallowance of bribes as tax-deductible expenses pursuant to Sec. 4(5) sentence 1 no. 10 of the German Income Tax Act (*Einkommensteuergesetz*) and the most recent corruption trials in Germany.[3] In cases in which taxpayers' documentation was found to be incomplete or the information furnished incorrect in the context of a tax audit, the frequency and severity of consequences for the relevant taxpayers increased significantly.

Overall, there has been an increase in the reasons for requiring adjustments to income in recent years and therefore in the tax exposure facing taxpayers. The tax administration's simultaneously acquired ability to exploit significantly more extensive sources of information for fiscal purposes is addressed below.

b) Improved Access and Investigatory Potential

As early as 2000[4], what is referred to as 'data access by the tax administration' was introduced in connection with tax audits. This was intended to take into account the increase in paperless bookkeeping records. For the first time, the tax authority received the right to access data for the purposes of auditing the taxpayer's accounts prepared by using data processing systems. This right applies to all tax-relevant data. The right to access data covers all electronic records (including accounts and related documents, inventories, annual financial statements, and bookkeeping vouchers) that must be stored in an orderly manner pursuant to Sec. 147(1) of the General Tax Code.

Section 147(6) of the General Tax Code enables the tax administration to exercise its right to access data in various ways. In practice, this usually involves access to data made available in the form of electronic storage media. The use of IDEA[5] analysis software gives the relevant tax auditor numerous ways of analyzing data once the relevant data inventory has been imported. Accounting entries can be examined for the presence of specific risk indicators. This makes it easier to identify errors and irregularities, which increases audit reliability and efficiency.

In 2009, the tax administration once again upgraded its resources by introducing the AIS TaxAudit module. With the basic version of IDEA, it was necessary to first prepare data and program or define the corresponding analytical application even for relatively simple analyses. This called for basic IT skills and was as a rule not possible without special training. In addition, the work this involved meant that valuable audit time was lost in practice. The new module that was introduced contains standard routines and 'audit macros', i.e. automated auditing routines. Data preparation thereby becomes significantly sim-

---

[3] See the following section.
[4] Tax Reduction Act 2000 (*Steuersenkungsgesetz*) of 23 Oct. 2000, Federal Law Gazette Part I, 2000, p. 1433 *et seqq*.
[5] Translation: Interactive Data Extraction and Analysis; official auditing software of the tax administration since 2002.

pler and faster, and the predefined audit macros also enable less experienced tax auditors to benefit from experience gained in the case of tax audits carried out with the use of IDEA. The predefined audit sequences provide indications of the presence of possible data irregularities and as a result justification for further audit procedures.

Such further audit procedures increasingly consist of electronic comparisons of the data received from the taxpayer with information assembled in central databases.

For example, the Federal Central Tax Office has since 1 Jan. 2001 maintained a central database that is referred to as 'ZAUBER' (*Zentrale Datenbank zur Auswertung und Speicherung von Umsatzsteuerbetrugsfällen und Entwicklung von Risikoprofilen*) for the purposes of evaluation and storage of cases of value-added tax (VAT) fraud and creation of risk profiles. Comparison with data previously keyed into IDEA permits relatively fast identification of similarities with cases of VAT fraud that have already been uncovered in the past. USLO (*Umsatzsteuer-Länder-Online*) and LUNA (*Länderumfassende Namensabfrage*) are further cross-border IT applications that can be used to curtail this type of VAT fraud.

The collection of data by the Information Center for Foreign Tax Relations, a department of the Federal Central Tax Office, is an important source of information in the context of tax audits. The Center collects information on foreign dealings of domestic residents as well as information on domestic dealings of non-residents. The data collected include e.g. information on legal entities in other countries and in particular on foreign letterbox companies (domiciliary companies) as well as on tax havens and low-tax countries. The sources for the collection of data include disclosures from taxpayers themselves, information received from German and foreign tax authorities and freely accessible databases such as foreign company registers. The financial authorities of the various German federal states can also access this database online ('ISI database').

The developments described using the area of tax auditing as an example show that the investigatory opportunities available to the tax administration have undergone significant improvement. On the one hand, the legislature is constantly authorizing access to new sources of data (see, for example, also automated data recall pursuant to Secs. 93(7) *et seqq.* and 93b of the General Tax Code); on the other hand, the tax administration is intensively involved in exploitation of the additional opportunities offered by domestic exchanges of information. Existing and new information is increasingly being networked to be used for the purposes of cross audits. The declared goal is 'cross-state integration of existing control segments'.

c) Limitation of Fiscal Confidentiality

The extensive disclosure and documentation duties involved in the taxation process are complemented by the provision on fiscal confidentiality contained in Sec. 30 of the General Tax Code. Section 30(1) of the General Tax Code requires that governmental officials maintain the confidentiality of tax information. They may not disclose information on business relations or commercial and trade secrets (Sec. 30(2) nos. 1 and 2 of the General Tax Code) of taxpayers or third parties, of which they become aware during their activity, without being authorized to do so. The provisions contained in Sec. 30(4) to (6) of the General Tax Code govern exceptions to this principle. According to Sec. 30(4) no. 2 of the General Tax Code, authority to disclose information exists e.g. if disclosure is explicitly allowed by law. In the course of the past ten years, the legislature has found itself compelled to make disclosure requirements more rigorous by replacing the authority to disclose information by mandatory disclosure requirements. Furthermore, additional mandatory disclosure requirements have become law and thus now limit fiscal confidentiality even more.

Disclosure pursuant to Sec. 31a of the General Tax Code, which became mandatory disclosure on 1 Aug. 2002[6], is one example that can be mentioned in this context. According to this provision, the tax authorities must disclose knowledge that can be used to combat undeclared work, illegal employment and unauthorized supply of temporary workers or that can be used to eliminate abusive receipt of social services or benefits. Such mandatory disclosure is not required only when compliance would entail unreasonable expense (Sec. 31a(2) sentence 3 of the General Tax Code).

Section 31b of the General Tax Code[7] contains another disclosure duty that was introduced in 2002. The tax authorities have since been obligated e.g. to forward any findings to prosecuting authorities that would seem to indicate the existence of a criminal offense pursuant to Sec. 261 of the Criminal Code (*Strafgesetzbuch*) (money laundering and related criminal offenses). This is intended to facilitate efforts to combat money laundering since the tax authorities are precisely the ones that would most likely encounter evidence of money laundering, especially in connection with tax audits or investigations.

What is important in the context described above is that the disclosure duties mentioned (at times) take the form of reciprocal duties to inform. The authorities that must be informed by the tax authorities must in turn inform the tax authorities of any evidence that could be relevant in connection with the preparation or conduct of (criminal) tax proceedings. This makes it clear that the legislature has recognized the importance of reciprocal support and cooperation in connection with implementation of a more stringent system of audits and controls to curtail undesirable economic conduct. It would therefore seem advisable to build on this realization when designing a company-wide tax compliance system. This basic idea is developed in greater detail below against the background of recent corruption scandals and the disclosure requirement con-

---

6 Act to Combat Illegal Employment (*Schwarzarbeitsbekämpfungsgesetz*) of 23 July 2002, Federal Law Gazette Part I, 2002, p. 2787 *et seqq*.

7 Inserted by Art. 18 no. 2 of the Fourth Financial Market Promotion Act (*Viertes Finanzmarktförderungsgesetz*) of 21 June 2002, Federal Law Gazette Part I, 2002, p. 2010 *et seqq*.

tained in Sec. 4(5) sentence 1 no. 10 sentence 3 of the Income Tax Act, which is especially relevant in this context.

2. Recent Corruption Scandals and Implications for Tax Law

a) Occasion for Investigation: Allegations of Corruption

Whether it be Daimler, Siemens, MAN or Ferrostaal, the investigative authorities have focused or are focusing on payments made in connection with efforts to obtain contracts.

In the case of Siemens AG, the prosecuting authority's press releases indicated that the authority had received information to the effect that funds 'were being diverted through front companies and offshore firms and their Swiss and Liechtenstein accounts' and therefore found itself compelled to ascertain 'whether and to what extent these funds were used for the payment of bribes'. As regards MAN, the press releases stated that there was a suspicion that 'a system for the promotion of sales of trucks and buses within the territory of Germany existed at MAN Nutzfahrzeuge AG' that involved 'payment of bribes' in order to ensure that 'purchasers entered into purchase or leasing agreements for truck or buses with MAN Nutzfahrzeuge AG for their respective employers and not with one of its competitors'. In addition, the prosecuting authority investigated allegations to the effect 'that commissions were paid not only in Germany, but also to employees and agents of foreign companies or to foreign officials'.

b) Tax Considerations

At the beginning of the MAN corruption affair, the Munich I State Prosecutor's Office announced that its investigation was triggered by notification of questionable payments from the tax authorities. The prosecuting authority stated that it had received two letters from the tax administration concerning what were considered 'problematic' payments. This indicates that a tax audit played a significant role, at least as regards the discovery of corruption in the case of the investigation of MAN. The reason for this is likely to have been the general disallowance of bribes as tax-deductible expenses and the fact that this provision of law allows deviation from the principle of fiscal confidentiality in this context.

Deduction of expenses incurred in connection with illegal acts of corruption (e.g. bribery in business transactions, Sec. 299(2) and (3) of the Criminal Code) is prohibited by Sec. 4(5) sentence 1 no. 10 sentence 1 of the Income Tax Act. If such payments are identified in the context of an audit, the prosecuting authority must be notified accordingly (Sec. 4(5) sentence 1 no. 10 sentence 3 of the Income Tax Act). The Federal Tax Court decision of 14 July 2008[8] makes such notification by the tax authority mandatory as soon as any reasonable suspicion arises. According to the Federal Tax Court, the tax authority must not

---

8 Federal Tax Court of 14 July 2008 – VII B 92/08, DStR 2008, p. 1734.

determine whether the act has become time-barred under criminal law or whether any exclusionary rules or bars to prosecution exist. Even taking into account the principle of proportionality, the Federal Tax Court comes to no other conclusion.

The fact that tax auditors' practice has departed from the previous opinion held by the administration[9] had already become apparent prior to this decision by the court. In the past, failure to name a recipient (Sec. 160 of the General Tax Code) could, in the absence of absolute proof that a payment of bribes had been conferred, constitute a ground for disallowance of deduction of such operating expenses for reasons of procedural expediency.[10] The fact that a taxpayer did not comply with a request to provide the name of the recipient and the tax administration resorted to the provision contained in Sec. 160(1) sentence 1 of the General Tax Code to disallow deduction as an operating expense did not in itself suffice as a basis for suspicion that would have made notification mandatory pursuant to Sec. 4(5) sentence 1 no. 10 sentence 3 of the Income Tax Act. However, it has recently been possible to ascertain that the threshold for such reasonable suspicion has been lowered significantly and, for example, that notification of the prosecuting authority was contemplated or took place even in the case of unclear situations, incomplete documentation or unusual payment channels.

To judge by the press releases mentioned above, such unusual payment channels, i.e. allusions to 'letterbox companies in Malta, the Bahamas, British Virgin Islands, Cyprus, London and New York' and 'payments in cash' also caused the tax administration to notify the prosecuting authority in the MAN case. It seems that the company could not furnish (sufficient) proof in the cases at issue to the effect that the commission represented appropriate remuneration for a service that was actually received and could also not show who ultimately received the commission. The purpose of the prosecuting authority's investigation was therefore e.g. to 'determine the occasion for and recipient of the payments'.

c) Inadequate Tax Compliance System

The MAN case exemplifies the fact that such transactions as those that triggered the investigation of the prosecuting authority can go undetected not only because of shortcomings in a business entity's internal system of controls, but especially also due to gaps or inadequate controls in the tax compliance system. Apart from the implications under tax law, the potential consequences in terms of criminal prosecution or fines in such cases also underscore the responsibility of tax departments for risk recognition on a systematic and ongoing basis as well as the importance of a company-wide approach that cuts across the various departments involved.

---

9 Guidance of 10 Oct. 2002 issued by the Federal Finance Ministry – IV A6 – S 2145 – Federal Tax Gazette Part I, p. 1031.
10 ibid., no. 36.

In-house audits conducted by the tax department (possibly involving internal auditors) modeled after the procedural approach of tax auditors enables a business entity to monitor the viability of its internal system of controls with the priority goal – from the point of view of the relevant tax department – of identifying tax risks and the equally important – not only in the case at issue here – additional benefit of preventing corruption.

This at the same time makes it obvious that a tax compliance system is not to be understood as a standalone process, but that interfaces (e.g. with accounting or controlling) resulting from a corresponding procedural and organizational structure must also be taken into account.

3. Increasingly Stringent Requirements in Corporate Governance

a) Legislative Reforms

As mentioned briefly above, a tax compliance system would be incomplete if it were to be limited exclusively to tax risks and measures to overcome such risks. Exclusive focus on tax risks could result in failure to recognize existing interdependencies with other risks (e.g. risks of corruption) and erroneous assessment of the overall risk exposure of the corporation. It is also necessary to take into account the fact that the reform process has resulted overall in more stringent managerial, oversight and disclosure duties for officers and directors in the past 15 years due to changes in corporate, accounting and capital market law.

For example, the new Sec. 91(2) of the German Stock Corporation Act (*Aktiengesetz*)[11] codifies the duty of the executive management of German stock corporations (*Aktiengesellschaften*) to take appropriate measures, including in particular measures to put in place monitoring systems to ensure timely detection of developments that could threaten the ability of their corporations to continue as going concerns. Such developments that threaten the ability of corporations to continue as going concerns can also result from tax risks, which is why a tax compliance system must satisfy the requirements that derive from Sec. 91(2) of the Stock Corporation Act as regards compliance with tax law.

In 2002[12], the provision contained in Sec. 161 of the Stock Corporation Act was introduced that requires that the boards of management and the supervisory boards of stock-listed corporations issue an annual statement to the effect that they have complied and will continue to comply with the recommendations contained in the German Corporate Governance Code and specify which recommendations were or are not applied, and make the statement permanently available to their shareholders ('comply or explain' principle). Statutory auditors are responsible for determining whether the officers and directors have is-

---

11 Introduced with Control and Transparency in Business Act (*Gesetz zur Kontrolle und Transparenz im Unternehmensbereich*) Federal Law Gazette Part I, 1998, p. 786 *et seqq.*
12 Transparency and Disclosure Act (*Transparenz- und Publizitätsgesetz*) of 19 July 2002, Federal Law Gazette Part I, 2002, p. 2681 *et seqq.*

sued and made permanently available a statement that formally satisfies the requirements of Sec. 161 of the Stock Corporation Act.

All in all, these and other changes in legislation (see e.g. the changes in business and corporate law[13] resulting from the corresponding EU Directives) have made the requirements that corporate management must satisfy as regards the treatment of risks significantly more stringent.

b) Recent Case Law

The additional organizational and oversight duties imposed on the members of corporate governing bodies by Germany's lawmakers in recent years have not yet been completely defined in case law.

For example, the extent of the scope and reach of a early-warning system within the meaning of Sec. 91(2) of the Stock Corporation Act remains a matter of dispute. Neither the wording nor the legislative history of this provision provides concrete information on the proper form of the early-warning system required by law. According to case law[14], however, 'documentation of the early-warning system also [belongs] to the central duties of executive management within the scope of operation of Sec. 91(2) of the Stock Corporation Act and the responsibility for preservation of the entity's ability to continue as a going concern expressed in this provision'. There is therefore a legal duty to document early-warning and oversight systems. Failure to document an early-warning system must therefore be considered a material violation of the law. In practice, this is unfortunately much too often ignored or taken into account only cursorily.

The criminal proceedings held in connection with the cases of corruption mentioned will also contribute to more precise definition of the compliance duties of corporate governing bodies. The judgment rendered by the Munich Regional Court on 10 Dec. 2013[15] deserves special mention.

This was the first time a German court had dealt in depth with the responsibility of a stock corporation's executive management for the implementation and oversight of a compliance organization and defined requirements based on responsibility for compliance. In the opinion of the court, executive officers must ensure that their corporations are organized and monitored so that no legal violations such as payments of bribes take place. Executive management can do this responsibility justice in a situation presenting such threats only if it has implemented a compliance organization designed to prevent damage and to control risks. Implementation of an inadequate compliance system and inadequate oversight of implementation constitute a breach of duty on the part of executive management. A functioning compliance system must meet stringent standards of care. All of a corporation's executive officers are required to come

---

13 See Sec. 107(3) sentence 2 of the Stock Corporation Act and Sec. 289(5) or Sec. 315(2) no. 5 of the German Commercial Code (*Handelsgesetzbuch*).
14 See Munich Regional Court I of 4 April 2007 – 5HK O 15964/06, AG 2007, 417 *et seqq.*
15 Munich Regional Court I of 10 Dec. 2013 – 5 HKO 1387/10, juris.

to a straightforward agreement as to which of the various executive officers will be primarily responsible for compliance. The oversight duty of management requires that each individual executive officer support implementation of a functioning compliance system at the level of executive management.

III. Structure of a Tax Compliance System

As shown above, general developments in corporate governance/corporate compliance have resulted in new requirements that must be met by corporations in general. Implementation of a system to ensure compliance with the requirements and prohibitions of tax law (and the desired implications for other areas of law or risk) is one aspect of these developments.

The duty to implement such a system affects in particular the range of responsibilities and activities of tax departments, which by virtue of the nature of their professional activities are most concerned with the issue of tax compliance. Changes in legislation covering corporate governance or compliance in recent years have, along with the increase in the complexity of tax law and the gradual internationalization of financial reporting, resulted in a dramatic increase in responsibility in terms of tax advice at the corporate level. It has gradually become recognized that systematic management of these risks must be considered an independent area of responsibility within tax departments.

In order to be able to do justice to these requirements, it is necessary to set up a tax compliance system with the following basic elements[16]:

1. Introduction of a Compliance Program

An effective compliance system presupposes the existence of the necessary corporate culture as well as a compliance program. Prevention policy within the entity and the resulting measures reflect the attitude of corporate management ('tone from the top') as regards what constitutes legally compliant conduct. This will also apply accordingly as regards compliance with tax laws. The attitude of management influences the conduct of employees and their willingness to obey the law. Taking into account concrete compliance goals and risks (e.g. avoidance of corruption), principles and measures must be introduced that are designed to facilitate avoidance of compliance violations.

2. Compliance Organization and Conduct Guidelines

The creation of clear organizational structures is an essential prerequisite for any compliance system. This area covers several sets of issues: Straightforward internal division of authority guarantees that activities, in particular unpopular activities, will not be shifted into the sphere of responsibility of other employees and that employees cannot coopt specific activities. Functional responsibilities must be clearly assigned and the individuals assigned such responsibilities

---
16 Modeled after IDW PS 980.

individually identified. In this context, it is also necessary to clearly define the lines of authority. The deployment and maintenance of such structures will vary as a function of corporate activity and size. What is critical is that it be possible in the individual case to determine without any great difficulty the parties responsible for specific tasks and the concomitant duties.

It is, however, necessary to determine not only the structure of the compliance organization, but also its 'procedural' organization. The compliance program must be translated into concrete recommendations for conduct. The introduction of conduct guidelines provides mandatory rules for each corporate unit. Abstract models, for example, in the form of anticorruption guidelines, do not take full advantage of the potential for prevention since they address only general values. Nevertheless, general rules of conduct can be initially adopted in guidelines that subsequently result in the concrete guidelines tailored to the needs of specific cases (e.g. awarding of contracts, invitations of business partners, etc.). These guidelines must be made available to employees. All employees must then confirm in writing that they are aware of and will comply with the conduct guidelines. The specific content will reflect the area of activity in which the corporation is involved. Finally, all guidelines must be regularly revised. They must be adapted to changes such as changes in legislation, current circumstances or the overall situation.

3. Communication

Once the organizational structures are put in place and documented, their existence must be made known within the organization to preclude any doubt or misunderstandings as regards responsibilities and authority. At the level of employees, is it necessary to cultivate an awareness of the fact that violations of the conduct guidelines expose not only the corporation and its management to not insignificant criminal sanctions but also the employee themselves. The guidelines may not be allowed to simply disappear into desk drawers without having had any influence on employee conduct. As a result, it is necessary to provide employee training related to the relevant topics to emphasize the importance of compliance with the conduct guidelines.

It is also necessary to determine how to deal with information on alleged and actual violations of rules within the corporation. Conduct guidelines should require that any violations be reported either to a special body established for such purposes (corporate compliance committee) or a corporate compliance officer. The compliance committee or the compliance officer forms an important interface for communication between executive management and employees.

Implementation of an anonymous reporting system ('whistleblower system') is also conceivable. It is necessary to take into account that management must ensure on the one hand that a report, regardless of how justified it might be, does not result in a defamatory smear campaign against the affected employee. In particular, if an allegation turns out to be unfounded, the ramifications in terms of the social integration of the person making the report can be fatal. On the other hand, a corporate culture that is conditioned by a certain sense of responsibility plays an important role in terms of fostering a willingness to make such reports. If this has been accepted by personnel and become a permanent part of everyday work, it will be a matter of course for employees to report irregularities or sources of danger to management.

4. Ongoing Control and Improvement

A permanently efficient compliance system presupposes ongoing controls. Appropriateness and efficacy must be monitored on an ongoing basis. This is the only way to identify weaknesses and achieve improvement. Precisely in the sphere of responsibility of tax departments, suitable controls would include data analyses such as those regularly carried out in tax audits (see above).

The necessary oversight is only possible if the principles and measures that make up the compliance system are appropriately documented. The importance of this aspect is reflected in the case law on documentation of early-warning systems (see above).

IV. Conclusions and Outlook

Today, no corporate officer or tax department can ignore the need for systematic avoidance of risks as regards tax and criminal law. The minimum requirements for an effective tax compliance system described above are of a general nature. Concrete implementation must take place as a function of the specific corporation. In this context, it is also necessary to keep in mind that any (tax) compliance system must be integrated into existing systems (early-warning system within the meaning of Sec. 91(2) of the Stock Corporation Act, system of internal controls, and risk management system) in order to avoid inefficient redundancy.

Jesco Idler

Public Auditor, Tax Advisor, Diplom-Kaufmann

Areas of Specialization

- Tax compliance/tax advisory services
- Internal investigations in order to identify tax risks
- Tax investigation and tax crime defense
- Voluntary disclosure of tax evasion
- Taxation of foreign artists, sportsmen, licensors and advertisers

Telephone (ext.) +49 228/95 94-641

Email: jesco.idler@fgs.de

Index

accounting for advertising spots 631 et seq.
– film and television funds 635
– film producer 632
– film rights 631
– intangible asset 631
– media decree 635
– 'real' commissioned production 632
– television and cinema films 637
– 'unreal' commissioned production 632

Base Erosion and Profit Shifting (BEPS) 321

business restructurings 187 et seq.
– claims of a sales agent 196
– contract manufacturer 190
– discounted cash flow method 192
– factual arm's length test 191
– first escape clause 193
– function 189
– hypothetical arm's length test 191
– low risk distributor 190
– range of mutual consent 191
– routine function 190
– second escape clause 193
– third escape clause 193
– transfer of goodwill 192
– transfer package 188

buyout investments - typical transaction structures 81 et seq.
– acquisition financing 85
– beneficial ownership 89
– debt pushdown 82
– downstream merger 83
– fiscal unity 83
– interest barrier rule 84
– Luxembourg 86
– management equity program 82
– management participation 87
– manager limited partnership 87
– private equity transactions 81
– vesting scheme 89
– withholding tax 86

codetermination 565 et seq.
– avoid codetermination 571
– codetermination by employees 565
– corporate codetermination 565
– cross-border merger 575
– foreign coporation & Co. KG 573
– legal forms 424
– partnership limited by shares (KGaA) 576
– SE 575
– SE & Co. KG 573
– Stiftung & Co. KG 572
– supervisory board subject to codetermination 568

contributions in kind of business units 215 et seq.
– branch of activity 216
– business units 216
– entire business 216
– interest in a partnership 216
– outbound cross-border contributions 222
– partners being resident in third countries 220
– retroaction 219
– tainted shares 220
– transferee 218
– transferor 217
– transfers 217

controlled foreign company (cfc) legislation 41 et seq.
– active income 44
– active income test 47
– CFC legislation and transparent entities 50
– control 42
– credit method 49
– de minimis test 47
– EU test 47
– financial investment income 43
– immigration and emigration of individuals 386
– losses 49
– low taxation 43

655

– passive low-taxed income 44
– publicly traded company test 48
– reorganizations 241
– subsequent dividends and capital gains 49
– tax treaty issues 50
– transactional approach 44
corporate and financial restructuring 513 et seq.
– chief restructuring officer 514
– Debenture Act 514, 518
– debt-to-equity swap 516, 517
– debtor in possession 514
– european insolvency regulation 513
– forum shopping 514
– in-court restructurings 513, 514, 517, 519, 520
– insolvency scheme 513, 516
– out-of-court restructurings 513, 514, 517, 520
– revision of insolvency law 513
– umbrella proceedings 515
corporate financing 139 et seq.
– crisis 152
– debt 139
– double taxation treaties 150
– equity 139
– financing 139
– hybrid financial instruments 145
– inbound investments 148
– interest barrier 140
– participation exemption 145
– shareholder loans 146
– thin capitalization rule 140
– waiver subject to restoration 152
corporate governance 501 et seq.
– comply or explain' principle 505
– corporate governance commission 502
– declaration of conformity 504
– executive board 506
– general meetung 508
– liability of directors and officers 504
– supervisory board 506
– transparency 510

– two-tier management system 506
corporate litigation 523 et seq.
– actions for annulment 524
– actions for disclosure 531, 536
– civil proceedings 526
– claims for compensation 532
– dismissal, action against 534
– partners' contributions 536
– predatory litigants 528
– release proceedings 526, 528
– restriction of transferability 536
– right of supervision 534
– right of termination 536
– special audit proceedings 530
– stock corporation 527
– valuation proceedings 524
corporations and partnerships, taxation by comparison 11 et seq.
– anti-treaty-shopping rule 16
– corporation 11
– credit method 19
– determining profits 12
– direct credit 17
– dividends 12
– exemption certificate 15
– exemption method 19
– holding company 16
– indirect credit 17
– interest and royalties directive 19
– interest barrier 19
– loss carryback 20
– loss utilization 21
– parent-subsidiary directive 16
– partnership 12
– subsidiary 11
– tax accounting 13
– tax losses 20
– thin capitalization rules 19
– trade tax 12
– withholding tax 15
criminal tax law 591 et seq.
– blanket provision 594
– company-related fine 598
– intent connected with tax evasion 599
– legal development 592 et seq.
– nonrecognition of expenses 595

– self-disclosure 598
– tax evasion 579 et seq., 593
– tax reduction 595
– unjustified tax advantage 595
– violation of tax notification obligations 597

cross-border reorganizations 453 et seq.
– change of legal form 455
– division 456
– employee participation 457
– merger 455
– merger directive 456
– merger examination 462
– merger reportmerger report 462
– transfer of assets 454

delisting 493 et seq.
– cold delisting 498
– DAT/Altana 498
– downgrading 497
– Frosta 496
– going public 493
– Macrotron 495
– regular delisting 495
– squeeze-out 494
– taking private transactions 493, 497

distribution 539 et seq.
– antitrust law 548
– authorized dealer 545
– choice of law 549
– claim for compensation 548
– commercial agent 540
– commercial broker 542
– commission agent 543
– franchisee 546
– general terms and conditions 547
– status-determination procedure 549
– statutory social-security regime 547
– types 539

financial statements 615 et seq.
– avoiding publication 625
– Disclosure Act 622
– format and content of published information 623
– partnerships with at least one natural person as a general partner 622
– publication exemptions 624
– publish consolidated financial statements 625
– sanctions 628
– scope of documents to be published 617
– timing of publication 624

foundation and trust in succession planning 353 et seq.
– add-back taxation 363
– current taxation 357
– dissolution of the foundation 359
– establishing the foundation 355
– establishment of a foreign EU/EEA (interim) foundation 363
– interim-beneficiary taxation 363
– substitute inheritance tax 357
– tax treatment 355
– taxation of trusts in germany 360
– types and advantages of foundations 354

group taxation 25 et seq.
– attribution of income 25
– controlled entity 25
– controlling entity 26
– dividend 28
– financial integration 26
– foreign controlling entity 30
– interest barrier 35
– invalid tax group 29
– losses 31
– partnership 26
– profit and loss transfer agreement (PLTA) 26, 33
– trade tax 27, 29
– valid tax group 27

immigration and emigration of individuals 379 et seq.
– commuter 382
– controlled foreign company (CFC) legislation 384

657

– dwelling 381
– exit taxation 380, 388
– extended limited tax liability 381
– extended unlimited tax liability 381
– foundation 386
– granny-flat 383
– guest house 384
– habitual abode 380, 382
– limited tax liability 380
– nationality 380
– physical presence 381
– residence 380
– summer cottage 383
inheritance and gift tax planning strategies 367 et seq.
– assumption of german gift tax 377
– changing the type of property 370
– characteristics of nonresident inheritance tax liability 367
– children buyout 369
– debt deduction strategy 373
– escape into resident german inheritance and gift tax liability 374
– graduated transfer of shares in corporations 376
– heir/legatee strategy 371
– holding company strategy 372
– objectives 368
inheritance tax liability 343 et seq.
– domestic assets 348
– domicile 346
– extended limited inheritance tax liability 351
– extended unlimited inheritance and gift tax liability 347
– Inheritance Tax Act 344
– limited inheritance and gift tax liability 348
– option to assume unlimited tax liability 350
– ordinary abode 346
– tax residents 345
– unlimited inheritance and gift tax liability 345
– Valuation Act 344

Investment Tax Act 155 et seq.
– AIF 155
– deemed distributed earnings 158
– distributed earnings 158
– interim profits 158
– investment company 156
– investment limited partnership 157
– investment stock company 157
– UCITS 155
joint audits 328
legal forms 415 et seq.
– Aktiengesellschaft (AG) 420
– codetermination 424
– control agreement 424
– corporate entities 415
– Gesellschaft bürgerlichen Rechts (GbR) 416
– Gesellschaft mit beschränkter Haftung (GmbH) 419
– insolvency 425
– Kommanditgesellschaft auf Aktien (KGaA) 422
– Offene Handelsgesellschaft (OHG) 417
– partnerships 415
– profit and loss transfer agreement 424
– Societas Europaea (SE) 423
M&A involving listed corporations 443 et seq.
– ad-hoc disclosure 445
– corporate actions 448
– delisting 447
– downgrading 447
– judicial valuation proceedings 447
– notification requirements 444
– public offers 445
– shareholder suit 446
– squeeze-out 447
– takeover legislation 445
M&A transactions, tax aspects 113 et seq.
– debt push-down 122
– deductibility of interest paid 118
– depreciation of acquired assets 117
– determination of capital gains 115
– incidental acquisition costs 121

- interest barrier 118
- loss carryforwards 123
- preferential tax rate 115
- supplementary balance sheet 115
- taxation-related technique 117
- trade-tax losses 118

matrix structures 553 et seq.
- compliance system 563
- controlling corporation 555
- cross-company steering models 563
- delegation 555
- dependent corporation 555
- direct steering models 554
- directional management 557
- function-oriented steering structures 553
- group-wide 'steering' 554
- indirect steering models 554
- organizational forms which are incongruent 553
- reporting system 555
- subject-specific instructions 558
- supervisory duty 555

nonprofit organizations 393 et seq.
- association 399
- charitable 393
- charitable purpose 394
- charitable purposes businesses 394
- donation 394
- european law 396
- foundation 394
- inheritance and gift tax 394
- Nonprofit-GmbH 397
- VAT 394
- withholding tax refund 394

private equity funds 67 et seq.
- capital gains 69
- carried interest 71
- co-entrepreneurship 70
- cross-border structures 72
- disproportionate profit share 61
- dividends 71
- interest 71
- non-german resident investor 71
- partnership 60
- private asset management partnerships 69

private M&A 429 et seq.
- APA 439
- asset deal 431
- change-of-control provision 436
- closing 431, 434
- confidentiality agreement 432
- corporate finance advisor 432
- Deutschland AG 429
- due diligence 431, 433
- investment bank 432
- letter of intent 432
- M&A laywers 431
- Mittelstand 430
- notarial recording 431
- share deal 431
- signing 431, 433
- SPA 439
- teaser 432

provisions 245 et seq.
- assumed provisions 251
- future obligation 248
- German GAAP 246
- legal framework 246
- present legal obligation 248
- provision for costs incurred for the authorization of plant protection products 250
- provision for future obligation to modify technical equipment to meet environmental standards 248
- provisions for refunds of excess fees charged by network operators 250

real estate transfer tax 293 et seq.
- accounting treatment 301
- changes of partner 298
- notification duties 302
- reversal of sale reversal of sale 302
- scope of application 293
- selected business transactions 303
- share aggregation 295
- share transfer 295
- structure 293
- tax assessment basis 299
- tax exemptions 298
- tax rate 300
- taxable events 294

– taxpayer 301
real estate, investments in 481 et seq.
– (no compete) covenant 489
– commercial leases 486
– easements 482
– incidental costs 487
– preemptive purchase right 484
– priority notation 483
– real-estate due-diligence 481
– rent security 489
– repurchase right 484
– written form requirement 486
real estate, taxation 125 et seq.
– G-REIT 135
– land tax 130
– non-PE structure 131
– open fund 135
– real estate transfer tax 127
– special fund 135
– value added tax (VAT) 129
reorganizations 199 et seq., 235 et seq., 467 et seq.
– branch of activity 208
– changes in form 210, 237, 470
– contributions 210
– controlled foreign company (CFC) legislation 241
– cross-border reorganizations 455 et seq.
– division 207, 208, 470
– hive-down 471
– losses 240
– merger 205, 207, 236, 470
– real estate transfer tax 240
– Reorganization Act 201, 469
– Reorganization Tax Act 202, 235
– spin-off 236, 471
– split-up 236, 471
– universal succession 470
repatriation 53
– anti-abuse rule 57
– anti-treaty-shopping rule 57
– corporation 53
– cross-border scenarios 53
– double taxation treaty 56
– eu parent-subsidiary directive 56

– foreign investors 53
– intragroup disposals 60
– investment 53
– partnership 53
– permanent establishment 53
– tax group 62
– withholding tax 54
ruling practice 331 et seq.
– advance pricing agreement 339
– advance ruling 332
– binding commitment 337
– binding effect 336
– obligation to pay fees 336
– wage-tax ruling 338
share-for-share transactions 225 et seq.
– applicant 231
– beneficial ownership 226, 228
– blocking period 230
– comparative type analysis 228
– contribution and subscription agreement 232
– cross-border qualified share-for-share transaction 227
– non discrimination 227
– nonvoting preferred stock 229
– qualified share-for-share transaction 226
– right to sue 233
– roll-over of the book value 231
– singular or universal succession 226
– third-party action for annulment 233
sportsmen and artists, taxation 403 et seq.
– advertising income 407
– certificate of exemption 404
– payments for appearances 407
– transfer fees 412
– withholding tax 404
tax accounting 257 et seq.
– accrual accounting 258
– beneficial ownership 258
– consistency 260
– digitization 263
– european harmonization 263

– provisions 263
– realization principle 259
– tax group 262
– taxonomy 263
taxation of partnership income
  93 et seq.
– attribution of tax criteria 97
– beneficiary owner 93
– check the box 91, 94, 96
– classification 91, 99
– conflict of classification 92
– GmbH 97, 98
– groups of individuals regarded as an entity 92
– KGaA 98
– partnership carrying on a trade or business 97
– pro rata 91, 92, 93, 97, 98, 99
– remuneration 93
– special business assets 91
– special business income 91
– taxable entity 91, 92, 93, 99
– transparent taxation 91
– treaty entitlement 92, 93, 96, 99
tax audits 321 et seq.
– audit procedure 324
– bounds of discretion 323
– digital data 326
– discretionary selection 323
– final meeting 327
– Gewinnabgrenzungsaufzeichnungsverordnung 327
– joint audits 328
– obligation to cooperate 325
– record-keeping duties 327
– records 327
– transfer pricing 178
tax classification of foreign legal entities 1 et seq.
– centralization of management 4
– check-the-box regulations 2
– comparability test 4
– discretion to access profits 5
– eight-factor test 6
– entity classification 2
– equity contributions 5
– free transferability of interests 4

– hybrid entities 2
– limited liability 4
– profit allocation 5
tax compliance 641 et seq.
– bribery 647
– compliance program 649
– compliance system 642, 648, 650, 651
– conduct guidelines 651
– corporate governance 641, 649, 651
– data access 644
– documentation duties 642, 645
– early-warning-system 650, 653
– fiscal confidentiality 641, 645, 647
– tax compliance system 646
– whistleblower system 652
tax disputes and litigation
  309 et seq.
– administrative appeal procedure 312
– appellate proceedings 315
– arbitration convention 319
– constitutional complaints 316
– European Court of Justice 317
– Federal Constitutional Court 316
– Federal Tax Court 315
– fundamental freedoms 317
– legal protection against double taxation 318
– lower tax courts 313
– non-admission complaint 316
– tax audit 312
– temporary legal protection 318
– termination of court proceedings 314
tax evasion, voluntary disclosure
  579 et seq.
– addressee 581
– blocking effect 585
– criminal code 580
– exemption from punishment 579
– federal court of justice 580
– infection effect 585
– limitation period 582
– notification of joinder 581
– partial voluntary disclosure of tax evasion 582

661

– requirement of completeness 582, 583
– system of adjustments 582
trade tax 281 et seq.
– corporation 286
– double taxation treaty 288
– Foreign Tax Act 290
– group taxation 285
– partnership 286
– permanent establishment 281
– real estate 284
– trading profit 282
trading partnership 103 et seq.
– anti-treaty-shopping provision 109
– asset deal 107
– branch profits tax 105
– check-the-box type rules 104
– classification 108
– rollover relief 110
– special business asset 105
– special business expenses 105
– special business income 105
transfer pricing 165 et seq., 177 et seq., 187 et seq.
– burden of proof 182
– business restructurings 187
– claims of a sales agent 196
– comparable uncontrolled price method 169
– contract manufacturer 190
– cost plus method 171
– discounted cash flow method 192
– documentation requirements 177 et seq.
– extraordinary business transactions 178
– factual arm's length test 191
– first escape clause 193
– function 189
– functional and risk analysis 180
– Goldscheider 172
– hypothetical arm's length test 191
– intangible assets 165
– Knoppe formula 172
– licensing 165
– low risk distributor 190
– penalties for documentation-related noncompliance 182
– range of mutual consent 191
– resale price method 170
– routine function 190
– second escape clause 193
– sublicensing fee 170
– tax audit 178
– third escape clause 193
– transactional profits method 171
– transfer of goodwill 192
– transfer package 188
– transfer pricing analysis 181
– withholding tax 173
valuation principles 603 et seq.
– business valuation 605
– capitalization rate 611
– control premium 612
– determining future cash flows 609
– income approach 607
– minority discount 612
– multiple-based methods 608
– standard of value 607
– standardized approach 609
– synergy effects 610
– valuation methods 607
VAT 267 et seq.
– autonomy 270
– close links 270
– economic integration 277
– entrepreneurial status 274
– financial integration 269
– financial link 276
– integration 270
– merger 272
– merger into a single taxable person 270
– non-taxable person 267
– organizational integration 269
– partnership 274
– subordinated person 272
– superordinate and subordinate relationship 267, 274
– taxable person 268, 271
– VAT fiscal unity 267